Dear Father in Heaven, we pray, that any error in this book may be over-ruled, and that the truth may find receptive hearts, and bring forth fruit unto life eternal.

Ashland, Ohio. 1907   C. F. Yoder.

"Whatsoever things are True, whatsoever things are Honest, whatsoever things are Just, whatsoever things are Pure, whatsoever things are Lovely, whatsoever things are of Good Report, if there be any Virtue, and if there be any Praise THINK ON THESE THINGS"

Presented to
Miss Charlotte Schutz
North Manchester, Ind.

With the compliments
of the author
Charles Francis Yoder

When you have read this book do not fail to test your reading with the closing questions.

The Old Church

I've been back to the country church I loved in days of yore,
I saw the horses hitched about the old familiar door,
And down the winding country ways where sweet the blossoms cling,
I found the faith of childhood such a fair and fragrant thing.

The robin's breast was red against the baby-blue of sky;
The little winds were blessed balm, the bloom was on the rye;
The veering ships of cloud were out and white was every sail,
And silvery came the song and sweet the piping of the quail.

And with it all the church of old—my mother worshiped there;
They led her to its altar as a bride so young and fair,
And through its windows came the light that fell upon her face,
When folded from the toil her hands, and reached the resting place.

There may be other churches that are grander to the eye,
There may be organs pealing out to shake the earth and sky,
But oh, to rest the soul, be sure no comfort do they bring
Like that in hymns that helped the heart the saints of old did sing.

I lingered in the morning light in that familiar place,
And seemed to hear the prayers of old and feel the tender grace,
I could not think of them away beyond the yearning heart,
For God is love and they are His, and we can never part.

And so I think of it today upon the city street,
The wind that ruffles up the grass where all the graves are sweet.
And, like a rose that will not fade, preserved by heavenly art,
The "old church" blooms and sweetens all the garden of my heart.

—W. Lomax Childress.

God's Means of Grace

A Discussion of the Various Helps Divinely Given as Aids to
Christian Character, and a Plea for Fidelity to
their Scriptural Form and Purpose

By C. F. YODER, A. B., B. D., Ph.D.

*Author of " Gospel Church Government," " Some Significant Tendencies
of the Times," and Various Tracts.*

ELGIN, ILLINOIS, U. S. A.
BRETHREN PUBLISHING HOUSE
1908

To my Christian Parents

*who taught me from my youth to love the Lord and
seek Him, to know His will and do it, and
to work for Him and with Him,*

This Book is Dedicated.

INTRODUCTION

By Amos H. Haines, A. M. D. D.,

Professor of Biblical Languages, History and Literature,
in Juniata College.

The merit of a book depends, for the most part, upon two things; first, the need and demand for the work, and second, upon the author's ability to put his thought in a straightforward and readable manner. This latter qualification usually results, if the author feels, down deep in his heart, that he has a message for his time and age.

The book entitled "God's Means of Grace," to which these few brief words are to serve as a preface, possesses, in my judgment, both of the above-named qualifications or marks of merit.

During the past two decades, many books have been written on theological, biblical and philosophical subjects. Some of these books will live, and the longer and more deeply studied, the more will they be appreciated and the greater good will they do. Others of these works will die before or with the author. The cause of this passing out is simply that the books are speculative in content and character, and therefore lack a basis of fact.

This work by Elder C. F. Yoder contains a practical message for a practical age. It is didactic and thoroughly biblical in tone. It is to be commended for its non-apologetic character and treatment. The Christian world to-day needs more direct biblical teaching and less of the surmising and speculative. This the book accomplishes in a most admirable manner. It may be said to be first and primarily biblical in character and content, rather than denominational. This is a wise discrimination to make and is doubtless just what the author set out to do. Entirely too many works on biblical and churchly topics put tradition, creed and church before the Bible, especially before the teaching of Christ and His apostles.

At this particular time of aroused and increasing interest in Bible study, I know of no work, outside of the Bible itself, that should prove more helpful and directive to the sincere and earnest seeker after truth. The author has given painstaking attention to the sources for his material.

As to the qualifications of the author, it may be said that there is perhaps no one of the Brethren Church to-day better qualified to write a work of this kind than he. Elder Yoder was born, so to speak, into the church. His experience and education have especially prepared him for his task. He has been a regular and careful student in academic, collegiate and university work, giving especial attention to theological and biblical study. He has proved his efficiency as a successful teacher, writer, editor, minister and missionary. His broad experience has brought him into contact with the world and the Church, and he has studied the conditions and needs of both.

I bespeak for the book a hearty welcome by all unprejudiced members and branches of the Church, also by all others who are interested in the fact and teaching of Christ.

Juniata College, Huntingdon, Pa., July, 1908.

"I was constrained to write unto you exhorting you to contend earnestly for the faith which was once for all delivered unto the saints"—Jude 3.

"For the time will come when they will not endure the sound doctrine; but, having itching ears, heap to themselves teachers after their own lusts; and will turn away their ears from the truth, and turn aside unto fables."—2 Tim. 4: 3, 4.

"If a man love me he will keep my word: and my Father will love him, and we will come unto him, and make our abode with him."—John 14: 23.

AUTHOR'S PREFACE

A leading professor of theology has recently said that Christianity is passing through the most serious crisis of its history, a crisis in which men are questioning the very foundations, and asking whether indeed Christianity be final. This crisis, he says, is not felt so much by the masses of believers as by the serious thinkers and investigators. He himself has been endeavoring to put the Christian faith in the terms of logic and find a rational basis for all its various phenomena, but in keeping clear of the pit of credulity he has fallen into the pit of doubt.

Christianity may indeed be passing through a crisis in the minds of many scholars, while the masses are unmoved. It has always been so. The little children enter into the kingdom while the wise and the learned argue about it. The modern theological seminaries are very much tainted with rationalism, and doubt cannot but result, because the things of the kingdom appeal to the heart rather than to reason alone. They are indeed grounded in the logic which God knows, but by men they must be received by faith, while understanding patiently waits. Who can explain the activities of life? Who can analyze the workings of love? "Who knoweth the mind of the Spirit?" It is enough to know that the Gospel has proven itself to be "the power of God unto salvation unto every one that believeth," and that by many infallible proofs, by the testimony of the millions of sinners redeemed from the power and the love of sin, and by the dawning of the millennial day toward which the Church is marching on.

There need be no fear because of serious investigation into

the merits of Christianity. The crisis that most truly threatens the church is due rather to indifference so great as to prevent investigation. Ministers of the Gospel who have spent their time in preparation, trying to trace the tracks of "J" and "P" and "E" through the Word instead of tracing the message of the Holy Spirit, and practicing in the actual use of the sword of the Spirit, are not able to protect their flocks from the enemies. The church leaders have been thinking too much of metaphysics and too little of the means of grace, and in consequence the ordinances of God have come to be replaced by the substitutes of men, which are barren of spiritual benefits. Rites unpleasant to human pride have been done away. Socials and lodges have usurped the place of the early love-feast, and the symbols that God gave for our instruction and help have been robbed of their meaning.

A generation ago it was popular to debate on doctrine. It is not so now. Competition is giving way to federation, and instead of making straight the way of truth, many are preparing the way for federation, by putting doctrine in the background with the simple assertion, "This way or that way is right for you, if you only believe."

It is not the purpose of this book to hinder the union of Christ's followers, but rather to promote it. Not, however, by disloyalty to the least of His commandments, but on the platform of fullest freedom to observe them all. The Gospel of united Christendom must be inclusive rather than exclusive. When pagan Rome first met the Church it was with the bloody sword of persecution. Failing thus to stay her progress, she federated with her, and by unholy alliance the fair robes were soiled in the filth of corruption. Whom Satan cannot kill he courts. Let the church beware lest in alliance of numbers she lose her power.

It is the observation of the author that the church of to-

Preface

day needs very much a new baptism of doctrinal conviction. She lacks that tremendous earnestness which sent the apostolic church through blood and fire with the message of the Gospel. She has numbers and wealth and opportunity, but she spends it mainly in amusement. This is largely due to the loss of that environment which was given the church for her protection, in the ordinances of grace. It is the plea of this book that God knew best the needs of the spiritual life; that His means are best to win His ends, and that therefore it is the part of wisdom as well as of love to retain unchanged, in form or meaning, the teaching symbols which He gave.

It will not do to say that these matters are obscure and therefore everyone should follow his own feelings or faith. " There is a way which seemeth right unto a man; but the end thereof are the ways of death " (Prov. 14: 12). That is feeling, and not faith, which causes conviction without investigation. The ordinances were not delivered obscurely, but have been obscured by false teaching. The Gospel is before us and we may not plead ignorance of the Master's will until we have done our utmost to know it. No individual and no church can be spiritually blessed by retaining error when it is known, or by being too indifferent to know when it is possible to do so. Among all the many denominations, there is need that *one* shall be promoted everywhere which shall give an opportunity, at least, to observe not only the spiritual teachings of Jesus, but the means of grace as well.

There are just two essentials to such a church. The first is that it be founded upon Jesus Christ as its divine and only foundation (Matt. 16: 16-18; 1 Cor. 3: 11), and the second is that it provide for the fullest obedience to Jesus Christ. Every type of life must have an environment suited to its needs. The Christian type of life is no exception. It requires its own peculiar protection and food and fellowship and exercise, such as Christ has supplied in the means of grace given to the church.

Far from being mere forms, these symbols are essential aids to the fullest Christian growth. It follows that the church which best observes them should also best exemplify the virtues which they teach. The proof of this is not lacking in the history of the church. The early church, which was most faithful to the means of grace, was the most blessed with the gifts and graces of the Spirit. And those modern Christians who are most loyal to these means of grace are likewise most in accord with Him who gave them. Travel the world over and one can find no more humble, sociable, Christly churches than those which stand for the full Gospel. It is the promise of the Lord and it is the verdict of experience.

Right here is the justification for this book. The best authorities in church history now acknowledge that the symbols contended for in this volume were found in the early church, but they do not regard them as binding upon Christians to-day. This position the Roman Catholics consistently take, because they teach that the church has the right to change the commandments of Christ; but for Protestants to take this position is utterly inconsistent. Grant the right of the church to alter the mode of baptism or to do away with any of the ordinances, and the door is open to any heresy or innovation. When the church once took this position, then came the image worship and priestcraft which has been the curse of Romanism.

The position is fundamentally false. The church is not a law-giver in the place of Christ, but the obedient bride of Christ, waiting for her Lord (Eph. 5: 25-33). She may not alter His commands, but must faithfully keep them till He comes. When the world is ready for a new dispensation, it will be ushered in with divine authority; till then the ordinances of God for this dispensation must be observed without change. Not in a formal way, to be sure, but according to both the letter and the spirit. Granting that the observance in the past has been largely formal, this is no reason for discarding the symbols which God has given for our good. *God's ways are best to win His ends.* This is the message we would proclaim to the world.

In this argument, the institutions given of God for this age, for the welfare of the race, are considered as " means of grace " without distinguishing those that are considered " sacraments " from the rest. " Sacrament " is not a scriptural term, nor do the Scriptures teach that some commands of God are to be held sacred and others not. Opinions differ as to what are sacraments and what are not, but there can be no question that all the institutions considered in this work may be called " means of grace," for they all minister to the welfare of the race and promote the graces of the Spirit.

The main argument of the book is implied in the title. The symbols or ordinances are helps to character and means of teaching, and because they are truly " God's means of grace " they have an intrinsic value which makes them worth contending for. The old apologetic made much of technical arguments and formal obedience. Such arguments now fail to appeal to thinking people so much as arguments based on utility. And, although the point has been much ignored in the past, here is the greatest reason for faithfulness to God's institutions. They are given for man's good, by Him who best of all knew man's needs and how to supply them. It is with this in mind that we have been constrained in these pages to " contend earnestly for the faith which was once for all delivered unto the saints." (Jude 3) In doing this we do not forget the many earnest Christian workers who have not so learned the Scriptures. They are lovable in their lives and sincere in their faith, and not for a moment would we cast reflection on their Christian character. Without having opportunity for thorough investigation for themselves, they have accepted the teaching given them. Their teachers have in turn been misled as to these means of grace, in the very seminaries which should have emphasized them. It is hard to break with home and church traditions and training, and we have only Christian compassion for those who are bound by it, but at the same time we have determined to be right as far as human endeavor and divine help can make us right. With others who share this desire we wish to share the results of our researches, that with slight cost they may know that which has cost years of labor to obtain.

We write with no sectarian spirit. God help us! There is too much of that in the world already. But to be loyal to the Gospel is not to be sectarian. The church must have its ordinances and officers, but it needs none other than a Gospel name, and none other than the Gospel for a creed. Within these limits there should be room for the coöperation of all the members of the body of Christ, if all have the spirit of Christ and heed the injunction, " Him that is weak in faith receive ye, yet not for decision of scruples " (Rom. 14: 1). In this work use has been made of the various books that have been written on doctrinal matters, but the quotations have been derived almost wholly from the original sources. The teachings of the Gospel have been supplemented by the writings of the early church only from the first centuries, because the coming in of errors vitiates the writings of later leaders.

The Scripture quotations are made from the American Revised Version because it is conceded by scholars to be the most faithful to the original. The dates of the early Fathers quoted are after *Stearn's Manual of Patrology*. They indicate the date of birth, rather than of writing.

Believing that all God's means of grace were wisely given, we have sincerely sought to know the truth concerning them, and now pass on the truth to others who wish the blessings of full obedience. The book is meant for study rather than for entertainment. Scripture references are given that all the positions taken may be verified by the Word of God. The author will be grateful for the pointing out of any errors that may have been overlooked. If the book is helpful to any reader let him make it known, that its help may be passed along " until we all come to the unity of the faith."

Just one closing caution: Obedience to the truth is absolutely imperative to the Christian. If the facts which follow reveal to any their errors, those errors must be given up; if they point the way of duty, that way must be followed; if obedience to the truth costs sacrifice, it is the price of life.

He that believeth on the Son hath eternal life; but he that obeyeth not the Son shall not see life, but the wrath of God abideth on him (John 3: 36). He that loveth father or mother more than me is not worthy of me; and he that loveth son or daughter more than me is not worthy of me. And he that doth not take his cross and follow after me, is not worthy of me. He that findeth his life shall lose it; and he that loseth his life for my sake shall find it (Matt. 10: 37, 38).

TABLE OF CONTENTS

CHAPTER

I. The Church.
   Necessity of Membership.
   Benefits of Membership.
   Value of the Ordinances.
   Relation of the Old and New Covenants.

II. Three Symbols as Means of Worship.
   The Bible.
   Prayer.
   Praise.

III. Three Symbols relating to the New Birth.
   Confession.
   Baptism.
   The Holy Kiss.

IV. Three Symbols Conducive to Christian Growth.
   Feet-washing.
   The Love-Feast.
   The Eucharist.

V. Three Symbols Relating to the Holy Spirit.
   Laying on of Hands.
   Ordination.
   Anointing the Sick with Oil.

VI. Three Symbols of Separation from the World.
   In Company: Special Reference to Lodges.
   In Dress: Non-conformity to the World.
   In conduct: Special Reference to Non-resistance.

VII. Three Symbols for the Welfare of the Race.
   Marriage.
   The Sabbath.
   The Tithe.
   The Return of our Lord.

CHAPTER I

THE CHURCH.

The Necessity of Membership—The Benefits of Membership—The Value of the Ordinances—The Relation of the Old and New Covenants.

* * * * * *

Christ also loved the church, and gave himself up for it; that he might sanctify it, having cleansed it by the washing of water with the word, that he might present the church to himself a glorious church, not having spot or wrinkle or any such thing; but that it should be holy and without blemish.—Eph. 5: 25, 26.

* * * * * *

They then that received his word were baptized; . . . And they continued stedfastly in the apostles' teaching and fellowship, in the breaking of bread and the prayers.—Acts. 2: 41, 42.

* * * * * *

Teaching them to observe all things whatsoever I have commanded you.—Matt. 28: 20.

If ye know these things, blessed are ye if ye do them.—John 13: 17.

* * * * * *

Till heaven and earth pass away, one jot or one tittle shall in no wise pass away from the law, till all things be accomplished.—Matt. 5: 18.

God, having of old time spoken unto the fathers in the prophets by divers portions and in divers manners, hath at the end of these days spoken unto us in his Son.—Heb. 1: 1, 2.

THE CHURCH.

It is common in these days to profess faith in Jesus Christ, and to depend upon that faith for salvation, without being connected with any church. Some, indeed, profess to belong to the true spiritual church while not observing the means of grace with any. A London preacher speaking in the streets was cheered when he spoke of Jesus, but hissed when he spoke of the church. This seems to be the attitude of a great portion of the unchurched masses. If it be true that the church may be discredited and discarded while retaining the salvation which the church preaches, it ought to be known so that all may be relieved of the burden which the maintenance of the church imposes; but if this be a delusion then it is high time that the trumpet of warning be sounded far and wide with no uncertain sound. What then is the will of God concerning the church? When He speaks let man be silent, and when He wills let man obey.

I. The Necessity of Church Membership.

1. THE CHURCH IS OF GOD.

Jesus said, " Upon this rock (Christian faith) I will build my church; and the gates of Hades shall not prevail against it " (Matt. 16: 18). When the first enemies of the church persecuted the apostles, Gamaliel, the wisest man of the Sanhedrin, said, " If this counsel or this work . . . is of God ye will not be able to overthrow them; lest haply ye be found even to be fighting against God " (Acts 5: 39). History has proven the wisdom of these words. Men have tried in vain to overthrow the church. Celsus tried it and Porphyry tried it and Nero tried it and Diocletian tried it and Julian the Apostate tried it, and hosts of others, but all have failed. Voltaire said, " It took twelve men to found Christianity, but I will show you that one man can tear it down." But Voltaire has passed into history and his press is now used to print Bibles, which are stored in his house. The Church is moving onward as an army with banners to the conquest of the world. The gates of hell shall not prevail against it because it is of God.

2. THE CHURCH IS BEING PREPARED AS THE BRIDE OF CHRIST. We read:

Husbands, love your wives, even as Christ also loved the church, and gave himself up for it; that he might sanctify it, having cleansed it by the washing of water with the word, that he might present the church to himself a glorious church, not having spot or wrinkle or any such thing; but that it should be holy and without blemish. Even so ought husbands to love their own wives as their own bodies. He that loveth his own wife loveth himself: for no man ever hated his own flesh; but nourisheth and cherisheth it, even as Christ also the church; because we are members of his body. For this cause shall a man leave father and mother, and shall cleave unto his wife; and the two shall become one flesh. This mystery is great: but I speak in regard of Christ and the church (Eph. 5: 25-33).

If then the church is to be the bride of Christ, how are they to share in the privileges of the bride who reject the church?

3. THE CHURCH IS TO BE UNITED WITH CHRIST IN THE COMING KINGDOM OF GOD. The Seer of Patmos looked across the centuries and beheld the scene and he wrote:

Hallelujah: for the Lord our God, the Almighty, reigneth. Let us rejoice and be exceeding glad, and let us give the glory unto him: for the marriage of the Lamb is come, and his wife hath made herself ready. And it was given unto her that she should array herself in fine linen, bright and pure: for the fine linen is the righteous acts of the saints. And he saith unto me, Write, Blessed are they that are bidden to the marriage supper of the Lamb (Rev. 19: 6-9).

Hear now the warning which Jesus uttered concerning this marriage supper:

> When the King came in to behold the guests, he saw there a man who had not on a wedding-garment: and he saith unto him, Friend, how camest thou in hither not having on a wedding-garment? And he was speechless. Then the King said to the servants, Bind him hand and foot, and cast him out into the outer darkness; there shall be the weeping and the gnashing of teeth (Matt. 22: 11-13).

Shall not this be the fate of those who "enter not by the door into the sheep fold," but like thieves and robbers try to climb up some other way? For, "Not every one that saith unto me, Lord, Lord, shall enter into the kingdom of heaven; but he that doeth the will of my Father who is in heaven." (Matt. 7: 21).

4. TO BE "ADDED TO THE LORD" MEANS TO BE "ADDED TO THE CHURCH." In Acts 2: 47 we read, "The Lord added to them day by day those that were saved," but in Acts 5: 14 the expression is, "Believers were the more added to the Lord." The two expressions mean the same thing, because to receive Christ is to receive also those whom He sends. "He that receiveth you receiveth me, and he that receiveth me receiveth him that sent me" (Matt. 10: 40). This does not mean that hypocrites in the church shall be saved, for, "the hope of the godless man shall perish" (Job 8: 13); nor does it mean that those converted and dying without opportunity to unite with the church shall be lost, for "if the readiness is there, it is acceptable according as a man hath and not according as he hath not" (2 Cor. 8: 12); but it does mean that to accept Christ we must accept the church also, for He is the "head over all things to the church which is his body" (Eph. 1: 22). Therefore, "in one Spirit were we all baptized into one body" (1 Cor. 12: 13), the body of Christ, the church,

and "as many of you as were baptized into Christ did put on Christ" (Gal. 3: 27). If this makes it appear that water baptism and church membership is necessary to the salvation of those able to receive it, remember that Jesus himself said, "Except one be born of water and the Spirit he cannot enter into the kingdom of God" (John 3: 5). Let those who will trifle with His words, but let us remember that He says, "The word that I spake, the same shall judge him in the last day" (John 12: 48).

5. TO REJECT THE CHURCH IS TO REJECT CHRIST ALSO. He said, "He that rejecteth you rejecteth me." However justly some things may be said in criticism of some church members, the church as a whole is the divine organization which bears the saving Gospel to the world. It is the body of Christ and His life is in the body, not floating around loose. He is "the Savior of the body" (Eph. 5: 23). How then will they receive life who refuse to be members of the body? And this life means health. The life that Jesus gives is not tainted or diseased. It is divine. It is the fountain of perpetual youth for which men sought in ages past. To those who receive it there comes a new light in the sky, a new beauty in the world, a new hope in the heart, a new ambition in the life, a new warmth in the hand, a new vigor to the feet, a new message to the lips, a new vision of duty and a new knowledge of divine love. And this is life eternal.

II. Benefits of Church Membership.

God's laws are all for man's good. To obey them is to live and be blessed; to disobey them is to perish. Since God commands church membership there must be resulting benefits which only the obedient may receive. What are they?

1. THE CHURCH PROVIDES SPIRITUAL FOOD. In the beautiful parable of the Good Shepherd, Jesus says of his own, that they shall go in and go out, and shall find pasture" (John 10: 9). Every species of life must have its special kind of food. So, spiritual people must have spiritual food. They cannot thrive on the silly and sinful stuff that the world feeds upon any more than a man can live on poison. We go to church worn by the cares of the week, and sometimes are sore discouraged, but in the church comes new inspiration and strength. The Word of God, the prayer and praise and fellowship, together afford a feast to the soul, and the thoughts of the week are better because of it. Here is a part of the menu of this spiritual feast in the church:

MILK.

Long for the spiritual milk which is without guile, that ye may grow thereby unto salvation (1 Peter 2: 2).

WATER.

Whosoever drinketh of the water that I shall give him shall never thirst; but the water that I shall give him shall become in him a well of water springing up unto eternal life (John 4: 14).

BREAD.

I am the bread of life: he that cometh to me shall not hunger (John 6: 35).

HONEY.

The ordinances of Jehovah are true, and righteous altogether. More to be desired are they than gold, yea, than much fine gold; sweeter also than honey and the droppings of the honeycomb. (Psa. 19: 9, 10).

He would feed them also with the finest of the wheat; and with honey out of the rock would I satisfy thee (Psa. 81: 16).

MEAT.

My meat is to do the will of him that sent me (John 4: 34).

The kingdom of God is not eating and drinking, but righteousnessand peace and joy in the Holy Spirit (Rom. 14: 17).

FRUIT.

He that reapeth receiveth wages, and gathereth fruit unto life eternal (John 4: 36).

The fruit of the Spirit is love, joy, peace, longsuffering, kindness, goodness, meekness, self-control; against such there is no law (Gal. 5: 22).

In the church is food for faith, and faith "is the victory that overcometh the world" (1 John 5: 4). In the church is food for hope, "which we have as an anchor of the soul, a hope both sure and steadfast" (Heb. 6: 19). In the church is food for love, and "God is love." "He that abideth in love abideth in God," but "Hereby we know that we love the children of God, when we love God and do his commandments" (1 John 5: 2).

2. THE CHURCH AFFORDS PROTECTION. The Good Shepherd who "layeth down his life for the sheep" will not suffer them to be harmed while they abide with him. He said, "My Father * * * is greater than all; and no one is able to snatch them out of the Father's hand" (John 10: 29). The very fact of being known as a Christian is a protection from temptation. The out and out, consistent church member is not invited to drink and dance and gamble and do a hundred other sinful things that the man of the world is invited to do. Even sinners respect the person who lives for Christ, but the one who refuses to do so opens the gate for the enemy of man-soul to come with all the fiery darts of sin. Who is so strong that he can afford to risk the loss of that protection which the church affords?

3. THE CHURCH AFFORDS SPIRITUAL FELLOWSHIP. Social beings crave companionship, but "Evil companionships corrupt good morals" (1 Cor. 15: 33). It is essential to spiritual life that the environment be helpful rather than harmful. The church affords an atmosphere in which the spiritual graces can flourish. It counteracts the evil that

must be met in the world. With all its weak members the church is still the best social group in the world. The very name church (Gr. *ecclesia*) means "called out," and they who are thus set apart are called "saints," which means "the holy." In the church we can say, "truly our fellowship is with the Father and with his Son Jesus Christ" (1 John 1: 3).

4. THE CHURCH PROVIDES SPIRITUAL EXERCISE. Its members are exhorted, "Exercise thyself unto godliness" (1 Tim. 4: 7). Without exercise life weakens and dies out. Any organ unused degenerates. Worldly people lose their spiritual faculties because they fail to use them; but church workers develop them by use. Have you ability to sing? The church calls you to exhort one another with "psalms and hymns and spiritual songs" (Eph. 5: 19). Can you preach the Gospel? The church bids you, "make disciples of all the nations" (Matt. 28: 19). Have you business ability? The church calls you to be "an overseer over the house of God," that all things may be done "decently and in order." Are you skillful in helping the afflicted? The church bids you "heal the sick" (Luke 10: 18) and "relieve the afflicted" (1 Tim. 5: 10). Whatever be your genius, the church teaches you to regard it as the gift of God (1 Cor. 12), and bids you consecrate it to His service. "Moreover, it is required in stewards, that a man be found faithful" (1 Cor. 4: 2).

5. THE CHURCH GIVES SPIRITUAL GUIDANCE. In this world of complex relations and manifold temptations we sorely need light on life's duties. This needed guidance the church affords; not by laws to cover every detail of life, not by priests to act as consciences and brains for us, but by the Word of God which is a lamp to our feet and a light to our pathway (Psa. 119: 105), by the Spirit of God, "whose anointing teacheth you concerning all things" (1 John 2: 27)

and by fellowship with the great Head of the church who "also suffered for you, leaving you an example, that ye should follow his steps" (1 Pet. 2: 21).

It is easy to rail at the church,—any fool can do that—but it is not so easy to provide something to take the place of it. One time Colonel Ingersoll and Henry Ward Beecher were together at a social gathering, and Mr. Ingersoll persisted in trying to argue with Mr. Beecher, until the latter said, "Mr. Ingersoll, I saw a horrible thing the other day. I was going down the street when I met a poor decrepit man hobbling along with a crutch under each arm, and a big, burly fellow came rushing along and knocked the crutches out from under him and left him lying helpless, without so much as looking back." Mr. Ingersoll said, "The brute! the brute!" but Mr. Beecher said, "Thou art the man! Here is poor, weak humanity, struggling along as best it can with the crutch of the Bible under one arm and the church under the other, and you strong son of a minister, would take them both away and give nothing upon which to lean in return."

Those who reject the church do more than that. They are careful to remain in a land which is civilized because of the influence of the church, yet do nothing to show a spark of gratitude for these blessings or to pass them on to the heathen or to posterity. The church with its Gospel is transforming the world, but they are content to stand by and enjoy the benefits while they rail at the workers who provide them. They know not what they do. The unconverted heart fails to understand the love of God or the motives of duty or gratitude. It is selfish and sinful and lost.

But it would make a great difference if the world could or would come to the church's point of view. The work of the church would appear in a different light. There was a man riding on a sleeping car who was annoyed by the

The Church

crying of a child. Finally he called out gruffly, "Why does not the mother of that child take care of it?" But it was a man's voice that replied, "My friend, the mother of that child is in a pine box in the baggage car, and I am doing the best I can for the poor little thing." When he heard this it was not long until the gruff man humbly apologized and he himself was carrying the motherless child, while the poor, tired, bereaved father was trying to get a little rest. If only the world would understand the church, instead of criticising it because of its weak members, it would join loving hands in trying to lift up the fallen, save the lost and bring back to God his wandering children. The church would not appear as a social club trying to get members for the sake of their support, but as an angel of God among men. Behold her now, as with one hand she holds aloft the light of truth and lights men to the city of God; and with the other hand she bears the healing ointment with which to mollify the wounds of these who have fallen among the thieves, the sins of this world. Ah, she keeps close to the side of him who said,

The Spirit of the Lord is upon me, Because he hath anointed me to preach the Gospel to the poor: He hath sent me to proclaim release to the captives, and recovering of sight to the blind, . . . to proclaim the acceptable year of the Lord (Luke 4: 18).

And with Him, the Son of God, the church, the white angel of the world, the bride to be, is calling out the people who have ears to hear and eyes to see and hearts to feel the love of God, and who will respond to the invitation to life eternal:

The Spirit and the bride say, Come. And he that heareth, let him say, Come. And he that is athirst, let him come: he that will let him take the water of life freely (Rev. 22: 17).

III. The Value of the Ordinances.

On most of the fundamental theological doctrines, the various evangelical churches are united, or at least there is liberty of conscience as to differences. The chief cause of division in organization is the matter of the ordinances. Because they are practiced outwardly there is need of uniformity. On this account there is a tendency to find excuse to do away with them altogether, and invite all to unite in the rest of the Gospel.

That, however, is a false unity, which must be purchased by disregard of God's commands. A true church of Christ must win adherents by its loyalty to Him, not by disloyalty. God does not give commands arbitrarily. When He bids us do something it is for our good (cf. Deut. 10: 13; John 13: 17). The ordinances of the church have an inherent value which makes them worth while, even if they had not the divine command back of them. God's word is wisdom. What, then, is the value of the ordinances, that we should be so conscientious in observing them?

1. THE ORDINANCES OF THE CHURCH AFFORD A TEST OF OBEDIENCE. "If a man love me he will keep my word" (John 14: 23). Christian experience is enriched and Christian character is strengthened by public tests, while by them false professors of Christianity are revealed and excluded.

2. THEY ARE A TESTIMONY OF FAITH. "Show me thy faith without thy works and I will show thee my faith by my works" (Jas. 2: 18). The observance of the ordinances puts one upon public record, and thus brings into play added motives for faithfulness. "I have washed my robes, how shall I defile them again?"

3. THEY ARE A WITNESS OF HOPE. "Ye proclaim the Lord's death till he come" (1 Cor. 11: 26). In our observance of these memorials we express our hope of meet-

ing again with Him who commanded them, "which hope we have as an anchor of the soul, sure and steadfast" (Heb. 6: 19).

4. THEY ARE A PROOF OF LOVE. "Hereby we know that we love the children of God, when we love God and do His commandments" (1 John 5: 2). Jesus repeatedly mentions obedience as proof of love to Him. How then shall we plead that we love Him if we seek excuse to dispense with what He commanded?

5. THEY ARE A MEMORIAL OF CHRIST. "This do in remembrance of me" (Luke 22: 19). They put in permanent and visible form a remembrance of the loving ministry, and sinless life, and vicarious death of our Lord, with all that that means for the world.

6. THEY ARE A BOND OF FELLOWSHIP. "Ye cannot partake of the table of the Lord and the table of demons" (1 Cor. 12: 12; 10: 18). Once baptized into Christ, we become united with the other members of his body. Once we sit together at the Lord's table, we are pledged to one another and may not go back to the table of sin. As we are united in these outward symbols, we are also bound together by the bonds of Christian love. The annual feasts of the Jews, with all their accompanying rites, were mighty forces to bind them together as a nation; and likewise the ordinances of the church bind the members together with bonds of the common hope and truth they represent.

7. THEY ARE A MEANS OF GRACE. "He that eateth my flesh and drinketh my blood abideth in me, and I in him" (John 6: 53-63; 1 Cor. 11: 30). The best proof of this is found in the fact that those who most faithfully observe them are richest in the virtues which they teach. The Brethren, for example, are often ridiculed for their manner of observing the ordinances, but the world agrees that they stand for sterling integrity of character, for peaceableness and hu-

mility, and for simple Christian living, such as any one might covet. They have the reward of their faithfulness, formal though it may be in many cases, in the fruit of Christian character.

8. THE ORDINANCES ARE SYMBOLS OF CERTAIN FUNDAMENTAL TRUTHS. Their full significance will be discussed later. See 1 Cor. 10: 16-18; John 13: 8; Rom. 6: 3-6. So important are these truths that our Lord thought it necessary to teach them in this form. Who then are we, that we should make our wisdom superior to His and say that they are not worth retaining?

9. THEY ARE A MEANS OF PRESERVING THE TRUTH. They are fixed in form and thus are unchanged in their teaching. See Rom. 6: 17; Matt. 9: 17; cf. Heb. 8: 5. As the bottles preserve the wine from wasting, so the ordinances preserve the truths they contain. And as the shell shows the shape of the kernel, so these symbols show the truth they represent. Therefore, to change the manner of observing the ordinances is to destroy to that extent their teaching by making it misleading. It were better to have no symbol than to have a misleading symbol. Verbal statements of truths may in time be lost or variously interpreted, but the unchanging symbol remains as a witness to the original truth taught. To embody truth in symbols is of the greatest value, but the symbol must be preserved unchanged.

10. THE ORDINANCES ARE AN AID TO THE UNDERSTANDING. Compare 1 Pet. 3: 21; John 13: 12-14; 1 Cor. 11: 29. All teachers recognize the value of pictures and actions in teaching. It is the principle of apprenticeship to learn by doing. The world has recognized its value and used it for ages. It is the earliest form of teaching. It is the common language of the world. It always has been and always will be the aid of the teacher of children, and of older people as well. It is used in every school in the world. It is the

inductive method of going from the known to the unknown, the method universally recognized by educators to-day as the true method of education. We must necessarily learn by this method. To illustrate: A little boy saw a turtle for the first time, and not knowing what to call it, he associated it with the nearest thing like it that he knew and called it a "big bug." Now God has taken some of the things that were familiar to men and has lifted them up into a higher realm, giving them a new meaning, and using them as connecting links to spiritual things. Thus the rainbow became a symbol of his unfailing promise. Circumcision, a rite practiced by many ancient nations, was made a seal of the covenant whereby the life was given to God. Sacrifice was made to signify vicarious atonement and point to the coming Savior of the world. So baptism, a rite familiar to Jews in Jesus' day, was given a new meaning for the church. Feet-washing, a custom common to eastern peoples, was lifted up and made a sacred symbol of the divine law of service and the spiritual cleansing necessary in preparation for it. The love-feast takes the world-wide custom of feasting together as a mark of hospitality and makes it a feast of love distinctively Christian. The eucharist likewise uses the natural to lead us into the spiritual, that thus we may learn the mystery of salvation by the blood of Christ and our union with Him. The value of these ordinances as means of divine education cannot well be overestimated. Certainly they should not be discarded. Even the secret societies employ various forms of initiation in order to impress indelibly the principles of the order. Abstract truths are hard for some to understand, but the lessons of the ordinances are so clear that even a child can see them. Thus they help to adapt the Gospel to all.

11. THEY STRENGTHEN THE MEMORY. Jesus said, "This do in remembrance of me" (Luke 22: 19). The ordinances

aid the memory by the accumulation of impressions. They come to the citadel of the soul through all the gates of the five senses—hearing, seeing, tasting, smelling, touching, and all of them are strengthened by action. There was formerly in Switzerland the custom of marking boundaries and then whipping a child at the marks, and ever after in case of dispute accepting the testimony of the child as expert evidence. The theory was that the child would not easily forget the spot. Thus the lessons taught by the ordinances, while not painful, yet are vividly impressed upon the memory. We may forget verbal teaching, but no one who ever understandingly goes through the ordinances will ever forget them or the lessons they teach.

12. THEY AROUSE THE EMOTIONS. "If ye know these things HAPPY are ye if ye do them" (John 13: 17 A. V.). It is a law of the mind that a feeling grows by expression. The truths taught by the ordinances, the virtues inculcated, the emotions aroused, are all intensified by participation. And inasmuch as life is influenced more by the emotions than by the reason or anything else, it is of the greatest importance that these means of arousing right emotions be retained in the church.

13. THEY REENFORCE THE WILL. "The bread which we break, is it not a communion of the body of Christ" (1 Cor. 10: 16)? Whatever touches the understanding or the emotions or the memory, affects the will. Poor, weak humanity needs to have the will to do right made as strong as possible, and to this end the ordinances are a great help. Who has ever sat at the Lord's table without being moved to resolve more strongly than ever to live worthy of the high calling of God in Christ Jesus? Who has ever come from the baptismal grave without resolving to show forth the new life received by being born from above? Who has stooped to wash his brother's feet without praying that his

own heart might be cleansed? These repeated and reënforced resolves give momentum to the decisions of the will in the trials of daily life. Let the ordinances have their blessed part.

14. THEY HOLD THE LIFE TO GOD. "As many of you as were baptized into Christ did put on Christ" (Gal. 3: 27; 1 Cor. 11: 25, 26). Life eternal comes through touch with God (John 17: 3) and at no time is this touch more real and impressive than when we observe the sacred symbols which He gave for the very purpose of revealing Himself to us more fully and of holding us to Him more closely. The time of communion is the time for reconsecration. All the other benefits of the ordinances merge into this reaction upon conduct which makes the disciple become as his Master.

15. THE ORDINANCES ARE A SEAL OR PLEDGE OF THE PROMISES CONTAINED IN THEM. Thus Abraham received circumcision as "a seal of the righteousness of the faith that he had while he was in uncircumcision; that he might be the father of all them that believe * * * for not through the law was the promise to Abraham or to his seed that he should be heir of the world, but through the righteousness of faith" (Rom. 4: 11-13). Thus also baptism is "not the putting away of the filth of the flesh, but the interrogation of a good conscience toward God" (1 Pet. 3: 21), and "the firm foundation of God standeth, having this seal, The Lord knoweth them that are his: and, Let every one that nameth the name of the Lord depart from unrighteousness" (2 Tim. 2: 19).

A seal is intended to keep safe the thing that is sealed, so the ordinances fortify us against the evils of the world. The very word "communion" in the Latin means "a fortifying together." A seal also shows the owner of the object sealed. So the observance of the ordinances is an outward sign of obedience, and if their lessons be learned there will also be the inward holiness which only God may fully see, as the mark of true children of the kingdom. Open obedience to Christ enables one to say with Paul, "Henceforth let no man trouble me; for I bear branded on my body the marks of Jesus" (Gal. 6: 17).

16. LASTLY, THE ORDINANCES ARE TYPES WHICH WILL FIND THEIR ANTITYPE IN THE KINGDOM OF GOD. "For Christ entered not into a holy place made with hands, LIKE IN PATTERN TO THE TRUE; but into heaven itself, now to appear before the face of God for us" (Heb. 9: 24). The new life we begin here will find its full development in heaven itself (Rev. 22: 1, 2). The cleansing for service we seek here will find its fulfillment in the day when, without spot or blemish, we shall serve in the beautiful city of God (Rev. 19: 8; 22: 3). The fellowship we enjoy here, as, without caste of any kind, we sit about the Lord's table, is but a foretaste of the marriage supper of the Lamb (Rev. 19: 9). And the memorials of His sufferings here, continually point us forward to the time when He shall again partake with us in the eternal kingdom of the redeemed (Luke 22: 16-18). Then we shall no longer need the church with its temple (Rev. 21: 22), its officers or its symbols; for faith will have become sight, our weakness will have become strength, our hope will have become lost in fruition, and "God may be all in all" (1 Cor. 15: 28).

IV. Symbols in the Old Testament.

It is a well-known scientific truth that each individual in his development in a general way recapitulates the history of the race. Without pressing the theory to an extreme, we may at least learn something of how to teach individuals at different stages of their growth by noting how God taught the chosen race at that corresponding stage.

In Old Testament times we find many symbols because

The Church

the race was in comparative infancy and needed more of such helps to the understanding of spiritual truths, and therefore more was given. In the patriarchal age we have examples of symbols in the flaming sword (Gen. 3: 24), the bow in the cloud (Gen. 9: 13) and in the rite of circumcision (Gen. 15). Significance was also given to visions and dreams. The race was in the kindergarten of morals. In the dispensation of the law, the Hebrews had reached a grade corresponding to that of charts, maps and manual training in school. There were many symbols to teach the many new truths which were revealed concerning God and duties toward God and men.

Examples:

1. God taught the people of His *power* by signs and wonders (Ex. 19: 16; Deut. 4: 7-14; Job 25: 14; Psa. 111: 6) and this resulted in *trust* (Psa. 20: 7).

2. He taught His *holiness* by such symbols as the burning bush (Ex. 3: 2), the preparation of the people to appear before Him by washing (Ex. 19: 11, 15), the separation of the clean and unclean (Gen. 7: 2; Lev. 11: 46, 47). The result of this was *righteousness* on the part of the people (Lev. 11: 44).

3. He taught His *justice* by symbolical acts of justice (Num 16: 30; Num 11, etc.). This brought forth *obedience* (Josh. 5: 6).

4. He taught His *mercy* by the mercy seat of the ark (Ex. 25: 17-22; 1 Chron. 28: 11). This was to teach the people also to be *merciful* (Luke 6: 36).

5. To teach God's *ownership* of all (Deut. 10: 14) a part (the tithe) was made holy to Him. The *Sabbath* (Ex. 20: 12, 20; Deut. 5: 15; Lev. 16: 31) and the *tithe* (Lev. 27: 30, 32; Num. 18: 26; Luke 11: 42) were symbols.

6. Vicarious *atonement* was taught by the offering of

blood (Lev. 16: 8-14; Ex. 30: 10) which was a symbol of the life.

7. *Cleansing* was also taught by means of various ablutions (Lev. 15: 5, 8, 11, 13, 21, 27; 16: 26, 28; 17: 15, 16).

Other examples might be given. The whole system of worship was ritualistic, that is, a system of teaching by means of symbols. The rites and ceremonies were of religious significance. They were (1) memorials of past events, (2) symbols of truths for the time then present, and (3) types which pointed to their fulfillment in the future. For this reason Moses was cautioned to be careful in the construction of the tabernacle. " See," said God, " that thou make all things according to the pattern that was showed thee in the mount " (Heb. 8: 5). To have deviated from the divine pattern would have destroyed its power to teach the truths intended. That is why the sin of Nadab and Abihu (Lev. 10) was so serious. The offering of strange fire, not taken from the altar, was a failure to recognize the truth of the atonement by blood for which the altar stood. Likewise the touching of the ark by Uzzah (2 Sam. 6) was a failure to recognize the holiness of God, whose presence was represented by the ark. If these men died because they dared to ignore the symbolism of the things of the old covenant, who are we that any of us should lightly alter the forms which have been set as sacred symbols in the church of God?

V. The Relation of the Old Testament to the New.

It will help us to understand the ordinances of the Gospel to trace their relation to the ordinances of the Old Testament. God's kingdom grows like the growing of a flower. There is the bud, then the blossom and then the fruit or ripened seed, which produces another plant with buds and flowers and fruit. So each dispensation has borne its fruit and passed away to give place to a new cycle, with better things.

1. THE LAW PREPARED THE WAY FOR THE GOSPEL. We read in Gal. 3: 24, 25 that "the law is become our tutor to bring us unto Christ." The word for schoolmaster is *pedagogos* (whence pedagog) and means literally, a " leader of children." The Greek pedagog was not the teacher, but a man who led the children to the teacher. So the law leads the way to Christ. It reveals our shortcomings and awakens a desire for righteousness, which only Christ can satisfy.

The book of Hebrews was written to show the relation of the old covenant to the new, and nothing would be more profitable at this point than to read that book carefully two or three times and write down the points the author makes. It will be seen that in speaking to us in these last days by His Son (Heb. 1) God has given us something that is final, and far superior to the law with its ceremonies.

2. THE LAW WAS A " SHADOW OF GOOD THINGS TO COME " (Heb. 10: 1; Col. 2: 14-17). The institutions of the law were not simply memorials of past events and symbols of truths for present guidance, but they pointed forward to their antitypes in the kingdom of God. Follow the word " better " through the book of Hebrews as the key word of the book and this truth will be made clear. Seven of the better things of the new covenant are thus pointed out, as follows:

(1) A *" better hope"* (ch. 7: 19). Instead of the hope of salvation by the law " which made nothing perfect," we have " hope of eternal life, which God, who cannot lie, promised before times eternal " (Titus 1: 2), and " it is not yet made manifest what we shall be. We know that, if he shall be manifested, we shall be like him; for we shall see him even as he is " (1 John 3: 2).

(2) A *"better covenant"* (ch. 8:6). The new covenant is better because it is made, not in the blood of beasts and of birds, but in the blood of Christ (Heb. 9; 1 Cor. 5:7); because its law is not written on tables of stone, but on the fleshly tables of the heart (2 Cor. 3:3; Heb. 8:1-13); because its seal is not the circumcision of the flesh, but the circumcision of the heart (Col. 2:11), and its members are not children of Abraham by blood, but by faith (Gal. 3:7, 27, 29). Under it we have, not the righteousness of the law, but the righteousness of Christ received by faith (Philpp. 3:9). Instead of guidance by signs (Ex. 28:30; Num. 19:21; 1 Sam. 28:6) we have the guidance of the Holy Spirit (1 John 2:27) and instead of a standard adapted to the time cf. Matt. 19:8; Heb. 7:19) we have the absolutely perfect standard in Christ (1 Pet. 2:21-24).

(3) A *"better High Priest"* (ch. 7). The new covenant has a better priest in Jesus because he is without sin (ch. 7:26), without change (ch. 13:8), without death (ch. 7:24, 25), and he appears, not in "a holy place made with hands, but in heaven itself" (ch. 9:24), where "he ever liveth to make intercession for us" (ch. 7:25), and, "to them that look for him shall he appear a second time without sin unto salvation" (ch. 9:28).

(4) *"Better sacrifices"* (ch. 9:23) because the old were made with birds and beasts, but the new is the Son of God, offered, not every year, but once for all (ch. 9:12-25). And believers are "crucified with Christ" (Gal. 2:20) that in offering themselves as a "living sacrifice" (Rom. 12:1), they may be "dead unto sin and alive unto God" (Rom. 6:11), and by open confession (Heb. 13:15) are marked as belonging to God (2 Tim. 2:19).

(5) A *"better country"* (ch. 11:16), because it is a heavenly country rather than one of earth, the new Jerusalem instead of the old (ch. 12:18-25).

(6) A *"better resurrection"* (ch. 11: 35), because it is a deliverance, not from temporal trials only, but deliverance from the eternal bondage of sin (Rom. 8: 2); a resurrection, not to the sinful pleasures of this life, but to joys that are from above (Col. 3: 1).

(7) *"Some better thing"* (ch. 11: 40). "God having provided some better thing concerning us, that apart from us they should not be made perfect." The promise which the saints of old received, but have not yet possessed, must be the spiritual fulfillment of their hopes in the kingdom of God. "When Jesus comes with all his saints" (1 Thess. 4: 14; Jude 14), then shall they with us walk in the light of the perfect day and "without us shall not be made perfect."

Even those institutions which are not for one dispensation but for all, Jesus unfolds in their eternal significance. Thus He taught the true purpose of the sabbath as based upon the needs of man (Mark. 3: 4; 2: 26, 27), and He provides the "heavenly rest" of which the Sabbath was a type (Heb. 9: 4; Matt. 11: 28-30). The tithe He shows "ought" to be paid (Matt. 23: 23), but not without the consecration of all (Luke 14: 33). Marriage He restores to its original purpose, making husband and wife one flesh (Matt. 19: 3-9) and the union indissoluble, because typical of the eternal union of Christ and the church (Eph. 5: 24-33; Rev. 19: 7-9).

3. THE OLD COVENANT IS FULFILLED AND DONE AWAY IN CHRIST. "Christ is the end of the law unto righteousness to every one that believeth" (Rom. 10: 4). He said, "One jot or one tittle shall in no wise pass away from the law, till all things be accomplished" (Matt. 5: 18), but now since all is fulfilled in Him, the law has passed. The prophet of whom Moses spoke (Deut. 18: 15) has come and the voice from heaven declared, "This is my Son, my chosen:

hear ye him" (Luke 9: 35). The blood of Jesus Christ has been shed for the sin of the world, therefore, "of how much sorer punishment, think ye, shall he be judged worthy, who hath trodden under foot the Son of God, and hath counted the blood of the covenant wherewith he was sanctified an unholy thing, and hath done despite unto the Spirit of grace?" (Heb. 10: 29). He was clothed with authority to institute new ordinances (Matt. 28: 18; John 13: 1-3) and is "Head over all things to the church, which is his body, the fulness of him that filleth all in all" Eph. 1: 22, 23).

Even the people under the old covenant were taught to look forward to the coming of the Christ, and not only did their ceremonies and institutions point to Him, but the inspired prophets in their most exalted moments spoke of Him in words that were as celestial shafts of light pointing afar to Calvary.

Now those things that were fulfilled in Christ have been done away that they might give place to the better things of the new covenant. The "gifts and sacrifices" with "meats and drinks and divers washings" are called "carnal ordinances imposed until a time of reformation" (Heb. 9: 10). Even circumcision was declared to be no longer binding (Acts 15) while Paul declares, "Let no man therefore judge you in meat, or in drink, or in respect of a feast day or a new moon or a sabbath day: which are a shadow of the things to come; but the body is Christ's" (Col. 2: 16, 17). To go back to the law and observe these types as ordinances for the present would be to deny their fulfillment in Christ and thus deny Christ, a fact which they ignore who would fasten the Jewish Sabbath upon Christians. "For freedom did Christ set us free: stand fast therefore, and be not entangled again in a yoke of bondage" (Gal. 5: 1-4).

4. THE NEW COVENANT IS BUT A FURTHER UNFOLDING OF GOD'S REVELATION OF HIMSELF. It is the bud opened into the flower. It is the substance of which the former things were the shadow (Heb. 10: 1). It is the fulfillment of the types and the prophecies, which were all a part of the one great river of water of life that flows with increasing volume down the ages (Ezek. 47).

If we have Christ as King and Priest, Israel had Moses, who was the lawgiver from God for them, and Aaron who was their priest. If we have the kingdom of God, they had the " righteous remnant " (Rom. 9: 27), the true Israel composed of the faithful. If we have the church, they had also the " church in the wilderness " (Acts 7: 38). If we are baptized unto Christ, they were " baptized unto Moses " (1 Cor. 10: 2), and if we receive life through Him, they also " drank of a spiritual rock that followed them: and that rock was Christ " (1 Cor. 10: 4). If they sinned, " these things happened unto them by way of example; and they were written for our admonition, upon whom the ends of the age are come " (1 Cor. 10: 11). Let us therefore beware lest we " fall after the same example of disobedience " (Heb. 4: 11).

5. THE NEW COVENANT HAS ORDINANCES AS WELL AS THE OLD. While Christ is the final Mediator between God and men, yet this is not the final dispensation. The kingdom which He founded is a growing kingdom, and its fullness will not be attained until the next dispensation when Christ shall come again. Therefore, just as the old covenant had its tabernacle with its forms, so the new covenant has the church with its ordinances. The ninth chapter of Hebrews explains this point. We read (v. 1), " Even the first covenant had also ordinances of divine service and a worldly sanctuary," thus implying that the second covenant has also. After naming the things in the tabernacle the author

says (v. 5), " of which things we cannot now speak particularly," showing that they each had their typical significance. In verse 8, he says expressly, " the Holy Spirit signifying that the way into the holiest of all was not made manifest while the first tabernacle is yet standing." If we can speak of the *first* tabernacle we must also have a second. In verse 9 (R. V.) these things are called a " figure for the time present," and therefore they are types of similar things in the second tabernacle, the church.

The eleventh verse reads, " But Christ being come an high priest of good things to come, by a greater and more perfect tabernacle, not made with hands, that is to say, not of this creation." The new tabernacle is the church, which is called the body of Christ (Eph. 1: 22, 23), and God's house, "But Christ as a son over his own house; whose house we are " (Heb. 3: 6). While therefore Christ has passed on into heaven (Heb. 9: 24) He is present by His Spirit (Matt. 28: 20) and is cleansing His temple, the church, which is preparing as a bride for her husband (Eph. 5: 25-33) and He is coming again to receive His bride (Heb. 9: 28) and to reign in His eternal kingdom.

6. THE OLD TABERNACLE WAS A TYPE OF THE NEW. In speaking of the tabernacle the inspired writers say that the things pertaining to it were a " figure for the time present " (Heb. 9: 9) and " copies of the things in the heavens " (that is, in the kingdom of heaven, of which the church is the outward, organized form); that they are " like in pattern to the true "(v. 24), and " a shadow of the good things to come " (ch. 10: 1). The light is Christ and the " good things to come " are the ordinances of His tabernacle, the church, and Christ shining through them is seen in the " shadows " thrown through the centuries of the old covenant. If we say that the ordinances of the old tabernacle were types of things in heaven above and not of

the church, we make the old better than the new. If the old represented heavenly things, much more do the new, and the two tabernacles must agree.

We can now understand why Bazaleel, the architect of the tabernacle, was inspired by the Spirit of God, (Ex. 31: 1-5) and was not as the ordinary builder of an ordinary house. As Dr. Torrey says, "There is nothing in the Bible that is more inspired than the tabernacle." We can also see why Moses was so particularly charged to make everything, furniture as well as tabernacle, according to the pattern showed in the mount (Ex. 25: 9). A change in the least particular would have made an error for the ages.

It is possible to press the typical significance of the tabernacle too far, but we are certainly safe in going as far as the Scriptures themselves go. The following parallel shows the features of the tabernacle which in Heb. 9: 1-9 are called "a figure for the time present," and their antitypes in the church.

OLD COVENANT TYPE.
1. The altar of Sacrifice Heb. 13: 10-13; Ex. 27: 1-9.
2. The laver. Ex. 30: 17-19.
3. Table of shewbread. Heb. 9: 2; Ex. 25: 23-30.
4. The pot of manna. Heb. 9: 4.
5. The golden candlestick. Heb. 9: 2; Ex. 25: 31-40.
6. The altar of incense. Heb. 9:4; Ex. 30: 1-10.

NEW COVENANT ANTITYPE.
1. Christ's atonement. (Heb. 13: 12) and our death with him (Rom. 12: 1).
2. Feet-washing. John 13: 1-17.
3. The Love-feast. 1 Cor. 5: 8; John 13: 34; Jude 12.
4. The cup and loaf. Luke 22: 19, 20.
5. The Holy Spirit. Zech. 4: 1-6; Acts 2.
6. Prayer. Rev. 8: 3.

7. The ark with the tables of the covenant (ten commandments). Heb. 9: 4; Ex. 25: 17-23.

7. The Gospel of Christ. Heb. 1: 1-3.

This dispensation is a step in advance of the old, and all believers are priests (1 Pet. 2: 5-9; Rev. 1: 6), and since the veil was taken away we may enter the holy of holies, while Jesus, our High Priest (Heb. 9: 24) has gone on into heaven (Heb. 9: 28). Meanwhile we must minister in the service of our tabernacle, the church, whose sacred symbols must not be altered or neglected, for they in turn point forward to the better things of the age to come. God, who planned the ages, gave them, and bids us guard them (Matt. 28: 19, 20). Let us do so.

7. THE TRUTHS REPRESENTED BY THE ORDINANCES ARE FUNDAMENTAL. If they were not they would not have been so carefully guarded. Birth, cleansing, nutrition and exercise,—these four things are fundamental to the natural life, and the corresponding laws are fundamental to the spiritual life. If then, God has embodied these vital truths in ordinances intended to teach and perpetuate them, what shall be the judgment of those who deliberately teach that they are " mere forms " and that it is of no consequence whether we observe them or not?

A man that hath set at nought Moses' laws dieth without compassion on the word of two or three witnesses: of how much sorer punishment, think ye, shall he be judged worthy, who hath trodden under foot the Son of God (Heb. 10: 28, 29)?

Jesus said, " He that shall break the least of these my commandments and shall teach men so, the same shall be called the least in the kingdom of heaven " (Matt. 5: 19).

Paul said, " I praise you that ye hold fast the traditions even as I delivered them unto you " (1 Cor. 11: 2).

The Church

John says, " Whosoever goeth onward and abideth not in the teaching of Christ, hath not God " (2 John 9).

James says, " To him therefore that knoweth to do good, and doeth it not, to him it is sin " (Jas. 4: 17).

With this, take the stern words of Heb. 10: 26. " If we sin wilfully after that we have received the knowledge of the truth, there remaineth no more sacrifice for sins."

If this seem to be a harsh fate for the disobedient remember that they have had plenty of warning.

Why call ye me Lord, Lord, and do not the things which I say (Luke 6: 46)?

Many will say to me in that day, Lord, Lord, did we not prophesy by thy name, and by thy name cast out demons, and by thy name do many mighty works? And then will I profess unto them, I never knew you: depart from me, ye that work iniquity (Matt. 7: 22, 23).

Not every one that saith unto me, Lord, Lord, shall enter into the kingdom of heaven, but he that doeth the will of my Father who is in heaven (Matt. 7: 21).

If ye love me, ye will keep my commandments. * * * He that hath my commandments and keepeth them, he it is that loveth me. * * * If a man love me he will keep my word: and my Father will love him, and we will come unto him, and make our abode with him. He that loveth me not keepeth not my words (John 14: 15, 21, 23, 24).

And this is love, that we should walk after his commandments (2 John 6).

Whatsoever things we ask we receive of him, because we keep his commandments and do the things that are pleasing in his sight (1 John 3: 22).

Hereby we know that we know him, if we keep his commandments. He that saith, I know him, and keepeth not his commandments, is a liar, and the truth is not in him; but whoso keepeth his word, in him verily hath the love of God been perfected (1 John 2: 3-5).

Know ye not, that to whom ye present yourselves as servants unto obedience, his servants ye are whom ye obey; whether of sin unto death, or of obedience unto righteousness? But thanks be to God, that, whereas ye were servants of sin, ye became obedient from the heart to that form of teaching whereunto ye were delivered (Rom. 6: 16, 17).

Bringing every thought into captivity to the obedience of Christ (2 Cor. 10: 5).

If ye know these things, blessed are ye if ye do them (John 13: 17).

Teaching them to observe all things whatsoever I have commanded you (Matt. 28: 20).

And ye are witnesses of these things; and so is the Holy Spirit, whom God hath given to them that obey him (Acts 5: 32).

We must obey God rather than men (Acts 5: 29).

The Lord Jesus shall be revealed from heaven with his mighty angels, in flaming fire taking vengeance on them that know not God, and that obey not the Gospel of our Lord Jesus Christ: who shall be punished with everlasting destruction from the presence of the Lord, and from the glory of his power: when he shall come (2 Thess. 1: 7-10).

BLESSED ARE THEY THAT WASH THEIR ROBES, THAT THEY MAY HAVE THE RIGHT TO THE TREE OF LIFE, AND MAY ENTER IN THROUGH THE GATES INTO THE CITY (Rev. 22: 14).

CHAPTER II

THREE SYMBOLS AS MEANS OF WORSHIP.

The Bible—Prayer—Praise.

* * * * * *

Search the Scriptures, because ye think that in them ye have eternal life; and these are they which bear witness of me (John 5: 39).

* * * * * *

Watch and pray, that ye enter not into temptation: the spirit indeed is willing, but the flesh is weak (Matt. 26: 41).

* * * * * *

Speaking one to another in psalms and hymns and spiritual songs, singing and making melody with your heart to the Lord (Eph. 5: 19).

THE BIBLE.

When Sir Walter Scott lay dying he said to those who stood by, "Bring me the Book." They said, "What book?" He replied "There is but one Book. Bring me the Bible." While it is true that "of the making of books there is no end," yet there is one Book which may be called THE Book because it is the story of God's revelation of Himself. As the natural man beholdeth his face in a mirror so through the printed page there shines the glory of the character of God. It is a part of the means He has taken to reveal Himself and to lead men to Himself, and as a means to that end is to be considered along with the church and its ordinances and forms of worship.

It is easier to believe in no God than to believe in an evil God. But if God is good He must love His creatures, and if He loves them He must desire their fellowship and their good. This is the supreme guarantee of revelation and immortality. If even an earthly parent, being evil, seeks in all ways to communicate with his little child, by gestures and baby talks, by smiles and cooings, attempting to translate the love of the parent into the understanding of the child, much more will our Father in heaven seek in all ways to reveal Himself to His children. But as the child learns to understand the parent only by using its senses and organs of understanding, so we must observe the means of grace that God has given and through which He speaks.

I. How God Speaks to Men.

1. GOD SPEAKS THROUGH NATURE.

The heavens declare the glory of God; and the firmament showeth his handiwork. Day unto day uttereth speech, And night unto night showeth knowledge. There is no speech nor language; Their voice is not heard (Psa. 19: 1).

It is sometimes said, Why has not God given His revelation to all the world, so that all may know of Him? The answer is, He has given His revelation to all the world, and in the universal language of nature, so that all who will may read of His wonderful wisdom and goodness and power in the works of nature about them.

For the invisible things of him since the creation of the world are clearly seen, being perceived through the things that are made, even his everlasting power and divinity; that they may be without excuse: because that, knowing God, they glorified him not as God, neither gave thanks (Rom. 1: 20, 21).

They who have eyes to see can read the message of God in the stars and in the flowers. They who have ears to hear may hear it in the songs of the birds and the voice of the thunder. But they whose hearts are blinded in sin understand none of these things. Therefore God has revealed Himself in other ways.

2. God speaks through His providence.

The goodness of God leadeth thee to repentance (Rom. 2: 4).

If a ship should be wrecked on a Labrador reef and those on board should escape through the icy water to the shore, and find there high and dry a cave with fuel and matches and food and clothing all nicely arranged, would they not say, "Some loving, thoughtful people have prepared this relief for such an hour as this"? Who would be so insane as to say, "All this is mere coincidence, the result of chance"? Just so, when we find this earth stored with everything needful for our temporal needs, and all things working together for the development of character and spiritual life, must we not also say, "This is not the work of chance, but of a Supreme Being who must be good and loving and wise"?

The Bible

But sometimes the development of character requires the rain of affliction as well as the sunshine of prosperity, and so in the good providence of God it happens that the message comes, " Hear ye the rod " (Micah 6: 9), and if we hear it aright we shall be able to testify with the psalmist, " It is good for me that I have been afflicted; That I might learn thy statutes " (Psa. 119: 71), and to believe with Paul, " Our light affliction which is for the moment, worketh for us more and more exceedingly an eternal weight of glory " (2 Cor. 4: 17). The providence of God is as a watchful parent who seeks in all ways the good of the child.

3. GOD SPEAKS THROUGH CONSCIENCE.

They show the work of the law written in their hearts, their conscience bearing witness therewith, and their thoughts one with another accusing or else excusing them (Rom. 2: 15).

Conscience is a creature of education, and hence is not an infallible guide, but it is a result of free moral agency, by which human beings perceive the right and wrong of things, and by obeying the right develop the power to perceive the right. Conscience is only a guide, but if followed faithfully will guide the life to God. If disobeyed, it may mislead and be lost, as creatures who live in the dark lose the power of sight. The world is lost, not because it has not had the Bible so much as because it has refused to follow the light it has had, until the very light within has become darkness.

4. GOD SPEAKS THROUGH PERSONAL WITNESSES.

Ye are my witnesses saith Jehovah (Isa. 43: 10).

Human language is better understood by human beings than the language of nature, because it is more definite, and is backed by human experience. Therefore the personal witness of those who have come to know God is more effective as a revelation than the universal language of nature. For this reason the prophets of all ages, who from the mountain tops of their own experience have caught glimpses of the truth of God and the goodness of God, have been as landmarks of history guiding the race in the way to God. These personal witnesses have interpreted the language of providence to the dulled consciences of those less spiritual, and have translated the leadings of the Spirit of God into the sermons which they have preached for the guidance of the people. Enoch, Noah, Abraham, Moses, David, and a host of others are as the light of the stars in the night which guide the wanderer toward the light of day.

5. GOD SPEAKS THROUGH HIS SON JESUS CHRIST.

God, having of old time spoken unto the fathers in the prophets by divers portions and in divers manners, hath at the end of these days spoken to us in his Son (Heb. 1: 1).

The supreme personal witness of God has been borne by Jesus Christ. Prophets before Him had caught visions of light from beneath, but he was the light itself come into the world from above. Others had taught fragments of truth, but he was the truth incarnate in life. Others had spoken of the attributes of divinity, but now we see "the light of the knowledge of the glory of God in the face of Jesus Christ" (2 Cor. 4: 6).

A missionary to San Domingo, in order to bring the slaves of that island to Christ, sold himself as a slave that he might work among them on equality and by his Christian spirit and teaching show them the way of life. He became incarnate in their sort of life and glorified it by the higher life which he knew. Even so Jesus came into the life of this world with the spirit and knowledge of the heaven above, and thus reveals to us the heavenly life. No one else has ever done this, and therefore He could say, " I am the way, the truth and the life: no man cometh unto the Father, but by me" (John 14: 6).

6. GOD SPEAKS THROUGH HIS SPIRIT.

And he, when he is come, will convict the world in respect of sin, and of righteousness and of judgment: of sin, because they believe not on me; of righteousness, because I go to the Father, and ye behold me no more; of judgment, because the prince of this world hath been judged (John 16: 8-11).

The Spirit of God has always been in the world striving to lead men into truth and right, but since the coming of Christ He is able to work with special power, because He can use the revelation of Jesus in leading men to God. He convicts of sin because Jesus in overcoming sin gave an example of the sinless or divine life, and they who believe not on Him will not believe in anything like Him divine and true. Therefore unbelief or rejection of Jesus is the greatest sin of the world, and they who boast of their honesty and other virtues while refusing to be Christians are worse off than the publicans and harlots who repent and receive Him. The Holy Spirit convicts of righteousness, because Jesus went to the Father and was accepted of Him. The Spirit urges this acceptance as proof of His divinity and consequent claims upon the world. He convicts the world of judgment, because in overcoming Satan Jesus judges all sinners. Because He overcame we also may overcome, and therefore if we remain in sin we are without excuse. And the sin against the Holy Spirit is the "sin unto death" (1 John 5: 16) for which there is no forgiveness (Mark 3: 29), because when He is wilfully disobeyed the very organ of moral discernment is destroyed. He it is who interprets to us the voice of nature and of revelation, and when He is gone we may no more understand the things of God than a cow can receive a college education. He who puts out his eyes, how shall he longer see? He who cuts out his heart, how shall he longer live? And he who destroys his power to perceive the divine leading, how shall he be divinely led? And if the very light within become darkness "How great is the darkness" (Matt. 6: 23). This condition is not the result of a single act, but of repeated and wilful sin (Heb. 10: 26-30). Such repeated rejection brings one to the condition of those Jews who at first *would* not believe in spite of the many miracles, and finally "*could* not believe" because their eyes were blinded and their hearts were hardened (John 12: 37-40). When God speaks to us by His Holy Spirit it is a fearful thing to reject that message.

7. GOD SPEAKS THROUGH THE BIBLE.

Every scripture inspired of God is also profitable for teaching, for reproof, for correction, for instruction which is in righteousness; that the man of God may be complete, furnished completely unto every good work (2 Tim. 3: 16).

The Holy Spirit interprets all things to the inner life, but the Bible puts a part of the message of the Spirit in black and white. It is the record of those who "spake from God, being moved by the Holy Spirit" (2 Pet. 1. 21). The apostle is even bolder and declares, "Which things also we speak, not in words which man's wisdom teacheth, but which the Spirit teacheth; combining spiritual things with spiritual *words*"(1 Cor. 2: 13).

Those who fail to see God in nature, or appreciate Him in providence, or hear His voice to the conscience, who reject Jesus as the Son of God, and grieve away the Spirit of God, will also fail to receive the Bible as the Word of God, but he that "willeth to do his will shall know of the teaching, whether it be of God" (John 7: 17), and by honest obedience will be able to say, "Thy Word is a lamp unto my feet and a light unto my pathway."

II. God's Two Books.

By God's two books we mean, not the Old Testament and the New, but the Book of Nature and the Bible. In considering the Bible as a means of grace, it will be helpful to compare it with the book of nature, that we may see the marks of its divine authorship the more clearly. When one author has written a number of books, by comparing one with another the personality of the author will be found to have shown itself in common characteristics. Let us note some of these marks that are common to the book of nature and the Book of Revelation, and which show that they have a common Author.

1. THE USE OF AGENTS. In the writing of the book of nature God has used the mighty physical and chemical forces. Gravitation and cohesion have shaped the earth; fire and flood have smoothed it; wind and rain have written upon it; life in all its forms has the autograph of God upon it. Nature's laws are God's laws and nature's forces are God's agents for writing His great book.

In writing the Bible, God has also used agents. The Mohammedans assert that the Koran existed in its present form from all eternity, laid up before the throne of God until sent down to Mohammed. The Bible makes no such claim for its origin. It is the product of agents whom God has used. They who have obeyed the conditions of spirituality, have discerned spiritual truths, and out of their own experiences have written the things of truth. God writes upon the skies with the pencil of the lightnings, but He has written the Bible with the pens of human agents. In either case we have the autograph of God.

2. DIVERSITY. In the book of nature the first characteristic to be noticed is that of diversity. The elements of nature, the manifestations of force, the forms of life and beauty are

all about us in such profusion that at first we think there is confusion. Nature is a rainbow of a thousand colors, a harp of a thousand strings, a book with a thousand chapters, a very dictionary of facts, unabridged.

The Book of Revelation is likewise marked by diversity. The land of Canaan itself is universal in its characteristics. It has all varieties of climate from the snows of Lebanon to the tropical valley of the lower Jordan, all varieties of surface, from the mountains piled against the sky to the plains stretched out as a carpet beneath; all varieties of plant and animal life to correspond to all zones of nature. And this small but universal bit of earth is so situated that across its borders surged all the traffic of the civilizations of antiquity; and the Hebrew race, from the hills of Judea and Samaria, came into touch with this march of nations and absorbed universal elements. So it came to pass that the writers of the Bible are cosmopolitan in character. They draw their illustrations from all forms of nature and betray familiarity with all kinds of human life. The result is a universal Book, which appeals to men of whatever zone or race or rank.

Here is a Book, which is not one, but sixty-six, written by some forty-four different authors, during an interval of a thousand years. And in these books we have cross-sections of all kinds of life scenes, and discussions of all kinds of subjects. Here we have facts from nature, from history and science, we have law and philosophy, biography, geography, prose and poetry, parables and proverbs, essays and allegories, politics and religion, morals and law, prophecy and apocalypse, dealing with time and eternity, God and man, life and death, duty and destiny, sin and salvation, heaven and hell, angels and demons, things personal and things social. From the Bible all the great writers of

The Bible

modern times have drawn in style and figures and ideas as from an unfailing well. It is the fountain source of pure literature and pure morals. In the Psalms alone there is said to be " a balm for every heart-ache and a fitting expression for every emotion that stirs the soul." Human books are adapted to particular peoples and times. A divine book must be universal. Such is the book of nature and such is the Bible.

3. UNITY. In the book of nature there is a marvelous unity. All forms of life can be grouped into varieties and species and orders and families branching as from a common tree. All forms of elements can be combined according to unchanging laws. All forms of forces can be transformed, the one into the other by some mysterious common multiple. The stars themselves, which seem like millions of lost sheep wandering about in the great blue pasture, are moving with exact precision according to their systems and laws. Nature is a unity, because the God of nature is One God.

But no less marvelous is the unity of the Bible. Here are the sixty-six books in orderly arrangement, the Old Testament grouped around the old covenant and the New Testament grouped about the new covenant, and all revolving about the cross of Jesus Christ. The prophet and the priest and the sage combine their teachings in fundamental harmony. Although the writers include in their number both the learned and illiterate, rich and poor, bond and free, Jew and Gentile, kings and peasants, men of almost every occupation and station; and though they deal with every variety of subject, with questions the most difficult, upon which the learned men of all ages have disagreed, yet there is an essential harmony in everything from the beginning of Genesis to the end of Revelation. Discrepancies and errors and absurdities which critics have asserted to exist have fled before investigation and proper interpretation. Every new discovery in archaeology confirms rather than disproves the accuracy of the Scriptures, and while there are such minor variations as are perfectly consistent with inspiration in fundamental revelations, the Book is a unity. It is many in one, but it is one. Towering at the beginning and at the end, like the mighty pillars of a suspension bridge, are two great groups of facts, the boundary marks of the two eternities. In the beginning there is the creation of the heavens and the earth; in the end we have the new heaven and the new earth. In the beginning man begins his mortal existence; in the end he begins his eternal career. In the beginning Satan enters to deceive and destroy; in the end he is bound and cast down to his doom. In the beginning man is driven from the tree of life and a curse is upon the ground for his sake; in the end there is no more curse, but once more a right to the tree of life in the paradise of God. And between these pillars of truth are woven the revelations of all these writers in one perfect cable upholding the bridge across the chasm of sin and death.

Suppose some forty lawyers should write sixty-six books on politics; or forty doctors, allopaths and homeopaths and osteopaths and hydropaths, etc., should write sixty-six books on medicine; or forty philosophers should write sixty-six books on ethics, where could leather be found strong enough to bind these books together? And suppose that each of these should deal, not with one but with many questions, would not confusion be worse confounded? Imagine further that these writers should be from a dozen centuries during which great progress in knowledge has been made, and the resulting chaos is almost beyond the imagination. Yet here is the Bible with a variety of authorship and subjects as great as that and yet as symmetrical as a palace. To use an illus-

The Bible

tration from H. L. Hastings: Suppose a stranger should come from a distant land and deposit a stone upon a lot. After some years another comes from another part of the country and deposits another. A third follows, and a fourth, until a thousand years have passed, and behold a beautiful temple, with every stone in place. What would you say? That the harmony of the work could only be due to the architect who supplied each builder with the design for his own portion and thus harmonize the whole. Even so, the only adequate explanation of the unity of the Bible is in the common architect, the Holy Spirit, who guided the writers from first to last. If the God of nature is a God of law and order, so also is the God of the Bible. The unity of both is the mark of a common Author.

4. SIMPLICITY IN PROFUNDITY. In the book of nature there are some things simple and some things mysterious. The great essentials of life, the sunlight and air and food and drink, are pressed upon us so simply that we cannot but receive them; but beyond these are the depths of the mathematics of astronomy of which the average mind has no conception whatever, the mysteries of the transformations of energy, the unseen and unknown forces, the secret of life and of ten thousand other things that show infinite wisdom somewhere.

So also in the Bible the path of duty is made so plain that a wayfaring man, though a fool need not err therein, and yet there are revelations so profound that they have never yet been fathomed. The little child or unlearned adult may find on every page some morsel of soul food, and on the same page the learned scholar will find a revelation involved which inspires him to write a book. The Bible has not only been quoted in more books, but has inspired the writing of more books than anything else in the world. That it is a simple book in its essentials is seen from the fact that the common people love it, and that it is profoundly true is seen from the fact that the most learned accept it. A convention of 250 scientists in 1903 declared their belief in it. John R. Mott, head of the Student Volunteer Movement, and himself one of the great men of the century, after visiting the colleges and universities of the world, declared that there is a larger percentage of Christians among the scientific students than anywhere else. The Bible is not only consistent with itself, but it is consistent with God's other great book, the book of nature, and they who have learned to read them both believe the most implicitly that both are books of God.

5. IMPARTIALITY. Nature is no respecter of persons. The fire that burns the rich will also burn the poor. The tornado stops not for palace or hovel, and the death angel knocks at every door. Nature is like her God, impartial (Acts 10: 34).

No less impartial is the Bible. Human books are wont to flatter the great and ignore the poor. A money king has reporters at his heels wherever he goes, but the laboring man who may be his superior in the sight of God, is left to pass on his way unnoticed. But the Bible makes no such distinction. The poor widow with her mite is mentioned as a greater giver than the rich, while the king himself is dragged from his throne and robed in sackcloth and ashes and the pen of the prophet writes down the story of his crime as a warning to the ages to come. Men do not commonly chisel the faults of their fathers upon their tombstones, yet in the Bible the writers spare not their own race or heroes. They tell the simple truth without fear or favor, and though some of them lost their lives for doing so, yet their fidelity to truth has given a value to their work that is imperishable. If the unchangeableness of nature is a mark of the majesty of the great Author of this book of truth, no less is the stern truthfulness of the Bible a witness to the same divine authorship.

6. DEVELOPMENT. The book of nature is an unfolding book. The buds on the trees or the nebulae of a star are only signs of a ceaseless operation that is unfolding the book of nature as an endless scroll. Age has piled upon age and geologists have read the records of the rocks concerning each, as the panorama of the world has been unfolded. This is a developing world, and the universe is a developing universe. We are moving from the chaos of the past to the city of God of the future.

And the Author who has set eternity in the heart of nature has also set eternity in the heart of man. The Bible is a partial unfolding of an eternal revelation. The light that shone as a distant star in the first promise that the seed of the woman should bruise the serpent's head moved on until on Calvary it became the Sun of Righteousness shining in His strength. The blood of ancient sacrifices led the way to the fountain opened for the sin of the world. What was foreshadowed in type was fulfilled in antitype, prophecy became history and promise became fruition. Each writer of the Bible contributes something new to the revelation of the Book, in harmony with its progressive revelation. The Word of God has grown, not as the stone pile grows as new stones are added, but as the tree grows as it enlarges its body according to the enlarging life within. The dispensations have moved on in succession as fixed as the procession of the equinoxes. The law, the Gospel, the consummated kingdom of God—these are the prints of the Divine Architect recorded in the Bible and unfolding in history—the bud, the blossom and the fruit of the divine type of life revealed to the world. In nature and the Bible alike may be seen the law of conformity to type and of succession of types. The Author of the one is the Author of the other, and the revelation of each when understood is so alike that Tennyson could write:

> "Flower of the crannied wall
> If I could pluck you out of the crannies,
> And know what you are root and all,
> I should know what God and man is."

7. A GOOD END. In the writing of the book of nature the progress has been from lower to higher forms, and this is a prophecy of the coming of the highest. As Paul says, "the earnest expectation of the creation waiteth for the revealing of the sons of God" (Rom. 8: 19). The law of "the survival of the fittest" is simply the gospel principle of judgment "according to works" (Rev. 22: 12). Because God is good "all things work together for good to them that love God" (Rom. 8: 28). For convenience we distinguish between the secular and sacred, the natural and spiritual, but in reality all God's laws are natural and all are moral. He is ruler of earth and heaven and hell, and if nature crowds out the hopelessly unfit, so the kingdom of God has no room for the sinner who rejects it for the sake of a lower type of life. If nature herself prophesies of a millennial day coming when the desert shall blossom as the rose and the wolf and the lamb shall lie down together, much more does the Word of God paint the glory of that day across the western sky. All other religions put the golden age in the past, but the Bible writers have put the night before the morning and set the star of hope in the ascension. From the lofty summit of their inspiration they saw the holy city and with zeal and eloquence they have tried to make the vision real. Martyrs they were for the vision's sake, but from their graves they speak as the vision lives and brightens and leads the way to the golden day.

There is no book like the Bible in its power to inspire hope and regenerate the life. Whoever heard of anyone who said, " I was lost in sin, discouraged and in despair, when I began to read a law book and found peace to my soul "? Or has anyone heard of any other book save the Bible, of which men say, " This book has been the means of my finding God. It has saved me from sin and is an unfailing lamp to my feet "?

A book that makes wholly for good must be a good book. Where is the nation or individual that has ever gone wrong through following the Bible? What husband ever beat his wife because of reading the Gospel? What thief carries a Testament in his pocket? One time two men sought lodging in a frontier hut, and being suspicious of danger, they agreed to take turns in watching that night. But soon the watcher began to disrobe as he said, " There is no need of watching here. I peeped through the keyhole and saw the man get down the Bible and begin to read." Would a deck of cards or a copy of Ingersoll's lectures have so calmed their fears? Ah, evil men hate the Book because it reproves their evil deeds, but good men love it as they love the sunshine, because it lights the path of an honest life. The book of nature begins with God and ends with God. Chaos becomes order, and order promotes life, and life moves on to its highest forms, the kingdom of God. The Bible begins with God and ends with God. It tells the story of moral chaos and of redemption. It ends with the union of Christ and the church. It is the love story of God in which " they got married at last." The pleasing end, not without its tragedy in the remaining outside of the wicked, is its song of joy. It lifts the race to its own ideal. It is the Book of God because it leads to God. Thus in its origin and in its nature, in its unity in diversity, in its simplicity in profundity, in its impartiality and truthfulness, in its organic development, in its glorious consummation, the Book of Revelation, like the book of nature, contains as it were in cypher the autograph of God. As only the fool hath said in his heart, "There is no God," so only the blind in heart have said, "There is no message from God." We leave off as we began, with the fact that the very goodness of God compels the revelation of God. It remains only for us to respond to His love, to listen to His message and to obey His will. In so doing we shall find eternal life.

III. The Purpose of the Bible.

No one criticises a locomotive headlight because it is not a parlor lamp. It serves its own purpose very well. So the Bible must be used according to its purpose or it will be used in vain. It was never intended to be a book of science or history or of amusement. It is interesting, to be sure, and it has allusions to facts in history and nature, but they are used only as a preacher uses such things for illustration, and such allusions must be so interpreted. They who hunt for errors in these lines as a ground for rejection might as well reject a pump because of some error in the writing upon it. If it pumps water well it serves its purpose.

Neither is the Bible a mere fetish or charm. When a fire was raging in Toronto some ignorant Catholics put Bibles before it to stop its progress. God works no such miracles through it. He is not pleased when young people place a key in it and tell fortunes, or when old people keep it upon the parlor table as sort of a superstitious sign of religion. Its mere presence is not like the blood of the doorposts of the Israelites. It is useful only as it is taken into the life.

Nor yet is the Bible intended to be a picture of the world to come. The ancient Egyptians had what they called the "Book of the Dead" which they placed in the coffin for the use of the deceased in the judgment, but the Bible is a book for the living. Its eschatology is the most obscure part of it. It takes it for granted that if we follow its light for this

The Bible

world we need not worry about the next. George Washington was not a poet but he was a very good general, so those who wish science may read books for that purpose, but they who ask, " Wherewithal shall a young man cleanse his way?" will find the answer true, " By taking heed thereto according to thy word." The Bible is a guidepost to duty. What it will do for those who heed it is best stated in its own words.

1. THE BIBLE IS A MEANS OF REGENERATION.

Having been begotten again, not of corruptible seed, but of incorruptible, through the word of God, which liveth and abideth (1 Pet. 1: 23).

As the teacher uses books as a means of leading the child out of the darkness of ignorance into the light of knowledge, and that new light is new life; so the Holy Spirit uses the Word to lead the sinner out of the darkness of his self life into the light of the higher life, and the coming in of that new ideal is the coming of a new life, and that is regeneration. As the living seed transforms the soil, and the flower and fruit appears, so the Bible brings the knowledge of Jesus into the soil of our hearts and the new life he gives springs up. Thus the saved can say, " Of his own will he brought us forth by the word of truth " (Jas. 1: 18).

2. THE BIBLE IS A MEANS OF FAITH.

Faith cometh by hearing, and hearing by the word of God (Rom. 10: 14, 17).

As light shining into good eyes cannot fail to be seen, so truth shining into honest hearts cannot fail to be believed. The Bible is self-authenticating. It conveys the impression to honest minds of its own truthfulness. It compels faith. Of course the wicked will refuse to believe it, the wilfully misled will fail to find its treasures, and the ignorant may wrest it in dealing with things too high for them, but that is nothing against its proper use. They who know it best believe it most. It is an unfailing fountain of faith and life.

3. THE BIBLE IS A MEANS OF JUSTIFICATION.

Abraham believed God, and it was reckoned unto him for righteousness (Rom. 4: 3).

It was the unwritten rather than the written word of God that Abraham received, but the act of faith was the same, and by his faith he was justified. So it is by the righteousness resulting from faith, rather than by formal works that we are saved (Rom. 10: 3-10). The Bible leads us into this righteousness of God which comes by faith.

4. THE BIBLE IS A MEANS OF SANCTIFICATION.

Sanctify them through thy truth. Thy word is truth (John 17: 17).

Other books reflect the morals of the times in which they are written, but the Bible reflects the righteousness of God. Its moral precepts are based, not on law or custom, but on the character of God. "Be ye holy for I am holy" was the decree of the law (Lev. 19: 2) and of the Gospel (Matt. 5: 48). This is the true and ultimate basis for all law and morality. It is so recognized by the highest courts. When Girard College was endowed by its infidel founder it was stipulated that no preacher should ever enter and that "only the highest standard of morality should be taught." When later a Y. M. C. A. was organized and the Bible was taught, an effort was made to prevent its use by the terms of the will, but the courts decided that the Bible is "the highest standard of morality" we know anything about, and therefore by the provisions of the will it may, it must be taught. As the darkness flees before the morning light, as error bows to truth, so he who beholds himself in this perfect law of liberty may see what manner of man he is, and measuring himself by Jesus Christ will fall down in sorrow for his shortcomings. Because the standard of the Word is the perfection of God Himself it is able to lead man to sanctification and fulness of life. "Every one when he is perfected shall be as his teacher" (Luke 6: 49). It is the law of conformity to ideal.

We all * * beholding as in a mirror the glory (character) of the Lord, are transformed into the same image from glory to glory, even as from the Lord the Spirit (2 Cor. 3: 18).

5. THE BIBLE IS A MEANS OF SPIRITUAL GROWTH.

Man shall not live by bread alone, but by every word that proceedeth out of the mouth of God (Matt. 4: 4).

Jesus exemplified this again when He said, "I have meat to eat that ye know not of." The psalmist realized it when he said, "Thy word have I hid in mine heart, that I might not sin against thee" (Psa. 119: 11). As the child grows in knowledge of arithmetic by the study of arithmetic, and in knowledge of history by the study of history, so the child of God grows in grace and in the knowledge of God by the study of His Word. Things of sin which were attractive before somehow lose their fascination after studying the Word of God. A young lady on becoming a Christian began to read the Bible and as she came to things which the Bible condemned she put them aside. She called this "pruning" herself. It would be a blessed thing if all people would prune themselves by the Bible. There would be a mighty heap of refuse resulting,—gold and pearls and costly array, cards and theaters and dances and all kinds of selfish indulgences,—but there would be multiplied beauty and joy instead.

The Bible is the "sword of the Spirit" (Eph. 6: 17), the only weapon of offense the Christian has. Let it be used, for it "is a discerner of the thoughts and intents of the heart" (Heb. 4: 12). A little time with the Bible in the morning will sweeten the life for the day. It is a source of strength. A certain woman whose life was one of toil became a proficient Bible teacher and of very Christly character. The secret of it was found in the little side-board in the kitchen, which she had made especially for her Bible, that in passing to and fro in her busy life she might now and then catch a sentence from the open Bible and have something better than tubs and brooms and dishes to feast her mind upon. She heeded the words of the Book which says,

Whatsoever things are true, whatsoever things are honorable, whatsoever things are just, whatsoever things are pure, whatsoever things are lovely, whatsoever things are of good report; if there be any virtue, and if there be any praise, think on these things (Philpp. 4: 8).

Thus feeding the soul on the Word of God rather than the gossip of the world, we grow into the things that are pure and true. As to live with a Mozart would be to become musical, or to live with Nero would be to become cruel, so to live with the saints of the Bible record, and most of all with Jesus who is there portrayed, is to become holy. It is the reward of abiding in the Word.

IV. How to Study the Bible.

A certain farmer purchased a binder, but soon discarded it and went back to the cradle, because he was too ignorant to regulate the binder. He was not unlike those who neglect the Bible because they have not learned to use it with profit. A few suggestions as to Bible study may help some young disciple to use it aright.

No one seeking medicine would think of going into an apothecary's shop and helping himself to the first bottle found, yet many read the Bible only when in fear of death, and then open it at random, not knowing what they may find. It has its food and medicine in order, and we need only to come to it aright to find just what we need upon any occasion.

1. BIBLE HELPS. In reading any book it is helpful to know something of the author and the purpose of writing. So in Bible study it is helpful to know something about the origin and history of the Bible. The preacher should study special books along these lines in his course of training, but the average reader will find in the helps of any good Teachers' Bible a great deal of information such as he needs. This is the kind of a Bible to buy. And it should be of the best possible binding so that just when it becomes the most valuable because of its markings it will not be worn out. A good concordance or subject index is indispensable to Bible study, and a good Bible dictionary is most helpful. Commentaries vary in value and must be taken for what they are worth. Rightly used they are of great help. Any good pastor or church leader will be glad to recommend the best up-to-date helps on Bible study. Pictorial Bibles are good for children and older people as well, as are also books of Bible stories, red letter Bibles and marked Bibles.

2. BIBLE MARKING. Some Bible marks betray irreverence, the worst mark being the dust from disuse, but some marks bear witness to the most reverent use. Such marks are like the labels on the goods in the store; they make it easy to locate what is wanted. The Bible can be marked by drawing a neat line underneath or beside the verse to be marked, or by going over the letters with a pen, making them stand out like bold type. The latter is the better method, but it takes more time. By using colored pencils, or broken lines of different kinds, each color or kind of line indicating some special subject, the most common subjects of study may be made to stand out boldly. The " railroad method " may be used in connection with the others, by drawing dotted lines

connecting related words or texts on the same page. There are many such. Many cross references can also be added to those already given, and many brief words of explanation or comment can be written upon the margins. Moody's Bible contained many sermon outlines in this way. It is the best plan to mark the verse when first it comes with special help, as otherwise its message may be lost. Preachers love to see their hearers with open Bibles and pencils, following through the Word as they preach. It means abiding good. God has given us the storehouse of good things, but we must provide the labels according to our own needs.

3. READING THE BIBLE. Sooner or later everyone should read the Bible through from beginning to end in order to have a good idea of the whole, but this is not the way to continue Bible reading. In a great store there are things for all kinds of people and all kinds of emergencies, and each may select what is needed at the time. Some parts of the Bible are like a doctor book for private reading, and some are adapted to public reading. A course of reading should be arranged according to the needs of the occasion. Some families use the home readings of the Sunday-school lessons in family worship, but these are so disconnected that they lose their value unless their relation to the lesson is explained. It is better to take devotional studies such as are given in the Y. M. C. A. Bible-class books or similar books which church leaders may recommend. The New Testament may be read consecutively with profit because it is more easily understood by the common people.

4. BIBLE STUDY BY BOOKS. There are some things in the Bible whose beauty and worth do not depend upon knowing the author or circumstances of writing, but there are other parts whose proper interpretation does depend upon these things. To study the Bible by books, it is necessary to know about their authors and the purpose of their

writing. The study of these things is called the "higher criticism," which in itself is a good thing and must not be confused with the writings of those destructive critics who put their own ideas above everything else and do away with the inspiration of the Bible. The study of the text of a book to make certain of what the author originally wrote is called the "lower criticism" and is also a most reverent and useful line of study. The ordinary reader cannot specialize in these things, but can learn something about the books studied, and may then proceed to get the outline of the book, the key verse or chapter, and the chief points of teaching. After making such an outline it will be helpful to find answers to such questions as, "What does this book teach about God? about Christ? about the Holy Spirit? about sin? about duty?" &c. The Bible should be used as a library rather than as an individual book.

5. BIBLE STUDY BY TOPICS. For practical help in everyday life, the best way to study the Bible is by topics. We wish to know what light it gives as to specific questions. How to pray, how to dress, how to choose life work, duties of husband and wife, how to win souls, and a hundred other such questions are ours to answer, and the topical method of study is the easiest way to find an answer. It involves the danger of misinterpreting some texts, for no passage should be interpreted apart from its context, but so much of the Bible has its meaning right on the surface that the common reader may get it without serious errors. It will be helpful to write on the blank pages of the Bible a few Bible readings on subjects which should be familiar,—as prayer, how to be saved, the ordinances, &c. Any reader may soon collect a large number of Bible readings from his own study, from papers and books and in other ways. It will be found that the Bible is in essential harmony on all subjects relating to duty.

V. How to Understand the Bible.

It is one thing to read the Bible and another to understand it. Pronouncing words is not appropriating ideas. It is the glory of the Book that it is for the common people as well as for the learned, but it must be used aright.

1. THE BIBLE SHOULD BE STUDIED DEVOTIONALLY. The botanist may dissect the flower and name its parts, but the artist who sees its beauty as a whole has perhaps the greater feast. The Bible critics have their work to do, but it is for the ordinary Christian to study the Book devotionally. One time Mr. Moody sat at a table with a skeptic, eating a fish. The skeptic said, "What do you do with the parts of the Bible you do not understand?" Moody replied, "I do just as we are doing with this fish. I feast on the good part and let any fool who wishes to do so choke himself on the bones." The bee will suck honey and the spider will suck poison from the same flower, even so the Gospel " is a savor of death unto death or of life unto life " (2 Cor. 2: 15, 16). Even preachers are tempted to miss its lessons because they seek applications for others rather than for themselves. The Bible speaks its richest message to those who come reverently asking, "What wilt thou have *me* to do?"

2. THE BIBLE SHOULD BE STUDIED LOVINGLY. A letter from a loved one has more between the lines than on them, and must be read and lingered over to be understood. Little Johnnie two years old can write a letter to his papa which no one else can understand, but papa knows the meaning of every mark. It takes love to understand the Bible. The love of God is shining through it and we must be keyed to love in order to understand it.

3. THE BIBLE SHOULD BE STUDIED WITH OBEDIENCE. Closing the eyes shuts out the light, and closing the heart to obedience to truths destroys also the will to believe and the pow-

er to understand. Professor Graham Taylor says that it is impossible to understand the Bible without obeying it. This is especially true with the more spiritual portions of it. He will never understand the words, "Love your enemies" who refuses to do so; nor will anyone understand how "it is more blessed to give than to receive" until by actual experience the truth is made real. A thousand other passages like these are meant to be proven, not by the cross examination of the critic, but by the test of obedience. They who best obey God's Word best understand it.

This truth is also applicable to the ordinances. There are differences of practice to-day, not so much because God has not made the commandments plain, as because leaders who have wished to practice otherwise have misled the people as to their meaning. They who are determined to practice one way will find it hard to understand the Bible any other way. But note the promises to the obedient: They shall know of the teaching (John 7: 17); they shall be called friends (John 15: 14); they shall abide in the love of God (John 14: 21-23); they shall have the guidance of the Holy Spirit (John 14: 16); they shall enjoy the manifestation of the Son and of the Father (John 14: 21-23); and have prevailing power in prayer (John 15: 16; 1 John 3: 22).

4. CHRIST THE KEY OF THE BIBLE. There was a little girl who was trying to put together the parts of a dissected map, but found it hard to do so. Her father turned it over and there was the picture of a man. It was easy to put all parts of the man in their proper place, but when this was done, lo, on the other side the map was properly arranged. So it is with the Bible. To study it simply with reference to history and geography and technical points, it will be comparatively barren, but to study it with reference to the man Christ Jesus it fits together perfectly. Foretold in

prophecy, foreshadowed in type, revealed in history, and coming in glory, He is the central thought of all things. To Him ancient history converges and from Him modern history dates. As in the British cordage there runs a scarlet thread, so throughout the Bible there runs the blood of Jesus Christ. From the promise in the garden of Eden (Gen. 3: 15) to the promise at the end of the Bible, Jesus is the subject of prophecy and song, the object of hope and the climax of revelation.

5. THE HOLY SPIRIT THE INTERPRETER. It is not to decry the historical method of Bible study to say that above all these side lights and technical helps in the help of the Holy Spirit in understanding God's Word according to its purpose. Language is not always adequate to express the ideas or spirit back of it, but the Holy Spirit in the life helps us to be in such a frame of mind that the message of love and duty God has for us in His Word will appeal to us, while otherwise it would be passed by. The Word is called the "sword of the Spirit" and it is His peculiar mission to guide into all truth, to bring to remembrance the words of the Master, and to glorify Christ. It is useless to try to get the full message of the Scriptures without Him. Other helps may not be accessible to all, but the humblest child of God may have the help of the Holy Spirit if he will (1 John 2: 27). He is the ever-present Interpreter, better than priest or pope. Because of His help the Bible may safely be trusted to speak its special message to anyone willing to receive it.

What has been said concerning Bible study will apply to private study, or study in the Sunday school or other gatherings. The Young People's Societies in general have used the topical method of study, but the Sunday school has been handicapped in the past by using disconnected passages without providing connecting outlines as a necessary part of the lesson. The temporary Sunday-school leaflet or quarterly should not supplant well-bound books as Bible helps to be studied and preserved. The pedagogical principles which are worked out with such care in the public schools should be utilized in the most important work in the world, the teaching of the Word of God.

The Sunday school is not for children alone. The command of the law was,

Assemble the people, the men and the women and the little ones, and thy sojourner that is within thy gates, that they may hear, and that they may learn, and fear Jehovah your God, and observe to do all the words of this law (Deut. 31: 12).

Note especially that the men come first, and that the visitor is to be taken along, instead of being made the excuse for remaining at home. The entire church should be in some department of Bible study. The adult Bible class movement is of special value, for this age needs the revival which will come from renewed interest in the study of the Bible.

The Word of God is backed by the power of God. There need be no fear lest the Bible be lost. "Truth crushed to earth will rise again." Better methods of interpretation may prevail, but the Bible will continue to be as it has been in the past, the "power of God unto salvation" (Rom. 1: 16). Other books may be in the public mind for a moment, but the Bible retains its hold from age to age. When in 1876 the Revised Version was completed, the entire New Testament was telegraphed from New York to Chicago in order to be used in the daily papers twenty-four hours sooner than steam could carry it. In 1904 the manager of a large department store in Chicago declared that more copies of the Bible, morocco bound, are sold every year than of the most popular of all other books. It has the persistence and the power of truth. The curse of the middles ages was in the keeping of God's Word from the masses of the people. Then heresy did its deadly work. But now the church of Christ is hasting to preach the Word as a witness to all nations ere He come again (Matt. 24: 14). God speed the work, for as the first angel flies " having the everlasting Gospel to preach unto them that dwell on the earth, and to every nation, and kindred, and tongue, and people " (Rev. 14: 6), the second prepares to proclaim, " Fallen, fallen is Babylon the great, that hath made all the nations to drink of the wine of the wrath of her fornication " (v. 8), and soon the revelator seizes his pen to write, " the tabernacle of God is with men, and he shall dwell with them, and they shall be his peoples " (Rev. 21: 3).

To My Bible.

Thou blessed Book, sweet gift of love,
I scan thy pages o'er and o'er:
I love thy precepts more and more,
As in my life their worth I prove.

Life is a journey, and thou art
A light unto my wandering feet;
My guide and compass and my chart,
My resting place and manna sweet.

Life is a school and thou the Book
From which I learn. Life is a field;
Thou art good seed. Life is a fight;
Thou art the sword my Master took.

May I as He win victory,
As He, bring from the Book of God,
Things new and old, which must be told,
To bring the world, my Lord, to Thee.

PRAYER.

In olden times the worshipers of the true God regarded the smoke of their sacrifices as a sweet savor which went up to God in their behalf. In the tabernacle holy place, there was the altar of incense which was kept burning every day that the fragrance might rise as prayer before God (Ex. 30: 1-11), and in Rev. 5: 8 we read that the incense is the prayers of the saints.

Prayer is to be classed with the symbols as a means of grace because the outward form of prayer is only the expression of the inward attitude of the heart. Words are but signs of ideas. Attitudes are the same. But as through words and gestures the race communicates and thus promotes knowledge and social life, so through the forms of prayer the race learns communion with God and advancement is made in spiritual knowledge. It is the most ancient, the most universal and most valuable of the forms of worship, and yet it is with the mass of the world a mere form, and even with Christians is fast becoming a lost art.

There is need of teaching concerning prayer. Men are giving their lives to patient toil, investigating the marvelous forces of nature that they may be able to utilize them in the activities of the world, but greater than electricity or any kindred forces is the power of true prayer. The man of science lays hold upon the physical forces and subdues them with bit and bridle, because by obeying the laws of their working he can make them obey him; but he who obeys the conditions of prevailing prayer puts himself into possession of all the infinite power of God. There is not a more stupendous revelation in God's Word than this, but it is absolutely true. "If ye abide in me, and my words abide in you, ye shall ask what ye will, and it shall be done unto you" (John 15: 7). These are the words of Him who never trifled, and whose own life is the sufficient proof of the truth of the promise. The prayer life of Jesus is a marvelous revelation of the possibilities of a child of God, but when we compare it with the prayerless lives of His professed followers we feel that the revelation needs to be made over again.

And yet the altar of incense is still in the church of God and the fires of true devotion have not gone out. Here and there are devout souls who in the rush of modern life are still taking time to pray. They are the salt of the earth. It was of them that Jesus must have thought when He committed the infinite interests of the kingdom, not to armies and navies, but to the prayers of His handful of followers. "Pray ye therefore the Lord of the harvest, that he may send forth laborers into his harvest" (Matt. 9: 38). The church has not yet learned the measure of responsibility that has been placed upon her because of the power that is at her command. She has been given the key to the infinite storehouse of energy, but has been carrying it without using it. The discussion which follows, it is earnestly hoped, may be the means of reviving to some extent the prayer life of those who may read it.

I. Can God Answer Prayer?

The Bible does not enter into scientific explanations of its revelations. It gives the facts and allows them to demonstrate themselves as facts to those who have faith enough to act upon them. They who lead lives of prayer are not troubled about the philosophy of it, but to those who are without experience of its power there come serious questions which may well be considered.

1. HAS GOD THE POWER TO ANSWER PRAYER? Unbelief staggers at miracles and says that all things must be accord-

Prayer 81

ing to natural laws, and therefore denies the supernatural. Does not the skeptic know that the existence of laws implies the existence of a Law-maker, and that the Law-maker is greater than the laws? And what do we know that we should assume to say what is natural and what is supernatural? In these days of wireless telegraphy, X-rays and other marvelous things, wise men are cautious about saying that the miracles of the Gospel are beyond the realm of the natural when once the natural is fully understood. He who holds the reins of all the forces has power to drive them all according to His own will. We know not what mighty forces await His bidding, which man has not yet discovered, but we know that one and all are known to God and one and all are touched by the key of prayer.

2. How is it possible for God to hear prayer? Here are thousands of people praying at once, and in all the five hundred or more languages of earth, how can God give attention to all? Ah, we must not judge God by our own finite powers. He who is able to keep every star in its place, and to guide the myriad forms of life on this planet and countless millions of others at the same time is able to perceive the cry of His children, whenever and wherever and however they cry. If the bunch of iron filings in the receiving instrument of the wireless telegraph is able to perceive and record the invisible messages that go in waves around the world, it is not wonderful that the living God should receive the thought messages from His children. The Holy Spirit is not less effective as a medium than electricity.

3. How can God give attention to such little things as the petty petitions of our prayers? How can He by the law of gravitation swing the mighty sun in his course, and by the same law take note of the tiniest speck of dust that floats in the sunlight? How can the ocean of

electricity about the world be so sensitive as to convey accurately the tiniest vibration that is flashed along the wires? If physical forces are able to operate in the greatest and the least of things, shall not spiritual forces also be able? And shall not the living God most of all be able?

4. How can God answer prayer without destroying the balance of forces? Here is the law of the conservation of energy according to which matter and force may change forms, but the sum total remains always the same. Now, it is said, if some external power, as prayer, is injected the balance will be destroyed. But hold. God is not an external force. He is not outside of nature ready to occasionally meddle in, but is in and through all. The spiritual forces are to be counted in the sum total of energy, so that in the interplay of forces the answer to prayer involves nothing more than the operation of natural laws.

5. How can God answer contradictory prayers? If one man prays for rain and another for sunshine, how can both be heard and answered? It is nowhere promised that God will answer prayer that does not fulfill the conditions laid down for true prayer, and one of these is that it shall be according to the will of God (1 John 5: 14). Prayers that are according to the will of God are not contradictory, either to one another or to the laws of nature. They cannot be, for God's will is the one supreme law correlating everything. When a great calamity comes, a city is destroyed by fire or flood or earthquake, what is it that sends the special trains speeding with relief? Do blind, unfeeling forces react in response to the cry of human need? Not at all. But human hearts are touched by human need, and hearts through heads give orders to hands, and forces are harnessed which carry the precious help. Is there any contradiction of forces because love and sympathy come in to work with these natural forces? Neither is there con-

tradition or confusion when the heart of the infinite Father is touched by the cry of His children and He sets in operation forces to respond. A family is seated at the table, when a faint cry is heard from the little bed upstairs. The baby is awake. Presently a hundred and fifty pounds of matter is rapidly ascending the stairway. Is there any contradiction in nature that so small a sound should move so large a body? Not if you count a father's love a part of nature. How much more is it possible for our Father in Heaven to respond to prayer because His love is in and over all.

II. Will God Answer Prayer?

If we grant the ability of God to answer prayer that fulfills the conditions, there still remains the question of willingness. But not to those who have learned to know God. Jesus answered that question once for all when He said,

If ye then, being evil, know how to give good gifts unto your children, how much more shall your Father in heaven give good things to them that ask him (Matt. 7: 11)?

To know that imperfect earthly parents delight to answer the requests of their children when it is for their good, and to deny that same willingness to our Father in heaven is to make Him worse than we who are evil. The difference is the other way. From the child which asks with confidence, let us learn to come with confidence to our Father when we ask for the thing that is right and are submissive to His will. If there is no question as to the power of God to answer proper prayer, much less can there be question as to His willingness. The only remaining question is as to our ability to fulfill the conditions of prevailing prayer.

III. Conditions of Prevailing Prayer.

A further proof that our Father will answer prayer is found in the fact that He has taught us how to pray.

Jesus was not only a living example of the life of prayer, but He taught us how to live the same sort of a life. We may accept His teaching as true, for He proved it true in His own career. What are the conditions He taught?

1. CONDITIONS AS TO ATTITUDE.

(1) *Sincerity.*

The hour cometh, and now is, when the true worshipers shall worship the Father in sincerity and in truth: for such doth the Father seek to be his worshipers (John 4: 23).

As the eye perceives light waves and the ear receives sound waves, so God being a Spirit they that worship Him must worship Him in spirit and in truth. As in wireless telegraphy the sending instrument and the receiving instrument must be in " tune," so the coming in spirit and in truth is the attuning of the heart to God. Without this inward attitude of earnestness the outward forms and expressions of prayer are but empty mockery.

(2) *Alone with God.*

When thou prayest, enter into thine inner chamber, and having shut thy door, pray to thy Father who is in secret, and thy Father who seeth in secret shall recompense thee (Matt. 6: 6).

Here is the condition of concentration. The vaunting Pharisees who love to be seen of men to pray have not their thoughts upon their prayers so much as upon the praise of men. Secret prayer helps to shut out the distractions and temptations to wrong motives which come from public prayer. For this reason private prayer is better than public prayer, save when for the sake of united prayer it is best to join in public petition. That Jesus endorsed public prayer is seen in His commendation of the publican who though he prayed in public " went down to his house justified" (Luke 18: 14), and by His own example at the grave of Lazarus when He prayed purposely that those standing about might hear (John 11: 42). Of course it is possible to have divided thoughts in secret prayer, and it is possible to concentrate the mind in public prayer. Being alone with God means shutting out the world wherever we are. It is like going into a telephone booth to talk. It is like taking a class of children into a room apart to teach them. It is like doing personal work with a man alone rather than in public. It is the exclusion of distractions and the concentration of the attention upon the petition desired.

(3) *Faith.*

All things whatsoever ye pray and ask for, believe that ye receive them, and ye shall have them (Mark 11: 24).

This daring promise seems to make faith the one condition of answer to prayer. And it is, in the sense in which Jesus speaks of faith, for " faith worketh through love " (Gal. 5: 6), and faith " is the victory that hath overcome the world; " not the faith that devils have when they believe and tremble, but the faith that is proven by works (Jas. 2: 17). "Without faith it is impossible to please God" because it is by faith that we recognize God as the giver and thank Him for the gift. Faith itself is the gift of God (1 Cor. 12: 9), through His Word (Rom. 10: 17), and though some may have a larger measure than others (Rom. 12: 3), yet the faith of all may grow (2 Thess. 1: 3) and we may pray the prayer of the disciples, "Lord, increase our faith" (Luke 17: 5). The possibilities of faith lie not so much in the quantity as in the quality. " If ye have faith as a grain of mustard seed " (Matt. 17: 20) means not so much *small* faith as *living* faith. A tiny seed because it lives may be planted in a crevice and split the rock.

A tree in Philadelphia was cut down because its roots were endangering a mammoth brick building, yet it came from a tiny seed.

Faith is the receptive attitude of the soul. It is the point of touch of the finite spirit with the infinite Spirit, and who can measure the possibilities developing from that touch? By faith we receive the adoption as children of God (John 1: 12) and become joint-heirs with Jesus Christ (Rom. 8: 17), and however hard it may be for the unregenerate to have faith, it ought to be easy for the children of God, for *faith in a promise is based upon faith in the promiser,* and when once we know God we cannot but have absolute confidence in Him. Because it is He who cannot lie that has promised we should rise to perfect faith in His promises.

(4) Repentance.

Let not that man think that he shall receive anything of the Lord; a double-minded man, unstable in all his ways (Jas. 1: 7).

True prayer cannot rise from an unrepentant heart. The man who was in danger of his life and began to pray "Good Lord, good devil," because, as he said, he did not know into whose hands he was going to fall, was not unlike many more who beg simply to be saved from the consequences of their sins without really being sorry for them. A Roman Catholic said, "It costs more to be a Catholic than a Protestant because when a Catholic gets drunk it costs $5 to get forgiven again, while a Protestant can repent for nothing." He did not know what repentance is. One cannot repent and wilfully do the same thing over again. And prayer that is without repentance from sin is as impossible of answer as for a rebel to receive pardon while continuing his rebellion.

(5) Obedience.

Whatsoever we ask we receive of him, because we keep his commandments and do the things that are pleasing in his sight (1 John 3: 22).

The spiritual forces have their conditions of working as well as the natural forces. Obedience is harmony with God, and that means harmony with all the forces of God, and that means power. (Paradoxical as it may seem, is absolutely true that the more laws of God we obey the more power we have. The stone that obeys only a few physical and chemical laws knows nothing of the power of man who in addition to these obeys the laws of life and spirit. Man cannot make a machine of any sort and say to electricity, "Now run it," but by conforming to the laws of that mysterious force he may cause it to run a hundred machines. And man cannot say, "I will do as I please and then call on God to help me out," but if he says as Jesus did, "Not my will but thine," he can also say, "Father, I will," for then his will and the Father's will shall be blended in one.

Henry Drummond calls obedience the "organ of spiritual vision," saying that it is in spiritual things what the eye is to the body. It leads the way into truth and the power of truth. "If any man willeth to do his will, he shall know of the teaching" (John 7:17). If these promises seem great, obedience is also great, and blessed is he who does His will, for he shall sit with Him on the throne of His power (Rev. 3:21). All the examples prove that men given to prayer have been men of righteous lives. There are no exceptions to-day, and there will be none to the end of time.

(6) *Forgiveness.*

Whensoever ye stand praying, forgive, if ye have aught against anyone; that your Father also who is in heaven may forgive you your trespasses (Mark 11:25).

Perhaps there is no condition of prevailing prayer more commonly violated than this. Anger has been called the besetting sin of church members. Those who would not be caught stealing for anything will shamelessly give way to temper and feelings of revenge. But, as Andrew Murray says, "Prayer and love are inseparable." Faith that holds the life to God will receive from Him the spirit of love. And obedience toward God is the proof of love toward men (1 John 5:2). "If a man say, I love God, and hateth his brother, he is a liar " (1 John 4: 20), but if any be conscious of love toward God and men, then " perfect love casteth out fear " and he may ask with assurance.

It should be noted that forgiveness is a condition of prayer, whether it be the one praying who holds the grudge (Mark 11: 25) or whether it be the other party (Matt. 5: 23, 24). It is common to say, " I have nothing against him, let him come to me," which is usually a lie, or the person would be willing to go first to be reconciled. The forgiveness must be " from the heart " (Matt. 18: 35) or it avails nothing. It should be easy, because although we were far less worthy yet " God for Christ's sake hath forgiven us " (Eph. 4: 32 A. V.).

(7) Righteousness.

The supplication of a righteous man availeth much in its working (Jas. 5: 16).

The barren tree is cut down lest it cumber the ground. The engine without steam is powerless when the throttle is opened. The life that is worldly is helpless when it comes to prayer. All the examples prove that men of power in prayer have been men of righteous lives. There are no exceptions to-day, and there will be none to the end of time, for it is as easy to operate a trolley line with a cotton rope as to prevail in prayer with a worldly life.

2. SEVEN CONDITIONS OF PROPER ASKING.

(1) With fasting.

This kind goeth not out but by prayer and fasting (Matt. 17: 14-21 A. V.).

Whether Jesus meant that that particular race of demons was specially hard to cast out, or whether he meant the kind of faith necessary to prevail is conditioned on prayer and fasting, is immaterial, for it makes fasting in either case an agency in attaining to power in prayer. If faith is laying

Prayer   89

hold on God, then fasting is letting go of the world, and both are essential. Fasting is an effectual means of cleansing the system of the poisons with which it is usually clogged from overeating. It crucifies the lusts of the flesh and strengthens the spiritual nature. It prepares the temple of God for His Holy Spirit and makes it a better instrument for His use. Far more than we realize, the church has lost its power in prayer because it has lost the earnestness which comes through fasting. It is given to feasting instead, and the oyster suppers and ice cream socials are crowded while the prayer meeting languishes. These things ought not to be so, but they will be so until the pastors with trumpet tones call back the people from their worldliness to fasting and prayer, that once more the heavens may be opened and a blessing poured out such as they shall not be able to receive. Fasting, like prayer, is to be in sincerity, not for show, and shall receive its recompense (Matt. 6: 16-18).

(2) *With definiteness.*

"What wilt thou?" (Luke 18: 41) is the question that comes to us as well as to the blind man of old. It is true our Father knows what things we have need of before we ask Him (Matt. 6: 8), but none the less He loves to have His children ask. Right asking is a proof of fitness to receive. A child is not given a pair of scissors until it is old enough to handle them, and when it is able to ask for them properly it is also able to use them properly. Definite asking is thus an evidence of the fitness to receive, which is the real condition back of the asking. Definite asking also enables us to mark the answer when it comes, and thus to glorify God, or to learn wherein we fail to ask aright, and thus to correct our prayer. Too often we are slothful, and instead of taking pains to find whether we are asking aright or not, we throw everything upon God and let it go. This is too much like the man who is said to have placed a printed prayer on the wall of his chamber, and when retiring would point to that, saying, "Lord, those are my sentiments," and jump into bed. The Lord is not pleased with such indifference. All the admonitions concerning prayer teach us to be definite, and while definite asking requires a more careful preparation and a larger faith, yet it brings results.

(3) *With submission.*

And this is the boldness which we have toward him, that, if we ask anything according to his will, he heareth us: and if we know that he heareth us whatsoever we ask, we know that we have the petitions which we have asked of him (1 John 5: 14, 15).

While we may generally know whether we are asking aright or not, yet our understanding is limited and we must submit ourselves to the will of God; for He knows best. A certain mother prayed for her child, "Anything, only spare his life!" The child lived, but was a helpless idiot the rest of its days. Far better it is to say, "Not my will but thine be done." Then if the thorn in the flesh be not taken away, there will be at least grace enough given to bear it (2 Cor. 12: 9); if we pass through the dark valley, His presence will go with us (Matt. 28: 20) and whatever comes we may be assured that "to them that love God, all things work together for good" (Rom. 8: 28).

(4) *With perseverance.*

And shall not God avenge his elect that cry to him day and night, and yet he is longsuffering over them (Luke 18: 7).

As children are prone to pluck unripe fruit, so we are eager to see answers to our prayers before conditions are fulfilled. The word translated "longsuffering" in the passage above is the same word that is used in James 5: 7.

Be patient therefore, brethren, until the coming of the Lord. Behold, the husbandman waiteth for the precious fruit of the

Prayer

earth, being patient over it until it receive the early and latter rain.

As the harvest cannot come until the conditions are fulfilled, and hence the farmer must be " longsuffering " over it as he sows and cultivates until the time comes, so we must be patient in prayer, working in the direction of our prayers, and waiting until all conditions are fulfilled, knowing that God is working with us as nature works with the farmer, and yearns to give more than we do to receive, if the answer is for our good. George Muller, whose orphanages in England are called " the standing miracle of Bristol " testified when he died at the age of ninety-three that though in some cases he prayed thirty years or more before receiving the answer, yet never had he prayed with assurance that he was in accord with God's will, that the answer did not sooner or later come. Perseverance does not mean vain repetition, but it does mean patience and abiding faith, accompanied with works toward the end for which we pray.

(5) *With unity.*

I say unto you, that if two of you shall agree on earth as touching anything that they shall ask, it shall be done for them of my Father who is in heaven (Matt. 18:19).

While private prayer has its advantages, yet when other conditions are fulfilled there can be far greater power in public prayer. Not that God changes His mind because a number join in prayer, but because the unity necessary serves to prepare the heart to ask according to God's will. Two or three cannot agree, save as they are gathered in Jesus' name and He is one in the midst (v. 20); and with Him in the midst the prayer is attuned to God's will. As an army must break step in crossing a bridge lest they break it by the accumulating vibrations, so the public prayer enables the many to reënforce one another. It is significant that on the day of Pentecost the disciples " *were all with one accord in* one place." Their contention was over and they were united in faith and love. Such are the conditions of power in united prayer to-day.

(6) *In Jesus' name.*

If ye shall ask anything in my name, that will I do (John 14: 14).

To ask in Jesus' name means more than to close with the words "in Jesus' name." To take His name means to take also His nature, for His name stands for Himself. When a bride receives the name of her husband she gives up her own, so when we take the name of Christ in prayer we must give up our own desires that we may be in harmony with Him. Thus asking in His name we are sure to ask according to the will of the Father, and to have the help of the Savior who has been received of the Father. "He ever liveth to make intercession" for us (Heb. 7: 25).

(7) *In the Spirit.*

Praying at all seasons in the Spirit (Eph. 6: 18).

Jesus taught us the beginning of prayer, but left it for the Holy Spirit to guide us into all truth. He it is who makes our bodies His temple, if only we are willing, and enables us to walk and talk and work and pray, all according to the will of God. Indeed,

We know not how to pray as we ought; but the Spirit himself maketh intercession for us with groanings which cannot be uttered (Rom. 8: 26).

Not that the Father loves us less, that the Son and the Spirit should both make intercession for us, for "the Father himself loveth you" (John 16: 27); but because of their own love for us the Son and Spirit join in helping us to the things for our good. Their intercession is "according to the will of God." If therefore we live in the Spirit we shall be able to pray in the Spirit and prevail.

The Example of Jesus.

All these conditions of prayer we find exemplified in the life of Jesus. Did He teach us to get alone with God? Lo we find Him many a time going apart to pray,—sometimes going into a solitary place (Matt. 14: 23) and sometimes rising early in the morning (Mark 1: 35). Did He teach us to come in faith believing? He was able to say in His own prayer, "I knew that thou hearest me always" (John 11: 42). Did He make obedience a condition? We hear Him say of Himself, "I do always the things that are pleasing to Him" (John 8: 29). Did He teach forgiveness? He prays for His enemies, "Father forgive them; for they know not what they do" (Luke 23: 34). Did He encourage fasting as a means of spirituality? He Himself gave the example (Luke 4). Does He teach us to be definite? We find Him asking definitely in all His prayers. Does He teach perseverance? We find Him continuing all night in prayer (Luke 6: 12). Does He teach submission to the Father's will? He illustrates it by His own submission. "Not my will, but thine, be done" (Luke 22: 42). He gave not a precept that He did not practice and made not a condition of power in prayer that He did not illustrate in His own life of prayer. If even He found it necessary to obey these conditions how much more must we do so. Why long to be like Him and then refuse to pay the cost? Why ask Him to teach us to pray and then refuse to follow His directions? If only the church would follow them it would be revolutionized at once and the world would speedily be evangelized and prepared for His coming again.

IV. The Externals of Prayer.

The foregoing scriptures deal with prayer as a real communion with God. There are others which deal with the external forms of prayer as a rite. These also have their place in preserving the spirit of prayer.

1. WHEN TO PRAY. The Scriptures give no rule as to how often to pray. They seek to guard against formality. Daniel prayed three times a day, but Jesus taught that men "ought always to pray and not to faint" (Luke 18: 1). This is in line with the injunction of Paul, "Pray without ceasing" (1 Thess. 5: 17). It means, not continual uttering of prayers, but a life lived in the spirit of prayer. Such a life will be given much to prayer even though the times be not set by formal rule. Jesus prayed at any time of the day or night. He always prayed before any important action in His life. He prayed for the sick and He prayed for the sorrowing.

Grace at meals. It seems to have been with Jesus a custom to always give thanks before eating (John 6: 11). This is a custom that Paul also followed (Acts 27: 35) and which every true Christian should follow. There is no responsible person who has not brains enough to formulate or commit a brief prayer of thanks for God's gifts when about to eat. And if there be ability to do so there should also be the grace to do so. If it be lacking there is need of praying for oneself. If the father is not a Christian the mother may lead the children in such devotion. The children themselves should be taught to offer such prayers that when they have homes of their own they may not neglect them.

Family worship. It will scarcely be possible to observe the Scriptures concerning prayer and to bring up the children in the nurture and admonition of the Lord without taking time for family worship. Even where there are no children the husband and wife cannot afford to miss the help which comes from prayers together. If there are children and they are taught to take a part in such worship it will be easy for them to conduct a family altar of their own. It is true that some children lose faith in religion because parents have family worship and then scold and quarrel in such a way as to discredit their religion, but to advocate a good thing is not to advocate its abuse. The family altar should stand for holy and loving family life, then its influence will always be a benediction, and though they wander far away they will never forget the old home altar. Two young men once visited their old home, and though father and mother were dead, they seemed to speak to them from the old familiar places. At last they paused by the well-worn spot on the floor before the fireplace, and one of them said, " There is where father used to kneel in family worship." Then they stood silent and the tears stole down their cheeks as they remembered the prayers that had there gone up for them. Then as if by common impulse they knelt again as they had done so long ago, and gave their hearts to their father's God. Truly, " train up a child in the way he should go, and when he is old he will not depart from it."

The morning watch. Thousands of earnest Christians throughout the world have come to observe the " morning watch," that is, the first few moments of the day are given to prayer and Bible study and meditation. Some spend half an hour in this way, some less, some more. They who take the time for this communion with God agree in their testimony, that far from being time lost in a busy life, it is time gained, for the morning watch somehow clears the mind, steadies the nerves, and prepares the heart for all that comes, so that as a result more and better work can be done in less time. Besides, the first and best of our time should be given to fellowship with the first and best of our friends. The morning watch may be observed alone or by friends or families together. The busiest of persons can find time for a few moments of communion with God which will sweeten the day and glorify the life. Try it and see.

The night watch is sometimes even more blessed than the morning watch, and many are the testimonies of God's saints to their seasons of blessing in their midnight meditations. See Psa. 16: 7; 42: 8; 77: 6; 119: 55; Acts 16: 9; 18: 9, &c. Prayer is the best cure for insomnia, and still better as a preventive than as a cure.

At night, when all is hushed and still, a wondrous peace my heart doth fill.
Then, Lord, as I commune with Thee, it bursteth into melody.
In that blest hour with solemn hush, so free from work's distracting crush,
I learn to know the Father's will,—at night when all is hushed and still.

The prayer meeting. The first regular meetings of the church were prayer meetings. The believers were holding a protracted prayer meeting when the Holy Spirit came and the Pentecost revival followed. The regular open meetings of the church were given to prayer and song and testimony. They were a means of fellowship as well as of worship and did much towards the upbuilding of the church. The modern church owes more than it realizes to the prayer meeting, and it will be a sad day for it when it allows the social or some other sort of pleasure party to drive out the prayer meeting. Though it be kept alive by the faithful few, yet it is the spiritual thermometer of the church. There may be improvements in the methods of conducting it but the primary purpose must remain. It is a meeting for prayer. In it every member of the church should be trained in prayer. Through it the various interests of the church should receive the help that comes from God. From it should go many a Paul and Barnabas, called of the Lord because of prayer for laborers (Matt. 9: 38; Acts 13: 1). It is never dull to those who have learned to love communion with the Father. Those who have not should there learn the same joy. It will probably continue to be sustained by the few saints who love to pray, but blessed are those few, for it is to them that Jesus comes.

2. WHERE TO PRAY. There was a time when men prayed at certain places, but Jesus said, "The hour cometh, and now is, when the true worshipers shall worship the Father in spirit and truth." Paul said, " I desire therefore that men pray in every place" (1 Tim. 2: 8). At home or at church, in the shop or store, in the fields or in the streets, the heart may be lifted in prayer. That place should be selected for extended prayer which will be least subject to distractions of any kind. Both private and public prayers have their place, and they who are accustomed to pray in private will also be able and willing to pray in public when necessary.

3. POSITION IN PRAYER. The Scriptures prescribe no one position for prayer. Kneeling seems to be the favorite mode. The Psalmist exhorts, "O come let us worship and bow down; Let us kneel before Jehovah our Maker" (Psa. 95: 6). This was the custom of Solomon (2 Chron. 6: 13), of Daniel (Dan. 6: 10), of Jesus (Luke 22: 41), of Stephen (Acts 7: 60), of Peter (Acts 9: 40) and Paul (Acts 20: 36) and Luke (Acts 21: 5). It is the mode which at once most fully expresses the feeling of humility and reverence, and shuts out the thoughts of other things. While Jesus endorsed the standing posture also (Mark 11: 25; Luke 18: 13) yet in practice it is unusually difficult to keep from seeing or hearing things which divide the attention, and when that is gone the prayer is lost. If it be said that big hats and fine clothing make it impracticable to kneel, then all the more should this posture be insisted upon so that pride may find it hard to sit at ease in the house of God.

4. THE " PRAYER COVERING." In 1 Cor. 11, Paul gives in-

structions to the Corinthian women to be veiled when praying or prophesying, but as this was a sign of subjection to the man as the head of the woman, as Christ is the head of the church, the question is considered in the chapter on marriage.

5. WHAT TO PRAY FOR. We nowhere find a list of things for which to pray, but we are taught to pray for anything that is according to the will of God (1 John 5: 14, 15), and here and there we are told of certain things that are the will of God. For them we may pray with confidence. Among these are the following: Pardon for sin (Luke 18: 13, 14), knowledge of God's will (Rom. 12: 1-3), for wisdom (Jas. 1: 5), for revival (Hab. 3: 2), for one another (Jas. 5: 16), for enemies (Matt. 5: 44), for workers (Matt. 9: 38), for the conversion of any who have not sinned unto death (1 John 5: 16, 17), for ministers (1 Thess. 5: 25), for healing (Jas. 5: 13, 14), for faith (Luke 22: 32), for rulers (1 Tim. 2: 1, 2), and last of all and best of all for the Holy Spirit (Luke 11: 13). Of course there are many more specific things for which to pray, the only limitation being that we seek to learn the will of God and conform our petitions to it.

V. The Lord's Prayer.

When the disciples came to Jesus saying, "Teach us to pray," He taught them a model prayer which is everywhere known as the Lord's Prayer. It is such a marvel of much in little that we should give it special study. As given by Matthew (6: 9-14 A. R. V.), it reads:

> Our Father who art in heaven,
>   Hallowed be thy name.
>   Thy kingdom come.
> Thy will be done, as in heaven, so on earth.
>   Give us this day our daily bread.

And forgive us our debts, as we also have forgiven our debtors. And bring us not into temptation, but deliver us from the evil one.

Note that there are six petitions, three concerning the things of God and three concerning the things of men, and that as in the ten commandments, the things of God come first. Let us notice the prayer in detail.

Our Father. It is interesting to note the development of the revelation of God by the different names that are revealed in the Scriptures. The first name used is Elohim, which is plural, "the Gods," and is used in the Genesis account of creation. It is a reference to the Deity without naming any of His attributes. Abraham knew God as El Shaddai, God Almighty, but not as Jehovah, the covenant-keeping God, by which name He was revealed to Moses (Ex. 6: 3). Never before Jesus were men taught to pray to Him as "Father," and even that term fails to reveal the fullness of His holiness and love, and we read of a new name that shall by and by be revealed (Rev. 3: 12).

Note that we are to address the Father in prayer rather than the Son or the Spirit. While we are to honor the Son even as we honor the Father (John 5: 23), yet the Son is subject to the Father (1 Cor. 15: 28), and the Spirit is subject to the Father and the Son (John 16: 13, 14). To call God "Father" means that we agree to live the relationship of children, and that means to do as Jesus would (1 John 2: 6). In a sense all men are children of God, "For we are also his offspring" (Acts 17: 29, 30), but prodigal children miss all the blessings of sonship, and only they who are "born again" (John 3: 5) are true children of God and joint heirs with Jesus Christ (Rom. 8: 16, 17). The Lord's Prayer was used at the World's Parliament of Religions by adherents of all religions, but not all are entitled to say "Our Father."

The Jews thought they were children of God, but Jesus called some of them "children of the devil" (John 8: 44) because they acted like him. They who would have God for their Father must obey the condition of adoption as children (John 1: 12).

If the expression "Our Father" teaches the fatherhood of God for believers, it teaches also the brotherhood of believers, that is, the kingdom of God. There is much talk of the fatherhood of God and the brotherhood of man that is unscriptural and misleading. Jesus said, "Whosoever shall do the will of my Father who is in heaven, he is my brother, and sister, and mother" (Matt. 12: 50). Then how about those who refuse to do the will of the Father in heaven? Are they not aliens from God and strangers to the kingdom? (Eph. 2: 3, 11-13). If we pray "Our Father" we must also live as brethren in the kingdom.

Hallowed be Thy Name. The name of God stands for Himself. To hallow the name is to reverence God, and reverence for God is a first step in coming to Him. They who pray this prayer cannot take the name of God in blasphemy or in irreverent jests or even in carelessness. Canon Boyle used always to pause before speaking the name of God. But to hallow the name means to live reverently at all times.

Thy kingdom come. The kingdom of God is "righteousness and joy and peace in the Holy Spirit" (Rom. 14: 17). It is already in the world but is not of the world. It is growing as the corn grows,—first the blade and then the stalk and then the full ear (Mark 4: 26-29). It is here in its beginning, but is coming in its fulness, and for that fulness we are to pray. But if we pray for the kingdom we must also work for the kingdom and we must live as children of the kingdom.

Thy will be done. Free will marks man from the animals, and choice of God's will rather than self-will marks the child of God from the rest of men. To pray that the will of God may be done on earth as it is in heaven, means that it shall be done perfectly, and that means the regeneration of society. It means the transformation of business and politics and the home life. It means that God shall be all in all. It means that we who pray this prayer must do the will of God ourselves, not merely talk about it, but do it, whether it send us to the heathen or not.

Give us this day our daily bread. "This day" does not mean provision at once for all the rest of life and for the children also, and "bread" does not mean luxuries. The expression literally is, "Give us for the coming day our little loaf." God wishes us to do our duty in the present and to trust Him for the future. The laborer is worthy of his wages, and we are laborers (Luke 10: 7). The soldier goes not to war on his own charges, and we are soldiers (1 Cor. 9: 7). The children lay not up for the parents, but the parents for the children, and we are children (2 Cor. 12: 14). If we live this relation we shall have boldness when we pray, and He who provides for the ravens when they cry will not leave us to suffer.

Forgive us our debts as we forgive our debtors. This phrase varies in the Gospels. Matthew uses "debts," and Luke uses "sins." The phrase refers not to loans of money, but to all manner of things which brotherly love demands that we forgive. The measure of our forgiveness is the measure of our fitness for heaven, and the forgiveness of God (Matt. 18: 21-33; Mark 11: 24, 25).

Lead us not into temptation. God tempts no man to do evil (Jas. 1: 13, 14), but He does allow us to be tested as a means of developing strength. "It is the stormy sea that makes the mariner," and "the dark night brings out the stars." The world in which by the providence of God we are placed is full of trials and temptations, and this prayer is a petition for escape from whatever might cause us to sin. "Woe to the world because of occasions of stumbling! for it must needs be that the occasions come; but woe to that man through whom the occasion cometh" (Matt. 18: 7). To pray this prayer means that we shall do our utmost to keep out of temptation. More than that it means that we will do our utmost to get temptations out of the world. It is hypocrisy to pray, "Lead us not into temptation," and then permit the embrace of the dance, the lewd suggestions of the theater, the seductive taste of intoxicants, the fascination of games of chance. He who prays this prayer and votes to license saloons is a hypocrite. We must work in the direction of our prayers or we pray in vain.

Deliver us from evil. The Revised Version reads, "the evil one." Evil has a cause, and our deliverance is from Satan, the active agent of evil. "For thine is the kingdom, the power and the glory, forever. Amen." These words are in the old versions, but not in the new, because not in the most ancient manuscripts. They form a fitting close to the prayer as they bring us back again from our present needs to the eternal kingdom and glory of the Father, and leave us with words of praise upon our lips.

If we turn to history for confirmation of what has been said concerning prayer, we find its pages covered with testimonies. From the time that Abraham interceded for Sodom until the closing words of the Gospel, "Amen: come, Lord Jesus," the sacred page is full of instances of answer to prayer. The most characteristic thing of the early church was its prayer. From this came the spirit of brotherhood and the spirit of missions and the enduement of power and the triumph of the cross. The believers prayed and the Spirit came (Acts 2) the prison doors were opened (Acts 12 and 16), the fields were prepared (1 Tim. 2: 1), the

Prayer

workers were sent forth (Acts 13: 2, 3), they were guided (Acts 10) and sustained and their witness was made fruitful (John 15: 16).

In subsequent times no less than in apostolic days has every step of progress made by the church been marked by prayer. It was while in prayer that Martin Luther received the guidance that opened the door of the reformation. Mary Queen of Scots used to say that she feared the prayers of John Knox more than an army of ten thousand men. Robert E. Speer after tracing the triumph of prayer in ages past says:

> It is only, therefore, in accordance with a very general truth that we trace the foundation of our present missionary organization to times of revival, which were also times of awakened prayer.

It was out of a revival of prayer that William Carey was called to open the door of modern missions. It was out of the famous haystack prayer meeting at Williams College that there came the American Board of Commissioners for Foreign Missions and the American Bible Society and the African School. Mr. Speer says further:

> And not only has prayer played the supreme part in the formation of missionary agencies, but it has been at the bottom of all revivals in missionary work. * * * Aye, and we may go a step further than this, and assert that through men who knew how to pray has every new departure and development of missions, which has borne in any real sense the marks of God's leading, been effected.

John G. Paton, the missionary whose work in the New Hebrides is no less marvelous than the acts of the Apostles, and Hudson Taylor, the founder of the great Inland and China mission, were both consecrated to missions by their parents before they were born. The Church Missionary Society in 1885 prayed for workers, and 100 students offered themselves for the work. A hundred more went to Inland China in 1887 in answer to prayer. Pastor Gossner alone sent out 144 missionaries and provided for them through prayer. It was said at his funeral:

> He prayed up the walls of a hospital and the hearts of the nurses; he prayed mission stations into being and missionaries into faith; he prayed open the hearts of the rich, and gold from the most distant lands.

The story of George Muller is even more wonderful. Through prayer he educated 95,000 orphan children, circulated 100,000,000 Bibles, and as many tracts, sent out over 250 missionaries, educated thousands of ministers and spent over $13,000,000 in the Lord's work, every penny of which came in answer to prayer. The first call for the observance of the week of prayer came from the mission field. The Student Volunteer movement resulted from prayer, and works by prayer. In 1902 the convention met at Toronto and prayed that during the next four years at least 1,000 students might volunteer to go where called in the mission field, and in 1906 John R. Mott announced at the convention at Nashville that in that time just 1,000 volunteers had enrolled. The present world-wide wave of evangelism may be clearly traced to prayer. For ten years there have been regular prayer meetings held in many places for the purpose of praying for world-wide revival. Out of one of these meetings Dr. Torrey received his call for his world tour which left 18,000 converts in his path. Out of another the great revival in Wales was born. Evan Roberts was so given to prayer that his landlady asked him to find another lodging place.

But why say more? Volumes might be written, have been written and will be written, only to be passed by with indifference by the mass of the church, which is neither cold nor hot. But some, perhaps, may read these things whose hearts may kindle and whose faith may burn, and whose prayers will ascend, and by the law of prayer will bring to pass yet other things that will mean the conversion of souls, the transformation of the world and the coming of our Lord in His glorious kingdom. Even so come Lord Jesus!

Prayer

Is there a God whom prayer may call?
And is it, is it true, that He
Is pleased to hear the cries of all
Who seek Him in sincerity?
Go ask the ravens when they cry,
If they are left to pine and die.
Go ask the stars, God's jeweled sheep,
Who guides them through their pastures steep.
Go ask the babe which sobs its prayer
To earthly parents; say if God
Is worse than they, or whether we
The babe's sure faith may justly share.

So teach me Lord, that I may pray.
Nay, more than that, inspire
This wilful, wayward heart of mine,
To seek thyself alway.
Thou art our Father, and I know
Thy love dost seek thy children, all;
Pass me not by, I would be thine;
I come, for Oh, I need Thee so.
Teach me to pray as Jesus prayed;
To live and love as He;
To work and watch and wait and come
By thine own Spirit's aid.

PRAISE.

True prayer is not without praise. The two go together like the two halves of a sphere. A stranger in a strange land, if he be wise, will learn the words for "please" and "thank you" first of all, for by these he shows that he is a gentleman and worthy of favor. If even courtesy among men demands the "thank you" as well as the "please," how much more should praise be a part of our communion with God. He does not overlook it. "Were there not ten cleansed? but where are the nine?"

I. Praise as a Symbol.

Praise as well as prayer, in its outward forms, is but a symbol, an expression of an inward attitude. It is a necessary symbol because the inward spirit of praise is a necessary attitude for a child of God. It is a most useful symbol, because emotion grows by expression, and the habit of praise therefore develops the spirit of praise. It is a joyful symbol, because it is the expression of gratitude for blessings received. It is an everlasting symbol, because it shall have its place in the eternal kingdom, where the redeemed of God shall sing His praise forever. (Rev. 5: 9; 14: 3; 15: 3).

II. Under the Old Covenant.

God's people formerly praised Him both by forms and songs. The very sacrifices were regarded as wafting praise to God from the worshiping people (Heb. 13: 15), and the offerings were the gift of grateful hearts. When Israel came into the Promised Land the people were required to dedicate all the fruit of the fourth year as a praise offering to God (Lev. 19: 24) and used none of it for themselves until the year following. In all their sacrifices and offerings, they were taught to give the first and best to God. Even the pagan nations have seen the fitness of this, and in some instances have been led to human sacrifices, for what more precious can be offered than the life of loved ones? The ignorant abuse of the principle God forbade (2 Kings 23: 10), but teaches us instead to present our bodies a living sacrifice, holy and acceptable unto God, which is our reasonable service (Rom. 12: 1).

When the temple was built David organized the song service with singers and players who gave their time continually to the service of praise. Under Solomon the temple choir numbered a thousand and the psalms were largely prepared for use in the worship of God in the temple. We lose much of their beauty and power in their translation, yet they still remain an inspiration to all who would find fitting words with which to voice their praise to God.

III. In the Church.

In the church, praise has had a prominent place from the first. When Jesus instituted the ordinances He closed the service with a hymn, which is mentioned as if such singing were a familiar custom with Jesus and the disciples. In the church the praise service developed as a part of its natural life. He who began his prayer with, "Father, I thank thee" (John 11: 41), who gave thanks at meals (John 6: 11; Luke 22: 19) and whose whole life was one of praise, inspired the like spirit in His church, even as it was prophesied, He shall give to them "the garment of praise for the spirit of heaviness" (Isa. 61: 3).

The first mention of the public worship of the church begins, "When ye come together, each one hath a psalm" &c. ,1 Cor. 14: 26), and the apostle further exhorts:

Let the word of Christ dwell in you richly; in all wisdom

teaching and admonishing one another with psalms and hymns and spiritual songs, singing with grace in your hearts unto God (Col. 3: 16).

The author of Hebrews also says:

Through him then let us offer up a sacrifice of praise to God continually, that is, the fruit of lips which make confession to his name (Heb. 13: 15).

Thus as the formal prayers help to inculcate the spirit of prayer at all times, so the service of song helps to inspire the spirit of praise at all times, so that we shall " do all to the honor and glory of God " and " in everything give thanks."

IV. The Use of Instruments.

The use of instruments in the song service of the temple began with David. In 2 Chron. 29: 25 we read:

And he set the Levites in the house of Jehovah with cymbals, with psalteries, and with harps, according to the commandment of David, and of Gad the king's seer, and Nathan the prophet; for the commandment was of Jehovah by his prophets.

This use of instruments was also encouraged by the inspired psalmists (Psa. 33: 2; 71: 22; 144: 9; 150: 4; Isa. 38: 20) and was never condemned of the Lord, unless the words of Amos (6: 5) are a condemnation. He denounces those who " invent for themselves instruments of music like David " (marg. " David's "), but he also denounces those " that sing idle songs to the sound of the viol." However, the use of instruments under the old covenant, with its means of grace adapted to the spiritual capacities of the people at that time, would alone be no authority for their use under the more advanced Gospel dispensation. In fact, there is no evidence that instruments were used in the apostolic church. However their absence be explained, the fact remains that the praise service of the church is said to have consisted of " psalms and hymns and spiritual songs," and the worshipers made melody *in the heart* unto God (Eph. 5: 19). It must be remembered, however, that the words and tunes of vocal music are only expressions in sound intended to voice the praise in the heart, and are therefore signs the same as the sounds of instruments used for the same purpose. The vocal chords are an instrument of the throat as the harp or organ is an instrument of the fingers, and the one may be used or abused the same as the other. Both vocal and instrumental music have been used for base ends in the vaudeville and other places of worldly amusement, and such abuse of both is condemned alike by the prophet (Amos 6: 5). There are those who in this dispensation love the inspiration that came from such instruments of devotion in the old, and there are those who cannot sing, but who can express sincere devotion by voicing the melodies of the same songs on instruments. In Rev. 15: 2 we read of the redeemed in heaven singing the song of Moses and the Lamb accompanied by " the harps of God." It would seem that if there are harps of God to lead the songs of heaven itself it certainly is not sinful to reverently use such instruments of praise on earth. There are many who can best express their emotions with the voice, and undoubtedly such praise should prevail in the church, but since God commanded these other helps in the Old Testament (2 Chron. 29: 25) and does not forbid them in the New, there should be liberty of conscience in their use, in so far, of course, as they are properly used. It cannot be denied that the use of instruments in the popular churches tends to increase the temptation to make the music a matter of entertainment rather than of worship, and this tendency must be most carefully guarded against. To sing " with the spirit and with the understanding " (1 Cor. 14: 15) as we are taught to do, is better than to seek the melody of instruments void of understanding, however entrancing that may be. And yet we see no reason why the spiritually minded may not be borne along "in spirit and in truth" by the reverent use of melody. Heaven with its harps shall be our judge.

V. The Spirit of Praise.

Praise is an act of worship as much as prayer or the preaching of the Word. Therefore the Holy Spirit, who assists in prayer (Rom. 8: 26) and in preaching (Acts 5: 32), also assists in the service of song. He is the "grace in your hearts" with which we are to sing. Without Him we cannot sing "spiritual songs" (Col. 3: 16) or with Paul "sing with the spirit and with the understanding also." (1 Cor. 14: 15). With Him we shall not make of the song service a mere exhibition of voice or of skill on instruments. The Holy Spirit in the early church caused the service of song to be spontaneous and free. There were no hired operatic singers or unconverted leaders to draw crowds by their entertainment. When once music descends to the level of entertainment it is no longer an act of worship. Henry Ward Beecher was quite right when he announced one day to his congregation, "We will now suspend our worship for a time while we have an exhibition by the choir." This is not to decry leadership in music, but to cry out against desecrating the worship of God with the spirit of formality and hypocrisy. It would be as consistent to call on an unrepentant sinner to pray or preach as to call on him or her to lead the worship of song. Such compromises, made for the sake of interesting the unconverted, serve to keep more away from Christ than they lead to Him. The service of song must be sincere or it cannot be "in the Spirit." If any join in the words of a song and do not mean them they make of them a hollow mockery, for they say and mean it not, they sing and they feel not, they promise and they obey not. For this reason the song books and the songs should be selected with a view to the soundness of their teaching as well as to the beauty of their melody, and the pastor or leader should explain the meaning of the songs that need explanation, that all may sing with the understanding as well as with the spirit.

If the spirit of praise be kept in proper condition in the church, it will reflect itself in the home life of the members as well. Christian homes should be marked by spiritual songs as well as the church. There is something wrong with the parents when the children are fed on " coon songs " and " rag time " music in the home instead of on music of an ennobling nature. If instruments are used let them be " instruments of righteousness rather than instruments of unrighteousness." Rightly used, music in the home is a powerful agency for good. Parents who provide for it and lead it in the proper channels can make it a means of holding their children to the right. Some have a song of thanks at meals; some sing at family worship, and some take time for singing at other times. The spirit of true praise in the heart will manifest itself in proper forms of outward expression. It is therefore the task of the church to teach to all the spirit of gratitude in such a way and in such a degree that it will have its proper place in the public worship and in the private life.

If anyone in the world has a right to use music to express joy and worship it is the Christian. Only they can sing the song of the redeemed and tune their music to the major key. Of all religions, Christianity is the inspiration of song, and while pagans have their songs they are of a doleful sound, while those of the church are of that triumphant chord which marks the moving of a victorious army. She moves with her banners aloft triumphant over the world, the flesh and the devil, toward the city whose streets are gold and whose gates are praise. There she shall join in singing the song of Moses and the Lamb and know the reality of the glory of which we here can only sing.

The Voice of Praise

Hear the song creation sings in oratorio,
Voicing praises unto God in language all may know,
Birds and beasts and flowers and stars, all things above, below,
Creatures and children together.

What is the theme that nature sings, and what the happy tune?
It is the theme of wondrous love of nature's God Triune.
Who knows it best may lead the rest, as all with Him commune,
Singing the song of redemption.

While the endless ages roll in glory round the throne,
Let the music of the spheres set free from sinner's groan,
Attuned to heaven's harmony blend voices with our own,
Praising our Heavenly Father.

CHAPTER III

THREE SYMBOLS RELATING TO THE NEW BIRTH.

Confession—Baptism by Triune Immersion—The Kiss of Peace.

* * * * * *

"With the heart man believeth unto righteousness; and with the mouth confession is made unto salvation."—Rom. 10: 10.

* * * * * *

"All authority hath been given unto me in heaven and on earth, Go ye therefore, and make disciples of all the nations, baptizing them into the name of the Father and of the Son and of the Holy Spirit: teaching them to observe all things whatsoever I have commanded you: and lo, I am with you always, even unto the end of the world."—Matt.28: 18-20.

* * * * * *

"Salute one another with a holy kiss."—1 Cor. 16: 20.

CONFESSION.

The first step toward the new life in Christ is to openly come to Him. There were many Jewish rulers who believed in Him, " but because of the Pharisees they did not confess it, lest they should be put out of the synagogue " (John 11: 42). Such faith without confession is dead. There is always something wrong when a believer is ashamed to confess. In the case of these rulers, " they loved the glory that is of men more than the glory that is of God " (v. 43). Jesus required an open confession, saying:

> Every one therefore who shall confess me before men, him will I also confess before my Father who is in heaven. But whosoever shall deny me before men, him will I also deny before my Father who is in heaven (Matt. 10: 32, 33).

I. The Value of Confession.

Of what value is public confession of Christ that it should be made a condition of discipleship?

1. CONFESSION IS AN EXPRESSION OF LOVE. What child loves its parents which does not rejoice in an opportunity to introduce them to friends? What friend loves a friend who is not likewise eager to make the friendship known? What servant even, in a royal family, is not proud to bear the marks of his high position? And shall they that serve the King of kings, not as servants merely, but as adopted children, be ashamed to own the Father in heaven, or His Son Jesus Christ, their Elder Brother?

> "Ashamed of Jesus, that dear friend
> On whom my hopes of heaven depend?
> No, when I blush be this my shame
> That I no more revere His name."

2. Confession is a symbol of coming out from the world. It therefore helps to separate the convert from the old life of sin. "Come out from among them and be ye separate" is the injunction of the Word. The church is called in the Greek *ecclesia,* which means "the called out." It will be of immense help to the disciple of Christ to let the old world know that he is no more of it.

3. Confession is a symbol of alliance with Christ and His people. It openly identifies us with the cause of Christ and allies us with all its friends. The help of these new friendships is valuable to the young disciple.

4. Confession is a sign of the indwelling Spirit.

Hereby know ye the Spirit of God: every spirit that confesseth that Jesus Christ is come in the flesh is of God (1 John 4: 2).

This does not refer to mere intellectual assent, but to confession that is born out of heart-faith (Rom. 10: 10). Such confession is evidence of a changed life, for "no man can say, Jesus is Lord, but in the Holy Spirit" (1 Cor. 12: 3).

5. Confession is a means of acceptance with Christ.

If we confess Him He will also confess us, but "if we deny him, he will also deny us" (2 Tim. 2: 12). This does not refer to hypocrites who "profess that they know God; but by their works they deny him" (Titus 1: 16), but to true confession; which is backed by a life lived openly and honestly for Christ. Confession of sin was a preparatory step to receiving the baptism of John (Matt. 3: 6), and continued to be a preparatory step for receiving Christian baptism under the apostles. When the eunuch desired baptism, Philip replied, "If thou believest with all thy heart thou mayest" and the eunuch replied "I believe that Jesus Christ is the Son of God" (Acts 8: 37). This passage has been put in the margin in the Revised Version, but it is

Confession

in harmony with the rest of the Gospel. The early church invariably required confession before baptism.

Chrysostom (347 A. D.) says:

What is more beautiful than the words with which we renounce the devil and enlist in the service of Christ, than both that confession which is before the baptismal laver and that which is after it?"—Hom. on Eph.

II. The Form of Confession.

There are just three things that the Scriptures seem to make essential to confession:

1. CONFESSION MUST BE OF JESUS AS LORD. This implies a recognition of His divinity as the Son of God, for the term Lord was never used by the apostles and the early church except with reference to a divine being. This acceptance of Christ as the Son of God was the essence of the good confession made by Peter (Matt. 16: 16-18), which marked him as a rock of the cliff on which Jesus builds His church. He says to him, "Thou art Peter ("Peter" is Greek for rock) and upon this rock (Gr., *petra,* a "cliff of rock") will I build my church." This confession of Peter was to be typical of all subsequent confessions. It was voluntary, made with the understanding, and by the Spirit of God.

2. CONFESSION MUST BE BEFORE THE WORLD. Jesus said, "He that confesseth me before men, him will I confess" &c. It is not enough to confess in private. Jesus calls us to public service. "Ye shall be my witnesses" (Greek, martyrs) (Acts 1: 8). If open confession means persecution or loss, well and good. "If we suffer with him we shall also reign with him."

3. CONFESSION MUST BE FOLLOWED BY LOVING OBEDIENCE.

Not every one that saith unto me Lord, Lord, shall enter into the kingdom of heaven; but he that doeth the will of my Father who is in heaven (Matt. 7: 21).

Even the demons confessed Jesus as the Son of God (Mark 5: 7), but it availed nothing because it was without love, which is the life of all forms of confession and service (1 Cor. 13).

There is absolutely no scripture which prescribes a certain way of taking the stand for Christ, whether by weeping at the mourner's bench, praying at the altar, coming forward to give the preacher the hand, making application to the elder or others, or any of the other forms that prevail. These various ways each have their merits and demerits and are to be considered as expediencies rather than essentials. The converts of the apostolic church were not required to come in a fixed and formal way. Wherever they were, they were allowed to make their confession of faith and repentance and go on to obedience. There should be like liberty today.

The *Apostolic Constitutions,* supposed to have been written in the second century and revised in the fourth, contain a copy of a form of confession of that early age, which we give herewith, not because it is of authority, but because it may be of interest as showing the general faith of the church at that time. It was the pledge taken by applicants for baptism. It reads:

I renounce Satan and his works, and his pomps, and his worships, and his angels, and his inventions, and all things that are under him.

And I associate myself with Christ, and believe and am baptized into one unbegotten Being, the only true God Almighty, the Father of Christ, the Creator and Maker of all things, and from whom are all things; and into the Lord Jesus Christ, His only begotten Son, the first born of the whole creation, who before the ages was begotten of the good pleasure of the Father, by whom all things were made both those in heaven and those on earth, visible and invisible; who in the last days descended from heaven and took flesh and was born of the virgin Mary, and did converse holily according to the laws of his God and Father, and was crucified under Pontius Pilate and died for us, and rose again from the dead after his passion the third day, and ascended into the heavens, and sitteth at the right hand of the Father, and again is to come at the end of the world with glory to judge the quick and the dead, of whose kingdom there shall be no end. And I am baptized into the Holy Ghost, that is, the Comforter, who wrought in all the saints from the beginning of the world, but was afterwards sent to the apostles by the Father, according to the Promise of our Lord and Saviour Jesus Christ; and after the apostles to all those that believe in the holy catholic church; into the resurrection of the flesh and into the remission of sins, and into the kingdom of heaven and into the life of the world to come.

BAPTISM.

I. The Old Testament Foreshadowings of Christian Baptism.

The revelation of God is a gradual unfolding of truth according to the capacities of the people. The truths of the Gospel which are so vital as to be taught and preserved by means of forms or rites, have their beginnings far back in the story of revelation, and were taught at other times by other forms that differed from the present forms, as the seed differs from the flower. Baptism is not known by that name in the beginning of God's revelation, but the truth for which it stands is taught in ways which foreshadow baptism in some points, while differing from it in others.

1. THE ARK.

Peter says,

While the ark was a preparing, wherein few, that is, eight souls, were saved through water; which also after a true likeness doth now save you, even baptism, not the putting away of the filth of the flesh, but the interrogation of a good conscience toward God—1 Peter 3: 21.

Here the point of likeness is the water as an agency of salvation to the obedient. (1) As Noah and his family left the old life with the ante-diluvian world, so the Christian dies to sin (Rom. 6: 11). (2) As the sinful world that then was lay buried in the flood, so " we are buried by baptism into death " (Rom. 6: 4). (3) As Noah and his family in the ark passed through the water to enter a new life in covenant relation with God, so we from the baptismal grave rise to " walk in newness of life " (Rom. 6: 4). (4) As Noah and his family proved their faith and love by their obedience, so baptism is " the answer of a good conscience

Baptism

toward God." The question of a triple action does not enter into the figure, because God was not revealed to Noah as "the Father, the Son and the Holy Spirit," as He is revealed to us in the command for Christian baptism (Matt. 28: 19).

2. THE PASSAGE OF THE RED SEA.

Paul says of the Israelites that they "were all baptized unto Moses in the cloud and in the sea" (1 Cor. 10: 1, 2). We have here the same points of likeness as in the figure of the ark: (1) leaving the old life in Egypt, (2) burying the sinful past in the sea, (3) emerging to the new life in covenant relation with God, (4) obedience to the conditions of this new life as the means of entering into it. As the Israelites had learned the new name, the covenant name of God, Jehovah, and went on to receive the law at Sinai, so Christians at baptism learn to know God as the Father, Son and Holy Spirit, and go on to obey the whole Gospel.

3. CIRCUMCISION.

Paul also speaks of circumcision as answering in a measure to baptism. He says:

In whom (Christ) ye were also circumcised with a circumcision not made with hands, in the putting off of the body of the flesh, in the circumcision of Christ; having been buried with him in baptism, wherein ye were also raised with him through faith in the working of God, who raised him from the dead. And you, being dead through your trespasses and the uncircumcision of your flesh, you, I say, did he make alive together with him, having forgiven us all our trespasses (Col. 2: 11-13).

Circumcision was a sacrifice of a part representing the seat of life as a token of God's ownership of all. Compare Rom. 12: 1, "Present your bodies a living sacrifice." It thus pointed to our being "baptized into death" with the accompanying burial and resurrection, and the idea of regeneration involved. It therefore stood at the entrance into the old covenant church as a "seal of the righteousness of the faith" (Rom. 4: 11), which Abraham exemplified when the rite was introduced, and for which baptism also stands to the spiritual seed of Abraham. "For we are the circumcision who worship by the Spirit of God, and glory in Christ Jesus, and have no confidence in the flesh" (Philpp. 3: 3).

4. BATHING BEFORE ATONEMENT.

In Heb. 10: 22 we read:

Having a great High Priest over the house of God; let us draw near with a true heart in fullness of faith, having our hearts sprinkled from an evil conscience: and having our bodies washed with pure water.

This is a reference to the atonement by blood which was by sprinkling, and the ceremonial cleansing by water on the day of atonement, which was by bathing (immersion) (Lev. 16: 4, 24, 26, 28). Thus the candidate for baptism accepts the atonement of Christ by faith and the regeneration represented by the baptismal bath. There is the inward work of grace and the outward representation of it, the cleansing of the heart and the bathing of the body.

There were many rites under the law to represent atonement by sprinkling blood (or ashes, or ashes and water) and to represent cleansing by bathing, but they were all summed up in the rites of the day of atonement referred to above. This came once a year, because the high priest himself being imperfect, needed often to make atonement, but Christ our High Priest has offered Himself once for all, and hence we are baptized once for all "into His death." It should be noted here that sprinkling was used only in rites signifying blood atonement. There is no command or instance in the Bible, of pure water alone being used to signify cleansing, save by immersion. Ezek. 26: 25 must be taken with Num. 8: 7 and 19: 17-20.

Baptism

5. JEWISH BAPTISM BY TRINE IMMERSION.

When later the Jews were carried captive and the temple was destroyed because of their sins, they could not keep all the ritual of the law, but even in exile they preserved the rites of circumcision and bathing as a symbol of cleansing, and the rites of atonement and purification came to be condensed into a triple bathing, mainly on the day of atonement, which was the next step in the coming of trine immersion as Christian baptism.

The *Jewish Cyclopedia,* which is the highest modern authority on Jewish customs, says under " Baptism " :

The natural method of cleansing the body by washing and bathing in water was always customary in Israel. The washing of their clothes was an important means of sanctification enjoined on the Israelites before the revelation on Mt. Sinai (Ex. 19: 10). The Rabbis connect with this the duty of bathing by complete immersion (" Tebilah," yebam 46b; Mek; Behodesh 3); and since sprinkling with blood was always accompanied by immersion, tradition connects with this immersion the blood lustration mentioned as having taken place immediately before the revelation (Ex. 24: 8), **these three acts being the initiatory rites always performed upon proselytes** " to bring them under the wings of the Shekinah " (yeb. 1. c.). This is what John preached to the sinners that gathered about him on the Jordan, and herein lies the significance of the bath of every proselyte. He is to be made " a new creature " (Gen. R. 39), " in the name of God." For this very reason the Israelites before the acceptance of the law had, according to Philo, On the Decalogue, as well as according to rabbinical tradition, to undergo the rite of baptismal purification (1 Cor. 10: 2).

The same cyclopedia says, under " Atonement," that the Persian Jews and the Samaritans also prepared for the day of atonement by a purification bath.

That this custom was familiar to the early church is shown by references to it. *Apostolic Constitutions* in prescribing the laying on of hands following baptism says that without this "the candidate does only DESCEND INTO THE WATER AS DO THE JEWS."

It is a fact also, not generally known, that the orthodox Jews continue to this day the *trine immersion* as a sign of renewing the heart. To this custom we have had the personal testimony of learned Jews who themselves have observed the rite. Rabbi Wise in the *American Israelite* said:

To the mikva, (bath) the Jewish women yet go according to Lev. 12 and 15, and to this goes every pious Israelite on the day of atonement.

These baths are invariably performed with three dips. Thus the three kinds of immersion commanded under the law, signifying the cleansing of the clothes, the body and the heart, were and are combined in one triune immersion. This was the Jewish custom which was considered as representing the heart of Jewish doctrine and the gist of the law, and was therefore imposed upon Gentiles wishing to accept Judaism. In Jesus' day is was called "proselyte baptism."

6. PROSELYTE BAPTISM.

Edersheim, a noted Jewish historian, in discussing John's baptism says:

What John preached, that he also symbolized by a rite which, though not in itself, yet in its application, was wholly new. Hitherto the law had it that those who contracted Levitical defilement were to immerse before offering sacrifices. Again, it was prescribed that such Gentiles as became "proselytes of righteousness" were to be admitted to full participation in the privileges of Israel by the threefold rites of circumcision, baptism and sacrifice—the immersion being, as it were, the acknowledgment and symbolic removal of moral defilement corresponding to that of Levitical uncleanness. But never before had it been proposed that Israel should undergo a "baptism of repentance," although there are indications of a deeper insight into the meaning of Levitical baptisms. The Talmud says, "A man who is guilty of sin, and makes confession, and does not turn from it, to whom is he like? To a man who has

Baptism

in his hand a defiling reptile, who even if he immerses in all the waters of the world, his baptism avails him nothing; but let him cast it from his hand, and if he immerses in only forty seas of water, immediately his baptism avails him."—Life of Christ, Vol. 1 Bk. 2. ch. 11.

Hastings' Bible Dictionary also says (Art. Bap.):

Every gentile, whether man or woman, who became a Jew, was purified from heathen pollution by immersion.

In the *Ethiopic Version* of the Gospel, Matt. 23: 15, reads: " Ye compass land and sea to IMMERSE one proselyte." We have already seen that this immersion was with triple action.

7. THE BAPTISM OF JOHN THE BAPTIST.

It was at this time, when the trine immersion of the Jews (especially on the day of atonement) and of proselytes on their conversion to Judaism, was familiar to all as a rite representing the purification of the heart, that John the Baptist came preaching and baptizing. He was of the sect of the Essenes, who, Josephus says, were accustomed to bathe frequently in cold water as a means of attaining holiness (B. J. 2: 8: 5). The Messianic hope of the Jews had ripened until the faithful among them were eagerly expecting the Christ. The fullness of the time had come, when the Father should speak through the Son and soon both be represented by the Holy Spirit. The kingdom of heaven was at hand and Judaism was to give way to Christianity, the law to the Gospel. The connecting link between the two was this baptism which represented the heart of both. It meant renewal of the heart, and this was the very thing essential to entrance into the kingdom (John 3: 5). John allowed only the repentant to receive it, promising that the King who was to come would give to them the Holy Spirit. Thus John took the people through the confession and repentance and water baptism that prepares the heart for the Holy Spirit, who works the inward change and makes the purified life His temple.

Concerning John's baptism *Edersheim* says:

May it not rather have been that as, when the first covenant was made, Moses was directed to prepare Israel by symbolic baptism of their persons and their garments (Ex. 19: 10-14 cf. Gen. 35: 2), so the initiation of the new covenant by which the people were to enter into the kingdom of God, was preceded by another general symbolic baptism of those who would be the true Israel, and receive, or take on themselves, the law of God? In that case the rite would have acquired not only a new significance but be deeply and truly an answer to John's call. In such case also, no special explanation would have been needed on the part of the Baptist, nor yet such spiritual insight on that of the people as we can scarcely suppose them to have possessed at that stage. Lastly, in that case nothing could have been more suitable, nor more solemn, than Israel in waiting for the Messiah and the rule of God, preparing as their fathers had done at the base of Mt. Sinai. This may help us even at this stage, to understand why our Lord, in the fulfillment of all righteousness, submitted to baptism. It seems also to explain why, after the coming of Christ, the baptism of John was alike unavailing and even meaningless (Acts 19: 3-5). Lastly, it also shows how he that is least in the kingdom of heaven is really greater than John himself (Luke 7: 28).

Thus Judaic baptism is linked with that of John in form and meaning, while it in turn prepared for the larger content of Christian baptism.

II. The Institution of Christian Baptism.

When Jesus began His ministry He was baptized by John, and John's disciples began to follow Jesus. Several of them Jesus called to be apostles, and as Jesus preached they baptized, presumably in the same manner as John, for there is no hint of any change at this time in form or significance. Jesus preached the kingdom as John did, except that He gradually explained its spiritual nature as John could not do. Then when He had finished His work and was ready to turn the evangelization of the world over to

His disciples, Jesus gave the commission to preach and to baptize "into the name of the Father and of the Son and of the Holy Spirit" (Matt. 28: 19). The Jews had taught faith in God the Father, faith in the coming Christ, the Son, and faith in the Holy Spirit. John had proclaimed the Christ as at hand, and the Spirit soon to come, and baptized his converts as a sign of their faith in this Gospel (good news), and now Jesus passes on this same triune immersion, but as a symbol of regeneration through faith in the Father, whose Fatherhood was now fully revealed; and in the Son whose work was now finished, and in the Holy Spirit who was now to accompany baptism with His own gracious work in the life.

That this baptism meant immersion in water, and not merely the gift of the Spirit, is shown by the practice of the apostles and the church (Acts 2: 38, 39; 8: 36; 9: 18, &c.). It is not credible that with the full directions received by the apostles from the Lord before His death, and by the Holy Spirit afterwards, that they should have been allowed to err so greatly as to fasten water baptism on the church as an ordinance when it was not intended by the commission. The "one baptism" of Eph. 4: 5 refers not to the baptism of the church by the Spirit, for He came once for all on Pentecost (Acts 2), but to that Christian baptism which was perpetuated as an ordinance in the church, the immersion in water being a symbol of the inner regeneration.

III. The Meaning of Christian Baptism.

Christian baptism is a symbol of regeneration. It represents the passing of the believer from the old life of sin into the new life in Christ, from the world to the kingdom. John 3: 5; Matt. 28: 19; 1 Cor. 12: 13; Rom. 6: 3-5. In this new birth there are several stages represented by corresponding acts in baptism.

1. BAPTISM MEANS THE DEATH OF THE OLD MAN OF SIN (Col. 3: 3). By a free act of the will we " reckon ourselves to be indeed dead unto sin " (Rom. 6: 11), and this crucifying of the old self is being " baptized into death " (Rom. 6: 3, 4), in the likeness of Jesus' death (Rom. 6: 3; cf. Gal. 2: 12, 20; Mark 10: 38; John 10: 17, 18). Jesus likens this death to a planting (John 12: 24, 32, 33), and Paul likens baptism to a planting (Literally " uniting by growth ") (Rom. 6: 5). And as Jesus voluntarily gave His life (John 10: 17, 18) so we are planted in the likeness of His death (See John 19: 30) by a voluntary, forward action in baptism.

2. NEXT IS THE BURIAL OF THIS CRUCIFIED "OLD MAN OF SIN," WHICH IS REPRESENTED BY PLACING HIM IN THE BAPTISMAL GRAVE. Rom. 6: 4; Col. 2: 12. This death and burial of the old self is also likened unto a cleansing or washing from sin (Acts 2: 38; 22: 16; 1 Pet. 3: 21). It implies salvation from, not only the penalty, but also the pollution and power of sin (Rom. 6: 6-11).

3. THE "OLD MAN OF SIN" BEING RECKONED DEAD AND BURIED IN THE BAPTISMAL GRAVE, THERE FOLLOWS THE COMING FORTH OR RESURRECTION OF THE NEW MAN IN CHRIST JESUS (Rom. 6: 4-10). This is called a *birth* (John 3: 5), and those regenerated are referred to as " babes " (1 Pet. 2: 2) and " new creatures " (2 Cor. 5: 17) who are henceforth to do the will of God (Gal. 6: 15; Col. 2: 10-13; 1 John 3: 9; 1 Pet. 1: 22; 2: 20, 21; cf. Rom. 12: 2). So important is the change of heart represented by this baptismal birth that Jesus says it is impossible to see the kingdom of God without it (John 3: 5). It is not the water, however, but the Holy Spirit who actually does the work of renewing the heart (Titus 3: 5).

4. BAPTISM HAS ANOTHER AND VERY VITAL SIGNIFICANCE WHICH IS COMMONLY OVERLOOKED. IT REPRESENTS

THE SAVING WORK OF EACH MEMBER OF THE TRINITY. The formula that Jesus gave is a Trinitarian, not a Unitarian, formula. It reads: "baptizing them into the name of the Father, AND OF the Son, AND OF the Holy Spirit" (Matt. 28: 19).

No one will claim that the terms "Father," "Son," and "Holy Spirit" are interchangeable. Whatever may be said about the unity of God, when we speak of the Father we do not mean the Son, and when we speak of the Son we do not mean the Holy Spirit. In some respects God is One, but in others He is Three, and it is with respect to the functions which mark the TRINITY that baptism is to be performed.

If Jesus did not mean that baptism should represent the acceptance of the distinctive saving work of each member of the Trinity, He would not have been so careful to word the commission as He did. He never used words carelessly. When He wished to refer to God in His unity He used the term "God," and when He used the terms "Father," "Son" or "Holy Spirit" He did so in order to distinguish the one from the other (John 15: 26, &c.). He so distinguishes here. If He had meant one name and one action He would have said so, but instead He commanded as clearly as words can do so, to baptize "into the name of the Father, and of the Son, and of the Holy Spirit,"—not into one name, but three. Therefore He must have meant each corresponding act in baptism to have its special significance. When He Himself was baptized, the Trinity was manifested. As the Son came from the water the Spirit descended upon Him, and the Father spoke from heaven (Matt. 3: 16, 17). And this distinction as to the Trinity is continually made by the inspired apostles. See 2 Cor. 13: 14; Eph. 6: 23, &c.

Moreover, saving faith must recognize this distinctive saving work of each member of the Trinity. There must be faith in the Father (Heb. 11: 6; Rom. 6: 23); there must be faith in the Son (John 14: 6; 8: 21-24; Acts 4: 12, &c.), and there must be faith in the Holy Spirit (Luke 11: 13; Gal. 3: 14; John 3: 5; 1 Cor. 6: 11; Acts 19: 1-6).

We are therefore ready to ask, What does it mean to baptize "into the name of the Father, and of the Son, and of the Holy Spirit"?

(1) It is the Father who accepts the faith of the penitent (John 3: 16), who forgives his sin (Eph. 4: 32) and who receives the new-born babe as His child (John 1: 12; Rom. 8: 15). To be baptized into the name of the Father, therefore, means the acceptance of His loving mercy and Fatherhood, Col. 2: 12, 13.

(2) It is the Son who is "the propitiation for our sins" (Rom. 8: 3; 1 John 2: 1, 2), the bearer of the divine life to us (1 John 5: 11, 12), and the head of the church, which is His body (Eph. 1: 23), therefore, to be baptized into the name of the Son means to have faith in Him, by which we "put on Christ" (Gal. 3: 27), become members of His body (1 Cor. 12: 13) and rise to walk with Him "in newness of life" (Rom. 6: 5-11).

(3) It is the Holy Spirit who convicts of sin (John 16: 8), who renews the heart (Titus 3: 5), who glorifies Jesus (John 16: 14) and enables us to live the Christ life (Gal. 5: 16-18), therefore, to be baptized into the name of the Holy Spirit means to receive by faith the Holy Spirit and His blessed work in regeneration (Gal. 3: 2, 14; John 3: 5).

Note, however, that just as the disciples received the Holy Spirit in regeneration and again in anointing for service (John 20: 22; Acts 1: 8) so the believer recognizes in baptism the regenerating work of the Spirit, but seeks a further anointing for service, symbolized by the laying on of hands (Acts 19: 1-6; Heb. 6: 2), which will be discussed later.

Being born of water and of the Spirit are linked together by faith (John 3: 5), and if faith be lacking, the first is not efficacious (Acts 8: 18-24) and the second cannot be (Gal. 3: 14). How simple and yet how beautiful is the symbol of baptism. We hear the Gospel and accept it. Penitent we come to the water. We bury the old life of sin. We bow the head to accept the gift of life from the Father (Rom. 6: 23), and again to show our faith in the Son whose blood "cleanseth us from all sin," and again to show faith in the Holy Spirit who makes our hearts His temple: we rise, redeemed, renewed, received, a child of God ready for enduement for service. How rich is the significance! How perfect the symbolism! How beautiful the service!

5. BAPTISM REPRESENTS THE ATTITUDE OF FAITH AND REPENTANCE AND OBEDIENCE ON THE PART OF THE BELIEVER.

He that believeth and is baptized shall be saved. (Mark 16: 16).

Repent and be baptized every one of you unto the remission of your sins (Acts 2: 38).

And now why tarriest thou? arise and be baptized, and wash away thy sins, calling on his name. (Acts 22: 16).

It is this attitude of the believer and not the mere immersion in water that is efficacious. The immersion is a test of this willingness of heart, without which God cannot and will not cleanse the life from sin and renew the heart. Baptism means more than a consecration or a cleansing, it represents the regeneration of the heart, and the saving inward work is so closely linked in the Bible with the formal outward representation of it because the inward attitude of obedience must be expressed in the outward acts of obedience. "Faith without works is dead." Professor Sandy, writing for the *International Critical Commentary* on Rom. 6: 3-5 says:

> Baptism has a double function. (1) It brings the Christian into personal contact with Christ, so close that it may fitly be described as union with him. (2) It expresses symbolically a series of acts corresponding to the redeeming acts of Christ.
> Immersion=Death.
> Submersion=Burial (the ratification of death).
> Emergence=Resurrection.
> All these the Christian has to undergo in a moral and spiritual sense, and by means of his union with Christ.

Professor Sandy might have added that the three dips of the head in baptism represent the faith of the candidate in the saving work of each member of the Trinity, as taught by Jesus (Matt. 28: 19) and also recognized by Paul (Titus 3: 4-8). To call baptism a saving ordinance is not to say that merely going through the form will save, but that baptism should have its place among the various agencies of salvation. Thus, for example, "By *grace* are ye saved" (Eph. 2: 5-8). *Confession* also saves, "For with the heart man believeth unto righteousness and with the mouth confession is made unto salvation" (Rom. 10: 9, 10). *Hope* also is said to save, "For we are saved by hope" (Rom. 8: 24). *Faith* also saves: "Believe on the Lord Jesus Christ and thou shalt be saved" (Acts 16: 31). The *Gospel* also "is the power of God unto salvation" (Rom. 1: 16). Now no one thinks of denying any of these agencies in salvation, even though we do not fully understand how it is that they work in us the change which brings salvation. Why then when we read: "He that believeth and is *baptized* shall be saved" (Mark 16: 16), and again, "Repent and be *baptized* every one of you unto the remission of your sins" (Acts 2: 38), and again, "were saved through water; which after a true likeness doth even now save you, even *baptism*" (1 Pet. 3: 21), should we make baptism less essential than the other agencies named? It has its part in aiding the understanding, enlightening the conscience and strengthening the will. To reject it or to alter it is to lose its benefits, and to do so wilfully is to show a readiness to break God's law at any other point, and thus being guilty in one point be guilty of all (Jas. 2: 10).

Baptism must not be isolated and then rejected, because none of the means of salvation are without the others. Thus if we read, "By *grace* are we saved," the words follow, "*through faith*" (Eph. 5: 2-8); and if we read that "faith is the victory" (1 John 5: 4), we also read that faith "worketh by *love*" (Gal. 5: 6); and if love is proof of being begotten of God (1 John 3: 13), then love itself is shown by *obedience:* "Hereby we know that we love the children of God, when we love God and *do his commandments*" (1 John 5: 2). Neither is love without *repentance,* for "no man can serve two masters" (Matt. 6: 24); nor is repentance without *confession,* for "if we confess our sins he is faithful and just to forgive" (1 John 1: 9). And all of these are in one passage or another vitally linked with *baptism,* so that we read:

When the **kindness** of God our Savior, and his **love** toward man, appeared, not by **works** done in righteousness, which we did ourselves, but according to his **mercy** he saved us, through the washing of regeneration (baptism) and **renewing** of the Holy Spirit, which he poured out upon us richly, through Jesus Christ our Savior; that, being justified by his **grace**, we might be made heirs according to the **hope** of eternal life. Faithful is the saying, and concerning these things I desire that thou affirm confidently, to the end that they who have believed God may be careful to maintain **good works** (Titus 3: 4-8).

IV. The Subjects of Baptism.

When we once learn the scriptures relating to the meaning of baptism there will be little question about the subjects, and on the other hand, the conditions laid down determinating the subjects of baptism confirm the statements concerning the meaning. Let us follow the evidence through from beginning to end.

1. ARGUMENTS FROM THE OLD COVENANT FOR INFANT BAPTISM REFUTED.

The chief argument of those who "baptize" infants is that they were included under the old covenant, and received the seal thereof (circumcision), and that they must therefore be included under the new and receive the seal thereof (baptism), and that if they had not received it there would have been an outcry by the early church, but as no such outcry is mentioned in the New Testament, therefore infants were baptized. There are several errors in this reasoning.

(1) If it proves anything it becomes absurd by proving too much. If baptism is to be applied to infants, because circumcision was, then it should be administered only to males, because circumcision was (Gen. 17: 9-14).

(2) If infants under the old covenant had to receive circumcision, and those under the new have to receive baptism to be saved, then all of them under eight days old under the law, and all unbaptized under the Gospel, are lost,—another absurdity.

(3) This argument for infant baptism overlooks the fact that the old covenant included all the natural descendants of Abraham (Gen. 17: 9-14), together with the proselytes (Deut. 23: 1-7), but the new covenant includes only those who are the "spiritual seed of Abraham" (Rom. 4: 13-16). Sinners to be counted in this number must be regenerated (John 3: 5), a process which involves faith (Heb. 11: 6), repentance (Luke 11: 3), confession (Rom. 10: 9, 10) and obedience (Matt. 7: 21). The conditions cannot apply to children, nor do they need the rite, for they are not sinners,

but are already included in the kingdom and the covenant. "Of such is the kingdom of heaven" (Matt. 19: 14). Indeed, baptism is to help to make adults like children in their guilelessness rather than to save children from damnation.

> Except ye turn, and become as little children, ye shall in no wise enter into the kingdom of heaven (Matt. 18: 3).

It is sometimes said that infants were considered members of the Jewish Church and therefore it is for those who oppose infant baptism to show when such church membership was abolished. The fact is that though infants (male) were circumcised on the eight day, that did not make them church members, else the girl babies would all have been excluded. Children were not admitted to the congregation until twelve years of age, and if the Jewish custom were to bind the church, that would be the age for admission now,—a very reasonable age. But Jewish custom is not binding, and the authority for doing away with it is in the voice from heaven directing obedience to Jesus Christ (Luke 9: 36). Again, "The law and the prophets were until John: since then the Gospel of the kingdom of God is preached" (Luke 16: 16). See also Col. 2: 16-18 and Heb. 8 and 9. Of the kingdom Jesus said, "Blessed are the pure in heart, for they shall see God." Surely this includes the infants without regard to circumcision or baptism.

What is sin? The Scripture tells us, "Sin is the transgression of the law," (1 John 3: 4), but in the case of infants there is no transgression of the law, for "where there is no law there is no transgression" (Rom. 4: 15). They know nothing of law or of sin and the symbol of regeneration is wholly out of place with them. When once they become sinners, it is time to treat them as such and bring them to regeneration, but until then they belong to God.

(4) Baptism is not for salvation from Adam's sin. To say that infants are accountable for "original sin" inherited from Adam, or even from their parents, is to fly in the face of both the Old Testament and the New. What saith the Scripture?

The soul that sinneth, it shall die: the son shall not bear the iniquity of the father, neither shall the father bear the iniquity of the son; the righteousness of the righteous shall be upon him, and the wickedness of the wicked shall be upon him (Ezek. 18: 20).

The "new Adam" completely atones for the sins of the old (Rom. 5: 18, 19):

So then as through one trespass the judgment came unto all men to condemnation; even so through one act of righteousness the free gift came unto all men to justification of life.

"So then each one of us must give account OF HIMSELF to God" (Rom. 14: 12). If infants must be regenerated by baptism to be saved from original sin it is of tremendous importance to know it, yet there is not one word in the Gospel to show it. Must we believe that the Holy Spirit made such a fatal omission? or is it better to reject the absurd doctrine of infant sin and infant damnation? Those who accept it should go the length of the mediæval church which deferred baptism not a moment from birth lest the child die unsaved. A doctrine so absurd is its own refutation.

(5) The absence from the Gospel of any record of complaint because children were not baptized by the apostles is probably because there was no such complaint to be recorded. The matter was so clearly understood that the parents did not expect their children to be baptized until old enough to come of themselves. The Jewish trine immersion, the proselyte baptism and the baptism of John with which they were familiar, were for adults only and for both

men and women. Being familiar with this fact, the people would hardly expect Christian baptism to be for infants. It may be added that in the New Testament parents are repeatedly instructed as to their duties to their children, yet never once are they given even a hint that it is their duty to have them baptized. After Philip carefully expounded the Gospel in the new field at Samaria, where the duty of infant baptism, if it were a duty, would naturally have been taught, only "men and women," according to the account, were baptized. Is it not likely that there were children in the households of these multitudes of believers?

2. THE TEACHING OF JESUS AND THE APOSTLES.

(1) *Jesus* said, "Go ye therefore, and make disciples of all the nations, baptizing them into the name of the Father and of the Son and of the Holy Spirit: teaching them to observe all things whatsoever I have commanded you." Here are three things commanded: (1) Making disciples, (2) baptism, (3) teaching; and none of these apply to infants under the age of accountability. Teaching is for those capable of receiving it and the symbol of regeneration (baptism) is for those who need regeneration. To be sure, Jesus blessed the children and said, "forbid them not to come unto me," but what has that to do with baptizing? Consecration of children is good, but baptism is a symbol of regeneration, not of consecration.

(2) *The apostles* taught the same conditions for baptism as Jesus, and *none* of them apply to infants. *Peter* said, "*Repent* and be baptized" (Acts 2: 38) to people who already believed. He also declared that baptism saves by being "the *answer of a good conscience* toward God" (1 Pet. 3: 21), but infants know nothing of conscience. *Philip* made *faith* a condition of baptism, for we read in Acts 8: 12, "When they *believed* Philip, preaching good tidings concerning the kingdom of God and the name of Jesus

Christ, they were baptized, both men and women." If infants were also baptized why were they not also specified with the rest? *Paul* also connects baptism and regeneration, —something not needed by infants. He says (Rom. 6: 3):

> All we who were baptized into Christ Jesus were baptized into his death. We are buried therefore with him through baptism into death: that like as Christ was raised from the dead through the glory of the Father, so we also might walk in newness of life.

Can these words apply to infants? The fact is, there is not one passage in the Bible that commands infant baptism or which even by inference permits it; neither is there one single example of it. This alone should be conclusive as evidence against it. The apostolic council decided against the continuance of circumcision (Acts 15), but said not a word of baptism taking the place of it, while Paul calls the children holy because of the faith of either parent (1 Cor. 7: 14) without a word about baptizing them. Why these incredible omissions if the baptism of infants prevailed? It is a serious charge that is brought against the Holy Spirit that He did not direct the Gospel writers to give one single clear word to justify the existence of an institution so essential (according to pædo-baptists) to the welfare of the millions of infants of all generations. We should fear to make such a charge or to take the liberty to add to the record we have.

HOUSEHOLDS.

It is asserted, however, that "households" were baptized, and that there were *probably* infants in these households. Let us see. There are just five instances of households being baptized, and two of these are doubtful. (1) *Lydia and her household* were baptized (Acts 16: 15), but she was a business woman over 120 miles away from home (v. 14) and it is not likely that she would be engaged in such business if she were a married woman with infant children. Her household was more probably composed of persons who helped her in her business of preparing and selling purple. (2) *The jailor and his household* were baptized, but in connection with that baptism " he rejoiced greatly, with all his house, having believed in God " (Acts 16: 33, 34). If infants were in that household and were baptized they must have " rejoiced greatly and believed,"—two things we have never seen infants do at their " baptism." (3) *The case of Cornelius* (Acts 10 and 11) is also claimed as an example, but the account says nothing of baptizing the household. It does say " We are all here present to hear " (ch. 10: 33), and " the Holy Spirit fell on all them that heard " (10: 44) and they spake with tongues and magnified God, and Peter said " Can any man forbid water that these should not be baptized who have received the Holy Spirit as well as we? " There is no room for infants in this account. (4) *Crispus* is referred to as another example, but it is not stated that the household of Crispus was baptized. It *is* stated that he " believed in the Lord with all his house " (Acts 18: 8). Where is the infant baptism in that? (5) *The household of Stephanus* (1 Cor. 1: 16) might be claimed as an example, in the absence of evidence to the contrary, but unfortunately for pædo-baptists, we read of this same household in 1 Cor. 16: 15, that " they set themselves to minister unto the saints," and thus again infants are ruled out. Search the Bible through and it will be found that not only is there no authority for infant baptism, but there is abundant authority for requiring faith, repentance and confession as essential conditions of receiving this sacred symbol of regeneration. When infants have become sinners and they by faith and repentance turn to the Savior, let not baptism be denied to them, but while they are without sin let not the symbol of regeneration be perverted from its purpose to be applied to them.

3. THE PRACTICE OF THE EARLY CHURCH.

The earliest testimony of church writers is against infant baptism. *The Didache,* or *"Teachings of the Apostles,"* written about 65 A. D., or a little later, says:

> Having first given all the preceding instruction, baptize into the name of the Father and of the Son and of the Holy Spirit, in living water. . . . But before baptism let the baptizer and the candidate fast, and any others who can. And thou shalt command him who is to be baptized to fast one or two days before.

It is very evident that this earliest and most authoritative document outside of the Scriptures did not contemplate the baptism of any but repentant believers, for imagine infants being commanded to fast one or two days preparatory to baptism!

Justin Martyr (150 A. D.) says baptism "is called illumination, because they who learn these things are illuminated in their understanding,"—*1st. Apol.* ch. 61. He was evidently not familiar with infant baptism for infants are not *illuminated* by baptism. *Tertullian* (160 A. D.), is the first to mention infant baptism, and he opposed it. He says of children, " Let them come while they are growing up * * * Why does the innocent period of life hasten to the remission of sins" (*De Baptism* ch. 18). He says also " All who became *believers* used to be baptized" (*De Baptism* ch. 13). By this time, however, the heresy was beginning to be taught, that infants are lost without baptism. The shocking heresy of infant damnation soon became the parent of infant baptism. It was carried later to such an extreme that the *Council of Cologne* decreed that if there were doubts of the life of the child it should be baptized during the process of its birth. From the rise of this heresy

Baptism

on to the present, it is easy to find supporters of infant baptism, but their words are of no value, because the *apostolic* church was free from both these heresies.

The first known advocate of infant baptism was *Cyprian,* Bishop of Carthage, in the middle of the third century and the *first authentic definite instance* of a child being baptized is that of the six-year-old son of the emperor Valens (375 A. D.) who demanded it. There is one passage in *Irenaeus* (130 A. D. *Ad Hereses* 22: 4) which is claimed by advocates of infant baptism as referring to that rite, but a careful study of the statement with the context fails to reveal any such reference. It is as follows:

Sanctifying every age, by that period corresponding to it which belonged to himself. For he (Jesus) came to save all through means of himself—all, I say, who through him are born again to God—infants, and children, and boys, and youths, and old men. He therefore passed through every age, becoming an infant for infants, thus sanctifying those who are of this age, being at the same time made to them an example of piety, righteousness, and submission; a youth for youths, becoming an example for youths, and thus sanctifying them for the Lord. So likewise he was an old man for old men, that he might be a perfect Master for all.

The passage scarcely needs comment, for there is no mention of baptism in it. The only point, and it is a good one, is that in passing through all ages Jesus became an example for every age. The word he uses for infants is often used of children six years of age or more. Irenaeus may not have had what we call infants in mind at all. But suppose he did, he says " born again to God," *not through baptism, but through Jesus.* How? " He therefore passed through every age," that is, became an example for each age. How was He an example for infants? By living as a perfect child. Infants then are saved by following His example as they do *by nature,* for He said " Of such is the kingdom," and that of unbaptized infants. When children are old enough to sin and repent, then it is time for them to come to baptism as Jesus did. Let each age imitate Jesus, as Irenaeus says, and He will save all who do so.

The Shepherd of Hermes, a writing of the apostolic age, perhaps the most popular of all the early writings, for it was by many received as a part of the Gospel, gives a statement concerning infants which indicates that baptism was not considered necessary for them. It is in Book 3, similitude 9:

> They are as infant children, in whose hearts no evil originates; nor did they know what wickedness is, but always remained as children. Such without doubt, dwell in the kingdom of God, because they defiled in nothing the commandments of God; for all infants are honorable before God and are the first persons with Him.

Origen (185 A. D.) has been quoted as an advocate of infant baptism because of "original sin," but in his reply to Celsus (8: 40) he denies that children are under condemnation for inherited sin. As this was the reason ascribed for infant baptism by those who first advocated it in the church, it must have originated later than Origen.

4. THE TESTIMONY OF MODERN AUTHORITIES.

John Calvin, founder of the Presbyterian Church, says, "It is nowhere expressed by the evangelists that any one infant was baptized."

Professor Stewart of Andover, the greatest exegete of his day, says, "In the New Testament I find no evidence of infant baptism."

The Episcopal Prayer-book requires faith and repentance before baptism, but infants are pledged by their sponsors, a custom which finds no support in the Gospel.

Neander, the great Jewish church historian, says:

> Infant baptism began in the north African church in the

middle of the third century, but was not generally prevalent until several centuries after. The coming of the idea of no salvation without baptism caused both infant baptism and infant communion.

Stanley (Of the Church of England) says:

The verdict in the apostolic age and three centuries after, is that those who came for baptism came of their own deliberate choice.

Bartlet says:

Infant baptism is not an apostolic usage. It is not only that there is no trace of it in the first century, but the very idea of baptism then universal, namely, as a rite of faith's self-consecration (afterward outwardly ratified by manifestations of the Spirit) is inconsistent therewith.—Apostolic Age,

Lange says:

Baptism of new-born infants was altogether unknown to primitive Christianity.—History of Protestantism.

Hastings' Bible Dictionary, Article on Baptism by Plummer says:

Not only is there no mention of infant baptism, but there is no text from which such baptism can be securely inferred.

Such quotations might be multiplied indefinitely. They simply show that candid historians admit that only *believers'* baptism is taught by the Gospel. The heresy of infant baptism crept into the church only gradually, but once in, it has found many who have felt bound to defend the custom of their church. They have labored in an unworthy cause, and their efforts have resulted in evil. Among the harmful results of infant baptism may be mentioned the following:

5. EVILS OF INFANT BAPTISM.

(1) *It introduces an unregenerate membership into the church.* Those " baptized " in infancy are received later on without further baptism and often without conversion. The catechism takes the place of conversion.

(2) *It causes such persons to be satisfied with the rite performed on them in infancy* and thus to miss the blessing which comes from true conversion and baptism.

(3) *It destroys the significance of the symbol* and tends to obscure the truths, for which it stands. The infant does not understand one thing about it at the time, and is not likely to investigate the meaning afterward. Thus baptism has been degraded into a mere form of consecration of babies, without reference to its original symbolism whatever. The next step has already been taken by some who advocate doing away with baptism and using a more appropriate form of consecration for infants.

(4) *It tends to make salvation a matter of form rather than of faith and repentance.* A sort of superstitious reverence is attached to the rite without reference to its meaning, and this is not far removed from the image worship of Romanists.

(5) *It keeps more out of the church than it brings in.* Many allow their infant baptism to take the place of active church membership later, and others are kept out by the unregenerated lives of such as trust in their infant baptism instead of going on to regeneration and true Christian living.

(6) *It destroys the distinction between the old covenant and the new,* which is better (Heb. 8: 6), because it is based upon faith.

> Know therefore that they that are of faith, the same are sons of Abraham. . . . that we might receive the promise of the Spirit through faith (Gal. 3: 7-14).

(7) *It tends to destroy the entire mission of the church.* This is easily seen by noting what would result if infant baptism should become universal. The *Christian Advocate*, official organ of a church which to a large extent practices

Baptism

infant baptism, points out the result of the universal adoption of the custom:

First, it would set aside believers' baptism. There would be no believers in that case to baptize.

Second, it would make void the great commandment, "He that believeth and is baptized shall be saved."

Third, there would be no need of preaching the Gospel, as all would be in the church before they could accept the Gospel.

Fourth, all would be in the church without faith.

Fifth, there would not, could not, be a converted person in the church; all would be in the church before they could be converted.

Sixth, if we were baptized in infancy, everybody would be in the church, hence the church would contain all the wicked people in the world.

Seventh, it would blot out the line between the church and the world. In truth there would be no world, all would be church members.

Eighth, there being no regenerated persons in the church, there could not be any Christians in such a church, hence such a practice would wipe out the church of Christ entirely.

The infant "baptism" error should be corrected. What is called infant baptism is not really baptism at all. Baptism is a divine ordinance given to symbolize certain great truths, none of which the babe can understand, and therefore to it there is nothing but the disagreeable water. There is no word in the Scriptures authorizing sponsors or substitutes to pledge faith and repentance for another. Therefore the rite for infants is a mere form of consecration which they should reverence as such, but which should never for a moment be allowed by them to take the place of believers' baptism when they are old enough to receive it. To receive true baptism, therefore, after having received so-called baptism in infancy, is not to be rebaptized. The child is not responsible for the error of the parents, but it should not be bound by it. It is not a mark of disrespect to them to render more perfect obedience to God than they understood, but it is disrespect toward God to allow the inherited error to usurp the place of the Lord's command. The pathway of duty is plain.

6. THE PROPER AGE.

There is no commandment in the Scriptures as to the proper age to receive baptism. The conditions of faith and repentance are laid down, and when they are fulfilled there need be no question as to age. Some children feel the pangs of conscience when five years old. Some have a clear understanding of their need of a Saviour at six or seven. Those who have made special study of the subject say that the examination of many thousands of cases supports the statement that the age of greatest religious susceptibility is from twelve to fourteen for girls and from fourteen to sixteen for boys. If they pass that age without conversion it will be difficult ever to win them. It is a safe thing to follow the injunction of Jesus, "Suffer the little children and forbid them not to *come* unto me." When they come of themselves and show that they really are seeking to serve Jesus they are ready to understand the symbol of baptism and receive it. Let us not forget that Polycarp was converted at nine; Baxter when eight; Matthew Henry at eleven; President Edwards at about seven; Dr. Watts at nine; Bishop Hall at eleven; Robert Hall at twelve and John Wesley at six. Dr. Edward Judson says:

> It is sometimes said that even a child can be converted; it should be said that even a grown person can be. The nearer the cradle as a rule, the nearer Christ. The most intelligent Christians are readiest to accept children.

Again, the beginnings of the conversion in adults may often be traced to seed planted in childhood days. As Horace Bushnell says:

> There was some root of right principle established in their

childhood which is here only quickened and developed as when Christians of mature age are revived in their piety after a period of spiritual lethargy, for it is conceivable that regenerate character may exist long before it is fully and formally developed.

Indeed, if it were not for the good influences of childhood there would be little hope of any adult ever being converted. Evangelist Munhall says that from tests in many large congregations he has found that the vast majority of Christians are converted before they are sixteen. If they wait until twenty the chances are only one in five thousand that they ever will be converted. If they wait until thirty the chances have diminished to one in twenty thousand. At forty the chances are only one in eighty thousand; at fifty only one in one hundred and fifty thousand. How terrible are these figures! how infinitely important that the children be brought to Christ while yet their spiritual faculties are sensitive to the Holy Spirit, for repeated rejection will sear the conscience and bring them to the condition of those Jews who " *could* not believe " (John 12: 39).

7. INFANT CONSECRATION.

There is no objection to be made to the consecration of infants. In fact, it would be a blessed thing if all parents would formally consecrate their children to God with prayer both at conception and birth, and then strive to keep them in the fold of the Good Shepherd, but the rite of baptism should not be used for this purpose any more than the Lord's supper. It was given for another purpose. What a pitiful blunder it has been to pervert this beautiful symbol so utterly that the form as well as the meaning has been almost wholly lost from the church, and the vital truths for which it should stand are fast being forgotten. There is a tendency on the part of very many in churches which teach infant baptism, to use some simple form of consecration instead and allow baptism to take its place as a symbol for the candidate rather than for others, and a mark of regeneration rather than a rite of consecration. On the other hand there is a tendency on the part of other churches to adopt the custom of consecrating infants to the Saviour. Let both these movements extend and they will help to bring all together on gospel ground.

We have seen that the giving of circumcision to children under the old covenant does not imply the giving of baptism to children under the new, because that was a covenant with an earthly nation, while this is with the members of a spiritual kingdom; that infants are members of this kingdom because they are sinless, and that others become members by regeneration, of which baptism is the symbol; that baptism is therefore only for those who come with faith and repentance as candidates for the kingdom; that this is what Jesus taught and the apostles practiced; that infant baptism was unknown in the church until in the second century the heresy of infant damnation arose; that this heresy has given rise to serious evils in the church ever since, and that it is the duty of all to help to rid the church of this error and go back to the pure Gospel. Surely there is a mission for a church that will help to deliver God's people from the wilderness of error into which so many have fallen.

V. The Mode of Baptism.

It is important to know and practice the right mode in baptism for several reasons. First, *obedience* requires care to be right. No one can show love to God and have contempt for His commandments (Matt. 28: 19; John 14: 21-25). Second, the *interests of truth* require the right mode, because to change the form of action destroys its power to teach the truth which baptism represents (cf. Rom. 1: 25; Heb. 8: 5). Third, the *interests of the king-*

dom require the right mode, because if the mode be changed the meaning of baptism will be perverted and the church will be hindered by unregenerate members. Baptism must represent, not mere consecration by proxy, but regeneration (John 3: 5; Titus 3: 5; Rom. 6: 3-5). Only the proper observance of the commandment will bring the blessings intended by it. God knows best what is for our good and it is presumptuous, to say the least, to discard His commands as useless or to alter His sacred symbols (John 13: 17).

There are several causes of confusion as to the mode of baptism. The first teaching of the churches was oral and when the epistles were written there was no need of full explanations as to the mode because the churches were already familiar with it, therefore we have only incidental references instead of full explanations. Other difficulties of the subject are due to the translation of the Gospel from the Greek to other languages, the adaptation of old words to new meanings, the confusion of baptism with the ceremonial cleansings of the Old Testament, and the heresies which arose in the church after the apostles. The apostles themselves insisted upon one mode of baptism, or else they would not have rebaptized those who were not rightly baptized (Acts 19: 1-6); therefore we should also seek to observe the one true mode. There is only one meaning to the commission, only one meaning to the rite, and only one thing to do to be right, namely; to obey the prescribed form. To ascertain conclusively the proper mode of baptism we have searched every known line of evidence, and they all lead one way. There is no contradiction or uncertainty, and the conclusion is backed by their combined authority.

To anyone not specially interested, the folloiwng pages may seem to tedious to read. They have not been written to entertain the slothful, but to guide those eekisng the truth.

Ten Arguments for Triune Immersion.

1. The meaning of the term "baptize" as used in Matthew 28: 19 is "to immerse."

2. The prepositions used in the Gospel in connection with baptism indicate immersion.

3. The plain meaning of the commission (Matt. 28: 19) requires triune immersion.

4. The symbolism of the rite requires triune immersion.

5. The New Testament examples prove immersion.

6. The early writers of the church testify to triune immersion.

7. Impartial modern authorities agree that triune immersion was the primitive mode.

8. Triune immersion has existed continuously from the days of the apostles to this.

9. The primitive baptistries prove the practice of forward immersion.

10. The beginning of sprinkling, pouring and single immersion is found on this side of the apostles, while the beginning of triune immersion cannot be thus located, but can be traced to Jesus.

1. Christian baptism must be immersion because the meaning of the term "baptize" as used in Matt. 28: 19 is "to dip or immerse." The word *baptize* is from the Greek word *baptizo* which is the frequentative or emphatic form of *bapto,* to dip. It is not translated in the English Bible because at the time King James' translation was made, in 1611, there was already a dispute concerning the mode. It is uniformly translated *immerse* elsewhere, but we must translate it in reference to baptism for ourselves. In doing so we give below the cumulative argument of seven sources of evidence, which combine to prove that *to baptize,* in Matt. 28: 19, *means to immerse.*

Baptism

(1) *This is the meaning of the word in classical Greek.*

(2) *This is the meaning also in biblical Greek.*

(3) *This is the translation everywhere else in the Bible.*

(4) *The Greek words which mean to sprinkle, pour, wash or purify are never used of Christian baptism.*

(5) *Wherever the term baptizo is translated in the versions of other languages it is translated by words which mean to immerse.*

(6) *The Septuagint version of the Old Testament translates the Hebrew words meaning to dip by the Greek, "baptizo."*

(7) *The figurative use of the word accords with its primary meaning, to dip or immerse.*

Surely this should be sufficient proof that this is its meaning. Follow the evidence carefully.

(1) *The only primary meaning in classical Greek is immerse or some derivative thereof.*

This is the testimony of all standard authorities. Compare the definitions of the following lexicographers and scholars:

(1) *Liddell and Scott,*—American Edition, "To dip, to dip repeatedly, to baptize." (2) *Sophocles.*—"To dip, to immerse, to sink, for the purpose of coloring or washing; to submerge, cleanse, wash." (3) *Robinson,*—"To immerse, to sink, a frequentative." (4) *Stephanus,*—"To immerse, dip, as we immerse." (5) *Schleusner,*—"mergo, to dip in." (6) *Rost and Palm,*—"To dip in." (7) *Donegan,*—"To immerse repeatedly into a liquid, to submerge, to sink; also to plunge, to cleanse, to wash." (8) *Parkhurst,*—"To dip, immerse or plunge in water." (9) *Schrevelius,*—"To immerse." (10) *Greenleaf,*—"To immerse, submerge, sink; in the New Testament, to wash, perform ablution, to cleanse." (11) *Adler's German Dictionary.* "Taufen, to dip." (*Taufen* is the German word used of

baptism). (12) *Wright,*—" Dip, Plunge, immerse." (13) *Leigh*—" The native and proper significance is to dip in water." (14) *Thayer,*—" As to the meaning of baptize, all reputable lexicographers are now agreed that its primary meaning is to immerse." (15) *Professor Humphreys* of the University of Virginia,—" There is no standard Greek-English lexicon that gives sprinkle or pour as meanings of baptize." (16) *Professor Tyler* of Amherst college,—" I do not know of any good lexicon which gives sprinkle as a rendering of *baptizo.*" (17) *Professor D'Ooge* of Colby University,—" There is no standard Greek-English lexicon that gives either sprinkle or pour as one of the meanings of the Greek *Baptizo.*" (18) *Professor Flagg* of Cornell University,—" I know of no lexicon which gives the meaning of sprinkle or pour for *baptizo,* not even the lexicon of the Roman and Byzantine periods of Professor E. A. Sophocles." (19) *Alexander de Stourdza,* Imperial Counsellor in France in a book published in 1816, says: " The very word *baptize* has in fact but one sole acceptation. It signifies literally and always to plunge. Baptism and immersion are therefore identical." (20) *Prof. Timayenis,*—" The Greek word *baptizo* means nothing but immersion in water. Baptism means nothing but immersion." (21) *Dr. Kyriasko* of the University of Athens, Greece,—" The verb *baptizo* in the Greek language never has the meaning of to pour or to sprinkle, but invariably that of to dip." (22) *Dr. Adolph Harnack,* one of Germany's greatest scholars,—" *Baptizein* undoubtedly signifies immersion (*eintauchen*). No proof can be found that it signifies anything else in the New Testament and in the most ancient Christian literature." (23) *Professor Delitsch* of Leipzig when asked the meaning of the Hebrew *tabhal* replied, " It means to immerse, the same as *baptizein.*" (24) *Dunbar,* —" *Baptizo* means to dip, submerge, immerse, plunge, sink, overwhelm." (25) *Wilke,*—"To immerse repeatedly, to bathe, to baptize." (26) *Cremer,*—"To immerse, submerge." (27) *Conant,* one of the number of scholars who translated the American Revised Version of the Bible, and who protested against leaving *baptizo* untranslated, cites the 175 examples of the classical use of *baptizein* and says:

> The ground idea expressed by this word is to put into or under water so as to entirely submerge; this act is always expressed in the literal application of the word and is the basis of the metaphorical uses. From the earliest of Greek literature down to its close, a period of about 2,000 years, not an example has been found in which the word has any other meaning. There is no instance in which it signifies to make a partial application of water by affusion or sprinkling, or to cleanse, to purify, apart from the literal act of immersion as the means of cleansing or purifying.—See Conant on Meaning and use of Baptizein.

(28) *Buttman* lays it down as a principle of the Greek language, that " a class of verbs formed from other verbs and ending in *izo,* have the signification of frequentatives. *Baptizo* is of this class. See *Buttman's Grammar,* see 119, 1, 2, 5. (29) *Rost* says the same thing. *Grammar* sec. 94; 2, 6. (30) *Stephens and Vosius* give like testimony, as do also, (31) *Burton,* (32) *Bretschneider,* (33) *Bullion,* and (34) *Dr. Robinson.* (35) *Professor Beery Ph. D.* of the University of Chicago says that *baptizo* is in form a frequentative of *bapto.* See also (36) *Handbook to the Grammar of the Greek Testament* by Green, sec. 1446. (37) *The Encyclopedia Britannica,* Vol. 1, p. 348 says " *baptizo* is the frequentative form of *bapto,* to dip or wash." (38) *Grimm* says, " *Baptizo* is the frequentative of *bapto.*" (39) *Green,* " *baptizo,* a frequentative of *bapto,* to immerse, submerge." (40) *Stokius,*—" *Baptizo*—Generally, and by the force of the word indicates the idea of simply dipping and diving, but properly it means to dip or immerse in water."

(41) *The Classic Greek-English Dictionary,* (published by Funk and Wagnalls) " *Baptizo,* to dip repeatedly, to dip under, to baptize." (42) *Passow,*—" To immerse often and repeatedly." (443) *Bretschneider,*—" Properly, often to dip." (44) *Komma,*—" To immerse, to dip repeatedly into a liquid." (45) *Gaza,*—" To dip repeatedly." (46) *Bars,*—" To dip, immerse, plunge in water, to bathe one's self." (47) *Richardson's* large *English Dictionary* defines *baptize* as anglicized from *baptizo,* to dip or merge repeatedly. (48) *Hastings' Bible Dictionary,*—" *Baptizo* is the intensive or frequentative form of *bapto,* to dip, and denotes immersion." (49) *The American,* one of the latest and greatest cyclopedias,—" Baptism, (from the Greek *baptizo,* from *baptizein,* to immerse or dip)." (50) *The Century Dictionary,* —" Baptism, from the Greek *baptizein,* to dip, to plunge in or under water, sink (a ship), drench, soak, draw (wine) by dipping with a cup."

The list of authorities is not by any means exhausted, but it is needless to quote further, because THERE IS NO STANDARD GREEK LEXICON OR AUTHORITY ON THE GREEK LANGUAGE THAT GIVES ANYTHING BUT IMMERSE OR DERIVATIVES THEREFROM AS THE PRIMARY MEANING OF BAPTIZO. There are some which add to the original meaning the modern meaning of baptize as derived from modern custom, but they never put these modern or derived meanings in the place of the primary meaning. The quotations given above are definitions of the primary meaning, and may be verified by any one who will examine the works quoted. Montfaucon gives sprinkle as one meaning of *baptizo,* but his work has been out of print for two hundred years. Grove and Pickering add " to cleanse, to purify " to their definitions, but these minor authorities are also out of print. Liddell and Scott in their first work gave such a meaning, but their revised lexicon omits it and gives only " to dip, to dip repeatedly,

Baptism

to baptize." THERE IS THEREFORE NOW NOT ONE STANDARD AUTHORITY THAT GIVES SPRINKLE OR POUR AS LITERAL OR PRIMARY MEANINGS OF BAPTIZO.

It is true that the word is sometimes used figuratively, but figurative meanings always involve the essential idea of the primary meaning, the context showing its figurative nature. Any attempt to substitute the figurative for the primary meaning involves absurdity at once. It is said, for instance, that because Jesus speaks of His baptism of suffering, therefore baptism is by sprinkling in imitation of the blood drops that trickled from Him, and that because we read of the baptism of the Spirit that baptism should be by pouring in imitation of the coming of the Spirit; and that because one classic writer speaks of a man "baptized (drowned) in his cups," therefore baptism means to get drunk. With such reasoning we might say that because a man may be "drowned in slumber" to "drown" means to sleep, or because we may "drink in a sermon" we may drink water in the same way. This secondary meaning argument is one of the main pillars of the affusion heresy, but it only shows the desperate weakness of the cause.

It has been said that there is a Greek word, *kata-bapto*, which means to immerse and nothing else and that the Savior should have used this if He meant baptism to be by immersion. But this is simply *bapto*, the weak form *of baptizo*, with the preposition *kata*, meaning down, added to it. Jesus used the strongest word, *baptizo*, which needs not the preposition "down" to make it mean immersion, for how can anyone dip without dipping *down*? This same preposition is used in Acts 8: 38 where it is said that "They went both *down into* (*katabaino eis*) the water, both Philip and the eunuch, and he baptized him." But lo, when here we have both the preposition *down* and the strongest word for immerse, yet affusionists halt upon the bank.

(2) *Biblical authorities give the primary meaning of "baptizo" as "immerse," the same as in classical Greek.*

Thayer's Greek-English Lexicon of the New Testament says:

Baptizo: 1. To dip repeatedly, to immerse, submerge. 2. To cleanse by dipping or submerging, to wash, to make clean with water; in the middle and first aorist passive, to wash one's self, to bathe. 3. Metaphorically, to overwhelm, to be overwhelmed with calamity. In the New Testament it is used particularly of the rite of sacred ablution, first instituted by John the Baptist, afterward by Christ's command received by Christians, and adjusted to the contents and nature of their religion, viz., an immersion in water.

Cremer's Biblico-Theological Lexicon of the New Testament Greek says: "*Baptizo,* to immerse, to submerge."

Green's Greek-English Lexicon to the New Testament says: "Baptizo, 1. primarily to dip, immerse."

(3) *Fifteen derivatives from bapto are used eighty-one times in the New Testament and in every case some form of "dip" or "immerse" can be substituted, while in many cases to substitute "sprinkle" or "pour" would cause absurdity.* For example try John 13: 26, "A sop when I have dipped (*bapso*) it." How would it sound to say, "A sop when I have sprinkled or poured it"? Or again, Luke 16: 24, "Send Lazarus that he may dip (*bapsa*) his finger in water and cool my tongue." Was Lazarus to apply his finger to the water or to apply water to the finger?

The latest discoveries of the archæologists in the lands of primitive Christianity have brought to light the writings of the common people of Jesus' day, and these have revealed the fact that the New Testament Greek is the language of the common people of the time, and therefore does not have secondary or sacred meanings for such terms as

Baptism

baptize. The fact that the word is used in the Gospel without explanation, and without any suggestion in the context of any secondary meaning, shows that it was intended to be understood in the simple, primary meaning, which every child of the day knew was "to dip or immerse." These same archæological discoveries prove that the Gospels were written during the first century as they claim to be, and that therefore the commission, which requires triune immersion was not a later addition. They further prove that the term "baptize" used in the commission had not a new religious significance, but the ordinary everyday meaning of "immerse." There is nothing in the context of Matt. 28: 19 to require a figurative meaning. WHY, THEN, SHOULD NOT BAPTISM IN THE COMMISSION BE TRANSLATED IMMERSION JUST AS IT IS IN SIMILAR CONSTRUCTIONS EVERYWHERE ELSE?

(4) *A fourth proof that immersion is meant by baptism is the fact that the Greek words which mean to sprinkle or pour or purify are never used in the Bible with reference to the rite of baptism.*

For example, *nipto* is the Greek word that means to wet, to wash the face, hands or feet, as in Mark 7: 3. "Except they wash their hands," and in John 13: 14, "If I have washed your feet," but this word is never used of baptism. *Cheo* means to pour and is used in Acts 2: 17, 18, but never of water baptism. *Raino,* means to sprinkle, but Jesus and the apostles avoid it when referring to baptism. Why did Jesus and the apostles avoid these words which mean to sprinkle or pour and use a word which always has the idea of immersion, when referring to the rite of baptism?

(5) *The translation of this Greek word "baptize" in the different versions or translations of the Gospel, is evidence that it means to dip or immerse.* The Bible is now translated into about four hundred and fifty different languages,

and whenever this word is translated at all it is translated by some form of dip or immerse. Some modern translations, however, transfer the word bodily and let the natives wrestle with it, just as the King James's translators did with the English. But in the ten great versions of the centuries the statement holds.

First, the Syriac version. This dates from the second century, and some scholars think that the first translation was made under the supervision of the apostles. It is a valuable version also because Syriac was the language Jesus used much in talking with the common people. We know this because He is quoted as using such words as *Epaphtha, Talithi cumi, mammon, abba,* &c., all of which are Syriac words. Now the Syriac word for baptize is *amad,* and means to dip. So says *Genesius' Hebrew and English Lexicon,* also Schaal, Schindler, Dr. Toy, Dr. Gottheil, Dr. R. Payne Smith, Prof. Noldeke, and other authorities.

Second, the Latin version, used by the early church in the West, made in the second century, uses the Latin word *tingo,* which, as any Latin dictionary will show, means to *dip.*

Third, the Egyptian version, dating from the third century, uses a word which means to dip or plunge.

Fourth, the Ethiopic version, dating from the fourth century, translates baptize by words which mean to dip or immerse.

Fifth, the Armenian version, in the fifth century does likewise.

Sixth, the Gothic version, also made in the fifth century, does likewise. This version includes the German which uses *taufen* to *dip;* the Swedish which uses *dopa,* to *dip;* and the Dutch, which uses *doopen,* to *dip.*

Seventh, the Slavonic version, of the fifth century which includes the Russian, Polish, Bohemian and kindred lan-

Baptism

guages, use the same root word, which means to *cross,* emphasizing the death symbolized in baptism rather than the burial.

Eighth, the Arabic version in the seventh century uses a word which means to immerse.

Ninth, the Persic version made in the eighth century uses a similar word.

Tenth, the old Anglo-Saxon version, uses *dyppan,* whence *dip.* If the *modern* English version had translated the word instead of transferring it, we would have "dip" in our English Bibles also, as indeed, we do have everywhere except when the sacred symbol is referred to.

(6) *The Septuagint translation of the Old Testament into Greek made by seventy Jewish scholars about 284 B. C., uses the word baptize to translate the Hebrew word "tabhal" which means to dip.* The case is that of Naaman who dipped himself seven times in the Jordan (2 Kings 5: 8-14). There is no question about this being a dipping rather than a sprinkling or pouring. Why then, did these seventy learned men nearly 300 years before Christ choose the word *baptizo* to express that *repeated dipping,* if *baptizo* is not the best word in the Greek language for that purpose? This same word *tabhal* occurs many other times in the Hebrew scriptures and *in every case is translated into our English version by dip or a kindred word, but into the Greek (Septuagint) it is translated by bapto,* whence *baptizo* and *baptize.* See Ex. 12: 22; Lev. 4: 6, 17; 9: 9; 14:6, 16, 51; Num. 19: 18; Deut. 33: 24; Josh. 3: 15; Ruth 2: 14; 1 Sam. 14: 27; 2 Kings 5: 14; Job 9: 31. In the last case it is translated "plunge." The Hebrew lexicons all agree with these translations and give the meaning of *tabhal* as "to dip or immerse."

Now is not the conclusion plain, that if *tabhal* means to dip but is uniformly translated into the Greek by *baptizo.*

(to express repeated dipping) or *bapto,* then baptize and dip mean the same? "Things equal to the same thing are equal to each other." Baptize=*tabhal;* dip=*tabhal;* therefore baptize=dip. This is a very important point, because it is said by opponents of immersion that the word *baptize* as used in the Bible had a different meaning from that of the classical Greek, that it had a secondary meaning of "to sprinkle," or "to pour." But mark you that this Septuagint version is *the very copy of the Scriptures which Jesus and the apostles used, and which they quote. They therefore used the word baptize in the common sense of the term as it is used in these scriptures, and that was the sense of "to dip."* If they had changed the meaning there would have been some notice of it. *Professor Sophocles,* a native Greek, and author of a Greek dictionary, says under *baptizo,* "There is no evidence that the New Testament writers put upon this verb meanings not recognized by the Greeks." No word of ours can be a stronger testimony than that of this learned Greek professor, who knew both biblical and classical Greek and speaks without prejudice. No attempt to show that a secondary or derived meaning, as, to sprinkle or pour, was used by Bible writers has ever succeeded. The most learned and elaborate attempt ever made was by Mr. J. W. Dale, the Goliath of the pædobaptists, who, in four labored volumes, tries to get rid of immersion in baptism and finally gives as his definition of the term the following:

Whatever is capable of thoroughly changing the character, state or condition of any object, is capable of baptizing that object; and by such change of character, state or condition does, in fact, baptize it.

If this be the true definition, then we may do away with water altogether and baptize people ("change their character, state or condition") by means of *argument* alone!

Baptism

What a pity that the apostles did not understand the Lord that way, so that we would not need to overcome their example of taking candidates into the water to baptize them!

Does "baptize" mean "purify"?

It has been suggested by some writers that the word baptism as used by Jesus should be given the meaning of "purify" because it carries with it the idea of purifying from sin. Others have cried, "Eureka! We have the solution here." Have we? It would be delightful indeed, if this were true, for Christendom is weary of the long dispute. But alas! on reflection we find difficulties, and see clearly that the matter cannot be settled by hiding behind a word that of itself means nothing as to mode, and will even permit of doing away with water baptism altogether. Here are some of the reasons why we cannot substitute "purifying" for "baptizing."

(a) There is a word *(katharidzo)* which means to purify, and is everywhere so translated. If Jesus had wished us to use that word He certainly would have used it Himself.

(b) *Baptizo,* the word that Jesus used, nowhere means to purify. It is never so translated anywhere else, and certainly would not have been used with that meaning here without precedent or a single word of explanation.

(c) The term *baptize* as used by the Jews (and, of course, by Jesus and the disciples also) was a familiar term and meant to immerse. It was constantly used with reference to proselyte baptism and John's baptism, both of which were by immersion. It violates common sense interpretation to drag in a new and extraordinary meaning without warning or explanation.

(d) The word *purify* means nothing as to mode, and if it had been used by Jesus He would have described the process by which it should be done. The directions for purifying under the law were very specific. See Lev. 15, &c. It is incredible that Jesus would institute so important a rite and say not a word or give not a hint as to *how* to obey it.

(e) The difficulty as to mode would only be increased, because Jewish symbolic purification was by immersion when water alone was used (Lev. 11: 32) and by sprinkling when purification by atonement was signified (Num. 19).

(f) Purification involves other elements than water baptism. For example, the purification by the sprinkling of blood. "And according to the law, I may almost say, all things are cleansed by blood, and apart from the shedding of blood there is no remission" (Heb. 9: 22). See also Acts 15: 1, "Purifying their hearts by faith," and 1 Pet. 3: 22, "Seeing ye have purified your souls by obedience to the truth." The word is too broad and indefinite to be used for the simple rite of immersion as a symbol of regeneration.

(g) If it be urged that the word be used in a spiritual rather than the literal sense, then we are confronted by the fact that the real or spiritual purification is not our work at all. It belongs to God, who only can cleanse the heart. To use the word in that sense would be to substitute the thing symbolized instead of the symbol.

How much better and simpler it is just to use the word that Jesus used, and in the sense in which He was accustomed to use it, and have the triune immersion He commands in the commission as a symbol, not of temporary purification, but of complete regeneration, by which we become new creatures by the working of the Triune God Father, Son and Holy Spirit, to whom be glory forever

(7) *The figurative use of the term "baptize" accord with its literal meaning to "immerse."*

Baptism

We have baptism spoken of as a *burial* (Rom. 6: 4) because it contains the idea of *covering* up; as a *birth* (John 3: 5) because it is a *coming forth* out of the water to a new life; as a *resurrection* (Col. 2: 12) for the same reason; as *regeneration* (Titus 3: 5) embodying the idea of the new birth. All these figures are consistently drawn from immersion, but they cannot be derived from sprinkling or pouring, for the resemblance is too slight.

We also have such expressions as "*baptized into* Christ" (Gal. 3: 27) and "*baptized into* one body" (1 Cor. 12: 13) which harmonizes with "*dipping into,*" but not with "sprinkling or pouring *upon.*"

We also have the baptism of suffering of which Jesus speaks, which was nothing less than death (Luke 12: 50), and so we are "*planted* in the *likeness of his death*" (Rom. 6: 5) but planting is covering up, nothing less. The Revised Version reads "united" instead of "planted" but the idea is the same. Dr. Parkhurst says in defining baptism, "Figuratively, it means to be plunged as it were into a sea of suffering." Thus Jesus was plunged, and thus our self-renunciation (Luke 14: 33) corresponds to our literal immersion in baptism.

Now, since all these figurative expressions are drawn naturally from immersion as baptism, but can only by unnatural straining be connected by resemblance with other modes, do they not show that the writers using these figures had the immersion scene in mind when they used them?

2. THE PREPOSITIONS USED IN THE GOSPEL IN CONNECTION WITH BAPTISM INDICATE IMMERSION.

The very fact that the term *baptizo* is used everywhere in the Scriptures with the prepositions *in* or *into* is proof that it means to immerse, for if it meant to sprinkle or to pour we would have the prepositions *on* or *upon* instead. The only seeming exception to this proof is the expression of John, "I indeed baptize you with water, but he shall baptize you with the Holy Spirit" (John 1: 33), but here also the Greek preposition used is *en* which corresponds to our *in* and is so translated in this very passage in the Revised Version. If it be said that *in* should not be used with reference to the Holy Spirit, we reply that the less must be baptized into or born of the greater and not *vice versa*. The argument is very clear: if baptism means sprinkling or pouring we would have the prepositions "on" or "upon" used in connection with it, which we never do; but since we *always* have "in" or "into" we must conclude that the action indicated is immersion.

3. THE GRAMMATICAL MEANING OF THE COMMISSION OF JESUS REQUIRES TRIUNE IMMERSION.

The commission reads:

All authority is given unto me in heaven and on earth. Go ye therefore, and make disciples of all nations, baptizing them into the name of the Father and of the Son and of the Holy Spirit: teaching them to observe all things whatsoever I have commanded you: and lo, I am with you always, even unto the end of the world.—Matt. 28: 18-20.

(1) *The importance of this command* can be seen at once when it is remembered that the Gospel everywhere closely connects baptism with salvation (See Mark 16: 16; Acts 2: 38, 39; 1 Cor. 12: 13; Gal. 3: 27, &c.) and yet this is absolutely the only recorded command of Jesus instituting it and giving us the mode of performing it, although Mark 16: 16 is an abridged reference to this same commission. Have we not a right to expect that the formula Jesus gave for such an important rite should be clear enough to be understood? It seems to have been understood by the apostles, for there was no dispute as to the mode of baptism until the fourth century, when the Arians introduced the Unitarian heresy.

Baptism

(2) The authenticity of the commission. Since then, the commission is of such vital importance to the subject, let us first be certain that it is a genuine command of our Lord, and not a later addition to His teaching, as a few destructive critics have asserted.

We find the commission quoted in the *Didache* or *Teachings of the Apostles,* written, Harnack says, between 70 and 140 A. D. Some recent authorities put the date as early as 65 A. D. If this early date is accepted it would be earlier than the date of Matthew's Gospel itself. At any rate it indicates the use of the commission right in the apostolic age, when if ever, it should have been and could have been and would have been disputed and refuted. But it is never once disputed in the early writings, in the Gospel or out. It is quoted by Ignatius, supposed to have been with Polycarp, a disciple of John. *Epistle to Philadelphia,* chapter 9.

Justin Martyr (130 A. D.) quotes it fully (*Apol.* 1: 6). *Tertullian* (160 A. D.) says it was used from the time of Jesus (*De baptism,* ch. 13). *The Apostolic Constitutions* (canon 49) prescribes that any bishop not using this formula "shall be deposed." Haefele says this canon is one of the oldest. The commission is frequently referred to by the early writers, and never once is its authenticity questioned, not even by the Eunomians who introduced single immersion and baptized into the death of Jesus. (See under X). It has been used continuously since the days of the apostles, and is accepted by every denomination of any consequence to-day.

Warren in "*Liturgy of the Ante-Nicene Church*" (p. 12) say:

There is no historical evidence for any formula being employed or approved in the Catholic Church except the Trinitarian formula enjoined by our Lord himself.

Hastings' Bible Dictionary says:

If from the first there was only one form (of baptism), that form was the Trinitarian. From the second century it certainly was the only form. Wherever Matthew's Gospel was received the Trinitarian formula would become obligatory, and that carries us back before Justin Martyr (130 A. D.).

When in the end of the third century the Eunomians shortened the formula and baptized " into the death of Christ," they were denounced as heretics and their converts on coming to the true church were rebaptized according to the commission. Surely, if there was any argument against the use of the Trinitarian formula of the commission they would have used it then. It is too late to try to overthrow it now.

(3) *The interpretation of the commission.* But how shall we interpret the commission? In the same way that we interpret anything else. There is no mystery about it. The words are plain and the construction simple. Take it as it reads. *Blackstone* says, " The words of a law are generally to be understood in their usual and most known signification, not so much regarding the propriety of grammar, as their general and popular use." *Greenleaf* says, " The terms of every written document are to be understood in their plain, ordinary and popular sense."

Let us interpret the commission according to this simple principle. Putting the Greek of it with the literal translation, it reads:

Edotha moi pasa exousia en ourano kai epi gas: poreu-
Is given to me all power in heaven and upon earth:
thentes oun matheteusate panta ta ethna, baptizontes autous
going therefore disciple all the nations, baptizing them
eis to onoma tou patros kai tou huios kai tou
into the name of the Father and of the Son and of the Holy
hagiou pneumatos, didaskontes autous tarein panta hosa
Spirit, teaching them to observe all things whatsoever

eneteilaman humin: kai hidou ego meth' humon enimi pasas
I have commanded to you: and behold I with you I am all
tas hameras eos tas sunteleias tou æonas.
the days until the end of the age.

Proof has already been given that *baptizontes* means "dipping" or "immersing." Now follows the proof that in this dipping three acts are required by the command.

(4) *Three names in the commission involve three corresponding dips.* The word "baptizing" (dipping or immersing) does not of itself indicate how many actions there are to be. In Naaman's dipping there were seven dips. The only thing in the commission to indicate the number of dips is the modifying phrase, "into the name of the Father and of the Son and of the Holy Spirit." This answers the question "How" and modifies "baptizing."

"Baptizing them," How? "*Into the name of the Father.*" Is the name of the Father a name distinct from the name of the Son and of the Holy Spirit? It must be, for we repeatedly read of "the Father's name," and know that it does not mean the Son or the Holy Spirit. For example: John 5: 43. "I am come in MY FATHER'S NAME." John 10: 25, "The works which I do I do IN MY FATHER'S NAME." John 12: 28, "Father glorify THY NAME." John 17: 11, "Holy Father keep them in THY NAME." Can words make it clearer that there is a special name here, which is not to be confused or identified with any other name? Be honest with your conscience and your God, dear reader, did not Jesus here recognize a distinct name belonging to the Father alone? If you say not, then tell us, pray, if He had wished to do so how could He have done so in stronger or clearer language than He does? But if He does *mean* "the name of the Father" when He *says* "the name of the Father," then baptism (immersion) must be first of all "into the name of the Father." *If the commission ended here would it not require one dip?*

But Jesus adds, *"and of the Son." What* of the Son? The *name* of the Son, of course. Does the Son have a distinct name also? To be sure He has. Where is the proof? In the Gospel. John 3: 18, "He that believeth not is condemned already, because he hath not believed *on the name of the only begotten Son of God."* Are you condemned because *you* do not believe on THE NAME OF THE SON? Do you show your unbelief by refusing baptism into this name, and allowing it only into the name of the Holy Spirit? Listen again. John 14: 13, "Whatsoever ye ask IN MY NAME that will I do, that the Father may be glorified in the Son." Do you *ask* "in Jesus' name" as He bids you ask when you pray? If so, why not *baptize* into the name of the Son also as He expressly bids you to baptize? If we need any further word we find it in 1 John 3: 23, "This is his commandment that ye *believe in the name of his Son Jesus Christ."* And why is this command? Because *"there is none other NAME given under heaven among men, whereby we must be saved"* (Acts 4: 12). Is it then a light thing to deny this name by saying, "It is all one with that of the Father"? When two things are all one and the same they can be substituted the one for the other, for it is an axiom long proven that "two things equal to the same thing are equal to each other." Can we substitute the name of the Father for the Son, or the name of the Son for that of the Father? But, you say, if the word "name" were only repeated so that we would not need to supply the ellipsis, then it would be clear, and we would believe that three names and consequently three dips are intended. Would you indeed believe in such a case? If there were an example in scripture where the word "name" is repeated, would you believe that there is more than one? Then read Rev,

Baptism

14: 1 (A. R. V.) and be no longer faithless, but believing. The revelator says, "And I saw and behold the Lamb (Christ, John 1: 29) standing on Mt. Zion, and with him a hundred and forty-four thousand, HAVING HIS NAME AND THE NAME OF HIS FATHER written on their foreheads." Do we have separate names for the Father and the Son here? Then we have them also in the commission.

But Jesus further commanded as to baptism that it should be *into the name " of the Holy Spirit."* Are we then to recognize the Holy Spirit in the same way that we recognize the Father and the Son? Certainly we are. Does not the Scripture use the personal pronoun with reference to the Spirit? Do we not read, " Who knoweth the mind of the Spirit "? Again, " The mind of the Spirit is life and peace " (Rom. 8: 6). And again (Mark 3: 29) " Whosoever shall blaspheme against the Holy Spirit hath never forgiveness." Would it not be a serious thing to slight the blessed Spirit? " Grieve not the Spirit " says Paul, " in whom ye were sealed unto the day of redemption " (Eph. 4: 30). But does He have a special name? He does in the same way that the Father has and the Son has. Did not Jesus say, " The *Comforter* whom the Father will send in my name "? (John 14: 26). Does He not in this one sentence recognize the Father, the Son and the Holy Spirit and show that the " name " of the Spirit is a private possession, not to be attributed to another? When we say the " Comforter," do we mean the Son or the Father? But now comes the old objection, " Does not the Bible say that 'these three are one'? " It does not. The old version of 1 John 5: 7 reads that way, but the statement is not in the best ancient manuscripts and is therefore omitted from the Revised Version. However, Jesus did say, " I and the Father are one " (John 10: 30), but that is far from saying that their *names* are one, and it is into the *name* of each that we are commanded to baptize (Matt. 28: 19).

Besides it is only in a limited sense that the Father, Son and Holy Spirit are one. They are one in character and will rather than in being and personality. We know this from the fact that Jesus prayed for the same unity to exist among His followers: He says:

That they may all be one; even as thou, Father, art in me, and I in thee, that they may be in us: that the world may believe that thou didst send me. And the glory which thou hast given me I have given unto them; THAT THEY MAY BE ONE, EVEN AS WE ARE ONE; I in them, and thou in me, that they may be perfected into one (John 17: 21-23).

Compare Gal. 3: 28, " Ye are all one in Christ Jesus." Who cannot see the truth taught here: that believers are to be one in spirit even as Jesus and the Father are one in spirit and character? But as each believer has his own name and personality, so the Father, Son and Holy Spirit have each His own name and being. Compare 1 Cor. 8: 6, " There is one God, the Father, of whom are all things, and we through him; and one Lord Jesus Christ, through whom are all things and we through him "; and 1 Tim. 2: 5, " There is one God, one mediator also between God and men, himself man, Jesus Christ." To make God one in every sense would do away with the Mediator, the one who said, " I am the way, the truth and the life; no man cometh unto the Father but by me " (John 14: 6). It would also do away with the Holy Spirit, against whom blasphemy is so grievous a sin that Jesus said:

Whosoever shall speak a word against the Son of man it shall be forgiven him, but whosoever shall speak against the Holy Spirit, it shall not be forgiven him, neither in this world, nor in the world to come (Matt. 12: 32).

If " these three are one " in every sense, why is this distinction made by Jesus Himself? Are single immersionists willing to be known as Unitarians and come under the condemnation of 1 John 4: 1-3? If not why will they not cease to be Unitarians in the matter of baptism? If the action need not represent the Trinity in the formula, then it need not represent the death, burial and resurrection either, and we may all take the position of the Friends. Certainly Jesus was wise in commanding baptism into the name of each member of the blessed Trinity, that the saving work of each might be represented and faith in the Trinity be perpetuated in the world. Since Jesus was so careful to guard this truth, should we not also be careful to guard it by perpetuating the only rite given to the church to teach it?

If one person uses the name of another he is liable to the law for forgery; is it less a sin to deny the ownership of the Father, the Son and the Holy Spirit, each of His own name, so explicitly referred to and consistently used? We may not understand the mystery of being or function in the Trinity. We do not need to. We need only use the term "name" in the simple, plain way that the Gospel uses it, and let it stand for whatever reality there is back of it. Be assured that there is enough of this reality. No human name can express the fullness of Divinity. The prophet who only caught a glimpse of the Messiah tried to give Him an expressive name by saying, "His name shall be called Wonderful, Counsellor, the Mighty God, the Everlasting Father, Prince of Peace." We are not told to baptize into all the titles or names ascribed to the Deity, but simply to use the formula as Jesus gave it and let each name there implied stand for all the fullness of Divinity back of it.

These names are not used in the sense in which members of a firm use a firm name, because in that case each member uses a *collective* name, while in this case there is *an intended distinction* and a recognition of each member of the Trinity in His own name,—as if each member of a firm should pledge himself to a promise by signing his own name as an individual, thus making himself individually responsible. In the commission Jesus purposely distinguishes between the Father and the Son and the Holy Spirit, because He would have us show faith in the saving work of each.

The difference is something like that between a "collective" and an "individual" note. If a firm signs a note as a firm, it is liable only as a firm, but if thee members sign as individuals, then each one is responsible for the full amount of the note. So in baptism the Father, the Son and the Holy Spirit have each their part in redemption, and this is pledged for each by the formula of the commission and must be recognized by the faith of the believer, which is therefore expressed in the act of baptism, by obeying this definite and express command to baptize into the name of each. It is true that the three are one in a sense, but in another sense they are as truly three, and it is the threeness rather than the oneness that is represented in baptism.

In the home there are the husband and the wife with the same family name. They are said to be "one flesh" (Matt. 19: 5), yet each has a special name, and when we call Mary we do not mean John too. We hear no such nonsense as that because they are one they are not also two, or that their individual names are all one.

Let us note this fact carefully, for right here is the stumblingblock of the single immersionist. For example, Ford says, "Trine immersion is really antagonistic to the law of the commission." "To justify such a practice," says Dr. Conant (another single immersionist), "the form should have been either 'in the names of,' or 'in the name of the Father, in the name of the Son, and in the name of the Holy Spirit.'" Let us see. There are two ways of expressing possession, one by use of the possessive case, and the other by use of the possessive phrase with "of." Any grammar will show this. Any intelligent person knows it without a grammar. For example, I may say "John's house," or "the house of John," and likewise, "the Father's name," or "the name of the Father." If I wish to show the separate possession, each of his own house, of—say, Mark, Luke and John, I can say "Mark's house, Luke's house and John's house," or I can say "the house of Mark, the house of Luke and the house of John." No one could mistake that language to mean one house instead of three, especially when it is well known that each has his own house, although in partnership in other things. But just so we say, "the Father's name, the Son's name, and the Holy Spirit's name," or we can say, meaning the same thing, "the name of the Father, and the name of the Son, and the name of the Holy Spirit"; and as we have seen that, whatever else they may have in common, each member of the Trinity is referred to as having "His own name" (see references above), it must be perfectly clear that this language recognizes the three names.

"But," you say, "the word 'name' is omitted the second and third times in the commission." Yes, but *the sign of possession is not,* and the second and third possessors are not, therefore we have a simple form of ellipsis, the word "name" being understood in the second and third cases just as if it were written. Knowing that the name of each is distinct from the name of the other, there should be not the slightest difficulty in seeing that the repetition of the possessive phrase "and of " necessitates the repetition of "the name" also, as the thing possessed in each case, and this gives us exactly the form which Dr. Conant says is necessary to require trine immersion in the commission.

Try the ellipsis in parallel constructions and it will be clear. Suppose I say, " Go along the street with these notices, taking them into the house of Mark and of Luke and of John." Now, knowing that each had his own house, would you wait until you got to the house of John and say "It is enough if I take one in here"? But that is exactly what they do who practice single immersion in baptism. Here is the scene. The convert is ready. The administrator says, " I baptize thee into the name of the Father," but he does not do it. Instead, he goes on to say, " and of the Son," but again he does nothing to correspond to his words; then finally he says, " and of the Holy Spirit," and then he dips once. He has baptized only into the name of the Holy Spirit. His actions have belied his words and he has dishonored the Father and the Son. He has played as false with the commission as if he had said, " I baptize (immerse) thee," and instead of immersing the candidate had sprinkled or poured a little water instead. He may protest that he is Trinitarian in faith, but certainly he is Unitarian in his baptism. His faith in the Trinity is dead because it is without works (James 2: 17).

If the possessive phrases "and of " had been omitted altogether, then the commission would read, " baptizing them into the name, Father, Son and Holy Spirit." These terms would then be in apposition as if meaning one and the same thing, and one dip might answer. But the possessive phrases *are not omitted*. If the commission read, " Baptizing them into the name of the Father, Son and Holy Spirit," the ellipsis would be so great as to make it uncertain whether one collective name would be meant or three individual names. But Jesus did not leave us in this uncertainty. He used the possessive phrase " and of " in each case to show that " the name " is not collective but individual. The three are equal in honor and coördinate in construction.

If, as Dr. Conant says, the word " name " were plural (" into the *names* of the Father " &c.) then it would imply that each member of the Trinity had several names at least, and that baptism should be into each and every one of them. Indeed, a number of names are applied to each, and we read of still a new name to be revealed (Rev. 3: 12), so that if the commission read, "into the names of the Father and of the Son and of the Holy Spirit," we would not know how many times to dip. But since the singular, "name," is used, we know that there is reference to one name for each, and one corresponding dip for each name. To make the matter clearer, suppose we know that Mark, Luke and John have each several houses on the street, and I say " Go down the street and take my friend into the *houses* of Mark, and of Luke, and of John," is it not clear that, however many the houses of each, you would have to go into all of them to obey the command? If it be said that Jesus should have expressly commanded to dip " three times " instead of " into the name of the Father and of the Son and of the Holy Spirit," we reply that such redundancy is not required in similar cases, as for example the following: "Ye believe in God, believe also in me" John 14: 1), or, "It was written in Hebrew and in Latin and in Greek" (John 19: 20). It is not necessary to say "believe twice," or "it was written three times," because every one understands the number from the words used. So the number of dips in baptism is clearly implied in the formula given. The early church understood this perfectly, and Tertullian, only a generation from the apostles, says candidates were immersed "three times, at each name, into each separate person" (*Ad. Prax.* c. 26). The *Didache,* which is, perhaps, as early as Matthew, commands "three times" in the action of baptism (c. 14). The fact is, if we were trying our best to command triune immersion by a brief commission we could not use a better word in the Greek for the act, or a better formula to express the three actions than Jesus used. The only way to make it clearer would be to supply the ellipsis and thus lengthen the formula, and when we have done that, lo, we have triune immersion as before.

(5) *The commission diagrammed shows clearly the ellipsis in the commission and the three names, involving three corresponding dips.* Study the following diagram and note that the three phrases which follow "baptizing them" are equal and alike, and that to show the action of baptism into each of the three names requires three immersions in the one baptizing.

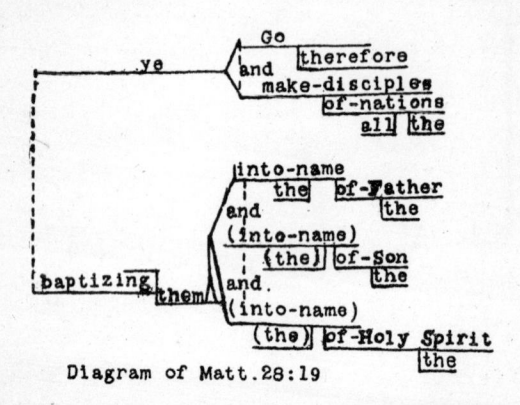

```
                    Go
         ye     \    therefore
                 \and
                  \make-disciples
                       of-nations
                          all  the

                  into-name
                     the  of-Father
                  and        the
                  (into-name)
                     (the)  of-Son
  baptizing them  and        the
                  (into-name)
                     (the)  of-Holy Spirit
                              the
```
Diagram of Matt. 28:19

Any furniture factory will furnish an illustration that will show the three actions of this construction clearly. It is common to finish certain grades of furniture by dipping it first into a tank of stain, then into a tank of "filler" and then into a tank of varnish. Now suppose we say, "Go ye, therefore, and polish tables, dipping them into the tank of the stain, and of the 'filler,' and of the varnish." How many dips would be required? Suppose you should say, "This is only a form: I will sprinkle or pour these tables instead of dipping them"! Or, being a single immersionist,

Baptism

you take the table to the tank of the stain, but dip it not; then to the tank of the "filler," but dip it not; then to the tank of the varnish and dip it once. Have you obeyed the command? Certainly not. Neither is it obeying the command to say, "I baptize thee into the name of the Father," and do it not; "and of the Son," and do it not; "and of the Holy Spirit," and then dip once. As there are three tanks for the one polishing so there are three names for the one baptism, and three dips in either case.

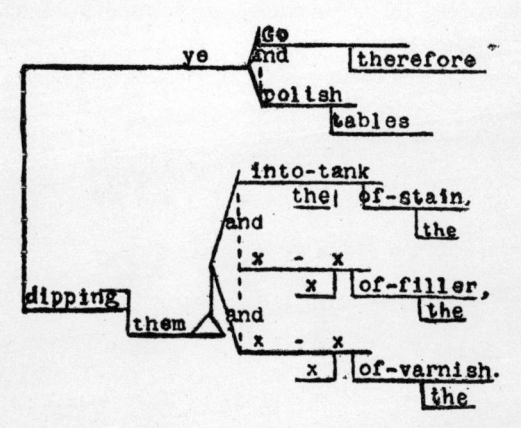

```
              Go
        ye   and        therefore
                  polish
                        tables

                    into-tank
                    the  of-stain,
                    and    the
                     x - x
                         x    of-filler,
                              the
   dipping  them   and
                     x - x
                         x    of-varnish.
                              the
```

(6) *The best authorities can be quoted to sustain this view*, which is merely a simple rule of grammar which scarcely needs to be argued, for every school child is taught it and understands it. But we will quote Dr. Myer, who is called by Schaff, the great church historian, "The ablest grammatical exegete of the age," and by the *Princeton Review*, "a master of the grammatical and historical method of interpretation." He ought to command attention. He says:

Had Jesus used the words, "the names" instead of "the name," then, however much he may have intended the names of three distinct persons to be understood, he would still have been liable to be misapprehended, for it might have been supposed that the plural was meant to refer to the various names of each separate person. The singular points to the specific name assigned in the text to each of the three respectively, so that "into the name" is, of course, to be understood both before the Son and before the Holy Spirit; compare Rev. 14: 1, "His name and the name of his Father."

Matt. 8: 11 is sometimes quoted as a parallel construction to prove single action. "Many shall sit down with Abraham and Isaac and Jacob in the kingdom." But the construction is not parallel and the meaning is totally different. One can sit down with a number of persons at once, but cannot call all their names with one word, or enter into each of their houses with one act, or be baptized into each of their names with one act.

It is also sometimes said, "We dedicate a church to the Triune God, but do not dedicate it three times, therefore we need not dip three times to dedicate the life to the Triune God." There are two fatal fallacies in this illustration. First, baptism is not a mere dedication of the life. They who baptize infants make it so, but the Scriptures make it a symbol of regeneration instead, and it is for us to follow the Scriptures. Second, the illustration compares a part of baptism with the whole of the dedication. Considering both as a whole there are a number of actions involved in each. Other misleading illustrations are sometimes used to discredit triune immersion, among which we should note the following: 1 John 2: 24, "Shall continue in the Son and in the Father." This example is not parallel, because to "continue in" is not the same as to "baptize into." One might continue in a room and in bed with one action, although to get into them would require (1) to go into the house, (2) to go into the room and (3) to get into bed. Baptism represents the *getting into* the divine life. "As many as have been baptized into Christ did put on

Christ" (Gal. 3: 27). Luke 9: 26, "He shall come in his own glory and the glory of the Father and of the holy angels." This example is like the first in that it represents a *continuance in* while baptism represents a *getting into*. The getting into the glory of the Father and of the holy angels must have been separate acts, because the glory of the Father is eternal while that of the angels is not. Matt. 23: 1, "He spake to the multitude and to the disciples." If this be taken to mean that Jesus addressed the multitude and the disciples together as one audience the case is not parallel, because baptism is not directed toward God in His unity but as a Trinity, for so the commission specifies. If, however, the speaking to the multitude and the disciples was in the sense of speaking to the multitude in parables and privately expounding the same to the disciples, as was His custom, then there is a point of similarity to baptism, but there is also a requirement of separate actions.

(7) *That the apostles and the early church understood the ellipsis in the commission is shown by the fact that they used it in its complete sense.* The *Didache*, written in the very days of the apostles, requires the trine action, expressly saying, "three times, into the name," &c.; and *Justin Martyr*, born only thirty years after John the disciple died, in describing baptism supplies the ellipsis and quotes the complete formula, explaining its meaning. He says:

There is pronounced over him who chooses to be born again, and has repented of his sins, **the name of God the Father and** Lord of the universe; he who leads to the laver (baptistry) the person that is to be washed, calling him by this name alone. For no one can utter the name of the ineffable God; and if any one dare say that there is a name, he raves with a hopeless madness. And this washing is called illumination because they who learn these things are illuminated in their understandings. **And in the name of Jesus Christ,** who was crucified under Pontius Pilate, **and in the name of the Holy Spirit,** who through the prophets foretold all about Jesus, he who is illuminated is washed.—1st Apol. ch. 71.

Gregory of Nyssa (335 A. D.) says, on the baptism of Christ:

> But coming to the element akin to earth, the water, we conceal ourselves in that as the Savior did in the earth; and by doing this thrice we represent for ourselves that grace of the resurrection which was wrought in three days. . . . Resist if you can those words of the Lord which gave to men the rule of baptismal invocation. What says the Lord's command? "Baptizing them into the name of the Father and of the Son and of the Holy Ghost." How into the name of the Father? Because He is above all. How into the name of the Son? Because He is the Maker of the creation. How into the name of the Holy Ghost? Because He is the power perfecting all. We bow ourselves therefore before the Father that we may be sanctified; before the Son also we bow that the same end may be fulfilled; we bow also before the Holy Ghost that we may be made what He is in fact and in name.

If it be objected that in order to be consistent we should immerse the entire body three times instead of only the head, we reply that we are commanded to baptize, not three times, but once; but the one baptism includes among the other actions necessary to it, the dipping of the head three times. For we are taught to recognize, not three separate Gods, but one God, with the Father, Son and Holy Spirit constituting the Godhead. We have a *triune* God and a *triune* baptism corresponding thereto. That this interpretation is correct is proven by the example of Philip, who did not take the eunuch into the water and out of the water three times in baptizing him, but "they went down into the water" once, and "came up out of the water" once, but while in the water "he baptized him" (Acts 8: 38). How did he baptize him? According to the commission which requires a dip into each of the three names mentioned. Triune immersion corresponds perfectly with the Gospel command and example.

Baptism

(8) *Paraphrasing or expanding the commission by including in it the other scriptures explaining baptism shows still more strongly that it teaches triune immersion.* The Trinitarian formula is in harmony with the Trinitarian practice or the other scriptures could not be fitted into it in harmony. Study the following explanation: " Since *all power is given unto me* as the Christ, *therefore go ye into all the world and disciple all the nations, BAPTIZING THEM,*" that is, immersing believers, as an outward sign (1 Pet. 3: 21) (1) of inward regeneration (John 3: 5) like to the death and burial of the sinful life, and resurrection of the eternal life (Rom. 6: 3, 5), and, (2) as a confession of faith in the Father and in the Son and in the Holy Spirit, who have each an essential work in this salvation; dipping first INTO THE NAME OF THE FATHER as a sign of entering into sonship through His mercy (Titus 3: 5) AND into the name OF THE SON as a sign of entering into the life that He gives (John 3: 16; 10: 10) AND into the name OF THE HOLY SPIRIT as a sign of entering into the renewing (Titus 3: 5) and enduing (Acts 1: 8) which He gives; thus coming into the church which is the body of Christ (1 Cor. 12: 13) and into the kingdom as children of God (2 Cor. 5: 17), having put on Christ (Gal. 3: 27) and being led of the Spirit, henceforth to be dead to the world and alive to God (Col. 3: 1-3), *and lo, I am with you always, even unto the end of the age* (Matt. 18: 20).

(9) *The spiritual significance of baptism implied in the Trinitarian formula involves triune action.* " Baptizing them into the name " here means more than " consecrating them by the authority of." It involves the passing from the natural to the spiritual life, from separation from God to union with Him, and that by faith in each member of the

Trinity. "As many of you as were baptized into Christ did put on Christ" (Gal. 3: 27) implies a like result of being baptized into the Father and into the Holy Spirit. *Kitto's Cyclopedia* says:

> The baptismal formula has sometimes been interpreted as meaning no more than that baptism is administered by the authority of the triune God; but this is now generally repudiated as philologically inadequate. The opinion now most generally received is that the name of the Father, Son and Holy Ghost means the revealed fact, lying at the basis of Christianity, of the Three-One-God, and to be baptized into (eis), for, with respect to or with a view to this, means that by submitting to this rite men acknowledge this revealed fact, receive God thus revealed as their God and profess willingness to be taught all that He enjoined.

(10) *That the commission requires a triple dipping is further proven by the use of the plural in Heb. 6: 2, "The doctrine of baptisms."* The Greek word here is *baptismone*, "dippings," the genitive plural of the regular word for the rite of baptism, and the term "enlightened" in verse 4 following is a common term for Christian baptism among the earliest writers. The author cannot by the plural mean to include anything but Christian baptism, because he is speaking only of "the first principles of *the doctrine of Christ*." And he cannot by the plural mean water baptism on the one hand and Spirit baptism on the other, because while these were not connected in John's baptism, they are parts of one and the same thing in Christian baptism (John 3: 5; 1 Cor. 12: 13). The only possible consistent explanation is that the passage refers to the triple dipping in the rite of baptism. The American Revised Version makes this still clearer, for it reads "The *teaching* of baptisms" (dippings) thus referring to the *significance* of the three dips in the symbol.

Thus every line of research leads to the conclusion that

the formula Jesus prescribed for baptism is a Trinitarian formula that involves triune action to correspond with it. The grammatical construction requires it. The separate names indicated by the sign of possession require it. The union with each of the divine persons referred to in the formula requires it. The use of the plural in Heb. 6: 2 confirms it, and the passages explanatory of the rite together with the practice of the apostles and the early church is in harmony with it. Illustrations, diagrams and comparisons by expansions with other Scriptures all help to make it clearer, and the more one studies the matter the higher piles the evidence that Jesus commanded triune immersion. It is little wonder that all churches accept it as valid. It *is* a wonder that anyone is not willing to receive it and set all doubts at rest.

4. THE MODE OF BAPTISM AS DETERMINED BY THE SIGNIFICANCE OF THE SYMBOL IS TRIUNE IMMERSION.

A symbol is a representation of something, and there must therefore be some likeness of the thing presented to be found in the symbol. For example, he is called a traitor who welcomes a friend with a kiss while he stabs him in the back, because the kiss means love, but the stab is different. So he is false to the commission of our Lord who says, " I baptize (immerse) thee," and at the same time does nothing, or does something different. The inward meaning and outward form of the symbol must correspond, else why have a symbol at all?

But mark this, if *any part* of the teaching of the symbol is to be expressed in the action, then *all of it* must be. The omission of a part is as much a perversion of the rite, and is as misleading, as the substitution of something different. By keeping this in mind we may learn from the different things represented in baptism, the sort of action that is required to represent them.

(1) *Baptism represents the* DEATH *of the old man of sin, and therefore requires a* FORWARD *action*. We read that we "are planted (R. V., united) in the likeness of his death" (Rom. 6: 5). If this means the literal, physical death of Jesus, then we have a bowing forward, for when He died He "bowed his head and gave up the ghost" (John 19: 30). But, if this means being planted or united with Him in the likeness of His death *figuratively*, that is, His self-renunciation, then we must still have the bowing forward, because the renunciation was voluntary (John 10: tt18), and only the forward action can represent the voluntary going forward of Jesus to the cross or our voluntary giving of the old life to death. God compels no one to be saved. Our coming is by choice of free will. Paul says, "Reckon ye yourselves to be indeed dead unto sin, but alive unto God" (Rom. 6: 11). This free choice of the candidate is expressed *by the forward motion in baptism*. Backward action means calamity. Eli fell backward and died (1 Sam. 4: 18), and the soldiers who arrested Jesus "went backward and fell to the ground" (John 18: 6). Backward action represents compulsion, but forward action is the proper action to show that the candidate says with Jesus of his life, "No one taketh it from me, but I lay it down of myself."

(2) *Baptism represents the* BURIAL *of the old man of sin* (Rom. 6: 4, 5), *and therefore requires* IMMERSION. Paul's words, (we are buried with him by baptism) would be meaningless and absurd if there were no resemblance between the act of baptism and the act of burial. How can a thing be a figure of another *totally* different? Where then is the resemblance here? In the going into the watery grave. But do we not bury backward? No, we let the body down by four corners. Other nations have different customs. The Romans usually burned their dead and buried the ashes.

The figure has just one point,—the thought of burial, but a body is buried when it is covered in the ground, no matter what its position. If we say, " He ran like a deer," we do not mean that he ran on all fours, but simply that he ran swiftly. So when we say, " buried with Christ in baptism," we mean simply covered out of sight in the baptismal grave. But it is impossible to get the likeness of a burial out of sprinkling or pouring. We should fear the resurrection of the same old man of sin if he were no more buried than those actions represent.

(3) *Baptism represents the* RESURRECTION *of the new man in Christ* (Rom. 6: 4, 5; John 3: 5) *by the* COMING FORTH *from the water*. We do not read the idea of this resurrection of the "new creature" (2 Cor. 5: 17) into baptism. The Scriptures themselves put it there, and we must therefore have something in the action to represent the truth, else we have no symbol of it at all. In sprinkling or pouring there is nothing to represent this resurrection, but in the coming forth from the water after immersion, we have it perfectly portrayed.

(4) *Baptism represents the* DISTINCTIVE SAVING WORK OF THE FATHER (John 3: 16) *and therefore requires* IMMERSION INTO THE NAME OF THE FATHER. If the commission read "baptizing them into the name of the Father," and ended there, would not one action be required? Then why not perform the action when we get that far, instead of saying, " I baptize thee into the name of the Father," and then doing nothing? The action to be right must correspond to the meaning and the formula.

(5) *Baptism represents the* DISTINCTIVE SAVING WORK OF THE SON (1 Tim. 2: 5) *and therefore requires* IMMERSION INTO THE NAME OF THE SON. The construction is precisely the same for the Son as for the Father, and as the Son is

equally recognized in the formula He must also be in the action.

(6) *Baptism represents the* DISTINCTIVE SAVING WORK OF THE HOLY SPIRIT (John 3: 5). This recognition is in the words of the formula and must also be in the action, *by immersion into the name of the Holy Spirit.*

Not only has the Father, the Son and the Holy Spirit each a special work in salvation, but the regenerated candidate is brought into a new relation with each. (1) He was before a sinner dead in sin (Rom. 6: 23); he is now *a child of God* (John 1: 12). (2) He was before a destitute prodigal; he is now restored, a *joint-heir with Jesus Christ* (Rom. 8: 17). (3) He was carnal before, but now lives "*in the Spirit*" (Gal. 5: 6-25).

Thus, the regenerated believer can say, "Truly our fellowship is with the Father and with his Son Jesus Christ" (1 John 1: 3) and all such may receive the benediction of the Triune God, "The grace of the Lord Jesus Christ, and the love of God, and the communion of the Holy Spirit be with you all." (2 Cor. 13: 14).

(7) *Baptism represents the* DEPENDENCE *of the believer upon God* for salvation, which is the free gift of God (Rom. 6: 23). "Not by works done in righteousness which we did ourselves, but according to his mercy he saved us, through the washing of regeneration and the renewing of the Holy Spirit" (Titus 3: 5). This complete *dependence* upon God is expressed in baptism *by the attitude of prayer.* In this we have the example of Jesus who prayed at the time of His baptism (Luke 3: 21).

This implies the forward action in baptism because all acts of worship are forward and not backward. Note, for example, the example of Abraham (Gen. 18: 2), Lot (Gen. 33: 3), Jacob (Gen. 47: 31), Joseph (Gen. 48: 12), Israel (Ex. 4: 31), Daniel (Dan. 6: 10), Jesus (Luke 22: 41),

Baptism

Stephen (Acts 7: 60), Peter (Acts 9: 40), Paul (Acts 20: 36) and John (Rev. 22: 8). In Psa. 95: 6 we are exhorted, "O come let us worship and bow down, let us kneel before the Lord our Maker," and in Philpp. 2: 10 we read "that in the name of Jesus every knee should bow." On the other hand, backward action is always associated in the Bible with evil. It is said, moreover, of the wicked that they shall "fall backward and be broken and snared and taken" (Isa. 28: 13). The example of Jesus in prayer at the time of baptism is reënforced by that of Paul, to whom it was said, "Arise and be baptized and wash away thy sins, calling on the name of the Lord." If Paul was "calling on the name of the Lord" during his baptism, he certainly was not falling backward at the time, but in the usual attitude of prayer, which was bowing forward. There can be no mistake in taking this reverent attitude in baptism.

Note the fact that these seven things included in the meaning of baptism are all important truths and should not by any means be ignored.

Note also that sprinkling and pouring fail to express the idea of death, burial and resurrection, while backward single immersion fails to express the idea of the Trinity, and free will, but forward triune immersion completely expresses every idea of the symbol. The evangelical churches profess to be Trinitarian and not Unitarian in doctrine, and to be consistent must be Trinitarian and not Unitarian in the practice of baptism. Single immersionists are inconsistent in that they profess to be Trinitarian in faith but in the act of baptism are Unitarian. Those who sprinkle or pour are likewise inconsistent in that they say one thing ("I baptize," i. e., immerse) and do another (sprinkle or pour). They should learn of *Martin Luther* who said "The *mode* of baptizing ought, therefore, to correspond to the *significance* of baptism."—*Opera Omnia,* Vol. 1. p. 319.

The following outline will help to show how the teaching of baptism is fully expressed by triune immersion, while it is only partially expressed by other modes.

	Teaching Intended.	Action Corresponding.	Mode or Modes Permitted.
Rom. 6:3. Gal. 2:20.	Death of Old Sinful Nature.	Bowing in Likeness of Jesus' Death. John 19:30 or John 10:18	Forward Immersion.
Rom. 6:4. Col. 2:12.	Burial or Planting.	Immersion.	Immersion, Single or Triune.
Rom. 6:5. Gal. 3:27.	Resurrection of New Life or Birth.	Coming Forth from the Water.	Immersion, Single or Triune.
Matt. 28:19. Rom. 6:4.	Faith in the Father.	Bowing the Head.	Trine Sprinkling, or Pouring, or Triune Immersion.
Matt. 28:19. 1 Cor. 12:13.	Faith in the Son.	Bowing the Head.	Trine Sprinkling, or Pouring, or Triune Immersion.
Matt. 28:19. John 3:5.	Faith in the Holy Spirit.	Bowing the Head.	Sprinkling, Pouring, or Triune Immersion.
Titus 3:5. Luke 3:21.	Dependence.	Bowing Posture	Triune Immersion.

Note that only three of the seven truths taught by the symbol, baptism, are represented by either sprinkling, pouring or single immersion, while *all of them are taught by triune immersion.* It is sometimes said that it is sufficient to recognize the Trinity by repeating the formula, but if that be true, then it is enough to recognize the other teachings of baptism by merely repeating the formula and have no action at all. If we have a right to change or do away with any part of the action, then we have the same right to do away with all of it. There is no middle ground between triune immersion and the position of the Friends, who reject water baptism altogether.

Combination of Modes. There are those who in baptism take the candidate down into the water and then pour water on the head three times. This comes more nearly fulfilling the symbol than any other form except triune immersion,

Baptism

but even this does not fully represent a burial and resurrection, while it also fails to fully conform to the meaning of the word " baptizo," to dip or immerse.

Water Baptism and Spirit Baptism. It is also argued that water baptism was meant to be a type of Spirit baptism, and that as the Spirit was *poured* out on the day of Pentecost, therefore only pouring can fulfill the symbol. At first thought this seems plausible, but on searching the Scriptures it soon appears that the prophecy, " He shall baptize you in the Holy Spirit," does not refer to Pentecost alone, for Peter quotes it also as being fulfilled at the home of Cornelius (Acts 11: 15, 16) where it is said, " the Spirit *fell* on on them " that heard the word. The gift of the Spirit was the regular accompaniment of Christian baptism as contrasted with John's baptism. See Acts 8; 19: 1-6. Jesus so connects it in His discourse with Nicodemus (John 3: 5) and speaks of the experience as a *birth* rather than a being sprinkled or poured upon. However, there is not one scripture which says that Christian baptism is to imitate or represent the coming of the Spirit. Indeed, it is said,

The wind bloweth where it will, and thou hearest the sound thereof, but knowest not whence it cometh or whither it goeth: so is every one that is born of the Spirit (John 3: 8).

At one time Jesus *" breathed on "* His disciples and said, " Receive ye the Holy Spirit " (John 20: 22). At another time Paul *" laid his hands on them "* and they received the Holy Spirit (Acts 19: 6). Repeatedly it is said, " They *were filled* with the Holy Spirit " (Acts 4: 8; 9: 17; 13: 9; Eph. 5: 18 etc.). The mystery of this coming of the Spirit of God to His temple cannot be fully represented in action. It is a *new birth,* and as the seed planted in the ground mysteriously gives up its old life that the new may spring forth, so we in baptism bury the old life that we may receive the new and rise to walk as children of God.

We cannot improve upon the symbol of this "renewing of the Holy Spirit" (Titus 3: 5) that Jesus gave. We are not to derive the mode of baptism from any *inferences* whatever, but simply to follow the commission, which is the only *command* concerning the mode. In doing so we shall find that every meaning of baptism is most fully taught by receiving the penitent believers on confession of faith in Christ and "baptizing them into the name of the Father and of the Son and of the Holy Spirit." This represents the regenerating work of the Spirit along with the saving work of the Father and the Son, and the further enduement of the Spirit is represented by the accompanying rite of confirmation by prayer and the *laying on of hands,* in imitation of the pouring out of the anointing oil under the old covenant, and the pouring out of the Spirit in the anointing of the new covenant. There is therefore no more reason for pouring water in baptism because the Spirit was, figuratively speaking, "poured out" than there is for drinking water and calling it baptism because they were all "*filled* with the Holy Spirit." If we really wish to know the right *mode* of baptism, why not go to the only command we have concerning it? The commission of Jesus (Matt. 28: 19) settles the whole matter.

5. THE SCRIPTURES REFERRING TO BAPTISM BY JOHN AND THE APOSTLES INDICATE TRIUNE IMMERSION.

Let us take them in order and consider both the objections and the positive evidence.

(1) *John the Baptist baptized by immersion.* Matt. 3: 11, "*I indeed baptize you in water unto repentance but . . . he shall baptize you in the Holy Spirit and in fire.*" See also Acts 1: 5 and 11: 16. The old version of 1611 reads "*with* water" instead of "*in* water," and for this reason it has been argued that "the element should be applied to the subject rather than the subject to the element," but the revised

Baptism

versions, both English and American, correct the error of the old and render the passage "*in* water."

However, it is still argued that we should say "with" because in the Greek the word for water is in the dative case. It is said that this is the "instrumental dative." It is true that there is such a use of the dative, but there are also other uses, and only the context shows which dative is used. In this case the context is against making this the instrumental dative and in favor of the translation "in." First, the verb *baptize* (immerse), implies motion of the subject toward and into the water, and verbs denoting approach take the dative (*Goodwin's Greek Grammar* p. 186). Hence it is just what we should expect here in case of immersion. Second, the case is strengthened by the fact that Matthew 3: 11 uses the preposition *en* which means "in." If the writer had meant "beside" he could have used *para* which means "beside," or if he had meant "with" he could have used *sun* which means "with." Since he used *en* he meant "IN." Third, we have a still stronger preposition used in Mark 1: 9. We read, "Jesus was baptized into *(eis)* Jordan by John." It is to be supposed that He was baptized in the same manner as the others, but *eis* with verbs of motion means "into" unless modified by the context. This is in perfect accord with the dipping implied in *baptize,* but it is grotesque if we attempt to substitute pour or sprinkle,—" Was poured or sprinkled *into* the Jordan by John! " The manifest purpose of the passage is to contrast the elements "water" and "the Holy Spirit" and the matter of mode is only incidentally implied. So in Ex. 12: 10, " That which remaineth * * * ye shall burn *with* fire,"—but the burning was by putting the material *in* the fire. *Brown's Biblical Dictionary* describing the baptism of proselytes says, " If males, they were circumcised, and then baptized *with* water by plunging them *into* a cistern." So John baptized both in and with water, but he did so by dipping the candidates "into" the water.

Mark 1: 4, *"John came, who baptized in the wilderness, and preached the baptism of repentance unto the remission of sins. And there went out unto him all the country of Judea, and all they of Jerusalem and were baptized of him in the river Jordan, confessing their sins."* See also Matt. 3: 6.

It has been argued that this baptizing could not have been by immersion because of the vast multitudes to be baptized— several millions at least according to the literal statement that "all Judea" went out and were baptized, but if any one is really so ignorant as not to be able to understand from this passage that only representatives from these places heard the preaching and were baptized, it is not worth while to try to explain the figure. It is equally idle to try to prove that "in Jordan" (literally, "in the Jordan River") means *in* the river rather than beside it. It is just as clear in the Greek as in the English. But if John baptized the people in the river Jordan it stands to reason that he immersed them, for sprinkling and pouring could have been accomplished as well on the bank. The expression "in the wilderness" manifestly means simply the region of the Jordan in the wilderness. He baptized "in Jordan" and "in the wilderness" through which the Jordan flowed, just as he would baptize "in a pool" and at the same time "in the city" in which the pool was located.

John 3: 23, *"John was baptizing in Aenon, near to Salem, because there was much water there."* To avoid the force of this passage some have said that the Greek "*polla hudada*" should be translated "many waters" instead of "much water," but the scholars who translated the revised version, although for the most part not immersionists, have felt obliged to retain the phrase "much water." It has also been said that John was attracted by the many springs whereat the multitudes might drink, but this idea is punctured by the plain statement of the Gospel that John was *baptizing* at Aenon because of the much water, not preaching there simply because of the much drinking water.

While the Scriptures do not say whether John baptized by single or triune immersion, yet the fact that many Jews even to this day baptize themselves on the day of atonement by thrice dipping themselves forward as a sign of renewing the heart, is no small evidence that it was this familiar triune immersion which John took up and made the symbol of birth into the kingdom. (See page 123.) This would account also for the fact that in giving the commission, which requires triune immersion, Jesus did not find it necessary to command any change in the mode of baptism to which the disciples were already accustomed.

(2) *The Apostles baptized by immersion.* It is fair to assume that the apostles knew better than any one else the mode of baptism which Jesus taught them to perform. The way they interpreted the commission is good authority for us. Let us then follow through all the references to examples of baptism given in the Acts and epistles.

Acts 2: 38-41, *"And Peter said unto them, Repent ye, and be baptized every one of you in the name of Jesus Christ unto the remission of your sins; and ye shall receive the gift of the Holy Spirit. . . . They then that received his word were baptized: and there were added unto them in that day about three thousand souls."* In this passage the only thing that indicates the mode of baptism is in the word itself, "be baptized." We have already seen that this means "be immersed." Peter had plenty of words meaning to sprinkle or to pour, had he desired to use them. Why did he not do so?

The phrase, *"In the name of Jesus Christ"* means simply " with the baptism Jesus commanded," rather than with proselyte baptism or that of John, both of which were familiar to them. In receiving Christ's baptism they would, of course, be baptized in the manner commanded in the commission which Jesus gave them just ten days before; and this, as we have seen, requires triune immersion.

If any added proof is needed of this, we find it in the *Didache or Teaching of the Twelve Apostles,* which was first written about 65 A. D., while most of the apostles were yet living. It expressly commands immersion, and three actions (Sec. 7), "into the name of the Father and of the Son and of the Holy Spirit," quoting the commission exactly, and yet in section 9 says: "Let no one eat or drink of your Thanksgiving (Lord's Supper), but they who have been *baptized into the name of the Lord.*" This clearly shows that the apostolic writers meant by the phrases, "into the name of Jesus," "by the authority of Jesus," for by His authority they baptized by triune immersion and called it baptism "into the name of the Lord."

The early writers of the church so understood it and so speak of it. *Cyprian,* Bishop of Carthage (220 A. D.) says:

Peter makes mention of Jesus Christ, not as though the Father should be omitted, but that the Son also might be joined to the Father.

Augustine (354 A. D.), the greatest theologian of the early church, says:

In this font, before we dipped your whole body, we asked you "believest thou in God the omnipotent Father?" After you averred that you believed we immersed three times your heads in the sacred font. YOU ARE RIGHTLY IMMERSED THREE TIMES; YOU WHO RECEIVE BAPTISM IN THE NAME OF JESUS CHRIST.—Sermo De Mysteria Baptismos.

Those who use this phrase against triune immersion reject their own arguments, for none of them use it in practice, but instead, the Trinitarian formula which Jesus gave.

It has also been objected that it would have been *impos-*

Baptism

sible to baptize three thousand persons by triune immersion in one day. It is not certain that they were all baptized that day, for it is common to count converts on their confession, even before they are actually baptized; but even if the three thousand were, it would have required only from five to ten hours for the apostles to do the baptizing, and it was only about nine o'clock in the morning when Peter preached his sermon (v. 15). Besides, there were other disciples, and doubtless many of these, especially the seventy (Luke 10), assisted in the baptizing. In any case, under favorable conditions, it takes only from one to two minutes to baptize by triune immersion, which is scarcely longer than is required by the other modes. There have been other examples of baptism by triune immersion, of large numbers, at a rate more rapid than the Pentecost account requires. Chrysostom tell of three thousand baptized in a single night (*Chrysostom.* Montfaucon's Edition Vol. 3, p. 618). Ford, *Studies in Baptism,* p. 190, mentions other instances.

It has also been said that there was *not water enough* in Jerusalem to admit of baptizing these people by immersion. But any Bible student knows that there were numerous large pools and canals in the city. It is absurd to assert that a city with water sufficient to supply the wants of over a million of people who were gathered there to observe the Passover, could not supply water enough to baptize three thousand of them, or that the disciples could not have access to them when they were allowed to preach for a time unhindered, and it is expressly said that they had "favor with all the people" (Acts 2: 47).

Josephus, in *History of the Jews,* p. 530, says:

There were moreover (in Jerusalem) several groves of trees and long walks through them with deep canals and cisterns.

Dr. Durbin, a traveler quoted by James Quinter in debate with Snyder (p. 180) says:

In almost every quarter, you may see some deep cistern, now dry and dirty, or some pool once furnishing pure water, now a mere sink for filth and rubbish.

The *Report of the Palestine Exploration Society* by Captain Warner, pp. 643-647, describes the abundant water supply of Jerusalem and says that there were three "Pools of Solomon" the largest of which was 600 x 200 feet.

It must be remembered that three times a year the male Jews from everywhere were required to gather at Jerusalem to observe *the feasts,* and that it was common to take their families along; and besides there were the scores of thousands of animals, to be provided with water during their protracted stay (the Passover and Feast of Tabernacles each lasting a week). And still further, these Jews were required to perform many ablutions and bathings preparatory to the observance of the feasts. In fact, "many went up to Jerusalem out of the country before the Passover, to purify themselves" (John 11: 55). Surely Jerusalem must have been, as *Strabo* calls it, a "well watered city." Indeed, so well watered was it that in that generation the several millions in it endured the long siege by the Romans without want of water. *Hastings' Bible Dictionary* says that there were porticos for the convenience of bathers, which were used for dressing rooms. Yet Dr. Dale says, "the difficulties in the way of this Pentecostal baptism are piled mountains upon mountains," and the mountain he seems troubled most about is the problem of what these baptized people did with their wet clothes! Inasmuch as hundreds of thousands were taking daily baths in that city at that time, there was probably some way for these comparatively few to change their raiment. Truly, unbelief imagines more difficulties than faith ever finds.

If any one wishes to investigate further the opportunities for baptism in Jerusalem, they can read of a number of

Baptism

pools in the Bible. See 1 Kings 22: 38; 2 Kings 18: 17; Isa. 36: 2; Isa. 22: 9; Neh. 3: 15; John 9: 7-11; Song of Solomon 7: 4; Neh. 2: 14; Isa. 7: 3; John 5: 2; 2 Chron. 32: 1-3; 2 Kings 20: 20. These are just a few incidentally mentioned. Remains of some of these pools are still to be found. Ford (*Studies in Baptism* pp. 393-402) quotes accounts of travelers describing pools and fountains and baths enough to accommodate many times the number baptized. Some of these were an acre or more in extent. Beyond all question Jerusalem had a perennial and abundant water supply.

Acts 8: 12-16, "*But when they believed Philip preaching good tidings concerning the kingdom of God and the name of Jesus Christ, they were baptized, both men and women. . . . Now when the apostles that were at Jerusalem heard that Samaria had received the word of God, they sent unto them Peter and John: who, when they were come down, prayed for them that they might receive the Holy Spirit: for as yet it was fallen upon none of them: only they had been baptized into the name of the Lord Jesus. Then laid they their hands on them, and they received the Holy Spirit.*"

Aside from the meaning of the word "baptized," which means "immersed," this passage is significant in that it shows that only believers were baptized. This confirms the statement that baptism is not a rite of consecration for infants, but a symbol of regeneration for believers; and that consequently it must conform in the act to the formula given and the truths it is intended to teach. It has already been shown that only triune immersion can fully do this. The passage also shows that water baptism is not a mere symbol of Spirit baptism, for these converts were not endued with the Spirit until confirmed by prayer and the laying on of hands. This was the case also of the twelve converts of Acts 19: 1-6.

Acts, 8: 36-38, *"And as they went on their way, they came to a certain water; and the eunuch saith, Behold, here is water; what doth hinder me to be baptized? And he commanded the chariot to stand still: and they both went down into the water, both Philip and the eunuch; and he baptized him. And when they came up out of the water, the Spirit of the Lord caught away Philip; and the eunuch saw him no more, for he went on his way rejoicing."*

This passage is so clear that even a child can see that the baptism was by immersion, for it would not be necessary for both to go down into the water for any other mode. Nevertheless, there are some who profess to see no immersion here.

First, they say that this baptism was in the desert (v. 26) and that therefore there was *not sufficient water for immersion.* Is it possible that in all the forty miles from Jerusalem to Gaza there was not this much water when the ordinary Bible map (which see) shows a dozen large towns and at least four large streams on the way? Against this absurd objection there is the plain statement of the Scripture, "They came unto a certain water." Moreover, it was large enough that they "both went down into it, both Philip and the eunuch, and he baptized (immersed) him."

But, it is said, *"into" does not mean into;* it means "at" or "near by." The Greek preposition is *eis,* which is translated "into" in both the authorized and revised versions of the Bible, and not only in this passage, but in others. For example: Matt. 13: 47, "a net that was cast into (eis) the sea;" Matt. 17: 15, "He falleth into (eis) the water;" Mark 5: 13, "The herd rushed into (eis) the sea and were drowned." (Imagine them drowning *beside* the sea!) It is true that there are rare instances where the meaning of the word is shaded by the necessities of the case, as, for example, "He went up into the mountain," or, "he ran

Baptism

into (eis) the sepulcher;" but in this last instance, lest the reader might think from the common meaning of *eis* that Peter went inside the sepulcher, the writer hastens to explain that he did not . When Paul says (Gal. 3: 27) "As many of you as were baptized (eis) into Christ did put on Christ," will any one say "into" means "at" or "near by?" It is beyond dispute that the ordinary, common, primary meaning of *eis* is *into* just as it is here translated, and according to the rules of interpretation quoted from Blackstone and Greenleaf, the leading authorities on law, we must adopt this ordinary meaning here.

There are other reasons for adopting it. First, the previous statement, "they came to a certain water," brings them *to* the water and it remained only to go *(kata baino eis)* "down into" it. Again, the preposition *eis* is strengthened in this meaning by the preposition *kata* (down) with the verb. "They went *down into* the water." The expression *kata-baino eis* is used ten times in the Gospel and always with the meaning *into*. See Rom. 10: 7; Eph. 4: 9; Acts 7: 15, etc. But as if to do everything possible to make it clear, the account goes on to say, "they came *up out of* the water."

"Hold," says some one, *"out of" does not mean out of,* but only "from." Well, if *ek* does not mean "out of," then there is no Greek word that does. While other words mean *beside* or *away from, ek* is the common word for *out of,* and from it we get our prefix *ex,* which with verbs of motion means so clearly "out of" that there is no need of argument. Witness: *ex-pel,* to put out of; *ex-it,* the way out of; and a host of other words.

To use any other meaning than "into" for *eis* and any other than "out of" for *ek,* especially when strengthened by the prepositions *kata* (down) and *ana* (up), is to substitute the extraordinary for the ordinary and violate the simplest rules of interpretation. This is especially true in this case because the very expression "he baptized (immersed) him" *requires* this meaning and the context bears it out. "But," says Binney's *Theological Compend,* "the statement 'he baptized him' proves nothing because it applies equally to Philip and the eunuch." This seems to be about the limit of sophistry in evading the truth. It is rebuked by the answer of a little child who was asked after reading this account, "Who was baptized here?" and replied, "Why, I suppose *the one who wanted to be.*"

To this may be added the old story of the Hollander who heard a sermon on this passage which explained that "into" means "beside" and "out of" means "from," and at the close he went to the preacher and said (in substance), "O I am so glad I was here to-night. Now I know that when it says the devils went into the swine they did not go into them at all, but only near enough to scare them. I never could believe that story before. And when it says that the wicked shall be turned into hell, it just means at or near by,—just close enough to be comfortable! But O Mr. Preacher, if you can only show me that when it says that the saved shall go into heaven and enter through the gates into the city, it *does* mean *into* and not at or near by—out in the cold, then I shall be so glad I was here to-night."

Acts 9: 18, *And he* (Saul) *arose and was baptized."* Advocates of sprinkling have argued that this means that Saul was baptized *standing* and therefore by sprinkling or pouring. Will they also say that when (in the next chapter) the messengers came to Peter from Cornelius and "he *arose and went forth* with them," that he "*went forth*" while *standing* in his room? The simple truth is that the statement "he arose and was baptized" does not indicate what preparation he made, or what position he took, for baptism. If he had been sprinkled or poured, Ananias could have done that without his arising to go to a suitable place for immersion.

Acts 10: 47, 48, *"Then answered Peter, Can any man forbid the water, that these should not be baptized, who have received the Holy Spirit as well as we? And he commanded them to be baptized in the name of Jesus Christ."*

The Greek order is, "He commanded them in the name of Jesus Christ to be baptized." Peter saw them filled with the Holy Spirit as a sign that God would receive the Gentiles by faith as well as the Jews, and he at once grasped the truth that the kingdom of God was not for those who were Jews by blood, but for those who are children of Abraham by faith, and that therefore these Gentiles who believed should be baptized and received into the church. It required this one instance of the gift of the Spirit in advance of water baptism to convince the disciples that Gentiles were to be received on faith and repentance as well as the Jews. The manifestation of the Spirit reminded Peter of the promise John made when baptizing, and since John's baptism was immersion the inference is that this was also.

It has been objected, however, that Peter's language, "Who can forbid water," indicates the bringing of water to the candidates instead of bringing the candidates to the water. This objection is removed by the Revised Version which reads, "Who can forbid the water," which is the most natural way to refer to the element to which they were to go for immersion. Compare the statement of Justin Martyr (150 A. D.):

They are led by us to where there is water and are regenerated in the same manner in which we ourselves were regenerated, for in the name of God the Father of all and Lord, and of our Savior Jesus Christ, and of the Holy Spirit, they then receive this bath in water.—Apol. 1: 61.

Compare also the example of the jailor cited below, in which "he *took* them the same hour of the night, and washed their stripes; and was baptized."

Acts 16: 15, *"And when she was baptized, and her household, she besought us saying, If ye have judged me to be faithful to the Lord, come into my house and abide there."*

This is the case of Lydia, whose native home was at Thyatira (v. 14) and who was at Philippi temporarily on business. The only indication of the *mode* of baptism in this passage is contained in the word *baptized,* which, we have seen, implies immersion, the number of dips being prescribed by Matt. 28: 19.

Acts 16: 33, *"And he took them the same hour of the night and washed their stripes and was baptized, he and all his immediately. And he brought them up into his house and set food before them, and rejoiced greatly, with all his house, having believed in God."*

This passage does not say where the jailor was baptized, but it does point to immersion, because if sprinkling were the mode there would doubtless have been water enough where they were, but instead "he took them" somewhere to an abundance of water, for "he washed their stripes" (Gr. *elousen,* he bathed) and then "brought them into his house" again. The fact that they were in the jail in the morning is in entire harmony with this going out for baptism and returning again in the night, according to the account.

A. D. Gnagey very graphically presents the scripture precedents and their teaching as to the mode of baptism by means of an outline, easily understood. See next page.

Let the reader find any other scripture reference, if possible, and indicate its teaching, and the mode of baptism that carries it out, and it will be found that triune immersion fulfills everything perfectly, while all other modes fall short.

ITEMS AND REFERENCES.	Trine Immersion: Forward.	Single Immersion: Backward.	Pouring.	Sprinkling.
1. Water, Acts 8: 36.	Water.	Water.	Water.	Water.
2. Much water, John 3: 23.	Much water.	Much water.		
3. Certain water, Acts 8: 36.	Unto Water.	Unto water.		
4. In Jordan, Matt. 3: 6.	In Jordan.	In Jordan.		
5. Went down, } Acts 8: 38. 6. Into water }	Went down Into water.	Went down Into water.		
7. Came up } Acts 8: 39 8. Out of water }	Came up Out of water.	Came up Out of water.		
9. Went up } Matt. 3: 16. 10. Out of water }	Went up Out of water.	Went up Out of water.		
11. Birth, John 3: 5.	Birth.	Birth.		
12. Burial, Rom. 6: 4.	Burial.	Burial.		
13. Holy Trinity, Matt. 28:19; Acts 22:16.	Trinity.		Trinity.	Trinity.
14. Washing, Titus 3: 5.	Washing.	Washing.		
15. Into death, Rom. 6: 5.	Into death.			
16. Likeness—death, Rom. 6: 5.	Likeness—death.			
17. Planted—death, Rom. 6: 5.	Planted—death.			

This ends the list of instances of baptism recorded in the New Testament. Taking them all together it may be seen that the following statements are true:

1. Wherever the conditions of receiving baptism are stated or implied, they involve faith and repentance, and there is no passage which indicates that these were not always required. There is absolutely no mention of infant baptism.

2. In every account of baptism some form of the word *baptizo* is used,—which is the intensive or frequentative form which invariably means to dip (and that repeatedly), unless the context requires a figurative or secondary meaning to make sense. Such a case occurs nowhere in reference to Christian baptism. Moreover, none of the various Greek words which mean a *partial* washing are ever used of Christian baptism.

3. In the one case where the act of baptism is described (Acts 8: 36-38), the simple meaning of the language requires immersion, while in no case is there a single word or circumstance that is inconsistent with this mode.

(3). *There is nothing in the Bible contrary to triune immersion.* In closing this line of evidence let us notice the proof texts commonly used against triune immersion and see if they are rightly so used.

Eph. 4: 5, " *One Lord, one faith, one baptism.*"

This passage is quoted by single immersionists to disprove the trine action, and by the Friends to disprove the use of water. However, a study of the context shows that Paul is not here speaking of the number of actions in baptism, or making a division between water and Spirit baptism. He is exhorting to Christian unity on the ground of the unity of faith. He says:

Giving diligence to keep the unity of the Spirit in the bond of peace. There is one body (the church, ch. 1: 22, 23) and

Baptism

one Spirit, even as also ye were called in one hope of your calling; one Lord (Christ, ch. 3: 11), one faith and one baptism (the baptism Christ commanded), one God and father of all, who is over all and through all and in all.

Now as the "one faith" means faith in the "Spirit," and in the "one Lord," and in the "one God and Father,"—three Persons expressly mentioned in this very passage as distinguished the one from the other, so the "one baptism" means baptism into the name of each, just as Jesus commanded. If "one faith" does not limit the exercise of faith toward one member of the Trinity, neither does the "one baptism" limit the immersion to one dip. Paul does not say "one dip" or one "immersion," if he had, the translators would have gladly translated the passage that way, for they were not triune-immersionists. But it cannot be so rendered. The word Paul uses is *baptisma* which is the name of the rite without specifying the number of actions in it. In the *Emphatic Diaglott* it is translated "dipping." It is used twenty-two times in the New Testament and is *never* translated in the singular, dip. The word being a Greek "frequentative" implies plurality of action, but the number of dips in the dipping is limited by the commission to perform the baptism "into the name of the Father and of the Son and of the Holy Spirit"—three names and three dips. *Ignatius,* who is said to have been with Polycarp, a disciple of John, quotes this same passage in his letter to the Philadelphians, ch. 4, and gives it the same interpretation we have given here. The author of Hebrews also refers to the rite of baptism with the thought of the triune dipping in mind, and uses the plural to express it,—"the teaching of baptisms (dippings)" (Heb. 6: 2).

That Paul does not mean by "one baptism" the baptism of the Holy Spirit is clear from the fact that he himself, along with the other apostles, practiced baptism in water (1 Cor. 1: 14, 15).

Finally, to say that Paul was here opposing triune immersion in favor of single, is to say that triune immersion was already introduced. But if so, by whom?

1 Cor. 12: 13, *"By one Spirit are we all baptized into one body."* The body here referred to is the body of Christ, which is the church, of which Jesus is the head (Eph. 1: 22, 23). By baptism we "put on Christ" (Gal. 3: 27) and become members of this one body (Rom. 12: 5), but there is no indication in the text as to the number of actions in baptism. That is determined by the commission (Matt. 28: 19). When we go into a house several steps may be required. When man and wife become one body (Eph. 5: 23-31) they do so by several steps, recognizing (1) love between themselves (2) the law of the land and (3) the law of God. So in being baptized into the one body by the one baptism we have the triple dipping of the head in recognition of the Triune God. To omit any one of the three actions would be akin to omitting one of the three essential steps in marriage.

Heb. 6: 1, 2, *"Wherefore leaving the doctrine of the first principles of Christ, let us press on unto perfection: not laying again a foundation of repentance from dead works and of faith toward God, of the teaching of baptisms (Gr. baptismone), and of laying on of hands,"* etc.

It is said that because "baptisms" is plural there was more than one mode of baptism. Let us see. The passage cannot refer to the Old Testament purifications instead of baptism, because the writer includes "baptisms" among the first principles *of Christ* (v. 1). The Syriac gives a better rendering as follows: "Will ye again lay another foundation for the repentance which is from dead works, and for the faith in God, and for the doctrine of baptism?" &c. That

Christian baptism is referred to is also indicated by the fourth verse, referring to those "once enlightened," which is a common phrase among early writers to designate those baptized. (Cf. Eph. 1: 18 and Heb. 10: 32, also Justin Martyr 1st. Apol. 1: 71 &c.). Indeed, the Syriac version has, "they who have once descended to baptism" instead of "they who were once enlightened," but in each case in the Syriac only the singular is used. The only plausible explanation of the plural in the Greek original is that the writer has in mind the *triple dipping* by which the rite was performed. The word used (*baptismone*) means simply "dippings," and while there may be plural *dippings*, yet assuredly none of them are *sprinklings* or *pourings*.

John 3: 5, "*Except one be born of water and the Spirit, he cannot enter into the kingdom of God.*"

That this passage refers to baptism is generally admitted by scholars. Inasmuch as John had been preaching for some time, and "there went out unto him all the country of Judea, and all they of Jerusalem; and they were baptized of John in the river Jordan, confessing their sins," it would be the most natural thing for Nicodemus and Jesus to begin their conversation with reference to John and his baptizing, and for Jesus to point out the fact that it is not sufficient to be born of the water merely, one must be born of the Spirit also in order to enter the kingdom. He does not discard the form, but shows that it only assists the real regeneration which is within.

This passage, however, has been used as an argument for single rather than triune immersion, on the ground that as a person is born only once into the kingdom he should be immersed only once. The fallacy of this argument lies in confusing one baptism with one immersion. We are indeed born but once into the kingdom and therefore baptism rightly administered is not repeated, but in the one baptism there are a number of actions, just as in the one birth there are a number of actions. The process of regeneration involves the being begotten *of the Father, through Jesus* the Son (1 John 5: 1) as well as being born *of the Spirit.* As a natural conception and birth involves both parents, so the spiritual birth involves the Trinity, and therefore baptism is in the name of each member of it and the outward form must represent the inward work of each. As in a marriage there is the promise of the bride and the promise of the groom and the pronouncement of the minister, each of these three actions being essential to one valid marriage, so in being united with Christ in baptism (Rom. 6: 5; Gal. 3: 27) there are the three dips of the head to represent the work of the Father and of the Son and of the Holy Spirit in the one regeneration.

Col. 2: 12, "*Buried with him in baptism.*"

The likeness of a burial is used to support single immersion, because, "we are buried but once and therefore should be immersed but once." The explanation of John 3: 5 given above will apply here also, with the additional note that baptism represents a great deal more than a burial. If that were all, one immersion might suffice, although even in one burial there is the putting of the body in the coffin, then in the box and then in the grave,—three movements, yet one burial; but baptism represents the Trinity as well as the burial of the old man of sin. The commission (Matt. 28: 19) says nothing of burial, but commands baptism into each member of the Trinity. To be complete therefore it must correspond in form to the formula, else why use the formula at all?

PASSAGES WHICH SPEAK OF "SPRINKLING" AND "POURING" AND "WASHING."

Under this head we will consider a number of passages which are often perverted by overlooking the fact that while

Baptism

sprinkling, pouring and washing are regularly associated with certain other ideas, they are NEVER connected in the Scriptures with baptism.

(1) *Sprinkling.* Under the old covenant the sprinkling of the ashes of sacrifice (Num. 19: 17-19), or of blood (Ex. 24: 8. cf. Heb. 9: 19, 20; Lev. 14: 50, 51) was a symbol of atonement. Under the new covenant this atonement by the sprinkling of the blood or ashes of animals was superseded by the atonement made by the blood of Christ, which was shed once for all (Heb. 9: 12). Therefore we have many passages which refer to cleansing by the sprinkling of the blood of atonement, but not once is the term " sprinkling " used with reference to baptism.

(2) *Pouring.* Under the old covenant the pouring of oil was a symbol of consecration and anointing of the Spirit. It pointed as a type to the coming of the Spirit on Pentecost, and His dwelling in the hearts of believers. Therefore, when the gift of the Spirit is referred to, we commonly have the word pour (See Prov. 1: 23; Zech. 12: 10; Ezek. 39: 29; Joel 2: 28; Acts. 10: 45), but the word "pour" is never used of Christian baptism. Under the new covenant the enduement of the Spirit is symbolized by the rite of the " laying on of hands " which represents the hands of God pouring out the gift of the Holy Spirit (Heb. 6: 2; Acts. 8: 17; 19: 1-6).

(3) *Washing with water,* was, under the old covenant, a symbol of ceremonial cleansing (Lev. 15, &c.), but these washings or bathings were not perfect types of baptism, for they were for those already under the covenant and were for repeated cleansing, and that ceremonial; but baptism is for those entering the covenant, and is given once for all, and then as a sign of regeneration. Therefore, while we have words meaning a partial washing referring to Jewish cleansings, yet none of them are ever used of Chris-

tian baptism. Thus in the Old Testament we have the sprinkling of blood, or of blood and ashes, or of water and ashes to represent atonement, the pouring of oil to represent the Holy Spirit, and the washing with water to represent cleansing, and we have New Testament references to these symbols, but never once do any of them refer to baptism. *Nowhere in the Bible is water alone commanded to be sprinkled or poured on any one.*

Let us next examine these passages separately.

Isa. 52: 15, "*So shall he sprinkle many nations.*" This passage is quoted as though it referred to baptism, and it is even said that the eunuch had baptism suggested to him by the reading of this passage as he journeyed (Acts. 8: 32). It need only be said that, far from seeing Christian baptism in what he read, he asked, " of whom speaketh the prophet this? of himself or of some other?" No, the knowledge of Christian baptism he had was what Philip preached to him. The entire verse quoted above reads, "Like as many were astonished at thee (his visage was so marred more than any man, and his form more than the sons of men)," and then follows the phrase, "*So* shall he sprinkle (margin, " startle ") many nations." The entire sentence clearly has reference to the suffering of the Messiah. Moreover, the eunuch, being from Africa, was no doubt reading from the Alexandrian version of the Septuagint, the version of the Scriptures in use in his country, which in common with other ancient manuscripts, and most modern commentators, and the margin of our Revised Version, reads, " so shall he STARTLE many nations." This accords with the "astonished " of the fore part of the sentence. However, the Gospel account (Acts. 8: 35) says Philip began where the eunuch was reading, which was not this chapter at all, but the 53rd. He preached baptism because of Jesus' command.

Baptism

In any case there is not the slightest reference to Christian baptism, in Isa. 52: 15, for the only sprinkling done by the Messiah was by His blood. " Unto the obedience and sprinkling of the blood of Jesus Christ " (1 Pet. 1: 2). The reference is to the blood of atonement and not to baptism. Dr. Milton S. Terry, a leading Bible teacher of the world, says of this last passage:

No faithful exegesis of this scripture can fail to recognize the obvious allusion to such atonement as was wont to be made by blood and sacrificial lambs. The entire passage is one of the most explicit on record for showing the propitiatory character of the death of Jesus Christ.—Biblical Theology, p. 386.

Ezek. 36: 25, *"I will sprinkle clean water upon you and ye shall be clean."* No scripture should ever be interpreted apart from its context. The context here shows that the prophet was speaking of Jews only, and of them only in the time of their return to their own land. Some think this meant the return from Babylonian exile and some think he prophesied the future return of the Jews at the end of this Christian dispensation, but in either case he does NOT refer to this age, and consequently the passage has no connection whatever with baptism.

It is said, however, that it at least contains the idea of purification by the sprinkling of water. Yes, by the " water for purification " (Num. 8: 7 A. V.) which was the only water used by the Jews for that purpose and which therefore *must* be the water meant here. But, mark you, it was *water mixed with ashes*. Directions for preparing this water are given in Numbers 19: 17-20. It was prepared by mixing running water with the ashes of the sin offering, which signified atonement by blood. There is not the slightest connection with Christian baptism, either in this sprinkling or in the immersion of the entire person which was commanded to follow it (v. 19). It may be well to note also that Dr. Clarke and others regard this verse as a reference to the Holy Spirit, who is frequently spoken of under the figure of water. See John 7: 38, 39; Ezek. 47.

Heb. 10: 22, *"Having our hearts sprinkled from an evil conscience and our body washed with pure water."* The sprinkling of this passage refers to the same sort of purification by the blood of atonement as that referred to above. The preceding verses (Heb. 10: 19, 20) make this very clear. First, there is a reference to the new covenant, just as in Ezekiel 36: 26, and then the statement, "Having therefore, brethren, boldness to enter into the holy place *by the blood* of Jesus, by the way which he dedicated for us, by a new and living way, through the veil, that is to say, his flesh; and having a great high priest over the house of God; let us draw near with a true heart in fulness of faith, having our hearts sprinkled (by the blood of atonement) from an evil conscience and our body washed with pure water (by immersion in baptism), let us hold fast the confession of our hope." Thus again we see that the sprinkling refers to the blood of atonement and not to baptism, and the passage simply means that instead of the sprinkling of blood of beasts by the high priest of old, Jesus our High Priest has once for all opened the way to God by His own blood, shed for us. Therefore the author of Hebrews goes on to say (ch. 12: 24) that we are come "to Jesus the mediator of the new covenant, and to the blood of sprinkling that speaketh better than that of Abel." The sprinkling refers to the blood and not to the water. There is absolutely not one passage in the Bible where Christian baptism is referred to as a sprinkling.

Heb. 9: 10, *"Being only (with meats and drinks and divers washings) carnal ordinances imposed until a time of reformation."* It is said that "divers washings" must mean different forms of baptism because the Greek word

Baptism

baptismois (dippings) is translated washings. But again, the context shows that the reference is not to Christian baptism at all, but to the purifications under the law such as are described in Lev. 15, and which were by bathing the entire body. Even the sprinkling described in Num. 19: 17-20 was followed by a bath in water (v. 20). These "dippings" were "divers" because they were for divers kinds of ceremonial uncleanness (Cf. Lev. 15 and Num. 19).

Votablus (as quoted by Quinter), a learned professor of Hebrew at Paris, says on Mark 7: 4: "They bathed their whole persons." *Maimonides,* a learned Jewish rabbi, says: "If a Pharisee touched but the garment of one of the common people, they were defiled and needed immersion." *Fry,* a converted Jew, says: "Every Jew knows that whatever is to be purified by water, cups, pots, &c., it must be by immersion." The learned Rabbi Wise in *The American Israelite,* July 26, 1876, says, "There were various kinds of ritual baths among the ancient Hebrews; all, however, in forty kab of flowing water. One was the bath of penitents, one the bath of proselytes. To the mikva (bath) the Jewish women yet go according to Lev. 12 and 15, and to this goes every pious Israelite on the day of atonement."

The *author of Hebrews* simply points out that all of these "divers dippings" have been done away because we are now cleansed by the blood of Christ. Read the entire 9th chapter and there will be not the slightest trouble in understanding the reference to these "divers washings" of the Old Covenant. But the passage has no reference to the Christian baptism of the New. The purifications of the Old were for those already members, but baptism is for those who wish to become members by the regeneration it symbolizes. The *repeated* symbol of cleansing for church members is that of feet-washing, the merit of which is derived from the blood of Christ which "cleanseth us from all sin" (1 John 1: 9).

Mark 7: 4, *"And when they come from the market place except they bathe themselves, they eat not; and many other things there are, which they have received to hold, washings of cups and pots and brazen vessels."*

It is argued from this passage that the bathing and washing referred to were not by immersion, and therefore *baptizo* does not always mean to immerse. Let us see. In this passage Jesus refers to three things. In verse three he speaks of washing the hands before eating and uses the word *nipsontai*, "to wash." He next speaks of bathing when they come from the market, but it is uncertain what Greek word was used in the original. Some ancient manuscripts have *rantisontai* and some have *baptisontai*. The old version follows the first word and translates "wash," while the Revised Version used the other and translates "bathe." Jewish writers say that the bathing place was in a little shed near the house, the huge water pots, such as Jesus used at the marriage feast (John 2: 6) being kept by the door filled with water for that purpose, and that the bathing was by immersion of the body, or the parts bathed, or of the vessels cleansed. It is said that the "baptizing" of pots, &c., was not immersion because "tables" are included. They are *not* included in the Revised Version, because they are not mentioned in the best ancient manuscripts.

In any case, the cleansing was by dipping in water, for this was the law of God in the matter, and the Pharisees were most careful to keep it to the letter. The law for the ceremonial purification of vessels, &c., reads, " Whether it be any vessel of wood, or raiment, or skin, or sack, whatsoever vessel it be, wherewith any work is done, IT MUST

BE PUT INTO THE WATER, and it shall be unclean until the even; then shall it be clean."—Lev. 11: 32, 33.

Eidersheim says: "Any contact with a heathen, even the touch of his dress, might involve such defilement, that on coming from the market the orthodox Jew would have to *immerse* . . . Earthen vessels that had contracted impurity were to be broken; those of wood, horn, glass or brass immersed; while, if vessels were bought of Gentiles, they were (as the case might be) to be immersed, put into boiling water, purged with fire, or at least polished."—*Life of Christ* Vol. II. p. 15. Thus this great Jewish authority (together with Grotius, Carson, Maimonides, Fry and other eminent authorities) confirms immersion and removes all difficulty from this passage. The fact is, there is no passage in the Gospel that is out of harmony with baptism by triune immersion, while there are many that cannot by any rational interpretation be made to admit of any other mode.

We have now considered all the passages which we have ever known to be used against triune immersion, and we have found that not one of them witnesses against triune immersion, but rather for it. We are willing to submit the case to the Scriptures themselves, for they are both clear and united. The Savior did not couch His instructions in mysterious language, but used everyday words, as did the apostles after Him. They all agree, and it only remains for us to agree with them.

6. THE EARLY CHURCH PRACTICED TRIUNE IMMERSION AS CHRISTIAN BAPTISM, BELIEVING IT TO BE COMMANDED BY THE LORD AND THE APOSTLES.

The testimony of writers of late date as to the customs of the early church are not worth as much as that of writers who lived near to the days of the apostles, before customs had time to be greatly altered by the heresies that crept in.

We shall therefore quote the earliest writers. It will be noted that they are *unanimous* in their testimony to triune immersion. This is not a result of selecting only favorable quotations, but is due to the fact that there is absolutely no other kind of testimony to be found among these early writers. Not one single early writer can be quoted in support of any other mode to the exclusion of triune immersion. Some understood the three actions to represent the Trinity and some the three days of Christ's burial, but all agree in ascribing the authority for the mode to Christ or the apostles or to both, and their cumulative testimony is very strong.

The First Century, or Apostolic Age.

The apostle John died about 98 A. D., therefore all writings of the first century may be considered as being in the apostolic age. From this period we have several testimonies to triune immersion, independent of the Scriptures.

The Didache. Among the documents of the early church none is more ancient or of greater authority than the *Didache* or *Teachings of the Twelve Apostles.* The manuscript was only discovered in 1873. Nearly all scholars agree in placing the date of the book not later than the first century. Harnack, who is perhaps the geatest living authority in that line, thinks it was written before the death of John the disciple of our Lord. Some recent writers place its first writing at 65 A. D., before many of the New Testament books were written. The simplicity of the teaching, the type of church life and government revealed, and the absence of reference to topics which absorbed the attention of later writers, all point to the apostolic date. What does the *Didache* say about baptism? This:

As regards baptism baptize in this manner: Having first

Baptism

given all the preceding instruction, baptize into the name of the Father, and of the Son, and of the Holy Spirit in living (running) water.

But if thou hast no living water, baptize into other water, and if thou canst not in cold, then in warm.

But if thou hast neither in sufficient quantities (for immersion) pour (Gr. éu-xeov, "pour copiously") water on the head three times,—into the name of the Father and of the Son and of the Holy Spirit.

But before baptism let the baptizer and the candidate for baptism fast and any others who can; and thou shalt command him who is to be baptized to fast one or two days before.

NOTE CAREFULLY THE FOLLOWING FACTS:

(1) The mode of the formula given in the commission (Matt. 28: 19) is the prescribed mode. It is not probable that this would have been the case at so early a day if it had not been in use by the apostles themselves. We have here proof outside of the Word for the apostolic use of this Trinitarian formula.

(2) The word baptize means immersion, as is shown by saying "baptize IN" rather than "WITH" water; and also by allowing the copious pouring three times, only in case of insufficient water for "baptism" (immersion).

(3) Note again that *three actions are required*. They are expressly commanded in the emergency of pouring, and must therefore have been considered essential also in the ordinary immersion, because the formula of the commission means the same in either case.

(4) Note again that there is not a word about infant baptism, but that the admonition about voluntary fasting one or two days by the candidate precludes infants.

(5) Note finally that the mode of baptism was *not* "a mere matter of convenience," as McGiffert says, because considerations of convenience would not cause the seeking of running and cold water in preference to other. Conven-

ience would not exclude sprinkling altogether and allow pouring (and that copiously) only when impossible to immerse for lack of water. The spirit that would take them to running water would also cause them to seek it in sufficient quantity for immersion, if it were to be found in any reasonable distance.

The Epistle of Barnabas, which was at first received by many as a part of the inspired Gospel, says (ch. 11):

We indeed **descend into the water** full of sins and defilement, but come up bearing fruit in our heart, having the fear (of God) and trust in Jesus in our heart.

Clementine Homilies, Second Century:

Being born again to God of water, by reason of fear you change your first generation, which is of lust, and thus you are able to obtain salvation. But otherwise it is impossible. For thus the prophet hath sworn to us saying, " Verily I say unto you, Unless ye be regenerated by living water, into the name of the Father, and of the Son and of the Holy Spirit, you shall not enter the kingdom of heaven . . . Wherefore flee to the waters, for this alone can quench the violence of fires."—Homily 40, ch. 26.

Recognitions of Clement (ch. 94):

For our first birth descends through the fire of lust, and therefore, by the divine appointment, this second birth is introduced by water, which may extinguish the nature of fire.

Clement also, describing the baptism of his mother says she was baptized by Peter " in the sea " at a sheltered place between the rocks.—*Recognitions* 7: 28 and *Homily* 14: 1.

The Pastor of Hermas was written about 160 A. D. By many it was thought to be written by the Hermas Paul mentions in Rom. 16: 24. By Clement, Origen, Eusebius, Jerome and others it was quoted as inspired. This most popular writing of the early church says (*Similitude* 9: 16) "*They descend into the water* dead and they arise alive." Again in Vision 3: 7: " Do you wish to know who are the others who fell near the waters, but could not be rolled into them? These are they who have heard the word and wish to be baptized into the name of the Lord; but when the chastity demanded by the truth comes into their recollection, they draw back." Again in Commandment 4: 3 he says: " I heard, sir, some teachers maintain that there is no other repentance than that which takes place when we *descended into the water* and received the remission of former sins. He said to me ' That was sound doctrine which you heard, for that is really the case.'" A note by *Harnack* on this passage says: " Immersion then continued to be the usage even in the west (the book was written in Rome) during this epoch."

A Treatise entitled *De Ecclesiastica Hierarchia,* quoted first in the 6th century but attributed to Dionysius the Areopagite (a convert of Paul, Acts 17: 3), says (ch. 2): "As Jesus remained three days and three nights in the heart of the earth, so the *three immersions* represent the three nights and the three emersions the three days." If this writer was the Dionysius baptized under the direction of Paul he should have known that the three immersions in baptism refer to the Trinity (Matt. 28: 19), but whether he understood this reason in addition to the one he mentions matters not; he knew at least that there were three dips; and whether he was the real Dionysius or not, we at least have here a voice for triune immersion from a very early date.

THE SECOND CENTURY.

Irenaeus (130-202) was a pupil of Polycarp (Eusebius, *Ecclesiastical History* 5: 20), and Polycarp was an associate of John the disciple, and for twenty-six years was contemporary with him. Irenaeus wrote five books against heresies, and being the greatest champion for the true Gospel in the age next to the apostles, he is good authority.

He says of certain heretics, "They have been instigated by Satan to a denial of that baptism which is regeneration unto God . . . for the baptism instituted by the visible Jesus was for the remission of sins."—*Against Heresies* 2: 1. This would seem to imply that baptism is not for infants, but for sinners. In the same chapter he denounces the heretics who "assert that it is superfluous to *bring persons to the water*, but mixing oil and water together, they place this mixture on the heads of those who are to be initiated."

That the bringing of candidates to the water was for baptism by dipping is shown by his statement in Book 3: 17: "Our bodies have received unity among themselves by means of that laver (baptismal pool) which leads to incorruption; but our souls, by means of the Spirit, wherefore both are necessary."

That *the immersion was triune immersion* is shown by his statement (Book 3: 17); that "giving to the disciples the power of regeneration unto God, He (Jesus) said to them 'Go and teach all nations, baptizing them into the name of the Father and of the Son and of the Holy Spirit.'" In a fragment also (34) *he speaks of the dipping of Naaman as a baptism* and says that we also "being lepers in our sins are cleansed by the holy water and invocation of the Lord, from our old transgressions, as newborn children spiritually regenerated, as the Lord too saith 'Except a man be born of water and of the Spirit, he cannot enter the kingdom of God.'"

Get the importance of this testimony. *There were doubtless many aged persons who knew Irenaeus who also knew some of the apostles, and Irenaeus is a witness to triune immersion.* If this form of baptism were not of the Lord this champion of the true Gospel would have denounced it instead of denouncing the pouring of oil and water which

Baptism

some heretics were attempting to substitute for triune immersion.

Justin Martyr (A. D. 150) was contemporary with Irenaeus. He is also a witness to triune immersion. He says:

> As many as are persuaded and believe to be true these things that are taught and spoken by us, and give assurance that they are able to live accordingly, are taught to pray, and fasting to implore from God the forgiveness of sins previously committed; we ourselves praying and fasting with them. Then they are led by us to where there is water and are regenerated in the same manner in which we ourselves were regenerated, for in the name of God the Father of all and Lord, and of our Savior Jesus Christ, and of the Holy Ghost, they then receive this bath in water.—Apology 1: 61.

He goes on to say in chapter 71:

> There is pronounced over him who chooses to be born again, and has repented of his sins, the name of God the Father and Lord of the universe; he who leads to the laver a person to be washed calling him by this name alone . . . and in the name of Jesus Christ, who was crucified under Pontius Pilate, and in the name of the Holy Ghost, who through the prophets foretold all things about Jesus, he who is illuminated is washed.

Note that Justin quotes the commission and *supplies the ellipsis* in it, speaking of being immersed " in the name of God the Father . . . and in the name of Jesus Christ . . . and in the name of the Holy Ghost." Here is just the form which single immersion authorities admit requires trine action, and thus we have in Justin Martyr a witness to nothing less than triune immersion, and that within hailing distance of the apostles. Irenaeus and Justin Martyr and the *Didache* are three witnesses in touch with the generation instructed by the apostles, and they all three quote the full Trinitarian commission and indicate three actions as the practice of the church as a result of it.

Apostolic Canons, an expansion of the *Didache,* written during the second century and revised in the fourth, on account of the beginning of heresies prescribes a penalty for deviating from the divinely commanded *triune immersion*. Canon 49 (which Hoefele, a leading authority, says is among the oldest) reads:

If any bishop or presbyter does not perform the three immersions, but only one immersion, let him be deposed.

Canon 50 also reads:

If any bishop or presbyter does not baptize according to our Lord's constitution, into the Father, the Son and the Holy Ghost, but into three beings without beginning, or into three Sons or three Comforters, let him be deposed.

This testimony may be of a little later date, but on account of its opposing the same heresies Irenaeus opposes, we believe that this canon was contemporaneous with him, and he was born only thirty-two years after the last of the apostles died.

Tertullian (160 A. D.) says:

The law of immersion has been imposed, and the form has been prescribed. "Go," said he, "teach all nations, baptizing them into the name of the Father and of the Son and of the Holy Ghost." Comparing this law with the limitation, "Except a man be born of water and of the Spirit, he cannot enter into the kingdom of God," we are forced to believe in the necessity of immersion. Therefore all who believed after these words were uttered, were immersed.—On Baptism ch. 13.

Note from this that Tertullian regarded the commission of Jesus as the law of baptism. He further testifies as to the mode as follows:

When we are going to enter the water, a little while before, in the presence of the congregation, and under the hand of the president, we solemnly profess that we disown the devil and his pomp and his angels. Hereupon we are thrice immersed, making a somewhat ampler pledge than the Lord in his Gospel has appointed.—De Corona.

Baptism

Some have seized upon the phrase "making a somewhat ampler pledge" and have tried to make out that it refers to the triune immersion rather than to the renunciation vow of which Tertullian speaks, therefore we quote the passage in the original Latin:

Aquam adituri ibidem, sed et aliquanto prius in ecclesia sub antistitis manu contestamur nos renuntiare diabole et pompae et angelis ejus. Dehinc ter mergitamur, amplius aliquid respondentes, quam Dominus in Evangelio determinavit.

Now note that the words in question are, *respondentes amplius aliquid,* "responding or promising somewhat more." *Respondentes* is not baptizing, as any one can see, even if they do not read Latin. *Ter mergitamur* (Thrice we are dipped) is the expression used for that. On the other hand *respondentes* means to covenant or vow. *White's Latin Dictionary* says: "To promise, to answer, to respond." It is clear that the "ampler pledge" was the lengthy consecration vow that came in that day to accompany baptism. (See page 118.)

Oehler's edition of Tertullian's works says that in four ancient editions the words of the quotation on baptism given above are: *amplius NON aliquid, not* anything more, but after reading the ancient pledge used, any one would agree that it was more ample than the Lord commanded. But not the baptism. Even the pledge bears testimony to being immersed into each person of the Trinity, and thus confirms Tertullian's testimony to triune immersion.

That in the passage in question Tertullian refers to the pledge, and not to the mode, as being "somewhat more ample" than the Lord commanded, is further conclusively shown that triune immersion was by his own plain statement *commanded by the Lord.* He says:

He commands them to baptize into the name of the Father and of the Son and of the Holy Ghost, not into a unipersonal

God. And indeed, it is not once only, but three times, at each name, into each separate person, that we are immersed.—Ad Praxeas, ch. 26.

This ought to settle the matter, but we add the testimony of James Chrystal of the Church of England, who, against the practice of his church says, after quoting these passages:

The above show:
1. That Tertullian believed that all the baptisms of the New Testament performed after the words of the commission were uttered, were performed by trine immersion.

2. That he believed that Christ enjoined this mode. In addition it should be remarked that, in the first five hundred years, the great bulk of orthodox testimony, so far as expressed, is in favor of both these views. The practice of the church for a thousand years coincides with them.—History of the Mode of Baptism. p. 62.

The only apology for discussing Tertullian's testimony at such length, is the importance of it. The great argument of single immersionists is that triune immersion came in to help refute the Arian heresy in the fourth century. Here, a century and a half before Arius, is a decisive witness to triune immersion BECAUSE THE LORD COMMANDED IT. Remember how this testimony connects with the apostles.—Tertullian (160 A. D.)—Irenaeus (130 A. D.)—the *Didache* (about 70 A. D.)—in the days of the apostles—Thus we have triune immersion, and that only, from Christ until the third century.

The Third Century.

Not many writings of the third century have come down to us, but those we do have add their testimony to triune immersion. After the second century there is an overwhelming amount of evidence for triune immersion, but it is important to connect it with the apostolic age.

Baptism

That there was no change from the apostles to Irenaeus (130 A. D.) is shown by his own testimony. He speaks of "the will of God delivered to us in writing, to be the pillar and foundation of our faith," referring to the written Gospels and epistles which they followed as their guide. In one place he names the bishops succeeding the apostles up to his own time and says: "This is the most abundant proof that there is one and the same vivifying faith which has been preserved from the apostles until now, and handed down in truth." He says of his teacher, Polycarp, that he "was not only instructed by the apostles, and conversed with many that had seen Christ, but was also by apostles in Asia appointed Bishop of Smyrna * * * and when a very old man gloriously and most nobly suffering martyrdom, departed this life, *having always taught those things which he had learned from the apostles, and which the church has handed down, and which alone are true. To these things all the churches of Asia testify, as do also those men who have succeeded Polycarp down to the present time.*"

This is clear testimony that there was no change in the ordinances during the first hundred years after Christ.

Consider with it the admission of Orchard, a Baptist historian, that no change took place in the second and third centuries. In his *History of Foreign Baptists* p. 26, he says:

Although unwarrantable customs and ceremonies began to prevail at the conclusion of this (the 2nd) century in some churches, yet the ordinances of religion were not altered from their original subject, which is supported by the best historians, as it does not appear by any approved authorities that there was any mutation or variation in baptism from the former century. It should be remembered that there exists a harmony among the churches on the mode and subject of baptism and all parties were regulated by the Scriptures.

Armitage, another Baptist authority, also says of the second century: "As to the act of baptism, there was no change in this age."—*History of the Baptists,* p. 160. Let us pass on then to hear the testimony of the third century. First we have one which connects the two.

Origen (185 A. D.) *supports triune immersion as follows:*

From all which we learn that the person of the Holy Spirit was of such authority and dignity, that saving baptism was not complete except by the authority of the most excellent Trinity of them all, i. e., by joining to the unbegotten God the Father, and to His only begotten Son, the name also of the Holy Spirit.—De Principiis, ch. 2.

We are therefore through this washing buried with Christ in regeneration.—Commentary on Matthew.

Monulus, Bishop of Girba (200 A. D.), in the Council of Carthage, said:

The true doctrine has always been with us, my brethren, and especially in the article of baptism, and the trine immersion wherewith it is celebrated, our Lord having said, "Go ye and baptize the Gentiles into the name of the Father, and of the Son and of the Holy Spirit," etc.

Monulus was followed by seventy-five other bishops, *none of whom disputed his words* on baptism. The speeches of each of the bishops in this council are preserved for us by Eusebius, the church historian of that period. Note that Monulus was partly contemporaneous with Tertullian and thus continues the chain of evidence unbroken from the apostles. He was as near to them as we are to the Revolutionary War.

Hippolytus (220 A. D.):

The Father's Word (Jesus), therefore, knowing the disposition and will of the Father,—that the Father seeks to be worshiped in no other way than this (as the Trinity), gave this charge to the disciples after he rose from the dead: "Go ye and teach all the nations, baptizing them into the name of the

Baptism

Father and of the Son and of the Holy Ghost." And by this he showed that whosoever omitted any one of these, failed in glorifying God perfectly. For it is through this Trinity that the Father is glorified. For the Father willed, the Son did and the Spirit manifested. The whole Scriptures, then, proclaim this truth.—Against Noetus.

After quoting Isa. 1: 16-19, Hippolytus says:

Thou sawest, beloved, how the prophet foretold the cleansing of holy baptism. For he who goes down with faith into the bath of regeneration is arrayed against the evil one and on the side of Christ: he denies the enemy and confesses Christ to be God; he puts off bondage and puts on sonship; he comes up from baptism (immersion) bright as the sun, flashing forth the rays of righteousness, but greatest of all, he comes up a son of God and a fellow-heir with Christ.

Cyprian (248 A. D.) says:

The Lord after his resurrection taught his disciples after what manner they should baptize when he said, "Go ye and teach all nations," etc.; when he delivered the doctrine of the Trinity, unto which mystery or sacrament the nations were to be baptized.

Then he argues against the heretics who baptized only in the name of Jesus, saying that Christ commanded baptism into the complete Trinity.

Athanasius (296 A. D.) says:

He that takes away any one person from the Trinity, and is baptized only in the name of the Father, or only in the name of the Son, or only in the name of the Father and the Son, without the Spirit, receives nothing, but remains void and uninitiated.—Epistle to Serapion.

In his oration against Arius he also speaks of baptizing into the three names, and in his discourse on the passover, speaking of those just baptized he says:

Thou didst imitate in the sinking down the burial of the Master; but thou didst rise again from thence before works, witnessing the works of the resurrection.

The Fourth Century.

Optatus (fourth century) calls baptism "the laver which Christ commanded to be celebrated in the name of the Trinity, and that holy water which flowed from the fountain of those three names."—*Op*. bk. 3, p. 85.

Cyril, Bishop of Jerusalem (315) says:

And ye professed the saving profession, and sunk down thrice into the water, and again came up . . . For as he who sinks down into the water, is completely surrounded on all sides by the waters, so also they were completely baptized by the Spirit.

Ambrose, (340 A. D.) Bishop of Milan says:

The water then, is that in which the flesh is dipped . . . So that the Syrian dipped himself seven times under the law, but you were baptized into the name of the Trinity. You confessed the Father. Call to mind what you did. You confessed the Son. You confessed the Holy Spirit. Mark well the order of things in this faith. You died to the world and rose again to God and as though buried to the world in that element, being dead to sin, you rose again to eternal life.

The Pseudo-Ambrose, writing about this time says:

Thou wast asked, Dost thou believe in God the Father Almighty? Thou saidst, I believe, and was dipt, that is, was buried. Again thou wast asked, Dost thou believe in the Lord Jesus Christ and in his cross? Thou saidst, I believe, and was dipt; therefore thou wast buried with Christ also; for he who was buried with Christ rises again with Christ. A third time thou wast asked, Dost thou believe also in the Holy Ghost? Thou saidst, I believe, and a third time thou wast dipt; that that threefold confession might absolve the manifold fault of thy former life.—De Sacramento, 2: 7.

Basil (329 A. D.):

In three immersion, then, and with three invocations, the great mystery of baptism is performed, to the end that the type of death may be fully figured.—De Spiritu Sanctu. ch. 1.

For other references from Basil, see under "Historical Objections answered."

Baptism

Gregory of Nyssa (335 A. D.) says:

And in like manner the grace is imperfect, if any one, whichever it be, of the names of the Holy Trinity be omitted in the saving baptism, for the sacrament of the regeneration is not in the name of the Son and the Father alone, without the Spirit; nor is the perfect boon of life imparted to baptism in the Father and the Spirit if the name of the Son be suppressed; nor is the grace of the resurrection accomplished in the Father and the Son if the Spirit be left out. For this reason we rest all our hope and the persuasion of the salvation of our souls upon the three persons recognized by these names . . . Having full assurance then, we are baptized as we were commanded, and we believe as we were baptized and we hold as we believe, so that with one accord our baptism, our faith and our ascription of praise is to the Father and to the Son and to the Holy Spirit.—Orations Cat. 35.

Note that Gregory says that triune immersion WAS COMMANDED, and for that reason was observed.

Augustine (354 A. D.), the greatest theologian of his day, whose influence is still seen in the theology of the Catholic Church and even among Protestants, says:

In this font, before we dipped your whole body, we asked you, "Believest thou in God the omnipotent Father?" After you averred that you believed, we immersed three times your heads in the sacred font, **You are rightly immersed three times you who receive baptism in the name of Jesus Christ** who rose the third day from the dead.—Sermon de Mysterio Baptismos.

After reading all these testimonies, the reader will understand what *Bingham* means when, after quoting many ancient testimonies to triune immersion, he says:

And to mention no more authorities, WHICH ARE INNUMERABLE, St. Augustine observes, that this was not only the general practice of the general church, but of most heresies also. For one might more easily find heretics that did not baptize at all than such as retained baptism without using those evangelical words, of which the creed consists, and without which baptism cannot be consecrated.—Antiquities p. 482.

Thus we might go on and quote Sozomen and Socrates, Church Historians of the fifth century, Pope Gregory of the sixth, The Synod of London of the seventh, Alcuin of the eighth, and other writers of every century since but the value of such testimonies diminishes with the distance from the apostles, because of the growth of heresies. We believe that if any one is not convinced by the array of testimony given he would not be affected by any number of testimonies of later ages. We turn therefore to consider the writers quoted against triune immersion.

HISTORICAL OBJECTIONS.

It is out purpose in this study to be perfectly honest. We shall not knowingly evade any evidence worth considering, which is opposed to the conclusion we have been compelled to form. We therefore give below all the historical statements of the early writers, which are quoted as against triune immersion.

The objection to Tertullian's testimony has already been answered. See page 223.

All the remaining quotations are from the first half of the fourth century, following the discussion over the Arian heresy, which consisted in denying the divinity of Christ. As a result of it his followers, led by Eunomius, changed the form of baptism from triune immersion to single immersion, because the Trinitarian form was a recognition of the divinity of Christ along with the Father and the Spirit. With this in mind it is easy to understand the references which follow:

Basil (329 A. D.), whose grandfather was a Christian born about one hundred and fifty years after John died, in arguing for the authority of apostolic tradition, says:

Moreover we bless the water of baptism and the oil of the chrism, and besides this the catechumen who is being baptized.

Baptism

On what written authority do we do this? Is not our authority the silent and mystical tradition? Nay, but by what written word is the anointing of oil itself taught? And whence comes the custom of baptizing thrice? And as to the other customs of baptism, from what Scriptures do we derive the renunciation of Satan and his angels? Does not this come from the unpublished and secret teaching which our fathers guarded in a silence out of the reach of curious meddling?—De Spiritu Sanctu ch. 27: 66.

Note that Basil does not deny that triune immersion was derived from the apostles. He simply argues that their *unwritten* commands were sufficient authority for it. There is indeed no express command of the *apostles* recorded, but *there is the command of Jesus, which Basil himself quotes as authority for the triune immersion* which they practiced. In a letter (210: 4) he says:

When it is said "Go and baptize into the name of the Father and of the Son and of the Holy Spirit" we must not suppose that here one name is delivered to us, for just as he who said "Paul and Sylvanus and Timotheus" mentioned three names and coupled them one with the other by the word "and," so he who spoke of the "name of the Father, and of the Son and of the Holy Ghost" mentioned three and united them by the conjunction, teaching that with each name must be understood its own proper meaning; for the names mean things. And no one gifted with even the smallest particle of intelligence doubts that the existence belonging to the things is peculiar to itself. For of the Father, Son and Holy Ghost there is the same nature and one Godhead, but these are different names setting forth to us the circumscription and exactitude of the meanings. For unless the meaning of the distinctive qualities of each be unconfounded, it is impossible for the doxology to be adequately offered to the Father, Son and Holy Ghost.

Does this sound as if Basil believed baptism by triune immersion to be a tradition of the apostles without the authority of the commission back of it? Indeed, Basil makes the authority of the commission his first means of perceiving the equality of the members of the Trinity. He says:

> To me nothing is more fearful than failure to fear the threats which the Lord has directed against them that blaspheme against the Holy Spirit. Kindly readers will find a satisfactory defense in what I have said, that I accept a phrase (the baptismal formula) so dear and familiar to the saints, and confirmed by usage so long, inasmuch as FROM THE DAY THE GOSPEL WAS FIRST PREACHED UP TO OUR OWN TIME it is shown to have been admitted to its full rights within the churches, and what is of the greatest moment, to have been accepted as bearing a sense in accordance with holiness and true religion. But before the great tribunal what have I prepared to say in my defense? This: that I WAS IN THE FIRST PLACE LED TO THE GLORY OF THE SPIRIT BY THE HONOR CONFERRED BY THE LORD IN ASSOCIATING HIM WITH HIMSELF AND WITH THE FATHER AT BAPTISM; AND SECONDLY BY THE INTRODUCTION OF EACH OF US TO THE KNOWLEDGE OF GOD BY SUCH AN INITIATION.—The Spirit, ch. 29.

Finally, in *Letters* 251, he says: "AS WE RECEIVED FROM THE LORD, SO WE ARE BAPTIZED."

If any one still thinks that Basil derived triune immersion from apostolic tradition rather than from the Lord's commission, let him read his book on *The Holy Spirit*, chapters seventeen and twenty-seven, and *Letters*, fifty-two and others, for in many places, with equal clearness, and at greater length, he presses this same point. He sees in triune immersion, not only the recognition of the three days' burial, which he mentions in one place, but much more, the recognition of the Trinity, which he mentions in many places, and which overwhelm the allusion to the authority of apostolic tradition which he uses in only one place.

Jerome (340 A. D.), in his letter to the Luciferians (ch. 8) likewise contends for some of the customs of the church on the authority of tradition, and says:

For many other observances of the church which are due to tradition, have acquired the authority of written law, as for instance, the custom of dipping the head three times in the laver and then after leaving the water, of tasting milk mingled with honey, in representation of infancy.

A careful reading of this passage shows that it may mean that after the triune immersion (which was all right) there followed the tasting of milk and honey, which grew out of tradition. In fact it must mean this or else Jerome contradicts himself, for he plainly ascribes triune immersion to the authority of the Scriptures. In his letters (69: 7) he says:

After his resurrection also, when sending his apostles to the Gentiles, he commands them to baptize these into the mystery of the Trinity.

He further says: " We are dipped in water that the mystery of the Trinity may appear to be but one, and *therefore though we be thrice put under the water to represent the mystery of the Trinity, yet it is reputed to be but one baptism.*"

Remember that the only thing that even single immersionists claim that Jerome does is to ascribe to tradition the *means of conveying the Lord's command* to observe triune immersion. He nowhere denies that it was a command of the Lord. On the contrary, he expressly affirms that it was. That being so, it was not so serious that the command for triune immersion should be *transmitted* by the tradition handed down from the apostles, even though it was not written by them. The apostles themselves considered their unwritten traditions worthy to be observed. Paul says, " Stand fast, and hold the traditions which ye were taught, WHETHER BY WORD OR BY EPISTLE OF OURS " (2 Thess. 2: 15), and again, " Withdraw yourselves from every brother that walketh disorderly and not after the *tradition* which they received of us." (2 Thess. 3: 6).

Surely it should take something worse than the fact that the commission was handed down by apostolic oral, rather than written, tradition to discredit triune immersion in the face of all the evidence given!

Chrysostom (347 A. D.) is sometimes quoted as casting doubt on triune immersion, because he says:

> Therefore in the case of baptism also the Trinity is included. The Father is able to effect the whole, as is the Son and the Holy Ghost, yet since concerning the Father no man doubted, but the doubt was concerning the Son, and the Holy Ghost, they are included in the rite, that by their community in supplying those unspeakable blessings we may also fully learn their community in one Divinity.—Commentary on John, Hom. 78.

It is said that this intimates that triune immersion arose because of the Arian heresy, but the Arian heresy is not mentioned, nor is it said that the triune immersion had its origin short of the apostles. Chrysostom may have had in mind the doubts of the Jews of Jesus' own day concerning him, and the consequent value of having his name included in the rite of baptism. That he in no way doubted the divine authority for triune immersion is shown by his own statements. In this same commentary on John (ch. 25) he says:

> As it is easy for us to dip and lift our heads again, so it is easy for God to bury the old man and to show forth the new, and this is done thrice that you may learn that the power of the Father, the Son and the Holy Ghost fulfilleth all this.

He says again: " CHRIST DELIVERED TO HIS DISCIPLES ONE BAPTISM IN THREE IMMERSIONS *when he said to them, 'Go and teach all nations, baptizing them in the name of the Father and of the Son and of the Holy Ghost.'* "—*On Faith*, Bk. 12, p. 290, Ed. Savil.

Since Chrysostom clearly ascribes triune immersion to

the command of Christ, we may not infer from his other statement that he believed it to be of later origin.

These are all the quotations that can be found that are used to cast doubt on triune immersion. It is no wonder that Ford, a leading Baptist author, says (*Studies in Baptism* p. 328), " Trine immersion is said by the fathers generally to be derived from the Lord and the apostles." So indeed it is. But note: (1) Even if they did not so testify, it is derived from the Lord anyway. (2) Not one of the early writers speaks of the origin of triune immersion as short of Jesus and the apostles. What a fine chance Eunomius and his followers would have had to sustain their single immersion, for which they were anathematized as heretics, if they could have shown that triune immersion was an innovation of men! But not a word of such an attempt do we find. Why not? Because there was no chance for such a thing. Triune immersion was so well established that they dared not even attempt to overthrow it by argument. Is it not too late to try to bolster up this Unitarian error now by an argument that the originators of it dared not use at the time they made the change?

(3) Only several writers, and they in the fourth century, even mention apostolic oral tradition as a means of transmitting the Lord's command for triune immersion, and *each of these in other places quotes the command of Jesus as authority for the practice*. They insist so strongly upon apostolic authority for it that they rebaptized those who repented of the Arian heresy and came with only their single immersion to join the orthodox church. May we not therefore truly say that *the testimony of the early writers is* UNANIMOUS *in supporting triune immersion as the regular, scriptural mode of baptism?*

7. THE LEADING MODERN AUTHORITIES IN CHURCH HISTORY AGREE THAT TRIUNE IMMERSION WAS THE PRIMITIVE MODE OF BAPTISM.

Modern testimony is not of as much worth as that of the centuries next to the apostles, but it has its weight as showing what conclusions impartial and learned investigators are compelled to reach. We might fill many books with testimonies, but we have selected those which have special weight because either they are written for all denominations (as cyclopedias) or else the authors are witnessing against the practice of their own denominations. Such testimonies cannot be said to be the result of sectarian prejudice. An admission against one's own interest is always regarded by courts as valuable evidence. We invite special attention therefore to the quotations which follow.

UNDENOMINATIONAL AUTHORITIES.

Smith,—Dictionary of Antiquity, Article on Baptism, says:

Triple immersion, that is, thrice dipping the head while standing in the water was all but the universal rule of the church in early times. Of this we find proof in Africa, in Palestine, in Egypt, at Antioch and Constantinople and in Cappadocia. For the Roman usage Tertullian indirectly witnesses in the second century, St. Jerome in the fourth, Leo the Great in the fifth, and Pope Pelagius and Gregory the Great in the sixth. Theodulf of Orleans witnesses for the general practice of his time at the close of the eighth century. Lastly the apostolic canons, so called alike in the Greek, the Coptic and the Latin versions, give special injunctions as to this observance, saying that any bishop or presbyter should be deposed who violated this rule.

Encyclopedia Britannica 9th edition of R. S. Peale & Co.), Article on Baptism, p. 51, says:

The council of Ravenna in 1311 was the first council of the church which legalized baptism by sprinkling by leaving it to the choice of the officiating minister. The custom was to immerse three times, once at the name of each of the persons of the Trinity.

Chambers's Encyclopedia: "A triple immersion was first used and continued a long time."

The American Encyclopedia, Art. Catholic Church, by Kendrick, says: "The original mode of baptism was immersion but the church claims the right to change the mode."

The Schaff-Herzog Encyclopedia says:

Baptism in the early church was a triple immersion. Various explanations were given. Some referred it to apostolic custom. Thomas Aquinas calls it a sin to immerse only once (1 c. qu. 66: 9). The Roman ritual enjoins trine affusion (pouring) on the head, as do the Lutherans.

The Cyclopedia of the Protestant Episcopal Church of America, Article on Baptism, p. 86, says:

As regards sprinkling, though it may be regarded as valid, yet it is irregular, there being no authority for its use. The rubric in the office of the American Prayer-Book orders that the minister taking the child "shall dip it in the water discreetly, or shall pour water upon it." In the English office there are two rubrics, the first ordering dipping in the water discreetly and warily, "provided that the sponsors shall certify that the child may well endure it." But if they certify that the child is weak, it shall suffice to pour water upon it. . . . There appears to be but little doubt that the usual custom of the early church was to lead the candidate into the water and there dip him three times while repeating the prescribed formula.

Smith's Dictionary of Antiquities, says:

While trine immersion was thus an all but universal practice, Eunomius (360 A. D.) appears to have been the first to introduce simple immersion "into the death of Christ." This practice was condemned on pain of degradation, by the apostolic canons, but it comes before us again about a century after in Spain, but then curiously enough it is a badge of orthodoxy in opposition to the practice of the Arians. These last kept to the use of triune immersion, but in such a way as to set forth their own doctrine of a gradation of the three persons.

The Americana, a recent cyclopedia of high authority, says:

In the primitive church the person to be baptized was immersed in a river or in a vessel, with the words which Christ had ordered, and a new name was generally bestowed at this time further to express the change. Sprinkling, or as it was termed, clinic baptism, was used only in the case of the sick who could not leave their beds. The Greek church and various eastern sects retained the custom of immersion.—Article on Baptism.

The new *International Encyclopedia* says:

In the primitive church the ordinary mode of baptism was by immersion. . . . The ancient practice of immersing three times has been neglected.

Wharton Marriot, one of the Anglican writers, says:

Triple immersion, that is, thrice dipping the head while standing in the water, was all but the universal rule of the church in early times. Of this we find proof in Africa, in Palestine, in Egypt, at Antioch and Constantinople, in Cappadocia. For the Roman usage Tertullian indirectly witnesses in the second century, St. Jerome in the fourth, Leo the Great in the fifth and Pope Pelagius and St. Gregory the Great in the sixth.

Neander, the great Jewish church historian, says:

In respect to the form of baptism, it was in conformity with the original institution and the original import of the symbol, performed by immersion.

Harnack, one of the most eminent of living authorities on church history, in a letter to C. W. Dobbs, 1885 (See *Schaff's Didache* p. 85), says:

Baptism undoubtedly signifies immersion. No proof can be found that it signifies anything else in the New Testament and in the most ancient Christian literature. The suggestion regarding a "sacred sense" is, out of the question. There is no passage in the New Testament which suggests the supposition that any New Testament author attached to the word baptizein any other sense than eintauchen, to dip in, or untertauchen, to dip under.

Schaff, Lessons from the Didache, p. 138, says:

Baptism was the rite of initiation into church membership and was usually administered by trine immersion in a river (in imitation of Christ's baptism in the Jordan), but with a margin for freedom as to the quality of water and the mode of application, and threefold pouring in case of scarcity of that element. Fasting before the act was required, but no oil, salt, or exorcism, or any other material or ceremony is mentioned. The Didache, the catacomb pictures and the teaching of the Fathers, Greek and Latin, are in essential harmony on this point and thus confirm one another. They all bear witness to trine immersion as the rule and affusion as the exception. This view is supported by the best scholars, Greek, Latin and Protestant.

Bapheidos, a Greek Historian (*Church History,* published 1884) describes the ancient mode as threefold immersion and restricts aspersion to cases of sickness. He says:

The orthodox church of Russia adopted from the beginning the same practice. The longer Russian catechism of Philaret defines baptism to be trine immersion in water and declares it to be most essential.

Pressence, Early Years of Christianity, p. 374, says:

Baptism was administered by immersion. The convert was plunged beneath the water and as he rose from it he received the laying on of hands.

Hastings' Bible Dictionary, a standard authority among the most advanced scholars, says of baptism:

The normal mode was by immersion of the whole body, as may be inferred from the meaning of the Greek baptizo which is the intensive or frequentative of the word bapto, I dip, and denotes immersion.

DENOMINATIONAL AUTHORITIES.

ALEXANDER CAMPBELL (*Founder of the Disciple Church*) *Debate with N. L. Rice,* p. 258, says:

Not only Mosheim, Neander, but all the historians, as well as Professor Stuart, trace trine immersion to the times of the apostles.

For some reason this statement has been expunged from late editions of the work, but it may be found in the original edition, certified by Campbell himself as correct, by calling for the volume in the Library at Washington, or writing to the Librarian of Congress concerning it.

Dr. Kurtz (Lutheran) says: " Baptism was performed by thrice immersing during which the formula of baptism was pronounced."—*Church History,* Vol. 1, p. 119.

Martin Luther (founder of the Lutheran Church), in 1530, giving directions for baptizing a woman, said:

Let her be placed in a bathing tub up to the neck in water; then let the baptist dip her head three times in water with the usual formula " I baptize thee," etc.—Walsches' edition of Luther's Work, part 10, p. 2637.

Luther also says:

The other thing which belongs to baptism is the sign of the sacrament, which is immersion in water; from whence also it derives its name; for baptizo in Greek is mergo (immerse) in Latin, and baptism is immersion. . . . Baptism is a sign both of death and resurrection. Being moved by this reason, I would have those who are to be baptized altogether dipped in the water, as the word doth express and the mystery doth signify, not because I think it necessary, but because it would be beautiful to have a full and perfect sign of so perfect and full a thing; AS ALSO WITHOUT DOUBT IT WAS INSTITUTED BY CHRIST.—Luther's Works, Vol. 2, pp. 272, 273, De Captivate Babylonica Ecclesiae.

John Calvin (founder of the Presbyterian Church) says in his *Institutes,* Vol. 4: 15, 19: " The very word signifies to immerse, and it is certain that immersion was observed by the ancient church." In his comments on John 3: 23 and Acts 8: 38 he makes similar statements.

Baptism

John Wesley (founder of the Methodist Church) believed in trine immersion. *Moore's Life of Wesley*, Vol. 1, p. 425, says:

> When Mr. Wesley baptized adults professing faith in Christ, he chose to do it by trine immersion if the person would submit to it, judging this to be the apostolic method.

William Cathcart (Baptist), author of *The Baptism of the Ages and Nations,* says:

> Trine immersion was the general practice of the Christians from the end of the second till the close of the twelfth century. The proof of this is overwhelming.

He produces no proof that it was *not* the practice in the first century also.

Conbeare and Howson (Episcopalian):

> This passage (Rom. 6: 4) cannot be understood unless it be borne in mind that the primitive baptism was by immersion.
> —Life and Epistles of Paul.

This interpretation of the reference of Paul to being buried in Christian baptism by immersion is confirmed by Dr. Barnes (Presbyterian), Dr. Bloomfield (Episcopalian), Tholuch (Lutheran), Lange (Lutheran), Clarke (Methodist), Chancellor Est (Roman Catholic), besides Meyer, Chalmers, Macknight, Lewin, Jowett, Colenso, Wordsworth, Reuss, Schott, Ellicott, Lightfoot, Pusey, Van-Oosterzee, Schaff, Olshausen, Tyndale and a host of others of all denominations.

Dean Stanley of the Church of England, in his *History of the Eastern Church* makes an especially clear statement as follows (p. 117):

> There can be no question that the original form of baptism, according to the very meaning of the word, was complete immersion in the deep baptismal waters, and that for at least four centuries any other form was at least unknown or disregarded, unless in the case of dangerous illness, as an exceptional, almost

a monstrous case. To this form the eastern church still vigorously adheres and the most illustrious portion of it, that of the Byzantine empire, absolutely repudiates any other mode of administration as essentially invalid. The Latin church has wholly altered the mode and with the two exceptions of the cathedral of Milan and the sects of the Baptists, a few drops of water are now the western substitute for the threefold plunge into the rushing rivers or the wide baptistries of the east.

One more statement may be added, which, like many others, is of especial value because it is a forced admission. *Rev. L. L. Paine,* D. D., Professor of Church History in the Congregational Seminary at Bangor, Maine, says in an article in the *Christian Mirror,* August 3, 1875, referring to the fact that immersion (which we have seen was the triune form) was the apostolic mode of baptism, says:

The testimony is ample and decisive. No matter of church history is clearer. The evidence is all one way and all church historians of any repute agree in accepting it. We cannot claim even originality in teaching it in a Congregational Seminary, and we really feel guilty of a kind of anachronism in writing an article to insist upon it. It is a point on which ancient, medieval and modern historians alike, Catholic, Protestant, Lutheran and Calvinist, have no controversy. And the simple reason for this unanimity is that the statements of the early Fathers are so clear, and the light shed upon these statements from the early customs of the church is so conclusive that no historian who cares for his reputation would dare to deny it and no historian who is worthy of the name would wish to.

No words of our own could be more clear or emphatic than these of a Congregational Professor to a church which practices sprinkling. The only plea for the practice of any other mode than triune immersion is that the mode is not important. But if there is any action at all required, then that action must be the right action, which will convey the meaning of the commission and the symbolical significance of the ordinance. Therefore, knowing the apostolic mode we must be true to it.

Quotations might be given from many other eminent authorities, but more would simply be a burden to read. Those who write history rather than sectarian prejudice agree with the statements already quoted. If any one wishes to consult further authorities, let them refer to the following: Dollinger, *History of the Church,* Vol. 2, p. 294; Waddington, *Church History,* p. 27; Dr. Wall, *History of Infant Baptism,* Vol. 2. p. 419; *Bishop Beveridge's Works,* Vol. 8, p. 336; Dr. Pengilly, *Scripture Guide to Baptism,* p. 73; Robinson's *History of Baptism,* p. 148; Mosheim, *Baptism of the First Century;* Dr. Chalmers, &c.

8. TRIUNE IMMERSION HAS BEEN PRACTICED CONTINUOUSLY FROM THE DAYS OF THE APOSTLES UNTIL NOW.

The practice of a large part of Christendom is a standing monument to the original mode of baptism, for it has never been changed among these churches.

The Greek Church includes four of the five ancient patriarchates and all but one of the churches mentioned in the Bible. It now numbers over 70,000,000. It includes, according to *Good and Gregory's Pantalogia;*

That part of the Christian Church which was first established in Greece and is now spread over a larger extent of country than any other established church. It comprehends in its bosom a considerable part of Greece, the Grecian Isles, Wallachia, Moldavia, Egypt, Abyssinia, Lybia, Arabia, Mesopotamia, Syria, Cilicia, and Palestine.

The same authors say, "It may be observed that they observe triune immersion, which is *unquestionably the primitive manner.*"

The Greeks certainly ought to know their own language best, and as the New Testament was written in Greek, their use of the word *baptizo* ought to be strong evidence. Although many superstitions crept into the Greek Church during the middle ages, yet so firm are they in their insistence that baptism means triune immersion, which they have practiced from the days of the apostles, that they will not accept any substitute. Missionaries laboring among them are obliged to yield to them in this point, and we have the unique spectacle of pædo-baptist missionaries among the Greeks baptizing their converts (or infants) by triune immersion.

The church at Philadelphia in Asia Minor, is mentioned in Rev. 3: 10 and is promised "Because thou hast kept the word of my patience, I will also keep thee in the hour of trial." That church continues to this day, the only one of the original apostolic churches, saved, as Gibbon the infidel historian says, "by prophecy or courage." And this church has preserved triune immersion in continuous practice from the days of the apostles until this.

The Catholics also at Milan have declined to make the change in baptism the rest of the church has adopted, and still practice the triune immersion which has been handed down in this church from Jesus without a break.

9. THE TESTIMONIES OF THE BAPTISTRIES OF THE EARLY CHURCH INDICATE THE PRACTICE OF FORWARD IMMERSION IN BAPTISM.

Some of these baptistries date back to the third century. They were frequently cut out of stone or marble. Some of them are very large, but others are just large enough for immersion in the kneeling, forward posture.

The American Cyclopedia says of them:

The center of the whole structure formed the baptismal basin, sometimes in allusion to Rom. 6: 4, being in the form of a grave with three steps leading down into it. . . . At first the baptistry was a structure outside of the church, but gradually as infant baptism became the rule in the church and aspersion took the place of immersion, there was less use for separate buildings, and after the ninth century they ceased to be built.

Baptism

. . . Occasionally we find the word kolumbathra, bath, and piscinia, fishpond, used as synonyms for baptistry.

Note the three steps, the usual number, leading down into the baptistry, significant perhaps, of the Trinity represented by the three actions in baptism.

Wolfred Nelson Cote M. D., formerly a missionary in Rome in his *Archæology of Baptism* describes a great many of these baptistries. Some of them, he says, were as much as twenty-five feet long and ranged from two and one half to four feet in depth by means of false wooden bottoms. (See *Baptism of the Ages,* p. 152).

Raffaele Garruci, a Jesuit who made a study of these ancient baptistries and wrote an elaborate work on Christian art, testifies as to the baptisms performed in them as follows:

The most ancient and solemn rite was to immerse the person in the water, and three times also the head, while the minister pronounced the three names, except in case of sickness or lack of water.

He says further that " immersion continued in the Latin or western half of the church until the thirteenth century."

In the chapel of St. Pudentiana in Rome there is a picture in mosaic, representing two persons in a family bath, kneeling, while one holds up his hands as if in prayer. The administrator has his right hand placed on the candidate's head as if to bow it forward into the water, while on the wall in Latin are the words: " Here in the living font the dead are born again."

Mr. Cote, in *Archæology of Baptism,* p. 324, gives a picture of one of the most ancient baptistries and says:

In company with Doctors H. C. Fish and H. Harvey of this country, we visited the ruins of the St. John cathedral at Tyre, and its ancient but recently discovered baptistry. The cathedral was built about 315 A. D. Eusebius preached the dedication sermon and pronounced it the most magnificent temple in Phoenicia. Professor Epp, under whose superintendence the excavations were made, pointed his visitors to the "old baptistry" and remarked, "they immersed people here"; and, to prove the feasibility of immersion, he at once went down into it, and lowered himself (by kneeling and projecting the head and shoulders forward) below the level of the top, saying "This is the way they baptized themselves."

Dr. Harvey (mentioned above) also describes this baptistry. He says:

It is made from a solid block of white marble. Steps descend into it from each end. The candidate evidently entered the pool from one end. **He then knelt down, and, according to the ancient usage, his head was bowed forward into the water by the administrator,** who stood outside, and pronounced the formula, and after being thus baptized he passed out by the steps at the other end.

The evidence of the later centuries is not important, because heresies crept into the church, but there is weight in the witness of these baptistries of the early centuries.

Dr. Robinson, when in Palestine measured some fonts belonging to old Greek churches now in ruins, which he thinks were too small for adult immersion. The measurements which he gives of the fonts of Tekoa and Gophna are "four feet on the inside, and three feet nine inches deep," and "five feet in diameter, two feet nine inches deep within" *(Biblical Researches,* Vol. 1 p. 486 and Vol. 2. p. 263).

Mr. Ford, a Baptist author *(Studies on Baptism,* p. 292), says:

One thing is certain in regard to these fonts: they are abundantly ample for infant immersion, while they are a thousand times too large for either adult or infant sprinkling. Our opinion is, that smaller fonts than these, even in depth, would be sufficiently large for adult immersion, if practiced according to Dunker method, viz.; in a kneeling posture, the subject being bent forward, instead of backward.

Here then we have the *unchangeable witness* of the rock-hewn baptistries to the kneeling, forward immersion, to which all the other lines of evidence also bear testimony. More than that, there are *pictures* on the walls of many of these ancient chapels which represent the administrator with his hand over the head of the candidate. Travelers unfamiliar with forward immersion have supposed that these pictures represent pouring water on the head with the hand, but to triune immersionists there is only the familiar scene of the administrator about to bend the head of the candidate forward into the water. One picture (the fresco-baptism of the St. Callistus cemetery, a copy of which is given in *Smith's Christian Antiquities,* p. 168) represents a youth standing in water while the baptizer's hand is resting on his head and a showery spray surrounds the youth. Of course, sprinklers see in this spray a proof of sprinkling, but triune immersionists ask why the youth should undress and go into the water to be sprinkled. They see in the spray the water flowing from a candidate who has received one dip and is about to receive another of the three commanded by Jesus.

J. P. Lundy, presbyter, in *Monumental Christianity,* says of this picture: " The child has received perhaps his third and last plunge and is receiving confirmation." And Hutchings concedes, " trine and nude immersion was preferred, and made obligatory by church authority as the regular mode of baptism, in all ordinary cases, say for the first one thousand years."—(*Ford* p. 297).

If authors who practice sprinkling and pouring and single immersion, make such admissions as these, because compelled by the truth, we may accept their admissions without further argument, except to show that since triune immersion as the mode is so evident, good Christians should *follow it* instead of teaching, as they do, that it is not necessary to do so.

It is true that there is a picture (but not of apostolic times) which represents John the Baptist baptizing by pouring water out of a shell as he stands with the candidate in the water, but it need only be asked, why, if this imagination of the artist is to be taken as a true picture of baptism, do not those who use it as an argument follow it themselves in their own practice?

10. THE ORIGIN OF SINGLE IMMERSION AND OF POURING AND OF SPRINKLING CAN BE DEFINITELY AND CERTAINLY LOCATED IN LATER AGES, BUT THE ORIGIN OF TRIUNE IMMERSION CANNOT BE FOUND THIS SIDE OF JESUS AND THE APOSTLES.

This is a strong statement, but if proven it should be conclusive. Can it be proven? Let us see. There are witnesses who know. Let them testify.

(1) *The origin of single immersion.*

First, *Gregory Nanzianzen* may take the chair.

When were you born?

330 A. D.

What was your office?

I was Bishop of Constantinople.

Where were you educated?

At Alexandria and Athens, the best schools of the day.

What did you write?

Sermons, poems, orations and letters.

Did you know Eunomius?

Yes, I was contemporaneous with him.

What do you say of him in your introduction to *Theological Orations?*

Eunomius was the first person heretically to discontinue the practice of threefold immersion in holy baptism. He also corrupted the form of that sacrament by setting aside the use

Baptism

of the name of the Father, Son and Holy Ghost and baptizing people "in the name of the Creator and in the death of Christ."

Does Eunomius or any of his friends or followers of that day deny this charge of Gregory? Not one of them. Therefore it stands. Call the next witness.

Philostargius may speak. Were you born while Eunomius was living?

Yes, I was born A. D. 364.

What was your standing in the church?

I was the author of a church history of twelve volumes.

What do you quote from a fragment preserved by Photius about Eunomius?

It reads as follows:

The Eunomians, not with trine immersion, but with one immersion, baptizing, as they said, into the Lord's death.

That will do. Who is the next witness?

Theodoret. When were you born?

386 A. D.

What was your standing?

Bishop of Cyrus and leading scholar of the century.

You lived close to Eunomius. What do you say of him?

He, Eunomius, subverted the holy law of baptism WHICH HAD BEEN HANDED DOWN FROM THE BEGINNING, FROM THE LORD AND THE APOSTLES, and made a contrary law, asserting that it is not necessary to immerse the candidate thrice, nor to mention the names of the Trinity, but to immerse only once, into the death of Christ.

Next, *Sozomen* may take the stand. When were you born?

400 A. D.

What do you say of Eunomius in your *Ecclesiastical History* (6: 26)?

Some assert that Euonimus was the first who ventured to maintain that divine baptism ought to be performed by one immersion, and to corrupt in this manner the apostolic tradition which has been carefully handed down to this present day. . . . He asserted that baptism ought not to be administered in the name of the Trinity, but in the name of the death of Christ. It appears that Eunomius broached no new opinion on the subject, but was from the beginning firmly attached to the sentiments of Arius. . . . After his elevation to the bishopric of Cyzicus his own clergy accused him of introducing innovations in doctrine. But whether it was Eunomius or any other person who first made these innovations upon the tradition of baptism, it seems to me that such innovators, whoever they may have been, were alone in danger, according to their own representations, of quitting this life without having received divine baptism, for if after they had been baptized by the mode recommended FROM THE BEGINNING, they found it impossible to rebaptize themselves, it must be admitted that they introduced a practice to which they had not themselves submitted.

Socrates (the church historian 440 A. D.) may next give his opinion.

What these nonsensical terms were, about which they (the Eunomians) differed, I consider unworthy of being recorded in this history, lest I should go into matters foreign to my purpose. I shall merely observe that they adulterated baptism, for they do not baptize into the name of the Trinity, but into the death of Christ.—Eccles. Church History, 5: 24.

Here now is the testimony of five witnesses who were contemporaneous with Eunomius or the generation following. They are witnesses who were leading bishops and authors of the church. They agree in stating that Eunomius, the disciple of the heretic Arius, who denied the divinity of Christ, altered the divine mode of baptism by triune immersion which was "handed down from the Lord and his apostles" and substituted single immersion instead. Is their testimony impeached by any one of that day? It is never questioned. What is more, it is said by these historians of his own day that the followers of

Eunomius themselves accused him of introducing innovations in doctrine.

Was the matter ever considered by the church as a whole in that day? Yes, it was considered by two of the General Councils of the Church, and they both decided against the heresy, and the Council of Nice, the first General or Ecumenical Council of the Church, A. D. 325, expelled Arius as a heretic. The Council of Constantinople, the second of the General Councils, met in 381 A. D., soon after Eunomius had started his heretical baptism, and decided in the 7th canon as follows:

> But the Eunomians, who only baptize with one immersion, and the Montanists, who are called Phrygians, and the Sabellians, who teach the doctrine of the Fatherhood of the Son (if they wish to be joined to the orthodox faith) we receive as heathen.

In spite of these decisions of councils against it, the Eunomian heresy persisted in certain parts of the church, and was denounced again and again. A prominent witness is Pope Pelagius, Bishop of Rome in the sixth century. In a letter (*Ad Guadentium* 4: 82) he says:

> There are many who say that they baptize in the name of Christ alone and by single immersion. But the Gospel command which was given by God himself and by our Lord and Savior Jesus Christ, reminds us that we should administer the baptism to every one in the name of the Trinity, and by triune immersion.

It was not until the Council of Toledo, 633 A. D., that single immersion was ever declared valid by any council of the church, and fifty-nine years after this the Council of Trullo reversed the decision and again denounced Eunomius for practicing single immersion.

(2) *First single immersion with Trinitarian formula.*
The Eunomian heretics perverted both the form of baptism and the formula as well. The first instance of single

immersion with the use of the Trinitarian formula is in Spain about 600 A. D. The Arian heresy had gotten this far, but the Eunomian had not. To get around the recognition of the Trinity (which Eunomius avoided by changing the form to a single immersion, and the Trinitarian formula to baptism into the name of the Creator and death of Christ) the Arians in Spain made the three dips represent three grades in the Trinity. *Leander of Sevil* wrote to Pope Gregory the Great about it and asked what to do. The Pope replied that since this Arian heresy caused the people to misunderstand baptism and confuse the trine immersion baptism with Arianism, it would be better to change and use single immersion instead. However the advice of the Pope did not prevail at once and in 633 there was held the Fourth Council of Toledo which decreed that either mode was right, but that the orthodox should practice only single immersion, so as to be different from the Arians. This council acted under the advice of the Pope. See *Beveridge's Works* Vol. 8, p. 336.

It was this advice of the Pope which gave to single immersion an impetus which caused it to spread. The Pope claimed the right to change the laws of the church, and still claims the right to do so. Therefore Catholics rest easy under the perverted mode of baptism practiced by the Roman Catholic Church, but they rightly charge the Protestants who baptize by other modes than triune immersion, with inconsistency. "You deny the authority of the Pope" they say, "and yet you follow the decree of the Pope in these things, instead of following the Gospel commands in the matter." It is for them to answer. The safe and right thing to do, the only consistent thing to do, is to pass by the Popes and Councils, on to the Lord himself and baptize according to the commission He gave. (Matt. 28: 19).

Baptism

A few Protestant advocates of the abridged forms of baptism, more consistent than the others, cling to the popish doctrine that the church has the right to alter the commands of the Lord, and thus allow the perverted forms of the symbol of baptism. At least such is the inference from *Dr. Robinson* in his *History of Baptists,* London edition, p. 545, who says:

> The very plain manner in which they (the English Baptists) baptize is a high degree of probability in their favor: but they appear to have varied a little from the original form which, however, the free constitution of their churches allows them any day to alter. . . . They baptize transversely by laying a person backward in the water.

(3) *First instance of backward immersion.*

The first instance of backward action in immersion is that of *Thomas Munzer,* a fanatic of the Reformation who led a half-religious and half-social rebellion in a German province until he and his forces were defeated. He was baptized backward March 1, 1522. His sect, on account of the custom of the country in burying by letting the body down back first, thought to make baptism more like such a burial by introducing the backward action. *Adoniram Judson,* a Baptist missionary, who visited Rome says:

> Previous to the seventeenth century the Baptists had formed churches in the different parts of the country, and having always seen infants, when baptized, taken into the hands of the administrator and laid backward in the water in the baptismal font, and not having much if any communication with the Baptists on the Continent, they thought, of course, that a candidate for baptism, though a grown person, should be treated in like manner and laid backwards under the water. They were probably confirmed in this idea by the phrase "buried in baptism." The consequence has been that all the Baptists in the world, who have sprung from the English Baptists, have practiced the backward posture. But from the beginning it was not so. In the apostolic times the administrator placed his right hand

upon the head of the candidate, who then, under the pressure of the administrator's hand, bowed forward, aided by that genuflection, which instinctively comes to one's aid when attempting to bow and then rise by his own effort.

(4) *Origin of pouring as a substitute for triune immersion.*

The first intimation of pouring being regarded as valid baptism under any circumstance is that in the *Didache* (65-140 A. D.) which says:

> But if thou hast neither (living or other water) in sufficient quantities (for immersion) pour water on the head three times, into the name of the Father and of the Son and of the Holy Ghost.

Some modern writers take advantage of this statement to say that at this early date the mode of baptism was a mere matter of convenience. If it was more *convenient* to pour than to immerse they poured. It seems to us that common honesty compels us to see that it was a matter of *possibility* rather than of *convenience*. The writer does not say "If it is more *convenient* to pour." Why does he not do so if that is what he *meant?* He does say "If thou *hast* neither." That does not mean "if it is not right at hand, convenient," for if it was convenience the writer had in mind he would not have insisted on baptism in *living,* that is *running,* water rather than other water.

The first actual instance of pouring in baptism is that of Novatian in the middle of the third century, recorded by Eusebius the church historian (250 A. D.). He says that Novatian was sick unto death and in this dire necessity was baptized by pouring. He afterward recovered and wanted to preach. In perplexity the church wrote to *Cyprian,* Bishop of Carthage, who replied: "In the saving sacraments WHEN NECESSITY REQUIRES, an abridgment confers the whole."

This is the only example of pouring known in the early

church. Such cases of baptism in sickness were called "clinics" from the Greek *klina* a couch.

Eusebius, the earliest church historian (250 A. D.) reflects the general feeling of the time in his remarks about Novatian. He says:

> But Satan, who entered and dwelt in him for a long time, became the occasion of his believing. Being delivered by the exorcist, he fell into a severe sickness, and as he seemed about to die, he received baptism by affusion, on the bed where he lay, —if indeed, we can say that such an one did receive it.—Euseb. 6: 43.

He adds that it was unlawful for such a one to enter into any clerical office. Novatian resented this rule and started a new sect which made a great deal of trouble.

The Council of Neo-Ceserea, early in the fourth century, in the 12th canon declared:

> If any man is baptized only in time of sickness he shall not be ordained as a presbyter, because his faith was not voluntary, but as it were of constraint, except his subsequent faith and diligence recommend him, or else the scarcity of men make it necessary to ordain him.—See Cyprian, Ep. 75: 19.

In the eighth century (753 A. D.), the king of the Lombards drove *Pope Stephen II* out of Rome, and he fled to France. While there the monks of Cresse of Brittany asked, "Is it lawful in sickness to baptize an infant by pouring from a cup or hand?" He answered, "Such a baptism performed IN SUCH A CASE OF NECESSITY may be accounted valid."

(5) *The origin of sprinkling.*

The first record of sprinkling passing for baptism is as follows: *Cyprian* (255 A. D.) in reply to a query says:

> You have asked my opinion of those who received the grace of God in a time of sickness, whether they are properly to be esteemed as Christians, because they are not washed, but only

sprinkled with the saving water? . . . I cannot apprehend how the blessings of heaven should descend upon any, maimed and imperfect, nor how they should suffer any diminution or abatement, where in the reception of them, neither giver nor receiver are at all deficient in their faith. . . . In cases of necessity, God will dispense with divers things, and will confer upon believers, in a more compendious way, all the benefits of his saving sacraments. . . or, if any one is persuaded that men in such circumstances have really nothing conferred upon them, because they are only sprinkled with baptismal water, and that all which is done for them in that way, is without effect, let them run no further risks; and therefore if they recover let them be baptized.

Here we have the origin of sprinkling in the middle of the third century, and then allowed only in cases of absolute necessity, and these to be followed by baptism in case of recovery in order to make sure of being right. Surely, if sprinkling had been considered baptism before this the learned Bishop would have known it and referred to the fact, but he does not, and therefore hesitates to start the precedent as well he might, for it was soon taken advantage of, and from being allowed only in case of sickness or necessity, it seeks to usurp the entire place of baptism.

The Edinburgh Cyclopedia says:

The first law for sprinkling was obtained in the following manner: Pope Stephen II fled to Pepin, who a short time before had usurped the crown of France. Whilst he remained there the Monks of Cressy, in Brittany consulted him whether in case of necessity baptism poured on the head of an infant would be lawful. Stephen replied that it would. But though the truth of this fact be allowed, which, however, some Catholics deny, yet pouring or sprinkling was admitted only in cases of necessity. It was not till the year 1311 that the legislature in a council held at Ravenna, declared immersion or sprinkling to be indifferent. In Scotland, however, sprinkling was never practiced in ordinary cases until after the Reformation about the middle of the 16th century. From Scotland it made its way to England in the reign of Elizabeth, but was not authorized in the established church.

Thus beginning in cases of necessity and growing with the heresy of infant baptism, the substitution of sprinkling for apostolic baptism has come to be so popular as to mock at the zeal of those who would cling to the triune immersion which Jesus instituted. But if one of His commands can be so altered and abridged by the Pope why not all of them be done away? And if Protestants follow the authority of the Pope in this respect how can they deny his authority in other respects?

(6) *Modern authorities on the origin of the compends of baptism*:

Brenner (Catholic) says:

For thirteen hundred years sprinkling and pouring as modes of baptism were disputed, nay, even forbidden.

Professor Norman Fox says:

Though affusion was used from the middle of the third century, yet the first formal sanction was the decree of the Council of Cologne in 1280.

This decree however prescribed immersion as the regular form and allowed aspersion only in the case of infants in danger of dying at birth.

The Encyclopedia Britannica (9th edition of R. S. Peale & Co., London) says:

The Council of Ravenna in 1311 was the first council of the church which legalized baptism by sprinkling by leaving it to the choice of the officiating minister. The custom was to immerse three times, once at the name of each person of the Trinity.

Professor Coleman in *Ancient Christianity Exemplified* says:

The introduction of infant baptism did not alter the mode from immersion to sprinkling.

(7) Combination of modes. In about the twelfth century we find the first mention of the combination of methods in baptism. The Roman ecclesiastic Gregory, in defense of affusion against Mark of Ephesus, in a council at Florence A. D. 1439 said:

> We do not immerse the infants' heads; for we cannot teach them to hold their breath, nor prevent water from going through their ears, nor close their mouths. But we so put them into the font as to omit nothing which is really necessary for carrying out the traditions (i. e., immersion, since he had previously stated that trine immersion was necessary, for thus it had been handed down by the saints to signify the three days' burial of the Lord). . . and that the head, the seat of the senses, and vehicle of the soul, may not be without holy baptism, we take water in the hollow of the hand, out of the font, and pour it over.

This double mode, however, was only used to avoid peril to the child. John, Bishop of Luttich, A. D. 1287, thus writes:

> When the baptizer immerses the candidate in water, he may say these words: "And that all peril to the one being baptized may be avoided, the head of the child may not be immersed in water; but the priest may pour water thrice on the crown of the child's head with a basin or other clean and fit vessel."

But these "compends" or abridged forms of baptism did not come to prevail without a struggle. Only gradually were they accepted.

Duns Scotus as late as the thirteenth century says (*Ford* p. 306):

> Trine immersion may be dispensed with by a minister in case he should be feeble in strength, and there should be a huge country fellow to be baptized whom he could neither plunge in nor lift out.

Quotations enough to fill many volumes might be given from writers all down through the ages, of every century, proving the continuous practice of triune immersion from the days of the apostles until this. But such quotations from medieval writers are of little worth. We have been concerned only to prove the apostolic mode as instituted by the Lord Himself. The historical testimony has been followed as far as it is of value to do this.

(8) *Triune immersion the dominant mode of the ages.* However, it is well to remember that, popular as affusion is among the Protestant churches of America, it is not the prevailing mode of this century, nor has it been of any century. More than nine-tenths of the Christians of the world have been baptized by trine action and nearly one-half of them have been immersed.

Not only did triune immersion predominate to the almost total exclusion of any compend or substitute in the early centuries, but it predominates to-day, in spite of the seeming prevalence of the various compends in our own country. Elder J. B. Wampler in *The Law of Baptism* has collected the statistics as follows:

THOSE WHO PRACTICE TRIUNE DIPPING.

The Greek Church,	98,616,000
Orthodox Hebrews,	7,000,000
Abyssinian Church	3,000,000
Armenian Church,	1,600,000
Moravian Church,	82,971
Seven Day Baptist (probably)	50,000
Brethren and others,	300,000
Copts, Nestorians, Spanish, and the Catholics at Milan (probably),	50,000,000
Liberal churches who give their subjects their choice (probably,)	10,000

Total observing sacrament by triune dipping, ...160,058,971

Those who practice trine pouring are:

Mennonites,	75,000
Roman Catholics,	180,000,000

Liberal churches, who give the subjects their choice
    (probably), ... 10,000

Total number who practice trine pouring, ... 180,085,000

Those who practice trine sprinkling are:

Lutheran Church, ... 50,000,000
Reformed, ... 20,000,000
The Church of England or Episcopalians, ... 23,253,000
Scotch Presbyterians and others (probably), ... 200,000
Covenanters, ... 200,000

Totol number of Trine Actionists, ... 433,896,971

Number of supposed Christians, ... 477,080,158
Total number of Trine Actionists, ... 433,896,971
    Leaving for Single Actionists, ... 43,183,187
Those who practice dipping are:
Baptists, Disciples and others, ... 9,220,000

Single Actionists by sprinkling and pouring, ... 33,933,187
Trine dipping above single dipping, ... 150,808,971
Trine Actionists above single, ... 290,713,984

From these approximate statistics the reader will readily observe that there are nearly eighteen times as many Trine Immersionists in the world as there are Single. There are also nearly ten times as many Trine Actionists as there are Single.

Now we have followed through the ten lines of evidence concerning the Gospel mode of baptism, and have found that they all agree together perfectly. They all lead to one conclusion, and their cumulative evidence is overwhelming. The very meaning of the term "baptize" requires immersion. The construction of the command of Jesus (Matt. 28: 19) requires triune immersion. The meaning of the symbol requires it. The New Testament examples prove the practice. The writings of the early church leaders show that triune immersion was universal except in

Baptism

cases of necessity. The testimony of modern historians agrees with this. The ancient baptistries and works of art confirm the testimony. Triune immersion has been continuously practiced since the days of the apostles, while the origin of sprinkling, pouring and single immersion has been definitely traced to later times, sprinkling and pouring arising from cases of necessity, and single immersion from the coming of the heresy of unitarianism.

If the evidence were such as to permit of reasonable doubt, then there would be room for the admission of choice of modes according to the conscience of the candidate, but since the evidence is so overwhelming, it becomes the duty of those who have gathered it together to give it as widely as possible to the world, that harmony among Christians in this respect may come, not by disregarding and perverting God's holy ordinance, but by observing it " according to the pattern " that He gave as His parting command. Evidence in harmony with the foregoing might be multiplied and testimonies increased, but surely these are sufficient. It only remains to remember the words of the Lord Jesus, how He said, " If ye love me, keep my commandments. . . . He that hath my commandments, and keepeth them, he it is that loveth me: and he that loveth me shall be loved of my Father."

VI. The Place of Baptism.

The place of baptism is of interest because the surroundings help or hinder the impressiveness of the baptismal service, according as they are appropriate or not.

1. *The Bible gives no directions as to the place* of baptism and it may therefore be assumed that there may be liberty in the choice of place. A study of Bible examples shows baptisms in the Jordan (Mark 1: 9), in Jerusalem (Acts 2: 37-40) where there was no stream, but abundant

water in pools and canals, and by the wayside (Acts 8: 34-40).

2. The *Didache,* however, (70-140 A. D.) insists upon baptism in a running stream if possible (*Didache* ch. 7).

3. *Soon after* the days of the apostles we find the church using *baptistries.* From earliest times the Christian writers speak of the "laver" or baptistry. It was sometimes called the "columbathra" or "bath." *Tertullian* (160 A. D.) says, "There is no difference whether one is washed in the sea, or in a pond, or in a river, or in a fountain, in a lake or in a canal."—*De Bap.* ch. 4.

4. *The clear, running stream, or lake* can better convey the idea of cleansing than a small or stagnant pool, but a baptistry is most suggestive of a grave. Preference should be given to the best place always. In any case the water should be as clear and pure and abundant as possible.

An editorial in *The Gospel Messenger,* Jan. 18, 1908, states the truth clearly as follows:

In this country there is more or less suffering where outdoor baptism is administered in the winter, when the weather is very cold, but we seldom hear of the experience producing unfavorable results. Where the applicant is properly dressed, is permitted to stand in the cold air before entering the water, and is then well wrapped in heavy blankets or quilts as soon as he, or she, comes from the water, no ill effects whatever need be feared. To get people, especially young people, who are not accustomed to water, to understand this, is not so easy. The work of the apostles was not hindered with conditions of this sort, for they did most of their preaching in countries where the climate is mild, even during the winter months, and where most of the people were accustomed to water. In our climate, and particularly in the northern States, it will be found wise to arrange for as many conveniences at baptism as practicable. A well-warmed building, by the side of a good stream or lake, is a great convenience. There should be a good place to enter the water, with as little mud as possible. Some churches have installed baptistries and use water with the chill taken off, while other churches have built pools in the yard. As a rule, baptism in a running stream, where the water is clean, is preferable, still the rite is just as valid when performed at other places, where there is plenty of pure water. Conveniences for the comfort of the applicant have nothing whatever to do with the validity of the rite. It may be performed in cold or warm water, in rivers, lakes, or pools. All this being true, there is nothing inconsistent in providing any necessary conveniences, with a view of making it pleasant for the applicant during the performance of the rite.

VII. The Time of Baptism.

The Gospel gives no commandment specially in regard to the time of administering baptism. There is not the least hint that there must be a certain season or occasion of the year for the rite.

1. *The commission* implies that baptizing accompanies the acceptance of the Gospel without unnecessary delay (Matt. 28: 19; Mark 16: 16).

2. *The New Testament examples* show that baptism was administered by the apostles as soon as possible after conversion. The outward sign accompanied the inward change. Peter said on Pentecost (Acts 2: 38), "Repent ye and be baptized." According to Acts 8: 36-38 Philip baptized the eunuch at once. That " same hour of the night " the jailor was baptized; and to Saul it was said, (Acts 22: 16) " Why tarriest thou? Arise and be baptized and wash away thy sins."

3. *There is no Gospel authority for any delay* in administering the rite when once there is the proper evidence of faith and repentance, and an opportunity to be baptized. Since, however, baptism in itself does not regenerate the heart, great care should be taken not to admit any one to the sacred rite who is not by sincere faith and repentance ready for it. Concerning this point *Chyrsostom* (347 A. D.) says (*Homily I* on Acts):

Let us then not wait for a set time lest by hesitating and putting off we depart empty and destitute of so great gifts. . . . I exhort you to leave all and draw near to baptism with great alacrity that having given proof of great earnestness in this present time we may obtain confidence for that which is to come.

In case of illness or other necessity, the church must act according to circumstances. No fixed rule can be given that will fit all cases, but in general it may be said that baptism should accompany faith and repentance as closely as possible. The outward symbol and inward reality should meet in point of time as well as in point of teaching.

VIII. The Administrator of Baptism.

1. *The Gospel nowhere specifies* definite persons in the church to perform the rite of baptism. The commission was given to the church as a whole. But in the church there are diversities of gifts and of ministrations (1 Cor. 12); God has called special persons for special work (Eph. 4: 10-12), and all things are to be done "decently and in order" (1 Cor. 14: 39). Paul felt called to preach rather than to baptize (1 Cor. 1: 17), but others did regularly administer the ordinances. This was done by the apostles and elders, but we find also Philip, one of the seven deacons (?) also baptizing (Acts 6 and 8). *Apostolic Constitutions,* Book 3, sec. 1: 9, 10, forbids women or any one but bishops or elders to perform the rite. These writings reflect early customs, but are not of binding authority.

2. *Must there be "apostolic succession"* in administrators? That is, must the administrator be some one who has been baptized by some one in direct line of baptisms clear back to the apostles? Decidedly no. Because:

(1) There is no command in the Gospel to that effect.

(2) There is no precedent or principle from which this doctrine can be inferred.

(3) If, as Jesus says, they are the true children of Abraham who do the works of Abraham (John 8: 30-44), therefore that is the true apostolic church which has the spirit and works of the apostolic church.

(4) The only churches which claim apostolic succession (Greek and Roman Catholic, Church of England, Armenian, &c.) are hopelessly antagonistic to each other and so lost in errors as to be farther from the Gospel than other Christian sects.

(5) The Lord has blessed with His Spirit the evangelical churches of to-day, and what God has blessed let no man curse.

3. *The true foundation is Christ.* But while there is no necessity for that false apostolic succession which consists only of outward organization, of bottles rather than the wine of the Gospel in the bottles, yet *there is necessity that there be true apostolic succession.* There can be no Christian baptism outside of the true church, which consists of believers everywhere who build on the one foundation, Christ Jesus (1 Cor. 3: 10-15; Matt. 16: 15-19).

In the early days the "demons" (heathen) imitated the baptism of the Christians in mockery, but their mock rites were not baptism. Any one so heretical as to give up the fundamental doctrines of Christ cannot administer Christian baptism.

4. *We have no example of women baptizing,* although they "did prophesy" (Acts 21: 9, 10) and otherwise assisted the apostles in teaching (Philpp. 4: 3; Acts 18: 26). The gifts of the spirit are without regard to sex and in Christ there is neither male nor female (Gal. 3: 28), but the principle of respect for common ideas of propriety so frequently urged by the apostles (1 Cor. 10: 32; Col. 4: 5, &c.) would seem to allow this work to women only in

cases of absolute necessity. It is a question of expediency rather than of special command (1 Cor. 6: 12).

5. *In case the administrator of baptism should prove to be unworthy in life,* that fact would not invalidate the baptism of those having received the rite from him in good faith and right understanding of the Gospel, but if the subject be unworthy, no virtue in the administrator can avail to make his baptism effectual. Witness the case of Simon Magus baptized by Philip and yet remaining "in the gall of bitterness and the bond of iniquity" (Acts 8: 13-24).

The rite of baptism however is a sign of putting on Christ (Gal. 3: 27) by becoming a member of His body (1 Cor. 12: 13) which is the church (Eph. 2: 21-23). Christian baptism cannot therefore be administered by any one who is not a member of the true church.

6. *As to the practice of the early church,* the *Didache* mentions no special person to baptize, but *Justin Martyr* a little later (130 A. D.), in a letter to Smyrna (8: 2) says: "It is not lawful without the elder either to baptize or to celebrate the love-feast."

Jerome (340 A. D.) says:

I do not deny that it is the practice of the churches in the case of those living far from the greater towns, to be baptized by presbyters and deacons, and for the bishop to visit them and by the laying on of hands to invoke the Holy Ghost upon them. . . . Hence it is that without ordination and the bishop's license, neither presbyter nor yet deacon has the power to baptize, and yet if necessity so be we know that even laymen may and frequently do baptize.—Ad. Luciferians, ch. 9.

IX. Attendant Ceremonies.

The early church in some way came to have a number of practices connected with baptism that have no command or precedent in the Gospel. Such was the custom of fasting as a preparation, both by administrator and candidate,

Baptism

disrobing the candidate for baptism, and of giving him milk and honey to taste on coming from the water as a sign of the blessing of the new life. It also became the custom to defer baptisms until a stated time, the Easter season, probably because of the connection of the idea of the new life of the baptized with the resurrection. These customs are all mentioned by various writers of the post-apostolic church, but none of them, save the fasting, is mentioned in the *Didache* or any writing of the earliest period, and since there is no mention of them in the Gospel they have no place among the ordinances. The tendency to multiply rites above those commanded should be avoided, lest the distinction between divine commands and human traditions be lost.

However, there were three ceremonies connected with baptism, which are symbols mentioned in the Gospels, and these are discussed accordingly in separate sections. These were (1) Confession, (2) The Laying on of Hands, and (3) The Kiss of Peace.

X. Rebaptism.

The introduction of irregularities in the form and purpose of baptism has involved the church in serious and complicated questions. The duty of adhering to the Gospel is clear, but the question of proper attitude toward those who are more or less in error is not so simple. The apostolic church was not divided into denominations, and consequently the Gospel does not directly deal with the question. However, there are general principles which can be applied.

1. BAPTISM PROPERLY ADMINISTERED SHOULD NOT BE REPEATED. The Old Covenant ablutions were for ceremonial cleansing, and as the need was frequent the rites were often repeated; but baptism means more than cleansing from sin. It stands for regeneration, and as the new birth is not re-

peated the symbol of it should not be. The Mormons rebaptize their members each time they repent of their backslidings, and if, as President Mullins says (claiming the endorsement of all Baptist and many Disciple ministers), baptism is simply for *ceremonial or symbolic remission* of sins, this is the proper thing to do. For this repeated cleansing, which is needed even by Christians, feet-washing has been instituted—which see. " Baptism for the dead " (1 Cor. 15: 29) is thought by some to refer to a repetition of the act in behalf of those dying without it, but Paul's argument seems to be simply that baptism into Christ (the dead) would be vain if Christ be not risen. There is nothing whatever to warrant the repetition of the rite once properly received.

2. Baptism not properly administered should be corrected. Many church members, finding themselves in error in regard to baptism, are willing to confess the truth, but not by submitting to rebaptism. Is it required that in order to correct their error they should do so? " We are Christians," they say, " and our sins have been forgiven. Why then should we appear in the attitude of sinners just converted? Do not the Scriptures say, ' Not laying again a foundation * * * of the teaching of baptism '?" We would not assume to say that such are not Christians, or that their sins are not already forgiven, for God alone is judge of that, but to correct one's baptism is not to appear as a sinner or to lay again the foundation of the teaching of baptism. It is simply to confess the teaching of baptism which had not been learned before, and there are a number of scriptural reasons why this should be done.

(1) *The example of Jesus*, who, though He was without sin, submitted to baptism to " fulfill all righteousness " (Matt. 3: 15) should teach us that the institution itself is of such importance that to preserve it as taught we should

submit to it, even though we have already been trying to live as children of God. Indeed, if we profess to have been Christians for some time we should be all the more ready to render that full obedience which Jesus requires in His disciples. We have no claim to discipleship if we halt in our obedience. Jesus said, "For their sakes I sanctify myself, that they also may be sanctified" (John 17: 19). We cannot be an example to others until our own example is made right.

(2) *The example of the apostles* also teaches us that it is so essential to preserve the true baptism that errors as to the rite should be corrected by rebaptism. We have only one instance of rebaptism, but that is enough to establish the custom. In Acts 19: 1-6 we read of twelve men who are called "disciples," and who had received the baptism of John, yet Paul rebaptized them according to the commission, and they received the gift of the Holy Spirit. It is true that Apollos (Acts 18: 24-28) also "knew only the baptism of John," and it is not said that he was rebaptized, but neither is it said that he was not rebaptized. When Aquila and Priscilla taught him the way of the Lord more accurately they may have included rebaptism just as Paul did. Besides, he had received the Holy Spirit, while the twelve had not. It is also true that it was probably not the form of baptism which Paul was correcting as much as the understanding of the meaning, but inasmuch as understanding of the meaning is so closely dependent upon obedience to the form we may not attempt to correct the one without the other. The perverted forms of baptism are all accompanied by misunderstanding of the meaning, and if Paul rebaptized to correct one only, much more he would to correct both together.

(3). *The example of the early church* is in harmony with the example of Jesus and the apostles. We find no such talk in the writings of the first centuries as, "It makes no difference how you are baptized; it is only a form anyhow." The *Didache* is so insistent upon the proper baptism that deviation is allowed only in case of lack of sufficient water. *Cyprian,* Bishop of Carthage, (200-256 A. D.) discusses the whole question at length, and while not rebaptizing repentant backsliders (Epistle 70: 2), nor those who in sickness received pouring or sprinkling (Ep. 75: 12), yet those having baptism from sects heretical in fundamentals were rebaptized (Ep. 69: 3), and that whether the previous mode was correct or not (Ep. 75: 7). In this he was opposed by Stephen, Bishop of Rome, but he quoted in his support the decision of a *council of seventy-one bishops* held many years before (Ep. 72: 3), and was also sustained by the Council of Arles 314 A. D. which said, "The baptism conferred by heretics is valid if administered in the name of the Holy Trinity," (which would be according to the commission) and also by the eighty-seven bishops of the *Seventh Council of Carthage* which said:

According to evangelical and apostolic testimony, heretics who are called adversaries of Christ, and anti-Christian, when they come to the church they must be baptized with the one baptism of the church, that they may be made of adversaries friends, and of anti-Christians Christians.

The Second General Synod, that of Constantinople 381 A. D., in its seventh canon declared:

But the Eunomians who only baptize with one immersion, and the Montanists (who taught the incarnation of the Holy Spirit in Montanus), and the Sabelliams, who teach the doctrine of the Fatherhood of the Son, we receive as heathen.

Apostolic Constitutions, Canon 447, says:

Let a bishop or presbyter who shall baptize again one who has rightly received baptism, or who shall not baptize one who has been polluted by the ungodly, be deposed.

(4) *The spirit of obedience* so often and so ardently insisted upon in the Gospel requires the right mode of baptism, even though rebaptism be necessary to secure it. Jesus said, "If a man love me he will keep my word" (John 14: 23).

(5) *Regard for the teaching of baptism* also requires the rebaptism of those improperly baptized. In Heb. 6: 1, 2 the "teaching of baptism" is named as a "foundation," one of "the first principles of Christ." Do we do more than the Gospel if we insist that this foundation teaching be preserved? But if any kind of baptism be accepted as valid how then can the teaching be preserved? Sprinkling and pouring fail to express the ideas of death, burial and resurrection, while single backward immersion is just as fatally defective in that it fails to represent the Trinity, the very thing specified in the commission. If these vital truths are to be preserved, the one baptism that the Gospel prescribes to teach them must also be preserved.

(6) *The leading of the Holy Spirit* will require rebaptism when necessary to fulfill the Gospel. God has promised the Spirit only "to them that obey him" (Acts 5: 32). He comes to lead into all truth, not away from the truth. We cannot expect to be led into more truth until we are willing to obey the truth that we have (John 7: 17).

(7) *Proper baptism is essential to peace of mind.* However much some preachers may say, "Peace, peace, let any baptism do," the conscientious believer hears above this lullaby the stern words of warning, "If we sin wilfully after that we have received the knowledge of the truth, there remaineth no more a sacrifice for sins, but a certain fearful expectation of judgment" (Heb. 10: 26). And however much the tempter may say "Peace, peace, you were sincere and 'if there first be a willing mind it is acceptable according as a man hath,'" he still remembers that "There

is a way that seemeth right unto a man, but the end thereof are the ways of death" (Prov. 14: 12), and he dares not claim the immunity of him who "hath not" when once "he hath" the truth. It is not superstitious or narrow to seek to obey God fully, and it is not irreverent to correct an error when once it is discovered. It is irreverent not to do so. It is not denying a former Christian experience to go on unto perfection by openly renouncing error and confessing the truth, and it cannot be wrong to follow the example of Jesus in submitting to a form to set an example of righteousness.

The following apt illustration is by Dr. J. D. McFaden:

The Golden Baptism.

I hold in my hand a piece of gold, a piece of silver and a piece of paper money; I am to give you one piece. As you are about to take it I tell you the piece of gold is genuine; it has been tested; there is no doubt about it; but there is doubt about the pieces of silver and paper. A great many who have investigated the matter say they are counterfeit. Now which piece will you take? "Why," you answer, "I will take the piece of gold, there is no doubt about that. Give me the gold piece."

Why not act this way when it comes to baptism? Here is baptism "In the name of the Father, and of the Son, and of the Holy Ghost," Matt. 28: 19; and there is single immersion and sprinkling. You ask, "Which shall I take?" Do just as you would with the piece of money. Take that about which there is no doubt. All admit—even those who practice differently—that triune immersion, or baptism according to the commission, is genuine. It has the clear apostolic ring. It passes current among all the churches. IT IS THE GOLDEN BAPTISM.

After this long and tedious consideration of baptism let us console ourselves for the effort by coming back to the fact that it is one of God's means of grace, vitally linked with salvation in the Gospel itself; that even as a symbol it is effective in realizing the spiritual life; that to preserve the teaching concerning the Trinity and the new birth for which it stands, the triune immersion form of the rite must be preserved. Let us stand upon the fact that what Jesus embodied in His last command cannot be unimportant, and though others are satisfied with traditions of men let us find peace in keeping the commandment of God.

Baptismal Birth.

As from the clay the crystal comes, as from the seed the flower,
So, praise the Lord, this heart of mine may be his throne of power.
As once upon the mystic cross eternal life was priced,
So I by counting self as dead am crucified with Christ.
With Him I bow the head in death; with Him go in the grave;
With Him I drink the Father's cup, and trust His power to save.

As from the tomb the Lord came forth, raised by the Spirit's power,
So from the blest baptismal grave I rise to sin no more.
Thrice hallowed be the Father's name, who counts me as His child,
Thrice hallowed be the name of Christ, through whom I'm reconciled.
Thrice hallowed be the Comforter, the Holy Ghost divine,
Through whom I realize the life of Christ my Lord in mine.

To each I bow, united now, in bonds of holy love,
And this I pray, that every day I may more faithful prove.
O wondrous death, by which I die! O wondrous wat'ry grave!
O wondrous birth, by which I live and know God's power to save.
May I, may you, to God be true, and all His Word fulfill,
That others thus may find through us the secret of His will.

THE HOLY KISS.

In the early church there was a symbol commanded by the apostles called "the holy kiss," or "kiss of love," which was observed on a variety of occasions, but because it was the custom to salute the newly baptized converts with this holy kiss as a "kiss of peace" on welcoming them into the church, it may properly be considered here. This was not its most frequent use, but it was its first use on the part of believers and marked their entrance into the brotherhood whose law was Christian love.

We read in the Bible of the kiss of reverence, as when Samuel kissed Saul (1 Sam. 10: 1); the kiss of idolatrous worship, as when the people kissed their idols (1 Kings 19: 18; Hos. 13: 2), and the kiss of carnality (Prov. 7: 13). From the most ancient times, however, the kiss has been a token of peace and love. In proof of this we have the example of Isaac and Jacob (Gen. 27: 26, 27), of Laban and his children (Gen. 33: 4), of Jacob and Esau (Gen. 48: 10), of Moses and Jethro (Ex. 18: 7), David and Jonathan (1 Sam. 20: 41), David and Barzillai (2 Sam. 19: 39), David and Absalom (2 Sam. 14: 38), and many others. This symbol was taken advantage of for the sake of treachery, as when Joab kissed Amasa and stabbed him (2 Sam. 20: 9), and Absalom kissed the people and plotted rebellion (2 Sam. 15: 5). In Jesus' day the Jews used the kiss as the common form of salutation. Jesus endorsed the custom by reproving Simon the Pharisee for neglecting it (Luke 7: 45). He accepted it from Judas as nothing strange (Matt. 26: 48), but, because of the

The Holy Kiss

elaborate and empty forms of greeting connected with it, he told the disciples when on their mission of haste to "salute no man by the way" (Luke 10: 4).

In the apostolic church, however, the kiss was made a symbol of holy love, and thus distinguished from the ordinary greeting. It is repeatedly commanded as if it were to be an emblem among Christians of the bond of love which bound them together.

I. The Holy Kiss not the Common Salutation.

For several reasons we cannot believe that these commands concerning the holy kiss refer merely to the observing of the common custom:

1. The custom was to greet all friends with a kiss; this was for the church only (Rom. 16: 16, &c.).

2. Jesus commanded to salute others than brethren, (Matt. 5: 47), but Paul commands this to "one another" only. "Salute all the brethren" (1 Thess. 5: 16). Since Paul received his Gospel from Jesus direct (Gal. 1: 12) they would not contradict one another.

3. The customary salutation was already familiar, being everywhere observed; but this had to be specially and repeatedly commanded.

4. The customary kiss was common, the general greeting, but this is uniformly called "holy." Why distinguish it in this way if it were not different from the ordinary greeting?

5. It matters not whether the Lord and the apostles took an old custom and gave it a new significance or whether they started a new custom, if they instituted a symbol to be perpetuated in the church, it ought to be so perpetuated.

II. The Holy Kiss a Sacred Symbol.

Since, then, we may not regard the "holy kiss" as the

ordinary greeting, let us see if it has the essentials of a symbol.

1. THE DIVINE COMMAND. Five times it is commanded in the Gospel. Rom. 16: 16, " Salute one another with a holy kiss." In 1 Cor. 16: 20 and 2 Cor. 13: 12 the same words are repeated. In 1 Thess. 5: 16 the command reads: " Salute all the brethren with a holy kiss." Peter varies a little by saying, " Salute one another with a kiss of love" (1 Pet. 5: 14).

Now note that this command is not made with the term " ought " to which the objection is made by critics in the case of feet-washing, but with the plain imperative mode. It is a clear command.

Note again that it is made by the apostle Paul who expressly says that he received his Gospel by direct revelation from Christ (Gal. 1: 12).

Note again that the command is given also by the apostle Peter, who was the leader among the apostles.

Note further that it is given in First Thessalonians, the earliest of the epistles, and in Peter, one of the latest.

Note still further that the command was given to the church at Corinth in the first letter, and repeated in the second; that it was given to the Thessalonians, and to the Romans; and that these churches were not Jewish, but Gentile. Why, if it were only a common greeting should this symbol be established among the Gentile Christians?

Note, lastly, that the command of Peter is in a general epistle to all the churches, and that the letters of Paul were exchanged by the churches (Col. 4: 16). This command is therefore not one of local adaptation or expediency, but for the entire church, both Jews and Gentiles. Moreover, the reasons for it are not those of local or temporary expediency, but of general and permanent significance.

2. A SPECIAL SIGNIFICANCE. The Holy Kiss has the

marks of a symbol in that it was given a religious meaning which was to be perpetuated.

(1) *It is called "holy"* to distinguish it from the formal greeting which was without any sacred significance. The term is the same in the original as that translated "saints." It might be called the "saints' kiss." It is a symbol which expresses the holy love which exists between holy brethren and sisters.

(2) *Peter calls it the "kiss of love"* (1 Pet. 5: 14), using for love the word *agape* which is used to designate the love-feasts of the church (Jude 12). The sin of Judas stands out in the greater blackness because he used the two most holy symbols to cover his base purpose. He ate bread as a pledge of friendship, and went immediately out to betray the Lord (John 13: 30). He then used the kiss, the sign of love, as a means of betraying the Master to the soldiers. Well may the feast of love and the kiss of love remind true Christians of the need of abiding in holy love, lest they lapse into such base perfidy.

(3) *The early church used the term "kiss of peace"* more than any other, and while this phrase is not found in the Gospel, yet there is reason to believe that the expression was apostolic. When Jesus sent out the seventy He told them on entering a house to be entertained, to say, "Peace be to this house" (Luke 10: 5). Since the salutation of the kiss was customary in such a welcome, it might easily come through this message of greeting to be called "the kiss of peace," and be a symbol of that true peace which Jesus promised: "Peace I leave with you; My peace give I unto you: not as the world giveth, give I unto you" (John 14: 27). This is "the peace of God which passeth all understanding" of which Paul speaks, and we sing, "Sweet peace, the Gift of God's Love."

III. How the Church Observed the Holy Kiss.

The early Christians understood the command to observe the "holy kiss" to lift it out of the level of the common greeting, and make it a distinctive Christian symbol. They used it as such in various ways.

1. As a salutation.

Tertullian speaks of it in this way (*Ad Uxorem,* Book 2, ch. 4), as does also Clement of Alexandria (153 A. D.). The latter reproves those who abused the custom. He says:

> There are those who do nothing but make the churches resound with a kiss, not having love itself within. For this very thing, the shameless use of a kiss, which ought to be mystic, occasions foul suspicions and evil reports. The apostle calls the kiss holy.—The Instructor, ch. 12.

It was not the intention of the Lord and the apostles to cheapen this symbol by making it common and public. Jesus denounced those who "love salutations in the market places" (Mark 12: 38), and thereby teaches us to avoid making a display of this symbol. It is to be used only when there is special occasion for it, and it must be sincere, and not a mere form. Witness the examples of Paul and the elders at Ephesus (Acts 20: 36, 37).

In the early church it was not given promiscuously on entering the place of worship, but at a signal from the bishop, following prayer. This is the witness of Tertullian (*On Prayer,* ch. 23) and of Augustine (*Homily on Col. 1: 20*).

2. THE HOLY KISS WAS ALSO USED WHEN WELCOMING NEWLY BAPTIZED CONVERTS INTO THE CHURCH. Chrysostom (354 A. D.) explains this custom by saying:

> For because before his baptism he was an enemy, but after baptism is made a friend of our common Lord, we therefore all rejoice with him: and upon this account, the kiss has the

name of peace, that we may learn thereby that God has ended the war, and received us into familiarity, and friendship with Himself. Hence it is, that to "give the peace" to any one, is the same thing many times in the writings of the ancients, as to "salute him with the holy kiss," in the phrase of the apostles. Sermons 50.

The new convert first received the kiss of peace at his baptism, and after that observed it in other ways with the rest as a custom peculiar to Christian believers.

3. THE HOLY KISS WAS ALSO GIVEN TO NEWLY ORDAINED ELDERS OR BISHOPS. It is so mentioned by Dionysius (*Hierarchia Eccl.* p. 5), and in the *Constitutions of the Apostles,* Book 8, ch. 5.

4. THE MOST FREQUENT MENTION OF THE HOLY KISS BY THE EARLY WRITERS IS AS A SYMBOL ACCOMPANYING THE LORD'S SUPPER.

Justin Martyr (150 A. D.) in describing the Lord's supper says: "Prayers having ended we salute one another with a kiss."

Apostolic Constitutions, prescribing the order for the Lord's supper says: "Then let the men give the men, and the women give the women the Lord's kiss."—Book 2, ch. 57.

Augustine (350 A. D.) says:

When the consecration is over we say the Lord's Prayer; and after that, "Peace be with you;" and then Christians salute one another with a holy kiss, which is a sign of peace, if that really be in your hearts, which they pretend with their lips.—Hom. 83. de Diversio.

Gregory Nazianzen (360 A. D.), on the Death of His Father, refers to the kiss of peace by saying of a Christian woman:

"She never grasped the hand or kissed the lips of any heathen woman, however honorable in other respects."

The proof of the observance of the holy kiss by the early church is so plain that modern historians are practically unanimous in teaching it, though they do not practice it.

Stanley (Church of England) says:

> The solemn service (the love-feast) opened with a practice which belongs to the childlike, joyous innocence of the early ages, and which as such was upheld as absolutely essential to the Christian worship, but which now has, with one exception, wholly disappeared from the west, and with two exceptions from the east. It was the kiss of peace. Justin Martyr mentions it as the universal mode of opening the service. It came direct from the apostolic times (1 Thess. 5: 26; 1 Cor. 16: 20; 2 Cor. 13: 12; Rom. 16: 16; 1 Peter 5: 14). Sometimes the men kiss the men and the women the women and sometimes it is without distinction. . . . In the Latin church it was continued till the end of the thirteenth century, and was then transferred to the close of the service.—Christian Institutions 3: 9.

Warren says:

> It is true that there is no liturgical position assigned to this kiss, but the epithet "holy" always applied to it by Paul, indicated that it was not merely the ordinary eastern mode of salutation, but that it partook of a religious character, and we find it from the very earliest post-scriptural times associated with the approach of the Holy Eucharist. Its eucharistic connection can hardly fail to have been suggested by Matt. 5: 23, 24.—Liturgy of the Ante-Nicene Church, p. 37.

Warren probably makes this inference from Matthew because the early church regarded the eucharist as a sacrifice, and peace (of which the kiss was the emblem) was made by Christ an essential preparation for offering a gift or sacrifice (Matt. 5: 23, 24).

Dr. Schaff says that the kiss as a symbol of love and peace was continued at love-feasts or communion services until the end of the thirteenth century.—*Church History*, Vol. 2, p. 237.

The Holy Kiss

We do not regard the precedents of the post-apostolic church as binding, but they have their value, when rightly estimated, in showing something of how the church understood the Lord and the apostles. The uses of the holy kiss which we have shown are certainly very appropriate. They are in harmony with the spirit of the command of the apostles and may well be imitated with profit by the church to-day.

The tendency to shrink from those things which distinguish Christians from the rest of the world is an unworthy tendency. While Christian love is the true badge of discipleship, yet these symbols which help to conserve the spirit of true love have their place and value and should not be neglected. They are a means of testimony open to all. By and by, when the Bridegroom comes for His bride, the union shall not be without the kiss of love, and who then will be ashamed?

CHAPTER IV
THREE SYMBOLS CONDUCIVE TO CHRISTIAN GROWTH.

Feet-washing,—The Love-Feast,—The Eucharist.

"He that is bathed needeth not save to wash his feet. . . . If I wash thee not thou hast no part with me. . . . If I then, your Lord and Master, have washed your feet, ye also ought to wash one another's feet. For I have given you an example, that ye should do as I have done to you."—John 13: 1-17.

* * * * * *

"Let us keep the feast, not with old leaven, neither with the leaven of malice and wickedness, but with the unleavened bread of sincerity and truth."—1 Cor. 5: 8.

* * * * * *

"This is my body which is given for you: this do in remembrance of me. And the cup in like manner after supper saying, This cup is the new covenant in my blood, even that which is poured out for you."—Luke 22: 19, 20.

THE LORD'S SUPPER, INCLUDING FEET-WASHING, THE LOVE-FEAST AND THE EUCHARIST.

1. OLD TESTAMENT TYPES.

Under the old covenant spiritual or ceremonial *cleansing* was represented by various ablutions (Lev. 15, &c.), with special washing of hands and feet for the priests at the door of the tabernacle when preparing for service (Ex. 30: 19-21). *Fellowship* with one another and with God was represented by the table of showbread in the tabernacle (Ex. 25: 23-28) and was inculcated by the three great feasts: the Passover with the feast of unleavened bread, commemorating deliverance from Egypt and pointing to Christ (Ex. 12): Pentecost, fifty days later, a celebration of first fruits, pointed to the first fruits of the Spirit on Pentecost (Lev. 23: 15-22): and the Feast of Tabernacles, a thanksgiving and fellowship feast of seven days (Lev. 23: 33), which many think, pointed also to the second coming of Christ. *Atonement* was represented by the altar of sacrifice before the tabernacle (Ex. 27: 1-8) and the various sacrifices (Lev. 23: 27; 17: 11; 19: 22; Num. 15: 22, &c.).

Under the new covenant these three great truths (cleansing, fellowship and atonement) are taught by the respective rites of *feet-washing,* the *love-feast* and the *eucharist* (John 13: 1-17; 1 Cor. 11: 17-34; Luke 22: 19, 20). They were instituted in the order named during the last evening that Jesus spent with His disciples before the betrayal and crucifixion, and together they form a simple but beautiful substitute for all the many purifications, feasts and sacrifices of the Jews under the old covenant. They are among the most important of the means of grace, because the cleansing, fellowship and forgiveness which they teach are among the most important doctrines of Christianity.

2. THE LORD'S SUPPER NOT THE JEWISH PASSOVER.

In the past, the Lord's supper has been commonly regarded as occurring at the time of the Jewish Passover supper, but more recent scholars are taking the position that the Brethren have always taken, viz., that it occurred a day before the Passover. See, for example, *New Light on the Life of Jesus* by Briggs, *Peloubet's Notes* and the changed title to the passage in the International Sunday-school lessons. When it is clear that this last supper was a special meal, and not the Passover, it will be easier to understand the institution of ordinances at that time.

(1) *The Jewish Passover was eaten at the beginning of the 15th of the month.*

First proof. The original command (Ex. 12: 6) says:

Thou shalt keep it (the passover lamb) until the fourteenth day and kill it in the evening (margin, between the two evenings).

The two evenings evidently meant are the natural evening which began at sunset, and the artificial evening which was reckoned from noon. Between the two would be three o'clock in the afternoon. *Josephus Antiquities,* book 3, ch. 10, part 5 says, "They (the Jews) slay their sacrifice from the 9th hour till the 11th hour"—i. e., from three to five o'clock P. M. As the first evening of the Jewish day began at sundown at the close of the fourteenth, this killing *must* be during the second evening and the eating following could not be before the beginning of the 15th. Ezra 9: 4-6 identifies the time of the evening sacrifice with the hour of prayer, and Acts 3: 1 shows that the hour of prayer was the 9th of the Jewish day or 3 o'clock in the

The Lord's Supper

afternoon, the very hour Jesus died. Since the Passover lambs were slain near the end of the 14th, the eating was at the beginning of the 15th.

Second proof. The Passover lamb was to be eaten the same evening it was killed, and nothing was to be left until morning (Ex. 12: 8-10). Josephus in the reference above says also of the Jews, "they leave nothing until the day following," therefore they must have eaten the meal in the evening of the end of the 14th and beginning of the 15th. The "morning" began at midnight. Compare Mark 1: 35.

Third proof. Israel left Egypt on the same night that the Passover was eaten (Ex. 12: 28-37), going in the night (Deut. 16: 1), but they left on the 15th day of the month (Num. 33: 3): therefore the Passover was eaten at the beginning of the 15th, the "morrow after the passover" being the next natural day, but part of the same Jewish day.

Fourth proof. By comparing Ex. 12: 6 and 18 we see that the seven-day feast of unleavened bread began with the Passover supper, which feast was in commemoration of the going out of Egypt (Ex. 13: 3-4), but it began on the 15th of the month (Lev. 23: 6): therefore the Passover supper must have been on the 15th, at the beginning. The fourteenth closed at sundown. No contradiction in the scriptures will be found if it be remembered that because the *killing* of the Passover and sprinkling of the blood was the most important part of the observance, and this was attended to toward sundown at the close of the 14th, therefore it is sometimes said that the Passover was "observed" on the 14th (Lev. 23: 5; Num. 28: 16; 2 Chron. 35: 1), although the meal was not *eaten* until after sundown, at the beginning of the 15th. Also, because on the 14th all leaven was removed from the houses, this day was called "the preparation" day (Matt. 27: 62; Luke 23: 54; John 19:

14). And because this putting away of the leaven on the 14th was accompanied by the preparation of the unleavened bread, which was eaten at the close of the 14th or beginning of the 15th, the 14th is sometimes called "the first day of unleavened bread" (Mark 14: 12).

Fifth proof. No leaven was to be seen in the houses during the seven days of the feast, and no work was to be done on the first day (Ex. 12: 16; 13: 7), but on the 14th, when leaven was put away, it *was* found and seen, and this was the busiest day of all. Therefore the *feast* was not on the 14th, but on the 15th.

(2) *Jesus ate the last supper with His disciples twenty-four hours before the Jewish Passover supper.*

First proof. Jesus did not eat the Jewish Passover, but at the wrong time. That was strictly against the law, and the penalty was death (Num. 9: 10-13). If He had done that the Jews would have needed no further charge to condemn Him to death, and that they did not charge Him with this is sufficient proof that they could not.

Second proof. Jesus did not eat the meal recorded in John 13 and then the Passover later. All four Gospels speak of the same meal. Each of the four accounts records in connection with the meal the revealing of the betrayer, Peter's denial and the going out from the meal into the garden. They must refer to the same meal.

Third proof. There are no scriptures which contradict this view. Several are used against it, but they are easily explained.

"*Now on the first (day) of unleavened bread the disciples came to Jesus, saying, Where wilt thou that we make ready for thee to eat the passover?*" (Matt. 26: 17.) This passage has caused trouble because the old version inserts the word "feast" which is not in the original Greek. It is therefore omitted in the Revised Version. The "day of unleavened bread" mentioned here was the 14th, for Mark 14: 12 says: "On the first day of unleavened bread, when they sacrifice the passover, his disciples say unto him." This "*first* day of unleavened bread" was the day before "the first day of the *feast* of unleavened bread" for two reasons: (a) During the feast no leaven was to be seen (Ex. 13: 7), but on this day it was seen and removed. (b) On the first day of the feast no work was to be done (Ex. 12: 16), but on the "first day of unleavened bread" there was all the work of preparation. The two expressions refer to different days. Keep this in mind and seeming contradictions vanish. When the disciples came to Jesus it was at the approach of the 14th, called "the preparation" or "first day of unleavened bread," which began at sunset, *eighteen hours before the lamb was to be killed* near the close of the same Jewish day.

"*They made ready the passover*" (Luke 22: 13) means simply that they prepared for the entire feast, so far as the law allowed at that time. They saw that the room was prepared, the leaven removed, the unleavened bread prepared, the lamb selected, &c. It does not mean that the lamb was killed, for that could not be done according to the law until three o'clock the next afternoon (which was eighteen hours later the same Jewish day). In 2 Chron. 35: 10, 11 we have another example of a Passover said to be "prepared" before the victims were killed.

"*When the hour was come*" (Luke 22: 14) means simply the hour for the evening meal as agreed upon. John expressly says that at the beginning of this meal it was "*before* the feast of the passover" (John 13: 1). It was twenty-four hours before. Matt. 26: 20 explains the expression by simply saying, "When even was come," that is, the late evening of darkness, rather than the early evening as the sun was getting low.

"*With desire have I desired to eat this passover*" (Luke 22: 15) means "this coming passover due to be eaten at the end of this same (Jewish) day (the 14th)." Compare John 7: 8-10 "I go not yet up unto this feast"—but Jesus was yet in Galilee, when He referred to the coming feast at Jerusalem as "*this* feast." Also in Acts 18: 21 A. V., Paul, although in Ephesus says, "I must by all means keep *this feast* which cometh at Jerusalem."

When Jesus said, "*I will keep the passover at thy house*" (Matt. 26: 18) He simply meant that He would go ahead to do so until the Father should lead otherwise. He was submissive to the Father's will, and the time had not yet come to reveal that He would be crucified at that very time. Compare the statement of Jesus in Matt. 8: 7, "I will come and heal him." This was said to the centurian concerning his son, but after talking with him and seeing his faith He did not go, but healed the lad without going. Did He therefore falsify? Verily no. Neither did He when He directed the disciples to prepare the preliminaries of the Passover although the observance was to be changed by the institution of a new feast, while He fulfilled the old by His own sacrifice.

Fourth proof. There are many scriptures clearly *against* the supposition that Jesus ate the Passover at this time.

(1) John 13: 1 says the meal was "before" the feast of the Passover, and it was,—the night before.

(2) John 13: 27-29 indicates that the Passover was yet future. While they were eating Judas went out and they supposed that he went to "buy what they had need of against the feast." J. W. Beer in his book on the Passover, suggests that it was because the 15th was a Sabbath or rest day and no work was to be done, that they thought Judas was hastening to complete his buying that evening.

(3) According to Ex. 12: 22, the people were not to

The Lord's Supper

go out of the house from the Passover feast until the morning (therefore midnight or after), yet Jesus encouraged Judas to go out, and with the disciples went out Himself, before that hour. Therefore they were not keeping the Passover feast.

(4) John 18: 28 says the Jews led Jesus to the palace of Caiaphas, yet "entered they not in * * * that they might not be defiled, but might eat the passover." Therefore, during the trial of Jesus the Passover was yet future.

(5) In Matt. 26: 2 Jesus Himself identifies the day of the Jewish Passover as the same day of His own crucifixion. He says, " Ye know that after two days the passover cometh, and the Son of man is delivered up to be crucified." In the next chapter (Matt. 27: 26) we read " But Jesus he (Pilate) scourged and delivered to be crucified," and then follows the account of the crucifixion at once. But the last supper was eaten with the disciples the evening before.

(6) In Matt. 27: 15 we read that " at the feast the governor was wont to release unto the multitude one prisoner, whom they would." This prisoner had not been released when Jesus was before Pilate, therefore the feast of the Passover was not past, but future at that time.

(7) John says (ch. 19: 14) that when Jesus was before Pilate " it was the preparation of the passover and about the sixth hour " (that is, the sixth hour of the trial, or perhaps, the sixth of the Roman day which began at midnight). This was the day for killing the Passover lambs (therefore the 14th), and the day of the crucifixion. Therefore the supper the evening before was not the Passover.

(8) In Mark 15: 42 we read that after the crucifixion " when even was now come, because it was the preparation, that is, the day before the sabbath, there cometh Joseph," &c. The Sabbath was on the 15th, therefore Jesus was crucified on the 14th, and therefore the meal the evening

before was not the Passover. This explains why the Jews were so anxious to get rid of the dead body of Jesus before their Passover supper and Sabbath, lest they be defiled by it.

(9) In Matt. 27: 62 we read that the priests asked that the tomb be sealed, but it was "the morrow after the preparation" and this also shows that the crucifixion was on the day of preparation (killing) and the last supper was therefore the day before the Passover supper.

(10) On the morrow after the weekly Sabbath day, on the first day of the week, Jesus appeared (Mark 16: 1, 2). The Sabbath ended at sundown, the 15th, and that same evening (after sundown) the women bought spices so as to be ready early in the morning for the anointing. But in the morning (the 16th) Jesus was risen, "the first fruits" (1 Cor. 14: 23), thus being the antitype of the first fruits which were waved on that day of the feast of unleavened bread. See Lev. 23: 10-11. The Sabbath during which Jesus was in the tomb was called a "high day" (John 19: 31) because it was the Passover Sabbath instead of the ordinary weekly Sabbath.

(11) The Jewish Passover was to be eaten with shoes on and standing (Ex. 12: 11), but Jesus and the disciples ate this meal without shoes, and reclining (John 13: 1-3), therefore this supper was not the Passover.

(12) Christ fulfilled the law (Matt. 5: 17) and therefore with it fulfilled the Jewish Passover, which was a part of the law, but this feast which He instituted with the disciples He says will not be fulfilled until it is fulfilled in the kingdom of God (Luke 22: 16). Therefore it cannot be the Jewish Passover.

Fifth proof. The typical significance of the Jewish Passover is evidence that the last supper was not the Passover. The foregoing scriptures make it clear that the

The Lord's Supper

Gospel accounts are not contradictory with one another or with the law. Jesus did not violate the law, and therefore He did not eat the Passover at this the wrong time. If any further proof is needed it may be found in the fact that Jesus was the antitype and the paschal lamb the type, and the two met in point of time, as Jesus expired on the cross at the very hour the lambs were being slain. Thus was Christ, our Passover, sacrificed for us. The following shows the likeness between the paschal lamb and Christ:

CHRIST OUR PASSOVER. 1 Cor. 5: 7.

1. A lamb. Ex. 12: 3.	1. Jesus the lamb of God, John 1: 29.
2. Of the first year, Ex. 12: 5.	2. The only begotten Son, John 3: 16.
3. Without blemish, Ex. 12: 5.	3. Without sin, 1 Pet. 2: 22-24.
4. Set apart on the 10th, Ex. 12: 3.	4. Entered Jerusalem the 10th, and was priced by the priests, John 12: 1, 12; Matt. 26: 15, cf. Zech. 11: 12.
5. Killed on the 14th, "between the two evenings, or 3 P. M. Ex. 12: 6.	5. Crucified the 14th, dying at 3 P. M.—the very hour, Matt. 27: 46-50.
6. Not a bone to be broken, Ex. 12: 46.	6. Not a bone broken, John 19: 33-36.
7. Killed by the whole assembly, Ex. 12: 6.	7. The multitudes cried "crucify," Luke 23: 18.
8. The blood sprinkled on houses, Ex. 12: 7, 13.	8. Saved by His blood, 1 Pet. 1: 2; 1 John 1: 7-9.
9. The flesh roasted with fire and feasted upon, Ex. 12: 10.	9. Jesus suffered; we partake of Him, John 6: 52-57; 1 Pet. 4: 12, 13.

10. All leaven to be removed, Ex. 12: 15.	10. All sin to be removed, 1 Cor. 5: 7, 8.
11. To be observed yearly, Ex. 12: 3.	11. To be approached continually, 1 Pet. 2: 3.
12. A sacred symbol, Ex. 12: 14.	12. The eucharist a sacred symbol, 1 Cor. 11: 26.

Dr. Torrey, one of the most learned and loyal Bible teachers of the age, bears strong witness to this point. He says:

The first day of the Passover week, no matter upon what day of the week it came, was always a sabbath (Ex. 12: 16; Lev. 23: 7; Num. 28: 16-18). The question therefore arises whether the sabbath that follows Christ's crucifixion was the weekly sabbath (Saturday) or the Passover sabbath, falling on the 15th of Nisan, which came that year on Thursday. Now the Bible does not leave us to speculate in regard to which sabbath is meant in this instance, for John tells us in so many words, in John 19: 14, that the day on which Jesus was tried and crucified was "the preparation of the Passover" (R. V.), that is, it was not the day before the weekly sabbath (Friday) but it was the day before the Passover sabbath, which came that year on Thursday. That is to say, the day on which Jesus Christ was crucified was Wednesday. John makes this clear as day.

The Gospel of John was written later than the other Gospels, and scholars have for a long time noticed that in various places there was an evident intention to correct false impressions that one might get from reading the other Gospels. One of these false impressions was that Jesus ate the Passover with his disciples at the regular time of the Passover. To correct this false impression John clearly states that he ate it the evening before, and that he himself died on the cross at the very moment the Passover lambs were being slain "between the two evenings" on the 14th of Nisan (Ex. 12: 6; Heb. and R. V. margin). God's real Paschal Lamb, Jesus, of whom all other paschal lambs offered through the centuries were only types, was therefore slain at the very time appointed of God."—Difficulties in the Bible, p. 102.

Note that only Luke and Paul mention the command to

The Lord's Supper

observe the eucharist as a symbol; John and Paul speak of the feet-washing; while Paul, Peter and Jude refer to the supper. If therefore the silence of one or more of the apostles concerning any ordinance invalidates it, they are all invalidated, but if it is enough to have the clear record of one or more of them then such record can be cited for each of these ordinances mentioned.

Note also that as Jesus gave the command to baptize into His spiritual body, the church (Eph. 1: 23; Gal. 3: 27), just as He was about to withdraw His earthly body, so now just as He is about to fulfill the old covenant types referring to His mediating work as the great High Priest, He institutes the symbols which represent the blessings of His continued spiritual presence. At the very hour that the paschal lamb was being slain for the Jewish Passover supper, "Christ our Passover" (1 Cor. 5: 7), "the lamb of God" (John 1: 36) was sacrificed for us.

The supper that Jesus ate with His disciples pointed, not to the exodus from Egypt and forward to the coming Messiah, but to the exodus from sin through the Savior already come and forward to His coming again in the fullness of His kingdom. Although the last supper Jesus ate with His disciples was not the Passover, it was a special meal of great importance, because at this time Jesus instituted the ordinance of feet-washing, the love-feast and eucharist. Here again we have a three-in-one symbol, the feet-washing taking the place of all the many ablutions of the law as a symbol of cleansing; the love-feast taking the place of the feasts as a symbol of fellowship; and the eucharist taking the place of the sacrifices as the symbol of our Savior, who saves us both by His death and by His life. We shall now study these three symbols separately.

THE LORD'S SUPPER.

	Authorized by	As a Memorial	As a Symbol	As a Type
Feet-washing	John 13: 1-17.	Of Jesus' ministry, John 13: 15.	Of cleansing for service, John 13: 8-10.	Of the wedding garment of righteousness, Matt. 22: 11; Rev. 19: 7-9; John 13: 8.
The Love-feast	John 13: 2; 1 Cor. 5: 8; 11: 17-34; Jude 12.	Of Jesus' love, John 13: 1, 34; Jude 12.	Of Christian love, John 13: 34; 1 Cor. 11: 34.	Of the marriage supper of Christ and the Church, Luke 22: 29, 30; Rev. 19: 7-9.
The Cup and Loaf	34; Jude 12. Luke 22: 19-22.	Of Jesus' death, 1 Cor. 11: 26.	Of union with Christ, 1 Cor. 10: 16.	Of the marriage of Christ and the Church, 1 Cor. 11: 26 with 1 Thess. 4: 16, 17; Luke 22: 18; Matt. 22: 2; Rev. 19: 7-9.

FEET-WASHING.

Feet-washing is observed as a symbol by all branches of the Brethren, by the Amish and Mennonites, by the "River" Brethren, the Nestorians, Armenians and some minor Baptist sects, by the Winebrennarians or Church of God, the Glassites or Sandemanians, the Waldensians, and in a perverted form by the Roman Catholic Church. It was formerly observed by many Methodist, United Brethren, Baptist and Disciple churches and by the Moravians and Jesuits. That an ordinance of such humiliating nature should ever be generally popular is not to be expected. Indeed, the very manner and record of its institution is such as to make it appeal, not to the worldly minded, or to those who seek only formal obedience, but to those who have the humble mind of Christ. Such ask, not, Is this popular? but, Is this right? That which Jesus blessed they are not willing to cast lightly aside. They have found in this humble rite one of the greatest of the means of grace, and in this experience find sufficient reason for literal obedience to Jesus' command, albeit the practice is sustained by other arguments as well.

Coming to the subject from an outside point of view, we find just three theories of the feet-washing recorded in John 13: 1-17:

I. That because the people wore sandals in that day and land, which they removed on entering the house, washing the feet at the door, this was done also by Jesus, who took the place of host or servant, to set an example to the disciples.

II. That because the disciples were quarreling about

rank, Jesus washed their feet to give them an object lesson in humility.

III. That Jesus instituted a symbol in connection with the love-feast and eucharist, to be perpetuated as a means of grace in the church.

Feet-washing as Performed and Commanded by Jesus in John 13: 1-17 Was Not the Customary Washing for Physical Cleansing.

The most common objection urged against feet-washing as an ordinance is that it was only the custom of hospitality which Jesus was enforcing by his example. Will this theory stand the test of the Bible record?

1. JESUS DID NOT TAKE THE PLACE OF THE ORDINARY HOST, BECAUSE IT WAS NOT THE CUSTOM OF THE HOST TO WASH THE FEET OF THE GUESTS. A study of Bible references to feet-washing will confirm this statement. In Gen. 18: 4 we read that Abraham said to the angels that he was entertaining, " Let now a little water be fetched, and wash your feet." When the angels came to the home of Lot he said, " Turn in now and wash your feet " (Gen. 19: 2). If these " saints " of the Old Testament did not even wash the feet of angels when acting as their host, it can scarcely be said to be the ordinary custom.

At the home of Laban the custom was the same, for when the servant of Abraham came he " gave water to wash his feet, and the feet of the men that were with him " (Gen. 24: 32). The custom was the same in the time of the judges, for we read in Judges 19: 21, " They washed their feet." The only reference in the Old Testament which allows even a suspicion of a different custom is the statement of Abigail in 1 Sam. 25: 41, " Behold thy handmaid is a servant to wash the feet of the servants of my Lord." This is simply an expression like that of Mark

1: 7, "Whose shoe latchet I am unworthy to unloose." It does not prove a custom. In the New Testament times the only reference we have is that of Luke 7: 44, from which we learn that Simon the Pharisee did not even furnish water for Jesus that He might wash His own feet. If Simon the prominent and scrupulous Pharisee, did not even furnish water, it is idle to maintain that it was the custom for the host to even wash the feet of the guests. The only reference to feet-washing being done by a host for his guests in the writings of the early church is in the second Clementine epistle on Virginity (ch. 3) in which the author calls himself a "holy man" and says that when pressed to stay with brethren "if there be a holy man with him we turn in and lodge, and that same brother will provide and prepare whatever is necessary for us; and he himself waits upon us, and he himself washes our feet for us, and anoints us with ointment."

Here the act is mentioned, not as the ordinary custom, but as the mark of the extraordinary love manifested by the holy brethren toward each other.

Mrs. Ghosn L. Howie of Schweir, Mt. Lebanon, Syria, is one of the best authorities on oriental customs. For years she has written "Oriental Lesson Lights" for *The Sunday School Times*. Writing on John 13 for this paper, April 11, 1908, she says:

Feet-washing of guests at a host's house is customary enough. But all that Abraham offered was that a little water be fetched (Gen. 18: 4), and that his guests (like Aaron and his sons later on) should themselves wash their feet. And no Oriental ever takes or understands Abigail's words literally when she said, "thy handmaid is a servant to wash the feet of the servants of my lord." (1 Sam. 25: 41). However, female slaves do wash the feet of their masters and those of their masters' guests. But it may be doubted whether a free man ever washed the feet of others in the ordinary course of Oriental life before or since the evening on which Jesus taught his matchless lesson of humility. On the Thursday before Easter Sunday, this act of Jesus is commemorated when a bishop washes the feet of twelve priests. This ceremony takes place in Jerusalem and in other parts of the East among Oriental Christians.

This distorted vestige of the original ordinance as practiced by the church, only further shows that the people among whom Jesus lived have not been able to reconcile His act with their ordinary customs.

The Jewish Encyclopedia says:

Among the Israelites it was the first duty of the host to give his guest water for his feet. To omit this was a sign of marked unfriendliness. It was also customary to wash the feet before meals and before going to bed.—Cf. Song of Solomon, 5: 3.

2. JESUS DID NOT TAKE THE PLACE OF A SERVANT. It was not a custom in Jesus' day for servants to wash the feet of guests, else why did not the servants of Simon the Pharisee wash the feet of Jesus when He was a guest at his house? Even if the rich did have slaves to perform this task, that proves nothing in this case, because the disciples were poor men, not accustomed to having servants; and furthermore Jesus did not encourage that sort of thing, for He taught equality among brethren. "One is your Master, even Christ, and all ye are brethren" (Matt. 23: 8, A. V.).

3. JESUS DID NOT TEACH THAT THE CUSTOMARY FEET-WASHING SHOULD BE DONE FOR ONE ANOTHER. This would have been to give the disciples a continual cause of dispute when together, as to who should be the one and who the other. If this had been the custom among them and they were now disputing about it, why had it not been settled long before this? Or why is there no record of any dispute about who should do it? They had washed feet hundreds of times together according to the custom, with-

out occasion for dispute, for the simple reason that it was the custom for each one to wash his own feet.

4. THIS WAS NOT A FEET-WASHING DUE TO A HOT, DUSTY JOURNEY, BECAUSE THIS WAS A TIME OF COLD. It was near the first of April and the account distinctly says that it was so cold that Peter warmed himself that night at a fire (John 18: 18). This proves little either way, but it at least weakens the assertion that they wore sandals instead of shoes at this time.

5. THIS FEET-WASHING WAS AT THE TABLE INSTEAD OF AT THE DOOR. If they did wash feet according to the custom, then according to custom it was done at the door before entering the house. That the customary ablutions had been attended to is indicated by the words of Jesus, " He that is bathed needeth not save to wash his feet, but is clean every whit" (v. 10). If Peter and the rest had bathed, it is probable that they had also washed their feet, and were rightly astonished when Jesus began to wash them at the table.

6. THIS WASHING WAS NOT THE CUSTOMARY WASHING FOR CLEANSING, BECAUSE THAT IS NOT THE REASON ASSIGNED FOR IT. In the introduction of it, John gives the thought Jesus had in mind when He began. Knowing that His hour was come, and that Judas had already arranged to betray Him; and that therefore as the old covenant types were fulfilled, it was time to institute the ordinances of the new; and knowing that He had authority to do so, for, " he was come from God and went to God," and " the Father had given all things into his hands,"—with this in mind He laid aside His garments and began the service. Why know all this to perform an ordinary everyday duty? The account says not a word, gives not a hint, of this being a washing for physical cleansing, but all the way through it is given a spiritual significance.

7. THAT THE WASHING WAS NOT THE CUSTOMARY PHYSICAL CLEANSING IS SHOWN BY THE FACT THAT THE DISCIPLES DID NOT UNDERSTAND IT. Jesus did not expect them to understand it, for He says, "What I do thou knowest not now, but thou shalt know hereafter" (v. 7). If it was the ordinary, everyday washing, it would not have required a special explanation. It was something new. Moreover, if the disciples had had the customary washing in mind, all that Jesus said as He proceeded would make greater confusion. "If I wash thee not thou hast no part with me," "Ye are clean, but not all,"—such references to a spiritual import cannot be harmonized with the customary physical cleansing.

8. THIS WAS NOT THE CUSTOMARY PHYSICAL CLEANSING BECAUSE JESUS MADE IT ESSENTIAL TO SALVATION. He said to Peter, "If I wash thee not thou hast no part with me" (v. 8). No part where? Not in this world, for Jesus was about to leave it. He must have meant in the coming kingdom. It is inconceivable that He who defended His disciples when they ate with unwashed hands (Matt. 15: 1-20) should now exclude one of them from the kingdom because of unwashed feet. But if He meant this as a symbol of the cleansing of the heart, it is plain, for none shall enter the city of God but they who have been cleansed from sin (Rev. 22: 14, 15).

9. THAT THIS WAS NOT A PHYSICAL CLEANSING IS FURTHER PROVEN BY THE FACT THAT JUDAS REMAINED UNCLEAN IN SPITE OF IT. The account reads, "For he knew who should betray him, therefore said he, Ye are not all clean" (v. 11). The thought of the betrayal was in the heart, and there the customary cleansing did not reach. Physically, Judas was as clean as the rest, but yet he was unclean, because the uncleanness which Jesus was now cleansing was spiritual, and not physical. Irenaeus was

the pupil of Polycarp, who was the pupil of John, and therefore Irenaeus should have known whether this was just the customary washing or not. He says of it, " He who washed the feet of the disciples sanctified the entire body and rendered it clean."—*Against Heresies,* Bk. 4: 2; 2: 1. He plainly teaches a spiritual cleansing and His Word is more than many modern commentaries.

10. THAT THIS WAS NOT FEET-WASHING ACCORDING TO CUSTOM IS PROVEN BY THE FACT THAT JESUS COMMANDS IT ONLY TO THE DISCIPLES (v. 14). If He had been merely enforcing a custom of hospitality, why should He so limit it? Would He contradict Himself? When He really was enforcing such duties He said, " If ye salute your brethren only what do ye more than others? Do not even the Gentiles the same?" (Matt. 5: 47.)

Furthermore, the disciples were at this time about to be scattered, and in a few days were to be sent to the uttermost parts of the earth to preach the Gospel. Jesus knew this, and therefore would hardly give them a command which He knew they would have no occasion to obey. But if this were to be an ordinance in the churches they were to found, then there would be opportunity to perpetuate it with them.

Therefore, since in every way this washing differed from the custom, since it was not by the customary persons, at the customary time or place, nor with the customary purpose, or results, it is impossible to hold to the theory that the rite is explained by the ordinary custom.

II. This Feet-washing as Performed and Commanded by Jesus Was Not a Mere Object Lesson in Humility.

There are those who acknowledge the spiritual significance of this action of Jesus, but yet deny that it is an ordinance. They say that the disciples had been having a quarrel as to who should be the greatest and to settle it for all time Jesus gave them this object lesson.

The account of this quarrel is in Luke 22: 24-29 and reads as follows:

> And there arose also a contention among them, which of them was accounted to be greatest. And he said unto them, The kings of the Gentiles have lordship over them; and they that have authority over them are called Benefactors. But ye shall not be so: but he that is greater among you, let him become as the younger; and he that is chief, as he that doth serve. For which is greater, he that sitteth at meat, or he that serveth? is not he that sitteth at meat? but I am in the midst of you as he that serveth. But ye are they that have continued with me in my temptations; and I appoint unto you a kingdom, even as my Father appointed me, that ye may eat and drink at my table in my kingdom; and ye shall sit on thrones judging the twelve tribes of Israel.

Now the argument is that Jesus heard this quarrel, and settled it by the washing of feet as an object lesson in humility; that the washing was not for physical cleansing, but for spiritual instruction; not because there was no host or servant to do it, but because there was a quarrel. Suppose, for a moment, this was the case. Does it not still follow that, because Jesus was the perfect Teacher, it is a wise thing to use His methods of teaching? Have we not similar quarrels among disciples to-day? Is there not need of such an object lesson now? And if, because customs have changed, this object lesson be discarded, what shall be substituted in place of it? If something *agreeable* to pride be used instead, where will be the resulting benefit? And if something as effective in destroying pride as this be used, who that rejects this will accept that? Is it not a fact that those who reject this symbol put no other effective substitute in the place of it? If they say that to " wash one another's feet" means for us to "black one another's shoes," and then fail to "black one another's shoes," do they not discredit their own theory?

But the theory is discredited in other ways.

1. THE CONTENTION IS NOT WHAT JESUS HAD IN MIND WHEN HE INSTITUTED THE FEET-WASHING. If the dispute were already on and Jesus was about to settle it by an object lesson in washing feet, we should expect that thought to be in His mind as He would begin the service. We are told what He did have in mind. Is it the dispute? There is not a word, not even a hint of it. Instead, we are told that He had something entirely different in mind, viz.: (1) That His hour had come, Judas having already plotted the betrayal, and (2) that He had all authority because He came from God and went to God, and the Father had given all things into His hands. Having in mind, then, that the time had come to fulfill the things of the old covenant, and to institute the new "in his own blood," and that He had authority to do so, "he riseth from supper and laid aside his garments and poureth water in a basin and began to wash the disciples' feet."—John 13: 1-5.

If there was nothing said as to what Jesus had in mind when He began the service, we might *imagine* that He had in mind to settle a dispute by an object lesson, but when we are plainly told that He had something else in mind which excludes that theory, we must give it up. Why would Jesus need to have in mind that His hour was come to be delivered up, and that He had all authority from God, in order to teach a little object lesson? If He were about to institute ordinances for the new dispensation He would need to know just this, but not for a mere object lesson.

2. JESUS' OWN EXPLANATION OF THE FEET-WASHING HAS NO MENTION OF THE QUARREL. Would it not be absurd to go through such an elaborate object lesson for the pur-

pose of settling a contention and then *fail to make the application?* Did not Jesus tell the inquiring disciples, " What I do ye know not now, but ye shall know hereafter " (when explained), and then when explaining the act make no mention of any contention at all? How account for this if the contention was the one thing He had in mind? Not only does He *not* mention any uncleanness of heart caused by quarreling, but He *does* say that at this time yet all were clean, except Judas. Was Judas the only one quarreling? There is no evidence that he was in the contention at any time. No, the uncleanness was not because of *disputing* as to who should be the greatest, but as the record says, " He knew who should *betray* him, therefore said he, Ye are not all clean " (John 13: 11). Because Jesus did not explain His act with reference to any dispute, but does explain it in an entirely different way, we must give up the theory of the dispute being the cause of it.

3. THE CONTENTION WAS NOT ABOUT WHO SHOULD WASH FEET, BUT ABOUT WHO SHOULD BE THE GREATEST. It is said that the dispute was because none of the disciples were willing to take the place of a servant and wash the feet of the others, and therefore Jesus set the example and thus stopped their quarreling about it. But these were poor men, not accustomed to having their feet washed by servants, but to washing their own feet. Besides, it would be strange indeed that if they were accustomed to do it for one another they should have been together several years, and have gone through the customary feet-washing hundreds of times, without deciding before this who should do it! If there were no cause for the contention given, it would still be incredible that this was the cause, but fortunately we are expressly told that the contention was as to who should be the greatest (Luke 22: 24). This is precisely what it had been about in every case before

this. Matthew (Matt. 18: 1-7), and Mark (Mark 9: 33-35) and Luke (Luke 9: 46-48) record a similar dispute as to who should be the greatest, and Matthew (Matt. 20: 20-29) and Mark (Mark 10: 33-45) relate how James and John wanted to be one on the right hand and the other on the left, in His coming kingdom, and this precipitated a quarrel. In either case, as in this case at the last supper, the dispute was in reference to rank in the glorious coming kingdom, and had nothing to do with a little thing like the customary feet-washing in the present world.

4. THERE IS NO RECORD THAT THIS CONTENTION WAS SETTLED BY JESUS WASHING THE DISCIPLES' FEET. Luke is the only writer that mentions the quarrel, and, being inspired, we should expect him to have the account straight. But not only does he *not* give the feet-washing as the method of dealing with the dispute, but he *does* give a different method. He says that Jesus used the illustration of the Gentiles whose kings have lordship over them, contrasting that with the kingdom in which the greatest shall be as the least; and then comforted them after this hard saying with the assurance that they should reign with Him in His kingdom. Of course, when He said, " I am among you as he that serveth," they would remember how He washed their feet only a little while before this, but that does not connect the two incidents as the one being the cause of the other. The fact remains that *the only record of the feet-washing explains the cause and purpose of it without reference to the contention, and the only record of the contention explains the cause and method of dealing with it without reference to the feet-washing and the only way to connect the two is by the imagination.*

5. THAT THE CONTENTION HAD NOTHING TO DO WITH

THE FEET-WASHING IS FURTHER PROVEN BY THE FACT THAT THE SPIRITUAL CLEANSING SYMBOLIZED BY THE FEET-WASHING HAD NO REFERENCE TO THE QUARREL. If the dispute were already on and the disciples were sullenly waiting for the explanation of Jesus' strange action in washing their feet, why did He say, "Ye are clean, but not all, for he knew who should betray him, therefore said he, Ye are not all clean" (John 13: 11)? If the feet-washing was to settle the contention, then the reference to the cleansing should connect with the quarrel, but it does not.

6. THAT THE FEET-WASHING WAS NOT A MERE OBJECT LESSON IN HUMILITY IS FURTHER PROVEN BY THE FACT THAT IT WAS NOT PERFORMED AS AN OBJECT LESSON IN HUMILITY, BUT AS A SYMBOL OF CLEANSING. Jesus did not say to Peter, "If you do not learn to be humble you shall have no part with me," but He did say, "If I wash thee not thou hast no part with me."

7. THAT THE FEET-WASHING WAS NOT ON ACCOUNT OF THE CONTENTION IS FURTHER PROVEN BY THE FACT THAT JUDAS WAS PRESENT AT THE FEET-WASHING, BUT NOT AT THE CONTENTION. We know that he *was* present at the feet-washing, because, after it was over and they were eating, Jesus pointed him out as the betrayer (John 13: 21-30), and we know that he was *not* present at the contention, because Jesus said at this time to all the disciples present, "Ye are they that have continued with me in my temptations; and I appoint unto you a kingdom, even as my Father appointed unto me, that ye may eat and drink at my table in my kingdom; and ye shall sit on thrones judging the twelve tribes of Israel" (Luke 22: 28-30). These words could not apply to Judas, for Jesus had just said a little while before this (v. 22), "Woe to that man by whom the son of man is betrayed!" And moreover,

John says that Judas went out when he was pointed out as the betrayer. Thus Luke and John agree in their accounts.

8. THAT THE FEET-WASHING WAS NOT A MERE OBJECT LESSON IN HUMILITY IS FURTHER PROVEN BY THE FACT THAT THE ACT ITSELF IS TO BE PERPETUATED. Jesus said, "If I then, your Lord and Teacher, have washed your feet, ye also ought to wash one another's feet, for I have given you an example (symbol or type) that ye should do as I have done to you." Now we have already seen from ten arguments that this example of washing could not have been the customary cleansing from travel, and therefore it was a symbolic washing. To this the advocates of the object lesson theory agree. *But if it was a symbolic washing, then we have a symbolic washing to perpetuate, for Jesus commanded His example to be followed.* Advocates of the second theory must either fall back upon the first, already discarded, or give up their own. Jesus did not make the feet-washing an illustration of humility and then command the virtue alone to be imitated, but commanded the act itself to be perpetuated as a means of teaching the truth back of it.

9. THAT THE FEET-WASHING WAS NOT A MERE OBJECT LESSON, BUT WAS TO BE PERPETUATED IS FURTHER PROVEN BY PAUL'S REFERENCE TO IT IN 1 TIM. 5: 10. "If she have washed the saints' feet." A mere object lesson might be referred to later, but not repeated. This was repeated and preserved as a symbol in the church, and that without any reference to this quarrel. Proof that this passage in Timothy refers to the ordinance rather than the custom will be discussed more fully later.

10. A FINAL AND FATAL OBJECTION TO THIS "OBJECT LESSON" THEORY IS THE FACT THAT THE FEET-WASHING TOOK PLACE BEFORE THE CONTENTION. Note the order

of events for yourself. The feet-washing was *before* the supper was eaten, for we find the meal proceeding afterward (John 13: 12, 26); and the bread and cup came *after* the supper, both according to the Gospels and to Paul (1 Cor. 11: 25), but the only account of the *contention* puts it *after the bread and cup* (Luke 22: 19-24). How then could the contention be the cause of the feet-washing? "Oh," says one, "Luke puts the account at the wrong place." Pray where is the proof? Imagination is not proof. The only scripture that suggests a connection between the two events is the statement of Jesus in settling the dispute, "I am among you as one that serveth," and even this implies that the feet-washing had preceded rather than followed the contention. There is absolutely nothing which contradicts Luke's order of events, but there are many things to prove that he is right. All the arguments given above are in favor of the account as it is, and in addition may be mentioned the following:

(1) Luke, the writer of this account, is the learned physician, the one, and only one of the Gospel writers, who says that he had "traced the course of all things accurately from the first, to write in order" (Luke 1: 3).

(2) The account is in perfect harmony with the accounts of the previous disputes. Once before this the disciples had come with the question as to who should be the greatest in the coming kingdom (Matt. 18: 1; Mark 9: 33-35; Luke 9: 46-48) and then again the mother of James and John came seeking the chief place for them (Matt 20: 20-29; Mark 10: 35-45). Now the third time the question comes up. A careful comparison of these accounts reveals the fact that Luke is right in giving the desire for the chief place in the coming kingdom as the cause of the contention, rather than such a trivial matter as who should wash feet. He is also in perfect harmony with the

other writers, in stating that to settle the question Jesus announced that in the kingdom the greatest should be as the younger; and this links this contention with the others, rather than with the feet-washing, at which entirely different language was used.

(3) It should be specially noted that in placing the account of the contention where he does Luke is in perfect harmony with John, who wrote long after the other Gospel writers, and adds things which they omit, and therefore, if Luke had made a mistake John would have shown it in his account. Instead he comfirms Luke.

(4) Let it be noted further that in putting the contention during the conversation after the supper, Luke is in perfect harmony with the other writers in associating the revelation of Jesus, as to His coming death and triumph and return, with the discussion. This had been the immediate occasion each time before (See references above), and now again at this last supper Jesus had given the memorials of His body and blood. He had revealed His betrayer (Compare Matt. 26: 26-29; Mark 14: 18-21; Luke 22: 21-23 and John 13: 18-30) and Judas had gone out. The disciples were sorrowful because of the statement that one of them should betray Him, and Jesus was comforting them by telling them more of His return (Matt. 26: 29; Mark 14: 25) and the mansions He was going to prepare for them. This naturally brought up the old question of preëminence, and Jesus rebuked it as He had done before by reminding them that in the kingdom the greatest is he who serves most. Luke puts the dispute exactly where John makes room for it, and John puts the feet-washing just where it belongs, and there is not one scripture that requires any change in the order.

(5) *The harmony of the Gospel accounts requires this order.*

The following order of events is in harmony with all four accounts:

1. Statement of authority and institution of ordinances.
    (1) Feet-washing, John 13: 1-17.
    (2) Love-feast, Matt. 26: 26; Mark 15: 22; Luke 22: 14; John 13: 18, 26.
    (3) The eucharist, Matt. 26: 26-29; Mark 14: 22-25; Luke 22: 14-20.
2. Revelation of the betrayer, Matt 26: 21-25; Mark 14: 18-21; Luke 22: 21-23; John 13: 18-30.
3. The dispute as to who should be greatest (Luke 22: 24-30) and the final discourses of Jesus, John 13: 31-ch. 18.
4. Peter's warning, as they were leaving for the Mount of Olives and the hymn, Matt. 26: 30-35; Mark 14: 26-31; Luke 22: 31-38; John 13: 36-38.

Matthew and Mark do not say that the betrayer was revealed before the eucharist, although they *speak* of it first. Likewise, John records the final discourse and prayer of Jesus without making it clear whether it was in the upper room or on the way to Olivet, or after arriving there, but neither of these points affects the order of the feet-washing and the contention. On the other hand, to drag the account of the contention out of its place and put it before the feet-washing makes absurd John's introduction to the feet-washing, denies Luke's cause of contention and substitutes another, denies his account of the method of settling the contention and substitutes another, goes contrary to the explanation Jesus gave of the feet-washing, and makes Judas present when Jesus promised to all present, "ye shall sit with me on thrones," thus contradicting John's statement that he had gone out before this last discourse. It would indeed have been a splendid object lesson to the contending disciples, and because of this it is easy to imagine that it was only that, but when we leave the imagination and follow the record, we find that the theory is wholly untenable and must be given up.

The only remaining explanation is that Jesus here instituted a sacred symbol as an ordinance of the church. Let us now consider it as such.

III. Jesus Instituted Feet-washing as an Ordinance.

1. THIS FEET-WASHING WAS THE FULFILLMENT OF A TYPE.

It was a symbolic cleansing preparatory to the communion service, foreshadowed by the washing of the feet of the priests at the laver in the tabernacle service.

Do you object to the thought of going to the law for obligation to keep a rite under the Gospel? We pray you, hear the evidence. Do you believe God's Word when it says that the things recorded of God's people under the old covenant "happened unto them by way of example (Greek, *typos,* type), and are written for our admonition" (1 Cor. 10: 10, 11)? Do you believe that the Gospel means what it says when it calls the things of the tabernacle worship "copies" (Heb. 9: 23) and "shadows" (Heb. 10: 1) and a "figure" for the time present (Heb. 9: 9)? But, if they were, then they pointed forward to their antitypes. Do you say we must not look for any antitypes of these things? Then you go against the Gospel which makes the antitypes more real than the types, for it says the types were but "*shadows* of good things to come" and gives this as the very reason why Moses was so strictly commanded to make "everything according to the pattern" showed him on the mount (Heb. 8: 5).

Now under the old covenant the priests (whose place believers now take) when they came to the service of communion with God, symbolized by the rites of the tabernacle, were obliged first to perform a symbolic cleansing by washing their hands and feet at the laver which stood before the door of the tabernacle (Ex. 30: 19-21). The prophet takes up the vital truth thus symbolized, and declares, "cleanse yourselves ye that bear the vessels of Jehovah" (Isa. 52: 11). Indeed, so important was this preparatory cleansing that death was the penalty of neglect (Ex. 30: 19-21), as it was also the penalty for the alteration of these copies which were to preserve the truths unchanged for a future age (Lev. 10: 1-3). Is it a little thing for us to alter or neglect them in this age of greater light?

Where is the laver in the popular churches of to-day? They have the priesthood of believers, and reject the Roman Catholic apostasy which puts a priesthood between believers and their Lord; they have the altar of incense (prayer); they have the golden candlestick (the Holy Spirit); they have the pot of manna, the bread from heaven (John 6: 31-34), in the eucharistic emblems; but they lack the laver and preparatory cleansing. Why? Is it less important that our hearts be cleansed when now we commune with God than it was then? Did Jesus make it less important when He said, "If I wash thee not thou hast no part with me" (John 13: 8)? If He made the feet-washing an essential preparation for communion, shall we toss it aside as nothing? Others may, but we would tremble to do so. The cleansing of God's servants, the priests, must have its antitype; Jesus puts it right where it belongs, and there we leave it lest we die.

2. THAT THE FEET-WASHING INSTITUTED BY JESUS WAS

Feet-washing

MEANT FOR A SACRED SYMBOL IS INDICATED BY THE MANNER OF INSTITUTING IT.

When some one attempts to change divine institutions or introduce new ordinances, what is the first question we ask? Is it not just what the Jews of old asked, " By what authority doest thou these things? " That was the question put to John when he came baptizing (John 1: 25), and to Jesus when He set things in order in the temple (John 2: 18, 19). And in each case there was a sign of authority. John had the sign of the dove, and Jesus gave the sign of His resurrection.

Now when He was about to institute the rite of Christian *baptism,* Jesus announced His authority to do so. He said "All authority is given unto me in heaven and on earth. Go ye therefore and make disciples of all the nations, baptizing them into the name of the Father and of the Son and of the Holy Spirit" (Matt. 28: 18, 19). Since it was death to trifle with God's types and ordinances without authority, it was right to announce such authority when instituting the new in place of the old. Should we not therefore expect the announcement of such authority when Jesus was about to institute the ordinances of communion? Indeed we do find it. But where? Just before the bread and cup? Not at all. Before the supper, but *after* the feet-washing? Not at all. We find it just *before* the institution of feet-washing.

Jesus, knowing that the Father had given all things into his hands, and that he came forth from God and goeth unto God, riseth from supper, and layeth aside his garments; and he took a towel and girded himself. Then he poureth water into a basin, and began to wash the disciples' feet.—John 13: 3, 4, 5.

If feet-washing was not intended to be an ordinance along with the supper and communion, why was this announcement of authority just before it? There is no adequate explanation of this declaration of authority and love and imminent departure, save that Jesus was about to institute the symbols for the church before He should be betrayed and crucified. The next afternoon He was to die at the very hour that the paschal lambs were being slain, thus bringing type and antitype together, and now He merges the types of the tabernacle into the symbols of the church, and makes them types of the spiritual realities in the age to come. Consider that Jesus included feet-washing with the other symbols, and this introduction fits in its place perfectly. We leave it there.

When God delivered to Israel the laws of the old covenant (the ten commandments, Heb. 9: 4) the people were commanded to sanctify themselves three days and wash their garments, and then were forbidden on pain of death to touch the mount (Ex. 19). Is not this a likeness of the cleansing Jesus instituted preparatory to the communion of which He said, " This cup is the new covenant in my blood " (Luke 22: 20)?

Likewise, whenever sacrifices were offered as symbols of atonement by blood, they were preceded by washings as symbols of cleansing. Is it strange then that symbols of the atonement of the new covenant, made in the blood of Jesus, should be preceded by a symbolic cleansing? He who said, "All things must be fulfilled, which are written in the law of Moses, and the prophets, and the psalms, concerning me " (Luke 24: 44) gave the ordinances in order, and we do well to receive them in order.

3. THAT FEET-WASHING IS A SYMBOL IS FURTHER INDICATED BY THE FACT THAT JESUS EXPRESSLY CALLED IT THAT WHEN HE COMMANDED AND EXPLAINED IT.

When He began to wash their feet and they in their astonishment objected, He said, " What I do ye know not now, but ye shall understand hereafter." Then when He came to explain He said, " I have given you "—what?—a "lesson in humility"? or "an object lesson"? He never said that. He said, "I have given you a SYMBOL." (John 13: 15.) "Hold on," you say, "the word is 'example'." It is so translated, but the Greek word in the original is *hupodeigma* which means primarily a symbol or sign. *Vincent's Word Studies* says it corresponds to our word "type." *Liddel and Scott* define it, "sign, token, mark." Why, then, did the translators use the word "example"? Because that is a *secondary* meaning of the word which they thought proper to use, because, evidently, they did not apprehend the sacramental character of the rite. It is the same word that is used in Heb. 8: 5 and translated "pattern." "See," said God to Moses, "that thou make all things according to the *pattern* that I showed thee." Now when Jesus says, "I have given you a *pattern*" (using the same word), do we dare to trifle with it any more than Moses did with the pattern given to him? Read Heb. 10: 28, 29:

A man that hath set at nought Moses' law dieth without compassion on the word of two or three witnesses: Of how much sorer punishment, think ye, shall he be judged worthy, who hath trodden under foot the Son of God?

This same word is used in Heb. 9: 23, "It was necessary therefore that the COPIES (hupodeigmata) of the things in the heavens should be cleansed with these; but the heavenly things themselves with better sacrifices than these." The "better sacrifices," the writer goes on to explain, is the atonement of Christ, whose blood was shed once for all, and is applied, not to a temple of wood, but to the human temple, our hearts. These "copies" therefore, pointed forward to something better, just as the "copy" or "pattern" or "symbol" or "example" which Jesus gave in feet-washing points to the spiritual cleansing of the heart and the holiness of the kingdom to come. This is the word

that Jesus uses when He says, " I have given you a symbol."
Let no man then say that it was only an example in hospitality, or an object lesson. The very sentence in which the word is found shows that it means more than an example of character. Jesus did not say, " I have given you an example that you should *be* as I have been " (humble), but he *did* say, " *do* as I have *done.*" Character is not *doing* but *being,* but this command is to *do*. It is not " be humble," but " wash feet." Of course the two go together, but Jesus is not here commanding to observe the spirit without the form, but to teach the spirit by means of the form. Therefore He uses a word which primarily refers to a form. He could not have used a better word to express the symbolic nature of the rite He instituted. Since, then, Jesus gave us a symbol to be observed as well as a virtue to be emulated, may we lay claim to the virtue while discarding the symbol? Jesus says, " If a man love me he will keep my commandments."

4. THAT FEET-WASHING IS A GOSPEL ORDINANCE IS SHOWN BY THE SPIRITUAL SIGNIFICANCE GIVEN TO IT BY THE LORD.

The customary feet-washing of Jesus' day had no special significance, save as a mark of hospitality, but this symbol which Jesus instituted was freighted with spiritual truth so vital that Jesus said to one of the leading apostles (Peter), " If I wash thee not thou hast no part with me." If it meant so much to Peter and the rest of the apostles it behooves us to learn what it means for us. After making the washing a matter of such vital importance we would scarcely expect Jesus to leave us in the dark concerning its meaning. Neither does He. The promise to Peter, " Thou shalt understand hereafter " (John 13: 7) was fulfilled (vs. 12-17). The ordinance is a memorial, a symbol and a type.

(1) *Feet-washing is a memorial of the pure and loving ministry of the Lord.*

"Know ye what I have done unto you?" said He. "Ye call me Teacher, and Lord; and ye say well, for so I am. If I then, the Lord and the Teacher, have washed your feet ye also ought to wash one another's feet. For I have given you an example (Gr. *Hupodeigma,* a symbol) that ye also should do as I have done to you . Verily, verily, I say unto you, A servant is not greater than his Lord; neither one that is sent greater than he that sent him" (vs. 12-16). There is, perhaps, no act in the ministry of Jesus that better expresses the very heart of it all than this washing of feet. The act was one unpleasant in itself, one which naturally no one would do for another, and yet one of real service. And it was performed voluntarily, gladly, by the Lord and Teacher, the Son of God, in the very face of disdain for that sort of service. To what else would the disciples look back with a greater sense of shame for their own pride and selfishness? What other act of Jesus would make a greater impression upon them, or be longer remembered? He had said before, "He that is greatest among you shall be your servant" (Matt. 23: 11), but they understood not the saying. He had said, "The son of man came not to be ministered unto, but to minister, and to give his life a ransom for many" (Mark 10: 45), but they still expected Him instead to reign in temporal glory. Now, in establishing this ordinance as a perpetual symbol for the church He gives the crowning example of His own spirit of humble service, His holy love and true glory. To be sure, the disciples so little understood it at the time that only a few minutes later they were disputing as to who should be the greatest in the kingdom, but after the resurrection when "their eyes were opened" (Luke 24: 45) and the Holy Spirit brought to their remembrance the words of the Lord (John 16: 14, 15) we find them following Jesus' example with wonderful fidelity. They all suffered many things for the sake of the Gospel, and Peter at his own request, when martyred, was crucified with his head downward because he did not feel worthy to die in the same manner as the Lord.

So deeply was the example of the humble ministry of Jesus impressed that we find in all the epistles continual allusions to it. Would Paul exhort the Philippians to service? He says:

In lowliness of mind each counting other better than himself; not looking each of you to his own things, but each of you also to the things of others. Have this mind in you which was also in Christ Jesus; who, existing in the form of God, counted not the being on an equality with God a thing to be grasped, but emptied himself, taking the form of a servant (Philpp. 2: 3-7).

Would Peter inspire to patient endurance in the Christian service? He says:

For hereunto were ye called: because Christ also suffered for you, leaving you an example, that ye should follow his steps (1 Pet. 2: 21).

And last of all, John, long after the others, confirms their exhortation, saying:

Hereby we know that we are in him: he that saith he abideth in him ought himself also to walk even as he walked (1 John 2: 6).

If there is any obligation expressed in the word "ought" in this passage, there is also obligation in the injunction of Jesus, "Ye ought also to wash one another's feet" (John 13: 14), for exactly the same word is used in both cases. In one instance it is used of an act, the washing of feet, and in the other of the spirit to be learned from the act; and the one is no more to be explained away than the other.

To many the literal observance of this ordinance is a matter for a smile or a jest or sigh of pity. Such are themselves to be pitied, for having eyes they see not and having ears they hear not, neither do they understand that in taking this humble form and lifting it from the common to the sacred, glorifying it by His own example and leaving it as a memorial of His own kingly life of service, Jesus gives to the church a symbol of the divine law of service which runs throughout the universe. It is one of the greatest and grandest of the laws of God. It is the law which leads the way to the very throne of God.

Scientists formerly wrote much of "The Struggle for Life" and "The Survival of the Fittest," but now they have learned to write of "The Struggle for the Life of Others" and "Making the Unfit Worthy to Survive." In Henry Drummond's *Ascent of Man* the chapter on "The Evolution of a Mother" is one of the most beautiful things in literature. He shows the working of the law of love in the mother instinct, but the mother's love is only a faint reflection of the love of God; and the human child is kept by its helplessness in the care of loving parents long after the animal child born at the same time is independent, because the human child must learn the multiform lessons of service which it needs as a citizen of a higher kingdom, preparing for citizenship in the kingdom of God. The fundamental law of progress is not a selfish fight for existence, but an unselfish law of service. Scientists call it "involution,"—the unfolding of the Divine in nature. Jesus referred to it when He said, "My Father worketh even until now and I work" (John 5: 17). Paul referred to it when he said, "It is God that worketh in you both to will and to do of his good pleasure" (Philpp. 2: 13). This increasing supremacy of the spiritual, this growing power of love in the world, is the working of the divine law of service. The lowest forms of life are individualistic, but the higher are social, and that means service. Among savages it is largely, "Every man for himself and the devil take the hindmost," but among Christians it is "Love one another as I have loved you" (John 13: 34).

The heaven to come is not a vast paradise filled with people, each seeking to satiate himself with pleasure, but it is a *city*. A CITY, what does that mean? It means complex relations. It means interdependence. It means service, as we read, "His servants shall do him service" (Rev. 22: 3). It means that service shall be mainly for others. In building homes and furnishing them, in securing food and clothing, each citizen in a city draws upon the labor of hundreds of others, and his own labor in turn is for others. All must work together or all must suffer together in consequence. But to work together means a yielding to this law of service. It means brotherhood. It means exactly what is taught by the example of Jesus in the ordinance of feet-washing which He instituted.

When we were in Tiflis, Russia, among the Mohammedans and Armenians, we asked the consul for Persia, a German, "Why do the Mohammedans and Armenians fight so much?" He replied, *Ach, sie sind Nachbars; das ist alles* (They are neighbors, that is all). These neighbors have not yet learned coöperation, the law of service. The disciples had not learned it yet when Jesus washed their feet. The world to-day has not learned it. Even the Christian world but partially perceives it, and a larger part of it rejects the very ordinance given to teach it. But it is a divine law, and it operates with increasing power from the lowest community of protozoans to the consummated city of God. It is inseparable from the holiness

Feet-washing

and love which inspire it and glorify it. It is a part of the expression of the divine nature, for "every one that loveth is begotten of God and knoweth God" (1 John 4: 7).

But it comes not by force or by law. It comes as the violets come when the sun kisses the valleys in the springtime. It comes as the image of the parents comes in the unfolding of the life of the child. It comes by the "law of imitation," which Professor Bryan, a leading authority in psychology, says is to the spiritual life what the law of heredity is to the natural life. Jesus taught it simply when He said, "Every one when he is perfected shall be as his teacher" (Luke 6: 40). He exemplified it perfectly when He stooped to wash the disciples' feet as an expression of that love wherewith "he loved them unto the end" (John 13: 1); and His followers simply conform to the same divine law when they follow His example. It is the simplest and sanest form of teaching. It is the bringing of the child into the life of the teacher in the most effective possible way. Who among those who scoff at feet-washing as an ordinance are really affected by the Gospel account of it? But who among those who properly observe it can fail to be transformed by it? When we act out this supreme example of the law of service, there enters into the life an ideal that is like the planting of a flower in the desert. And it comes with such power that it transforms the desert into a garden. It is the coming of the divine by incarnation into the human, the transforming of the common into the sacred. It is the making real of the spirit of Christ in these weak lives of ours. "Verily, verily, if ye know these things happy are ye if ye do them."

(2) *Feet-washing is also a symbol. It is a symbol of spiritual cleansing: first as a preparation for the communion service, and second, for the daily life.*

That which was in Jesus which caused the Father to

say, " This is my beloved Son in whom I am well pleased," Jesus wished to pass on to His disciples. He said in His prayer, " The glory which thou has given me I have given unto them; that they may be one, even as we are one, that the world may believe that thou hast sent me " (John 17: 22, 23). Feet-washing was therefore given, not merely as a memorial, but as a symbol, that the truth it represents may become real in the lives of all believers.

First. It is a symbol of cleansing preparatory to communion. In the service of the tabernacle only the high priest went into the holy of holies, and that only once a year. It was a solemn moment preceded by ceremonial cleansings on the part of the priests and the people (Lev. 16). This was the copy of our going into the holy of holies to commune with our Lord. " The bread which we break is it not a communion of the body of Christ? The cup of blessing which we bless is it not a communion of the blood of Christ?" (1 Cor. 10: 16.) It is a solemn moment when we enter into this union with our Lord. Shall we do it with uncleansed hearts and thus eat and drink judgment to ourselves? (1 Cor. 11: 29.) Nay, rather, let us be reminded by the solemn symbol of feet-washing, that the heart must be pure when we appear before God.

The Jewish Encyclopedia, in explaining the feet-washing at the laver before the tabernacle (Ex. 30: 17-20), says:

Just as no one is allowed to approach a king or prince without due preparation, which includes the washing of the hands and feet, so the Israelites, and especially the priests, are forbidden in their unclean condition to approach Jehovah, for he who comes defiled will surely die.

If the Jew with his imperfect knowledge of God must so cleanse himself before approaching God in worship, is it strange that Christians should be given also a symbolic cleansing at so sacred a season as that of communion?

If we count this preparatory cleansing of no consequence shall we not be guilty of the sin of Nadab and Abihu who put no difference between things sacred and profane (Lev. 10)? We have seen church members partake of the bread and cup, clothed in the height of fashion and giggling with frivolous irreverence. The rite of feet-washing would seldom allow such a spirit at the communion. It is a needful preparation.

Second. Feet-washing is a symbol of that cleansing which the Christian needs daily in his service of God. Jesus said when instituting the rite, "He that is bathed needeth not save to wash his feet, but is clean every whit, and ye are clean, but not all. For he knew who should betray him, therefore said he, Ye are not all clean." Almost all scholars agree that the first part of this sentence is a reference to baptism. Just as, according to the customs of the times, a person bathed in the bath house and then washed the feet on entering the house, because soiled on the way, so he that is baptized once for all and has been regenerated, needeth not save by this feet-washing to symbolize the cleansing from sins on the way from baptism to the heavenly home. The promise of this cleansing is clearly expressed in 1 John 1: 8, 9, "If we say that we have no sin we deceive ourselves and the truth is not in us. If we confess our sins he is faithful and righteous to forgive us our sins and to cleanse us from all unrighteousness."

Discussing the words of Jesus, "He that is bathed needeth not save to wash his feet," Jamieson, Fausset and Brown in their *Commentary,* say:

Of the two cleansings the one (baptism) points to that which takes place at the commencement of the Christian life, embracing complete absolution from sin as a guilty state. . . .

This cleansing is effected once for all and is never repeated. The other cleansing, described as that of "the feet" is such as one walking from the bath quite cleansed still needs, in consequence of his contact with the earth (Cf. Ex. 30: 18, 19). It is the daily cleansing we are taught to seek; when in the spirit of adoption we say, "Our Father who art in heaven—forgive us our debts"; And when burdened with the sense of manifold shortcomings, as what tender spirit of a Christian is not? is it not a relief to be permitted thus to wash our feet after a day's contact with the earth? This is not to call into question the completeness of our past justification. Our Lord, while graciously insisting on washing Peter's feet, refuses to extend the cleansing further, that the symbolical instruction intended to be conveyed might not be marred.

Thus far there is no trouble, for this explanation is almost universally accepted without controversy. It is when the symbol of cleansing (feet-washing) is perpetuated that there is a halt. But why? If, as the learned commentators agree, there is a reference to literal baptism in the words of Jesus "he that is bathed," then there is a reference to a literal rite also in the remainder of the sentence, "needeth not save to wash his feet." If the one is literal the other is literal, and if baptism is to be perpetuated, feet-washing is also to be perpetuated.

Perhaps some one, seeing that the authorities in accepting "bathed" as referring to baptism put themselves under obligation to observe feet-washing, will reject this explanation. But this will not do, for the authorities are here supported by the Word of God. Jesus uses the same word here as Paul uses in Titus 3: 5, "the washing of regeneration." This could not refer to an ordinary bath, for that is not a spiritual regeneration. Jesus must have referred to a spiritual cleansing in both cases, and because the spiritual regeneration represented by baptism is taught by the literal rite as a sacred ordinance, so the spiritual

Feet-washing

cleansing represented by the feet-washing is to be taught by the literal rite.

Again, Jesus said, "Ye are clean," yet He washed their feet. To wash something already clean is to perform a symbol, and this is exactly what Jesus said He did. "I have given you a symbol (translated "example"), that ye should do as I have done to you." Feet-washing is then the symbol of cleansing of the heart, and is connected by Jesus Himself with baptism as a necessary ordinance in the church. However, since baptism represents regeneration, it is received once for all by each believer, for we are born but once into the kingdom; but since feet-washing represents cleansing preparatory to each communion service, and from the sins of daily life, after being baptized, it is, like the eucharist itself, a symbol whose teaching is constantly needed, and which should therefore be often repeated.

Very frequently backsliders, on being "turned again" as Peter was (Luke 22: 32), request to be rebaptized because, as they say, "I have sinned since being a Christian, and that openly, and now in coming back I feel that I ought to do something to show my new start." To be sure they ought, and the Lord has provided for just this need. Baptism represents too much to be repeated, but feet-washing represents exactly what they wish. It is a sign of repentance and cleansing from sins committed after conversion, and a public pledge to renewed devotion to Christ in holy and loving service. The strongest possible testimony to this truth is borne by writers who have been taught to spiritualize this ordinance. Thus two leadings writers in the *Sunday School Times,* April 11, 1908, commenting on the statement, "He that is bathed needeth not save to wash his feet," bear witness to the need of this symbol in the church.

S. D. Gordon says:

The second thing Jesus is teaching indirectly is this: that slips and bad breaks, no matter how serious, can be forgiven. He who has been bathed might get his feet badly dirtied in returning home from the public bathhouse. The feet must then be washed, but their condition does not affect the fact that all the rest of the body is clean.

A man may make some terrible breaks in his loyalty to Jesus, but these do not destroy his real relation to Jesus. They must be forgiven before he can be in full touch again, but then they can be forgiven; the way back into fellowship is open. Peter's moral feet got badly messed up in the courtyard that same night, but he had learned his lesson, and came back to have them washed.

W. H. Ridgeway says:

He that is bathed needeth not save to wash his feet (v. 10). Did you ever go in swimming and in getting into your clothes get your feet all dirty? Well, you don't have to undress and jump in again just to wash the sand off your feet. This is what Jesus means. So if you are living the Christian life don't get discouraged if you make a little slip—just wash your feet. You don't need to be converted all over again. As some one has said, "Christ's act did not typify cleansing from the guilt of sin, but from the defilement of the daily walk (Rom. 6: 18-23).

So far so good. But if it is so important to preserve the truth back of the symbol, was not Jesus wise in commanding the symbol itself to be perpetuated as a means of teaching it? And will it not be wise for the church to-day to practice it just as He taught it?

In giving this symbol to the church, Jesus established the true Gospel doctrine of holiness, which includes both regeneration and growth in grace. It avoids on the one hand the error of claiming such complete and absolute goodness as to be incapable of sinning; and on the other hand it avoids the error of supposing such weakness of the flesh, in spite of the indwelling Spirit, as to be obliged to continue wilful sinning. These extremes, both of which are errors, have wrought great harm in the world, and between them the blessed Gospel doctrine of holiness has been brought into disrepute.

The true doctrine of holiness, as taught by the rite of feet-washing, includes three things: (1) the perfect ideal, the example of Jesus, (2) a recognition of human weakness, and therefore the need of repeated cleansing, and (3) the means of bringing the life up to the ideal, and therefore the means of grace are given, including feet-washing. First, there is the perfect ideal. That the Christian is to strive for no less a standard than perfection is clear from such passages as the following:

"Ye therefore shall be perfect, even as your heavenly Father is perfect" Matt. 5: 48. "Follow after sanctification without which no man shall see the Lord."—Heb. 12: 14. "Whosoever is begotten of God doeth no sin, because his seed abideth in him: and he cannot sin because he is begotten of God."—1 John 3: 9. This last passage is very strong, but it requires an explanation. The verb translated "doeth no sin" is in what is called the "imperfect" tense, which has no equivalent in English. It denotes continued or repeated action. This passage therefore means that the person who is born of God cannot go on sinning wilfully. It does not mean that he is henceforth infallible. Of the wilful sinner we read, "If we sin wilfully after that we have received the knowledge of the truth, there remaineth no more a sacrifice for sins" (Heb. 10: 26); but of the one who in human weakness comes short of the glory of God it is said, "These things write I unto you that ye may not sin. And if any man sin, we have an advocate with the Father, Jesus Christ the righteous" (1 John 2: 1). This is the glorious promise brought to remembrance in the rite of feet-washing. " He that saith he knoweth him ought himself also to walk, even as he walked " (1 John 2: 6), but if in walking " in his steps " we make missteps and soil our wedding garment (Rev. 19: 8), we may claim the promise, " If we confess our sins he is faithful and just to forgive us our sins and to cleanse us from all unrighteousness " (1 John 1: 9).

That the best of mortals do fall short of the absolute standard of perfection is certain from the testimonies of the Spirit-filled apostles. Paul says, " Not that I have already attained, either am already perfect " (Philpp. 3: 12), and again, " For I know nothing against myself; yet am I not hereby justified " (1 Cor. 4: 4). James also says, " In many things we all stumble " (Jas. 3: 2). And, to settle the matter finally, Jesus said, " None is good save one, even God " (Mark 10: 18).

But though we may not possess absolute holiness, we may at least be perfect in will or desire, for that is under our own power. The sin that condemns is wilful sin. From that there is always a way of escape (1 Cor. 10: 13). Peter, after naming certain conditions, says, " If ye do these things ye shall never stumble " (2 Pet. 1: 10). Paul says, " Walk by the Spirit and ye shall not fulfill the lust of the flesh " (Gal. 5: 16). So then, as we go on our pilgrim journey, we will " press toward the mark of the prize of our high calling in Christ Jesus " (Philpp. 3: 13), and come often to " the living Rock " and to the " sincere milk of the Word, that we may grow thereby " (1 Pet. 2: 2), but lest we lose sight of our standard and the means of attaining to it, we will remind ourselves of our weakness and of Christ's help, by the ordinance of cleansing, and thus forgiven and strengthened, we may go on our way rejoicing.

(3) *Feet-washing is also a type. It is a type of the " wedding garment "* (Matt. 22: 11) *which is " the right-*

eousness of the saints" (Rev. 19: 8), *required at the coming "marriage supper of the Lamb."*

There are a number of scriptures which indicate this. First, there is the fact that as the laver at the tabernacle, at which the priests washed before ministering in the service of God, foreshadowed the priesthood of all believers (Heb. 9; 1 Pet. 2: 9), who must be spiritually cleansed before they can acceptably serve (Rom. 12: 1); so the feet-washing foreshadows the time when, as Jesus passed on to heaven itself (Heb. 9: 24), so we shall follow after, and enter into the service which is eternal and without sin (Rev. 22: 3, 5, 14).

Then, second, Jesus Himself revealed this typical significance when He instituted the rite. He said, "If I wash thee not thou hast no part with me." Where? In the place He was going to prepare (John 14: 3), and at the supper in the kingdom at which He would again sit down with them and serve (Luke 12: 37), and drink anew of the fruit of the vine (Luke 22: 18, 29; Mark 14: 25; Matt. 26: 29). This occasion is the "marriage supper of the Lamb" when the church, which is the bride, shall be united with Him, the Lord. True, believers are now said to be united with Christ, but that is in accord with eastern custom which counts the marriage from the engagement rather than from the formal union. The church is now the waiting bride, but the marriage supper in the kingdom is to come. We read that Christ "loved the church and gave himself up for it; that he might sanctify it, having cleansed it by the washing of water with the word, that he might present the church to himself a glorious church, not having spot or wrinkle or any such thing; but that it should be holy and without blemish" (Eph. 5: 24-27). Then the faithful church shall have prepared herself "as a bride adorned for her husband," and shall enter into the eternal union with Christ, of which we have only the preparation here. As the substance is more real than the shadow, so shall the joy of that time be more blessed than the hope of this. " Blessed are they that are called to the marriage supper of the Lamb " (Rev. 19: 9). No wonder John adds, " And he saith unto me, These are true words of God."

But in the parable of this marriage supper (Matt. 22: 1-13), Jesus says:

When the king came in to behold the guests, he saw there a man who had not on a wedding garment; and he saith unto him, Friend, how camest thou in hither not having a wedding garment? And he was speechless. Then the king said to the servants, Bind him hand and foot, and cast him out into the outer darkness; there shall be the weeping and the gnashing of teeth, For many are called, but few chosen.

Now, if we ask, What is this wedding garment which is so essential? We have the answer in Rev. 19: 8:

The marriage of the Lamb is come, and his wife hath made herself ready. And it was given unto her that she should array herself in fine linen, bright and pure: for the fine linen is the righteousness of the saints.

If we ask further, What is there in the church to represent, typically, this cleansing which clothes the bride with purity as with a garment of fine linen? We have the answer in the ordinance of feet-washing which stands for this very thing. It is a *memorial* of that quality in Jesus, a *symbol* of it in the church, which is His bride, and a *type* of the consummation of it in the kingdom of God. When Peter declined the feet-washing and Jesus said, " If 1 wash thee not thou hast no part with me " He was in perfect harmony with what He said about the wedding-garment, and with what the Revelator later was told to write about it. Jesus has gone to prepare a place, but He is coming again to receive His own to Himself. Happy then will they be who are ready; whose adorning is not that outward adorning which worldly prides prepares, but the "inward adorning of a meek and quiet spirit" (1 Pet. 3: 4); who "have washed their robes and made them white in the blood of the lamb" (Rev. 7: 13), for they "shall have a right to enter in by the gates into the city" (Rev. 22: 14).

5. THE OBLIGATION TO OBSERVE FEET-WASHING IS EXPRESSED IN THE STRONGEST POSSIBLE FORM.

It is sometimes said that because Jesus did not use the imperative mode He did not mean His words to be taken as a command. On the contrary He expresses a stronger form of obligation than the use of the simple imperative could express. It is stronger for several reasons.

(1) *The word "ought" is the strongest word to express binding obligation.* Jesus said, "If I then, the Lord and the Teacher, have washed your feet, ye ought also to wash one another's feet" (v. 14). Note that Jesus does not base the obligation upon the courtesy of custom, but upon His own example, which was not according to custom. He puts back of the word "ought" the authority of His own act, and this "knowing that the Father had given all things into His hands." He says, You *ought,* that is, you are indebted, are under binding obligation, to do this because I have instituted it by My example, backed by My authority to establish the church with its ordinances. The word ought implies a duty involved in the very nature of things, which needs no imperative command to make it more binding. For example, when God said, "Remember the sabbath day to keep it holy" that command was enough to make obedience obligatory without further explanation, but when Jesus said, "The sabbath was made for man" He taught that there is the further reason for keeping the Sabbath holy, in that it is essential to the welfare of the

race. So also when the apostle says that "men ought to love their wives," he grounds the obligation on a duty inherent in their relation, and that is stronger than an arbitrary command. Even so this command to wash one another's feet is grounded on the inherent value of Jesus' example and the consequent duty of imitating it.

(2) *This obligation is further enforced by the statement of a blessing for obedience and a penalty for disobedience.* "If ye know these things, blessed are ye if ye do them" (v. 17), but "If I wash thee not, thou hast no part with me." We do not say that all Christians who fail to observe this ordinance will be lost, for we believe that God will take into account their opportunities and training (Luke 12: 47, 48), but certainly, "If we sin wilfully, after that we have received a knowledge of the truth, there remaineth no more a sacrifice for sins" (Heb. 10: 26).

(3) *The obligation to observe this ordinance is further enforced by the example of Jesus,* who first washed the feet of the disciples and then said to them "do as I have done to you" (v. 15).

There is nothing lacking, therefore, which an ordinance should have. We have the command, the example, the penalty or blessing, and the spiritual significance. It is the most completely buttressed in these respects of all the ordinances of the church.

6. Feet-washing as a symbol was practiced by the apostolic church.

(1) *Paul enjoins it. In 1 Tim. 5: 10 he states certain conditions of being enrolled as a "widow" (an order of aged deaconesses in the church) and among them, "If she have washed the saints' feet."*

Those who discard feet-washing as an ordinance will say that this refers to the act of hospitality because it is mentioned in connection with such duties, but before accepting such an assertion it will be well to study the passage more carefully. Does the mention of feet-washing in connection with Christian duties preclude its being an ordinance? For an answer let us turn to 1 Cor. 5: 7, 8 and ask whether the connection of the supper with " sincerity and truth " discredits the ordinance. Let us also turn to Heb. 6: 2 and ask whether the mention of ordinances with principles there discredits the ordinances. Let us turn also to Matt. 23: 23 and ask whether the mention of the tithe with justice, judgment and mercy does away with the tithe as an institution. Jesus at least did not think so, for He immediately adds *" these ought ye to have done and not to have left the other undone."* It must be clear that if the mention of ordinances with other duties does not discredit the ordinances in other passages it does not in this.

On the other hand, we have here a command to wash the feet of others, while we have seen that the custom was for each person to wash his own feet. More than that, the rite was to be performed for " saints," that is, for church members only. Jesus never limited hospitality that way. More than that, this cannot be the mere duty of hospitality, because that duty had already been mentioned in the phrase before this (" if she have lodged strangers "). Lodging strangers would imply the furnishing of water for washing their feet as custom required, but this phrase is not connected with strangers at all, but with " saints." It is coördinate with the other duties mentioned here, and therefore is not a repetition.

(2) *The evidence of early church writers sustains this interpretation.* In the second *Epistle on Virginity* attributed to *" Clement the disciple of Peter "* we read (ch. 3): " Nor do women wash our feet for us." Clement greatly denounces one who allowed that, saying: " Alas

for this effrontery and folly, which is without fear of God." Even though this passage may indicate that, among the heathen, females performed this service for men, it also shows that it was *not* the custom of the church to allow it. Paul especially would have been on his guard against this sort of reproach, because he was a "Hebrew of the Hebrews" (Philpp. 3: 5), among whom, according to the *Talmud,* it was part of the sacred duties of the wife to "prepare her husband's drink and bed and wash his face and feet" (*Talmud, Ket,* 61 a). Hence for a Jew to allow another woman to take the place of the wife in this respect would have been a cause of reproach to both. Would Paul command as a duty so important as to be a condition of enrollment as a widow, something which the conscience of his converts (Clement was one, Philpp. 4: 3) rejected as grossly improper? In other words, if it caused scandal for Christian men to allow women to wash their feet as an act of hospitality, it is scarcely credible that that is the thing that Paul commanded that women especially consecrated should do. Did he not command the church, " Give no occasion of stumbling, either to the Jews or Greeks or to the church of God " (1 Cor. 10: 32)? Did he not say of himself, "We bear all things that we may cause no hindrance to the Gospel of Christ" (1 Cor. 9: 12)? Would Paul command in others what he at such great sacrifice avoided himself? Nay, finally, does he not, in introducing this very statement concerning the washing of the saints' feet, make it impossible to consider it the custom which was a mark of heathen effeminacy in the eyes of the church? He says in verse seven, "These things command that they MAY BE WITHOUT REPROACH," and then he goes on to name the essential conditions in being enrolled as a " widow," or supported servant of the church, and among them puts the condition of having washed the saints' feet, a thing of reproach if it referred to the custom of hospitality, but perfectly proper if it referred to the ordinance preparatory to the communion service, the beautiful symbol in which the men served the men and the women the women.

That this is what he did mean is further proven by the statement of Tertullian (160 A. D.) to the effect that women only offered water for visiting saints to wash their own feet. In arguing against marrying unbelievers, he mentions things to which such an unbelieving husband would object, and among them "to offer water for the saints' feet." (*To his wife,* ch. 4.) Putting all these things together it seems morally certain that Paul refers to the symbol of feet-washing rather than the act of hospitality, and likely did so because it was the symbol of humble and holy service such as these widows were expected to perform, and which they would show their willingness to do by their observance of the ordinance.

The Pope of Rome is said to wear on his crown the words, "THE SERVANT OF SERVANTS," but on the brow of one who lives in luxury and pomp the words are an idle mockery. The sentiment, however, is good. Jesus said of Himself, "I am among you as one that serveth." When we are trained by this symbol to do the most menial service for one another, we will not refuse the other forms of service that may come to us.

7. THE RITE OF FEET-WASHING WAS OBSERVED BY THE EARLY CHURCH.

The practice of the post-apostolic church is of little authority as against the command of the Lord, because even at an early date weak human nature began to tamper with the ordinances, adding to or taking from, but as a side light on the Scriptures the practice of the church is of some value. To those who ask for historical proof, we would reply in a favorite phrase of Dr. Torrey, "It's in the Book; what are you going to do about it?" However, let us examine the historical evidence.

(1) *The Gospel of John itself is historical evidence, because it was written at Ephesus near the end of the first century.* The account which John gives implies the existence of the rite. How did it get to Ephesus, a Gentile city so far from Jerusalem, and remain there to the end of the century, if it was not taught by the apostles and practiced by the church? John's Gospel was written long after Paul's epistle to Timothy, hence Paul's injunction was from a source independent of John. He received his Gospel from the Lord Himself (Gal. 1: 12).

(2) *The first centuries after Christ.*

But other testimonies soon follow. *Irenaeus* (A. D. 130) (and remember that he was the disciple of Polycarp, who was the disciple of John) says:

Now in the last days, when the fullness of the time of liberty had arrived, the Word himself did by himself "Wash away the filth of the daughters of Zion" (Isa. 4: 4) when he washed the feet of the disciples with his own hands. For this is the end of the human race inheriting God; That as in the beginning, by means of our first (parents) we were all brought into bondage, by being made subject to death; so at last, by means of the New Man, all who from the beginning were his disciples, having been cleansed and washed from things pertaining to death, should come to the life of God. For he who **washed the feet of the disciples sanctified the entire body,** and rendered it clean.—Ad Heresies Bk. 4: 2; 2: 1.

To be sure, this reference does not clearly describe a church ordinance, but it does clearly show that Irenaeus knew that Jesus washed the disciples' feet as a symbol of cleansing from sins rather than to teach them humility, or to serve one another in physical cleansing according to a custom of the times, and this is the essential point in the contention. If feet-washing was neither of these things, then it must have been a symbol of cleansing to be so observed by the church. *Clement of Alexandria* (about 153 A. D.) may have a reference to this cleansing when in the *Stromata,* Book 4 ch. 22 he says:

> So it is said that we should go washed to sacrifices and prayers, clean and bright; and that this external adornment and purification are practiced for a sign.

The "sacrifices and prayers" referred to are the love-feasts of the early church, which are commonly spoken of in this way. For example, *The Teaching of the Apostles,* written in the days of the apostles (65-100 A. D.), in chapter 14 calls the Lord's supper a "sacrifice" and enjoins prayers in connection with it, models for which are given. See also Cyprian on *Works and Alms* ch. 15; Tertullian *Ad Faustus* 20: 20. For the Gospel idea of spiritual sacrifice connected with this service see Rom. 12: 1; Philpp. 2: 17: Heb. 13: 15; 1 Pet. 2: 5.

Here, then, we have a washing preparatory to the Lord's supper, and practiced, not for physical cleansing, but *"for a sign."* What can this be but the feet-washing with its symbolic meaning? But if so, then we have this rite in Egypt as well as in Asia Minor, within the century following its institution.

Tertullian (160 A. D.). This testimony of Clement is confirmed by the still clearer statement of Tertullian, who in the same country a little later in speaking of the utensils used in the church worship says:

> I must recognize Christ, both as he reclines on a couch, and when he presents a basin for the feet of his disciples, and when he pours water into it from a ewer, and when he is girt about with a linen towel—a garment specially sacred to Osiris. It is thus in general that I reply upon the point, admitting indeed that we use along with others these articles.—De Corona, ch. 8.

In his description of the love-feast in *Apology* ch. 39, Tertullian also speaks of *"manual ablutions"* in connection with it. These statements of Tertullian are in harmony with the belief that feet-washing was practiced in Tertullian's day, and he was only a century from the death of the apostles. Later, however, the rite became perverted, as most of the ordinances did, and we read of the washing of hands instead of the washing of feet. This was no doubt more congenial to human nature then as now.

(3) *Perversions of the rite.*

Cyril, Bishop of Jerusalem (315 A. D.) says:

Ye have seen the deacon bring water to the bishop or presbyters standing about the altar, to wash their hands. Did he give it to wash the filth of their bodies? By no means. For we do not go into the church with bodies defiled: but that washing is a symbol, that you ought to be pure from sin and transgression of the law.

Apostolic Constitutions (200-400 A. D.) prescribe:

Let one of the sub-deacons bring water to wash the hands of the priests, which is **a symbol of the purity** of those souls that are devoted to God.

Chrysostom (347 A. D.) also bears witness to this washing preparatory to communion, which was regarded as an essential. He says: "Thou wouldst not dare to touch the holy Sacrifice with unwashed hands, however pressing the necessity might be. Approach not then with an unwashed soul." The question naturally arises why feet-washing is not mentioned here if practiced, but it is met by the similar question, why do not the other writers mention this washing of hands which was considered so essential? Feet-washing may have ceased with the *agape* or love-feast, long before this, but absence of direct mention of it in such passages is no proof of it. Its essential idea, that of cleansing, was perpetuated for a time in this symbolic washing of hands, but even this was later discarded, even as the original true baptism has been discarded by many.

In some places also the rite of feet-washing became united with the ordinance of baptism, and we find *Ambrose* (340 A. D.) explaining it as the symbol of cleansing from hereditary sins. He says:

Peter was clean, but he must wash his feet, for he had sin by succession from the first man, when the serpent overthrew him and persuaded him to sin. His feet were therefore washed, that hereditary sins might be washed away, for our own sins are remitted through baptism. Observe at the same time that the mystery (of feet-washing) consists in the very office of humility, for Christ says, "If I, your Lord and Master, have washed your feet, ye ought also to wash one another's feet." For since the Author of salvation Himself redeemed us through His obedience, how much more ought we, His servants to offer the service of humility and obedience.—De Mysteries, ch. 6.

It must be remembered also that the feet-washing was a part of the love-feast in the early church, and that this feast itself came to be prohibited, first by the state because of suspicions and then by the church itself because of real abuses, and this tended to do away with feet-washing with it. When once it was lost it was not long until writers also lost the proper understanding of the scriptures referring to it, and hence do not always interpret them rightly.

Athanasius (296 A. D.) says:

The Bishop shall eat often with the priests in the church that he may see their behavior; whether they do eat in quietness and in the fear of God. And he shall stand there and serve them, and if they be weak he shall wash their feet with his own hands. And if he be not able to do this he shall cause the arch-priest or him that is after him to wash their feet. Suffer not the commandment of the Savior to depart from you, because for all these things shall ye be answerable, that they likewise may see the holiness of the Savior in you.—Canon 66.

But although there was confusion and misunderstanding as to the rite, yet it did not entirely die out. *Augustine* (354 A. D.), the great theologian of the church, commenting on John 13, says:

> Nor should the Christian think it beneath him to do what was done by Christ. For when the body is bent at the brother's feet, the feeling of such humility is either awakened in the heart itself, or is strengthened if already present. But apart from this moral understanding of this passage we remember that the way in which we commended to your attention the grandeur of this act of the Lord's was that in washing the feet of the disciples, who were already washed and clean, **the Lord instituted a sign** to the end that on account of the human feelings that occupy us on the earth, however far we may be advanced in righteousness, we might know that we are not exempt from sin. . . . And if he forgives us, whom we have nothing to forgive, how much more ought we, who are unable to live here without sin, to forgive one another. **For what else does the Lord apparently intimate in the profound significance of this sacramental sign** when he says, "For I have given you an example that ye should do as I have done to you."

In his *letter to Januarius* Augustine says:

> As to the feet-washing, since the Lord recommended this because of its being an example of that humility which he came to teach, as he himself afterward explained, the question has arisen, at what time it is best by literal performance of this work to give public instruction in the important duty which it illustrates, and this time (Lent) was suggested in order that the lesson taught by it might make a deeper and more serious impression. Many, however, have not accepted this as a custom lest it be thought to belong to the ordinance of baptism.

This objection was due to the fact that at that period most baptisms were performed just before this Easter feast.

The Synod of Toledo (694 A. D.) decided that the rite should be observed on Maundy Thursday (the Thursday before Easter), the day on which Christ observed it.

Feet-washing

This synod expelled from communion those who refused to participate in the feet-washing.

(4) *First opposition.* The first opposition recorded to feet-washing as an ordinance is a canon of the *Council of Elvira* A. D. 307, which forbids the practice. This was probably because abuses had crept in and destroyed the spiritual value of the ordinance. It will be remembered that on account of the decree of the Roman emperor the entire service had come to be held secretly at night, and this led to temptations and scandals.

Note, however, that this council was one of the earliest and that the practice of feet-washing as an ordinance must have been widely prevalent in order to cause a council to act upon it. But to become widely prevalent must have required a long time, especially for so humble a rite. It is scarcely conceivable that any leading teacher should have introduced it as an innovation without some of the writers of the period saying something about it. During the preceding century lived Cyprian the Bishop of Carthage, who was quick to resent an innovation; Eusebius, the church historian, who would have mentioned it if some heretic had introduced a new ordinance; Athanasins, the champion of orthodoxy; Clement of Alexandria, Hippolytus and others, whose writings remain as witnesses of the faith and customs of the time. The coming in of single immersion and of other innovations can be clearly traced. When did feet-washing as an ordinance originate if not with the Lord and the apostles? The very fact that so early a council tried to do away with it confirms the statements quoted from Clement, Irenaeus and Tertullian concerning it. In spite of the decision of the Council of Elvira, the church continued in places to observe feet-washing as an ordinance, and we find a later council, that of Toledo, 694 A. D., making it an essential to communion.

8. MANY MODERN WRITERS ACKNOWLEDGE THAT FEET-WASHING WAS AN ORDINANCE IN THE EARLY CHURCH.

Modern writers are not unanimous in their opinions of feet-washing, any more than on anything else, but many of them, while not practicing it, concede that it was observed as an ordinance in the early church and that there is scriptural authority for such observance.

Kitto, says:

Feet-washing became, as might be expected, part of the observances practiced in the early church. The real significance however was soon forgotten or overloaded by superstitious feelings or mere outward practices.—Biblical Encyclopedia.

McClintock and Strong say:

There was also a general celebration of the Lord's supper, at which the ceremony of washing of feet was connected. The origin of this practice is generally referred to the 7th century but Riddle (Christian Antiquity, p. 669) contends that it appears to have been of much earlier origin.

In the Greek church, feet-washing came even to be regarded as a sacrament. In the Catholic church, Bernard of Clairvaux strongly recommended it as a sacrament for the remission of daily sins. Yet it did not become a general practice in either church. The church of England at first carried out the letter of the command.—Biblical, Theological and Ecclesiastical Cyclopedia, Art. "Maundy Thursday."

Alford says:

This feet-washing represented to them, besides its lesson of humility and brotherly love, their daily need of cleansing from daily pollution, even after spiritual regeneration at the hands of their divine Master.—See 2 Cor. 7: 1; Jas. 1: 21; Acts 15: 8, 9; 2 Peter. 2: 22.—Greek Testament Commentary on John 13: 10.

The new *International Cyclopedia* says:

In memory and imitation of the example of Christ at the last supper (John 13) the earliest Christians were accustomed to regard foot-washing as an act of piety. By the end of the fourth century it was specially connected with the observance of the Thursday before Easter, when, at least in the churches of Africa, Gaul and Milan, it was the custom for the bishop to wash the feet of the newly baptized with solemn ritual observances. When infant baptism became the rule, foot-washing was dissociated from the administration of the sacrament; but as a liturgical custom observed on Maundy Thursday, it became more and more generally practiced.

Schaff says:

Besides baptism and the Lord's supper, mention is made in the apostolic literature of other sacred usages which come at least very near to sacraments and may therefore be designated as in a certain sense sacramental acts.

1. The washing of feet, as described in John 13: 4-16, seems to answer fully to the conception of a sacrament, combining all the three elements; an outward sign, the visible act and the express command, "I have given you an example that ye should do as I have done to you."—Apostolic Church, p. 583.

Next came Maundy Thursday, in commemoration of the Holy Supper, which on this day was observed in the evening—and was usually connected with a love-feast and also with feet-washing.—Church History Vol. 2, p. 402.

Jackson says:

Feet-washing became a ceremony in the primitive Christian church and continued through the middle ages. Bernard of Clairvaux even thought of making it a sacrament, but Luther denounced it. The early Jesuits adopted it.—Concise Dictionary and Gazetteer, p. 261.

Smith and Cheatham say:

The old Gallican ritual after baptism had feet-washing with the words, "While washing his feet thou shalt say, I wash thy feet as our Lord Jesus Christ did unto his disciples. So thou like to pilgrims and strangers wash that thou mayest have eternal life."—Dictionary of Christian Antiquities, Art. Baptism.

Godfried Arnold says:

Among the services or duties which were observed by the

first Christians, that of feet-washing was included.—History of Primitive Christians, bk. 3, ch. 2.

John Calvin says:

For the observation of Augustine, that some churches in his time rejected the custom of washing the saints' feet as a solemn imitation of Christ, lest the ceremony might be supposed to have any reference to baptizing, implies that there was no other kind of washing then practiced which bore any resemblance to baptism.—Institutes, vol. 3, p. 210.

The *Martyr's Mirror* (p. 320) quotes an ancient *Waldensic Confession of Faith* as follows:

We confess that feet-washing is an ordinance of Christ, which He Himself administered to His disciples, and recommended by example to the practice of believers.

Schmidt, professor of theology at Strassburg, says of the Albigenses:

They had adopted the custom of washing one another's feet in imitation of the example of the Savior, who had washed the feet of His disciples to give them a lesson of humility.—History of the Albigenses, p. 26.

Henry Ward Beecher in a sermon declared that he could not understand why feet-washing never was made an ordinance. He said:

It sinks deeper than the ordinance of the Lord's supper. It has a profounder grip upon man's nature, duty and destiny.

Lyman Abbott in writing about Henry Ward Beecher and this teaching said:

Is the Lord's Supper (the eucharist) commanded? The language is not one-half so explicit as that which accompanied the rite of feet-washing, which the church discarded because it ceased to be profitable.

Mrs. Catherine Booth says:

If we were to have any binding form in the new and spiritual

Feet-washing

kingdom, in which all forms find fulfillment, it seems to me that there is a great deal more ground for insisting on washing one another's feet, than for either of those already referred to, and in this we can see a great practical lesson on the human side, which our Lord actually laid down. How comes it, I wonder, that many of those who regard the former with such sanctimonious reverence can utterly, and without scruple set aside the latter? I fear that human pride and priestly assumption must be held largely responsible.—Popular Christianity.

Dr. J. M. Buckley, Editor of the *Christian Advocate,* the leading Methodist paper, one of the keenest men of the country, in an editorial related an interesting controversy he got into with a "foot-washer" whom he met on the train while snowbound in one of the New England States. He says that when it came to history his friend had not much to say, but when it came to Scripture he "planted his feet squarely on John 13 as sufficient proof to establish feet-washing as a church ordinance," and, says Dr. Buckley, "I COULD NOT DISLODGE HIM, AND NO ONE ELSE CAN WITHOUT RESORT TO TRADITION." Verily not. The same arguments that would dislodge feet-washing from the Gospel as a church ordinance, would dislodge all the other ordinances. However, will not Jesus say, "Why do ye transgress the commandment of God with your tradition?" (Matt. 15: 2.) There are thousands in other churches to-day who really believe in the ordinance of feet-washing and would be glad to practice it if their denomination did so. They do not obey the command because their churches give them no opportunity. There are yet other thousands who would readily believe if only their preachers would give them the Gospel teaching on the matter, and the preachers might also believe were they to investigate the subject in the seminaries. By investigation, evidence is accumulated rather than dissipated.

9. THERE ARE NO FATAL HISTORICAL OBJECTIONS TO FEET-WASHING.

All the historical objections that have been raised against feet-washing are of the inconclusive, negative type, being based on what history does not say rather than on what it does say. They embrace such questions as the following:

If feet-washing is a rite why is it so described and commanded in only one of the Gospels?

We answer by asking, why is baptism commanded in only one Gospel? And why is the eucharist only commanded in one Gospel? From Luke and John we would never guess that baptism was to be a rite in the church. From Matthew, Mark and John we would not know that the eucharist was to be continued. Why is this? The Holy Spirit honors the apostles' witness by counting one as sufficient. We ask no special favors for feet-washing, but let the rite be judged by the same tests that are applied to the other rites.

Again, if feet-washing is a rite why is it not so described in the apostolic letters? Again we answer by asking, Why is baptism only incidentally referred to in these letters? And why is the eucharist only incidentally mentioned? And why is the love-feast mentioned only in connection with abuses that the apostles were correcting? Nowhere do the apostles write with the purpose of instituting or describing these ordinances. Were it not for the special incidents which suggest the ordinances what would we know of them from the epistles? The reference to feet-washing in 1 Tim. 5: 10 is as clear as the reference to the eucharist in Acts 20: 7, which is considered sufficient authority for weekly communion by one large denomination. The apostles instituted churches in person, not by letter. The letters came afterward when the churches were organized and the rites established, and there was no occasion for more than incidental mention of them. In this way some of the rites escaped mention more than others.

If feet-washing was instituted as a rite, why is there not more and clearer mention of it by the early writers? For the same reason that there is not more explicit description of the other ordinances in the apostolic writings. There was no special occasion to mention it. Besides, inasmuch as customs differed in other things it is likely that this rite was not universal. Pride then as now would seek many excuses to do away with it. Again, we have seen that the apostles, and leaders immediately following them, were accustomed to speak of the entire service with one term. Thus "breaking of bread," "Lord's supper," "Lord's table" and "lovefeast" meant the same thing and included the entire service. Likewise among the fathers the terms "Thanksgiving," "festival," "eucharist," "agape," "passover," "festival" and "feast" were used at different times and by different writers to refer to the same "Lord's supper" which included the feast and eucharist with the preparatory rite of feet-washing. The quotations given from Clement, Irenaeus, Tertullian and Augustine show that the Fathers saw in the feet-washing a "sacramental sign."

Besides, we have seen that scarcely had the last of the apostles died before the Emperor Trajan forbade these feasts, suppressing them in some places and driving them into secret in others, so that the entire service was largely abandoned through no fault of the Lord or the apostles, and consequently many writers show seeming ignorance of the rite in these succeeding centuries. For example, Chrysostom, in his commentary discussing John 13, says nothing of feet-washing as a rite, but he prepared for the ministry in retirement in Syria, and later was located at Constantinople, the eastern capital, and hence was not in a position to know of the early rite in the church. On the other hand, Augustine, of the same period, lived in Africa, at Hippo, in touch with an apostolic church, and he mentions the rite as prevailing as an ordinance. In the same way, our posterity may read authors of to-day, and from some of them conclude that triune immersion, the love-feast and feet-washing were nonexistent in our day because not mentioned; whereas if they should happen to read others they would learn all about them. We could wish for more historical testimony on feet-washing, but since the Gospel itself is more clear and explicit on this rite than on any other, the loss is not so great. It is to the Lord Jesus and the Book that we must go for authority for all the ordinances of the church.

10. FEET-WASHING IS SUSTAINED AS AN ORDINANCE BY ITS GREAT PRACTICAL VALUE AS SUCH.

This statement will seem absurd to those who scoff at the ordinance; it will seem erroneous to honest persons who have never properly practiced the rite; but those who have obeyed the Savior's command will bear witness to the truth of His words, "If ye know these things blessed are ye if ye do them."

(1) *In the first place, the truth which enriches this symbol is one of the most important of the Gospel.* "If I wash thee not, thou hast no part with me," said the Savior. Jesus is the Head and the Church is the body, therefore it must be pure. Jesus is the Groom and the Church is the bride, therefore it must be pure. The members of the Church bear the name of Christ before the world, therefore they must be pure. Heaven is holy, therefore there shall not enter into it anything that defileth. What virtue does the virgin Church need to remember more than this, that she must be pure? Yet she dwells in the midst

of a sinful world and must of necessity be tempted by it. What rite, then, is needed more than this which enforces in such an impressive way the necessity of coming often to the Savior for the cleansing we may claim through Him?

(2) *Again, the rite is needed now as much as ever.* The world has not grown less proud since the days of Jesus, however much it may be better in other ways. Lift up your eyes and see, for behold, prides goes about the streets, and sits in public assemblies, and lodges in the homes of the people. Selfishness claims even the throne of the heart. If ever the church needed something as a test to keep out of it the unregenerate, and to help those in it to walk humbly before God, it needs it now. Feet-washing is such a rite. It does make the churches that properly practice it unpopular with those who are proud in heart. It does test those within the fold and help them to exemplify the virtues which it teaches.

(3) *It is effective now as then in perfecting the bond of Christian love.* Let the candid reader say if the denominations which practice the ordinances are not noted for their simplicity of life, their humility of character, their devotion to the Word of God and their love for one another. In them the rich and the poor, employer and employee, mingle on equality in a lowly service. Think you that the rich employer who stoops to wash the feet of his employee in the church, preparatory to the communion, will the next day grind down that same employee? Think you that the mistress who washes the feet of her servant will next day be haughty toward that servant? The rite is a leveler which is of vast utility to the church. If the Pharisees of old had practiced it, they would not have despised the common people as they did. If the rich and popular denominations of to-day would practice it they would have fewer hypocrites in them, and more power. If the reader

who has never practiced or witnessed the rite, will attend such a service and listen to the testimonies there given he will be convinced that the participants receive great blessing, which others miss.

(4) *Of course the rite may be perverted now as it was in the early days.* It may be kept in the letter only and not in the spirit. It may be observed without discerning the cleansing of the heart or the spirit of humble and loving service. It may bring condemnation instead of blessing. But all this does not in the least detract from the value of the ordinance when rightly observed. Let it be studied. Let its lessons be explained. Let them be meditated upon. Let the service be as nearly as possible in the spirit of the Master in that upper room in Jerusalem. Let it not be needlessly public. Let it be free from irreverence or petty factions. Let it be directed wholly toward the purpose for which Jesus instituted it and in every case His words will prove true, " IF YE KNOW THESE THINGS BLESSED ARE YE IF YE DO THEM."

TIME AND MANNER OF OBSERVANCE OF FEET-WASHING.

(1) *The Gospel gives no directions* as to the time of year or frequency of observance. *Augustine* says that the church observed it at the time Jesus did, that is, on the Thursday before Easter and in connection with the love-feast held at that time. *Clement of Alexandria,* and also *Tertullian,* mention it as observed in connection with the love-feast. It would seem proper to observe the rite in connection with the supper and eucharist, just as it was instituted. That it was before the supper is shown by the fact that they were yet eating when Jesus gave Judas the sop (John 13:26), but this was *after* the feet-washing. The expression " during supper," in v. 2, R. V., means during the entire course of the supper, including the preparation, and " riseth from supper " in v. 4 means from the table where they were already seated.

(2) *The only hint as to manner of observance* is in the words of Jesus, " Ye also ought to wash one another's feet." The essential idea is carried out when each person participates in the washing of another's feet. Of course, Christian propriety requires that men and women observe the rite separately. The rite should not be given more than its proper proportion of time in the Lord's supper.

(3) *Meditation and teaching* should accompany the observance of the rite. It is no time for argument directed to unbelievers. All the surroundings should be such as will contribute to the purpose of the occasion. The talk should impress the lesson of the symbol. If others than participants are present, they will be convinced of the value of the rite by seeing it properly observed, rather than by arguments accompanying a merely formal observance. The service should cause all to pray the prayer of the song,

A Clean Heart.

" One thing I of the Lord desire, for all my path hath miry been,
 Be it by water or by fire, O make me clean, O make me clean.
 If clearer vision thou impart, grateful and glad my soul shall be;
 But yet to have a purer heart is more to me, is more to me.

" Yea, only as this heart is clean may larger vision yet be mine,
 For, mirrored in its depths are seen the things divine, the things divine.
 I watch to shun the miry way, and stanch the springs of guilty thought,
 But, watch and struggle as I may, pure I am not, pure I am not.

" **So wash me Thou, without, within, or purge with fire if that must be,**
 No matter how, if only sin die out in me, die out in me."

THE LOVE-FEAST.

By the love-feast is meant the full evening meal which Jesus ate with the disciples, which was preceded by the feet-washing and followed by the eucharist, and which was perpetuated with these symbols in the apostolic church. The question is, Was this meal to be thus continued as a symbol and if so with what significance?

1. THE LOVE-FEAST MUST HAVE ITS PLACE AS AN ORDINANCE IN THE CHURCH AS THE ANTITYPE OF THE SHOWBREAD IN THE FIRST TABERNACLE.

By reference to a diagram of the tabernacle it will be seen that on the table of showbread there were twelve loaves, representing the twelve tribes of Israel (Lev. 24: 5-9), besides frankincense and utensils for both eating and drinking (Ex. 25: 29); that this bread was renewed every week and was eaten by the priests (Matt. 12: 4). In the new tabernacle, the church, all believers are priests (Rev. 1: 6) and have access to the "table of the Lord" (1 Cor. 10: 21) where they have communion together with Him.

The feast of the Passover also was connected with the seven-day feast of unleavened bread, as the eucharist is connected with the love-feast. The paschal lamb was a type of Christ (analagous to the eucharist) and the feast of unleavened bread corresponded to the love-feast. Paul so speaks of them when he says, "For our passover also hath been sacrificed, *even* Christ: wherefore let us keep the feast, not with old leaven, neither with the leaven of malice and wickedness, but with the unleavened bread of sincerity and truth" (1 Cor. 5: 7, 8). Here we have clear proof that

The Love-Feast

Jesus was the antitype of the Passover and clear authority for keeping the feast connected with the eucharist. The various other feasts of the old covenant also served to promote fellowship among God's people, which need is met in like manner by the love-feasts of the church.

2. THE LOVE-FEAST IS AN ORDINANCE BECAUSE IT IS INSEPARABLY CONNECTED WITH THE FEET-WASHING AND EUCHARIST IN ITS INSTITUTION.

In John 13: 1-3 we have the introduction to the institution of these ordinances in the statement that Jesus knew (1) that His hour was come to depart, and (2) that He was come from God and went to God, and (3) that all authority was given Him in heaven and on earth. Knowing this He proceeded to establish the ordinances which were to be observed in His church after He left. First He instituted feet-washing by precept and example, then the supper while He taught the disciples, and then instituted the eucharist and commanded its observance. It does not stand to reason that He would make the revelation as to His departure and authority, institute one ordinance, and then leave this work of instituting ordinances and eat just an ordinary meal, and later take up the matter again and institute another ordinance. The supper is between the two ordinances that are commanded, and is vitally connected with them. It must also have been commanded.

3. THE LOVE-FEAST IS VITALLY CONNECTED WITH FEET-WASHING AND THE EUCHARIST IN ITS SIGNIFICANCE. The eucharist represents communion with our Lord, but the love-feast represents fellowship with one another as brethren and sisters in Christ. If the eucharist inculcates the first of the great commandments, " Thou shalt love the Lord thy God," the love-feast exemplifies the second, which is like unto it, " Thou shalt love thy neighbor as thyself."

If love to one another is proof of being born again (1 John

4: 7), then love to God is proof of love to one another (1 John 5: 2), and the two cannot be separated. "If a man say, I love God, and hateth his brother, he is a liar" (1 John 4: 20). Neither can these symbols be separated without violence. They belong together, and the feet-washing, symbol of cleansing and humble service, is preparatory to both the others. They are united in their significance, and Jesus must have commanded the second as well as the first and third.

4. THE APOSTLES OBSERVED THE LOVE-FEAST AND TAUGHT THE CHURCHES TO OBSERVE IT. Jesus gave them no authority to originate ordinances and we have no evidence that they did. They simply carried out the things which Jesus first taught them (Matt. 28: 19). When, therefore, we find the apostles speaking of this love-feast as a regular, well-known, undisputed Christian institution, it is evidence that it had the authority of the Lord. Thus they refer to it.

First, *Paul speaks of it*. In 1 Cor. 5: 7 he says:

For our passover also hath been sacrificed, even Christ: wherefore **let us keep the feast,** not with old leaven, neither with the leaven of malice and wickedness, but with the unleavened bread of sincerity and truth.

A bit of bread and a sip of wine is not a "feast." Paul was not referring to the eucharist alone, but to the entire love-feast, and he bids the church to keep it. He calls it THE feast as if it was well known as one of the institutions given by the Lord.

That this "feast" which Paul exhorts the church to keep was not the Jewish Passover is shown by Paul's *contrasting* it with that institution. Can one contrast a thing with itself? Christ takes the place of the Jewish paschal lamb, and we partake of Him in the emblems of His flesh and blood, while the love-feast takes the place of the feast of unleavened bread. Leaven was a type of sin, because it represented fermentation and decay. Therefore Paul exhorts that instead of putting away leaven as the Jews were doing, the Christians should put away malice and wickedness and keep the Christian "feast" with pure hearts.

That he refers to the ordinance of the love-feast is made clear beyond cavil, by his reference to it in 1 Cor. 11: 17-34, where he corrects certain abuses which had crept into the church at Corinth. The passage reads:

(17) But in giving you this charge, I praise you not, that ye come together not for the better, but for the worse. (18) For first of all when ye come together in the church, I hear that divisions exist among you; and I partly believe it. (19) For there must be also factions among you, that they that are approved may be made manifest among you. (20) When therefore ye assemble yourselves together, it is not possible to eat the Lord's supper: (21) for in your eating each one taketh before other his own supper; and one is hungry and another is drunken. (22) What, have ye not houses to eat and to drink in? or despise ye the church of God, and put them to shame that have not? What shall I say to you? shall I praise you? In this I praise you not. (23) For I received of the Lord that which also I delivered unto you, that the Lord Jesus in the night in which he was betrayed took bread; (24) and when he had given thanks, he brake it and said, This is my body which is for you; this do in remembrance of me. (25) In like manner also the cup, after supper, saying, This cup is the new covenant in my blood: this do, as often as ye drink it, in remembrance of me. (26) For as often as ye eat the bread, and drink the cup, ye proclaim the Lord's death till he come. (27) Wherefore whosoever shall eat the bread and drink the cup of the Lord in an unworthy manner, shall be guilty of the body and blood of the Lord. (28) But let a man prove himself, and so let him eat of the bread, and drink of the cup. (29) For he that eateth and drinketh, eateth and drinketh judgment unto himself, if he discern not the body. (30) For this cause many among you are weak and sickly, and not a few sleep. (31) But if we discerned ourselves, we should not be judged. (32) But when we are judged, we are chastened

of the Lord, that we may not be condemned with the world. (33) Wherefore, my brethren, when ye come together to eat, wait one for another. (34) If any man is hungry, let him eat at home; that your coming together be not unto judgment. And the rest will I set in order whensoever I come.

Now note carefully:

(1) There is not one word against the *fact* of the observance of the supper, but only a correction of disorders connected with it. To correct merely the abuse of a thing is to endorse the thing itself.

(2) The term "Lord's supper" is introduced and used as a familiar term, implying a familiar, existing institution. Tertullian, born less than a century later, (160 A. D.) also so uses it with reference to the love-feast. (*Ad Uxorem* Book 1, ch. 1). It must have been known among all the churches, for Paul planted most of them.

(3) The church is urged to observe the supper, not for the gratification of appetite, but for the spiritual teaching, that is, *as a symbol* (vs. 20, 21, 22, 23, 24). "This is not to eat the Lord's supper," Paul said, because each one in greed ate privately instead of waiting to eat together as one body in Christ. Therefore he said, "If any hunger, let him eat at home." The supper in the church is not to satisfy hunger, but to teach brotherly love and equality, fellowship with one another and with the Lord. Since the supper was to symbolize truth rather than satisfy hunger, it must have been an ordinance.

(4) The supper was connected with the eucharistic emblems (vs. 23, 24, 25). This was precisely as Jesus instituted it, and therefore indicates the perpetuation of the entire service according to the pattern given in the upper room.

(5) The church was commanded to tarry one for another, so that being one body in the Lord, they might eat a com-

The Love-Feast

mon meal in fellowship (v. 33). This was to preserve the teaching of brotherly love and equality which the supper symbolizes, and which the Corinthian church was perverting.

This passage, therefore, shows clearly that the apostolic church perpetuated the meal which Jesus ate with His disciples, at which He washed their feet and gave them the emblems of His body and blood. To this many of the learned commentators agree, although they do not practice their belief. For example, *Lange,* one of the best known of modern commentators, in explaining this passage in 1 Cor. 11: 19 says:

By this the apostle designates neither the agapæ (Jude 12) the so-called church feasts; (as Romanists interpret who would thus elude the argument furnished by this passage against their sacrificial theory of the eucharist): nor yet the Holy Supper by itself (v. 23); but the combination of the two as it was to be found in the Christian Churches, according to the original apostolic custom, and in accordance with the first institution of the supper, which, as we know, followed upon a regular meal.

The Jewish Encyclopedia regards the Lord's supper as a full meal. It says:

In rabbinical literature reference is made to a similar feast, where "the table spread by the rich in front of their doors is likened to an altar which atones for the sins of the rich" (Targ. yer. ex. 40: 6). Every table at which portions were reserved for the poor is called the "table that is before the Lord" (Ezek. 4: 22; Ber. 55a; cf. ab. 3: 6): hence the term "Lord's Supper" (1 Cor. 11: 20) which originally did not refer to Jesus.—Art. Agape.

The early writers also understood Paul's rebuke in this chapter to refer to the abuse of the love-feast. See Cyprian (248 A. D.) *Instructor,* Book 2, ch. 1. Two other apostles speak of these same love-feasts and of the same disorders which Paul corrects, and thus we have the evidence of three apostles who confirm one another. *Peter* warns the church against the hypocrites in it, saying of them, " men that count it pleasure to revel in the daytime, spots and blemishes, revelling in their deceivings while they feast with you " (2 Pet. 2: 13). Note the words "*revelling*" and "*while they feast with you*" and compare them with those of Paul denouncing those who were drunken while others were hungry. Manifestly they refer to the same thing, although Paul calls it at one place a " feast " and at another " the Lord's supper " while Peter calls it the " love-feast." *Jude* also calls it the " love-feast " and says these same greedy church members (v. 12), "*These are spots in your love-feasts.*"

Since, then, the apostles regarded the love-feast as an institution of the Lord to be perpetuated and guarded against abuse, we may safely follow their example.

5. THE SCRIPTURES SHOW THAT THE LOVE-FEAST IS AN ORDINANCE, BECAUSE THE MEANING OF THE TERMS APPLIED TO THIS RITE INDICATE A FULL MEAL, RATHER THAN A SIP OF WINE AND A BITE OF BREAD.

(1) *It is called the Lord's supper.* John (John 13: 2) and Paul (1 Cor. 11: 20) refer to this sacrament as a "*supper*" using the Greek word *deipnos,* which regularly means a full evening meal. *Liddell and Scott's Greek Lexicon* defines the word as a " meal." *Smith's Dictionary of Antiquity* describes it as " the principal meal. Usually eaten rather late in the day, frequently not before sunset." Tertullian (160 A. D.) calls the feast " the Lord's supper " (*Ad Uxorem* ch. 4) and describes it as a full meal.

The same word, *deipnos,* when used elsewhere in the Gospel is always translated " feast " or " supper." Examples: Matt. 23: 6, " Love the uppermost rooms at feasts " (*deipnois*); (Luke 14: 12, " When thou makest a feast (*deipnon*) "; John 12: 2, " Made a feast (*deipnon*) and Martha served."

It is not necessary to give further examples because scholars agree that this is the meaning of the term. But if *deipnos* means a supper, a full meal, then what right have we to abridge the Lord's feast to a mere mouthful? That is as bad as condensing *baptizo,* to immerse, into a few drops of water. Let us be consistent. Not only does the term mean a supper, a full evening meal, but it is distinctly stated that it is not to be identified with the eucharistic emblems, for we read " as they were yet eating Jesus took bread and blessed it " &c. They had been eating during that long discourse. Paul describes the institution of the eucharist " after supper " (1 Cor. 11: 25). Moreover, it is not the bread and wine alone that are spoken of as sacred, but the supper is called " the Lord's supper " (1 Cor. 11: 20). The supper itself is an institution of the Lord as well as the emblems after it.

This is further proven by the fact that Paul refers to the service as " the Lord's *table* " (1 Cor. 10: 21). Why use a table if there was only the bread and wine passed about as in most modern churches? To find a scene that corresponds to the Gospel descriptions and the early church pictures we must go to where the love-feast is observed with the eucharist, sitting about a table. In the Scriptures the *eucharist* is referred to as the bread and cup, and is never called the Lord's supper. See 1 Cor. 10: 16.

(2) *Love*-FEAST. In Jude 12, we have the term *agape* or love-feast used. This is a term which, all scholars agree, referred to a real feast or full meal, which was not the eucharist, but a part of the same service. It is used scores of times by the early writers and always with the same meaning. The word Paul uses in 1 Cor. 5: 7 is *heortazomen,* which means, " let us keep the *feast,*" just as it is

translated. The word Peter uses in 2 Pet. 2: 13 is *suneuokoumenoi,* to *feast* with, just as it is translated. If the Lord's *feast* is to be simply a bit of bread and wine why did the Holy Spirit direct the use of words which mean a feast rather than words which mean a taste? If it means what it says, then "let us keep the *feast.*"

6. ANOTHER REASON FOR BELIEVING THAT THE LOVE-FEAST IS AN ORDINANCE IS FOUND IN ITS SPECIAL NAME—"LOVE-FEAST" (Greek *agape*).

Where did the name originate? Jude uses it (v. 12) in reference to the meal as if it were familiar to all his readers, and he was one of the apostles. Where did he get it? Jacobs, an Episcopalian, and author of *Ecclesiastical Polity of the New Testament,* says (p. 287):

"Agape," used over 100 times in the New Testament, did not exist in classical Greek, though the kindred agapao did. Neither of the Greek words eros and phileo were as appropriate for expressing the holy love to God and the disinterested love to man which was to hold so prominent a place in the Christian religion: **a new word therefore was employed,** which from the Latin caritos has been often translated "charity" in our English Bibles.

It is a pity that this new Greek word, which has no exact equivalent in English, was not retained with all the significance which Jesus gave it when He instituted the supper. There was far more reason for doing so than for retaining *baptize* untranslated.

But we have answered the question. Where did this term originate? Jesus taught it. Turn to John 13: 34 and read, "A new commandment I give unto you, that ye love one another; even as I have loved you, that ye also love one another." It is no wonder that Jacobs says that the classical Greek had no suitable word. Their love was something different. They knew not the holy love with which Jesus loved the disciples. Three times in this new commandment Jesus uses this root word *agapao*, and then the new word *agape* in the statement, "By this shall all men know that ye are my disciples if ye have love (*agape*) one to another." This holy love that Jesus taught to the disciples was to be the badge of their discipleship. Is there anything more important to be taught by the symbols? Vincent in *Word Studies of the New Testament*, says: "*This new commandment embodies the essential principles of the whole law.*"

After the resurrection, Jesus tested Peter to see if he had learned this lesson. He said (John 21: 15) "Simon, son of John, lovest thou me (*agapas me*) more than these?" Peter was too humble to use that word. It was too high and holy. He replied, "Thou knowest that I love thee" (*philo se*). A second time Jesus asked him, using the same word, and the second time Peter humbly kept to his first answer. The third time Jesus changed and used Peter's word, and Peter retained it in his answer. He had learned the lesson of the feet-washing at least, and was humble in the presence of the Master Whom he had denied. But also, he learned the meaning of *agape*, that *holy love* which the Master wished him to confess, and in his letter (1 Pet. 1: 22) he uses it in his exhortation, "Seeing ye have purified your souls in your obedience to the truth, unto unfeigned love of the brethren, *love (agapasate) one another with a pure heart fervently.*"

Over one hundred times the Gospel uses this word, this new word, taught by the Lord, and given to the feast which He instituted to inculcate the holy love which is to mark His disciples and bind them together, and to Him. Again we ask, Where did the name "love-feast" originate? And now we think it is easy to answer, The dear Lord Jesus taught it when He instituted the blessed *love*-feast, to be a feast as distinct in its character from the Jewish sacrificial feasts and the heathen drunken and licentious feasts, as the holy Christian love is higher than the love of the world. How holily should we "keep this feast" for it is "*the Lord's agape.*"

This evidence derived from the new name, *agape,* to the original institution of the love-feast as an ordinance, has not, to our knowledge, been used before, although it appeals to us with a great deal of force. It is therefore with delight that we may note that one of the most scholarly and valuable works of recent Christian literature, just fresh from the press, —*The Dictionary of Christ and the Gospels,* in an article on the Lord's supper, gives the following testimony:

> There can be no doubt that the common meals of the primitive Christians and the table fellowship which the Corinthian church abused, answer to the later agape. A new name was given to what was really a new thing, for there is nothing elsewhere like the spirit of love which called into existence and pervaded the common intercourse of brotherhood. The occasion for the origin of the name may be found in John 13: 16, though the technical term probably did not come into use till long after the brethren had been enjoying the reality.

The love-feast which the Lord instituted was so different from the social feasts of that day that a new name had to be coined to distinguish it from them, and it is so different from the social feasts of popular churches to-day that the name should be preserved. It is not the abbreviated sacrament of the eucharist, wrongly called the Lord's supper by many churches, nor is it akin to the ice cream festivals and oyster suppers which have usurped its place. It is a sacred meal because it represents and promotes the sacred love of God in the hearts of His people.

7. THE SYMBOLIC MEANING OF THE LOVE-FEAST, GIVEN TO IT BY THE SCRIPTURES, IS PROOF THAT IT WAS INTENDED TO BE PERPETUATED AS AN ORDINANCE.

The Love-Feast

If this were an ordinary meal eaten in an ordinary manner there would be no reason for treating it otherwise, but if it appears that Jesus first, and the apostles after Him, taught the churches to see in the love-feast a religious significance, we have good reason to believe that the feast was to be continued in order to teach and perpetuate the truths that are back of it. What then does the Gospel teach as to the religious significance of the love-feast?

(1) *The love-feast is a memorial of the love of Christ.* We know this, because in the introduction to the entire service in John 13: 1 special reference is made to this love of Jesus: "Having loved his own which were in the world, he loved them unto the end," and then when Jesus was teaching the disciples during the supper He gave special commandment to perpetuate this type of love: "A new commandment give I unto you, that ye love one another; *even as I have loved you*" (John 13: 34). The feast at which this commandment was given is a means of teaching and enforcing it. The love-feast, with this new name expressing this new type of love, which the world first saw in Jesus, is a standing memorial of Jesus' love. This explains why Paul exhorts the church to "tarry one for the other" in order that they may "eat the *Lord's* supper," that is, the supper which is a memorial of the Lord and His love which endured unto the end. It also explains why Peter and Jude denounce those hypocrites who spoiled the significance of the love-feast by their own revelings. Such selfishness was contrary to the spirit of the feast as a memorial of Jesus' love. These admonitions are as applicable to-day as ever. The world is prone to forget. It needs this memorial by which it may be frequently reminded of the love of God as it was manifested in Christ Jesus. There is nothing greater than this love, and nothing sweeter than the feast of love by which it is commemorated.

(2) *The love-feast is also a symbol—a symbol of the love which should characterize the followers of Jesus.*

It was as He was instituting this feast that He said: "By this shall all men know that ye are my disciples, if ye have love one toward another" (John 13: 35). As the feast commemorated the love of Jesus, so it teaches His disciples to manifest that same love one toward another. It was at the close of this feast that Jesus prayed, to the Father, "That the love wherewith thou lovest me may be in them, and I in them" (John 17: 26). Thus by example, by commandment and by prayer did Jesus give to this love-feast the significance which made it such a bond of love in the apostolic church, and which should make it of like blessing to-day.

This Christian love implies unity, equality and fellowship. It implies unity because the church assembled at this feast is "one body in Christ" (Rom. 12: 4, 5), and the body is a unity, made so by the common life which Jesus gives.

But speaking the truth in love, may grow up in all things into him, who is the head, even Christ; from whom all the body fitly framed and knit together through that which every joint supplieth, according to the working in due measure of each several part, maketh the increase of the body unto the building up itself in love (Eph. 4: 15, 16).

It implies equality because in this body of Christ all the members have equal honor.

But God tempered the body together, giving more abundant honor to the part which lacked; that there should be no schism in the body; but that the members should have the same care one for the other. And whether one member suffereth, all the members suffer with it; or one member is honored, all the members rejoice with it (1 Cor. 12: 24-26). There can be neither Jew nor Greek, there can be neither bond nor free, there can be no male and female; for ye are all one in Christ Jesus (Gal. 3: 28).

The Love-Feast

At the ordinary feasts the disciples had been prone to seek the chief places, but this feast was a corrective of that desire for preëminence. Jesus said, "One is your Teacher and all ye are brethren" (Matt. 23: 8). This equality was destroyed in the love-feast at Corinth by the eagerness of some who did not wait for the rest. Therefore Paul rebuked them, saying, "Each one eateth before other his own supper * * * Shall I praise you in this? I praise you not." He closes his rebuke by saying, "When ye come together to eat (that is, in future love-feasts) tarry one for the other" (1 Cor. 11: 33).

The breaking of bread together has in all ages and countries been a symbol or pledge of brotherly love. On this account the words of Jesus concerning Judas are very keen, "He that eateth bread with me hath lifted up his heel against me" (John 13: 18). This was a prophecy quoted from Psa. 41: 9, which shows that this same symbol was known in ancient times, but was given its special significance for the church because of the special type of love it teaches from the example of Jesus.

There are many Bible examples of eating together as a pledge of friendship or love.

Note the example of Melchizedek and Abraham (Gen. 14: 17, 18). Religious feasts were also common in connection with family events as marriages (Judges 14: 10), birthdays (Gen. 40: 20), meeting of friends (Gen. 24: 33), &c. Our own travels in the East brought many illustrations of this custom of eating together as a pledge of friendship. At one time in the Caucasus, after eating with several Mohammedan travelers, they put themselves out continually to show kindness and friendship.

Among the Jews of Jesus' day there was the sect of the Essenes, of which John the Baptist is thought to have been a member, which had common feasts very similar to the *agapae* of the Christians. They are mentioned by Josephus (B. J. 2: 8: 5), and Philo (*Quod Omnis Probus Liber*) and Hyppolytus (*Ref. Heres.* 9: 18-28).

Keating says:

Again and again Jesus uses the image of a supper to symbolize His kingdom. His miraculous feeding of the multitude, with the connected discourses, presents the same idea in a different form. Not only in connection with the Last Supper, but again and again He is represented as sitting at meat with His disciples—taking His place as head of the household, which consisted of His immediate followers. His fellowship with His disciples was, in a word, to a large extent a "table fellowship." Accordingly, after His resurrection He appears to have been recognized by His manner of breaking bread (Luke 24: 30, 31; John 21: 13). Accordingly we can understand that, even apart from the memorial of His passion instituted at the Last Supper, His followers would continue these meals with a conscious recollection of their relations with Him, and of the union constituted by Him. It might, further, under the new dispensation in some sense be a type and evidence of the kingdom of God (Luke 22: 30) as existing among them, and ruling and transforming their whole social life.—Agape and Eucharist, p. 37.

Probst says:

The religious devotion which sanctified the whole life of the early Christians was connected with these meals. Particularly the effect of the High Priestly prayer entered in, "Preserve them in thy name that they may be one."—Liturgie, p. 18.

(3) *The love-feast is also a type. It is a type of the coming marriage supper of the Lamb.*

Jesus referred to this event when, as He was instituting these ordinances, He said:

"I will not drink henceforth of the fruit of the vine until I drink it new in the kingdom of God" (Matt. 26: 29).

The time of the fulfillment of this prediction is described in Rev. 19: 7-9:

The Love-Feast

Let us rejoice and be exceeding glad, and let us give thanks unto him: for the marriage of the Lamb is come, and his wife hath made herself ready. And it was given unto her that she should array herself in fine linen, bright and pure: for the fine linen is the righteous acts of the saints. And he saith unto me, Write, Blessed are they that are bidden to the marriage supper of the Lamb.

Just as the table of showbread in the tabernacle, which represented the twelve tribes of Israel, and was partaken of only by the priests, was a type which pointed to this time when we all as priests (Rev. 1: 6) are permitted to sit " in the heavenly places in Christ Jesus " (Eph. 1: 3) and have " fellowship with the Father and with his Son Jesus Christ " (1 John 1: 3), so the love-feast is a type which points to the time when this foretaste of heavenly fellowship (Eph. 1: 14) shall give way to the fulness of the heavenly life. All the earthly gifts and possessions shall pass away. Faith itself shall become sight, hope shall become fruition, and love, the eternal, abiding love of God shall be an eternal feast. It is this love that shines through the love-feast as a memorial, a symbol and a type, and gives it an abiding glory. Jesus Himself refers in a number of places to this coming feast. He speaks of the time when the children of God shall gather from the east and from the west and shall sit down with Abraham and Isaac and Jacob in the kingdom of God (Matt. 8: 11). He speaks of the time when the faithful servants shall gather at that feast, and He, the Lord, shall make them to sit down and shall Himself once more gird Himself and serve them (Luke 12: 35-38). But in that marriage feast the " wedding-garment " is required, and " many are called, but few chosen " (Matt. 22: 1-14), and they that depend upon borrowed oil shall fail to enter in to the feast (Matt. 25: 1-13). One of the clearest references to the typical nature of the love-feast is the statement of Jesus when He instituted it. He said:

> Ye are they that have continued with me in my temptations; and I appoint unto you a kingdom, even as my Father appointed unto me, that ye may eat and drink at my table in my kingdom (Luke 22: 29, 30).

It is with confidence therefore, that, as we partake of the *agape* together, we may look forward to the time when we shall sit with Christ at the heavenly feast to which this one points, and reign with Him in His eternal kingdom.

Is it not strange that this ordinance, so rich in its significance, should be discarded by so many denominations? The early Christians regarded it so highly that when forbidden by the emperor to observe it they continued to celebrate it in secret, although in danger of death. Jesus regarded it so highly that He makes the love which it teaches the one badge of discipleship, by which the world may know that we are truly His. "By this shall all men know that ye are my disciples, if ye have love (*agape*) one toward another" (John 13: 35). John even says this love is proof of our love to God (1 John 4: 20, 21), which in turn is proof of being born of God (1 John 4: 7), "Beloved, let us love one another, for love is of God; and every one that loveth is begotten of God and knoweth God." Paul says that "love is the fulfillment of the law" (Rom. 13: 10), and that without it, though we be eloquent in testimony and rich in gifts, we are nothing (1 Cor. 13). It is the crowning virtue. It is the nature of God, for "God is love." Thank God for the "love-feast" of the new commandment, by which we are enriched in this love of God. There is no grander revelation of our possibilities than in the prayer of Jesus: "That the love wherewith thou lovest me may be in them and I in them" (1 John 17: 26).

The Love-Feast

8. HISTORICAL EVIDENCE PROVES THAT THE LOVE-FEAST WAS OBSERVED AS AN ORDINANCE BY THE EARLY CHURCH.

The observance of the love-feast can be clearly traced in history to the very time of its institution by Jesus and the apostles. The references to it in the writings of the apostolic period and the years immediately following are ample and decisive. They cannot be disputed, and they establish the fact that the Scripture references given above have been interpreted rightly as proving that the love-feast was instituted by our Lord as an ordinance.

(1) *References to the original love-feast.* *The Didache* (65 A. D. or soon after) in chapter nine gives a model for prayer before the meal, and in chapter ten for the prayer after eating. Chapter ten begins "*but after ye are filled, thus give thanks*"; &c. This passage clearly indicate a full meal and is testimony next in authority to the Scriptures, for it was written prior to some of the Scriptures. Chapter ten closes by saying, " But permit the prophets to make Thanksgiving (i. e., appoint a communion) as much as they desire." That a full meal is referred to here is proven by the further direction following, " Every prophet who *ordereth a meal* in the Spirit eateth not from it, except indeed he be a false prophet." The translator's note on this passage says: " Probably a love-feast commanded by the prophet in his peculiar utterance." Chapter 9 also, closes by saying: " Let no one *eat or drink of your Thanksgiving* (eucharist) but they who have been baptized." *Dr. Schaff,* the great church historian, says in discussing the *Didache,* that in order to understand it we must remember that the early writers were accustomed to speak of *the whole love-feast as a sacrifice or eucharist.*

Ignatius (69 A. D., martyred at Rome 110 A. D.) says:
Let that be deemed a proper eucharist which is administered by a bishop or some one whom he has entrusted to it. It is

not lawful without the bishop either to baptize or to present sacrifice (the eucharist) or to celebrate a love feast."—Ad. Smyrna, ch. 8.

In a letter to Dognetus which scholars generally concede to be genuine, Ignatius says of the Christians: "They have a common meal."

This testimony of Ignatius is very important, because he lived contemporaneous with the apostles and died only twelve years after John. Both the *Didache* and Ignatius, under the very supervision of the apostles, before whom they would not have dared to speak falsely, refer to the love-feast as a regular religious institution of the church. They refer to it without prejudice or controversy, and their words must be accepted as proof that the apostolic churches observed the feast as an ordinance of the Lord.

Pliny (111 A. D.). This testimony of the *Didache* and Ignatius is reëchoed by a pagan writer, the Roman governor and noted author, Pliny. Reporting his province to the emperor Trajan in A. D. 111 he says:

They (the Christians) had been wont to assemble on a stated day before dawn and recite responsively a hymn to Christ as to God and bind themselves with a religious vow, not to the commission of any crime, but against theft, robbery, adultery, breach of trust, or denial of a deposit when claimed. This over, it was the custom to separate and again to meet for a meal of an open and innocent nature, which very thing they had ceased to do after my edict in which by your orders I forbade club meetings.—Epistles 96, 97.

Here is independent testimony from a Roman author of high rank, within twenty years of the apostle John. It points out the religious nature of the meal, and also the reason for its being forbidden. The Roman empire at this time was being endangered by the many secret societies, some of which became instruments of political intrigue. The love-feasts of the Christians, being attended by the

The Love-Feast

church members only, came under the suspicion of honest Roman officials, because the Jewish and pagan enemies of the Christians falsely accused them of doing evil things in secret in connection with these feasts.

West's Ancient History says:

> The Jews themselves accused the Christians of horrible orgies in the secret love-feasts or communion suppers. . . . All secret societies were feared and forbidden by the empire on political grounds.—Vol. 1, Sec. 507.

Although Pliny says that his order was obeyed, yet we know from the writings of the Christians that they regarded this sacred institution of the Lord so highly that instead of giving it up they met in the late hours of the night and celebrated it in secret as far as possible. But the edict of Trajan made it difficult to continue the love-feast, and in many places it was separated from the eucharist proper. Where it was celebrated in the night there were accompanying dangers and temptations, and in some cases, scandals, so that the church itself, in order to avoid criticism, gave up in large measure the love-feast, but continued the eucharist.

Clement of Alexandria, on the love symbolized by the *agape,* says:

> For the supper is made for love, but the supper is not love (agape); only a proof of mutual and reciprocal kindly feeling. "Let not then your good be evil spoken of; for the kingdom of God is not meat and drink," says the apostle, in order that the meal spoken of may not be conceived as ephemeral, "but righteousness and peace and joy in the Holy Ghost." He who eats of this meal, the best of all, shall possess the kingdom of God, fixing his regards here on the holy assembly of love, the heavenly church.—The Instructor 2: 1.

Clement in Stromata 3: 3 also refers to the abuse of the love-feasts, and the translator explains by saying:

> The early disappearance of the Christian agapæ may probably

be attributed to the terrible abuse of the word here referred to, by the licentious Carpocratians. The genuine agapæ were of apostolic origin (2 Pet. 2: 13; Jude 12), but were often abused by the hypocrites, even under the apostolic eye (1 Cor. 11: 21).

In his epistle to the Corinthians (ch. 44) Clement speaks of bishops as "those who have offered the gifts of the bishop's office unblamably and holy," and these gifts the learned bishop Lightfoot explains as referring to the "alms, eucharistic elements, contributions to the *agape* (love-feast) and so forth."

Minucius Felix (second century) says:

We practice sharing in banquets which are not only modest, but also sober; for we do not indulge in entertainments nor prolong our feasts with wine. . . . Thus we love one another, to your regret, with a mutual love, because we do not know how to hate. Thus we call one another, to your envy, brethren, as being men born of one God and Parent, and companions in faith and fellow-heirs in hope.—Octav. 31.

Tertullian (160 A. D.) says:

Our love-feasts are rather a substitute for the sacrifices spoken of by our Lord in the words already quoted, "I will have mercy and not sacrifice." At our love-feasts the poor obtain vegetable or animal food, and so the creature of God is used, as far as it is suitable for the nourishment of man, who is also God's creature. . . . Because in our love-feasts flesh is often given to the poor, you compare Christian charity to pagan sacrifices.—Reply to Faustus, Bk. 20: 20.

Our feast explains itself by its name. The Greeks call it **agape,** i. e., love. Whatever it costs, our outlay in the name of piety is gain, since with the good things of the feast we benefit the needy . . . If the object of our feast be good, in the light of that consider its further regulations. **As it is an act of religious service** it permits no vileness or immodesty. The participants, before reclining, taste first of prayer to God. As much is eaten as satisfies the cravings of hunger; as much is drunk as befits the chaste. They say it is enough, as those who remember that even during the night they have to worship God; they talk as those who know that the Lord is one of their auditors. After manual ablutions, and the bringing in of lights, each is asked to stand forth and sing, as he can, a hymn to God, either one from the Scriptures or one of his own composing—a proof of the measure of our drinking. As the feast began with prayer, so with prayer it is closed. —Apology ch. 39.

We take also in congregations, before day-break begins, and from the hands of none but the presidents, the sacrament of the eucharist, which the Lord both commanded to be eaten at meal times and enjoined to be taken by all alike. As often as the anniversary comes around we make offerings for the dead as birth day honors.—On the Crown, ch. 3.

Origen (185 A. D.) says:

His wish is to bring into disrepute what are termed the "love-feasts" of the Christians, as if they had their origin in the common danger.—Reply to Celsus, Bk. 1, ch. 1.

Apostolic Canons (200-500 A. D.):

If any bishop or presbyter, otherwise than our Lord has ordained concerning the sacrifice, offer things at the altar of God, as honey, milk, or strong beer instead of wine, any necessaries, or birds, or animals, or pulse, otherwise than is ordained, let him be deprived; excepting grains of new corn, or ears of wheat, or bunches of grapes in their season.— Canon 4.

This passage clearly shows that when we have the term "sacrifice" in the early writings it refers to the entire Lord's supper and not to the eucharistic emblems only.

Chrysostom (345 A. D.), says:

You are rich and wealthy, and think you that you celebrate the feast of the Lord, who are altogether negligent of the offering; who come into the Lord's house without a sacrifice, and take part out of that sacrifice which the poor has offered.— Works and Alms, ch. 15.

In Epistle 54 he warns against allowing certain heretics to share in the feasts.

The Canons of Hippolytus of the fourth century are similar to the Apostolic canons and give similar directions concerning the love-feast.

The synod of Laodicea (A. D. 343) canon 28 decreed, " Beds shall not be set up in churches nor shall love-feasts be held there." This prohibition came because of the temptations which arose from the celebration of the love-feast in the late hours of the night. The custom began because of persecution, but brought evils in its wake.

Cyprian, Bishop of Carthage (248 A. D.), says:

Since therefore this custom (the **agape**) was broken through, a custom most excellent and useful; (for it was a foundation of love and a comfort to poverty, and a corrective of riches, and an occasion of the highest philosophy, and an instruction in humility:) since, however, he (Paul) saw so great advantages in a way to be destroyed, he naturally addresses them with severity.—Homily 27 on 1 Cor. 17.

In another homily (*22 Oported haereses esse*) Chrysostom speaks of these same love-feasts and of their benefits. Theodoret (386 A. D.) and the pseudo-Jerome (on 1 Cor. 11: 16) make similar statements.

Julian the Apostate in the fourth century represents the Galileans (Christians) as taking advantage of the neglect of the poor by their own heathen priests to lure them into Christianity. He says:

In the same manner, beginning with their agape (love-feast), as it is called amongst them, and their entertainment and ministry of tables . . . they have led the faithful into atheism.—Fragment Epistolæ, 49.

Being a heathen, Christianity was to him atheism.

Thus friends and enemies of the church alike agree in attesting the fact of the observance of the love-feast or Lord's supper in the apostolic church as a sacred symbol, which was only given up when Roman law drove it into secret and temptations and abuses followed. After being forbidden in churches it continued for centuries in private houses. For a full historical discussion see *"The Agape and the Eucharist,"* by Keating.

(2) *Substitute for the love-feasts.* Instead of the primitive *agape* or love-feasts when they were forbidden there seems to have come the custom of bringing offerings of food in the churches which were then distributed as an oblation. The Council of Trullo (692 A. D.), Canon 28, prescribed that grapes thus brought should be consecrated and distributed apart from the eucharist, instead of with it as several churches were accustomed to do.

Socrates (440 A. D.) says of Chrysanthus, Bishop of the Novatians at Constantinople that " he would receive nothing of the churches but two loaves of the consecrated bread every Lord's day."—*Eccl. Hist.* 7: 10.

Narrating the difference of practice among the churches he says:

The Egyptians in the neighborhood of Alexandria, and the inhabitants of Thebais, . . . after having eaten and satisfied themselves with food of all kinds, in the evening making their offerings, they partake of the mysteries (eucharist). . . . The practice in Alexandria is of great antiquity, for it appears that Origen most commonly taught in the church in those days.

(3) *Pictures of the early church.* There is historical evidence also in favor of the love-feast in the pictures of the ancient church.

Dr. Schaff, commenting on the *Didache* (p. 58) says:

The earliest eucharistic pictures represent chiefly the **agape** or supper which preceded the actual communion.

Christian Archaeology by Bennet gives many pictures of frescoes and other works of art in the early church. One of these is a fresco of the oldest part of Santa Domatilla,

Rome, dating from near the death of John. It represents a fish on the table, and the author says in explanation:

> The meal here celebrated must be regarded as having a eucharistic significance. The table of the householder becomes the table of the Lord, and the proper priestly character of each private person is here asserted. Herein is fulfilled the prophecy (Isa. 61: 6) of the old dispensation as it was witnessed and affirmed by the apostles of the new (1 Pet. 2: 5, 9). . . . Other mural paintings from the catacombs of Rome confirm the correctness of this interpretation. Some of them bear unmistakable evidence of the eucharistic character of the feast, in which the fish is the central figure.—page 79.
>
> Nearly all the early frescoes confirm this view of the social character of the supper. A table around which are couches on which sit or recline the participants is the ordinary method of representing the celebration of the Lord's supper. . . . Each contributed a share of the food necessary, the community of love and fellowship being herein shown. . . . To this unifying power of the eucharist Paul evidently refers (1 Cor. 10: 16, 17). . . . It seems that during the early apostolic period the method of keeping the supper recalled the last meeting of Christ with the disciples. It was accompanied with prayer and hymns, and was connected with a social meal, the **agape,** to indicate that its purpose was an expression of brotherly love. The offering of thanks and praise was probably followed with the holy kiss. **In the earliest notices of the Lord's supper a simple and almost literal imitation of the meal as instituted by Christ is prevalent.**—pp. 462-464.

The catacomb of San Calisto and also frescoes from Christian catacombs in Alexandria show the last supper with loaves and fishes. In the offerings for these feasts, which were called "oblations," and from which distribution was made for the clergy and the poor, gifts from extortioners, usurers and corrupt persons were excluded.

9. MODERN AUTHORITIES AGREE THAT THE LOVE-FEAST WAS OBSERVED BY THE APOSTOLIC CHURCH.

Jacobs (Episcopalian) says:

The Lord's supper as then administered was immediately

preceded by the agape or love-feast, and in Christian brotherhood, in which distinctions of rank and social position were laid aside, all met and sat down together with that free acknowledgment of equality in Christ, which has been before described. Immediately after this, and as a concluding part of it, bread and wine were laid on the table. And the bread was then broken and distributed with the wine among the guests after Christ's example and appointment; the very words of thanksgiving and of presentation which Jesus had originally used being doubtless repeated by an apostle, or whoever presided at the meeting. Hence the name "Lord's Supper," or the more simple appellation of "the breaking of bread" was given to this ordinance, **including at first the whole social meal, the agape itself as well as the sacramental celebration with which it closed. The agape itself was evidently an apostolic institution;** and was at first, no doubt not only an evidence of the existence, but also a powerful means for the promotion of a strong feeling of union and Christian brotherhood.—Ecclesiastical Polity p. 227.

Kitto says:

In the first age of the church the eucharist was celebrated after the agape, but in Chrysostom's time the order was frequently reversed. (Homiletics, 22, 27). When Christianity was introduced among the Anglo-Saxons by Austin (596) Gregory the Great advised the celebration of the agape in booths formed of branches of trees at the consecration of churches.—Bible Encyclopedia, p. 80.

Cruden's Concordance says:

Love-feasts or feasts of charity were used among the primitive Christians in the public meetings of the church to show their unity among themselves, to promote and maintain mutual charity, and for the relief of the poor among them. At the close thereof they administered the Lord's supper (Jude 12).—Art. on Feasts.

Hastings' Bible Dictionary, one of the most authoritative Bible Dictionaries published, says:

In Scripture there is no trace of the eucharist being separated from the joint evening meal or agape; and the "breaking of bread" covers the whole.—Art. Lord's Supper.

Neander, the great Jewish historian says:

After the model of the Jewish passover and the first institution of this rite the celebration of the Lord's supper originally was always joined with a general meal and both together formed one whole, and because the communion of believers with their Lord and their brotherly communion with each other, were represented by it, the two together were called the "supper of the Lord." It was the daily rite of the Christian communion in the first church at Jerusalem. We find both connected together in the first Corinthian church, and one is inclined to suppose that this was the simple, innocent meal of the Christians of which Pliny speaks in his report to the emperor Trajan.—Church History Vol. 3, p. 461.

The view held by Neander is worth noting. He says in his Life of Christ:

Jesus foresaw that he would have to leave the disciples before the Jewish passover, and determined to give a peculiar meaning to his last meal with them, and to place it in a peculiar relation to the passover of the old covenant, the place of which was to be taken by the meal of the new covenant.

Bingham describes the love-feast of the early church and says: "This was a ritual always accompanying the communion."—*Antiquities* Bk. 15, ch. 7.

Gibbon, the infidel historian, in his *History of Rome,* under the fifth cause for the rise of Christianity says:

A sufficient sum was allotted for public worship, of which the feasts of love, the "agapæ" as they were called, formed a very pleasing part.

Professor James Orr says:

The crowning act of the New Testament religious service was the Lord's supper with which in this age was always combined the agape, or love-feast. The two indeed formed one sacred meal in the course of which, after blessing, the bread was broken and wine drunk after the example of our Lord. (1 Cor. 11: 23, 24). Different types of observance may however be distinguished. In Gentile churches the service tended to be adapted to the free model of the Greek feast (hence the abuses at Corinth, 1 Cor. 11): in Jewish churches there was a closer adherence to the ritual of the passover. The eucharistic prayers of the Didache are on the latter model.—Apostolic Church.

Stanley says:

The eucharist in those early times was the common festive gathering of the rich and poor in the same social meal, to which, as Paul enjoined, every one was to bring his portion. . . . There was united from earliest times the practice of collecting alms and contributions for the poor, at the time when our Christian communion and fellowship with each other is most impressed upon us. So we see them in the catacombs and in a bas-relief in S. Ambroglio in Milan, sitting around a semi-circular table, men and women together, which so far was an infringement on the Greek custom, where the sexes were kept apart. . . . Finally the meal itself fell under suspicion. Augustine and Ambrose condemned the thing itself as the apostle had condemned its excesses, and in the fifth century that which had been the original form of the eucharist was forbidden as profane by the councils of Carthage and Laodicea. It was the parallel of the gradual extinction of the bath of baptism.—Christian Institutions, ch. 4.

Allen says:

The agape was not an institution devised or created by the early church, but must be regarded as the continuation as well as the commemoration of Christ's last supper with his disciples. It is first mentioned by Paul in 1 Cor. 11, who seeks to correct the abuses of the rite.

The first intimation of the Lord's supper as a rite distinct from the agape is contained in the apology of Justin Martyr about the middle of the second century (Apology 67, p. 82).—Christian Institutions, p. 518.

The Edinburgh Review says:

It is apparent from all the paintings of Christian feasts, whether the agape or the burial of the dead or the holy sacrament, that they were celebrated by the early Christians while sitting around a table.—Art. Roman Catacombs, Jan. 1859.

Robinson says:

Agape, feasts of friendship, love or kindness, were in use among primitive Christians. It is very probable that they were instituted in memory of the last supper of Jesus Christ with his disciples, which supper was concluded before he instituted the eucharist. These festivals were kept in the assembly of the church towards evening, after prayers and worship were over.—Bible Encyclopedia, p. 27.

Guericke says:

The administration of the holy communion was originally combined with a feast or meal which was a symbol of brotherly love, and was called the agape.—Manual of Antiquities, p. 245.

Zenos (Presbyterian) says:

Whether on special occasions or in connection with each weekly service of worship it is not possible to tell, the Lord's supper was celebrated. This was in the earliest times associated with a meal as at its first institution. This meal, called a love-feast (agape) was liable to abuse as we learn from Paul rebuking such abuse in the Corinthian church.—Church History.

Kurtz says:

At first the Lord's supper was always connected with an agape but when Trajan published a stringent edict against club feasts (heteræ) the Christians intermitted the agape of which the prohibition was implied in the edict, and connected the observance of the Lord's supper with the ordinary homiletic public worship. This continued the practice even after the celebration of the agape was again resumed.—Church History, p. 21.

Canon Farrar says:

The expression "breaking of bread" refers to the sacramental character given by the early Christians to their daily meals—the agape and holy communion (Acts 2: 48).—Texts Explained, p. 139.

Bartlett says:

The same feast was at once a social meal and the communion of the body and blood of Christ, i. e., the feeding upon his word and spirit, symbolized first by his body and blood and then by the elements of daily food. There was then but one sacred meal or feast, having various aspects, the emphasis on which seems to have varied in different circles, and it was held like the last supper in the evening. Such was the case at Troas about 56 A. D. So it was half a century later when Ignatius used the terms "eucharist" and "agape" as synonymous (See letter to Phila. ch. 4 and to Smyrna 8: 1). Pliny's letter shows it to have been in the evening.—Apostolic Age.

Mosheim says:

This most holy ordinance (eucharist) was followed by sober repasts, which from their design were denominated agapæ, feasts of love. . . . the earliest Christians did not everywhere celebrate this or other institutions in the same manner.—Institutes of Eccl. Hist., p. 87.

Bishop Lightfoot says:

In the apostolic age the eucharist formed part of the agape. The original form of the Lord's supper as it was first instituted by Christ, was thus in a manner kept up. This appears from 1 Cor. 11: 17 ff (cf Acts 10: 7) from which passage we infer that the celebration of the eucharist came, as it naturally would, at a late stage in the entertainment. In the Didache (Teaching of the Apostles, 10) this early practice is still observed. In after times however, the agape was held at a separate time from the eucharist. Had the change taken place before Ignatius wrote (100-118 A. D.)? I think not.

Weizaker says:

The great practical importance of these meals in the primitive church could only be increased by the poverty of a section of the church. In 1 Cor. 11 Paul implies that the practice was beyond question.—Apostolic Age, Vol. 2, p. 204.

Moxom says:

As early as the persecution under Pliny (110 A. D.) in Asia Minor the Lord's supper, which still at that time had been celebrated in the evening in connection with the "love-feast" was joined to the preaching service, and **the love-feast was abandoned in order to avoid the appearance of violating the law against secret meetings.** The danger to which the church was exposed afterwards caused the exclusion of all heathen from the preaching service.—From Jerusalem to Nicea, p. 69.

Fisher says:

They (the early Christians) met in their own place of assembly or in a private house. There they joined in a common meal which concluded with a solemn partaking of bread and wine, **the whole being a commemoration of the last supper of the Lord with his disciples.** This meal accompanied with prayer and song, which at a later day received the name of agape, or love-feast, was the original method of celebrating the Lord's supper. It was one great family gathering about a common table and signifying by this means so natural and familiar in all ages, their union with one another and the absent head of the household.—Beginnings of Christianity, p. 546.

Pullan says:

While the agape or love-feast was retained it was of a strictly **religious character.**—History of Early Christianity, p. 289.

Henson says:

There can be no doubt that the Lord's supper was preceded by the common meal or agape, and that the shocking abuses denounced by Paul belonged primarily to the latter. The association seems to have continued far into the sub-apostolic age. The name "eucharist" seems to have extended both to the agape and the Lord's supper.—Apostolic Christianity p. 152.

Keating says:

The separation of the agape from the eucharist does not seem to have taken effect during the apostolic age, nor for some time afterwards.

The Eucharist

In this work (for which he was given the degree of Doctor of Divinity by the Cambridge professors, England) he says (p. 44), "*The union of the eucharist and love-feast at first is practically undoubted.*"—*The Agape and Eucharist,* p. 53.

Many other authorities may be quoted, as historians all agree on this point. See Adam Clarke, *Commentary,* on Jude; *Henry's Christian Antiquities; Brown's Bible Dictionary* under Agape; Coleman, *Ancient Christianity Exemplified;* Cave, *Primitive Christianity;* Lange, *Commentary,* on 1 Cor. 11: 20, &c., &c.

A survival of the early love-feasts continues in the Gallican church in the " hallowed bread "; and in the Greek churches in the " eulogia " distributed to noncommunicants at the close of the Eucharist, from the loaf out of which the bread of oblation is supposed to have been cut. The Christian or Disciple Church formerly observed it, as did also the United Brethren, and many Baptist churches. The Methodist Church also has what it calls a " love-feast " although it consists only of bread and water, taken in the morning, preceding the observance of the eucharist in the evening. It is celebrated also by the Brethren, the River Brethren, the Church of God, the Mennonites and Amish.

10. THE PRACTICAL BENEFITS RESULTING FROM THE OBSERVANCE OF THE LOVE-FEAST IS PROOF OF THE DIVINE WISDOM IN ESTABLISHING IT.

In the apostolic church it was the means of bringing rich and poor together in equality so that none suffered through poverty (Acts 2: 43-47; 6: 1-4). In the sub-apostolic church it had the same effect, so that even the *Emperor Julian,* who fought Christianity harder than any one else, attributed the success of Christianity mainly to the fact that it had this care for the poor. (*Julian,* Epistle 49).

Tertullian (160 A. D.) witnesses also to this brotherly love which the love-feast taught and enforced. He says:

> They (the heathen) are wroth with us, too, because we call each other brethren. Our presidents are the men of age and standing amongst us, who have gained their distinction, not by money, but by merit. For money counts not in the things of God. Even though we have a kind of treasure chest, it is not made up as in a religion that has its price. Every man places there a small contribution on one day of the month, or whensoever he will, so he do but will, and so he be but able; for no man is constrained, but contributes willingly. These are, as it were, the deposits of piety. For expenditure is not incurred therefrom upon feasting or drinking, or on disgusting haunts of gluttony; but for feeding and burying the poor, for boys and girls without fortune and without parents, for old men now confined to the house; for the shipwrecked likewise, and any who are in the mines, or in the islands, or in prison; provided they are there for the sake of God's way, they become nurslings of their creed.—Apology, ch. 39.

Chrysostom (347 A. D.) witnesses to the same good results from the feast in the early church. He says:

> And so from this fellowship in eating and the reverence for the place, they were all strictly united in charity with one another, and much pleasure and profit arose thence to them all; for the poor were comforted and the rich reaped the fruit of their benevolence, both from those whom they fed and from God.—Operted Haereses esse, 22.

Bingham, in his monumental work *Christian Antiquities,* says:

> Happy it had been for the Christian religion, if Christians had never had occasion to object more against their own feasts of charity than Julian, their bitterest enemy, could find to object to them! They might then have gone on with innocence and glory and have continued a useful and beautiful rite to this day.—Vol. 2, p. 835.

The same results may be observed to-day. The churches which properly observe the love-feast are characterized by a larger sense of brotherhood than is found in those that have discarded it. A single instance will illustrate the point. A woman said, " A peddler stopped here to-day and inquired if there was a Dunkard settlement near, ' because,' he said ' If I can only find a Dunkard settlement I am sure of kind treatment and a place to stay.' " On the other hand those churches which do not observe the love-feast find a want in their lives unsupplied and seek to provide for it in all kinds of social affairs, oyster suppers, ice-cream socials, festivals, box suppers and many other things which pander to the flesh rather than minister to the spirit, and work evil to the church rather than good. Concerning this, *The Christian*, edited by H. L. Hastings, says:

> The primitive churches had their "agape" or "feasts of charity" or love, where social intercourse of a strictly religious character was enjoyed by the disciples of the Lord. Instead of these ancient and pious festivals, we are now accustomed to a class of social gatherings of an entirely different character which are inaugurated and perpetuated for the special object of getting money and making cheap and poor fun which crowds closely upon absolute sin.

Thus:
> "Mirth doth into folly glide
> And folly into sin."

It is ever the devil's delight to masquerade in the guise of things sacred. The use of the counterfeit in the place of the true is his favorite way of getting rid of things which he hates, and in the modern church amusement gatherings he surely has a burlesque upon the love-feast which the Lord instituted to meet the social needs of the church by teaching it the true fellowship of the kingdom of heaven.

THE EUCHARIST, OR CUP AND LOAF.

Although the eucharistic emblems have been preserved in almost all denominations, yet there has been as much discussion of the meaning and purpose of this ordinance as anything else. If a symbol is to be dropped because it is not so clearly commanded and explained in the Bible as to prevent disagreement concerning it, then baptism and the eucharist would have to go as well as feet-washing and the supper, but if the controversies of men are to be passed by, and the Gospel itself accepted on all these points, there will be little difficulty in accepting all.

1. OLD COVENANT TYPES OF THE EUCHARIST.

(1) *The various sacrifices* of the Old Testament were typical of the Christ who was to come and give Himself for the salvation of men. Several of these are especially mentioned as types. Paul says, referring to the eucharist, "For our passover also hath been sacrificed, *even* Christ" (1 Cor. 5: 7, 8). As the blood of the lamb, a spotless lamb of the first year, was sprinkled on the doorposts of the houses as a sign to the destroying angel to "pass over" (Ex. 12), so Christ is "the Lamb slain" from the foundation of the world (Rev. 5: 6), "in whom we have our redemption, through his blood" (Eph. 1: 7). The memorial of the broken body and atoning blood of Christ is the "bread which we break" which is "a communion of the body of Christ," and the "cup of the new covenant" which is "a communion of the blood of Christ" (1 Cor. 10: 16). As the Passover proper and the feast of unleavened bread were joined together as one feast, sometimes

called "the passover" as a whole, and sometimes "the feast of unleavened bread" (Luke 22), so the eucharist and love-feast together form one service, pointing as a whole to the marriage supper of the Lamb (Rev. 19: 6-9).

(2) *In the symbols of the tabernacle also,* which were "copies" of the things to come in the church (Heb. 9), there was kept in the ark a *pot of manna* as a memorial of the "bread from heaven" that God gave His people in the wilderness. This manna was a type of Christ, as He said,

Your fathers ate manna in the wilderness and they died. This is the bread which cometh down out of heaven, that a man may eat thereof and not die. I am the living bread which came down out of heaven: if any man eat of this bread he shall live forever (John 6: 49-51).

In the bread and the cup we have the emblems of the body and blood of our Lord. Again, as in the tabernacle there was the showbread in the holy place and the manna in the holy of holies, so in the Lord's supper there is the love-feast representing God's people in His presence, and the eucharist representing God's presence in Christ, who gave His life for the world. As the veil separating the holy place from the holy of holies was done away in Christ (2 Cor. 3: 14; Matt. 27: 51) we have both these sacred emblems together, and one "Lord's Supper" and one "table of the Lord" and one blessed fellowship with Him.

2. THE EUCHARISTIC EMBLEMS WERE INSTITUTED BY THE LORD IMMEDIATELY FOLLOWING THE SUPPER ON THE NIGHT OF THE BETRAYAL.

The accounts of the institution are found in Matt. 26: 26-29; Mark 14: 22-24; Luke 22: 19, 20; 1 Cor. 11: 23-27. Only Luke and Paul quote the command to continue the symbol, "Do this in remembrance of me," but it will be remembered that only John and Paul mention the feet-washing and only Matthew quotes the command for baptism. However, in the case of the eucharist there is little question among the evangelical churches but that the eucharist should be observed as a perpetual memorial until Jesus comes.

The writings of the early Christians contain many references to the eucharist, which show that the church understood its meaning and continued it as Jesus commanded.

The Didache or *Teaching of the Twelve Apostles,* which some recent authorities put as early as 65 A. D., gives directions for observing the eucharist, together with model prayers for it.

Ignatius, born 69 A. D. and martyred at Rome only twelve years after John died, says:

I exhort you to have one faith and one kind of preaching, and one eucharist. For there is one flesh of the Lord Jesus Christ, and his blood shed for us is one:—one loaf also is broken to all and one cup is distributed to all.—To Philadelphia, ch. 4.

Justin Martyr (150 A. D), says:

Those whom we call deacons distribute this eucharistic bread and wine and water to every one present to partake of them, and they carry it to the absent. This food is called the eucharist which is partaken of by none but the believing and the baptized who live according to the commands of Christ.—First Apology, ch. 66, 67.

3. THE MEANING OF THE EUCHARIST.

All the Christian sacraments were instituted because of their symbolic teaching. The eucharist has been retained by churches which have discarded the rest of the original communion service, because its meaning is so rich and the truths taught are so vital.

(1) *A memorial of atonement.* The eucharistic bread and wine are a memorial of the atoning work of Christ. " This is my body, which is given for you." (Luke 22: 19,) " As often as ye eat this bread and drink the cup, ye proclaim the

The Eucharist

Lord's death till he come" (1 Cor. 11: 26). All the sacrificial blood of the Old Testament (covenant) pointed forward to this atonement, but especially the Passover lamb. "Our passover also hath been sacrificed *even* Christ" (1 Cor. 5: 7). The memory of this sacrifice for us is the means of arousing the higher nature in us in such a way that it becomes dominant, and thus we "are conformed to his image" and are ready to make like sacrifices for others (1 John 3: 16 with John 3: 16).

(2) *A symbol of divine life.* The eucharistic bread and wine, representing the body and blood of our Lord, convey to us the realization of His sinless nature and help us to share in it. The Passover lamb was to be without blemish. So Jesus was without sin. "Which of you convicteth me of sin?" was the challenge He gave to the world, and it has never been successfully taken up. He is the Lamb of God, the immaculate offering, the bread which gives eternal life. "I am the living bread which came down from heaven. If any man eat of this bread he shall live forever" (John 6: 51). Not the literal flesh indeed, by some priestly miracle made real from the symbolic bread, for "It is the spirit that giveth life. The flesh profiteth nothing. The words that I have spoken unto you are spirit, and are life" (John 6: 63).

We know not how it is that the bread we eat is transmuted into brain and muscle and again into thought and action, but we know that this occurs. We do not know just how it is that contemplating the life and death of the Son of God begets in us a longing to be like Him which becomes a reality, but we know that it is a fact that "We all, with unveiled face beholding as in a mirror the glory of the Lord, are transformed into the same image from glory to glory, even as from the Lord the Spirit." (2 Cor. 3: 18). It is what Drummond calls the "alchemy of influence," and this Professor Bryan says is as great in the spiritual world as heredity is in the physical world. Whatever aids us to realize vividly the character of Jesus helps us to become like Him, and there is no time that we come so near to Him as when we feed upon the emblems of His very self and say "Whom having not seen, ye love" (1 Pet. 1: 8).

The spiritual health resulting from feeding on Christ reacts in physical health. The mind is superior to the body as the agent is superior to the instrument. It is no wonder that such an observance as they had fallen into at Corinth where some were hungry and others drunken, caused also that some should be weak and sickly and not a few to sleep (1 Cor. 11: 30). But if we "discern the Lord's body," if we remember that He is the vine and we are the branches (John 15), or in the figure of Paul, that He is the Head and the church is the body (Eph. 1: 22, 23), then we shall strive to "walk even as he walked" (1 John 2: 6) and love as He loved (John 17: 26).

The "church in the wilderness" was not without this spiritual food, for we read that they "did all eat the same spiritual food; and did all drink of the same spiritual drink: for they drank of the spiritual rock that followed them, and the rock was Christ" (1 Cor. 10: 3, 4). Much more may we, having Christ in reality, and not in type only, partake of Him and live.

(3) *The cup and loaf are a type of the union of Christ and the Church.* "As often as ye eat this bread, and drink the cup, ye proclaim the Lord's death TILL HE COME" (1 Cor. 11: 26).

To regard the eucharist as both a memorial and a type is not to strain it with a double meaning, for it represents Christ, "who is and who was and who is to come" (Rev. 1: 4). It only represents Him more perfectly as it reminds

The Eucharist

us both of His blood that was shed for us, His presence with us in spirit now, and His coming again in person.

Soon we shall hear the words, "Rejoice and be exceeding glad, * * * for the marriage of the Lamb is come, and his wife hath made herself ready" (Rev. 19: 7-9). This hope is the "anchor to the soul, both sure and steadfast" (Heb. 6: 19). This is the rainbow of beauty that shines resplendent over this service. This is the purifying hope for, "every one that hath this hope *set* on him purifyeth himself even as he is pure" (1 John 3: 3). This is the comfort which sustains in the hour of trial. The Lord is coming again, and that at any time. It would be a beautiful custom in all churches, as it is in some, to place a vacant chair at the head of the Lord's table on communion occasions, ready for the Lord Himself should He come, as a reminder of this "blessed hope" (Titus 2: 13).

(4) *A testimony of faith.* In observing the eucharist understandingly, we acknowledge the deity of our Lord. He said, "I am the living bread which came down from heaven" (John 6: 53, 54). He is therefore divine. In eating these emblems we proclaim our faith in Jesus as the Bread of Heaven, the Son of God.

(5) It is also a *confession* of our sin. When we say "The bread which WE BREAK" (1 Cor. 10: 16) we confess to a share in the breaking of the body of Christ, represented by the bread. Our sins still rend His heart, and when we make confession of them in the communion service it should be with sincere repentance.

(6) It is also a *covenant* with our Lord to live the life He gives. "This is the new covenant in my blood" (1 Cor. 11: 25). A covenant is an agreement between two parties, and involves mutual obligation. Jesus gives us eternal life on condition that we accept Him, with all that

that acceptance implies. In the communion service we publicly pledge ourselves to do this.

(7) It is an *earnest or foretaste of heaven*. The church is already the bride of Christ (Rev. 22: 17) and is being prepared that she may be spotless at His coming (Eph. 5: 25-32), and while waiting, sits down on these occasions of the Lord's supper, "in the heavenly places in Christ Jesus" (Eph. 1: 3). Jesus is with us always in spirit (Matt. 28: 20), but when we take of the emblems of His body and blood we have a reminder of His coming personal presence.

Conditions of Sharing in the Lord's Supper.

1. *The Lord's supper is for Christians only, that is for regenerate believers in Christ, because:*

(1) It was instituted by Jesus when with the disciples only.

(2) It was commanded to be observed by believers only.

(3) There is no record of any but church members participating in the apostolic age.

(4) The church is rebuked for even allowing hypocritical church members to partake (1 Cor. 5: 11; 2 Pet. 2: 13; Jude 12).

(5) The term "Lord's table" implies that it is for only those who are the Lord's (1 Cor. 1: 10: 21).

(6) It is the communion of the body of Christ and therefore only members of His body (1 Cor. 12: 13) may commune (1 Cor. 10: 16).

(7) It represents Christian truths which only Christians can accept or obey.

2. *Since baptism is the symbol of putting on Christ* (Gal. 3: 27; 1 Cor. 12: 13) *it follows that baptism is regularly a prerequisite to the communion.* However, the principle of 2 Cor. 8: 12 may permit, in rare cases, a person to com-

mune who has been converted but has not found it possible to be baptized before communion, but who means to do so at the earliest opportunity, for "if the readiness is there it is acceptable according as a man hath, and not according as he hath not."

The same principle allows us to admit that there are Christians who are evangelical, but who have been mistaken in regard to some of these Gospel doctrines, who, if they are honestly seeking more light and are willing to obey Christ, may therefore be recognized as having Christ as their foundation (1 Cor. 3: 11) and be admitted to communion with Christ's people. "Him that is weak in faith receive ye, but not to decision of scruples" (Rom. 14: 1). *Justin Martyr* (150 A. D.) says:

> This food is called the eucharist, of which no one is allowed to partake, but those who believe that the things which we teach are true, and have been washed with the washing which is for the remission of sins, and unto regeneration, and who is living as Christ has enjoined.—Apology 1: 66.

3. Communion should not be neglected because of doubts as to some part of the service.

There are those who have honest doubts as to some details of the manner of observing the ordinances. Such should be taught rather than excluded. It is the Lord's table. He it is who gives the invitation, and the blessing or judgment. If we should exclude all who differ from us in minor doctrines we might shut out those whom God has accepted. The twelve disciples were not perfect either in faith or practice, yet they shared alike in that first supper, and we may well follow the example of charity which our Lord gave when He instituted the ordinance. "But," says one, "He that doubteth is condemned if he eat." That was spoken of meat offered to idols, not of the Lord's supper. A wilful doubter, to be sure, is unworthy, but one seeking the truth in sincerity, is not a doubter to be excluded, but a disciple to be helped. A person may misunderstand baptism and yet be clear as to the communion service. Or some may understand one part of this service better than another. Let their faith grow by experience.

4. *Heart preparation is required.* We are taught to "examine" ourselves and each partake according to his own conscience (1 Cor. 11: 28-33). We must not refuse to participate because there is some one else at the table whom we believe to be sinful. We may be deceived, but "the Lord knoweth them that are his" (2 Tim. 2: 19). If the church is properly disciplined, and this service properly conducted and explained, there will be few, if any, who will ever sit at the Lord's table who have no right there.

5. *An understanding of the meaning of the service is essential to receiving from it the blessing intended.*

To eat and drink not "discerning the Lord's body" (1 Cor. 11: 29) is to eat and drink condemnation, because it is to sit in the presence of spiritual teaching and be blind to it. Note that this requirement precludes the giving of the communion to infants.

6. *Neglect of the Lord's Supper involves vital spiritual loss.* The physical life requires food; no less does the spiritual. Jesus spent much time in communion with the Father; much more should we. While there is no Gospel command or precedent for excommunicating church members simply for missing a communion service, yet those who willfully and persistently reject it will by such a course cut themselves off from Christ and prove in other ways unworthy of fellowship. But those who feel their unworthiness and sincerely repent and seek to be better, should have the help afforded by this means of grace. The Lord's supper is for the strengthening of all, both weak and strong. The very word "communion" means literally a "fortifying to-

gether." Those who miss it because they feel unworthy only add disobedience to other sins and increase their unworthiness.

If any have received Christ as their Savior and are building upon Him as their foundation, they may be received at the Lord's table as fellow-Christians, even though they may differ in some minor items of faith, for "No one can call Jesus Lord, but by the Spirit of God" (1 Cor. 12: 3), and "As many as are led by the Spirit of God they are the sons of God" (Rom. 8: 14). The church in the past has burned at the stake those who were called heretics because of dissent from its errors. It has now grown more tolerant and Christlike. The Savior suffered even Judas at the table, and bore with the contentious disciples" (Luke 22: 24) because He knew they were learners and would grow in both grace and knowledge.

While, therefore, we should do our utmost to make the church of Christ spotless as a bride adorned for her husband, yet Christ and not we, is Lord of the feast which He has provided. If He refuses none who come to Him (John 6: 37) we should be slow to close the door to any true Christians who seek to share communion with Him.

7. The customs of the post-apostolic churches differed in regard to the communion service.

The *Apostolic Constitutions* say:

Let them (penitents) not be admitted to the communion until they have received the seal of baptism and are made complete Christians.—Bk. 2, Sec. 5, ch. 39.

Cyprian (200-258 A. D.), advised the rebaptism of heretics as a condition of communion, but did not refuse to commune with those not so rebaptized (Epistles 71: 1, 12). But since the Scriptures themselves are so clear in regard to the observance of this rite we should not confuse the matter by following the variations which crept into the church later.

The Time of Observing the Lord's Supper.

1. *Jesus, so far as the record shows, gave no command as to the time of observing the communion service.* He simply said, "This do in remembrance of me" (Luke 22: 19). The frequency of the observance thus seems to be left to the desire of the church.

2. *The apostles give no command in regard to the matter.* Paul says "As oft as ye eat this bread and drink the cup ye proclaim the Lord's death till he come" (1 Cor. 11: 26). This also leaves it with the conscience of the church. His exhortation in 1 Cor. 5: 7, 8, "Let us keep the feast," may imply a set time for observing it, but gives no certain clue as to whether it was observed annually or occasionally.

3. *The example of the apostolic church affords no fixed rule as to time.*

(1) *Daily observance.* The believers at first had all things in common. They ate their meals together and at these common meals partook of the eucharistic emblems daily in little groups in connection with their daily meals. "And day by day continuing steadfastly with one accord in the temple and breaking bread at home they took their food with gladness and singleness of heart." (Acts 2: 44-46). The expression "breaking of bread" became a common term referring to the sacrament of the eucharist (Cf. Acts 20: 7; 1 Cor. 10: 16).

That this custom of daily celebration of the eucharist continued in some sections of the church for a long time is shown by the testimonies of the Fathers. *Augustine* as late as the fourth century, in Tract 26, describes the eucharist and says it was observed in some places, especially in the east, daily, and in others at intervals. In his first letter to Januarius, ch. 3, Augustine says:

> Some one may say the eucharist ought not to be taken every day. You ask on what grounds . . . Perhaps a third party interposes with a more just decision of the question, reminding them that the principal thing is to remain united in peace of Christ and that each should be free to do what according to his belief he conscientiously regards as his duty.

Cyprian (200-285 A. D.) *De Oration Dominica opera,* p. 421, speaks of daily taking of the eucharist.

(2) *Weekly observance.* As the disciples multiplied it was not convenient or even possible for them to have daily common meals, and then the love-feast became a part of the weekly worship on the first day of the week. " On the first day of the week when the disciples came together to break bread Paul preached unto them " (Acts 20: 7). It should be said that some deny that this refers to the Lord's supper, and it cannot be proven conclusively either way.

Pliny (111 A. D.) speaks in *Epistles* 96 and 97 of "a stated day" on which the Christians had a common meal together in the night. Historians commonly think this stated day was the Lord's day.

Socrates (440 A. D.) says:

> There are several cities and villages in Egypt where contrary to the usages established elsewhere, the people meet together on the **Sabbath evening** and although they have dined previously, partake of the mysteries.—Ecclesiastical History, 7: 19.

The Didache (65-140 A. D.) says:

> But **every Lord's day** do ye gather yourselves together and give thanksgiving after having confessed your transgressions, that your sacrifice may be pure.—ch. 14.

Justin Martyr (130 A. D.) describes the observance of the Lord's supper following baptism, and also regularly on

Sunday, which he calls also the Lord's day. He uses the term eucharist or thanksgiving of the entire service. See Apol. 1: 65, 66.

Apostolic Constitutions (300-500 A. D.) say:

And on the day of our Lord's resurrection, which is the Lord's day, meet more diligently. . . . in which is performed the reading of the prophets, the preaching of the Gospel, the oblation of the sacrifice, the gift of the holy food.—Sec. 7: 59.

(3) *Occasional observance.* As the believers multiplied it was no longer expedient to have daily meetings together. Persecution had scattered the workers, and the apostles were also widely separated preaching the Gospel. While they were present there were frequent meetings and frequent observance of the Lord's supper, and wherever they went they instructed their converts in these things. Their coming to any church was the occasion of preaching services and a love-feast. The scripture references already quoted (1 Cor. 11: 17-34; 2 Pet. 2: 13; Jude 12) imply occasional observance of the love-feast, while the statements of the *Didache,* written about the same time confirm the inference. The *Didache* says (ch. 10), "But permit the prophets to make Thanksgiving (i. e., appoint love-feasts) as much as they desire." Their coming brought the church together and afforded a suitable time for a love-feast. Chapter 11 says, "Every prophet that ordereth a meal eateth not from it unless indeed he be a false prophet." Why this statement? Because a true prophet used the love-feast occasion for teaching rather than for feeding himself.

(4) *Private observance.* There are references also to the observance of this feast in private families, especially on the occasion of the visit of saints from a distance. The statement in Acts 2: 46, "and breaking bread at home,

they took their food with gladness and singleness of heart," seems to imply the observance by families.

With this view accords the statement of *Tertullian* (200 A. D.) *De Corona* ch. 3. "Which (the eucharist) the Lord ordained to be eaten at meal times."

The *Clementine Homilies* (14: 1) ascribed to Clement, the pupil of Peter, after describing the baptism of his mother Matthidia " in the sea," tells how they then observed the eucharist. He says:

We went then to our lodging, and while waiting for Peter's arrival, we conversed with each other. Peter came several hours after, and breaking the bread for the eucharist, and putting salt upon it, he gave it first to our mother, and after her, to us her sons. And thus we took food along with her and blessed God.

The Synod of Gangra (end of 4th century), canon 11, says:

If any one despises those who in the faith solemnize the agape for the honor of the Lord and invite their brethren to it, and will take no part in these invitations because he lightly esteems the matter, let him be anathema.

(5) *Anniversary observance.* From the very first the entire service as instituted by Jesus was observed on the anniversary of its institution, that is, on the Thursday evening before Easter. However, there was an early movement to observe it instead, on the Sunday evening following, in order to have it on the day of resurrection. Over this matter raged one of the longest and fiercest disputes of the early church.

Irenaeus (130 A. D.), who was connected through Polycarp with the apostles, says that Polycarp, who was associated for twenty-six years with the apostle John, always as bishop, insisted on observing it on the 14th day of April (the anniversary date) *because John so observed it.* John was for many years bishop at Ephesus and there gave his example. Polycarp was so earnest in preserving the example of John that he walked a thousand miles to be present at a council to prevent, if possible, any change from that date. Irenaeus further mentions many other leading men of the church of his day who insisted on the same custom. He says that while Polycarp could not persuade the church at Rome to follow the eastern custom received from the apostles, yet they all remained in harmony in other matters. See *Fragments* from Irenaeus.

In the fragments of writings attributed to the *apostle Peter* (*Ante-Nicene Fathers* Vol. 6, p. 282) there is a lengthy argument to show that Jesus was the antitype of the paschal lamb and therefore took the place of the Passover eaten by the Jews.

Anatolius, (270 A. D.), being a great mathematician, wrote a learned treatise as to how to determine the proper time of Easter which closes by saying:

> We should keep the solemn festival of the passover on the Lord's day, and after the equinox, and yet not beyond the limit of the moon's twentieth day.

Tertullian (160 A. D.), says:

> If the apostle has erased all devotion absolutely, "of seasons, and days, and months, and years" why do we celebrate the Passover by an annual rotation in the first month?—On Fasting, ch. 14.
>
> But how shall we assemble together say you; how shall we observe the ordinances of the Lord? To be sure, just as the apostles did also, who were protected by faith, not by money. —On Flight from Persecution, ch. 14.

Origen (185 A. D.) says:

> If it be objected on this subject that we ourselves are accustomed to observe certain days, as for example, the Lord's day, the Preparation, the Passover, or Pentecost, I have to answer, that to the perfect Christian, who is ever in his thoughts,

words and deeds, serving his natural Lord, God the Word, all his days are the Lord's, and he is always keeping the Lord's day.—Reply to Celsus, ch. 22.

Theophilus, Bishop of Ceserea in Palestine, (A. D. 169), writing on the question of the date of the Christian Passover Feast says:

> We would have you know, too, that in Alexandria also they observe the festival on the same day as ourselves. For the Paschal letters are sent from us to them, and from them to us: so that we observe the holy day in unison and together.

Melito (170 A. D.) wrote two books on the Paschal Feast and one on the Lord's Day. A fragment remaining from one of these books says:

> When Servius Paulus was proconsul of Asia, at the time that Sagaris suffered martyrdom, there arose a great controversy at Laodicea concerning the time of the celebration of the Passover, which on that occasion had happened to fall at the proper season; and this treatise was then written.

This was about 162 A. D. when Marcus Aurelius was emperor.

Claudius Apollinaris, Bishop of Hieropolis (160-180 A. D.) also wrote a book of which a fragment remains, in which he opposes holding the Christian Passover at the same time as the Jewish, because Jesus died at the time the lambs were to be slain for that feast. He says the contrary opinion is contrary to the law and the Gospels, and that "The fourteenth day (of the month of Nisan) is the true Passover of the Lord; the great sacrifice, the Son of God instead of the lamb."

Polycrates (130-196 A. D.), after mentioning Philip and John, the apostles, Polycarp, Sagaris, Papirus, bishops and martyrs, and Melito, says:

> These all kept the Passover on the 14th day of the month, in accordance with the Gospel, without ever deviating from it.

An unknown writer of that period quotes *Hyppolytus* as saying:

> Christ kept the supper, then, on that day, and then suffered; whence it is needful that I, too, should keep it in the same manner as the Lord did.

The same writer goes on to say that " when Christ suffered he did not eat the Passover of the law. For He was the Passover that had been of old proclaimed, and that was fulfilled on that determinate day."—(*Ante-Nicene Fathers* Vol. 5, p. 240).

The Constitutions of the Apostles (200-500 A. D.) say:

> It is therefore your duty, brethren, who are redeemed by the precious blood of Christ, to observe the days of the passover exactly, with all care, after the vernal equinox, lest ye be obliged to keep it twice in a year. Keep it only once in a year for him that died but once.

It is further directed to keep it on Sunday and " at the same time as your brethren of the circumcision," but while the Jews were keeping their Passover to " fast and pray for them."—Book 5: 3: 17.

Augustine (354 A. D.) says that many observed the " feast on the anniversary of the institution without fasting previously as they did when observing it at other times." —*Ad Januarius* 1: 7.

Eusebius (265 A. D.), in his *Life of Constantine,* quotes the Emperor as saying to the General Council of the Church assembled at Nice, 325 A. D.:

> For their (the Jews') boast is indeed absurd, that it is not in our power without instruction from them to observe these things (the celebration of the anniversary of the Lord's supper). . . . For our Savior has left us one feast in commemoration of the day of our deliverance, I mean the day of his most holy passion.

Eusebius further says that the eastern churches retained

The Eucharist

the custom of observing the anniversary, while the western churches kept the Sunday evening following.

The Council of Antioch, A. D. 341, said:

Whosoever shall presume to set aside the decree of the holy and great Synod which was assembled at Nice in the presence of the pious Emperor Constantine, beloved of God, concerning the holy and salutary feast of Easter; if they shall persist in opposing what was then rightly ordained let them be excommunicated and cast out of the church.—Canon 1.

Chrysostom (347 A. D.) says:

Many partake of this sacrifice once in the whole year, others twice; others many times.

Many more quotations might be given. So many have been given simply to show how great is the multitude of witnesses to the truth of the statement that there was no uniform rule as to the time of observing the Lord's supper. Since then the Gospel gives no directions in the matter of time, and the apostolic and later church used liberty of conscience in the matter, we conclude that the church of to-day may do the same. Perhaps the best way is to have a regular anniversary observance, and then such other occasions of observance as the church may wish.

Suggestions on the Lord's Supper.

1. *The Lord's supper, including feet-washing, the love-feast, and the eucharist, is a unity and should not be divided.*

(1) The service was a unit in its institution. The announcement of the near departure of the Lord, and the full authority He possessed to institute ordinances, is made at the beginning of the entire service and applies to each of the three symbols. The one followed the other in orderly and immediate succession, and the whole closed with a common benediction. There is no evidence that they were

ever separated in the apostolic church, and although the service became separated later, that is nothing to us. We must follow the Lord rather than the customs of men.

(2) The service is one in significance. It includes three of the four great truths of physical or spiritual life. Baptism represented the new birth and this service represents cleansing, exercise and nutrition. The first provides the beginning of life, and the other three have to do with its growth and continuance. They belong together. Feet-washing represents cleansing for communion and service. The love-feast represents the exercise of Christian love, and crowning all, the eucharist represents our union with God. Peace having been made through the atonement, we are sustained by the divine life as the branch is sustained by the vine. Service, fellowship, worship,—these three agree in one. The service is a unit.

(3) The service is a unit as a type. It is the type of the marriage of Christ and the church. The feet-washing represents the purity of the bride, the sanctification "without which no man shall see the Lord" (Heb. 12: 14), the "wedding-garment" without which there is no admission to the feast (Matt. 22: 11-13). The love-feast represents the wedding supper. Blessed are they that are called to partake (Rev. 19: 9). The eucharist represents the mystic union of bride and groom, the Church and her Lord, henceforth never to be separated again (Rev. 19: 7, 8). Which of these three things, think you, can be omitted in the antitype, the real marriage feast in heaven? But if not in the antitype, then neither in the type may either one be omitted. The service is a unit.

This figure of the heavenly marriage feast is a representation of the heavenly life, of which we have the earnest here (2 Cor. 1: 22; Eph. 1: 14), but the fullness hereafter (Rev. 22: 17). It is a representation of the kingdom of God, and what is that? It is "not eating and drinking, but righteousness and peace and joy in the Holy Spirit" (Rom. 14: 17). First, righteousness by faith (represented by the rite of cleansing), then joy, the joy of fellowship (represented by the supper), and then peace, the peace of God that passeth all understanding (represented by the eucharist). "For he is our peace who hath made both one." Which of these three, think you, should be omitted, either in reality or in type?

Lastly, since righteousness is by faith (Rom. 3: 21, 22), and "faith worketh through love" (Gal. 5: 6), and "love is of God, for God is love" (1 John 4: 7), the service of cleansing exercises *faith;* the supper inspires hope for the heavenly feast, and the cup and loaf unite us with Christ in love. Faith, hope, love, the abiding things of God,—which of them, think you, should be omitted, in reality or in symbol? This blessed service is one, one in form, one in significance and one in spirit. "What God hath joined together, let not man put asunder" (Matt. 19: 6).

2. *The Lord's Supper should always be preceded by spiritual preparation.* There should be special services to explain the reasons for the service, so as to strengthen faith, and induce proper preparation on the part of the members. This should be accompanied by visitation of all the members by the pastor and others appointed for the work. Every effort should be made to have the church in love and harmony, so that all the members will commune if possible, and that worthily. The early church prepared by a period of fasting, which was not at all a bad idea. If the modern church would fast a little more and feast a little less it would enter into the spirit of the service a little better.

3. *The early church was accustomed to give the "holy kiss"* (Rom. 16: 16) *or "kiss of love" or "peace"* (1 Peter 5: 14) at the Lord's supper, and it seems certain that the

custom was derived from the apostles. This was usually given just following the prayers preceding the supper and was a beautiful symbol of love and harmony. It is more fully discussed in a separate chapter and is therefore passed here with the mere mention of the fact that, while there is no express mention of it in the accounts of the institution of the Lord's supper, yet the spirit of the service not only allows it, but almost requires it. Love seeks to express itself, and grows by expression, and there is no symbol so universally used as this sacred symbol of love. The holy kiss of the children of God stands for a type of love so much higher than that which the world knows, that it should be continued as an outward witness of the "love which is the bond of perfectness." Col. 3: 14.

4. *The communion loaf should be unleavened and the communion cup should be unfermented.*

We use the term "loaf" instead of "bread" because the Greek word *artos,* uniformly used, means literally "loaf" (in the plural, "bread"). The customary loaves were small, round cakes about six inches long.

UNLEAVENED BREAD.

(1) The communion bread should be without leaven because leaven is a symbol of sin. The Jewish Passover, which was a type of this feast, was required to be eaten without leaven, and included the seven-day feast of unleavened bread (Ex. 12: 15; 34: 25). To the Israelites it represented the haste with which they came out of Egypt, but to the Christian, Egypt represents the bondage of sin, and both Jesus and the apostles use leaven as a type of sin. See Matt. 16: 6, 11; Mark 8: 15; Luke 12: 1; 1 Cor. 5: 6-8; Gal. 5: 9. Since the communion bread represents to us the body of our sinless Lord, it should not contain the element which represents sin. The strong may overlook this Gospel

The Eucharist

significance of leaven, but the weak may be affected by it.

(2) The exhortation of Paul in 1 Cor. 5: 7, 8, "Let us keep the feast with the unleavened bread of sincerity and truth" occupies much the same position as his phrase "buried with Christ in baptism" occupies with reference to that rite. He mentions both the rite and the thing signified, and the two should correspond.

UNFERMENTED WINE.

(3) Nowhere in the Gospel is there any command to use wine for the communion cup. There is not even any mention of wine in this connection, nor any definite precedent in the Gospel of its being used. Moreover, even if it were used, the word commonly translated "wine" in the Gospel, is *oinos* which means either fermented or unfermented wine. It is only *supposed* that Jesus used wine.

(4) What Jesus did use was "the fruit of the vine" (Luke 22: 18). Now the fruit of the vine is the pure blood of the grape. What is fermented wine? It is the fruit of bacteria, the product of decay, the poison of alcohol. We cannot have fermented wine without a rotting of the liquid through the action of the bacteria that get into it. Let us not substitute the poisonous product of decay for the pure "fruit of the vine" which Jesus used. It is no wonder that the *Apostolic Constitutions* (canon 3) forbade its use.

(5) The communion cup represents the blood of the sinless Christ. How can fermented (rotten) wine do that? Where is the reason for using that curse of the ages denounced from the beginning of God's Word to the end of it, to represent that which is most sacred and holy? It is out of reason to do so. The very thought of it is repulsive.

(6) Even if there were no Scripture for it, the fitness of things would be against the use of fermented wine. It is associated with the saloon, the low dance hall and the

brothel. It is the destroyer of homes and lives. The very smell of it in the communion cup might (as it has) renew in some converted drunkard the demon of appetite for alcohol. Let not the church of God be guilty of such a sin.

(7) *Not only should the communion cup be unfermented, but we believe that it should be a mingled cup, that is, mingled with water.* Certain it is that such was the cup used by the early church. Justin Martyr (130 A. D.) distinctly testifies to this. He says, " there is brought a cup of wine mingled with water."—*Apology* 1: 65.

It was the tradition of the church that the cup which Jesus gave to His disciples was the pure blood of the grape mingled with water. The Council of Trullo (692 A. D.) in forbidding the omission of water from the cup said that James the brother of Jesus had commanded it, and quotes also from Basil and the Council of Carthage, which based its action on the command of Jesus. See canon 32.

Whether the tradition was true or not, the significance of the mingled cup is worthy of such a command. The wine and water mingled represented the blood and water that came from the side of Jesus as they thrust in the spear. Physicians say that this flow of blood and water proved that the heart had burst, and Jesus was dead before ever they thrust in the spear, but the thieves were still alive. It was not the cross that killed our Lord. It was the agony of bearing the sin of the world. When He, the Son of God, loving the Father with an infinite love, found that in taking the sinner's place He must bear the sinner's doom of separation from God, in that most awful moment He cried, " My God, My God, Why hast thou forsaken me?" Matt. 27: 46. They were no words of weakness which mark the climax of the awful tragedy when the Son faced separation from the Father. Then burst His mighty heart. It burst because of the sin of the world which He bore. Well may

The Eucharist

we mingle water with the wine to remind ourselves of that burst heart, the fearful penalty which sin involves for Him or us. Dear Lord Jesus, help us to be true to Thee!

5. *The Lord's Supper should be for the Lord's people, and not an exhibition for the world.* The first service by Jesus and the disciples was private, and the service continued to be private in the early church. The revelers who crept in were members of the church, not scoffers from the world. So strict was the post-apostolic church that they came to have a doorkeeper to admit only those who were to participate. This was partly on account of the persecutions which drove the church to observe the feast in secret, but even where there was liberty the unbelieving world was not admitted. There are other services for the instruction and conversion of unbelievers; this is the one service above all others which is for the church. There may be spectators of the marriage feast in heaven who are not participants, but they will be on the other side of the impassable gulf (Luke 16: 19-30).

Chrysostom explains the thought of the church of the fourth century by saying:

For the mysteries we too therefore celebrate with closed doors, and keep out the uninterested, not for any weakness of which we have convicted our rites, but because the many are yet imperfectly prepared for them. For this reason Jesus himself also discoursed much unto the Jews in parables "because they seeing saw not."

Since the first institution was private, and there is not the slightest indication that the apostles changed it in this respect, the burden of proof should be upon those who would make it public to-day. Where is the proof in the Scriptures that it should be public? Do you quote Jesus who said. " In secret have I done nothing " and again " Let your light shine; then what will you do with Jesus' example in this?

To make the service for the church only is not to make it secret, nor is it to hide the light. The church will have more influence for good if it guards this sacred service from the distractions incident to the presence of a large crowd, out of sympathy with the whole thing. The young people, especially, are embarrassed by the winks and grins of their unconverted acquaintances who sit back. They should have their minds on the lessons of the service instead.

It may not be expedient to forbid the coming of any but members, or even to announce the service as for the church only, but if it is announced as a service intended for only those who love the Lord, and then is conducted solely with reference to the participants, as it ought to be, it is not likely that scoffers will continue to come. It may be difficult to reform the customs in some places, but the service should be made to conform as nearly as possible to the original pattern given in the upper room in Jerusalem. If the marriage supper of the Lamb is for the bride and invited guests only, the pattern of that supper here should not violate its function as a type.

6. *The Lord's Supper should be made a blessing to others than participants as far as possible*. It was the custom of the early church to send portions remaining from the feast to the absent, especially to the sick and poor. There is a hint at this custom in 1 Cor. 11: 33 where Paul commands the church to tarry one for the other, lest some be hungry and others drunken. He would have a proper distribution so that all would have their share.

Justin Martyr (130 A. D.) says that the deacons attended to the distribution of portions to those absent, and to the poor. From the *Didache* as well as from later testimonies it seems that offerings were made in abundance at these feasts, and were called "oblations." Some of them went to the ministry.

It may be more practical to have an offering of money for the poor at such occasions, but the spirit of love inculcated by the service should be given a chance for practical expression. It is a law of psychology that an emotion aroused but not expressed causes a reaction that makes it more difficult to arouse that emotion again. Let the tide of brotherly love which floods the feast of love be made to overflow until all the needy in the community are made to realize its reality, and there will be faith in the service, far greater than that inspired by allowing skeptical witnesses of a service purely formal.

7. There is no commandment as to what materials shall compose the supper. There was liquid food of some sort at the time of its institution, for we read of Jesus dipping a sop (John 13: 26), but there is no intimation that soup is therefore *required,* although, of course, it eases the conscience to have the copy as nearly as possible like the original. In any case the food should be wholesome, and abundant enough to constitute a true supper or feast, with plenty remaining to send to the absent or give to the poor.

Tertullian (160 A. D.) mentions both meat and vegetable food as being used. The table of showbread in the tabernacle contained utensils for both food and drink (Ex. 25: 29) and Jesus when instituting the Lord's supper spoke of both eating and drinking in the antitypical supper of the kingdom (Luke 22: 30), but as to just what to eat and drink there is left liberty of conscience.

The lamb which was so essential to the Passover feast met its antitype in Christ (1 Cor. 5: 7), who is present in this feast in the emblems of His body and blood, and therefore to contend for lamb in the supper is unscriptural. Let the feast be an ample but plain meal, such as befits the modest bride who is watching for the coming of her Lord.

8. The custom of visiting neighboring congregations at

such a time is apostolic and helpful. The presence and testimony of fellow Christians strengthens all and widens the spirit of love and fellowship.

9. *The supper as Jesus instituted it included conversation and instruction.* It will add much to the value of the service to have an open season of testimony. There will be many public confessions made, which will strengthen the persons making them and others as well, and there will be new resolves made and blessed experiences related, which will help to clothe the entire service with flesh and blood and make it a season of blessed memory.

10. *The occasions of the Lord's Supper should be given to learning the lessons of the various symbols employed.* During the feet-washing the minds of the people should be directed to the necessity of cleansing from sin and to the spirit of humble and loving service. During the supper the thought should be directed toward the lessons of fellowship and brotherly love and equality. During the eucharist the lessons of the giving of our Lord for us and of our union with Him, should be the subject of meditation and prayer.

Controversy is out of place at this time. The world should be instructed at other times in the reasons for the forms observed; this is the one occasion for the spiritual direction of the members. If their minds are simply filled with arguments for the form they will not receive the lessons taught by the forms. Thus they will " strain at a gnat and swallow a camel " (Matt. 23: 23, 24). Every effort should be made to remove distractions and make the communion real rather than formal.

In the discussion of these ordinances we have tried to be true to the Scriptures, to history, and to the experience of the churches which observe them as here described. They only of all the church are qualified to speak of their worth. Their general spirit of humility and brotherly love and their

The Lord's Supper

devotion to the Gospel are living evidence of the value of these sacred ordinances, even when largely spoiled by the spirit of formality. If we are wise we will not stumble at the formality, but seek to correct it. When the supper was abused at Corinth, Paul did not abolish what the Lord had commanded, but only the abuses which would have destroyed all if they had remained. We do not reject all money because of counterfeits, or all the church because of hypocrites. Let us not give up God's blessed means of grace because of man's perversions of them. God knows best. His teaching methods are best. His ways are best to win His ends. Are we wiser than He? If not, let us obey Him in all these things.

The following are just a few sample testimonies taken as uttered, all at a single service. They show that the statements concerning the inherent value of the service are supported by the actual experiences of the people.

This service is of such blessing to me that I would not want to give it up even if it were not commanded in the Gospel.

I am glad for a church in which I can practice these ordinances, from which I get so much strength.

The older I grow the more precious do these occasions become to me.

Every Lord's Supper seems more blessed than the last. I used to say, " O how foolish! " Now I say, " O how blessed."

It is a blessing to me to think that I am following the example of Jesus. My life has not been what I would wish it, but I am trying.

What would we do without this service? When my burdens seem like mountains, this removes them all.

This service revives my faith in our common humanity. It brings us back to Christ and unites us in Him.

This is the most solemn and blessed service that I ever passed through.

Agape

John 13: 34; 1 Cor. 5: 7.

How happy the feast of the children of God!
One Master, our Savior, as onward we plod;
All brethren and sisters, united in love,
Our feast is a foretaste of heaven above,
Whose glory is love, the glory of God.

Love seeketh the lost ones wherever they flee;
Love shareth their sorrows, whatever they be;
Love healeth the wounds that ingratitude makes;
Love cheereth the heart when all courage forsakes;
Love lifteth the world, blessed Father, to Thee.

Love gildeth the cross and maketh it bright;
Love lifteth the burden and maketh it light;
Love stirreth the heart to compassionate beat;
Love warmeth the heart and hasteth the feet;
Love maketh all service a source of delight.

Come feast on the love that in Jesus we share;
Come help to make earth like to heaven so fair;
Come learn by the symbol; come join in the song;
Come share in the service, God's praises prolong;
Come feast on God's love and for heaven prepare.

CHAPTER V

THREE SYMBOLS RELATING TO THE HOLY SPIRIT.

The Laying on of Hands—Ordination for Special Service—Anointing the Sick with Oil.

"The teaching of baptism and of laying on of hands."—Heb. 6: 2.

"If ye then, being evil, know how to give good gifts unto your children, how much more will your heavenly Father give the Holy Spirit to them that ask him."—Luke 11: 13.

"And when they heard this, they were baptized into the name of the Lord Jesus. And when Paul had laid his hands upon them, the Holy Spirit came on them."—Acts 19: 5, 6.

* * * * * *

"But ye shall receive power when the Holy Spirit is come upon you: and ye shall be my witnesses, both in Jerusalem, and in all Judea and Samaria, and unto the uttermost part of the earth."—Acts 1: 8.

"Neglect not the gift that is in thee, which was given thee by prophecy, with the laying on of the hands of the presbytery."—1 Tim. 4: 14.

* * * * * *

"And into whatsoever city ye enter, and they receive you, eat such things as are set before you: and heal the sick that are therein, and say unto them, The kingdom of God is come nigh unto you."—Luke 10: 8, 9.

"Is any among you sick? Let him call for the elders of the church; and let them pray over him, anointing him with oil in the name of the Lord. And the prayer of faith shall save him that is sick, and the Lord shall raise him up; and if he have committed sins it shall be forgiven him."—James 5: 14, 15.

THREE SYMBOLS RELATING TO THE HOLY SPIRIT.

There is need of teaching concerning the Holy Spirit, for, while the Gospel itself contains many references to Him, yet until of recent years there has been little taught in sermon or in song. One Sunday-school teacher, typical we fear of many, declared to his class that the Holy Spirit is only an influence or emanation akin to electricity. Many preachers, even, have confused the Spirit with the Word, and the church for ages has lacked in power because it has lacked faith in the enduement of the Holy Spirit. The awakening of faith in the promise of enduement has been accompanied by a quickening of the church and a mighty, world-wide wave of evangelism.

1. THE HOLY SPIRIT IS A PERSON. The personal pronoun is used in Scripture references to Him (John 15: 26; 16: 7, 8, 13, 14, etc). The Revised Version rightly capitalizes the pronouns referring to Him in the Old Testament. Personal qualities are attributed to Him, such as knowledge (1 Cor. 2: 10, 11), will (1 Cor. 12: 11), mind (Rom. 8: 27), love (Rom. 15: 30), grief (Eph. 4: 30). Personal acts are also ascribed to Him. He "searcheth" (1 Cor. 2: 10), "bears witness" (John 15: 26) and "teaches" (John 14: 26).

The Holy Spirit is also said to possess the attributes of Deity. He is eternal (Heb. 9: 14), omnipresent (Psa. 139: 7-10), omnipotent (Luke 1: 35; Rom. 15: 19), and omniscient (John 16: 12, 13). He is called God (Heb. 3: 7-9; Acts 5: 3, 4) and yet is distinguished from the Father and the Son (Luke 3: 21, 22; Matt. 28: 19; John 16: 7; Acts

2: 33), being sent by the Father and the Son (John 14: 26; 15: 26) and speaking the message from them (John 16: 13, R. V.; cf. John 7: 16, 18; 8: 26, 40).

In considering the enduement of the Spirit it is not necessary to attempt any metaphysical discussion of the Trinity. It is enough to know that we have in our own experience the manifestations of the Trinity, and know God as the Holy Spirit in His manifestation to the spiritual capacities of our own lives. The Holy Spirit has always been in the world, but only the spiritually minded have been able to perceive Him. "The natural man receiveth not the things of the Spirit of God: for they are foolishness unto him; and he cannot know them because they are spiritually judged. But he that is spiritual judgeth all things, and he himself is judged of no man" (1 Cor. 2: 14, 15). Just as steam or electricity must have proper mediums or instruments through which to work, so the Holy Spirit must have spiritual minds to which to reveal Himself. The blind perceive no light and the deaf perceive no sound, and the worldly minded know not the voice of the Spirit of God. He labored with the antediluvian people with little response (Gen. 6: 3), but He touched the hearts of the prophets, and "holy men of old spake as they were moved by the Holy Spirit" (2 Pet. 1: 21). He breathed the spirit of song into the heart of the psalmist and gave the words of the Gospel to the apostles (1 Cor. 2: 13).

In His work He is sometimes represented as a purging fire (Isa. 4: 4), sometimes as a reviving wind (Ezek. 37: 9, 10, 14), sometimes as the refreshing rain and dew (Hosea 6: 3; Psa. 133: 3) and sometimes as water for the thirsty (Isa. 44: 3, 4) or a river of water of life (Ezek. 47). They who receive Him are said to be born of the Spirit (John 3: 5), then to have the upspringing life eternal (John 4: 14), and then the outflowing life of blessing (John 7: 38).

The Holy Spirit

He is called "the Spirit of the Lord" (Isa. 11: 2), "the Holy Spirit" (Luke 11: 13), "the spirit of burning" (Isa. 4: 4), "the spirit of holiness" (Rom. 1: 4), "the spirit of truth" (John 15: 26), "the spirit of life" (Rom. 8: 2), "the spirit of grace" (Heb. 10: 29), "the spirit of glory" (1 Peter 4: 14), and "the Comforter" (John 14: 26).

2. OLD TESTAMENT TYPES. In the tabernacle types of the church there was first the anointing of the priests with the sacred oil (Ex. 30: 23-33) representing their anointing by the Holy Spirit for their special service. Kings were also so anointed (1 Sam. 10: 1; 16: 1, 13). There was also in the holy place a candlestick, seven-branched to represent divinity (compare Rev. 1: 4), and daily renewing of oil to represent the daily renewing of the Holy Spirit (cf. Zech. 4: 1-6; 2 Cor. 4: 16). Then finally, in the holy of holies there was kept Aaron's rod that budded as a sign of the authority of the priesthood in the office to which they were called and consecrated by the Holy Spirit (Num. 17: 10). These three symbols represented sanctification by the Spirit for service, for worship and for administration, and pointed to the corresponding work of the Holy Spirit under the new covenant, represented and perpetuated in the church by appropriate symbols, which we are now to consider.

3. THE HOLY SPIRIT IN THE CHURCH. This is the age of the Holy Spirit. The prediction of Joel (Joel 2: 28-32) and of John the Baptist (Matt. 3: 11) and the promise of Jesus (Acts 1: 5) was fulfilled on the day of Pentecost, when the Holy Spirit came to the church nevermore to depart. This coming to the church was more than the enduement of the twelve apostles; for others than the twelve were endued,— as Stephen (Acts 6: 8), and Philip (Acts 8: 4-6) and Paul (Acts 19: 7). The gift was given to the believing Samaritans (Acts 8: 14-17) and to the Gentiles (Acts 10: 44-48), to women as well as to men (Acts 2: 17). Peter, filled with

the Holy Spirit, said " To you is the promise, and to your children, and to all that are afar off, *even* as many as the Lord our God shall call " (Acts 2: 37-39). Paul under the same inspiration commanded, " Be filled with the Spirit " (Eph. 5: 18). More than all, Jesus himself taught us to ask for the Holy Spirit, saying, " If ye then, being evil, know how to give good gifts unto your children, how much more will your Father in heaven give the Holy Spirit to them that ask him " (Luke 11: 13).

The baptism of John was accompanied with the promise that the Holy Spirit should come, but after Pentecost Christian baptism was regularly confirmed by the gracious work of the Holy Spirit (Acts 19: 1-6). John speaks of the work of the Spirit in believers as if it were sevenfold, as follows: (1) Regeneration (John 3: 3-6), (2) indwelling (ch. 4: 14; cf. Eph. 3: 16 and Gal. 5: 22), (3) outflowing (John 7: 38), (4) comforting (John 14: 16), (5) teaching (John 14: 26; 1 John 2: 27), (6) guiding (John 16: 13), and (7) convicting of sin, of righteousness and of judgment (John 16: 8).

Aside from baptism, which was the rite of induction into the church (1 Cor. 12: 13; Gal. 3: 27), there are three Gospel symbols to represent the work of the Holy Spirit in the church: (1) The laying on of hands, to represent the enduement of the Spirit for service (Heb. 6: 2; Acts 19: 1-6), (2) ordination, to represent anointing for special service (1 Tim. 4: 14), and (3) anointing the sick with oil to represent the work of the Holy Spirit in healing (Jas. 5: 14).

THE LAYING ON OF HANDS THE SYMBOL OF ENDUEMENT.

1. ENDUEMENT FOR SERVICE IS MORE THAN REGENERATION. The enduement of the Spirit for service is something more than the regeneration symbolized in baptism. We are said to be "born of water and of the Spirit," but this spiritual birth is not accomplished by the Spirit alone, but by the Father who begets (1 John 5: 18), the Son who brought the life (1 John 5: 11, 12), and the Holy Spirit who enables us to receive it (Titus 3: 5), hence the triune form of the commission (Matt. 28: 19) and of the act of baptism. Through this regeneration we become members of the body of Christ (1 Cor. 12: 13), which is the church (Eph. 1: 22, 23) and are thus "added to the Lord" (Acts 5: 14), which is infinitely more than to be added merely to a human organization.

But the Christian life is not simply a keeping free from evil. It is a life of service, and we are called to labor while it is day (John 9: 4); it is a vineyard, and we must render the fruits in their season (Matt. 21: 34); it is a stewardship, and we must be faithful (1 Cor. 4: 2); it is a fight of faith, and we must be good soldiers (2 Tim. 2: 3). The field is the world, and to the church as a whole is given the marching orders. "Ye shall be witnesses of me," was spoken to the church, as was also the promise of enduement of power (Acts 1: 8; 2: 39). The gifts of the Spirit may differ, but there is some gift for all. "All these (gifts) worketh the one and the same Spirit, dividing to each one severally even as he will" (1 Cor. 12: 11).

2. ANOINTING FOR SERVICE UNDER THE OLD COVENANT. Under the old covenant the anointing for service was only for priests and kings, but now all believers are called to be

"kings and priests unto God" (Rev. 1: 6), and therefore require the anointing for service. Jesus received the Spirit at baptism as He prayed (Luke 3: 21, 22). Then He taught by the Spirit (Luke 4: 18), gave commandments by the Spirit (Acts 1: 2) healed by the Spirit (Matt. 12: 28), and by the Spirit offered Himself a sacrifice for sin (Heb. 9: 14). The church was likewise endued for its work of witnessing, and this enduement was continued by repeated blessings. Peter and others were filled with the Spirit in Acts 2: 4, and again in Acts 4: 8, and again in Acts 4: 31, and with the disciples again in Acts 13: 52.

3. SPECIAL GIFTS OF THE APOSTLES. In the case of the twelve, and some others, there were special gifts (1 Cor. 12, 28, 29) by which they were enabled to perform "signs" as proof of their authority (Luke 10: 19), even as the miracles of Jesus were proofs of His authority (Acts 2: 22), special miracles being wrought by Paul (Acts 19: 11), because of his special call to the apostleship, but these signs were special rather than regular (1 Cor. 13: 8) and therefore are now not a necessary part of the enduement of the Spirit, although in modern times, especially in mission fields, there are authentic instances of the wonderful works of God, not less miraculous than those recorded of the apostolic church. The apostles also were inspired as to the deep truths of God (Eph. 3: 5), and as to the language by which to teach it (1 Cor. 2: 13; 1 Peter 1: 10, 11, 12).

While not all are called to be apostles yet all are called to be witnesses, and it is for the work of witnessing that the enduement of the Spirit specially prepares. This work includes: (1) The help of the Spirit in understanding the Word of God, "Interpreting spiritual things to spiritual men" (1 Cor. 2: 13 R. V. margin); "The anointing ye have received teacheth you all things" (John 2: 27);

(2) help in prayer. "Praying in the Spirit" (Eph. 6: 18); "We know not how to pray as we ought; but the Spirit himself maketh intercession for us with groanings which cannot be uttered" (Rom. 8: 26, 27; see also Jude 20); (3) help in song (Eph. 5: 18-20; Heb. 13: 15); (4) help in preaching (John 15: 26, 27; Acts 4: 31; 5: 32, &c.).

Before the disciples were endued they were quarrelsome, timid and doubting, but after they were endued they immediately began "with great power to bear witness of the resurrection of Jesus Christ from the dead," and soon filled Jerusalem with their doctrine (Acts 5: 28) and then carried it to the regions beyond (Col. 1: 23). In this the lay members had a part as well as the apostles, for while the latter were yet in Jerusalem "they that were scattered abroad went everywhere preaching the Word" (Acts 8: 4). If the church to-day would obey the commission of our Lord and all the lay members would assist in winning souls and spreading the Gospel would there not be a larger enduement of power for the glorious work?

4. THE CONDITIONS OF ENDUEMENT. The Holy Spirit may be received just as we receive salvation through Christ.

(1) There must be *faith*. "Received ye the Spirit by the works of the law or the hearing of faith?" (Gal. 3: 2, 14).

(2) *Repentance*. "Repent and be baptized, every one of you in the name of Jesus Christ, unto the remission of your sins and ye shall receive the gift of the Holy Spirit" (Acts 2: 39).

(3) *Obedience*. "The Holy Spirit whom God hath given to those that obey him" (Acts 5: 32).

(4) *Prayer*. "How much more will your Father in heaven give the Holy Spirit to them that ask him" (Luke 11: 13).

5. LAYING ON OF HANDS THE SYMBOL OF ENDUEMENT.

As a symbol of this enduement of the Spirit the apostolic church was given the "laying on of hands." In Heb. 6: 2 this is called one of the "first principles of the doctrine of Christ." The six principles mentioned are: (1) repentance, (2) faith, (3) baptism, (4) the laying on of hands, (5) resurrection, and (6) judgment. The laying on of hands is mentioned as distinct from, but coördinate with baptism. These six principles are "first" in the Christian life, and hence the other ordinances connected with later development are not here mentioned.

While we have no record of the command to lay on hands after baptism being given by Jesus, before the ascension, yet He must have given it at some time, for all the apostles practiced it. Jesus Himself gave the *example* of laying on hands as a symbol of imparting the Spirit in healing or blessing (Matt. 19: 13; Mark 6: 5; Luke 13: 13), and commanded the disciples to do likewise (Mark 16: 18). Even if this last passage be rejected, the rest are sufficient to give His authority to the rite.

6. TIME AND MANNER OF OBSERVANCE. As a "first principle" the laying on of hands comes at the beginning of the Christian life. In the case of the Samaritans, there was a delay until the sanction of the apostles could be received upon the work done at Samaria (Acts 8: 12-17), but in the case of the men at Ephesus, the laying on of hands followed baptism at once (Acts 19: 1-6). In every case it was accompanied by prayer, but whether the prayers always preceded the laying on of hands it is impossible to say.

7. THE PRACTICE OF THE EARLY CHURCH. The symbol thus derived from the Old Testament types and practiced by Jesus and the apostles, was continued in the early church.

Tertullian, who was born only sixty-three years after John died, says:

The Laying on of Hands

In the next place (after baptism) the hand is laid on us invoking and inviting the Holy Spirit through benediction.—De Baptism, ch. 8.

Apostolic Canons (second and fourth centuries), say:

Let him say these and like things, for this is the efficacy of the **laying on of hands,** for unless there be such a recital made for every one of these, the candidate for baptism does only descend into the water as do the Jews, and he only puts off the filth of the body and not the filth of the soul.—Canon 44.

Cyprian (200 A. D.), in arguing for the rebaptism of those who had received only single, forward immersion, says:

Or if they attribute the effect of baptism to the majesty of the name, so that they who are baptized anywhere and anyhow in the name of Jesus Christ are judged to be renewed and sanctified, why among them are not **hands laid upon the baptized persons in the name of the same Christ, for the reception of the Holy Spirit?**—Epistles, 70.

Jerome (340 A. D.) says:

Do you not know that the laying on of hands after baptism and the invocation of the Spirit, is a custom of the churches? Do you demand Scripture proof? You may find it in the Acts of the apostles. And even if it did not rest upon the authority of the Scriptures, yet the consensus of the whole world in this respect would have the force of a command.—To the Luciferians, ch. 8.

That this apostolic rite persisted in the church much longer than this is shown by the statement of Pope Urban First, in the eighth century. He says:

For all the faithful ought to receive the Holy Spirit after baptism by imposition of the hand of the bishops, so that they may be Christians fully.

Modern church historians need not be quoted, because there is no dispute as to the practice of the apostolic church. *Hastings' Bible Dictionary* says: " In the post-apostolic church the practice was universal." "There is nothing," says *Dr. Wall,* "more frequently mentioned in antiquity than this anointing and laying on of hands of the bishop in order to implore the graces of the Spirit on the baptized."

If, then, we find the rite typified in the Old Testament and the type fulfilled in the coming of the Spirit, and this "earnest of the Spirit" (2 Cor. 1: 22) pointing to the fuller blessings of the next dispensation, symbolized in the practice of Jesus and the apostles and the church by the laying on of hands, we are certainly right in continuing the symbol as one of the helpful means of grace which God has given. Modern churches have almost wholly discarded it, but they have also largely lost the enduement of the Spirit for service, and the witness of the church is not what it was in the days of the apostles. The passing of the symbol has been marked by the neglect of the truth back of it, so that if the apostle should come to the churches of to-day and say to the members, "Did ye receive the Holy Spirit when ye believed?" only a few of them would be able to answer, "Praise God, I did!"

But is it not the duty of the church to seek this enduement for service? The command is clear: "Be ye filled with the Spirit." If we heed it, by obeying the conditions of enduement, we should soon find the joy of soul-winning. The church would be engaged in spiritual occupations rather than be continually trying to entertain itself, and often running with the world into all kinds of frivolity in order to do so.

It is not for us to choose our gifts (1 Cor. 12: 11), but to allow the Spirit to divide to each as He will, nevertheless we are to "covet earnestly the best gifts" (1 Cor. 12: 31), and to use what we have in service. Especially the members of churches which have the teaching of the laying on of hands should show to the world that this is

The Laying on of Hands

no empty form, but that in preserving the symbol they also receive the promise and bear the witness to which the Savior calls, and for which the Holy Spirit prepares.

ORDINATION: THE SYMBOL OF ENDUEMENT FOR SPECIAL SERVICE.

1. SOME GIFT FOR ALL AND SPECIAL GIFTS FOR SOME. Besides the enduement of the Holy Spirit for service, which it is the privilege of all Christians to receive, there is a further special enduement for special service to which some are called, which has its appropriate symbol in the rite of ordination.

"There are diversities of gifts, but the same Spirit" (1 Cor. 12: 4) and to all there is a gift of some kind, for "all these worketh one and the same Spirit, dividing to each one severally even as he will" (1 Cor. 12: 11). Not all are apostles, or prophets (v. 29), but those that are have their special gift from God and are responsible for it. Paul says, "I thank God who ENABLED ME putting me into the ministry." Part of this divine preparation may be by nature, as in the case of Timothy, who inherited a disposition to faith (2 Tim. 1: 5); and part of it is the gift of the Spirit received in ordination (1 Tim. 4: 14), but whatever the gift, and however received, it is to be developed by study and use. "Neglect not the gift that is in thee" (1 Tim. 4: 14). "Give diligence to present thyself approved unto God, a workman that needeth not to be ashamed" (2 Tim. 2: 15).

2. ORDINATION A SYMBOL OF SEPARATION FOR SPECIAL SERVICE. In the service of the "church in the wilderness" there was the ordination of priests and kings by the anointing with oil as a symbol of the anointing of the Holy Spirit, and in the tabernacle Aaron's rod that budded was preserved as a symbol of the authority of the priesthood in their special work. Joshua was ordained as the

successor of Moses by the laying on of hands and giving a charge (Num. 27: 18-23). Jesus was anointed by the Spirit for His mission. He said, "The Spirit of the Lord is upon me, because he hath anointed me to preach the Gospel to the poor" &c. (Luke 4: 18). Persons so ordained were called "The Lord's anointed" (Zech. 4: 14; 1 Sam. 12: 3, 5, &c.). In the church the six men who were chosen to look after the poor were set apart by prayer and the laying on of hands (Acts 6: 6), as if such ordination were already familiar. Paul and Barnabas were similarly set apart for their missionary labors (Acts 13: 2). Timothy received his gift "by the laying on of hands of the presbytery" (1 Tim. 4: 14), and was told in turn to "lay hands hastily on no man" (1 Tim. 5: 22). When Titus was told to "appoint elders in every church" (Titus 1: 5) he doubtless did it in the regular way with prayer and the laying on of hands. This was not a mere form of consecration to special work, but an outward symbol of the inward enduement of the Holy Spirit for that work. Whom the Lord calls He also qualifies if the person called has faith to receive the gift.

3. THE DUTY OF CALLING WORKERS TO THE MINISTRY. Just as it is the duty of the entire church to "be filled with the Spirit" and thus endued for service, so it is the duty of the church to seek out those who may be fitted for special service and call them to such work. Under the Old Covenant, the tribe of Levi was separated for the work of the priesthood as a substitute for the firstborn of every family, to whom God made claim as His own in recognition of His ownership of all. He has not relinquished His ownership. He still says to us in emphatic tones, "Ye are not your own; ye have been bought with a price" (1 Cor. 6: 20). The children all belong to Him (Psa. 127: 3), and therefore parents have no right to

plan for their children as if God had no claim upon them for their life work. Instead of setting apart one in ten, or the firstborn, the Gospel calls for every one to labor as he may. It says, " Pray ye therefore the Lord of the harvest that he may send forth laborers into his harvest " (Matt. 9: 38). We are taught that the " gift of prophecy," that is, the teaching or preaching of the Gospel, is the greatest of the spiritual gifts (1 Cor. 14: 5), and we are therefore commanded to " desire earnestly to prophesy " (1 Cor. 14: 39) and to " covet earnestly the greater gifts " (1 Cor. 12: 31). The church at this age stands greatly condemned. Instead of being concerned for the ripe harvest fields of the Master, perishing for want of workers, God's people are almost wholly concerned with their own. Instead of praying that God may give them children who may become ministers or missionaries, Christian parents endow their children with the lust of the flesh at conception and with the lust of gold from infancy up. Instead of teaching them the blessedness of the ministry, they tell them of its hardships and so criticise the ministry that the children are turned from it. And the church, instead of diligently seeking out those who may be useful in the higher callings, sees her bright young men and women turn to the world to struggle for money and honor, because she has not laid her hands upon them to claim them for the work of God. Although God has given her wealth, she spends it upon her pleasures, while those who would be willing to spread the Gospel are left to struggle as they may without call or financial encouragement. The church is corrupted by the poison of the world. O that the ministry would with the trumpet of God call her to prayer! But alas, the ministry itself is largely to blame, for how few are the preachers that are doing their duty and recruiting the ranks of the workers; and that although the most important part of their work

Ordination for Special Service

is the finding and training of other workers. Jesus so regarded it, for He made the training of the disciples the great work of His ministry, and it was this work that bore fruit in the spread and permanence of the Gospel.

4. THE DUTY OF SEEKING THE CALL TO THE MINISTRY. It is not only the duty of the church to call the workers to the fields, or rather, to allow God to call them through her, but it is the duty of every Christian to desire the ministry as life work. Far from its being presumptuous to seek the ministry, we are encouraged to do so. " Faithful is the saying, If a man seeketh the office of a bishop he desireth a good work" (1 Tim. 3: 1). Is not this the exercise of the greater spiritual gifts? and are we not to covet earnestly the greater gifts? It follows that instead of waiting to think of the ministry until the slothful church issues a call, young Christians should not think of anything else as their life work until they first learn whether they may not be able to do this. Though many be called and few chosen, yet all should present themselves in readiness for whatever calling God assigns, earnestly desiring this the best.

The call to the ministry is not simply for those who are gifted and prepared for it, but for those also who have the capacity to receive preparation. Timothy was first called and then told to study, to neglect not his gift, but to give attention to reading, to exhortation and to doctrine. " Stir up the gift that is in thee " says Paul; and Jesus Himself would say to us, " Let the dead bury their own dead, but go thou and preach the kingdom of God " (Luke 9: 59, 60). That is, let those who cannot fit themselves for the higher work take care of the raising of corn, the building of houses and handling of goods, but you who have the ability and opportunity to understand and teach the Gospel, will sin against your highest self as well as against your lost brothers in the world, and against the Savior who died for all, if you turn from the winning of souls to eternal life to engage in the work which perishes with the world.

Do you say that the ministry is poorly paid? Yes, in money, but in true reward it is the most richly paid of all callings. For this life there is enough, and for eternity, reward beyond the imagination of the carnal mind to conceive. Must you leave home and lands for the sake of the Gospel? Perhaps, but Jesus said, "There is no man that hath left houses or brethren, or sisters, or father, or children, or lands, for my sake and the Gospel's sake, but he shall receive a hundredfold, now in this time, houses and brethren, and sisters, and mothers, and children, and lands, with persecutions; and in the world to come eternal life" (Mark 10: 29, 30). Do you fear that you will not be successful? It is not what the world calls *success* that the Lord requires. It is *faithfulness*. Paul says, "Let a man so account of us, as of ministers of Christ, and stewards of the mysteries of God. Here, moreover, it is required in stewards that a man be found *faithful*" (1 Cor. 4: 1); and again "Necessity is laid upon me; for woe is unto me if I preach not the Gospel. For if I do this of mine own will I have a reward: but if not of mine own will I have a stewardship intrusted to me" (1 Cor. 9: 16, 17). Christians have a stewardship in the talents and time and opportunities and life energies that God has given them. The parents have a stewardship in the children whom God has given them to train for His service. The church has a stewardship in all the members with their various gifts. They are not to be allowed to stand idle all the day long, loitering in the market place of the world when they should be in the harvest field of the Lord. The symbol of ordination by the laying on of hands is a reminder to the church that the Holy Spirit is calling for those who may do special service, and it is for the church to respond with her best. Will she do it?

Christ's Call.

"Leave the dead to bury their own dead; but go thou and publish abroad the kingdom of God" (Luke 9: 60).

I saw a youth stand in the road where the way of life divides:
And I saw the conflict in his soul surge like opposing tides.
There to the left he saw the world, a vision fair to see;
For there were parks and palaces of aristocracy;
And there were multitudes at ease, and multitudes at toil,
And there were huts and haunts of sin, as well as palace royal.
"What shall I do?" the youth inquires. "What shall I be, and where?
"What shall I seek? Shall it be wealth? or ease? or power?"
"Beware!"
A voice exclaimed in tender tones,—it seemed to call his name:
"Beware! a dungeon lies beneath the things of earthly fame."
He turned. Again he heard the voice: "Lift up your eyes, behold,
The way of life lies to the right; seek not the crown of gold."
His eyes were opened and he saw a world of human need.
He saw the bloody prints of sin, and Oh, his heart did bleed.
"Is there no help, no hope, no way by which to save these lost?"
Once more the voice said: "Lift your eyes. Behold, I paid the cost."
He looked. He saw the cross, the tomb. He saw the Savior stand,
With heavenly light upon His brow, with nail prints in His hand.
"My child, " said He, "come, follow me, and I will give you rest;
And I will give you wealth and joy, and make you truly blest.
My rest is found in righteousness; my wealth is life and truth;
My joy,—it is the harmony with things divine,—O youth,
Come with me. Let the dead in sin the things of sin attend.
Go thou and preach salvation, and be faithful till the end.
The field, the forum and the mart, have each enough,—to spare;
Thy Father's harvest field is ripe, and few the lab'rers there.
"What is it worth to add a few more farms or houses, or amass
More coins or cattle, in a world which soon itself must pass?
What matter if the world may hate you, as it hated me;
Or that it calls a "sacrifice" the life of ministry?
It is enough to know that souls are saved from sinful strife,
And that your names are written down in heaven's book of life."
O Christian youth, who read these lines, to you it is, Christ calls.
What answer will you give Him now, ere night, fast coming, falls?

ANOINTING THE SICK WITH OIL: THE SYMBOL OF ENDUEMENT FOR HEALING.

The third symbol of the Holy Spirit given to the church is that of the anointing with oil for the healing of the sick.

I. The Authority of Jesus for the Rite.

This is found in the fact that He commissioned His disciples to heal as well as to preach, and in obeying His command the disciples anointed the sick with oil for their healing.

> And he sent them forth to preach the kingdom of God and to heal the sick . . . and they departed, and went through the villages, preaching the Gospel and healing everywhere.—(Luke 9: 2, 6).

> And they cast out many demons, **and anointed with oil** many that were sick, and healed them.—(Mark 6: 13).

That this command was not for the temporary mission of the disciples only, but was a part of their world-wide work, is shown by the fact that it is included in the last great commission as recorded by Mark, and was observed by the church following.

> And he said unto them, Go ye into all the world, and preach the Gospel to the whole creation. He that believeth and is baptized shall be saved; but he that disbelieveth shall be condemned. And these signs shall accompany them that believe: in my name shall they cast out demons; they shall speak with new tongues; they shall take up serpents, and if they shall drink any deadly thing it shall in no wise hurt them.—(Mark 16: 16-18).

Grant that this passage is not found in a few of the ancient manuscripts, and that the "signs" promised as proof of authority in establishing the Gospel (Acts 2: 22) were destined to cease when no longer needed (1 Cor. 13: 8) and that the spiritual work of the Gospel is greater than its physical benefits (Compare 1 Cor. 14: 1 and 39), it remains true that the healing mission of the Gospel was intended to continue and did continue. The physical is inseparable from the spiritual in this life, and the material benefits of faith are borne out of and are the natural fruit of the spiritual blessings. Therefore we find the command:

Is any among you sick? let him call for the elders of the church; and let them pray over him, anointing him with oil in the name of the Lord: and the prayer of faith shall save him that is sick, and the Lord shall raise him up; and if he have committed sins, it shall be forgiven him (James 5: 14, 15).

II. Anointing a Healing Agency as a Symbol.

The anointing with oil was not the means of healing in itself, but was a symbol of the anointing of the Holy Spirit who did the healing. Jesus Himself professed to heal "by the Spirit of God" (Matt. 12: 28), and the disciples after Him prayed, "Grant unto thy servants to speak thy word with all boldness, WHILE THOU STRETCHEST FORTH THY HAND TO HEAL" (Acts 4: 30).

It is true that oil was used as a medicine in that age, but that this rite of anointing was as a symbol rather than a medicine is shown by the plain statement, "The *prayer of faith* shall save the sick" (v. 15). The anointing is an aid to the understanding and to faith, just as the other Gospel symbols are aids.

The anointing with oil is not for the forgiveness of sins merely, or a preparation for death. The Roman Catholic Church has wholly perverted the rite in making it the rite of "extreme unction." The command does not read, "Is any sinful among you? let him call for the elders of the church and let them anoint him," but "is any SICK" and the regular word for sickness is used. In fact, it is implied that the sickness may not have any connection with personal sins at all, for the passage reads, "IF he have committed sins they shall be forgiven." If he has not committed sins, the meaning is, the promise for healing from the sickness remains.

The question of physical healing, however, involves a number of points which should be considered.

III. Questions Concerning Healing.

1. WHAT CAUSES SICKNESS? The Scriptures recognize a number of causes for sickness.

(1) The *natural infirmity* of the flesh.

Thou rememberest that we are dust (Psa. 103: 13-16); The flesh is weak (Matt. 26: 41).

(2) *Unavoidable dangers*. The people killed by Pilate, and those killed by the tower of Siloam were not sinners above others, but chanced to be in positions of danger (Luke 13: 1-5).

(3) *Sin*.

Visiting the iniquity of the parents upon the children unto the third and fourth generations (Ex. 20: 5).

If thou wilt not hearken unto the voice of Jehovah thy God. . . . Jehovah will make the pestilence to cleave unto thee. Jehovah will smite thee with consumption and with fever, and with inflammation and with fiery heat (Deut. 28: 15-25).

See also Lev. 26: 15, 16; 1 Cor. 11: 30; Psa. 107: 17.

(4) *Satan*.

Ought not this woman, whom Satan hath bound, lo these eighteen years, to have been loosed from this bond on the sabbath? (Luke 13: 16); Even Jesus of Nazareth, how God anointed him with the Holy Spirit and with power; who went about doing good, **and healing all that were oppressed of the Devil;** for God was with him (Acts 10: 38).

(5) *God may send* disease as the *penalty of sins,* as in

the case of Jehoram (2 Chron 21: 18), but it is not His will that any should thus suffer. He seeks rather to save all both from sin and from suffering.

(6) *The present evil world* involves the innocent with the guilty. "That upon you may come all the righteous blood shed on the earth" (Matt. 23: 35). Not only are the innocent subject to the violence of the wicked, but they are more or less exposed to the diseases spread by them. Thousands of women suffer because of the impurity of their husbands, and thousands of others are afflicted because of the evil environment in which they are cast.

(7) "*That the works of God may be made manifest,*" there are cases like that of the man born blind (John 9: 3), of whom Jesus said, "Neither did this man sin nor his parents." We may not understand the deep things of the providence of God, but we may be sure that the divine order is working out what is best, and the hardships of the present world are overruled by Him for the spiritual good of His children. Such cases as this last find their further explanation in the considerations which follow.

2. How to use afflictions for good.

(1) *Sickness and other afflictions should teach us God's laws.*

It is good for me that I have been afflicted; That I might learn thy statutes (Psa. 119: 71).

The experience with and study of diseases leads to knowledge of God's laws both natural and spiritual, so that many diseases can be thus prevented.

We burn our fingers and avoid the fire. We have a fall and avoid the precipice. We suffer from fever and learn to guard our food and drink from impurity. We are afflicted in other ways and in this school of affliction learn how to keep others from similar suffering.

(2) *They teach humility.*

And by reason of the exceeding greatness of the revelations, that I should not be exalted overmuch, there was given to me a thorn in the flesh, a messenger of Satan to buffet me, that I should not be exalted overmuch (2 Cor. 12: 7).

(3) *When rightly borne, they develop the glory of Christian character.*

For our light affliction, which is for the moment, worketh for us more and more exceedingly an eternal weight of glory; while we look not at the things which are seen, but at the things which are not seen: for the things which are seen are temporal; but the things which are not seen are eternal (2 Cor. 4: 17).

We spend years of time and hundreds of dollars of money to secure the blessings of education, but these without Christ become a curse, for education enables the rascal to do more evil. It pays much better sometimes to learn in God's school of affliction. They who graduate in it have power and glory, not for this life only, but for eternity.

(4) *They may be used to help others.*

Who comforteth us in all our affliction, that we may be able to comfort them that are in any affliction, through the comfort wherewith we ourselves are comforted of God (2 Cor. 1: 4).

How it helps us to hear Jesus say to us, " Be comforted. I know all about it, for I too have suffered." How it gives us power to sympathize and help if we have had a common sorrow.

(5) *They may be used as warnings.*

Now these things were our examples, to the intent we should not lust after evil things, as they also lusted (1 Cor. 10: 6-12).

(6) *They may be used as opportunities to glorify God.*

Neither did this man sin or his parents: but that the works of God should be made manifest in him (John 9: 3).

The afflicted person should learn to say, " I will not only use this affliction to learn its cause and cure, but will use

Anointing the Sick

my suffering as an opportunity to show how patient Christ can enable me to be, or what he can do through my faith.

(7) *They may be used to develop appreciation of salvation.*

Blessed are they that mourn: for they shall be comforted (Matt. 5: 4).

If they that are forgiven much also love much, then they also who suffer much will rejoice the more in the bright world that is free from pain.

3. SHOULD WE DO WHAT WE CAN TO RELIEVE SICKNESS OURSELVES?

Many teach that trust in God for healing precludes the use of natural remedies, but we do not so believe. The Scriptures do not condemn the use of remedies. The only passage usually so quoted is 2 Chron. 16: 12, " In his disease he sought not to the Lord, but to the physicians. And Asa slept with his fathers." Asa's fault was in NOT seeking unto the Lord, rather than in supplementing that with what he could do for himself.

On the other hand, there are many passages which commend the use of remedies such as human beings can apply for themselves. Isaiah used a poultice of figs in the healing of Hezekiah (Isa. 38: 21); Jesus used an ointment of saliva and clay (John 9: 6; Mark 8: 23). Edersheim says that this was a common remedy of the time for eye diseases. Grant that Jesus used it simply to increase the faith of the blind, doctors also administer most of their remedies to-day with the purpose of easing the mind of the patient and increasing faith in recovery. Jesus also commends the good Samaritan who bound up the wounds of the man whom he found half dead by the roadside, " pouring in oil and wine," and says, " Go thou and do likewise " (Luke 10: 34-37). Paul advises Timothy " Be no longer a user of water, but use a little wine for thy stomach's sake and for thine often infirmities" (1 Tim. 5: 23). Any one who has traveled in the East and knows the wretched impurity of most of the supply of drinking water, can easily understand Paul's advice without making capital of it for modern drinking in this country, which is wholly without excuse. Paul also calls Luke "the beloved physician" (Col. 4: 14) long after his conversion, showing that there was nothing in the profession out of harmony with Gospel principles. Oil itself was a common remedy of the time. It was used in the Old Testament times (Isa. 1: 6) and in the New (Mark 6: 13). Pliny, the Roman writer of 110 A. D., mentions its medicinal use (*Pliny's Writings,* 15: 4, 7; 23: 3, 4). Dion Cassius (15: 29) says it was used externally and internally. The rabbinical literature of the Jews says it was used as a remedy for skin diseases, and Josephus also speaks of it as a medicine (*Antiquities* 17: 6; 5). In fact, it is still highly regarded as a home remedy and enters into the composition of many medicines.

To supplement our prayers and faith in God with our own efforts to help ourselves in the matter of healing is in harmony with all the Scriptures in other matters. Are we taught to pray for sinners (1 John 5: 16)? We are also taught to try to win them by our personal efforts (Matt. 28: 19). Did Jesus pray for His disciples (John 17: 9)? He also said, "I have given them thy word" (v. 14). Are we taught to pray, "Give us this day our daily bread" (Matt. 6: 11)? We are also taught, "If any man will not work, neither let him eat" (2 Thess. 3: 10). Are we taught to pray, "Thy kingdom come" (Matt. 6: 10)? We are also taught, "Make ye ready the way of the Lord" (Matt. 3: 3). Are we taught to trust God for the forgiveness of sins? We are also taught that "faith if it have not works is dead" (James 2: 17). Are we taught to pray for the sick and to trust God for healing (James 5: 14)?

We are also taught to do those things which contribute to health (Acts 27: 34; Mark 6: 31; 1 Tim. 5: 23). Not to do so would be to tempt God. Jesus Himself refused to ask God to manifest His power when it was not necessary to do so, saying, "Thou shalt not make trial of the Lord thy God" (Luke 4: 12). If we are praying according to the will of God, it is our duty to work in the direction of our prayers, and if they are not according to the will of God, we have no right to utter them. God's moral and natural laws are in harmony, and must work together. The working of natural remedies is no less divine than the working of faith. It is true that many people sin against God as Asa did, by resorting to remedies without recourse to God at all. It is true that many Christians dope themselves with drugs entirely too much, and true that many drugs are used which are an injury rather than a blessing. It is true that many of the best physicians admit, with Dr. Osler of Johns Hopkins University, that "The best doctor is the one who knows the utter worthlessness of most drugs." All this and more might be said against the common resort to doctors and drugs, and especially to patent medicines with unknown ingredients, but at the same time the principle holds that self-effort should supplement prayer. All forms of knowledge must advance, and in advancing will make blunders. Medical science has made its blunders, but it has also greatly blessed the world. It has made civilization more sanitary; it has stamped out some of the most malignant diseases; it has greatly reduced infant mortality, abated the horrors of surgery and prolonged the average length of life. The blessing of God has been upon it and it is not for man to curse. Medical science has yet much to do in promoting proper diet, proper dress, proper exercise, proper marital relations, and many other things. Let it advance, but not alone. It is only beginning to learn that it must work with God and not without Him.

4. TO WHAT EXTENT HAVE WE A RIGHT TO PRAY FOR HEALING?

There is one limitation which affects all prayer: It must be according to the will of God. "If we ask anything according to his will, he heareth us" (1 John 5: 14). Even Jesus conformed to this limitation and prayed, "If it be possible * * * nevertheless not my will but thine be done" (Matt. 26: 39). There are other conditions—faith (Mark 11: 24), love (Mark 11: 25), obedience (1 John 3: 22), perseverance (Luke 18: 7), in Jesus' name (John 14: 14)—but none of these can be fulfilled without this submission to the will of God.

(1) *The prayer for the forgiveness of sins is limited by the possibility of the "eternal sin"* (Mark 3: 29 R. V.) for which we are not to pray (1 John 5: 16), and likewise the prayer with the anointing with oil is limited by the fact that there is a sentence of death upon the race until Jesus comes (1 Cor. 15: 25, 26) and there comes a time for every one of us to die. When that time comes it is for us to say, "Father, into thy hands I commit my spirit."

(2) *There are also infirmities which are for our good, and therefore should be received as the chastening of the Lord.* Among this number was the thorn in the flesh for the removal of which Paul prayed thrice and in answer received, not its removal, but grace enough to bear it (2 Cor. 12: 8). Sometimes the affliction is for a time and will be removed when it is best. Of this class Trophimus may be an example, for instead of being healed as many others were at the hands of Paul (Acts 19: 11) he was left sick at Miletus. (2 Tim. 4: 20).

The anointing with oil being "in the name of the Lord" must be in submission to His will, and having fulfilled all

Anointing the Sick

known conditions of healing the patient should rest in perfect peace of mind, knowing that thus blessing will result, for, "We know that to them that love God all things work together for good, *even* to them that are called according to his purpose" (Rom. 8: 28). For this reason confession of sins and prayer, getting right with God, precedes healing (Jas. 5: 16). A study of the examples of healing by Jesus confirms this. See Mark 5: 29-34; Matt. 9: 2; 13: 15; Acts 28: 27, &c. Man is not body alone or spirit alone, but spirit and body, and therefore the prayer, "that thou mayest prosper and be in health, even as thy soul prospereth" (2 John 2).

5. WHAT IS THE BASIS FOR TRUSTING IN GOD FOR HEALTH?

(1) First, there is the *natural basis*. There is no question but that God *can* heal if He wishes to do so, and, being a loving Father, there is no question but that He wishes to do so whenever it is best. It is in God that "we live and move and have our being" (Acts 17: 28). If then His Spirit envelops us more closely than the very atmosphere we breathe, must we not believe that health as well as life may be from Him? We are to be "temples of the living God" (1 Cor. 3: 16): shall not then God have a care for His temple? "We are members of Christ's body" (Eph. 5: 30). Shall He then not be concerned for His own body? Hear the apostle say, "Christ liveth in me" (Gal. 2: 20), and again "I can do all things through Christ who strengtheneth me" (Philpp. 3: 20).

(2) Second, there is the *revelation of God's Word*. Even in the Old Testament there are many passages which are bright with this promise of healing.

If thou wilt diligently hearken to the voice of Jehovah. . . . I will put none of the diseases upon thee, which I have put upon the Egyptians: For I am Jehovah that healeth thee (Ex. 15: 26).

See also Ex. 23: 25 and Deut. 7: 15, and note the testimony of the fulfillment of these promises in Psa. 105: 37, "He brought them forth with silver and gold, and there was not one feeble person among his tribes." It is a matter of common observation that the Jews to-day, although they only imperfectly follow the commandments of Moses, are free from many of the Gentile diseases. Read also the 91st Psalm. Even though we allow for poetic language, these promises remain strong and true.

Because God lives and reigns in His world, we have a right to expect progress toward the supremacy of the spiritual, and therefore a greater dominance of the spirit over matter in this age than in former ages. We are taught to beware of the sins of Israel which brought upon them various afflictions (1 Cor. 10: 6-11).

The New Testament not only teaches the anointing with oil with the prayer of faith for the sick (Jas. 5: 14-16), but also teaches direct prayer (Jas. 5: 13), intercessory prayer (Acts 4: 30) and the laying on of hands by those who have the "gift of healing" (1 Cor. 12: 9, 30; Mark 6: 5; Acts 28: 8), which is one of the gifts of the Spirit not given to all, for He giveth "to each one severally as he will" (1 Cor. 12: 11), but which, since "the gifts and calling of God are not repented of" (Rom. 11: 29), we have a right to expect in the church to-day whenever and wherever God considers that there is occasion for it.

(3) *The atonement of Christ* is also a basis for faith in divine healing. It was predicted that His atonement should cover both the guilt of sin and the consequences of sin. Isaiah says "Surely he hath borne our griefs (Heb. sicknesses. See R. V. margin) and carried our sorrows" (Isa. 53: 4) and Matthew says, "He cast out the spirits with a word, and healed all that were sick: that it might be fulfilled which was spoken through Isaiah the prophet,

Anointing the Sick

saying, Himself took our infirmities and bare our diseases" (Matt. 8: 17). Luke says that Jesus went about "healing all them that were oppressed of the devil" (Acts 10: 38), and John says that "he was manifested that he might destroy the works of the devil" (1 John 3: 8). If the Scriptures teach us the glorious fact that Jesus bore our sins (1 Pet. 2: 24) they also state the fact that He bore our sicknesses (Matt. 8: 17). If He who was without sin could bear our sins, so He who was without sickness could bear our sicknesses, and give to us the life which is free from both sin and sickness. This does not mean that we shall enter into the full heritage of this life at once. We have only the beginning of it here. "God hath given to us the earnest of the Spirit" (1 Cor. 1: 22). We yet have need to be reminded, "If we say that we have no sin we deceive ourselves and the truth is not in us" (1 John 1: 8), but we may claim the promise that follows, "If we confess our sins he is faithful and just to forgive us of our sins, and to cleanse us from all unrighteousness." So also we are yet compelled to struggle with the weaknesses of the flesh, the diseases of the world and the wiles of the devil, but we may also claim the promise, "the prayer of faith shall save the sick" (Jas. 5: 14). Because we find ourselves guilty of sin, shall we give up Christ as our Savior? And because we find ourselves sick, shall we give up Christ as our healer? Now we must be content with such things as we have, while we are patient "for the coming of the Lord is at hand" (Jas. 5: 8), and then we shall look for both the "sanctification of the spirit" (2 Thess. 2: 13) and the "redemption of the body" (Rom. 8: 23).

To the end he may establish your hearts unblamable in holiness, before our God and Father at the coming of our Lord Jesus with all his saints (1 Thess. 3: 13). For our citizenship is in heaven, whence also we wait for a Savior, the Lord Jesus Christ who shall fashion anew the body of our humiliation, that it may be conformed to the body of his glory, according to the working whereby he is able to subject all things unto himself (Philpp. 3: 20, 21).

(4.) *The indwelling Spirit of God* is a basis for faith in healing. " Know ye not that ye are a temple of God, and *that* the Spirit of God dwelleth in you " (1 Cor. 3: 16) ? It is the Spirit who is the active agent in healing in all the Gospel miracles. The gift of healing is only one of the gifts of the Spirit (1 Cor. 12: 9, 30) and are we not to ascribe more power to the Giver than to the gift? If then the Giver of the gift of healing dwell in us may we not believe in Him for healing? If the Spirit can change our vile body and fashion it after the likeness of Christ's glorious body (Philpp. 3: 21) can He not now work such slight changes as are necessary to healing? If He can raise us up at the last day (John 5: 28, 29) can He not raise up the sick now (Jas. 5: 15) ? If then Christ dwells in our hearts by faith (Eph. 3: 17) and " is the same yesterday, to-day and forever " (Heb. 13: 8), may we not trust His compassion as did the afflicted of old, and by faith receive the blessings of healing He freely bestowed according to the will of God?

If the Spirit of him that raised up Jesus from the dead dwelleth in you, he that raised up Jesus from the dead shall give life also to your mortal bodies through his Spirit that dwelleth in you (Rom. 8: 11). For we who live are always delivered unto death for Jesus' sake, that the life also of Jesus may be manifested in our mortal flesh (2 Cor. 4: 11).

6. How did the early church understand the anointing of the sick with oil?

It has already been shown from the Scriptures that the mission of healing was practiced by the entire church dur-

Anointing the Sick

ing the apostolic period. It remains only to show that it continued longer and may continue to-day.

Irenaeus (130 A. D.) says:

That some cast out demons is a matter that cannot be called in question, since it is attested by the experience of those who have been thus delivered and are now in the church. Others still heal the sick by laying hands upon them and they are made whole again.—Against Heresies, 2: 4.

Clement of Rome, (second century), says:

But in the present life, washing in a flowing river, or fountain, or even in the sea, with the thrice blessed invocation, you shall not only be able to drive away the spirits which lurk in you, but, no longer sinning, and undoubtedly believing God, you shall drive out evil spirits and dire demons, with terrible diseases from others.—Hom. Bk. 9, ch. 8.

Justin Martyr (150 A. D.) to the Roman Emperor says:

For numberless demoniacs throughout the whole world and in your city, many Christian men by exorcising them in the name of Jesus Christ who was crucified under Pontius Pilate, have healed and do heal, rendering helpless and driving out the possessing demons, though they could not be cured by other exorcists and those who used incantations and drugs.—Apology 2: 6.

Tertullian (160 A. D.) says:

For the clerk of one who was liable to be thrown down upon the ground by an evil spirit was set free from his affliction, as was also the relative of another, and a little boy of a third, and how many men of rank, to say nothing of the common people, have been delivered from demons and healed of diseases.—Letter to Scapula 4: 4.

Origen (185 A. D.) says:

And some gave evidence of having received through their faith a marvelous power by the cures they perform, invoking no other name over those who need their help than that of the God of all things, and the name of Jesus along with the mention of his history, for by those means we too have seen many persons freed from grievous calamities and distractions of mind and madness and countless other ills which could not be cured by men or devils.—*Against Celsus* 3: 24.

Clement of Alexandria (220 A. D.) in giving directions to the sick says:

Let them therefore with fasting and prayer make their intercessions, and not with the well-arranged and fitly ordered words of learning, but as men who have received the gift of healing, confidently to the glory of God.—*Epistles* 100: 12.

Augustine (354 A. D.) says:

For even now miracles are wrought in his name, whether by sacraments or by prayers.—*Works* 5: 299.

That the rite of anointing with oil for healing was perpetuated throughout these early centuries is a clear record of church history. Tertullian (*Ad. Scap.* 4) says that Proculus anointed Severus and healed him. In the third century it was decided that only a bishop might prepare the oil, but that anyone might use it.—*Innocent Decentia* 3: 8. In the fifth century its use was restricted to priests.—*Labbe and Cossart, Concilla* 9: 419. By the twelfth century the idea of healing had become obsolete and the anointing was simply a preparation for death.—*Council of Florence,* 1439. The *Council of Trent* later made this rite one of the seven sacraments of the church and called it "extreme unction."

By the *Waldensians,* however, who were the means of preserving others of the apostolic doctrines, the rite of anointing was practiced as taught by James, and has been more or less in use among modern denominations. It is true that the testimonies quoted from the early Fathers may not be wholly reliable, just as many modern testimonies are not, but they are to be taken for what they are worth. There are many modern testimonies that are also true. The

Anointing the Sick

true must not be rejected because of the false. Volumes of specific instances might be given, proving the fact of healing through faith in God to-day.

7. WHAT OF THE HEALING IMPOSTERS AND HERESIES OF TO-DAY? Counterfeiting is the favorite device of Satan. He loves to parade as an angel of light. He uses the truth as a sugar coating with which to administer the poison of error. Thus through imposters and delusions he secures the acceptance of error or else discredits the truth.

Christian Science.

So-called Christian Science is an example. This modern fad takes the glorious truth of healing through faith from the Gospel and mixes it with a lot of absurdities and vital heresies, thus deceiving those who do not discriminate between the two. There is no question but that many have been healed through the teaching of " Christian Science," but it is equally true that they should have had the same healing through the church, without endorsing the anti-Christian and anti-scientific teachings of " Christian Science." The church is partly to blame for this, because it has not taught the Gospel healing by faith as it should, nor perpetuated the symbol given as a witness of that truth, the anointing with oil, but there is no need of anyone turning to heresy to receive what they may have in the church. That Christian Science does teach heresies which no Christian can accept may be seen from the following parallel passages taken from Mrs. Eddy's book, and the Bible.

MRS. EDDY'S ERRORS.	BIBLE TRUTH.
The atonement denied: One sacrifice, however great, is insufficient to pay the debt of sin (p. 23).	Now once in the end of the ages hath he appeared to put away sin by the sacrifice of himself (Heb. 9: 26).

452 God's Means of Grace

Jesus' death and resurrection denied: He (Jesus) had not died (p. 45).

Christ died and lived again (Rom. 14: 9).

The Holy Spirit denied: The Comforter I understand to be Divine Science (p. 55).

The Comforter, even the Holy Spirit, whom the Father will send in my name (John 14: 25).

Evil denied: The supposition that there are good and evil spirits is a mistake. . . Evil has no reality (p. 70, 71).

In that hour he (Jesus) cured many of diseases and plagues and evil spirits (Luke 7: 21). Abhor that which is evil (Rom. 12: 9).

Miracles denied: Miracles are impossible to science (p. 83).

Many believed on his name beholding the signs that he did (John 2: 23).

Matter denied: God never created matter (p. 355).

In the beginning God created the heavens and the earth (Gen. 1: 1).

The Trinity denied: The theory of three persons in one God—that is, a personal Trinity—suggests heathen gods rather than the ever-present I Am (p. 256).

Baptizing them into the name of the Father and of the Son and of the Holy Spirit (Matt. 28: 19).

Man's mortality denied: man coëxists with God and the universe (p. 266).

God created man (Gen. 1: 27).

The body denied: Spirit and matter no more commingle than light and darkness: when one appears the other disappears (p. 261).

Your body is a temple of the Holy Spirit which is in you (1 Cor. 6: 19).

The judgment denied: No final judgment awaits mortals (p. 291).

It is appointed unto men once to die and after this cometh judgment (Heb. 9: 27).

Sin denied: Because soul is immortal, soul cannot sin (p. 468).

The soul that sinneth it shall die (Ezek. 18: 4).

Anointing the Sick

The Coming of Christ denied: The second appearance of Jesus is unquestionably the spiritual advent of the advancing idea of God in Christian Science (Autobiography, p. 96).	Many deceivers are gone forth into the world, even they that confess not that Jesus Christ cometh in the flesh. This is the deceiver and the anti-Christ (2 John 7 A. R. V.).

Other quotations might be given, but these are sufficient to show that this heresy is neither Christian nor scientific. With a single Christian truth, the power of faith, it deludes its followers into denying the very fundamentals of Christianity. We do not deny that many Christian Scientists live beautiful moral lives, but as is the case with lodge membership, Satan is not so much concerned about that as he is to subvert faith in Jesus Christ his conqueror.

One good thing, however, is resulting from the spread of this and similar heresies,—the church is giving more attention to its mission of healing. It has rightly considered the teaching of the Gospel as a greater work than the healing of the sick (1 Cor. 14: 5), but it has had no right to neglect the sick. True, it has been the means of promoting hospitals and asylums, but it has turned these over too largely to doctors and drugs, and has not taught the healing agency of faith and the Holy Spirit. Now it is realizing more fully the Scripture teaching that man is both body and spirit, and is giving care to the whole man. Some churches are establishing homes where the sick may come and receive the spiritual treatment which they need in coöperation with the natural remedies used. Concerning one of these Eld. Samuel Dick, pastor of the Wesley Church, Boston, says:

I cannot give you all instances where cures have been effected, but I could tell of scores of cases that would make you think we had stolen them from patent medicine ads. . . . This system will cure ten where Christian Science will cure one, and it can be used in any church.—Current Anecdotes, March, 1908.

Concerning another church that has taken up such work, the *Homiletic Review* of February, 1908, says:

The Boston Clinic is now taxed to its utmost resources, and we are compelled to turn a deaf ear to many appeals for help, heart rending as many of them are, which reach us from all parts of the United States and even from other countries. The principle (of faith as a healing agency) is . . . supported by such scientific authorities as James, Munsterberg, Prince, Forrel, and many highly distinguished men.

Dr. Francis E. Clark in the *Christian Endeavor World*, April 2, 1908, says:

One of the happy developments of modern times is the new alliance between the church and the medical profession, between the minister and the doctor. Not that there have not always been devout physicians on the one hand, and, on the other, ministers who have brought the healing consolations of the Gospel to the bedside of the sick, but until recently each has kept to his own side of the line, and there has been little avowed coöperation. . . . The work done in Emmanuel Episcopal Church in Boston is an indication of this new alliance.

Already in Chicago under Bishop Fallows' lead, in New York, at Clifton Springs, and in other places a similar work is carried on, while at least one college (Tufts) has established courses in "psychotherapy," this "new" science of healing. Many physicians have been non-Christians (partly because they see the hypocrisy of some Christians), but the best physician is the one who knows best how to use the spiritual forces that make for health as well as the physical, and the greatest force of all is the Spirit of God.

While other churches have discarded the divinely given symbol of healing, the anointing the sick with oil, the Waldensians and the Brethren and perhaps others have perpetuated it, and while not teaching it as prominently as it should be taught, yet it is in the church for those who will avail themselves of it. Should it not be given its rightful place and retained?

The Rose's Thorn.

Have you considered, troubled dears, why every rose must have its thorn?
Why with our joys are sorrows born, and every life must have its tears?
Some evil beast might else devour the tender rose, and selfish joy,
Unchecked by pain, might soon destroy thy sympathy and love and power.

Were life one long unending day, these bodies would full soon recoil,
Beneath the wear of ceaseless toil, and turn again to senseless clay.
Could summer's sun forever shine, undimmed by cloud or passing night,
Fair earth would soon be parched and blight, and all life perished,—even thine.

Did fortune smile upon thy lot continuously, thy human heart
Might also sear and cease its part, and all thy duties be forgot.
But God knows best, who sends the rain and freezing cold upon the earth,
And mellowed soil reveals their worth, when tempered by the sun again.

Couldst thou but see through Calvary's tears; for blasted hopes and vacant chairs,
There stands a cup of blessing there, which sweeter grows with passing years.
Then fret not for the passing pain, but bless the cup—the Master's cup—
Which teaches thee to e'er look up, and count thy loss as richest gain.

CHAPTER VI

THREE SYMBOLS OF SEPARATION FROM THE WORLD.

Separation in Customs: Nonconformity to the World.
Separation in Company: Special Reference to Lodges.
Separation in Conduct: Special Reference to Nonresistance.

* * * * * *

"Wherefore come ye out from among them, and be ye separate, saith the Lord."—2 Cor. 6: 17.

"And be ye not fashioned according to this world, but be ye transformed by the renewing of your minds."—Rom. 12: 2.

* * * * * *

"Proving what is well-pleasing unto the Lord; and have no fellowship with the unfruitful works of darkness, but rather even reprove them."—Eph. 5: 11.

"Swear not at all. . . . but let your speech be, Yea, yea; Nay, nay: and whatsoever is more than these is of the evil one."—Matt. 5: 33-37.

* * * * * *

"Put up again thy sword into its place: for all they that take up the sword shall perish with the sword."—Matt. 26: 52.

"And they shall beat their swords into plowshares and their spears into pruning hooks; nation shall not lift up sword against nation, neither shall they learn war any more."—Isa. 2: 4.

THREE SYMBOLS OF SEPARATION FROM THE WORLD.

I. The Principle of Separation.

The symbols of separation from the world are to be considered among the means of grace, but the principle that is back of them is not peculiar to Christianity. It is one of the laws of God enforced in all His kingdoms.

1. IN NATURE. The working of this principle may be observed in nature in what scientists call the "law of conformity to type." Each type of life must obey the conditions necessary to its own development. Therefore no two widely different types of life may amalgamate. Hybrids cannot reproduce themselves, while even the crossing of "varieties" results in "freaks."

2. IN THE KINGDOM OF GOD. Spiritual life is so different from the merely natural life that it must be gotten from God. It cannot assimilate or unite with the sinful nature. To attempt to unite it with the worldly type of life is to lose it. For its environment it needs the means of grace that God has given.

To develop this type of life God has selected in each age the most spiritual representatives of it. Therefore we have the successive covenants with Noah (Gen. 9: 12), Abraham (Gen. 17), Israel (Ex. 34: 28), David (Jer. 33: 25, 26) and the "righteous remnant" (Rom. 9: 27) through whom came at last the Bible and the Christ. This process of selection was to the kingdom of God what the law of natural selection and the survival of the fittest is to the lower kingdoms.

The chosen people, Israel, were required to be separate from the world in various ways.

(1) They were forbidden to even *inquire* into the heathen religions lest they should be led to imitate them (Deut. 12: 30).

(2) They were commanded to utterly *drive out* the Canaanites, when their iniquity was full (Gen. 15: 16) and were forbidden to make any league with them lest they be corrupted by them (Judges 2: 2).

(3) They were not allowed to *intermarry* with other peoples lest thus they be corrupted in blood and ensnared by alliances (Deut. 7: 1-6).

(4) They were required to perform many *ceremonial cleansings* to teach them purity and separation (Num. 19 &c).

(5) Most of all they were to regard themselves as *missionaries* to the world to witness of God (Gen. 22: 18; Deut. 32: 8); and while other nations perished in their corruption by the way, Israel, by negative commands designed to enforce the principle of separation, and by a positive mission designed to develop the godly type of life, was led from height to height in character, on toward the city of God. This was not due to arbitrary partiality, for " God is no respecter of persons " (Acts 10: 34), but to the superior responsiveness of Abraham and his descendants to God's call to separation from the wicked world. Such separation has been shown in various ways, some true and some false.

II. What Separation is Not.

1. CHRISTIAN SEPARATION FROM THE WORLD IS NOT MONASTICISM. The rise of monasticism did good as well as evil in its day, because of the corruption of the church through its alliance with the State; but it is not the ideal of Christianity to hide away in the wilderness, or seek holiness in a cloister. Jesus did indeed fast forty days in the

wilderness, but only to prepare for the busy life of service in the world. He said, "I pray not that thou shouldest take them from the world" (John 17: 15). He taught that Christians are to be the light of the world, but light must shine where it is needed, not be hid under a bushel. Christians are to be salt, but salt must be used where otherwise there would be decay. Christians are to be leaven, but leaven must be mixed through the meal. Christians are to provide for their own, not flee from them to the peace of a cloister. The principle of self-renunciation (Luke 14: 33) is to be worked out in the street, in the home, in the busy world. When Jesus looked upon the multitude he did not flee in horror because of their sins, but wept with compassion because " they were as sheep not having a shepherd. And he preached the word of God unto them."

2. CHRISTIAN SEPARATION IS NOT ASCETICISM. It sends no one to needless self-torture after the manner of the Hindu holy man. Neither Christianity nor science inspired Mrs. Eddy to say:

It is morally wrong to examine the body in order to ascertain if we are in health. The daily ablutions of an infant are no more natural or necessary than it would be to take a fish out of the water once a day and cover it with dirt, in order to make it thrive more vigorously thereafter in its native element.

Jesus cared for the needs of the body. He "came eating and drinking" (Matt. 11: 19), thus fulfilling the precept of Deut. 26: 11, "Thou shalt rejoice in all the good which Jehovah thy God hath given unto thee." Christianity seeks the use but not the abuse of the good things of this world.

3. CHRISTIAN SEPARATION IS NOT MERELY CEREMONIAL. The Scribes and Pharisees made broad their phylacteries and prolonged their public prayers; they bathed on returning from market to remove the possible pollution of touch

with Gentiles; but inwardly they were full of extortion and adultery (Matt. 23). No class of sinners received more bitter rebuke from Jesus than did these hypocrites who said, "I am holier than thou," who displayed the outward forms of faith, but lacked the inward graces of the Spirit. One church member said to another, "Are you a Christian?" "Yes." "Well, you don't look like one." The other replied, "Are you a Christian?" "Yes." "Well, you don't *act* like one." To be sure the inward graces will reveal themselves in outward signs, but to seek the signs only is like placing artificial roses on the bush. First give life to the bush and the real roses will come of themselves.

4. CHRISTIAN SEPARATION RESULTS IN FUNDAMENTAL UNIFORMITY.

There are "diversities of gifts," but "the same Spirit" (1 Cor. 12: 4). God did not give to all flowers the same color, nor to all birds the same song, nor to all people the same spirit; but flowers and birds and people each have the fundamental characteristics of their respective kingdoms, and by them are easily classified. The personality of each of us will be manifested after conversion as well as before, but only in agreement with the personality of Christ. "To me to live is Christ." An attempt to create absolute uniformity among Christians would be like the act of the king in the fable, who decreed that all his subjects should be like himself; those who were longer to be cut off, and those who were shorter to be stretched out; but, on the other hand, to have no uniformity is to reject the unifying spirit of Christ. There are the "least" and the "greatest" in the kingdom as "one star differeth from another in glory"; and in agreement with this unity in diversity, manifest in all the works of God, we must expect a certain amount of diversity, and yet a fundamental unity among Christians.

Methods and expediencies for securing this unity are not to be confused with the principle itself.

III. Principles of the Christian Type of Life.

The Christian life is a type of life as much higher than the worldly life as the human, but worldly, life is higher than that of the animals. It is characterized by choosing the will of God rather than the will of the flesh or of the world. "Not every one that sayeth unto me, Lord, Lord, shall enter into the kingdom of heaven, but he that doeth the will of my Father who is in heaven" (Matt. 7: 21). Jesus exemplified this life and testified, "I do always the things that please Him" (John 8: 29). It follows that such a life cannot assimilate the evil things of the world." "We know that whosoever is begotten of God sinneth not; but he that was begotten of God keepeth himself, and the evil one toucheth him not" (1 John 5: 18). Thus we read of Jesus, the perfect exemplification of this type of life, that He was "separated from sinners" (Heb. 7: 26). This was not in form, for He was blamed for eating with publicans and sinners (Matt. 9: 11), but in spirit. He sought them, not to share their sins, but to save their souls. "The son of man is come to seek and to save that which was lost." In conformity to this example of Jesus the Gospel gives us a number of principles which may guide us in our contact with the world.

1. THE CHRISTIAN IS A CHILD OF GOD. He must therefore show the love and obedience of a child.

As many as are led by the Spirit of God these are the sons of God" (Rom. 8: 14). He that saith he abideth in him ought himself also to walk even as he walked (1 John 2: 6).

2. THE CHRISTIAN IS A STEWARD. He must therefore be faithful as one that must give an account.

Let a man so account of us, as of ministers of Christ, and

stewards of the mysteries of God. Here, moreover, it is required of stewards that a man be found faithful (1 Cor. 4: 2). See also Matt. 6: 24; 25; 14-30.

Note that it is not required that we be famous or successful, but FAITHFUL, but that faithfulness is not merely suggested or requested but REQUIRED. How little is the principle of stewardship preached or practiced! What a gasping there will be by the unfaithful stewards when the day of accounting comes!

3. THE CHRISTIAN IS A MEMBER OF THE BODY OF CHRIST. He must therefore be guided by Christ the Head.

And he is the head of the body, the church: who is the beginning of the firstborn from the dead; that in all things he might have the preëminence (Col. 1: 18).

This does not mean obedience when we please, or when our friends please, but obedience that is above all worldly influences. Paul says:

To me to live is Christ (Philpp. 1: 21). For whom I suffered the loss of all things, and do count them but refuse that I may gain Christ (Philpp. 3: 8).

4. THE CHURCH IS THE BRIDE OF CHRIST. Its members must therefore be faithful as a bride expecting her betrothed.

Christ also loved the church, and gave himself up for it; having cleansed it by the washing of water with the word, that he might present the church to himself a glorious church, not having spot or wrinkle or any such thing; but that it should be holy and without blemish (Eph. 5: 26, 27).

With what eager expectancy does a true bride look forward to the day of marriage! How carefully she lives that she may be without reproach in that day! So ought the church to live with the hope of the coming of the Lord, who may appear at any time to take His waiting bride to Himself. Alas for those who shall be found flirting with the world at that day!

5. THE KINGDOM OF GOD IS A BROTHERHOOD. The children of God are one family; the Christian must therefore avoid anything that might cause stumbling in others.

Let us not therefore judge one another any more: but judge ye this rather, that no man put a stumbling block in his brother's way, or an occasion of falling (Rom. 14: 13).

No one accepting this principle will say, "I do not drink, therefore I will do nothing against saloons," or, "Tobacco does not harm me, therefore I may use it regardless of the effect of my example on others."

The essence of the sin of Cain was in his words, "Am I my brother's keeper?" but this is precisely the sin of those who assert their personal liberty when to do so causes injury to others. They who would be of the family of our Father in heaven, must learn the love of heaven here. "Love worketh no ill to his neighbor, therefore love is the fulfillment of the law" (Rom. 13: 10).

6. THE CHRISTIAN IS A SOLDIER. He must therefore give himself to the "fight of faith" (1 Tim. 6: 12).

Suffer hardship with me, as a good soldier of Christ Jesus. No soldier on service entangleth himself in the affairs of this life; that he may please him who enrolled him to be a soldier (2 Tim. 2: 3).

This means buckling on "the whole armor of God" (Eph. 6) and entering into the fight with sin. It sometimes means the dividing of households (Matt. 10: 34-39). It always means an overcoming of sin rather than living at peace with it. It means that the one business of the Christian is to conquer this world for Jesus Christ. "And this is the victory that hath overcome the world, even our faith" (1 John 5: 4).

7. THE CHRISTIAN IS A BRANCH OF THE TRUE VINE, CHRIST JESUS. He should therefore avoid anything that might hinder the fullest fruitfulness (John 15: 1-10).

"Ye did not choose me, but I chose you and appointed you, that ye should go and bear fruit, and *that* your fruit may abide, and that whatsoever ye shall ask of the Father in my name he may give it you" (John 15: 16).

There are many things in which some church members indulge, such as dancing, theater going, card playing, and pleasure seeking of the selfish kind, which do not seem to them to be very wrong, but which hinder both their influence for good among men and their power in prayer to God. A wealthy man took his pastor with him on a pleasure excursion and together they indulged themselves in worldly ways, but when the man became ill he asked the colored servant, who was a devout man, rather than his pastor, to pray for him. All the pleasures of this world cannot repay such loss of spiritual power and influence.

And if thy right eye cause thee to stumble, pluck it out, and cast it from thee: for it is profitable for thee that one of thy members should perish, and not thy whole body be cast into hell (Matt. 5: 29).

Therefore let us also, seeing we are compassed about with so great a cloud of witnesses, lay aside every weight, and the sin which doth so easily beset us, and let us run with patience the race that is set before us, looking to Jesus the author and perfector of **our** faith, who for the joy that was set before him endured the cross, despising shame, and hath sat down at the right hand of the throne of God (Heb. 12: 1-3).

SEPARATION IN CUSTOMS: NONCONFORMITY TO THE WORLD.

There was once a poor Christian family which moved from Chicago to a small village. The two little girls entered school with cheap, red calico dresses, but the other children made fun of their dresses and they came home crying. Their mother said to them, " Go back again and tell the other girls that we did not come down here from Chicago to follow the style, but to set the style." They did as they were told, and lo, it was not long until the other little girls in school appeared in red dresses also.

So it should be with the Christian. He is not in the world to follow the style but to set the style. He has received a new type of life and must manifest it to the world or lose it. " He that is ashamed of me or of my words in this adulterous and sinful generation, the Son of man shall also be ashamed of him when he cometh in the glory of the Father with the holy angels " (Mark 8: 38).

There is no such thing as secret discipleship. Those who are Christ's must live for Him openly, and the love in the heart will reveal itself in the conversation, in the occupation and in the adornments of life.

1. IN CONVERSATION THE CHRISTIAN SHOULD LEAD RATHER THAN FOLLOW. Jesus said, " Every idle word that men shall speak they shall give an account thereof in the day of judgment" (Matt. 12: 36). Paul commanded Timothy to be " an example in word " (1 Tim. 4: 12). Much of the conversation of the world is mixed with vulgarity or gossip that is not only useless, but positively harmful. The Gospel says:

All uncleanness or covetousness, let it not even be named

among you, as becometh saints; nor filthiness, nor foolish talking, or jesting, which are not befitting; but rather giving of thanks (Eph. 5: 4).

One time a man was about to tell a smutty story in the presence of General Grant. He first looked about and said, " I see there are no ladies here." General Grant replied, " No, but there are some gentlemen here." The story was not told. If Christians would always remember that Christ is present in spirit and hears all their conversation, how different much of it would be! Should we not remember?

2. IN OCCUPATION THE CHRISTIAN SHOULD REMEMBER THAT GOD IS SENIOR PARTNER. We are workers together with Him (2 Cor. 6: 1). We must therefore seek the highest calling and the best gifts (1 Cor. 12: 31) and trust the promise, " Seek ye first the kingdom of God and his righteousness, and all these things shall be added unto you " (Matt. 6: 33).

A certain preacher said, " Modern business is so conducted that a strictly honest man must fail. Therefore a Christian man must keep from the common dishonesty on the one hand only as far as the line of failure will permit him on the other." In other words, " Steal no more than you must to succeed." This is not the message of the Gospel. It says, " Let him that stole steal no more: but rather let him labor, working with his hands the thing that is good " (Eph. 4: 28). We do not believe that it is necessary in legitimate business for a good Christian business man to be dishonest in order to succeed, but if so, it is better to give up business than to give up honesty. Christian principles were meant to be applied in business as well as elsewhere, and the world awaits the Christian business men with courage to so apply them. The revival wave now sweeping

Separation: Nonconformity

the world is resulting in just such civic righteousness. It has been long in coming. May it ever abide.

3. IN DRESS THE CHRISTIAN SHOULD CONFORM TO THE SPIRIT OF CHRIST WITHIN RATHER THAN TO THE FASHIONS OF THE WORLD WITHOUT.

Jesus said, " Consider the lilies how they grow, they toil not neither do they spin; yet I say unto you, Even Solomon in all his glory was not arrayed like one of these."

What is the lesson here? Consider the lilies HOW they grow." How do they get their beauty, surpassing all the artificial glory of Solomon? By simply growing and allowing the lily life within to express itself. Even so if Christians will allow the Christian spirit within to express itself unhampered by the weight of worldly notions, it will clothe itself in a way more beautiful than worldly artists can devise. It is a mistake, a sad, inexpressibly sad mistake, which despoils the looks of the fair bride of Christ, that the church should think it necessary to follow the styles of the world rather than to set a style of its own. The worldly spirit clothes itself in the vanities of the world, but the Christian spirit should be allowed to clothe itself in harmony with its own beauteous graces. If they who seek to be beautiful were only wise they would know that plain and modest attire contributes far more to beauty than all the gorgeous foppery that is foisted by fashion upon her foolish devotees. The church should seek to bring its members up to the Gospel principles in this as well as in other matters.

(1) *Men and women should dress as befits their nature and position without attempting to imitate each other.*

It was written in the law:

A woman shall not wear that which pertaineth unto a man, neither shall a man put on a woman's garment; for whosoever doeth these things is an abomination unto Jehovah thy God (Deut. 22: 5).

Grant that the law has passed away, God has not changed, and the evil of immodesty is still an abomination in His sight. The "good fellow" girl who apes the men in dress and manners is trifling with fire. Whatever tends to destroy the distinctions which God in nature has ordained tends to destroy also the one who yields to it. God's commandments are for our good, and they who love God will obey them. As Cyprian, one of the early church Fathers, said:

Let chaste and modest virgins avoid the dress of the unchaste, the manners of the immodest, the ensigns of the brothels and the ornaments of harlots.—Treatise 1: 12.

(2) The adornment of the Christian should be that of character rather than of costume. The Gospel says:

Whose adorning, let it be not that outward adorning of braiding the hair, and of wearing jewels of gold, or of putting on apparel; but let it be the hidden man of the heart, in the incorruptible apparel of a meek and quiet spirit, which is in the sight of God of great price (1 Pet. 3: 3, 4).

This command, with all others, is to be interpreted and applied according to the spirit of it rather than the mere letter, "For the letter killeth, but the spirit giveth life" (2 Cor. 3: 6), and the specific things mentioned are not by any means all the things included by the spirit of the command. Pride in the heart has many ways of showing itself, and there are adornments of house and harness as well as of hair and raiment.

Christianity does not draw the line vertically and say "You may lavish money in every other way after the customs of the world, except in this and this," but it draws the line transversely and says, "You must avoid excess in all things." One with the Christian spirit will be asking, not so much, "Is this the style or not?" but, "Is this the way in which I can do the most good with this money which is entrusted to me as a steward?" Plain clothes and twenty-thousand-dollar houses do not go well together. Hooks and eyes on the clothes must make the tobacco in the mouth only more nauseating in the sight of God. As much of God's money is spent for costly furniture and needless bric-a-brac as is spent for jewels and plumage. One who really has the spirit of Christ will not strain at a gnat and swallow a camel in these things. If Christianity means anything it means the renunciation of self with all selfish desires. Jesus said, "Whosoever he be of you that renounceth not all that he hath he cannot be my disciple" (Luke 14: 33).

(3) *Where the Christian spirit and worldly customs conflict, Christ must have the preëminence.*

Be not fashioned according to this world, but be ye transformed by the renewing of your minds (Rom. 12: 2).

This does not mean that everything the world has is evil and must be avoided; it means only, as Jesus prayed, "that thou wouldst keep them from the evil *one*." There is on record the testimony of *Mathetes* (130 A. D) who calls himself a disciple of the apostles, who in a letter to Diognetus, ch. 5, says:

For the Christians are distinguished from other men neither by country nor language, nor the customs which they observe. . . . But inhabiting Greek as well as barbarian cities, according as the lot of each of them has determined, and following the customs of the natives as respects clothing, food, and the rest of their ordinary conduct, they display to us their wonderful and confessedly striking methods of life.

But while the Christians retained all that was good and useful in the world, they rebelled at the evil customs. *Jerome* rebukes the worldly women of his day in words which might well be sounded in the ears of all those whose chief study is the fashion plates to-day. He says:

> You may see numbers of these—their faces painted, their eyes like those of vipers, their teeth rubbed with pumice stone, raving and carping at Christians with insane fury. One of these ladies,
>
> "A violet mantle round her shoulders thrown,
>   Drawls out some mawkish stuff, speaks through her nose,
>   And minces half her words with tripping tongue."
>
> What place have rouge and white lead on the face of a Christian woman? The one simulates the natural red of the cheeks and lips; the other the whiteness of the neck and face. They only serve to inflame young men's passions, to stimulate lust and to indicate an unchaste mind. How can a woman weep for her sins whose tears lay bare her true complexion and mark furrows on her cheeks? Such adorning is not of the Lord. A mask of this kind belongs to anti-Christ. With what confidence can a woman raise features to heaven which the Creator must fail to recognize? It is idle to allege in excuse for such practices girlishness and youthful vanity.—Letters 14.

Cyprian also takes up the cudgel against hydra-headed pride, which threatened the church then as now. He says:

> You say that you are wealthy and rich. But not everything that can be done ought to be done; nor ought the broad desires that arise out of the pride of the world to be extended beyond the honor and modesty of virginity; since it is written, "All things are lawful, but all things are not expedient: all things are lawful, but all things edify not." For the rest, if you dress your hair sumptuously and walk so as to draw attention in public, and attract the eyes of youth upon you, and draw the sighs of young men after you, nourish the lust of concupiscence, and inflame the fuel of sighs, so that, although you yourself perish not, yet you cause others to perish, and offer yourself as it were, a sword or poison to the spectators; you cannot be excused on pretense that you are chaste and modest in mind. Your shameful dress and immodest ornament accuse you; nor can you be accounted now among Christ's maidens and virgins, since you live in such a manner as to make yourselves objects of desire.—Treatise 2: 8.

Separation: Nonconformity

It is said that over in Paris there are several Jews who manage the large clothing houses where the styles for the world are prepared. Here the wealthy women come for the latest ideas, and the milliners for the fashions they must display to be up with the times. Here the changes are made from year to year so as to do away with the last season's clothing, whether worn out or not, and sell a new supply. And the Christian women of the world bow down with the rest and say, "We must be in style. It is better to be out of the world than out of style"; and the Lord's money is poured out at the feet of the goddess of fashion. It is all wrong. It is silly as well as sinful. If Christians would renounce the world as they profess to do, they could set the style instead of following it, and would be all the more beautiful because clothed in the garments that betoken modesty and humility and consecration to the Lord Jesus. While they would not all need to dress exactly alike yet they would all dress modestly and economically.

This does not mean the despising of beauty. No one appreciates true beauty more than the Christian. He sees the glories of nature more than the worldling, but back of these he sees the glory of God and seeks that first of all, —the glory of character. The love of God in the heart gives a new view point of beauty. They who love God see no beauty in a hat adorned with plumage which has cost the lives of God's dear little innocent birds. They see no beauty in a mansion that represents a sum of money that might comfortably house the owner in a more modest home and leave a goodly sum to send the Gospel to the heathen. They find no pleasure in adornments of walls or table that tell a tale of selfishness rather than of love for the souls of men. Those who love God see beauty in the modest apparel at which the world laughs, and find pleasure in the simple life which the world rejects, but in the new life they find a full reward. It may be that in showing to the world the evidences of their separation from it they will be subjected to some ridicule and ostracism, but they will rejoice even in this when they remember the Scriptures:

> Because ye are not of the world, but I have chosen you out of the world, therefore the world hateth you. Remember the word that I said unto you, A servant is not greater than his lord. If they persecuted me they will also persecute you . . . but all these things will they do unto you for my name's sake, because they know not him that sent me.—John 15: 19-21.
>
> Yea, all that would live godly in Christ Jesus shall suffer persecution (2 Tim. 3: 12).
>
> But if a man suffer as a Christian, let him not be ashamed; but let him glorify God in this name—1 Pet. 4: 16.
>
> If we endure, we shall also reign with him: if we deny him he will also deny us (2 Tim. 2: 12).

4. THE REWARDS OF THE SEPARATED LIFE. Jesus promised to those who would renounce the world for His sake, an hundredfold in this life, with persecutions, and in the world to come eternal life (Mark 10: 29). The testing of this promise shows it to be true.

1. *Separation means power.* It is the locomotive that holds to the narrow track that crosses the continent with speed and power. It is the person who sits on an insulated stool that can be charged with the electric energy. It is the Christian whose life is hid with Christ in God who can say with Paul, "I can do all things through Christ who strengtheneth me" (Philpp. 2: 20).

2. *Separation means fellowship.* Not indeed with the world, but with the citizens of the heavenly kingdom. Jesus said, "Ye are not of the world even as I am not of the world." Separation from the world means fellowship with Him. It means fellowship with Paul who said, "God forbid that I should glory save in the cross of Christ my Lord,

through which the world hath been crucified to me and I unto the world" (Gal. 6: 14). It means fellowship with that "great cloud of witnesses" spoken of in Heb. 12: 1 and the chapter before. It means fellowship with those who shall be heirs of the eternal kingdom because they have "washed their robes and have made them white in the blood of the lamb."

SEPARATION IN COMPANY: SPECIAL REFERENCE TO LODGES.

Separation from the world involves important questions concerning associations, which, if the principle is to be maintained as a means of grace, must be answered by the Gospel. The following discussion is one of Gospel principles rather than of organizations or persons. The question of lodge membership is dealt with specially because it involves all the others connected with Christian companionship, being itself perhaps the most important. Some members of secret orders and other associations of the world say that there is nothing evil in them, but others come out from them and declare that they are evil. The testimony of ministers and other Christian workers in the lodges is not fully reliable, because initiation ceremonies are sometimes altered to suit the consciences of those entering. Such persons (who enter by altered initiations) become either blind guides of others or else share in the deception which brings others in by the regular way because of their example. It is not enough either to depend upon the published apologies or explanations of the orders, because these must only deal with the open work and teaching, while it is the secret oaths and secret favoritism that is most opposed.

If Christians know the Gospel principles which apply, they will know for themselves how far to go in their relations with lodges. The Gospel is not a law book with specific directions to fit all cases. Rather it inspires a type of life which instinctively shuns all forms of evil. Christ in the heart is the Christian criterion of conduct. He binds no human being to the conscience of another. When the

Separation: Non-secrecy

candidate at the door of the lodge agrees to trust the word of another that his obligation to secrecy will not involve any wrong, he binds himself by the conscience of another even more fatally than the Romanist who goes to confessional and allows the priest to be conscience for him, to the destruction of his own moral independence. Christ seeks rather to develop the moral sense in men by giving us the ideal and then the responsibility of seeking it. He recognized the fact that His followers must be more or less in contact with the wicked world, yet declared that they should be "not of the world." He prayed, "not that thou shouldst take them from the world, but that thou shouldst keep them from the evil *one*" (John 17: 15). All His precepts are in line with this principle:

(1) He allowed certain *political and business dealings* with the world when He said, "Render therefore unto Caesar the things that are Caesar's" (Matt. 22: 21).

(2) In His *social contact* with the world Jesus dined with publicans and sinners as well as Scribes and Pharisees, but always to save them,—never to be partakers of their sins.

(3) In the matter of *charity* Jesus taught His disciples to do good even to their enemies. This brings touch with the needy who are of the ungodly world. He therefore puts a certain responsibility upon the individual conscience in deciding duty in specific cases.

But liberty of conscience does not mean license to set aside plain principles of right and wrong which Jesus has taught. Where He says stop we must stop and where He says go we must go. His words are of final authority because they are truth. "The words that I speak the same shall judge you at the last day." What then does Jesus Christ say to us concerning participation in secret or oath-bound or worldly organizations?

I. Principles by Which to Judge Worldly Organizations.

1. CHRISTIANS MUST AVOID ALL SINFUL UNION WITH THE WORLD.

I pray not that thou shouldst take them from the world, but that thou shouldst keep them from the evil one (John 17: 15).

Ye are an elect race, a royal priesthood, a holy nation, a people for God's own possession, that ye may show forth the excellencies of him who called you out of darkness into his marvelous light (1 Pet. 2: 9).

This is one of the most repeated principles of the Gospel, and it is violated in worldly associations in various ways. Let us look at its application more in detail.

(1) *Christians should not seek the fellowship of non-Christians for the sake of social pleasures.*

Know ye not that the friendship of the world is enmity with God? Whosoever therefore would be a friend with the world maketh himself an enemy of God (Jas. 4: 4). The time past may suffice to have wrought the desire of the Gentiles, and to have walked in lasciviousness, lusts, wine-bibbings, revellings, carousings, and abominable idolatries: wherein they think it strange that ye run not with them into the same excess of riot, speaking evil of you: who shall give an account to him who is ready to judge both the living and the dead (1 Pet. 4: 3-5). Be not unequally yoked together with unbelievers: for what fellowship hath righteousness with iniquity? or what communion hath light with darkness? And what concord hath Christ with Belial? or what portion hath a believer with an unbeliever? And what agreement hath a temple of God with idols? for we are a temple of the living God; even as God said, I will dwell in them, and walk in them; and I will be their God, and they shall be my people. Wherefore, Come ye out from among them, and be ye separate, saith the Lord, and touch no unclean thing; and I will receive you, and will be to you a Father, and ye shall be to me sons and daughters, saith the Lord Almighty—(2 Cor. 6: 14-18).

When Christian members of the oath-bound secret societies go to dances and card parties, the "big-eats" and other worldly pleasures of their lodges to mingle with the unconverted just for the sake of their company they certainly fly in the face of these Scriptures and must stand their judgment.

(2) *But again, Christians must not become subject to the control of non-Christians in moral matters.* "One is your teacher, even Christ" (Matt. 23: 8). In lodges the non-Christians may be in the majority and vote for a dance or some other worldly pleasure, over the heads of the Christians, who still, by virtue of their being voluntary members of the lodge, must bear the blame of sharing in these sins. If the church *as a church* should get up a dance every member in it would share the blame and disgrace of it before the world, and where lodges do such things the members all share the responsibility, because membership is voluntary and any one not approving the conduct of the lodge may remain out of it.

(3) *Christians must not share in the propagation of a moral standard incompatible with Christ.* He says: "I am the way, the truth and the life" (John 14: 6). So far as we know, none of the oath-bound secret societies preach Christ as the only way of life eternal, while some of them use burial rituals which imply salvation without Christ. Do not Christian members of such lodges lend their assent to such heresy?

(4) *Christians must not take obligations which are in violation of loyalty to Christ.* "No man can serve two masters" (Matt. 6: 24). If Christ is our Master we dare not pledge supreme allegiance to any other. "He is the head of the body, the church: who is the beginning, the firstborn from the dead; that in all things he might have the preëminence" (Col. 1: 18). The oath is a bond which binds, not to Christ, but to another, and the honorary

titles, "Master" or "Grand Master," &c., imply allegiance to these others.

(5) *Christians must not be party to any organization that overrides the family and the church.* Do not the lodges hide their secrets from them and erect a barrier between them? Do they not take time and money which should go to them? Say not that membership is necessary for the sake of insurance, for there are accident and life insurance companies which do not ask their patrons to spend an evening a week in a guarded lodge room. If the church is to be in spotless raiment as she waits for her Lord (Eph. 5: 25-32), she must not accept another as her master in anything. Toward all such proposals she must turn with the words, "Get thee behind me, Satan, for thou savorest not of the things that be of God, but of the things that be of men" (Matt. 16: 23).

2. CHRISTIANS MUST BE OPPOSED TO OATH-BOUND SECRET SOCIETIES BECAUSE OF THEIR OATHS.

(1) *Their oaths are an insult to Christian honor.* When a Christian says "Yea, yea," or "Nay, nay," that should be the end of it, but the oath-bound order says, "Your word is unreliable. Your honor is insufficient. You cannot satisfy us without taking an oath."

(2) *The oath is an appeal to superstition.* It conjures with the sacred names in the oath to cause fear; but he who does not fear to break his simple word has no true reverence for God, and only blasphemes when he makes the honor of God depend upon his own weak vow.

(3) *The oath is a direct violation of the explicit and emphatic command of Christ.* No appeal to the law can break His words, for He is superior to the law and the prophets, and we are to "hear him" (Luke 9: 35). What can be plainer than His words,

Ye have heard that it was said to them of old time, Thou

shalt not forswear thyself, but shalt perform unto the Lord thine oaths; but I say unto you, Swear not at all; . . . But let your speech be, Yea, yea; nay, nay: and whatsoever is more than these is of the evil one (Matt. 5: 33-38).

If oaths are of the evil one, Christians must oppose them, for Jesus' word is final.

(4) *The oaths of secret societies are to be opposed because some of them at least, have penalties attached which no Christian could help in enforcing.* Some of them involve murder in horrible forms. Published exposures of Blue Lodge Masonry, admitted by some Masons to be substantially true, give as the penalties of the first three degrees for violations of the oaths,

To have the throat cut from ear to ear, the tongue torn out, the heart and vitals taken out and buried by the sands of the sea, the body cut in two, the bowels burned in the middle and scattered to the four winds of heaven.

Higher degrees are said to have even worse oaths, and whether they be taken literally and seriously or not, familiarity with them in frequent initiations cannot help but prepare the heart for murder. Such oaths assume to threaten for disloyalty to the lodge, penalties reserved by the State for only the capital crimes of treason and murder and thus imply that the lodge is more important than the State.

(5) *They obligate the member to keep secret some things of which he is still in ignorance, and as to which he is therefore guilty.* (Lev. 5: 4, 5). What if some lodge friend or officer assures the candidate that there will be nothing to interfere with "those high and holy duties which he owes to his family, the State or to God," what right has any man to make himself slave to the conscience of another? And who knows what he is pledging to keep secret when he says, "I promise to conceal and never to reveal any of

those secret arts which have already been revealed, are now about to be revealed or which shall hereafter be revealed?" According to president Blanchard of Wheaton College, there is a case on record at Hartford, Connecticut, of a Mr. Jackson, who was compelled by the State to witness against a fellow Mason who had admitted to him as a brother Mason that he had committed arson, and *because he did not perjure himself to the State to keep his wicked oath to the lodge and protect the criminal lodge member, the supreme lodge of the State expelled him from membership.* That is what it was to promise to keep secret things yet unknown. Even if everything in the society were good, then the vow to keep what is good a secret is itself wrong, for it is the duty of all to pass along every good thing as much as possible.

3. Christians must also be opposed to oath-bound secret societies because of their secrecy.

It will not do to say that the secrecy is only such as business men must have to prevent being imposed upon, for a system of membership cards kept up to date would be far more effective and would render oaths and secret meetings wholly unnecessary. Witness the example of the Y. M. C. A.

(1) *Secrecy is contrary to Christ* who said, "Men do not light a lamp and put it under a bushel * * * Let your light so shine before men; that they may see your good works, and glorify your Father who is in heaven" (Matt. 5: 15, 16).

(2) *Secrecy is wrong in principle.* If a doctor discovers a remedy for a disease he is in honor bound to give his discovery to the world. If a scientist discovers a new truth he hastens to make it known. If secret societies have good principles they should teach them to the world, even as the church proclaims the Gospel to all nations (1 Cor. 9: 16).

Separation: Non-secrecy

(3) *Secrecy is harmful in practice.* It causes husbands to have a shrine in the heart which not even the wives may enter. It places these secrets of the lodges above the family and the church and makes closer confidants of non-Christians in the lodges than of one's own pastor or family. This alienates both from the family and from the church (Col. 1. 18).

(4) *Secrecy puts one in a bad light before the world.* It causes suspicion of evil, for why should good be kept secret? Paul speaks of evil companies in his day, saying, "the things done of them in secret it is a shame even to speak of" (Eph. 5: 11, 12). It is repeatedly charged by those who have renounced the orders that they assist their members to political office and to escape the consequences of crimes when committed. At this time there is an Ohio banker who was sentenced to the penitentiary, but instead of working inside he has an easy clerical position near by. A public official who has seen him repeatedly, said to us "He has never seen the inside of the penitentiary, and never will, and *no other Mason ever will.*" Such charges are denied by lodge members, but they are so numerous and so direct that they put the odium of suspicion upon all who join in secret work. That many lodge members are opposed to such practices may be admitted, but the very foundation principle of such organizations encourages such work. Only a few years ago (according to President Blanchard) a man named Keith at Belvidere, Illinois, committed seduction and murder. Judge Whitney of that place sought to bring him to justice, but the murderer was a Mason and an Odd Fellow, and the sheriff being a fellow lodge member "could not find him." A deputy was appointed who did, but fellow lodge members caused the jury to disagree in each trial and the villain went free. More than that, *Judge Whitney was expelled by the*

grand lodge of the State for disloyalty to the order and unmasonic conduct in seeking to prosecute a fellow member. Readers may judge for themselves if this is an exceptional case or whether it is the natural fruit of a vicious favoritism fostered by the lodge principle.

(5) *Secrecy as well as the oath helps to estrange the lodge member from his family and from the church.* It divides his interest, his support and his affections. It hides his doings from those who have a right to his fullest confidence. It violates his sacred relations to his family and to Christ. The Christian must be as the Lord who could say, " In secret I spake nothing " (John 18: 20), and must therefore oppose union with all organizations which violate this principle. When Jesus cast the demons out of the man with the legion He said to him, " Go home to thy house." He had been dwelling among the tombs and in the mountains. If the Master were to walk in the midst of men today and should see the sad-hearted wives and mothers at home while their husbands spend night after night at the lodges, and the children roam the streets, is there any doubt but that He would say to these men, " Go home to thy house! You have taken upon you sacred vows in marriage, which now you break. Your wife whom you pledged to love, you now desert in the evenings for the lodge. Your children you mislead by your example. She whom God hath ordained should be ' as one flesh ' with her husband, you separate for the sake of your oath of secrecy. The church which is the bride of Christ you treat as a thing inferior. Go home to thy house. The home and not the lodge is the place for Christian men." Men who go to lodges because they have no homes should establish homes of their own instead. No decent man need be forever without one. They who shirk the responsibilities of a home are largely responsible for the existence of the brothel.

God established the home: let not man establish substitutes for it.

4. CHRISTIANS SHOULD NOT SUBSTITUTE A LOW OR PARTIAL MORAL STANDARD FOR THE GOSPEL STANDARD.

This is exactly what most lodges do, and the resulting tendency is to do away with the Gospel standard altogether. For example, it is said that "there is honor even among thieves," so that one thief will not steal from another. This is in effect the lodge standard. The Mason is said to swear that he will not rob or wrong a brother Mason knowing him to be such. What does this mean if it does not give him liberty to wrong one not a Mason? Again he is said to swear "not to have carnal intercourse with the wife or sister or mother or daughter of a brother Mason, knowing them to be such." What is this but to expose every other woman in the world to the lust of the Masonic libertine?

It is needless to deny that this is the implication, for every school boy who has studied Civil Government knows that it is a principle of law that when a person specifically deeds away certain of his things he retains full possession of all the rest. For example, in America, whatever rights the States do not give to the Federal Government by specific mention in the Constitution, they retain. Now, when the lodge member deeds away by his oath his "right" to violate the wife or sister or mother or daughter of a fellow Mason, he by this well-known principle of law assumes to *retain* the "right" to commit adultery with any other woman. The lodge leaders may not so explain it, nor the befogged members so understand it, but that is the implication of such an oath, and no intelligent Christian can stoop to its plane. If it be said that the lodge does not recognize the right to commit adultery or to rob at all, but seeks only to impress the *special* obligations to Masons, or other fellow lodge members, we reply that the very act of limitation *assumes* that a person has a right to do such things to others. How can one deed away a *part* when he does not possess *any?* How can one swear away his (assumed) right to wrong fellow members, if he does not pretend to have the right to wrong them or any one else? The position is absurd, and not only absurd, but wicked. The Gospel principles are universal and not partial, and no Christian can assume to possess the right to limit his moral obligations as lodges in general do. Their moral standard is not Christ and the Gospel, but a sham substitute which is sugar-coated to deceive the Christian who is won to the lodge, but which confirms the wicked in their wickedness. It may be granted that some lodges teach some principles that are good and true, but where even the Golden Rule is made the way of salvation rather than the Christ who gave the Golden Rule, it becomes an anti-Christ. That some lodges do put their principles in the place of Christ as the way of salvation can be noted by any one who will take the trouble to listen to one of their burial services and note how hope of meeting " in that grand lodge above " is *not* based on faith in Christ and obedience to His Gospel.

EVEN IN THEIR BOASTED " CHARITY " THE LODGE SUBSTITUTES A LOW STANDARD OF BENEVOLENCE FOR THE GOSPEL STANDARD.

(1) *Their " charity " is only insurance to members whereas Christians are taught to " do good to all men "* (Gal. 6: 10; Rom. 12: 20).

(2) *It is delegated instead of voluntary.* When our brow is fevered let it be smoothed by some loving fellow-Christian rather than by some man of the world sent by a lodge. " If I bestow all my goods to feed *the poor* * * * but have not love, it profiteth me nothing " (1 Cor. 13: 3).

Separation: Non-secrecy

(3) *Lodge members pay their dues hoping to receive as much again,* while Christians are taught to "do good and lend hoping for nothing again" (Luke 6: 35 A. V).

(4) *Lodge charity is of the standard of the world* because, "if ye do good to them that do good to you, what thank have ye? for even sinners do the same. But love your enemies and do *them* good" (Luke 6: 34, 35).

(5) *Lodge "charity" is not in the name of a disciple, nor does it give glory to God.* It is true that no one shall give a cup of cold water and lose his reward, but it must be "in the name of a disciple" (Matt. 10: 42). "Whatsoever ye do in word or in deed, *do* all in the name of the Lord Jesus" (Col. 3: 17). The lodges, instead, take all glory to themselves and to their principles, and thus seek to exalt themselves rather than the Savior who gave to the world the example of true love. When the Good Samaritan helped the man who fell among thieves he took him to the inn and provided for all his needs, not because the man was a fellow lodge member and had paid his dues, but because he had Christian compassion. The Good Samaritan is Jesus, not lodge members, and the inn is the church, not the lodge, and the help given is not dependent on ability to pay dues. If lodge members really wish to help the cause of love and friendship, why do they not give their individual devotion to the church which has in Christ the only model of true love, rather than to a halfway substitute?

5. CHRISTIANS MUST OPPOSE OATH-BOUND SECRET SOCIETIES BECAUSE IN GREATER OR LESS DEGREE THEY ARE FALSE RELIGIONS.

That lodges assume the functions of religion is more true of some than of others, and it is denied altogether by some members of all, but by others it is admitted, and still others make a boast of it. We have heard many lodge members say, "My lodge principles are good enough religion for me." As proof that the lodge does usurp the place of true religion note the following:

(1) *The lodge has an altar but not a Christian altar.* In all ages the altar has been the symbol of worship. What is a family altar? The institution of family worship. What is the church altar? The place of worship. What is the lodge altar? The place of religious ceremonies. Is the lodge altar Christian? It cannot be in those lodges which treat Christianity as simply one religion of many in the world. The lodge altar is simply a symbol of religion in general, pagan, Mohammedan, Christian, or any other. The lodge altar therefore represents the lodge religion, and is to be classed with the altars of Baal or Buddha and the rest, all of which Christianity came, not to affiliate with, but to overthrow. Christianity is not hostile to truth or to any good principle but it has no compromise with any of Satan's substitutes for the Gospel.

(2) *The lodge has prayer, but not Christian prayer,* because it cannot be in the name of Christ. This is true of even the order of Odd Fellows, which is thought by many church members, and even ministers, to be in harmony with the Gospel because it makes so much of the incident of the Good Samaritan. The Grand Lodge of Massachusetts, says the *Christian Cynosure,* asked the Sovereign Grand Lodge of the World for the Order of Odd Fellows, the following question, the answer to which authoritatively sustains the point we make.

Question,—Is it lawful for a chaplain to commence and finish his prayers in the name of Christ?

Answer: Our order only requires a belief in the existence of a Supreme Being as a qualification for membership, and has no affinity with any religious sect or system of faith. Hence anything savoring of sectarianism is not to be tolerated. The words, "system of faith or sect," do not have reference to sects within the pale of Christianity, but have a far broader significance, and include all the religions of the world. In this sense, Christianity is a sect; hence it is inexpedient, and I think, unlawful, to make prominent reference to it in lodge work.

Donneldson's Pocket Companion of Oddfellowship also says that none other than the prescribed forms of prayer may be used (p. 166), and these bar the name of Christ, the only name in which there is assurance of answer (John 16: 26). Can a Christian join in such Christless prayers?

The fact that lodges use some of the truths and incidents of the Bible, while rejecting the vital things of the Gospel, as the atonement, regeneration, &c., only makes them the more dangerous when posing as substitutes. Satan is most to be dreaded when he "transforms himself into an angel of light," and thus seeks to sidetrack worship from the true God to himself.

(3) *The lodge uses the Bible, but simply as a part of its "furniture."* In Hindoo, Buddhist or Mohammedan countries, the so-called sacred books of those religions are used by the adherents instead of the Bible. Lodge religion, therefore, is not Bible religion.

(4) *Some lodges have religious rites and symbols,* such as facing the altar to the east, kneeling, being half dressed, with left side bare, going through a mock burial and resurrection, &c. If the lodge is not considered religious, why is it that these religious rites are made an essential part of the ritual?

(5) *All, or nearly all, lodges have religious rites for the dead, but they are not Christian.* The ritual prayers may be read by a lodge chaplain who is himself an unregenerate, vile man. They may include the dropping of a sprig of evergreen as a symbol of the resurrection, but they do not base the hope of salvation on the atonement of Christ. They do not include faith and repentance, but every lodge member, whether regenerate or not, is buried

with the hope of meeting again " in the grand lodge above." If this does not put the lodge as a substitute for the church and make it a false religion, what can make it so?

The following is a sample of their funeral odes:

> Though in the Grand Lodge above
> We remember thee in love.
> Till life shall end—then hear the voice,
> Depart in peace from earth to heaven.
> And now he quits our weary train,
> And marches o'er the heavenly heights.
> —Manual of Oddfellowship by A. B. Grosh, p. 408.

Compare this with the declaration of Jesus,

I am the way, . . . no man cometh to the Father but by me. . . . I am the door, . . . he that entereth not by the door, but climbeth up some other way, the same is a thief and a robber (John 10: 1).

With such a system calculated to inspire a false hope it is no wonder that *it is the testimony of all earnest pastors that as a rule the lodge tends to become a substitute for the church.* There are church members, to be sure, who are also active lodge members, but it remains true that the energy and time and money and thought that is spent upon the lodges is that much taken from the church. And in the majority of cases, as those who read these lines may know for themselves, the waxing of zeal for the lodge causes a waning of zeal for the church, and while some men have been brought to the church through the lodge, yet on the other hand, many more have been led away from the church by the lodge. Who ever heard of a church member being more devoted to the prayer meeting because of joining a lodge? Let it be remembered, however, that what has been said is in reference to lodges in general, and not of the exceptions; of the tendency of lodge principles, not of members who retain the Christian spirit in spite of them.

Separation: Non-secrecy

6. CHRISTIANS MUST NOT VIOLATE THE SCRIPTURES CONCERNING TITLES OF HONOR.

Jesus said, " Be not ye called masters, for one is your Master even Christ " (Matt. 23: 8-10 A. V.), but the secret orders with scarcely an exception heap high and mighty titles upon their various officers and members of advanced degrees, all of which encourage that vanity and worldly pride which is directly contrary to the spirit of Christ and the church. Jesus said, " He that is greatest among you let him be your minister," but the lodge says, " Let him be your ' Royal chief ' or ' Supreme Grand Chancellor ' or ' Worshipful Master ' or some other superior person." If these titles are empty they are mockery, and if they are taken as they mean they are blasphemous. That some take them as child's play is no excuse for them. The Christian has no business with them, for they savor of the anti-Christ.

7. CHRISTIANS MUST OPPOSE THE PROMOTION OF UNCHRISTIAN CASTE SPIRIT.

The Gospel teaches us to be " no respecter of persons " (Acts 10: 34; Jas. 2: 1-10), but the lodges are so continuously guilty of helping their own members in preference to others equally or more worthy, that it is idle for them to deny that they do such things. Some members may not, but the system as a whole fosters that sort of thing. The open fact that so many men join lodges in order to get office or position or practice, is incontestible proof that this unjust favoritism exists. Some men by joining a great many lodges get such a " pull " that they can secure almost any position over the heads of far more worthy persons. Space need not be taken for specific instances, although volumes of such might easily be given, because every reader will know of such instances for himself. They are a part of the " secret work " which is not all behind closed doors, and thousands of such cases of injustice escape general observation. Thus the very foundations of the lodge system are based on error and wrong. Whatever divides humanity on artificial lines and bestows favor without merit, or withholds it from the deserving because of being alien to the lodge, is wrong. Again we admit that many lodge members, because of their Christian teaching, oppose such favoritism and caste distinctions, but the very nature of the lodge caste tends to foster and encourage it. We have known even preachers to be so blinded to right as to join lodges for the sake of gaining positions and emoluments that they could not otherwise obtain. Whether they deserved them or not, in either case the lodge is wrong in helping or hindering on the basis of lodge membership rather than on the basis of merit. Christianity breaks down evil caste, but the lodge builds it up, therefore the lodge is no place for a Christian.

Imagine now a minister of the Gospel, fired with an ambition to become prominent in the community, who has been called to preach that besides the name of Christ there is none other "name under heaven that is given among men, whereby we must be saved" (Acts 4: 12), as a candidate for membership in a lodge which excludes that name from its ritual lest it offend its infidel or Jewish members. He leaves the wife whom he has vowed to treat as "one flesh" with himself, and announces himself as ready to receive secrets as yet unknown, and forever conceal them from the companion of his bosom. He leaves the little children whom God commands him to rear "in the nurture and admonition of the Lord" to seek pleasure with infidel and other members of a caste which binds its members for time and eternity. He knocks three times, the guard calls out "Who's there?" and he replies, "A man poor and blind and naked, seeking light and shelter,"—thus at the very door repudiating his Christianity as if he were a sinner coming to a Savior. He passes the closed and guarded door, and,

Separation: Non-secrecy

trampling upon the Master's words, "swear not at all," he proceeds to take an oath accompanied with penalties which belong only to the State, and which must mean murder if enforced, or mockery, if evaded. He kneels in prayer, but not "in the Spirit," or in the name of Christ (John 15: 16). He uses the Bible which says "Have no fellowship with the unfruitful works of darkness, but rather reprove them" (Eph. 5: 11), only as a means of enforcing his oath to cherish and protect and conceal them. He goes through rites of which he may never speak to his wife or children, or in the pulpit. He faces his superior officers and salutes them as "worshipful master" or something similar, forgetting Him who said, "Be ye not called masters, for one is your Master, even the Christ" (Matt. 23: 10 A. V.). He is seated in the company and sees it vote to have a dance the following week and is powerless to prevent it. He hears a committee report that in its "benevolent" work the lodge had paid so much to such members during the month, but not in the name of Christ (Col. 3: 17; Matt. 10: 42). He hears the lodge arrange to attend the funeral of a non-Christian member who has died, and learns that he must put on the lodge regalia and march in line to the funeral or give a good excuse for not doing so. He marches to the grave and hears a chaplain of unclean life read from the lodge ritual words which imply that the deceased unbeliever shall share heaven with the rest, and then he drops his sprig of myrtle in the grave to show his own assent to this lodge hope; and after the funeral he returns to his home to prepare to preach from the pulpit, the Gospel, the whole Gospel, and nothing but the Gospel. *Think you he can do it?*

Grant that this is putting the worst possibilities forward, are these things not possibilities? And could Satan work a worse deception than to cause a Christian to feel that in doing such things he is embracing an opportunity for good? Grant also that most lodges encourage morality and most lodge members live according to law, yet Satan seeks not so much to cause sin directly as to cause unbelief. In breaking down the atonement made by Jesus is the great sin of the lodge system.

II. The Church Should be a Complete Substitute for All the Good Done by the Lodge.

1. THE SOCIETY OF THE CHURCH SHOULD BE SUPERIOR TO THAT OF THE LODGES. Professor Henderson, the great sociologist, says it is infinitely superior. "At best," he says, "the lodges are only stag parties." In the church, the family is united instead of divided. In the church, there is no division of wealth, the poor who cannot pay dues being excluded altogether. Promotion to office does not depend upon ability to pay costs of a higher degree In the church there is no exclusion of either sex. All are one family in the household of God. In the church there is worship with helpful means of grace instead of a lot of nonsense like riding the goat, leading candidates through perils of darkness, blindfolded and undressed. In the church, the one purpose is to help the kingdom of God rather than to build up a temporal society. In the church, Christ is the head rather than some "worshipful master" who may be a child of the devil. Let the church be sociable. Let it seek the lost and help the weak. Let it be a home for the homeless and an earnest of the heaven above, and its members will not be tempted to seek more congenial company in the lodges. It is pride—sinful, selfish pride that is making of some churches merely aristocratic clubs where the poor are not welcome. The New Testament church must furnish a fellowship that is pure, and leave the societies of the unregenerate to themselves. The church is far more

than a society. It is the body of Christ (Eph. 1: 22, 23) and members of it are "new creatures," whose hope of life eternal is in the new life that they receive from Christ (John 3: 36). Let the church hold high her standard and it will not be confused with that of the world.

2. IN MORAL TEACHING THE CHURCH SHOULD NEVER CONSENT TO THE LODGE SUBSTITUTE.

(1) *Morals and religion must not be separated.* "If any man hath not the spirit of Christ he is none of his" (Rom. 8: 9). The lodges have their rules for morality, and treat religion as if it were a separate and indifferent matter. But unless morality spring out of true religion it shall perish as a branch separated from the vine. Paul said, "If any man preacheth to you any Gospel other than that which ye received, let him be anathema" (Gal. 1: 9). The lodges preach another Gospel which assumes to unite their members "in the grand lodge above" regardless of faith in Christ. Ritual prayers and burial rites which are the same for Christians and unbelievers, and thus override Christianity, can never be accepted by Christians without sin.

(2) *Christ rather than the lodge book rules must be exalted as the criterion of life.* Moral life springs from the new Christ-spirit within rather than from lodge rules forced upon one from without. The church has the only hope of eternal life and must so insistently hold up Christ that not for one moment may men be tempted to say, "The lodge is good enough for me." However good some of the principles of lodges may be, they are mere broken branches which cannot save. The life-giving vine is the Christ whom the church exalts and for whom there can be no substitute.

3. IN THE CARE OF THE NEEDY THE CHURCH SHOULD BE A COMPLETE SUBSTITUTE FOR THE LODGES. Here is the one point where the lodges claim an argument. They say they

are doing the charity work that the church is neglecting. If that is true, it is no reason for lodges, but the more reason for a return of the church to the New Testament rule.

(1) *The church should have a fund for the needy.* This fund should be fed by gifts and bequests such as were brought to the apostles by the first converts (Acts 2: 45), and by regular weekly offerings as God has prospered, such as were commanded by the apostle in 1 Cor. 16: 2 ff. Note that this fund for the poor was arranged for in advance and collected systematically. It was not for the support of the ministry, as many suppose, but for the poor. God ordained the tithe for the support of the ministry (1 Cor. 9: 14). Let the church get into line with the Gospel and both the ministers and the poor will have care.

(2) *The church officers should superintend the distribution of this bounty to the needy.* See Acts 6: 1-6. It is the duty of the deacons and elders to see that the church is keeping up its fund for this purpose and that it is properly distributed.

(3) *There should be a test of worthiness so that no wrong be done.*

If any will not work neither let him eat (2 Thess. 3: 10). Let the elders that rule well (Gr. wear themselves out) be counted worthy of double honor (Gr. support). 1 Tim. 5: 17.

Testimonies.

The foregoing propositions are plain Gospel statements which need no other authority to back them, but it will be of interest to know that the experience of eminent and good men is in line with them, and many churches are loyal enough to the Gospel to oppose the mightiest organizations that violate its principles.

Wendell Phillips, one of the greatest and noblest of Americans, said:

Separation: Non-secrecy

Secret societies are not needed for any good purpose, and may be used for any evil purpose whatsoever; such organizations should be prohibited by law.

Daniel Webster, a statesman and orator known to all the world, said:

In my opinion, the imposition of such obligations as Freemasonry imposes should be prohibited by law.

Wm. H. Seward, "Anti-slavery Champion;" *Charles Sumner,* "The Scholar in Politics;" *Millard Fillmore,* President of the United States; *John Marshall,* Chief Justice of the United States; *William Wirt,* Attorney-general of the United States; all united in condemnation of secret societies.

Oath-bound secret orders have also been condemned by many honorable bodies of Christians, among whom are the sturdy *United Presbyterians,* the *Wesleyan Methodists,* the *Brethren,* and by far the larger part of the *Lutheran* church, including three great general bodies, viz.: the General Council, the Synodical Conference, commonly called the Missouri Synod, and the Joint Synod of Ohio and other States.

With only kind respect for sincere lodge Christians, we ask, Does it pay for Christians, and especially for ministers, to identify themselves with secret societies, in order to gain influence for good over the members there? Do the ministers who do this also go to the saloons and play poker in order to gain an influence over the poker players? Do they go to dances in order to win the dancers? If it is right to take oaths and engage in secret mystic rites for the sake of influence, why for the sake of influence is it not right to do other things that the Gospel forbids? "Shall we do evil that good may come? God forbid." The testimony of D. L. Moody covers this point so well that we shall let him speak the final word.

Moody Against Secretism.

I do not see how any Christian, most of all a Christian minister, can go into these secret lodges with unbelievers. They say they can have more influence for good, but I say they can have more influence for good by staying out of them, and then reproving their evil deeds. Abraham had more influence in Sodom than Lot had. If twenty-five Christians go into a secret lodge with fifty who are not Christians, the fifty can vote anything they please, and the twenty-five will be partakers of their sins. They are unequally yoked together with unbelievers. "But," says one, "what do you say about these secret temperance orders?" I say the same thing. Do not evil that good may come. You can never reform anything by unequally yoking yourself with ungodly men. True reformers separate themselves from the world. "But," say you, "You had one of them in your church." So I had, but when I found out what it was I cleaned it out like a cage of unclean birds. They drew in a lot of young men of the church in the name of temperance, and then they got up a dance and kept them out until after twelve at night. I was a partaker of their sins, because I let them get into the church; but they were cleaned out, and then they never came back. This idea of promoting temperance by yoking one's self up in that way with ungodly men is abominable. The most abominable meeting I ever attended was a temperance meeting in England. It was full of secret societies, and there was no Christianity about it. I felt as though I had got into Sodom, and got out as soon as I could. A man rescued from intemperance by a society not working on Gospel principles gets filled with pride and boasts about reforming himself. Such a man is harder to save than a drunkard. "But, Mr. Moody," some say, "if you talk that way you will drive all the members of secret societies out of your meetings and out of your churches." But what if I did? Better men will take their places. Give them the truth anyway, and if they would rather leave their churches than their lodges, the sooner they get out of the churches the better. I would rather have ten members who are separated from the world than a thousand such members. Come out from the lodge. Better one with God than a thousand without Him. We must walk with God, and if only one or two go with us, it is all right. Do not let down the standard to suit men who love their secret lodges or have some darling sin they will not give up.

SEPARATION IN CONDUCT: SPECIAL REFERENCE TO NONRESISTANCE.

The essence of all sinful conduct is found in selfishness. It is to secure more for self than the good of all allows that men sin in all ways. The ancient slavery and the modern merciless competition are both forms of the same evil. Lawsuits and wars are but individual and national aspects of the same spirit. Since these embody in themselves the elements of most other questions of Christian conduct, and are the most common and virulent forms of selfish aggression, we may well consider them specially in the light of the Gospel. A proper attitude toward them will help to guide Christian conduct in all the affairs of life, and thus become a means of grace.

The Gospel Against Lawsuits with Brethren.

One of the marks of conduct by which Christians are to show themselves Christians before the world is their avoidance of lawsuits with one another. This principle does not prevent the use of the law as a police power to restrain the lawlessness of wicked men. The law is good and courts are good, but Christians should have little need of either in their dealings with one another. The passage specifically setting forth the principle that Christians should arbitrate their questions among themselves rather than resort to law, is found in 1 Cor. 6: 1-12, and needs but little comment.

1. *Lawsuits among Christians are inconsistent.*

1. Dare any of you, having a matter against his neighbor, go to law before the unrighteous, and not before the saints?

That lawsuits between fellow-Christians is meant is seen

by reference to verses 5 and 6. The inconsistency of seeking the right at the hands of the unrighteous appears at a glance. The Roman law courts were very corrupt and justice was rare. Ours are better, but justice is still uncertain. It should be sought at the hands of the just rather than the unjust.

2. *Christians best qualified to judge Christians.*

2. Or know ye not that the saints shall judge the world? and if the world is judged by you, are ye unworthy to judge the smallest matters? 3. Know ye not that we shall judge angels? How much more, things that pertain to this life? 4. If then ye have to judge things pertaining to this life, do ye set them to judge who are of no account in the church?

Paul has reference here, no doubt, to the revelation that in Christ we are exalted above the angels (Heb. 1: 13, 14; 2: 5, 16), and shall reign in the kingdom of God (Rev. 2: 25-27). Christians because of their common Christian experience and hope are best fitted to pass upon matters between themselves.

3. *Arbitration the better way.*

5. I say this to move you to shame. What, cannot there be found among you one wise man who shall be able to decide between his brethren?

Going to law before the world is a confession of weakness on the part of Christians, as if the principles of the Gospel were insufficient to guide them in such matters.

4. *Christian lawsuits disgrace the church.*

6. But brother goeth to law with brother, and that before unbelievers?

Compare the words of Paul in 1 Cor. 10: 32, " Give no occasion of stumbling, either to Jews or to Greeks, or to the church of God." If we give Christ the preëminence, as we ought (Col. 1: 18), then we will have His cause at heart more than our own petty matters.

Separation: Nonresistance

5. *To suffer is better than to sue.*

7. Nay, already it is altogether a defect in you, that ye have lawsuits one with another. Why not rather take wrong? why not rather be defrauded?

The doctrine that it is cowardly to suffer wrong rather than to resent it is not Christian. The truest courage may be shown in suffering wrong, for the sake of the kingdom which is "righteousness and peace and joy." There are limitations, to be sure, but the principle is clear that it is our duty to suffer loss rather than in maintaining our rights to cause a greater loss to the kingdom. Jesus said, "If any man sue thee at the law and take away thy coat, let him have thy cloak also." Paul taught this principle when he testified, "Nevertheless we did not use this right; but we bear all things, that we may cause no hindrance to the Gospel of Christ" (1 Cor. 9: 12).

6. *Lawing unfits for the kingdom.*

8. Nay, but ye yourselves do wrong, and defraud, and that your brethren. 9. Or know ye not that the unrighteous shall not inherit the kingdom of God? Be not deceived: neither fornicators, nor idolators, nor adulterers, nor effeminate, nor abusers of themselves with men. 10. Nor thieves, nor covetous, nor drunkards, nor revilers, nor extortioners, shall inherit the kingdom of God.

If Christians are not to go to the world to avenge themselves against their brethren much less are they to be the party in the wrong. The apostle mentions some of the causes of lawsuits and gives the warning that they who are guilty of such things shall not inherit the kingdom of God.

7. *Christians should be better than the world.*

11. And such were some of you: but ye were washed, but ye were sanctified, but ye were justified in the name of the Lord Jesus Christ, and in the Spirit of our God.

Because Christians have come out from the world and have their citizenship in heaven (Eph. 2: 19) they should live according to the love of God, and not according to the wickedness of the world. If they descend from this their high calling to act as does the unregenerate world, they must expect to end up with the world.

This principle of expediency needs application in our day. Shall not churches and preachers be called to account if they do not teach and practice it? Such a course will mark God's people from the world, to be sure, but are we not called to be " an elect race, a royal priesthood, a holy nation, a people for God's own possession" (2 Pet. 2: 9)? Separation from the world in this evil custom of lawing will aid consecration to God. It is worth while.

The Gospel Against War.

"I am war. The upturned eyeballs of piled dead men greet mine eye,
And the sons of mothers perish—and I laugh to see them die—
Mine the demon lust for torture, mine the devil lust for pain,
And there is to me no beauty like the pale brows of the slain.

"Pagan, heathen and inhuman, devilish as the heart of hell,
Wild as chaos, strong for ruin clothed in hate unspeakable—
So they call me, and I care not. Still I work my waste afar,
Heeding not your weeping mothers and your widows—I am war!"

What has been said concerning non-resistance on the part of individuals applies also to governments, for the same Gospel is over all, and governments shall be judged by it as well as individuals. God announces to the nations through His prophet:

At what instant I shall speak concerning a nation, and concerning a kingdom, to pluck up and to break down and to destroy it; if that nation concerning which I have spoken, turn from their evil, I will repent of the evil that I thought to do unto them. And at what instant I shall speak concerning a

Separation: Nonresistance

nation, and concerning a kingdom, to build and to plant it; if they do that which is evil in my sight, that they obey not my voice, then I will repent of the good, wherewith I said I would benefit them (Jer. 18: 7-9).

These words of the prophet are confirmed by the testimony of all history. The ruins of Egypt and Babylon and Greece and Rome bear witness to the judgment of God upon the kingdoms of men. It will be a great day for the world when the governments learn that the Gospel code of morals must be obeyed by nations as well as individuals, for then the present beastly biting and devouring of one another shall give a place to the universal kingdom of peace. The members of this kingdom are now its representatives before the world that knows not God and must stand true to its principles of peace. Will the world ridicule and persecute them because they "are not of the world"? Even so, yet, "blessed are the peacemakers, for they shall be called the children of God." The open stand we are required to take under the banner of love becomes itself a source of strength. "Stand therefore, having shod your feet with the preparation of the gospel of peace" (Eph. 6: 15). "The *powers* that be are ordained of God" (Rom. 13: 1), therefore they are subject to God and must bear the sword according to the will of God. Therefore it is written :

Rulers are not a terror to the good work, but to the evil. And wouldst thou have no fear of the power? do that which is good, and thou shalt have praise from the same: for he is a minister of God to thee for good. But if thou do that which is evil, be afraid; for he beareth not the sword in vain (Rom. 13: 3-5).

The principle of this passage justifies not only the exercise of police power in maintaining law and order at home, but in all places where the government has rightful authority. It was clearly the duty of America to put a stop to the atrocities in Cuba, although it is not clear that a war was necessary to do it. It was in accordance with this principle that the Israelites were used to punish the Canaanites, whose cup of iniquity had been filling for more than four hundred years (Gen. 15: 16). As the neighbor of an individual is anyone whom he may help (Luke 10: 36), so the neighbor of a nation is any people whom that nation may help. And if the giving of help require that the sword be borne against the thieves, as well as caring for their victim, the nation must then be "a terror to the evil." But Christian nations have no right to resort to the sword merely to settle their contentions. Though war may be inevitable among the barbarous nations, which like the animals know no better than to fight for what they want; yet nations that have heard the Gospel of the love of God have no excuse for savagery. The same principles that forbid individual Christians to go to law with one another forbid Christian nations to war with one another.

1. MIGHT IS NOT RIGHT. If the chances for justice in a worldly law-court are uncertain, much more is it folly to expect that justice is to be won by war. Justice is not shielded by the grim dogs of war, but by the everlasting arms of Almighty God. If she steps forth from the battle field unbound, it is because God rules and overrules and not because one nation happened to be stronger to fight than another. Was it a matter of justice that Cortez in Mexico and Pizarro in South America massacred the confiding Indians to satiate their lust of gold? And have not most of the wars of history been wars of conquest, wars of passion, wars for glory or revenge, in which justice has no part save to weep and wait until the folly of men be past?

2. WAR IS SHAMEFUL. When a big dog pounces on a little dog and fights him the bystanders cry, Shame! and stone the big dog out of the fight. When two men fight, the officers separate them and take them to jail in dis-

grace. But when nations let loose their war dogs at one another's throats there is talk of patriotism and glory of battle, as if among Christian people justice and right can only be secured by the methods of the beasts! Doth not the Almighty say to the nations, "What, have you not one wise man or committee of men among you who shall be able to investigate your trouble and judge according to justice? Nay, ye yourselves do wrong and fight *and that before the heathen.* What shame upon your profession of civilization and knowledge of right!"

3. WAR GIVES AN EVIL EXAMPLE TO THE HEATHEN. What must the heathen nations think of Christianity when they see professed Christian nations, from which missionaries come to them with the Gospel, resort to murdering one another at wholesale, in order to settle some dispute? Is this the way to promote the kingdom of God? or to use aright the stewardship entrusted to nations? Is it any wonder that Japan in emerging from paganism is thought by many to have become a menace to the peace of the world because she has copied our principles of war more rapidly than our principles of peace? Is it any wonder that China is rapidly following in her steps? And if Christian nations continue to set the example of trusting in war, shall not all the world continue to whet the sword and train their armies? Let the Christian nations be ashamed. Let them set the example of common sense and Christian love. They have abolished slavery, and intemperance is even now being driven to cover. Let the dogs of war be chained in the pit with him who was a murderer from the beginning, and let Christian nations know that Christian living is the surest guarantee of the peace of the world.

4. IT IS BETTER TO SUFFER THAN TO FIGHT. If Christians must suffer themselves to be wronged rather than to hinder the cause of Christ by disgraceful lawsuits, much

more should Christian nations be willing to suffer loss rather than to set the example of war before the eyes of the non-Christian millions of the world, and that at the frightful loss which goes with war. We speak, of course, of war in which no vital moral principle is at stake. Righteousness is above all, and no nation can afford to compromise with sin for the sake of peace. But ordinary wars are not for principle so much as for plunder, and they cost more than all they obtain is worth. The *cost in money* is the least of all, yet even here figures mount up until they appall the imagination. As Charles Sumner said:

> They seem to pant, as they toil vainly to represent the enormous sums consumed in this unparalleled waste. Without making allowance for the loss sustained by the withdrawal of active men from productive industry, we find that since the adoption of the Federal Constitution there has been expended from the National Treasury for expenses incident to war the inconceivable sum total of more than $2,000,000,000.—more than seven times as much as was set apart during the same period for all purposes whatever.

That was before the Civil War which cost $7,500,000,000.00. What would Sumner now say when this amount has been vastly multiplied and we are spending as much to keep the pace with other Christian nations in times of peace as it formerly cost in times of war?

The *withdrawal of men from useful industry* is not the least item in the cost of war. A million men engaged in fighting might be earning their several million dollars a day if engaged in useful labor. And then there is the *destruction of commerce and the demoralization of agriculture and manufacturing interests* everywhere. Surely it must be a pearl of great price that would justify such loss to obtain it. And little wonder is it that the great business firms of the world are coming to be mighty peace factors,

Separation: Nonresistance

because they are realizing how closely are their temporal interests bound up with the peace of the world.

But what are business interests compared with *human life?* How can the cost of war be measured when over against it are weighed the tears of widows and orphans, the groans of dying men, the blood of the innocent slain, the precious life that is the gift of God, and not the right of man to spill? It has been estimated that in all the wars of historic times more than fourteen billion lives have been lost, which, according to Burke, would make blood enough to fill a lake seventeen miles in circumference and float all the navies of the world, or a globe of flesh three miles in diameter, sacrificed to the god of war. What shall they say who are responsible for all this when the God of love shall call them to account?

5. WAR IS DEMORALIZING. But that is not all. The life is more than meat and the body more than raiment. Blood is less than character and life is less than morals. If we gasp at the cost in money and close our eyes at the horrors of blood, what shall we do before the *loss that is eternal!* War is itself a ferocious monster that knows no pity. It devours without mercy all who come in its path. And it begets in all its devotees a kindred spirit.

And what shall be said of Christian nations that deliberately place their millions of men into a school of butchery? Is it surprising that many men and boys who were noble before, are left by war worse wrecks in morals than in health? What is the significance of recent reports of army officers showing that ninety per cent of the soldiers in the Philippines have passed through the hospital on account of diseases caused by vice, and that many of the officers are so corrupt as to desire the selling of liquor in the army canteen? What must be the effect upon the soldiers when (as was formerly the case and would be again if the canteen were restored) young men who have been carefully trained by Christian parents are compelled in the army to take their turn in selling liquor in the canteen? This is only a part of the discipline of the Government in training its soldiers in Satan's school of war.

Everybody knows that the handling of deadly weapons begets a desire to use them, and that the taste of bloodshed arouses the old animal nature which thirsts for gore. There was a man who raised a tiger from a cub and thought it safe and tame. But one day while he was sleeping the huge beast licked his hand until it tasted blood, when instantly its tiger nature was aroused and the man awoke horrified to find himself facing, no longer a pet, but a glaring monster ready to spring upon him. Only the weapon at his hand saved his life. It is so with the tiger in men. The taste of war arouses the monster and it will not down until satiated with blood. The ancient Romans grew so depraved through their gladiatorial combats that the most refined ladies would at last refuse to give "thumbs down" to spare the fallen fighter, but when the blood spurted from his death wound would cry, "*Hoc habet! Hoc habet!*" (He has it! He has it!) Such is the effect of familiarity with scenes of blood. Many generations cannot efface from the blood of the race the taint of a single war.

And this is not all. War not only stirs the animal nature in man and trains him in all the black arts of deception and murder, but it *withholds the ordinary means of grace*. Men are withdrawn from the tender and uplifting influences of home and church and placed in the hell of war. What though they sing patriotic songs and talk of fighting for principle; the principles of the Gospel are not to be taught by Christian nations fighting one another. If nations rise from the ruin of war to better things it is because they sicken of the horrors it brings, rather than learn from any virtues it teaches. The cause of temperance had made such strides before the Civil War that half the country was under prohibitory laws, but in that fearful strife the cause went back and has had to be fought all over again. Other reforms have been hindered rather than helped by war. The greatest reform the world can ever know will be the abolition of war itself.

6. WAR IS UNNECESSARY. Whatever may be said in apology for the wars of the world during the times of its ignorance, there is no excuse for war between Christian nations ever to show his gory hoofs again. And why? Because there are so many millions in every Christian nation who have vowed allegiance to the Prince of Peace that it is possible to arbitrate any difficulty that may arise. Governments exist only by the consent of the governed, and it requires only that public sentiment shall express itself generally enough and forcibly enough, and the most autocratic government must yield to it. The mass of the people do not want war. The governments are to blame that Christendom is like an armed camp in time of peace, with seven million under arms and twenty-nine million more ready to be armed at a word. The government officials must be taught to arbitrate rather than declare war.

If a tithe of the money that is now spent in maintaining large armies and navies were spent in diffusing the principles of peace throughout the world, such a sentiment might be aroused in all the great Christian nations that it would be impossible for any ruler to get the consent of his people to engage in war. The fifteen million dollars that go into a single new battleship of the modern type would scatter a great many million peace tracts all over Europe and Asia and the Americas. The cost of a large standing army would engage an army of ambassadors of peace that could bring about sentiment among the people of any of the great powers, such that the rulers, however backward themselves, would be bound to adopt arbitration and abandon their barbarous war policies.

7. BETTER THINGS ARE EXPECTED OF CHRISTIAN NATIONS. It is not for Christian nations to hide behind the sins of the savage. There will be no danger of invasion from the uncivilized tribes of earth if the Christian powers will agree to arbitrate their own differences and maintain only such a force as may be sufficient, all united, to guarantee the peace of the world. Let them then use the surplus that is now wasted in trying to outdo their Christian neighbors in the most destructive instruments of murder, in evangelizing and civilizing the non-Christian nations, and there will be no danger of any future invasion by barbarian hordes. But let the so-called Christian nations continue their policy of war, and at some future day God may use some barbarian horde to wipe them out to make room for more obedient people. Men have inscribed upon their cannons the motto, *"Ultima ratio regis"*—the last argument of kings,—but God's last argument was the gift of His Son (John 3: 16; Matt. 21: 37). Love could do no more. And to this example God called the individuals and the nations of the world.

And at the last *the voice of God* is above all as He thunders against war and calls His people to peace. From the time that the first murderer was called to account so sternly that he said, " My punishment is greater than I can bear," until the closing vision of the city of God coming down from heaven, the Word of God is an anthem of peace. The descendants of Abraham were restrained from entering their promised land until they could occupy it without injustice to the inhabitants. Four hundred years they waited until the iniquity of the Amorite was full (Gen. 15:

16) and then were sent to dispossess them. Among themselves they had their cities of refuge to provide justice from the avenger of blood (Num. 35: 13). Continually they were taught to trust in God for protection rather than in the power of arms or crafty treaties with other powers. They were forbidden to multiply horses and chariots lest they be lifted up with pride and led by them to lust for war. From age to age their poets sang and prophets prophesied of the reign of peace, when the sword should be turned to a plowshare and the spear to a pruning hook and nations should not learn war any more (Isa. 2: 4). In their clearest visions they saw the coming of the Prince of Peace who should found an everlasting kingdom, not of the skulls of enemies conquered, but in the hearts of subjects won by love. He came. He lived the life of peace. He taught the doctrine of non-resistance. He made love, even to enemies, the badge of discipleship. He said, "My kingdom is not of this world * * * else would my servants fight * * * but now is my kingdom not from hence" (John 18: 36). He warned the nations, "All they that take the sword shall perish by the sword" (Matt. 26: 52). He died, but He rose again and He lives; and He reigns, and His kingdom is absorbing the kingdoms of the world. He lives and He calls His people to peace.

For though we walk in the flesh, we do not war according to the flesh (for the weapons of our warfare are not of the flesh, but mighty before God to the casting down of strongholds) 2 Cor. 10: 3, 4.

It is enough. Our King is coming, and He comes to reign. And the peace, which was heralded by angels at His coming, and left by Him at His death as His legacy to the world, is finding at last a haven in the hearts of men. Long driven hither and thither by the storms of war, and with plumage wet with the tears of centuries, she asks an abiding place. Will the church respond to her voice, and cause the nations also to hear it and respond?

I am Peace. The olive branch from heaven I bring to sinful men.
O'er the storm of war I wave it, and the rainbow shines again.
Mine it is to bear the message, "Peace on earth," thus saith my King,
Mine the anthem of the angels; yours to join them as they sing.
I am the dew upon the desert; I am the blue athwart the sky;
I am the golden-ribboned morning of the day that cannot die.
Righteousness doth march before me; joy doth follow; sin doth cease.
Let the nations bid me welcome, Child of Heaven, I am Peace.

The Tempted Bride.

The Church of Christ walked forth one day, in modest garb attired.
In humble, loving ministry, her heart was then inspired.
She met the world: he said to her, "Quite fair you are; but now
Come walk with me, and I will give new beauty to your brow.
For I have many handsome gowns, and jewels, all for you;
And I will teach you how to show your charms as others do.
The church at first drew back, alarmed, and then was pleased, and then,
She timidly consented, and—he led her to his den.
He gave to her a gorgeous robe, adorned her head as well,
Displayed her charms in latest style,—then turned his face toward hell.
"Come on," said he, "and I will be your sponsor as we go.
I'll show you how to reach the lost, for all their haunts I know."
She went with him to haunts of sin, altho her robes were soiled,
From sight of sin to taste of sin, from which she once recoiled,
From taste of sin to depths of sin, she plunged, as Satan smiled;
The gates of hell he opened now and claimed her for his child.

* * * * * *

Is this a dream, a horrid dream, and this the fearful end?
Praise God that faith may see afar, another scene attend.
The Bride of Christ walks forth with Him in modest garb attired;
With Him she seeks to save the lost; with love for Him inspired.
Then Satan comes arrayed as light, and speaks with pious word.
"I've found a way to reach the lost, and thus to please the Lord.
It will not do to be so queer: a fool does little good.
If you would win the worldly-wise, join with them as you should."

She turned to Him who by her side, and yet within the veil,
Had promised true to be her guide, whose word can never fail.
Then to the tempter in disguise she turned and said, "Not so,
For I belong to Christ my Lord, and with Him I will go.
If sinners railed at Him, much more must I be counted queer,
But be it so, I stand aloof from all that sin holds dear."
He fled, and lo the Bride-to-be was clothed with light and power.
And in her faithful ministry she found her bridal dower.

CHAPTER VII

THREE SYMBOLS FOR THE WELFARE OF THE RACE.

Marriage—The Sabbath—The Tithe.

* * * * * *

"It is not good that the man should be alone. I will make him an helpmeet for him."—Gen. 2: 18.

"For this cause shall a man leave father and mother, and shall cleave to his wife; and they two shall become one flesh. . . . What therefore God hath joined together, let not man put asunder."—Matt. 19: 5, 6.

* * * * * *

"And God blessed the seventh day, and hallowed it; because that in it he rested from all his work which God had created and made."—Gen. 2: 3.

"The sabbath was made for man."—Mark 2: 27.

"There remaineth therefore a sabbath rest for the people of God. . . . Let us therefore give diligence to enter into that rest, that no man fall after the same example of disobedience."—Heb. 4: 9-11.

* * * * * *

"All the tithe of the land, whether of the seed of the land or of the fruit of the tree, is holy unto Jehovah."—Lev. 27: 30.

"Render therefore unto Caesar the things that are Caesar's; and unto God the things that are God's."—Matt. 22: 21.

"All things that are mine are thine and thine are mine."—John 17: 10.

MARRIAGE.

One of the first institutions which God ordained for the welfare of the race was marriage. None other has He ever more carefully guarded, and none should be more carefully studied. It is important for the contracting parties, because it affects their happiness, fortune and destiny for time and eternity. It is important for their children and for their friends. It affects the State because it is made up of families. The home is the unit of civilization, and when it is destroyed there is a reversion to barbarism. No nation has ever fallen which preserved the sanctity of the marriage relation, and no nation has ever long survived that lost it. The question is therefore one which concerns the kingdom of God, for there is perhaps nothing that hinders the kingdom so much as the social sin, and there is no way, save by the preaching of the Gospel, that the kingdom can be helped more than by making proper use of the laws of influence involved in the marriage relation.

I. Marriage is an Institution.

1. MARRIAGE IS A DIVINE INSTITUTION. It was ordained in Eden by the Creator Himself. "Therefore shall a man leave his father and his mother and shall cleave unto his wife: and they shall be one flesh" (Gen. 2: 24). However, it is only for this world, for in heaven they "neither marry nor are given in marriage" (Luke 20: 34). Since marriage is of God it is sacred and inviolable. They who degrade it by vulgar jesting, by impure thoughts or licentious deeds, set themselves against God Himself and must bear their judgment.

2. MARRIAGE IS FOR MAN'S GOOD. "It is not good that

the man should be alone" (Gen. 2: 18). The institution is based upon the needs of human society and cannot be degraded without destroying society. "Whoso findeth a wife findeth a good thing, and obtaineth favor of Jehovah" (Prov. 18: 22), and marriage is to be "had in honor before all" (Heb. 13: 4). Free love is therefore condemned in the most unmeasured terms, and the teaching of it is a mark of the last apostasy through the antichrist (1 Tim. 4: 1-3).

Jesus hallowed the marriage institution by performing His first miracle at a wedding, and by hedging the institution about with the strictest of regulations (Matt. 19: 3-12). So strict, indeed, was He, that the disciples said "It is not expedient to marry," and Jesus acknowledged that not all men can rise at once to the divine standard, but instead of lowering the standard, He allows celibacy to those who can receive it "for the kingdom of heaven's sake."

3. MARRIAGE IS GUARDED BY THE MOST SOLEMN RESTRICTIONS. There are some unions that are not of God. True marriage must be according to the laws of God.

(1) *There should be no marriage by those physically unfit.* The Gospel teaching is that the body is the temple of God. "If any man destroyeth the temple of God, him shall God destroy" (1 Cor. 3: 16, 17). The marriage of the physically unfit tends to destroy the temple of God. There are those with hereditary insanity, or with venereal diseases which pollute the innocent partner and taint the blood of the innocent children, and such should be prohibited by civil law, as they are already disqualified by divine law, from entering the marriage state.

(2) *There should be no marriage without love.* Husbands are commanded to love their wives (Eph. 5: 25), and wives to love their husbands (Titus 2: 4), and without such love there can be no true marriage. Without love

Marriage

the marriage state is only legalized harlotry. "It is better to dwell in the corner of the housetop than with a contentious woman in a wide house" (Prov. 21: 9); and likewise it is better for a woman to live a virgin until death than to be bound to a living death through marriage to a brute of a man who uses her only for a convenience, and who will curse their offspring with his own besotted character. They who make themselves slaves to their vile habits cannot love their wives above these habits, or the Lord Jesus above all, and therefore are unfit for the marriage bond. If all women would be as sensible as Frances E. Willard, who rejected her lover because he refused to give up a bad habit, there would be a mighty revolution among men that would bring the kingdom in. It is the folly of hasty marriage that is mother to the tragedy of the divorce mill.

(3) *Marriage is forbidden to adulterers.* It was forbidden under the law to priests (Lev. 21: 7), and it is forbidden under the Gospel (1 Cor. 6: 16). Not, indeed, to those who have repented of their sins and have been forgiven, cleansed and regenerated, for this sin is not the unpardonable sin, but to those who wilfully persist in this sin. And the simple reason is that no one can keep the marriage covenant and break it at the same time. By the very faithlessness the bond is ignored, and becomes a mockery.

(4) *Marriage of near relatives is forbidden.* In Lev. 18 and 20 may be found the restrictions of the law on this line, and because they are based on the laws of physical being which are the same to-day, they are just as essential to the welfare of society to-day as in that day. Experience has proven their wisdom. They who marry relatives pay the penalty in sorrow because of insanity in the children. Royal families have so much inherited insanity because they break this law in their intermarriages.

(5) *Marriage should be "only in the Lord"* (1 Cor.

7: 39; 1 Cor. 9: 5). The first marriages of "the sons of God" with the "daughters of men" resulted in a generation of sinners that had to be destroyed. The laws of Moses were very strict on intermarriage (Deut. 7: 3, 4) and the Gospel raises rather than lowers the standard. Besides the positive precept to "marry only in the Lord" (1 Cor. 7: 39) we have an equally strong negative command, "be ye *not* unequally yoked with unbelievers" (2 Cor. 6: 14). If it be objected that this command refers to business associations or something of that kind, we reply that if it applies to such unions it applies much more to marriage, for that union is the closest and most sacred of all. In the very nature of the case it is impossible for a true union to exist between one who makes Jesus preëminent in all things, and another who hates him. It is true that there are some happy marriages with those who have made no public profession of faith, but never between real unbelievers and true Christians. The neglect of observing the Gospel on this point has been the cause of much sorrow in the world.

(6) *They should not marry who for any reason cannot or will not fulfill the duties of the marriage relation.* Paul advised the unmarried of his time to remain so "because of the present distress" (1 Cor. 7: 27-30), a warning which Jesus also gave beforehand (Matt. 24: 19). There are also those, who like Paul, are called of the Lord to labor in travels and dangers such that it is inexpedient to be cumbered with the cares of a wife and family. They therefore, should forego the blessings of that institution for the sake of the larger work of the Gospel.

(7) *Polygamy is forbidden.* The original institution of marriage was for one man and one woman (Gen. 2: 23-25). God never abolished that law. He did indeed bear with the people under the old dispensations "because of

the hardness of their hearts" (Mark 10: 2-10), but Jesus goes back of this temporary provision and puts marriage for this age upon the original plane of monogamy. His word is final.

4. THE RELATION OF HUSBAND AND WIFE. There is a story of a certain man who said to his wife, with whom he quarreled a great deal, " My dear, why cannot we live together as peaceably as the cat and dog there by the fire?" She replied, " Just tie them together and you will see how they fight." There is philosophy in the answer, but not enough. Christ in the home makes it possible to have love and harmony. The Gospel gives us the proper relations of Christian companions.

(1) *The husband is the " head" in the home.* " For the husband is the head of the wife, as Christ also is the head of the church " (Eph. 5: 23). This means that the maintenance of the home is the husband's responsibility (1 Tim. 5: 8), but it does not mean that he may be an arbitrary " boss." If we read, " as the church is subject to Christ, so *let* the wives *be* to their husbands in everything," the words follow, " Husbands love your wives, even as Christ also loved the church." If we read of the man ruling his own house (1 Tim. 3: 4) we read also in the same letter of the woman ruling the household (1 Tim. 5: 14). Both husband and wife have their spheres for which they are fitted by nature and to which they should keep and be faithful. In doing so there will be harmony.

(2) *How the principle of " headship" is to be shown.*

In 1 Cor. 11: 1-17, Paul admonishes the church to recognize this principle of headship in dress and conduct. The passage follows:

The principle announced.

3. But I would have you know that the head of every man

is Christ; and the head of the woman is the man; and the head of Christ is God.

The application enjoined.

4. Every man praying or prophesying having his head covered, dishonoreth his head. But every woman praying or prophesying with her head unveiled dishonoreth her head; for it is one and the same thing as if she were shaven.

The veil required by modesty.

6. For if a woman is not veiled, let her also be shorn; but if it is a shame for a woman to be shorn or shaven, let her be veiled.

The principle taught by nature.

7. For a man indeed ought not to have his head veiled, forasmuch as he is the image and glory of God; but the woman is the glory of the man. 8. For the man is not of the woman; but the woman of the man. 9. For neither was the man created for the woman, but the woman for the man:

Because of the angels.

10. For this cause ought the woman to have a sign of authority on her head, because of the angels.

The principle not to be abused.

11. Nevertheless, neither is the woman without the man, nor the man without the woman, in the Lord. 12. For as the woman is of the man, so is the man also by the woman; but all things are of God.

Harmony with nature enjoined.

13. Judge ye in yourselves: is it seemly that a woman pray unto God unveiled? 14. Doth not even nature itself teach you, that, if a man have long hair, it is a dishonor to him? 15. But if a woman have long hair, it is a glory to her: for her hair is given her for a covering.

The custom not to cause contention.

16. But if any man seemeth to be contentious, we have no such custom, neither the churches of God.

Marriage

If we search for historical side lights upon this passage we find the following facts:

First. In Paul's day the Jewish men wore their hair long (as, witness the pictures of Jesus), while the Gentile men (except the effeminate, vs. 4, 14) wore theirs short.

Second. The women, both Jew and Gentile (except the unchaste) wore long hair, and in addition, a veil when in public places. Concerning this veil Geike says:

> In antiquity, as in the east and in some old-world portions of many European countries still, each locality has its distinctive dress, which marked not only the nationality of the wearer, but in many cases more or less recognized, was identified with modesty. To vary from it was as grave a revolt from propriety as similar innovations would now be in Turkey. Among the most settled and unalterable of these fashions was that which Greece, with the exception of Lacedaemonia, honored in common with oriental nations, of women appearing in public, only with heads covered with a "peplum" or shawl, ordinarily worn on the shoulders, but thrown over the heads in the streets or when they went to public gatherings.—New Testament Hours, Vol. 3, p. 175.

Tertullian, (160 A. D.) opposed any attempt by Christians to abridge the customary covering. He says:

> Some with their turbans and woolen bands, do not veil the head, but bind it up; protected, indeed, in front, but where the head properly lies, bare. Others are to a certain extent covered over the region of the brain with linen coifs of small dimensions. . . of such small dimensions do they imagine their heads to be. . . . Let them know that the whole head constitutes the woman.—On the Veiling of Virgins, ch. 17.

This shawl or veil not only was a sign of fidelity to the husband, but it helped to distinguish women from men, for in other respects the appearance of their dress was very similar; and also protected the women from the gaze of evil men, who were tempted the more because an unveiled face was then an unusual sight.

Third, the early churches varied somewhat in their customs in this respect. For example, *Clement of Alexandria* says:

> Woman and man are to go to church decently attired. . . . Let the woman observe this further: let her be entirely covered, unless she happen to be at home.—Instructor, Bk. 3: 11.

Tertullian (160 A. D.), advocating the veiling of virgins as well as married women, says:

> But I will not, meantime attribute this usage to Truth. Be it for awhile custom: that to custom I may likewise oppose custom. Throughout Greece and certain of its barbaric provinces, the majority of churches keep their virgins covered. There are places, too, beneath this African sky, where this practice obtains.—On the Veiling of Virgins, ch. 2.

Cyprian, however, because among the Romans the veil was used in pagan worship, commends the Christian women who refused it.

> Your head has remained free from the impious and wicked veil with which the captive heads of those who sacrificed there were veiled. Your brow, with the sign of God, could not bear the crown of the devil, but reserved itself for the Lord's crown. —Treatise 437.

The entire Scripture passage quoted has been found so difficult that no two authors entirely agree upon it. Any one who loves the truth must be willing to consider views which differ somewhat from his own. We therefore shall state as fairly as possible the various theories.

First, there is the literal interpretation which would mean the same sort of a veil as Paul had in mind when he wrote to the Corinthians.

Second, there are those who regard the veil as a religious symbol intended to teach and preserve the Gospel doctrine of "headship": man the head of woman, as Christ is the head of the church and God the head of Christ (1

Cor. 11: 3); but, remembering that we are "ministers of a new covenant; not of the letter, but of the spirit; for the letter killeth, but the spirit giveth life" (2 Cor. 3: 6), they regard the symbol as fulfilled when the veil is coincident with the hair as a covering of the head.

Third, there are others who believe that Paul meant the veil to represent, not the idea of the subjection of the woman, but the Christian idea of her spiritual equality and authority; that when Paul says in v. 10, "for this cause ought the woman to have *a sign of* authority on her head, because of the angels," he means the veil to be a sign of woman's power or authority to exercise in religious services on an equal plane with man, as stated in Gal. 3: 28; and that this sign of authority is to prevent abuse of the law stated in v. 3. While man remains the "head" he must yet respect the new spiritual place and authority of woman, safeguarded by the sign.

Fourth, there are still others who believe that the principle of "headship" as taught in the Gospel should be applied to costume and conduct in general, and not alone to head dress and public worship. They simply give the teaching a wider application and maintain that the outward signs of the Christian relations of men and women should be consistent throughout, each keeping in the sphere in which God through nature put them, and showing this fidelity to the divine order both in dress and conduct. They believe that verse 16 must refer to the custom of veiling, since "but" is adversative, and that therefore the passage was not intended to prescribe one particular application of the principle to the exclusion of others; and especially that it could not intend to fasten the cruel subjection of the heathen women of that day upon the Christian women of all time.

Since all the theories agree as to the principle itself, and differ only in the details of its application, surely the spirit of Christ will lead those who reverently hold to one form of application to grant liberty of conscience to those who as reverently hold to another. All will doubtless grant that, when worn in the spirit which Paul intended, the veiled head of woman in worship is not only a mark of modesty, but a real means of spiritual power, which gives it intrinsic value as a means of grace. A minister of a popular denomination on witnessing a service in which the custom was observed broke down and wept as he said, " I am sad when I think of the power we have lost since we discarded this custom."

In these days the appearance of the headdress of the women in most congregations in the popular churches indicates the subjection of the man rather than of the woman and prevailing pride rather than prevailing prayer. And when we consider the vast sums of the Lord's money entrusted to His people as a stewardship, which is poured at the feet of the goddess of fashion, while the cause of missions goes begging, we cannot but pray that the Lord may raise up a church which will be brave enough and humble enough to break with the fashions of the world and set the example of the simple life, with plain attire and loving subjection to one another and to God. Nearly all the colleges and universities, and many high schools, have adopted caps and gowns for commencement occasions to prevent a lavish display of clothes and thus give the poor an equal standing with the rich. If this is wise on the part of the world, why should it be counted foolish for the church to have a similar method of promoting Christian truth and virtue? And though it be counted foolish, yet we hear the apostle saying:

> Would that ye could bear with me in a little foolishness: but indeed ye do bear with me. For I am jealous over you with a godly jealousy: for I espoused you to one husband,

Marriage

that I might present you as a pure virgin to Christ. But I fear, lest by any means, as the serpent beguiled Eve in his craftiness, your minds should be corrupted **from the simplicity and the purity that is toward Christ** (2 Cor. 11: 3).

(3) *The husband and wife are equal and one in Christ and in duties to one another* (Gal 3: 28). If wives are to love their husbands (Titus 2: 4) and submit to them (Col. 3: 18), husbands are also to love their wives (Eph. 5: 25) and honor them (1 Pet. 3: 7). Some one has said of the creation of woman:

Woman was taken from man, not from his head to be his superior, not from his feet to be his inferior, but from his side to be his equal, under his arm to be protected and near his heart to be beloved.

In some ways men excel women and in some ways women excel men. Each have their own sphere and should fulfill their mission in it. Where there is mutual love there will be a common purse, a common devotion to all the interests of the home and a common voice in their direction. This principle involves the right of suffrage, because every interest of the home is as dear to the woman as to the man and she is as capable of deciding what is best. Jesus taught that husband and wife are "one flesh": let them so abide. They are united and equal in Christ: let them be divided and opposed in nothing. Their relation is said to be like that of the Son and the Father (1 Cor. 11: 3), and we are taught to honor the Son even as the Father (John 6: 23). In the flesh the earthly limitations give each a limited sphere, but in the spirit there is equality in Christ.

(4) *Should women be silent in the church?*

It is sometimes taught that the Bible proclaims the spiritual superiority of the man, because Paul enjoined the women to "keep silence in the churches: for it is not permitted unto them to speak; but let them be in subjection, as also saith the law" (1 Cor. 14: 34).

To understand this passage it must be taken in connection with the entire teaching of the Gospel on the subject. It may be safely assumed that since the Gospel does not contradict itself, no meaning should be taken from this passage which cannot be harmonized with the rest of God's Word. Now, if we trace the matter through from beginning to end, we shall find that everywhere else in the Scriptures women are encouraged to use their spiritual gifts. We have the example of the Old Testament prophetesses: Miriam (Ex. 15: 20), Deborah (Judges 4: 4), and Huldah (2 Kings 22: 14), and in the New Testament, Anna (Luke 2: 36). It was predicted of the Gospel age that in it God would pour out the Holy Spirit and the daughters as well as the sons should prophesy (Joel 2: 28). On the day of Pentecost Peter, filled with the Spirit, declared this prophecy fulfilled (Acts 2: 18). But to prophesy means to publicly teach. Paul says, " He that prophesieth speaketh unto men edification, and exhortation, and consolation" (1 Cor. 14: 3). That women did so teach in the apostolic church is shown by the example of the four daughters of Philip " who did prophesy" (Acts 21: 9). And that Paul himself did not object to such work under the proper circumstances is shown by his own injunction, " Greet Aquila and Priscilla, my fellow helpers in the Lord" (Acts 18: 26; Rom. 16: 3). And again, he calls Phoebe a servant of the church at Cenchrea (Rom. 16: 1), using a word translated in the Revised Version margin " deaconess," but which is regularly used elsewhere of the ministry, and since Paul speaks of her as his own helper she must have been an assistant in the ministry. In the early Christian literature we read that there were such assistants who did for women what the men did for the men. Women are limited in their service by the natural capacities and proprieties of their sex; but so also are men, and neither should transgress the principle of pro-

Marriage

priety which Paul in so many places insists upon. Concerning women he says again, " Help those women who labored with me in the Gospel " (Philpp. 4: 3). That there were others also who took part in public worship is implied in his words concerning the veil, " Every woman praying or prophesying with her head unveiled dishonoreth her head " (1 Cor. 11: 5) Paul also teaches that " in Christ there is neither Jew nor Greek, male nor female," &c. (Gal. 3: 28), and in all references to the spiritual gifts they are promised without distinction as to sex (Acts 2: 18; 8: 12, 17; 1 Cor. 12: 13, &c.), but if they are given to women as well as to men they should be used by women as well as men, for *no talent is given to be buried.* Many quotations might be given from the writings of the early church sustaining this position.

Therefore the injunction that women should keep silence in the churches must be construed with reference to the *abuse* of the privilege which the women enjoyed in the church, of which the women of that region were guilty. In order to guard against reproach in breaking with the pagan customs which the doctrine of spiritual equality contradicted, it was necessary to go slow. The heart of the command is in the words " I suffer not a woman to usurp authority over the man." This interpretation of the passage gives us a principle which is in harmony with all the rest of the Scriptures, and which should be applied in all ages, varying in details of application according to the proprieties of the time and place.

5. THE RELATION OF PARENTS TO CHILDREN.

(1) *Parents should love children.* The command of God to the first husband and wife was, " Be fruitful and multiply and subdue the earth." This is the prime purpose of marriage. Spiritual fellowship might be enjoyed without it. Children therefore are a " heritage of the Lord " (Psa. 127: 3).

Those who seek the carnal pleasures of the marriage state while shirking its duties are criminals in the sight of God. Parents are commanded to love their children (Titus 2: 4) and if they love them they will not murder them before they are born. Neither will they turn their children over to some negro nurse while they themselves go into the nauseating business of fondling poodle dogs or puking cats. If there is one sin which should cause the eternal burning of shame in the judgment, it must be that of substituting for the dear little children in the image of God the offspring of brute beasts, all for the sake of standing in "society." Heaven has no society for such.

(2) *Parents should provide for the temporal needs of their children* (1 Cor. 12: 14; 1 Tim. 5: 8). This does not mean that parents are to toil all their lives in order to keep her children from toiling. It does not mean that they are to lay up luxuries for them. It means simply that they are to provide the necessities of life for them while helpless. The way to curse a child is to rear it in idleness and give it plenty of money with which to gratify its desires. Thousands of children have gone to destruction under such indulgence, and the parents must answer for it in judgment.

(3) *Parents are commanded to rear their children "in the chastening and admonition of the Lord"* (Eph. 6: 4). This means that they must be taught to obey. If they are not, the parents must answer for it. The house of Eli was judged with destruction, "because his sons made themselves vile and he restrained them not" (1 Sam. 3: 12). It is tiresome to hear strong parents talk of not being able to control their children. If they control them while still infants they will as a rule have little trouble when they are older. Of course, parents are not to be arbitrary or brutal to their children, but are to teach them to obey (Eph.

Marriage

6: 1; Col. 3: 20, 21). To do this they will need the help of the family altar, of grace at meals, and the constant attitude of trust and devotion toward God.

(4) *While parents are responsible for the right teaching of their children, yet every one must give an account of himself toward God.* Children inherit tendencies from their parents, but they cannot inherit sin. (Ezek. 18: 20). Far from being condemned by "original sin" they, in the innocent period, belong to the kingdom (Matt. 19: 14) and have the care of special angels (Matt. 18: 10). They should grow up in the kingdom without ever getting out of it.

6. MARRIAGE AND THE STATE. While marriage is a divine institution, yet because it so vitally affects the interests of society, it is right that the civil law should guard it from the abuse of those who regard not God or man. The State therefore, as representative of God (Rom. 13: 1), requires certain things: as the securing of license, being of proper age and of proper condition. The State should guard against the marriage bond even more closely than it does, and prevent the marriage of any persons ineligible according to the law of God. (See under 2, p. 517).

However, since the institution is divine, the rite should be performed by the representatives of religion rather than the State. The divine law should thus be recognized outwardly and obeyed in all the relations of marriage.

7. MARRIAGE IS A TYPE OF THE UNION OF CHRIST AND THE CHURCH (Eph. 5: 28-31; Matt. 9: 15; Rev. 19: 7-9). The love that should exist in the home, therefore, is not that sensual desire or instinct which the animals know, but that pure and holy love which Christ showed toward the church. Thus home becomes a type of heaven and the blessings of the marriage relation prepare for the blessings of heaven.

II. Divorce.

1. DIVORCE IS CONTRARY TO THE WILL OF GOD. It was not contemplated as a part of the marriage institution and no provision was made for it when God ordained marriage (Gen. 2: 24). It is true that the laws of Moses allowed it (Deut. 24: 1), but Jesus explains that that was "because of the hardness of heart" (Mark 10: 2-10. He goes back of this temporal provision to the original intention "What God hath joined together let no man put asunder (Matt. 19: 6).

2. WHAT THEN DOES JESUS MEAN BY ALLOWING SEPARATION BECAUSE OF ADULTERY? Matt. 5: 31-32. The word He uses here is *porneia* which denotes a harlot. Jesus forbade this sin, but when one becomes such a character the marriage bond is already destroyed and the sin cannot be covered by merely living together. While therefore, He recognizes the separation which has already occurred He forbids the remarriage of such (Matt. 14: 3-9; Mark 10: 2-12).

III. Separation.

The Gospel recognizes the expediency of separation in some cases, though not of divorce. Jesus Himself permits separation in the case the marriage bond is already broken by harlotry (Matt. 5: 31, 32). Paul recognizes a like condition in the case of the Christ-hating unbeliever who deserts his companion, and says that the believer " is not under bondage in such *cases*" (1 Cor. 7: 11-15). There are doubtless other situations in which the marriage bond is as surely severed as in these, and Jesus, who placed human needs above the letter of the law, would doubtless judge such with the spirit of mercy, yet it is not for erring mortals to begin to catalogue exceptions lest soon the law be buried beneath the alleged exceptions.

IV. Remarriage.

Since the marriage bond is for life it cannot be broken by remarriage during life. Death may break it and the surviving companion be left free to marry again (Rom. 7: 3), but those merely separated, are still held by the sacred bond, and may not remarry without sin (Matt. 19: 3-9; 1 Cor. 7: 11). If this divine law were enforced by civil statutes there would be much less resort to the divorce courts. In the case of those who have married or remarried contrary to the Scriptures, but have repented and wish to serve God, the only way to obey all the Scriptures is to provide for those dependent upon them because of their relations (1 Tim. 5: 8), but live as Jesus advised to those who cannot receive the high standard which He taught (Matt. 19: 12). By exercising self-control they can "make themselves eunuchs for the kingdom of heaven's sake." They must not expect to sin without paying a penalty. There are many complexities connected with different cases which must be dealt with in Christian charity, and yet the Gospel principle must be upheld. The church dare stand for nothing less.

The foregoing are Gospel principles. They are the ideal standard. In their application, the State must take into account the hardness of heart that still exists (Mark 10: 2-10) and judge by the spirit of the law as occasion demands (2 Cor. 3: 6). It is not to be expected that the world will attain to the high standard of the Gospel at once, but the representatives of the Gospel should uphold it and do all in their power to bring the world to it.

V. The Practical Value of the Marriage Institution.

In the minds of depraved men, marriage is a subject for vulgar jest, but in the mind of God the institution is a vital means of grace. Its blessings are both physical and moral.

1. PHYSICAL BLESSINGS. The history of the race shows that the marriage bond has tended to physical development. The nations which guard it are physically superior to those who do not. Licentiousness strikes at the very fountain of life with the poison of the viper. The marriage state is for normal people the normal state. It is according to nature and therefore makes for health. Life insurance statistics are said to show that the married live longer than the celibate. Proper regard for the marriage bond results in care for the home, the endowment of children with their rightful heritage of energy, their proper care and development, and the guarding of society against the cancer of the social sin, which has sent many fair nations to Sheol. It inspires men to wear in their hats and in their hearts the sentiment:

> "And have I not a right to be
> As wholesome and as pure as she,
> Who through the years so glad and free,
> Moves gently forward to meet me?"

2. MORAL BLESSINGS. If physical health aids morality, much more does moral health aid physical strength. The marriage institution begets, first, a sense of responsibility. This is the turning point from barbarism. The savage is an animal unrestrained; the Christian lives according to the will of God. The restraint of the animal passions involved in monogamy is but the beginning. Marriage begets a sense of responsibility in protecting and providing for the wife and family and in maintaining properly the social relations involved. Training in responsibility is training for the kingdom of heaven.

Second, marriage develops the spirit of love, and thus leads the race to God, who is love. It begets love in the selecting and wooing of companions, in the concentrating of the affections, in the constant and long-continued association, and in the enforced coöperation involved in family relations. As Tennyson says:

> "O we fell out, my wife and I,
>   O we fell out,—I know not why,
> And kissed again in tears.
>   'Twas there beside a little grave
> We made in other years,
>   Yes there beside the little grave,
> We kissed again in tears."

Lastly, the maintenance of the Christian home on earth is a preparation for the heavenly home above. The relation of husband and wife is like that of Christ and the church. The relation of parents and children is like that of our heavenly Father and His children. The relation of children with one another is like that of the inhabitants of heaven. The home is a type of heaven and all the relations of the home should be ruled by the will of Him whose will obeyed makes heaven what it is. Such is the sacred institution of marriage. Given of God as a means of grace, it must be preserved by all the race until it be fulfilled in the eternal kingdom.

Heaven and Home.

Where shall we find in all the world, a picture, fair and bright,
Of heaven above, with all its love and peace and joy and light?
'Tis not upon the battle field where nations clash in sinful strife;
'Tis not in forum or in mart where competition crushes life;
'Tis not the giddy social whirl; 'tis not the palace dome:
—It is the charmed circle which we love to call " Sweet Home."

'Tis there that man and wife are one, as God is One in heaven;
'Tis there the bond of love unites the children He has given.
There is the pureness of the child, there is the parents' love;
There is the fellowship divine, the type of that above.

'Tis there we train for heaven; and tho the wide, wide world
   we roam,
'Tis there and only there we find the joy of Home Sweet Home.

Shall beastly lust with horns and hoofs destroy the picture
   fair?
Shall selfish greed or haughty pride load it with worldly care?
Please God may you whose hearts are true, like gallant knights
   of old,
Stand forth to fight for truth and right, and home's dear
   sheltered fold.
Till morning breaks and earth awakes 'neath heaven's beauteous
   dome,
Let paradise beneath the skies be found in Home Sweet Home.

THE SABBATH AND THE LORD'S DAY

When God created man and ordained marriage as an institution vital to his welfare in the world, He also commanded the observance of every seventh day as a day of rest and worship. The name "Sabbath" is the Hebrew for "rest" and expresses the purpose of the day. Man rests from the labors of this world, and in his worship comes into the eternal rest which the Sabbath prefigures. The temporal rest is an absolute necessity to the physical well-being of the race, and the worship is just as necessary to its moral welfare. The Sabbath is a means of grace.

In this book the term Sabbath is used in its general sense, while dispensational Sabbaths are so designated. Some have been confused as to which to keep by failing to distinguish between the creation Sabbath and the dispensational Sabbaths. Both the Saturday Sabbath of the dispensation of the law, and the first day Sabbath or Lord's day of the Christian dispensation regard the seventh day after six days of labor, in keeping with the law of the creation Sabbath. In each age the Sabbath has had its dispensational significance and requirements, but the fundamental law remains the same. It is the law of human need.

I. The Creation Sabbath.

1. INSTITUTION. The creation Sabbath was instituted at the beginning of human history. Gen. 2: 1-3, "And God blessed the seventh day and hallowed it; because that in it he rested from all his work which God had created and made." The six days of creation need not be taken as solar days of twenty-four hours each, because the word "day" in the Bible is used with various meanings, as: a generation

(Job 14: 6), a short indefinite season (Heb. 3: 8), a day of twenty-four hours (John 1: 39), the twelve hours of daylight (1 Thess. 2: 9), or a special set time (2 Pet. 3: 12). In Gen. 1, it evidently means the indefinitely long periods of creation. Six of these were given to the creation of the material universe and life, up to man, but the seventh is the day of humanity. God labored until He created the human spirit, and now in this seventh or Sabbath period He is developing the human race. That He is not resting by idleness is shown by the revelation of Jesus: "My Father worketh even until now, and I work" (John 5: 17).

Note that the creation Sabbath is the seventh day after six days of labor. It is a part of the divine law of sevens which is seen so much in nature. The French revolutionists tried to abolish it and have one day in ten as a day of rest instead, but the effort failed and the divine appointment of one day in seven was restored.

2. SIGNIFICANCE OF THE SABBATH.

(1) *A memorial.* The creation Sabbath is a memorial of this rest from creation labor. Gen. 2: 2, 3.

(2) *A symbol.* It is also a symbol to all ages, of rest in God. Just as God labored six days and brought forth man, in His own image, with whom He now enjoys fellowship; so "the whole creation groaneth and travaileth in pain together until now." Why? "Waiting for the revealing of the sons of God" (Rom. 8: 19-24). The sons of God belong not to bondage, but to the day of rest. "Thou wilt keep *him* in perfect peace *whose* mind *is* stayed *on thee*" (Isa. 26: 3). "There remaineth therefore a sabbath rest for the people of God" (Heb. 4: 9). Of this rest in God the creation Sabbath is a symbol. We keep it by turning from material labors to spiritual things.

(3) *A type.* It is also a type which points forward to that eternal rest of heaven. "That they may rest from their

labors; for their works follow with them " (Rev. 14: 13). This is for the righteous, for the wicked reject the Sabbath rest here and likewise the rest of salvation there.

3. CONTINUANCE. Since the creation Sabbath is made for man (Mark 2: 27), being based upon his natural needs, it must continue during the age of man on the earth. It spans the period from the creation of the earth until the new heavens and the new earth (Rev. 21 and 22).

II. The Old Covenant Sabbath.

1. INSTITUTION. The Jewish Sabbath was the sign of the special covenant with Israel.

Wherefore the children of Israel shall keep the sabbath, to observe the sabbath throughout their generations, for a perpetual covenant. It is a sign between me and the children of Israel forever. Ex. 31: 17; Ezek. 20: 12.

Note that this Sabbath is only for Israel and to continue throughout " THEIR " generations. Their generation ceased when " the times of the Gentiles " came in (Luke 21: 24). In Lev. 23 the weekly Jewish Sabbath is expressly listed with the other dispensational Sabbaths.

2. SIGNIFICANCE OF THE OLD COVENANT SABBATH.

(1) *A memorial.* The Jewish Sabbath was a memorial to Israel of their deliverance from the bondage of Egypt.

Thou shalt remember that thou wast a servant in the land of Egypt, and Jehovah thy God brought thee out thence by a mighty hand and an outstretched arm: therefore Jehovah thy God commanded thee to keep the sabbath day ((Deut. 5: 15).

This passage is a part of the ten commandments as quoted by Moses, and the Sabbath mentioned is therefore the dispensational weekly Sabbath so often referred to under the law. Its dispensational character is clearly declared in this commandment.

(2) *A symbol.* The Jewish Sabbath was a symbol to

Israel of the rest promised them through obedience to the covenant of Jehovah with the nation. He had said, "My presence shall go *with thee* and I will give thee rest" (Ex. 33: 14). "On the seventh day is a sabbath of solemn rest, a holy convocation" (Lev. 23: 3). On this day the people were reminded of the good promises of the covenant of which the Sabbath was the sign, but which they forfeited through disobedience. We read that "they to whom the good tidings were before preached failed to enter in because of disobedience" (Heb. 4: 6).

(3) *A type.* The Jewish Sabbath was also a type which pointed forward to the true rest of the people of God, which came, not under the law, but under the Gospel, and not through Moses, but through Christ.

There remaineth therefore a sabbath rest for the people of God. For he that is entered into his rest hath himself rested from his works, as God did from his. Let us therefore give diligence to enter into that rest, that no man fall after the same example of disobedience (Heb. 4: 3-11).

The Jews themselves were ardently looking for the coming of the Messiah who should give them rest from their enemies and make them a glorious nation, but they grossly misunderstood the true nature of His kingdom, and when He came they rejected and crucified Him, and with Him they rejected the true rest which He gives. "Come unto me all ye that labor and are heavy laden and I will give you rest" (Matt. 11: 28). In Christ the type met the antitype and the old was done away. Instead of the type and shadow we have the true "sabbath rest for the people of God."

3. CONTINUANCE.

(1) *Since the Jewish Sabbath was a dispensational sign it belonged only to the dispensation of the old covenant.* Jeremiah predicted that the old covenant would be superseded by a new and better covenant (Jer. 31: 31-35), and in Hebrews 8 we have the full account of the

The Sabbath

doing away with it to make room for the new and better covenant in the blood of Christ. The terms "Old Testament" and "New Testament" mean simply "old covenant" and "new covenant." The old was the law; the new is the Gospel.

That the Jewish Sabbath was included in this old covenant, and therefore passed away with it, is very clear from the Scriptures. It is expressly called a covenant (Ex. 31: 16) but only for the Jews and for "THEIR generations." The command to keep this dispensational Sabbath is the fourth of the ten commandments, which are also called the covenant (Deut. 5: 1-22). The stones on which the commandments were written are called the "tables of the covenant" (Ex. 32: 15), and the ark in which they were carried is called "the ark of the covenant" (Num. 10: 33; Heb. 9: 4).

More than that, the Jewish Sabbath is expressly named among the old covenant institutions which passed away. Paul says in Col. 2: 16, "Let no man therefore judge you in meat or in drink, or in respect of a feast day or a new moon OR A SABBATH DAY: which are a shadow of the things to come; but the body is Christ's." That the weekly Sabbath is not to be classed apart from the other Jewish Sabbaths is clear from the fact that it is listed without distinction among the dispensational feasts or Sabbaths in Lev. 23. It is therefore dispensational with the rest.

(2) *The law was a "tutor to bring us unto Christ"* (Gal. 3: 24), *and therefore was only in force until Christ did away with it.* He is our King and Lawgiver. He therefore had a right to do away with the dispensational law when He stood up and said, "Ye have heard that it hath been said of old time," &c., "but I say unto you," &c. He did not indeed, destroy, but He fulfilled by giving the new in place of the old, and thus the old gives way to

the new. See Matt. 17:5; 28:18; Luke 16:16; John 13: 1-3. Since He was clothed with authority to introduce a new dispensation He went back of the law (Matt. 5:21, 22, 27, &c.; 19:8) and taught the new Gospel. He gave no command to observe the Jewish Sabbath, and for us to return to it would be to go back and be debtors to the whole law (Gal. 5:3) and therefore be under the curse, for it is written of those under the law, " Cursed is every one that continueth not in all things that are written in the book of the law to do them" (Gal. 3:10-14. And again, "Ye are severed from Christ, ye who would be justified by the law; ye are fallen away from grace" (Gal. 5:4).

(3) That the Jewish Sabbath was done away is further shown by the fact that all the moral duties of the ten commandments and the rest of the law are taught in the Gospel in higher form, but *the Sabbath command is not in the Gospel.*

Compare the following:

THE TEN COMMANDMENTS

1. Thou shalt have no other Gods before me.
Ex. 20:1-17; Deut. 5:6-22.

2. Thou shalt not make unto thee any graven image, &c.

3. Thou shalt not take the name of the Lord thy God in vain.

4. *Remember the sabbath day to keep it holy.*

THE GOSPEL

1. Matt. 22:37, Thou shalt love the Lord thy God with all thy heart and with all thy soul and with all thy mind.

2. 1 John 5:21, Little children, guard yourselves from idols.

3. Matt. 5:34, Swear not at all.

4. *Col. 2:16, 17. Let no man therefore judge you in meat or in drink, or*

The Sabbath

	in respect of a feast day or a new moon, or a sabbath day, which are a shadow of things to come.
5. Honor thy father and thy mother.	5. Eph. 6: 1, Children obey your parents in the Lord.
6. Thou shalt not kill.	6. Matt. 5: 22, Every one who is angry with his brother shall be in danger of the judgment.
7. Thou shalt not commit adultery.	7. Matt. 5: 27, 28, He that looketh upon a woman to lust after her hath committed adultery.
8. Thou shalt not steal.	8. Eph. 4: 28, Let him that stole steal no more.
9. Thou shalt not bear false witness, &c.	9. Col. 3: 9, Lie not one to another.
10. Thou shalt not covet, &c.	10. Luke 12: 15, Keep yourselves from all covetousness.

Who can find a commandment of the Gospel to correspond to the fourth of the ten? There is none. Instead we read, " Let no man judge you * * * in respect of a sabbath day " (Col. 2: 16), and again, " One man esteemeth one day above another: another esteemeth every day alike. Let each man be fully assured in his own mind " (Rom. 14: 5).

It is true that just as Jesus went back of the law which allowed divorce and placed marriage upon the creation standard of God (Matt. 19: 8, 9), so He went back of the Jewish law and declared of the creation Sabbath, " The sabbath was made for man and not man for the sabbath "

(Mark 2: 27), thus implying that the observance of one day in seven is for man's good and therefore should be continued. But He did not continue the dispensational features of the Sabbath, for He said, " It is lawful to do good on the sabbath " (Matt. 12: 12), while the law said " Thou shalt do NO work," making no exception of good works. The creation Sabbath which Jesus recognized as of perpetual good, is perpetuated in the Lord's Day just as much as in the Saturday Sabbath of the Jews, but the Jewish features that were added to it have been done away, and Christian features have been added instead.

(4) Finally, we are clearly taught that the ten commandments as a part of the law have been done away. Paul says:

If the ministration of death, written and engraved on stones (the ten commandments, Ex. 32: 15; Heb. 9: 5), came with glory, so that the children of Israel could not look stedfastly upon the face of Moses for the glory of his face: which glory was to be done away; how shall not rather the ministration of the Spirit (The Gospel Age, Acts 2) be with glory? . . . For if that which passeth away was with glory, much more that which remaineth is in glory (2 Cor. 3: 6: 11).

The ten commandments graven on stones have been done away, and we have the will of God for us in the Gospel, which remains, and we are therefore " ministers of the new covenant (v. 6).

Christian parents and teachers should beware, lest in teaching the ten commandments they fail to explain that as a covenant they are done away, and that we are under the Gospel instead, which gives us the eternal principles of these commandments in the form of life instead of law. It is better to teach the positive precepts of the Gospel than the negative precepts of the law. The ten commandments are brief and convenient for memorizing, but they should be explained in the light of the Gospel, which teaches us to live holily every day and to consecrate all that we have.

III. The New Covenant Sabbath or the Lord's Day.

1. INSTITUTION. It must not be thought that because the Jewish Sabbath was done away the creation Sabbath was also done away. The creation Sabbath is for all dispensations of man. It is the seventh day as a day of rest and worship after six days of toil. As such it was observed in the Jewish Sabbath, and is also observed in like manner in the Lord's Day, which is a day of rest and worship after six days of toil. Jesus recognized and observed this Sabbath, but taught its true significance for all ages as a day for the spiritual good of man. He therefore allowed on it works of necessity (Mark 2: 23-28), of mercy (Mark 3: 1-6) and of worship (Luke 4: 16-20). But having fulfilled the types of the old covenant He established the new in His own blood (Heb. 8) and gave us the sign of the Lord's Day, with its special significance because of its coming on the first day of the week instead of the seventh. This significance was given in several ways:

(1) *The various types of the Old Testament pointed to the Lord's Day of the New.*

As the creation Sabbath was the first day of the life of our first parents, so the Lord's Day (also the day of rest after six days of labor) is the memorial of the first day of the resurrection life of the New Adam, Christ.

The feast of Pentecost under the law was a type of the true Pentecost of this age of the Spirit, and both came on the first day of the week (Lev. 23: 16; Acts 2: 1). The jubilee year was the first after the sabbatical year (Lev. 25: 8-11) and pointed to its fulfillment in Christ, who proclaimed release to the captives (Luke 4: 18), and thus to the Lord's Day, the first after the Sabbath.

(2) *The first day of the week began to be observed by the appointment of Jesus Himself.* He arose from the dead on that day (Mark 16: 1-8) and appeared to His disciples five times on that day (Matt. 28: 1, 9-18; Mark 16: 9, 12, 14; John 20: 19-26). How does it happen that He met with them so much on this day unless He wished to have them meet then, rather than on the old Jewish Sabbath? Since He began these meetings for prayer and religious teaching on the first day, it is not strange that the apostles and the church kept them up.

(3) *The Holy Spirit came on the first day* (Acts 2: 1). This also was by divine appointment in honor of this day, which had been foreshadowed in the feast of Pentecost. The appointment of Jesus with His disciples on the first day prepared them for this day of blessing, which helped to confirm them in their observance of the day.

(4) *The inspired apostles continued to observe the first day as a day of rest and worship.* " The first day of the week when we were gathered together to break bread, Paul preached," &c. (Acts 20: 7). "Upon the first day of the week let every one of you lay by him in store as God has prospered" (1 Cor. 16: 2). That this laying by for the poor was to be done in connection with the first day religious services rather than in connection with the secular business of the week is shown by the writings of the early church which speak of such offerings as a regular custom. See *Teachings of the Apostles* ch. 14, *Constitutions of the Apostles.* Bk. 2, ch. 57 and 59, &c.

To be sure, the apostles preached also on the Jewish Sabbath, not because they believed it binding, but because the Jews met on that day to worship, and they thus had a convenient opportunity to preach to them. It was not strange that they should use such opportunities, but it would be strange that they should make their own appointments on the first day of the week had they not been divinely commanded to do so.

(5) *The writings of the early Christians show that the observance of the Lord's Day instead of the Sabbath began with the apostles and continued from that time on.*

The most constantly reiterated assertion of Saturday keepers is that the change from Saturday to Sunday was made by decree of the Emperor Constantine 321 A. D., and that he did it at the behest of the Pope, who arrogantly assumes to change times and seasons and thus shows the "mark of the beast" (Rev. 13: 16-18), since they regard the Pope as the antichrist. They fondly quote from the *Douay Catechism* a statement citing the change of the Sabbath as an illustration of the exercise by the papacy of the right to change times and seasons, but a little research reveals the fact that the Lord's Day, Sunday, was observed from the very days of Christ. The following quotations are taken from the writings of the Ante-nicene Fathers, which are accessible to all, through publishers or libraries, and the extracts may be verified. *The Teachings of the Apostles* was written in the apostolic age. Some of the best recent writers put it as early as 65 A. D., before the death of the apostles. It says (ch. 14):

But **every Lord's day do ye gather yourselves together** and break bread, and give thanksgiving, after having confessed your transgressions.

Ignatius, who was appointed Bishop of Antioch A. D. 69 says:

After the Sabbath let every friend of Christ keep the Lord's day, the queen and chief of all the days. Looking forward to this the prophet declared, "To the end of the 8th day," on which our life both sprang up again and the victory over death was obtained through Christ.

The prophecy of the eighth day referred to is the inscription of the 6th and 12th Psalms, in the original. Ignatius further says:

> Wherefore if they who were brought up in these ancient laws (Jewish) came nevertheless to the newness of the hope; **no longer observing sabbaths, but keeping the Lord's day,** in which also our life is sprung up by him. &c.—To the Magnesians.—3: 3.

The Epistle of Barnabas was written, if not by Barnabas, at least by some one near his day, as it was for a time regarded as a part of the Gospel. It must have been highly regarded, and that very widely, to hold such a place. It says (ch. 15):

> The Sabbaths that now are, hath God said, are not pleasing to me. The beginning of the eighth day I will make to be a Sabbath, which is the commandment of another world. Wherefore we keep the eighth day as a day of joy; on it Jesus arose from the dead, and after he had showed himself, ascended into heaven.

In *Recognitions,* an ancient document ascribed to *Clement,* Bishop of Rome next after Peter, and mentioned by Paul in Philpp. 4: 3, says that Peter converted Faustinianus and "the NEXT LORD'S DAY he baptized him."

Justin Martyr (150 A. D.) says:

> And **on the day called Sunday** all who live in the cities or country gather together to one place, and the memoirs of the apostles or writing of the prophets are read as long as time permits. Then when the reader has ceased the president instructs verbally and exhorts to the imitation of those good things. . . . Sunday is the day on which we all hold our common assembly, because it is the first day in which God, having made a change in the darkness and matter, created the world, and Jesus Christ our Savior rose from the dead. —Apology 1: 6.

> Is there any other matter, my friends, in which we are blamed than this, that we live not after the law, and are not circumcised in the flesh, as your forefathers were, and **do not observe Sabbaths** as you do?—Dialogue with Trypho, ch. 10.

The Sabbath

As, then, circumcision began with Abraham, and the Sabbath with Moses. . . . so it was necessary in accordance with the Father's will, that they should have an end in Him who was born of a virgin.—Dialogue with Trypho, ch. 43.

Irenaeus (130 A. D.) says:

The custom of not bending the knee on Sunday is a symbol of the resurrection through which we have been set free. Now this custom **took its rise in apostolic times.**

Origen (185 A. D.) says:

If it be objected to us on this subject that we ourselves are accustomed to observe certain days, as for example, **the Lord's day.**—Reply to Celsus, 8: 22.

Tertullian (160 A. D.) says:

But if we, like them (the heathen), celebrate Sunday as a day of rejoicing, it is for a reason vastly different from that of worshiping the sun; for **we solemnize the day after Saturday in contradistinction to those who call this day their Sabbath.**—Apology, ch. 16.

Again in answer to the Jews, ch. 4, he says:

The observance of the Sabbath is demonstrated to have been temporary.

Apostolic Constitutions, written in the second century and revised in the fourth, prescribes as follows:

Every Lord's day hold your solemn assemblies and rejoice, for he will be guilty of sin who fasts on the Lord's day, being the day of the resurrection.—Bk. 5, ch. 3.

And on the day of our Lord's resurrection, which is the Lord's day, meet more diligently, sending praise to God that made the universe by Jesus, and sent Him to us, and condescended to let Him suffer, and raised Him from the dead. Otherwise what apology will he make to God who does not assemble on that day to hear the saving word concerning the resurrection, on which we pray thrice standing in memory of Him who rose in three days, in which is performed the reading of the prophets, the preaching of the Gospel, the oblation of the sacrifice, the gift of the holy food.—Bk. 2, ch. 59.

It is true that quotations may be found indicating that some of the Christians continued to meet also on the Jewish Sabbath, but some also met every day (*Apostolic Constitutions* 2: 59), and some continued for a time to observe circumcision, but the fact remains that from the first the Lord's Day was observed as the special day of worship of the Christians.

Bardesanes, writing about the middle of the second century, says:

Wherever we be, all of us are called by the one name of the Messiah, Christians; and upon one day, which is the first day of the week, we assemble ourselves together, and on the appointed days we abstain from food.

Dionysius, Bishop of Corinth, in a letter to the Romans about A. D. 170, says:

We are to-day keeping the Lord's holy day.

Mileto, Bishop of Sardis, is said to have composed a treatise on the Lord's Day about this time.

Cyprian (190 A. D.) in a letter written about 250 A. D. connects the Lord's Day with circumcision and with the resurrection.

Peter, Bishop of Alexandria, A. D. 300, says:

We keep the Lord's Day as a day of joy because of Jesus who rose thereon.

Thus, from the days of the apostles until now, the chain of evidence is complete. The Lord's Day has been observed, not because of Constantine's decree, or later councils or popes, but because the Spirit of God so led the apostles and the church to observe this day, from the time of the resurrection on to the present.

(6) *The first day of the week is called the "Lord's Day" in writings of the apostolic age.* It is so called in the *Didache* or *Teaching of the Apostles* (ch. 14), a document

older than some of the Gospels, in *Apostolic Constitutions* (5: 3), in the *Recognitions* of Clement, and many other writings. This name (the Lord's Day) is distinctly linked with the first day of the week, being called also Sunday or the resurrection day, but it *is never used of the Jewish Sabbath,* and the term Sabbath is never used of the Lord's Day in the early writings until after the Judaizing sect of the Christians had died out. This faction, which made so much trouble by insisting on circumcision (Acts 15: 1-3), the Jewish Sabbath (Rom. 14: 5), and other ordinances of the law (Col. 2: 16) was severely denounced by the apostle. See Gal. 2 to 4, Col. 2, &c. Their leaders followed him up and incited controversy wherever they went, but, being in error, the sect died out. Modern sabbatizers are less consistent in that although they try to get under the law in one point they reject it in the others.

(7) *The apostolic term " Lord's Day" as applied to the Christian Sabbath is a prophecy of our Lord's return.* An ancient Syrian writing introductory to *The Teaching of the Apostles* and purporting to be written by Addaeus, one of the seventy (Luke 10: 1), gives in addition to other reasons for observing the Lord's Day the last and most interesting as follows:

And on the first day of the week He will appear at last with the angels of heaven.—Ante-Nicene Fathers, Vol. 8, p. 668.

This day of the coming of the Lord is repeatedly called in the Scriptures "the day of the Lord" (1 Cor. 5: 5; 2 Cor. 1: 14; 1 Thess. 5: 2; 2 Pet. 3: 10, &c.) and in Rev. 1: 10 it is called " the Lord's day," which is the same thing. The name Lord's Day, given to the Christian Sabbath seems to be due to the tradition that the Lord will come on that day. At any rate there will be no more fitting time for His appearing than when the thousands of the faithful are worshiping in His name. Thus from first to last in Gospel history the first day of the week is "the Lord's Day" and should be kept holy unto Him.

2. Significance of the Lord's Day.

(1) *A memorial.* The Lord's Day is a memorial of rest from the bondage of sin through the resurrection of Christ. As under the creation Sabbath we have the labor of creation, the making of man in the image of God, and then rest; and as under the Jewish Sabbath we have the labor in Egypt, the covenant with Israel, and its memorial the seventh-day Sabbath; so now we have the battle of Jesus with sin, His deliverance from the grave and following rest on the first day, which is a type of our bondage of sin, our deliverance through Christ, and our rest in Him. Therefore the first-day Sabbath is to the church as a memorial.

(2) *A symbol.* The Lord's Day is a symbol of the new life which we have in Christ. The Jewish Sabbath pointed forward to rest in Christ, but we possess this rest through faith and obedience. See Heb. 4: 3-11; quoted above. See also 1 Pet. 1: 3-10:

Blessed be the God and Father of our Lord Jesus Christ, who according to his great mercy begat us again unto a living hope by the resurrection of Jesus Christ from the dead, unto an inheritance incorruptible, &c.

Every Lord's Day we are reminded of the resurrection, and thus of the risen life that we should live (Rom. 6: 5). "If ye then, were raised together with Christ, seek the things that are above" (Col. 3: 1). We are also reminded of the coming of the Spirit on that day to make this life possible to us. "Walk by the Spirit and ye shall not fulfill the lust of the flesh" (Gal. 5: 16). This is true rest, of which the rest of the Jewish Sabbath was only a faint type. To us, therefore, who rest in Jesus (Matt. 11: 28), the lying of Jesus in the grave on the Jewish Sabbath day

The Sabbath

is a symbol of that grave into which the law puts us as a penalty of sin (Rom. 6: 23), and on the first day we thank God that we are not under the law, but under grace and thus have life, eternal life, of which the Lord's Day has become a symbol.

(3) *A type.* The Lord's Day is also a type. This dispensation is not the final one, and the types of one dispensation point forward to their fulfillment in the next. The Lord's Day reminds us of the millennial rest, when the Lord Himself shall come again. In that day the whole earth shall have rest, for Satan shall be chained in the abyss (Rev. 20) and righteousness shall cover the earth as the waters cover the sea.

3. CONTINUANCE. As the Jewish Sabbath continued during the old covenant, so the Christian Sabbath or Lord's Day shall continue during the new covenant. In the new earth and heaven types and shadows shall have passed away, for we shall have the Lord Himself with us.

> There remaineth a rest for the people of God.
> Though here we be blest with a bit of earth's sod,
> And a handful of years,—how soon they are gone,
> And the sob of eternity's billows comes on,
> And leaves us bereft, unless we have left
> The sweet Sabbath rest of the people of God.
>
> There remaineth a rest for the people of God.
> Now pilgrims confest as onward we plod,
> Soon, soon shall our pilgrimage journey be o'er,
> Soon, soon shall we rest in the bright evermore,
> Nor sorrow, nor pain shall we suffer again,
> In the sweet Sabbath rest for the people of God.

4. TEXTS EXPLAINED.

Matt. 5: 17-20, I came not to destroy but to fulfill.

When Jesus fulfilled the old covenant, then it gave place to the new. He continues, "One jot or one tittle shall in no wise pass away from the law *till all things be accomplished."* That is to say *it shall pass when all is accomplished.* This came to pass when Jesus said *"it is finished"* (John 19: 30). The law was not destroyed, but like ripe fruit that falls in due season, it passed away that it might give place to the Gospel.

Matt. 24: 20, Pray that your flight be not in the winter, neither on a sabbath.

This refers not to the weekly Sabbath, but to any of the Sabbaths. If it proves that the Jewish Sabbath is to be observed it proves that the *winter* is also to be observed. The fact is, it simply points out the hardship of flight at those seasons, because of the cold, and because of the lack of the ordinary means of travel when the Jews were keeping Sabbath, and the gates of the city were closed.

James 1: 25, He that looketh into the perfect law, the law of liberty, and so continueth, being not a hearer that forgetteth, but a doer that worketh, this man shall be blessed in his doing.

The "perfect law" to which James refers is not the Mosaic law, for we are told that it was not perfect (Heb. 8: 7, 8) and could make no one perfect (Heb. 7: 16-19), but the law of Christ does (Rom. 8: 1-4), "for the law of the spirit of life in Christ Jesus hath made me free from the law of sin and death." This is the perfect law of liberty (Gal. 5: 1; John 8: 36). Happy are they who continue in it instead of going back to the curse pronounced by the old law (Gal. 3: 10, 11).

Ex. 31: 17, It (the Sabbath) is a sign between me and the children of Israel forever.

One needs only to compare this with other scriptures to see the meaning of "forever." Ex. 12: 14, "Keep it (the Passover) a feast and an ordinance forever." Do Saturday keepers also keep the Passover "forever"? "He (the servant) shall serve him forever" (Ex. 21: 6). Does this mean all eternity? Not so, for on jubilee year all slaves went free, and in Christ we are free, which jubilee freedom we celebrate by the Lord's Day of the new covenant.

Acts 18: 4, He (Paul) reasoned in the synagogue every sabbath.

This passage is used to prove that the apostles observed the Jewish Sabbath. It shows simply that they took advantage of the assembling of the Jews on that day to preach the Gospel to them, just as they embraced like opportunities on any other day. The case of the meeting by the riverside in Philippi is no exception, for there were Jews in all the cities, whom Paul sought on their Sabbath as there was opportunity.

Rom. 14: 5, One man esteemeth one day above another: another esteemeth every day alike. Let each man be fully assured in his own mind. He that regardeth the day regardeth it unto the Lord. . . . So then each one of us must give an account of himself unto God.

In this passage we have a clear proof that the Jewish Sabbath is not binding on Christians, but at the same time liberty to observe it is granted to those "weak in the faith" (v. 1). We must bear with them patiently, but we must not allow them to entangle us again in the "yoke of bondage" (Gal. 5: 1), or cause us to deny our Lord by denying that he fulfilled the old covenant and established the new in its place.

IV. The Practical Value of the Sabbath.

"The Sabbath was made for man," therefore it is not for man to unmake the Sabbath. It was made to be observed, not to be broken, because its observance works good and not evil. Civil laws enforcing Sabbath observance are not to be classed with religious persecution, because it is the duty of the State to preserve the social welfare, and the social welfare depends upon preserving the Sabbath as a day of rest and worship. This is not a law of man, but a law of nature and of nature's God.

1. THE VALUE OF THE SABBATH TO THE PHYSICAL LIFE. It has been said that because the lower animals observe no Sabbath, therefore it is not needful for man. The argument is false, because the animals do rest a larger proportion of their time than even man with the Sabbath, and not being moral creatures they have no need of the Sabbath as a moral force. For man the Sabbath is a physical as well as a spiritual necessity. Medical experts testify that there is an excess of waste from the wear and tear of labor each day, which is not made up in the ordinary nightly rest, but which is equalized by the Sabbath rest every seventh day. When this periodic rest is not observed there is an accumulation of poisonous, burned up cells in the blood which destroys vitality. May it not be that the sluggishness of heathen nations is largely due to their disobedience of this law of nature? Even among the animals this law of sevens may be observed in the development of life. Eggs, for example, hatch according to periods of seven days. The period of gestation in the mammalia is marked by similar periods, while the life of man himself is in line with the law throughout. Thus at seven the child becomes a youth, at fourteen passes to the age of adolescence, at twenty-one is counted an adult, at forty-nine enters old age and at three score and ten reaches the allotted time of man. He may discard this law of periodicity if he will, but if in doing so he brings on typhoid fever his life depends upon the changes which occur at the end of each seven days.

Whatever may be the scientific explanation of this, history proves it to be a fact. Anyone with eyes to see may know that they who observe the Sabbath do more work in the six days than they who break it do in seven. When in 1847, gold was discovered in California, and there was a rush across the western deserts and mountains they who rested themselves and their beasts according to the commandment, reached their goal in safety, while those who in avaricious greed pressed forward on the Sabbath and every day, whitened the plains with their bones. Men may bank upon their surplus energy for a time, but when the Angel of Life wound up the springs of man's vitality he turned over the key to the Angel of Death, and he who squanders his life, interest and all, must come the sooner to senility and the grave.

2. THE VALUE OF THE SABBATH TO THE SPIRITUAL LIFE. If this life were all it would be necessary to observe the Sabbath, but it is not all. The most important feature of this life is the development of a character which is to endure for eternity. It follows that whatever contributes to the development of good character is of great value. The Sabbath contributes to this end far more than we appreciate. It is an aid to morals because it contributes to health and strength, and people in health have more power to resist temptation than those with debilitated systems. It contributes to the good because it affords an opportunity to engage in works of mercy and kindness, to visit the sick and the needy, and to cultivate that human interest which comes from social touch. But most of all, the Sabbath aids the kingdom because it reminds the race of the Great King, the Creator, "whose we are and whom we serve." If the nightly rest is insufficient to repair the waste of the labor of the day, much less is the hasty devotion of each day sufficient to meet the needs of the spiritual life. He who neglects the Sabbath worship sooner or later becomes a

spiritual bankrupt. They who inherit strong spiritual tendencies may bank upon them for a time, but the strongest character without God's means of grace will dwarf and die. Let the nations hearken to the sepulchral voices of the past which warn them of the folly of forgetting God. Let them learn from Israel seventy years in captivity, "until the land enjoyed her Sabbaths" after four hundred and ninety years of Sabbath-breaking (2 Chron. 36: 21). The sinner may mock at the preacher, and at the religious institutions which the preacher proclaims, but in the end he will find that God's means of grace are bound up in the book of life, and he who belittles them in doing so writes his own doom.

"O day of rest and gladness, O day of joy and light,
O balm of care and sadness, most beautiful and bright;
On thee the high and lowly, through ages joined in tune,
Sing Holy, Holy, Holy, to the great God Triune.
To-day on weary nations the heavenly manna falls;
To holy convocations the silver trumpet calls,
Where Gospel light is glowing, with pure and radiant beams,
And living water flowing with soul-refreshing streams,
New graces ever gaining, from this our day of rest,
We reach the rest remaining to spirits of the blest."

THE TITHE A SYMBOL OF CHRISTIAN STEWARDSHIP.

Of all the great truths taught by Jesus and recorded in the Gospel, the one that came nearest to oblivion,—being quoted, not by the four Gospels, but by Paul,—is perhaps one of the best of them all, "It is more blessed to give than to receive" (Acts 20: 35). Of all the Christian graces the one that seems to be most in danger of now being lost is the "grace of giving" (2 Cor. 8: 1-9). And of all God's means of grace the one that is most neglected to-day is the symbol of stewardship, which was established along with marriage and the Sabbath in Eden itself. "Will a man rob God?" cried the prophet, "yet ye have robbed me. But, ye say, wherein have we robbed thee? *In tithes and offerings*" (Mal. 3: 8). Strange as it may seem, in seeking wealth for themselves, men reject the very thing which would give them the greatest prosperity. It is the old story which Jesus put in the saying, "He that seeketh his life shall lose it." "Ye are cursed with a curse," said the Lord, "for ye have robbed me, even this whole nation," and that curse upon the evil steward who used his Lord's portion for himself, is burning throughout Christendom to-day. The very church which ought to give to the world an example of faithful Christian stewardship, for the most part denies the very symbol of it, and gives back to the Lord only the paltry remnant left after satiating itself. The first sign of backsliding is usually seen in this repudiation of God's ownership. The servant acts as if he were Lord instead of steward.

The people themselves are not so much to blame for this

as the pastors who fail to teach them the Gospel of giving. Many seem to be too indifferent even to study the subject for themselves. They are like the pastor to whom a rich man who was dying said, " I am dying and I am lost, for I have hoarded all my wealth when I should have used it for the Lord. I am lost and it is your fault, for you never taught me my duty in giving. You who never prayed with me about my money, pray for my lost soul now." Is it not true that in most churches, while the people are taught that their souls belong to God, they seldom hear that their bodies and their money or other property, and their time and their talent, and their children and all belong also to Him? And yet, as some one has forcibly said, " Unless Jesus Christ is Lord of all He is not Lord at all." And would it not be strange if God, who has embodied all the other great truths of His revelation in appropriate teaching symbols, should leave the doctrine of stewardship to be forgotten? He has not so left it, but in all ages has required the holy tithe as a sacred symbol. This Christian dispensation is no exception. The Gospel increases rather than diminishes our obligations to God, and woe to us if we care not for its message.

I. Money and the Kingdom.

1. THE GREAT POWER OF MONEY. By money one may, though crippled or tied up in business, yet transform himself into a missionary of the cross and then multiply himself many fold, and speak with a hundred tongues to a hundred audiences, or fly with the wings of ten thousand tracts, or bear the message of a thousand Bibles to as many homes. It makes it possible for *all* (and the command was given to all) to help " make disciples of all nations " Matt. 28: 19.

2. THE GREAT NEED OF MONEY. The whole world is passing through a crisis. History and prophecy are touching

a converging point. False faiths are crumbling. Highways through heathendom are opened, while anon there is world-wide apostasy and our Christianity must mightily assert itself. Time and again Dr. Lyman Beecher fervently said: "Now is the nick of time! One dollar *now* is worth fifty dollars fifty years from now." That appeal has been reëchoed with increasing power by every leader who has come into touch with the mighty throb and rush of events with which this century is opening. Great times call for great efforts. And workers are not wanting. Hosts of young men and women whom God has called to go are knocking at the doors of our colleges only to find them barred because other hosts whom God has called to *give* are *embezzling* the wealth over which He has made them *stewards* and *not owners*. In the hour of victory, mission boards are compelled to retrench under the gloom of the shadow of enormous debts. Church reports are poorest here. Work in every department is crippled here, not because times are hard or the church is poor, but because *it does not practice the gospel of giving*.

3. OUR GREAT WEALTH. Charles Brandt, in *The Key to the Kingdom,* has shown that the wealth of church members in the United States alone is $23,000,000,000, while the annual increase is $725,000,000. Of this the unspeakably paltry sum of about forty cents for each church member is given each year for the evangelization of some eight hundred million souls for whom Christ died, while an *equal number* of sinners with no more wealth, spend two hundred and twenty times as much for liquor and one hundred times as much for tobacco! Yea, hide your head in shame, nor lift it up again until *your giving* has helped destroy this infamous fact from the earth. While only $7,500,000 is spent annually for foreign work and $250,000,000 for home church work, Americans spend $11,000,000 for chewing

gum, $178,000,000 for confections, $700,000,000 for jewelry and plate, $750,000,000 for tobacco and $1,643,000,000 for liquor. The problem is not lack of wealth but *lack of consecration*. It is of thrilling significance that God has put the power of this enormous wealth into the hands of the church just at this crisis, and of added significance that as never before He is rousing His faithful few to a right conception of their duty in giving. The triumph of the kingdom is sure, but woe to that man who, when the King cometh, shall have buried his Lord's money (Matt. 25: 30), though it be but one talent. Mission boards may cry " Retrench," but God commands, " Go forward," and His commands are enablings.

4. THE GREAT PROMISE. If some one should say to us, " If you will observe a few simple conditions which are entirely possible, I will guarantee that you shall always be happy and free from want," how quickly we would close with the offer. In all seriousness God presents to us a proposition no less than this. It was made over and over again to Israel (Deut. 28: 1-68; 7: 12-16; 11: 13-18; Jer. 26: 4-6, &c.) and verified in their checkered history—prosperous when obedient, cast down and in captivity when disobedient. It was made to the disciples and the church and has been verified by its career to this day. Jesus gave us the very heart of it when He said, "All things that are mine are thine, and thine are mine." (John 17: 10). See also Zech. 4: 6, " Not by might, nor by power, but by my Spirit, saith Jehovah of hosts." " Bring ye the whole tithe into the storehouse. . . . and see if I will not open you the windows of heaven and pour you out a blessing such as there shall not be room enough to receive it" (Mal. 3: 10). "And my God shall supply every need" (Philpp. 4: 19).

Read the daring promise to the disciples (Luke 10)

when Jesus sent them out, and their testimony on returning (Luke 22: 35), "When I sent you forth without purse, or script, lacked ye anything? and they said, Nothing." Is God's arm shortened? or His favor withdrawn? or has the law of faith become inoperative? Time would fail to tell of Spurgeon and Simpson and Morris and Judson and Blumhardt and missionaries in every land, who in our own day, through faith, have wrought miracles of transformation and healing, and have subdued kingdoms and wrought righteousness and stopped the mouths of cavilers. The whole world knows of Müller and his work, "the standing miracle of Bristol," who in his lifetime until 1872 had fed, clothed and educated 24,788 orphans, given away 75,392 Bibles, 148,739 portions of Scriptures, 42,500,000 tracts, sent out 47 missionaries, and in these and other ways expended over *seven millions* of dollars for the Lord, and every penny was received *in direct answer to prayer*. He asked no man for a penny nor did he give public credit to gratify pride, but from meal to meal the Lord supplied the need. *There was no debt.* He wrote: "Faith is above circumstances. No evil, no war, no panic can touch it." Read his *Life of Trust* and be not faithless but believing. There is another home at Halle, and there are missions in New York and Chicago and other places which stand as witnesses to the proposition that if we obey the conditions God will supply the need, however hard the times or poor His people. Let us, therefore, "Lift up the hands that hang down" (Heb. 12: 12), and search and see if we have not sinned (Dan. 9: 8-16; Mal. 3: 8). The promises of God are conditional. *He will* do his part and *we can* do our part.

5. THE GOSPEL OF GETTING. "*Seek ye first his kingdom and his righteousness and all these things shall be added*" (Matt. 6: 33). There are three lessons in this text:

(1) *Seeking implies action.* There is no comfort for the lazy man or church or nation. "In diligence not slothful" (Rom. 12: 11). "Redeeming the time" (Eph. 5: 16). "We commanded you, If any will not work, neither let him eat" (2 Thess. 3: 10). At least one talent has been given to each, not for burial, but for use. "Trade ye herewith till I come" (Luke 19: 13).

(2) *"The kingdom first" are the key words of Christian getting.* The expression means that amid perplexing questions as to the use of time, talent or money, our constant criterion must be, not, "How may I have the most pleasure or gain?" but "How may I do the most good?" Such a rule will prevent a dishonest use of one's talents in preaching, or song, or whatever they be, by disuse or bad use, or less than the best use; of one's time by squandering it in pleasure-seeking, frivolous reading, idle games or useless work; of money by using it in any selfish way. It will exclude dishonest dealings between individuals and ungodly licensing of evil by the public. It will exclude such church methods as work more spiritual harm than financial good. Mr. Aked lays down three principles on money:

(1) No money is honestly owned which is not a return for service rendered. (2) No money is honestly owned which is gotten by the toil of one simply to enrich another. (3) No amount of giving can atone for stealing.

(3) *"All these things shall be added"* is not an empty promise, else all God's promises are vain. Mark its shining proof in the history of every nation. Mark how to-day the scepter of power and wealth is passing from heathen to Christian peoples. As the billow upon its trough, so prosperity rides upon the heels of obedience and is inseparable from it. No legislation can bring enduring prosperity upon evil, but "Honor Jehovah with thy substance * * * so shall thy barns be filled with plenty." Prov. 3: 9, 10.

II. The Principle of Stewardship.

1. THE PRINCIPLE OF STEWARDSHIP BELONGS TO ALL AGES. It is not for this dispensation merely. It is not a new teaching with Jesus. He simply unfolded it from the bud into the flower, as He did many other Scripture teachings.

(1) *In the patriarchal age the principle of stewardship was recognized.* It is hinted at in God's rebuke of Cain as quoted in Heb. 11: 4; " By faith Abel offered unto God a more excellent (Gr. *pleiona,* " fuller ") sacrifice than Cain." It is recognized in God's command to Abraham in calling him away from his home and in promising him and his posterity a land of their own (Gen. 12: 1, 7), which yet was only a stewardship, for the patriarchs all " confessed that they were strangers and pilgrims on the earth " (Heb. 11: 13).

(2) *Uuder the law the principle of stewardship is still more clearly taught.* God claims the people (Deut. 7: 6-8; Ezek. 18: 4), the land (Lev. 25: 23; Ex. 19: 5), the silver and gold (Haggai 2: 8), and the cattle (Psa. 50: 10), while the people were taught to regard themselves as " pilgrims and strangers " (Lev. 25: 23). Everything belonged to God and they were simply stewards.

(3) *In the Gospel, the principle of stewardship is brought to its fulness.* Jesus continually teaches it and devotes several of His greatest parables to explaining it,—the parable of the talents (Matt. 25: 14-30), and the parable of the pounds (Luke 19: 11-27). Paul declares with emphasis, " Ye are not your own; for ye were bought with a price " (1 Cor. 6: 19, 20). We read that " Every good gift and every perfect gift is from above, coming down from the Father " (Jas. 1: 17). We therefore, like our fathers, " Have here no abiding city, but we seek after *the city* which is to come " (Heb. 13: 14). We are stewards.

2. THE PRINCIPLE OF STEWARDSHIP IS NOT ANNULLED BECAUSE WE ARE ACCOUNTED CHILDREN OF GOD (John 1: 12) RATHER THAN SERVANTS. Jesus was the beloved Son, yet was most of all devoted to the Father's will (John 5: 30). He said, "The servant knoweth not what his Lord doeth," but must obey without understanding; how much more gladly must they obey who as children know the loving purpose of God's commands?

3. THE PRINCIPLE OF STEWARDSHIP INVOLVES THE SUPPORT OF THE STEWARD. Jesus said, "The laborer is worthy of his hire" (Luke 10: 7), while Paul declares, "If any provideth not for his own, and specially they of his own household, he hath denied the faith and is worse than an unbeliever" (1 Tim. 5: 8). *This does not mean the providing of luxuries,* for Jesus denounced the stewards who took advantage of the delay of their Lord to indulge themselves (Luke 12: 45, 46). He taught us to pray, "Give us day by day our daily bread (literally, our little loaf) Matt. 6: 11. We are not to take anxious thought for the future to the neglect of the kingdom of God in the present (Luke 12: 13-40). Therefore, "Godliness with contentment is great gain: for we brought nothing into this world, for neither can we carry anything out; but having food and covering we shall be therewith content" (1 Tim. 6: 6-8). There are other, and far greater rewards for the faithful steward, but they are not of this world (Rev. 22: 12).

4. THE PRINCIPLE OF STEWARDSHIP MEANS THE USE OF EVERYTHING ACCORDING TO THE WILL OF GOD. He is the Owner and Lord. To him we must give an account of ourselves (Rom. 14: 12), of our works (Rom. 2: 6), of our energy (Matt. 21: 28), of our property (Luke 19: 12-19), of our time (John 9: 4), of our opportunities (Matt. 25: 14-30), of our children (Psa. 127: 3), of our spiritual gifts (1 Cor. 12: 11), of our use of the Gospel (Matt. 28: 19), and of

our words (Matt. 12: 36). God is our senior partner (1 Cor. 7: 24) and we are foolish indeed if we fail to consult Him in all our affairs. "If any man lack wisdom let him ask of God (Jas. 1: 5).

III. The Tithe: A Symbol of Stewardship.

Not very many Christians have ever given the tithe any serious study. People do not naturally incline to follow a line of study that will lead them to an unwelcome duty. Even ministers of the Gospel are blind leaders of the blind in many cases when dealing with the tithe. Those who oppose usually content themselves by saying, "Tithes are of the law which passed away. We are of the Gospel, and tithes are not commanded in the Gospel, and that is the end of it." Is it really a *fact* that the tithe is only of the Mosaic law? Or is it *true* that there is no ground for observing the tithes under the Gospel? What if we shall find the tithe, like the creation Sabbath (not the Jewish Sabbath), ordained for all dispensations, with special adaptations and significations for each? If the Jews were cursed with a curse because they "robbed God" in tithes and offerings (Mal. 3: 8-10), and this under the law, does it not behoove us who have the greater light of the Gospel to search carefully for the will of God in the matter, lest we also sin?

1. THE TITHE AN INSTITUTION FOR ALL AGES.

(1) *From creation to the law God required the tithe.* In the very first family we find men bringing their offerings unto God (Gen. 4: 3). Who taught them to do this if God did not? Cain's offering was rejected. Why? The Septuagint version of Gen. 4: 7 reads, "If thou hast offered aright, but hast not divided aright, hast thou not sinned?" This thought is sustained by the Greek of Heb. 11: 4, which reads, "By faith Abel offered a *fuller* (Gr.

pleionas) sacrifice than Cain." How could Cain sin in giving the wrong proportion in his offering if God had not taught them to tithe?

This interpretation is confirmed by the fact that almost immediately after the flood we find Abraham, faithful servant of the true God, giving tithes to Melchizedek who was a priest of the true God (Gen. 14: 20), and doing it as a matter of course, as if he were accustomed to do it. The custom must have been handed down through all the line of worshipers of the true God (Heb. 7: 1-10). It was further observed by Jacob (Gen. 28: 20-22), and is first mentioned by Moses as an institution already existing and well known (Lev. 27: 30). The practice of all the nations of antiquity is added evidence that the tithe was a divine institution derived from the very beginning.

Grotius, the sacred historian, says:

"From the most ancient ages the tenth has been regarded as the portion due to God."

Montacutius, one of the most learned men of his day, says:

Instances are mentioned in history of some nations which did not offer sacrifices, but in the annals of time none are found that did not pay tithes.

EGYPTIANS.

Mospero says that the Egyptians before the time of Joseph set apart a regular proportion for religious worship.—*Dawn of Civilization,* p. 303.

BABYLONIANS.

Dr. Sayce says of the Babylonians:

The temple and priests were supported by the contributions of the people,—partly obligatory and partly voluntary. The most important among them were the "tithes" paid upon all produce. The tithes were contributed by all classes of the population from the king to the peasant; and lists exist which record the amounts severally due from the tenants of an estate.—Social Life among the Assyrians and Babylonians, p. 121.

CANAANITES AND PHOENICIANS.

Madam Ragozin, says of the Canaanites and Phoenicians:

They gave at least the male firstborn of every domestic animal, the first fruits of every crop, and a portion,—generally a tenth,—of all the products both of the soil and of men's industry, was to be paid in at stated intervals.—Assyria, p. 119.

ARABIANS.

Dr. Robertson Smith, professor of Arabic in Cambridge University, is witness for Arabia. He says:

The agricultural tribute of first fruits and tithes is a charge on the produce of the land, paid to the gods as Baalim, or landlords.—Religion of the Semites, p. 439.

PERSIANS.

Cyrus, the "shepherd of Jehovah" (Isa. 44: 28) when he conquered Persia gave a tenth of the spoil.—*Struggle of the Nations,* p. 36.

GREEKS.

Of tithing among the Greeks there are many witnesses. Agesilaus, King of Sparta and the Spartan General Lysander, both of the fourth century B. C., were accustomed to tithe. *Herodotus* tells of a woman of Thracia who sent a tenth of her gains to the temple of Apollo.—*Herodotus* 2: 152. He also says that certain islanders of the Ægean tithed their gains from gold and silver mines. 2: 57.

Xenophon, the Greek general and historian, was not specially religious, but he observed the tithe. See *Anabasis* 5: 8.

Thucydides, describing the division of the Island of Lesbos, four hundred years before Christ, says a tenth was consecrated to the gods.— *Thucy.* 3: 50.

Romans.

Among the Romans there are records of tithing as early as 395 B. C. The augurs of the temple reported that the gods were displeased and Camillus publicly declared that he was not surprised, for the country had greatly neglected tithing.

Varro, in the second century B. C., testifies that Roman farmers carefully tithed the fruits of the ground, and *Pliny* says that the Romans never tasted their new produce until the gods were first given the first fruits or tithe.

So essential was the custom regarded among the Romans that *Ulpian,* a prominent jurist of the third century, argued that the heirs and executors of one deceased were obliged to pay the tithe he owed.

Very many more quotations might be given adding testimony from other nations. For a lengthy and learned discussion of the point let the reader refer to *The Sacred Tenth* by Dr. Lansdell from which part of these quotations are taken.

How was it that this institution was uniformly observed among the ancient nations? *Dr. Kennicott* says:

Such a custom must be derived from some revelation, and this revelation must be antecedent to the dispersion at Babel.

The Missionary Visitor says:

The law of God is specific on this point if we will but open our hearts to it just as in the case of other laws. In reference to the Sabbath no one is in doubt about how much time is to be given. It is the seventh. This is holy unto the Lord. Yet this was commanded at the beginning. Or marriage. In the beginning it was declared that "they two shall become one flesh." There is no doubt as to the limitations in this law. The marriage tie is holy unto the Lord. Both these laws were in the beginning. And when in scanning the history of nations, not in contact with God's peculiar people, we find tithing so uniformly prevalent,—when we find in Sacred Writ

The Tithe

that Abraham and Jacob tithed, and that later Moses reduced those laws to writing so as to be preserved for the people, it looks very much as if the giving of the tenth is a law just as obligatory as is the law of the Sabbath or of marriage. In the light of this reasoning, no one but he who would reject God and his true relations to Him, can say there is no regulation in giving, and that each one is left to do just as he pleases.

(2) *In the dispensation of the law the creation tithe which had been handed down from the beginning, is carefully distinguished from the dispensational tithes.* It is called "holy" while the others are not (Lev. 27: 30). It is first mentioned as already existing and well known. In fact, announcement is simply made, as if it were already recognized, that "all the tithe of the land is holy unto the Lord" (Lev. 27: 30). This is similar to the first mention of the creation Sabbath, and the commandment "*Remember* the Sabbath." Neither of these institutions originated with the Mosaic dispensation, nor did they end with it.

The fact that the Sabbath was made a memorial of a special day for the Jews (Deut. 5: 15) and that there were other Sabbaths besides THE Sabbath, did not at all destroy the creation Sabbath. Neither does the fact that the tithe is included in the laws of Moses with other tithes do away with it or make it dispensational.

There were other regulations for giving that were dispensational. Besides the holy tithe which was used for the support of the Levites, God's representatives before the people (Num. 18: 21-24), the Jews were required to leave the corners of their fields for the poor (Lev. 19: 9), then the first fruits (Deut. 26: 1-10), then the festival tithe for the expenses and offerings of the annual feasts (Deut. 14: 22), then every third year a tithe for the poor (Deut. 14: 28), also free will offerings (Deut. 16: 10), vows

(Lev. 27: 9, 28), allowing the land to rest every seventh year (Lev. 25), remission of debts on jubilee year (Lev. 25: 28), redemption of the firstborn (Ex. 13: 15), and many other offerings. But remember, of all these only one is called " the holy " tithe and that it stood then as it stands now, a symbol of God's ownership of all, being used for the support of His representatives.

(3) *The observance of the tithe in all previous dispensations is presumption for its continuance in this dispensation.* All will admit that the tithe was binding under the law, but many deny that there is Gospel authority for it. Let such follow the evidence carefully.

The fact that the tithe was observed by all nations, and seemingly from the beginning, and is distinguished from the dispensational tithes under the law, is evidence that it belongs, not to one, but to all dispensations, and therefore to this.

This same fact should cause us not to expect a specific command in the Gospel to observe it. We have no such command in the Gospel concerning the creation Sabbath. We have no such command concerning marriage. And why? Because these sacred institutions, handed down from the beginning, needed no such command to reëstablish them. Neither did the holy tithe. It is in exactly the same position, and the logic that will annul either of these three because not expressly commanded in the Gospel will exclude all of them.

(4) *Jesus Himself enjoined the tithe and made it binding.* He said to the Jews, " Ye tithe mint and anise and cummin * * * these ought ye to have done " (Matt. 23: 23). When He made changes in the interpretation of the law He said, " Ye have heard that it hath been said of old time * * * but *I* say unto you." He never spoke this way of the tithe. When He said " Render to Caesar the

things that are Caesar's and to God the things that are God's" (Matt. 22:21), He must have had in mind the tithe, for He was speaking of taxes, and the tithe was the portion for God, the only tax designated as "holy unto the Lord." Here then is a command to give to God that which belongs to God, the sacred tithe.

That Jesus Himself observed the tithe must be apparent from the fact that the Pharisees never accused Him of not doing so. They were keen as hawks to detect any flaw in His life. They quibbled about His nonobservance of the Sabbath and of His not washing His hands as much as they, but they never once found occasion against Him in the matter of the tithe.

All the recorded teaching of Jesus concerning giving is in harmony with this observance of the tithe. As He enlarged the interpretation of other moral duties, so He did of this. He put the spirit of the law above the letter and made "justice, judgment and mercy" greater than mere payment of tithes, because the greater will include the less. First have love and love will fulfill the law. Thus Jesus taught:

" Freely ye have received, freely give." " Sell that ye have and give alms; make for yourselves purses that wax not old, a treasure in the heavens that faileth not." " Take heed and beware of covetousness, for a man's life consisteth not in the abundance of the things that he possesseth." " IT IS MORE BLESSED TO GIVE THAN TO RECEIVE."

(5) *The apostles also taught the tithe.* Not one of them is accused of opposing it, while two of them clearly teach it.

In 1 Cor. 9: 7-14 *Paul* announces God's law for the support of the ministry. In doing so he quotes the law for the support of the priests (which was the tithe), (Num. 18: 21-24) and says "EVEN so hath God ordained that they who preach the Gospel should live of the Gospel." "Even so" means "in like manner," and that means the tithe. And mark, He says that God Himself has so ordained or commanded, and this command is for the Gospel dispensation.

Again, *the author of Hebrews* draws an argument from the payment of tithes by Abraham to Melchizedek. Abraham was "the father of the faithful," a type of those who have the righteousness of faith rather than of works (Rom. 4), that is, of *Christians,* and Melchizedek was a priest of the true God and a type of Christ (Heb. 7: 17). The argument is that Abraham in paying tithes to Melchizedek recognized the priest as greater than himself, but as Melchizedek was a type of Christ, Abraham thus prophetically recognized the supremacy of Christ over the Levitical priesthood (Heb. 7: 1-20). Therefore this paying of tithes by Abraham foreshadowed the like homage of Christians to Christ.

If then we count the example of Jesus and the apostles as worth anything, if we count the "ought" of Jesus in Matt. 23: 23 as binding, as it is in John 13: 14 or in Luke 18: 1, or Acts 5: 29, where it is said, "We must (A. V. "ought to") obey God rather than man"; if we count the commands and arguments that undoubtedly refer to the tithe as authoritative, we must admit that the one tithe is considered holy and binding by the Gospel as well as by the law.

(6) *The leaders of the early church considered the tithe a Christian obligation.* They were so unanimous in their faith and practice, and the liberality of the early church was so great, that there was little occasion to mention the tithe, and yet the testimony recorded is unanimous for it. The early church discarded circumcision, and the Jewish Sabbath, while they kept the creation Sabbath, in the Lord's

The Tithe

Day; and likewise discarded the dispensational regulations as to giving, but they never gave up the holy tithe, God's tenth of the ages. It remained for the apostate church of the Dark Ages to do that. Should the modern church follow the church of the Dark Ages rather than that of the apostles?

The Teaching of the Apostles (A. D. 65) says:

Every first fruit therefore, of the products of the wine press and threshing floor, of oxen and of sheep, thou shalt take and give to the prophets, for they are your high priests. But if ye have not a prophet give it to the poor.—Ch. 13.

Constitutions of the Apostles (second and fourth centuries):

Those which were then first fruits, and tithes and offerings and gifts, now are oblations, which are presented by holy bishops to the Lord God through Jesus Christ.—Bk. 2, ch. 25.

Irenaeus (130 A. D.) says:

We ought to offer to God the first fruits of his creatures, as Moses says, "Thou shalt not appear before the Lord empty." Christ came not to diminish, but to increase our obligations.

Chrysostom (345 A. D.) says:

O what a shame! that what was no great matter among the Jews should be pretended to be such among Christians! If there was danger then of omitting tithes, how great must be that danger now.

Augustine (354 A. D.), the greatest theologian of the early church says:

Tithes ought to be paid from whatever be your occupation. Tithes are required as a debt. He who would procure either pardon or reward, let him pay tithes, and out of the nine parts give alms. God who has given us the whole has thought it meet to ask the tenth from us, not for His benefit, but for our own.

Quotations might also be given from Origen, Jerome and many others of the early writers. *Bingham* in his great work, *Christian Antiquities,* says, " This is the unanimous judgment of the Fathers, and the voice of the Church uncontradicted for more than a thousand years." These are not isolated testimonies, for *the entire church assembled in councils declared the same thing.* The tithe was held to be binding to the Word of God by the Council of Ancyra, A. D. 314; by that of Gangra, A. D. 324; Orleans, A. D. 511; Tours, A. D. 567; Toledo, A. D. 633; Touen, A. D. 650; Fimili, A. D. 791; and London, A. D. 1425.

(7) Of modern writers John Calvin, John Knox, Thomas Chalmers and many others were fearless advocates of the tithe.

Dr. Owen says:

The payment of tithes (1) before the law, with (2) the like usage among all nations living according to nature, (3) their establishment under the law, (4) their express relation in gospel appointment unto that establishment, (1 Cor. 9: 13, 14)— do make that kind of payment so far pleadable that no man can, with any pretense of a good conscience, consent to this taking away.

Max Müller, one of England's greatest scholars, says:

Can there be any lower or simpler test of sincerity than the giving of the tenth of one's income? And yet when one thinks what this world would be if at least this minimum of Christianity were a reality, one feels that you are right in preaching this simple duty, in season and out of season, until people see that without observing it every other pretense of religion is a mere sham.

C. C. McCabe says:

The old standard of one-tenth for the Lord's treasury would flood the world with salvation.

Alexander Grant says:

If the principle here advocated were adopted, even by the

truly converted and spiritual of the members, it were well within the reach of the churches to evangelize the world in twenty years, and actually to preach the Gospel to every creature under heaven.

James Sunderland says:

The universal adoption of this principle of giving would furnish such means as the church has not known in its history, and enable it to prosecute its great missionary and educational enterprises with such strength and vigor as their importance demands.

According to the interpretation of others *the obligation of the tithe will not end with this dispensation,* but as it has been handed down from former dispensations, so it will be observed by the converted and restored kingdom of Israel in the millennial dispensation to come. So says Jeremiah (Jer. 33: 13) and so says Ezekiel (Ezek. 20: 37), if these prophecies refer to that period, as many think. These prophets speak of "passing under the rod" because that was the way of counting the tithe of the flocks, each tenth animal being marked as it passed under.

Now we believe that without wresting the Scriptures from their real meaning they have been shown to establish the tithe as a sacred obligation in recognition of the stewardship of man, not for one dispensation only, but for all. It can be traced through precisely as the Sabbath or marriage or any of the great moral obligations can be traced through. It is true, it is not in the decalogue, but no more is marriage. Nevertheless, the preamble to the decalogue implies the stewardship of which the tithe is the symbol. "I am Jehovah thy God, that brought thee out of the land of Egypt, out of the house of bondage" means that as a consequence God has a right to give commands and exact the tithe as recognition of His Lordship over all.

2. THE SYMBOLISM OF THE TITHE. The tithe is none the

less a divine symbol because it has been neglected and perverted by many in all ages. All God's ordinances have been perverted. The tithe is a symbol, because God Himself has no need of man's gifts; they cannot enrich Him, but He requires them as a means of teaching men their stewardship and accountability.

(1) *In the patriarchal dispensation* we find God exercising His ownership in the case of Abraham (Gen. 12: 1), who recognized it by paying tithes (Gen. 14: 18-20); thus the patriarchs confessed that they were pilgrims and not owners (Heb. 11: 13, 15). But this giving of the tithe to God was also an expression of faith in the heavenly possessions to come (Heb. 11: 16).

(2) *In the dispensation of the law* the tithe was given a special significance because Israel belonged to God in a special way, for He had redeemed them from the bondage of Egypt. Yet in the promised land they were to pay the tithe as a symbol of the fact that God was owner and they were strangers (Lev. 25: 23). The tithe was to them a symbol, but it was also a type, for it pointed to the spiritual possessions of the kingdom of Christ (Eph. 2: 19).

(3) *In this Gospel dispensation* the consecration of the tithe as holy to God has a special significance because we have been redeemed from the bondage of sin by the precious blood of Christ (1 Cor. 6: 20). The giving of a tenth is a symbol of His ownership of all. It is also a type, for we also are pilgrims here, having no abiding city, but are reminded (or should be) of the city to come, the new Jerusalem (Heb. 13: 14), in which we shall receive the reward of our stewardship (Rev. 22: 12).

(4) *The use of the tithe for the support of God's ministers was a further enforcement of its symbolism.* As the tithe of possessions was required as a recognition of God's ownership of all, so from among the people the consecration

of the firstborn was required as a similar sign (Ex. 13: 2). The sign was required of the nation as well as of families, and in Num. 3: 12, 13 we read, " I have taken the Levites from among the children of Israel instead of the firstborn, and the Levites shall be mine."

The Levites became the priests and had no inheritance or income other than the holy tithe. This was given to them as the representatives of God (Num. 18: 21-26). This use of the tithe belongs to it as a part of its significance. It was also in the unwritten law observed by Abraham (Gen. 14: 18-20) in the patriarchal dispensation, and is further enjoined upon the church in this dispensation (1 Cor. 9: 7-14). If only the churches would obey the Gospel in this, how easy it would be to provide for the support of the ministry.

Instead of giving the tithe the majority of churches excuse themselves by a resort to a misinterpretation of 1 Cor. 16: 2. " Upon the first day of the week let every one of you lay by him in store as God has prospered." They take this weekly offering for the support of the church whereas Paul commanded it *for the help of the poor* (v. 3), and that not as a substitute for the tithe, which he elsewhere enjoins for the support of the ministry (1 Cor. 9: 7-14), but as a free-will offering. If the churches would only obey the Gospel in this also, there would be an ample fund for the relief of the poor and no occasion for any church member to say, " I must join the lodge in order to make sure of help in time of sickness or need." Disobedience in one point causes sin in others as well. God's way is best. Why not accept it?

3. THE PRACTICAL VALUE OF THE TITHE.

(1) *All history bears witness to the fact that the tithe was made for man, and not man for the tithe.* God has not one law for morals and another for business. The tithe

being an institution of God is also a blessing to man. Why is it that just a *seventh* part of time is essential for rest and worship? Yet it is so, and no human law can change it. The French revolutionists tried one day in ten, but failed and had to change back. Why is it that one tenth of one's income is the healthful proportion to give to the Lord? History proves that it is so and that is enough. The curse followed neglect of the tithe (Mal. 3: 8-10), just as for neglect of the Sabbath (2 Chron. 36: 21), while blessing followed obedience (Isa. 58: 13, 14; Mal. 3: 10; Prov. 3: 9, 10).

Dr. Miller, one of the ablest scholars of this country, says:

It was a proverb among the Jews—" pay tithes and be rich." The heathen made the same observation that he who paid most to his gods did receive most from them. They saw God's judgment upon them for not paying him his tenth; they repented, restored the tithe and were delivered. But we Christians remain the only incurable infidels, and we refuse to pay God that which by a universal decree, he has reserved unto himself.

This unbelief is the more inexcusable because we have before our eyes the fact that the Christian nations are the most prosperous, together with the testimony of the ages to the blessing of observing the tithe. Abraham, of whom tithes are first recorded, was immensely rich in consequence (Gen. 13: 2). Malachi, the last of the prophets of the Old Testament, said:

Bring ye the whole tithe into the store house, that there may be food in my house, and prove me now herewith saith Jehovah of hosts, if I will not open you the windows of heaven and pour you out a blessing such that there shall not be room enough to receive it (Mal. 3: 10).

Our Savior said, " It is more blessed to give than to receive " (Acts 20: 35), and yet the church remains indifferent or hostile to this blessed institution of God.

If it be said that the tithe was fulfilled and done away, we reply that the record does not show it. The stewardship of which it was and is the symbol has never been done away; and besides, obligations resting upon the very nature of our being are not ceremonial and dispensational. The tithe is such an obligation. It is not arbitrary, but is for man's good, just as the Sabbath, or marriage, or worship, or honesty. These things are right, therefore they are also profitable, and are to be perpetuated during all the age of man on this earth. Volumes of testimony from those who practice tithing now might be given to sustain this verdict of the Scriptures and of history. The late Thomas Kane of Chicago for over thirty years collected testimony in answer to the question, "Do you know of any exception to the rule that God prospers in their temporal affairs those who honor Him by setting apart one-tenth of their income?" Although the question was put to many millions of people he says that almost no testimony against tithing worthy of the name was received. On the contrary many thousands have eagerly testified to the great increase of temporal blessings which followed the observance of this law of God.

(2) *If God blesses even in temporal affairs those who honor Him with the tithe, how much more will spiritual blessings follow.* The stingy Christian is a powerless Christian. When Israel robbed God the light of the nation waned. The testimony of the church to-day might be multiplied in power many fold by a return to God's law of giving. When Jesus was on earth He sat over against the treasury and watched the people give, and judged their hearts by the giving (Luke 21: 1-4). Does He not behold His treasury to-day? Does He not know when we rob Him? Does He not bless when we are faithful? Can we play the part of Ananias and Sapphira and escape judgment (Acts 5)? Nay, nay. But if we give as did the

early church, we, like they, shall take our food "with gladness and singleness of heart, praising God and finding favor with all the people" (Acts 2: 47).

4. TITHING IS PRACTICABLE IN THIS AGE. It is often said, "Tithing was adapted to that day, but not to this, and therefore we may modify the method of giving." We beg to ask, Why is tithing less practicable now than then? Are farmers more stupid that they cannot count their income? Are business men more ignorant of methods of bookkeeping? Are we not able to keep our other accounts with accuracy? Why not the tithe account as well? The matter is simple when we get the principle right and the heart ready. Only remember that the amount to be tithed is the income remaining after deducting cost of conducting the business, but not deducting cost of living. Increase of wealth is also to be tithed. Such increase can be reckoned at convenient intervals. Rigby, in *Christ Our Creditor* explains as follows:

First, all debts and expenses incurred in order to produce an income are to be deducted from the gross receipts. In other words, all money expended for wages, rents, insurance, taxes, advertising, traveling, or other **necessary expenses,** is to be counted as capital invested, not as increase, and therefore not to be tithed. Second, no debt or expenses incurred for other than business purposes are to be deducted from the increase before it is tithed; that is to say, no person in any pursuit, may deduct any sum for home, or living, or personal purposes of whatever sort, from the profits of his industry, until he has deducted the Lord's tenth. He may not feed or clothe himself or his family, pay his house rent, insurance or taxes, educate his children, speculate in property, or otherwise use money which does not belong to him. For all right and reasonable uses God has graciously allowed us so much of nine-tenths as may be essential to our well-being and comfort, but the first tenth is God's tenth, just as the first day of every seven days is now the Lord's day—neither of which is ours to use for our own selfish or sacrilegious purposes.

The Tithe

It is idle to say that the church is following a better standard in giving without any definite rule. A very few may be giving more than the tenth, but the vast majority are giving scarcely a tenth of a tenth. Recent statistics show that the average income of American families is about six hundred dollars. Now suppose a congregation has only fifty families in it, the tithe would yet amount to three thousand dollars a year. How many churches of this size are giving anything like this amount? Men with incomes of six hundred dollars instead of giving sixty dollars make their subscription five dollars and think they are shining lights! Churches are pastorless and mission fields are unoccupied because they who claim to be God's people rob God of His sacred tenth and excuse themselves by saying, "It is not practicable in this age!" What shall He some day say to them?

IV. Offerings: An Application of Stewardship.

The observance of the tithe is not the end of giving. The tithe is a debt, a symbol of God's ownership of all. It must be paid as a matter of rent. Over and above that, our love for God will find expression in free will offerings. The Jews in the dim light of the law had many of these. Should we in the light of the Gospel have less?

It is sometimes said that tithing does not bear equally on rich and poor, but that matter is equalized by the further duty of offerings. The principle of stewardship requires that, not only shall the rental of one tenth be paid, but all the nine-tenths must be used as the owner directs. Is it the will of God that the nine-tenths shall be spent selfishly? Have the rich a right to live in luxury just because they "can afford it"? When Jesus demanded self-denial as an essential condition of discipleship, He made no exceptions of the rich. Self-denial means the denial of self, and that means the cross,—death to selfishness. John Wesley set the right example for all in his practice. When his salary was thirty pounds a year he lived on twenty-eight and gave the other two. When later he received a hundred and fifty he still lived on twenty-eight and gave all the rest. It will never do to substitute a bequest for the living example of self-denial. Jesus said, "If any man would come after me, let him deny himself and take up his cross daily and follow me" (Luke 14: 33). When in the baptismal grave we buried the old self, we rose a "new creature" (Col. 3: 1-10) with "affections set on things above," and not on fun and feasting and selfish pleasure-seeking, including many such things "of the which I tell you before that they which do such things shall not inherit the kingdom of God" (Gal. 5: 21, 24). Reason a moment. The price of that big Sunday dinner, or those fine ornaments, or year's supply of tobacco, &c., would pay for so much preaching, by voice or tract, which would result in conversions. You know this, and when you spend your time or money uselessly do you not in reality say, "Rather than deny myself of this pleasure I will see my brother die in his sins"? Is this being "faithful over a few things"? (Matt. 25: 23). "Is it a time for you to dwell in your ceiled houses and this house lie waste?" (Hag. 1: 4.) Some one has said, "What I spent for self is lost; what I save I have for the present, but what I give aright is treasure laid up in heaven to be mine forever." Not spasmodic giving, but daily self-denial is required by the gospel of giving.

This custom of offerings was also universal in the apostolic church. In Acts 2: 44, 45, we read that when the Spirit came to the church the resulting liberality was so great that "they had all things common; and they sold their possessions and goods, and parted them all, according as any man had need," and in ch. 4: 34 we read:

For neither was there any among them that lacked; for as many as were possessors of lands or houses sold them, and brought the prices of the things that were sold, and laid them at the apostles' feet; and distribution was made unto each, according as any one had need.

In the *Didache* (65-100 A. D.) the command is to give the first fruits for the support of prophets and teachers, or, if the church were without these, for the poor. (*Didache* 13.) In this period such offerings were so large that they covered and included the tithe, but later they diminished, and then the church leaders insisted on the law of the tithe being observed, even if the spirit of giving did not prompt the church to liberal offerings in addition.

Proof that the church at first included the tithe with the offerings, but was so free in giving that they called the whole " offerings " rather than " the tithe " is shown by the directions of the *Apostolic Constitutions,* which are a later expansion of the *Didache,* written in the second and revised in the fourth centuries. In directions to the bishop we read:

Let him use those **tenths and first fruits** which are given **according to the command of God,** as a man of God; also let him dispense in a right manner the **free-will offerings** which are brought in on account of the poor, to the orphans, the widows and the afflicted, and strangers in distress, as having that God for the examiner of his accounts who has committed the disposition to him.—Bk. 2, Sec. 4: 1.

V. The Spirit of Stewardship.

It would be a lamentable thing if the acceptance of the tithe should cause any one to give as if impelled by law rather than by love, or to be content with fulfilling the letter rather than the spirit of the command. A little boy was given a small piece of ground to farm and when the things were ripe which he planted on it he joyfully brought the first as a gift of love to his father who gave the ground. He had the spirit of stewardship. When the church has it giving will not be a burden, but a delight. Then several other teachings of the Gospel in regard to giving will come naturally and easily.

1. THE LORD'S WORK SHOULD BE SUSTAINED BY GIVING, NOT BY BEGGING. The Gospel says, "Taking nothing of the Gentiles" (3 John 7). God has ever emphatically insisted upon the separation of His people from the world (Judges 2: 1, 2; 2 Cor. 6: 14-18) and taught them not to depend upon the Assyrian (Hosea 5: 13), or Egyptian (Isa. 30: 1-4), or Gentiles (3 John 7), or human power alone (2 Chron. 16: 12, 13; Zech. 4: 6). See also Abraham's example (Gen. 14: 21-24). Paul received voluntary offerings (Acts 28: 2-10), such as Christ sustained (Luke 10: 7), but there is absolutely no Scripture warrant or precedent for begging the world to support the church of the living God. Nor is there any need of it; but half practice the gospel of giving and there will be full treasuries of consecrated gifts.

2. THE CHURCH SHOULD AVOID DEBT. The Gospel says, "Owe no man anything, but to love one another" (Rom. 13: 8). Whatever be our thought on this text, the fact remains that Müller, Spurgeon, Simpson and others, whom God greatly blessed, refused to go into debt, relying upon the Scripture promise of support. It is nice to have a fine church, but many a fine church is a monument of folly, from whose expensive pillars grins the spectre of debt. It is better to dwell in the wilderness than ride on the beast of worldly power. It will help the kingdom more to turn money into Bibles or preaching than into a needless pile of brick. The great work of the church is to evangelize the world, not to build costly cathedrals (Matt. 24: 14; Acts

15: 14-17). If the church will stick to its mission and give as God ordained there will never be need of debt.

3. GIVING SHOULD BE UNIVERSAL. The Gospel says, " Let EVERY ONE of you lay by him in store " (1 Cor. 16: 2). It is as much the duty of all to observe the grace of giving as it is to observe any other virtue. Children should be taught to observe it from their youth up. The poor members of the church should be like the poor widow whom Jesus commended (Mark 12: 42). No one is poorer by observing the Sabbath. Instead, those who keep it faithfully are most prosperous and get the most work done in the end. So the poor should observe the tithe as a means of overcoming poverty. Many are poor and " cursed with a curse " because they have robbed God to feed their own base appetites. Of course there are worthy poor and there are times of special need when the tithe should be used for family necessities. These are cases of pulling the ox out of the ditch. They are exceptions, not the rule. God forbid that we should allow such exceptions to usurp the place of God's rule.

4. THE GOSPEL OF STEWARDSHIP SHOULD BE PRACTICED CHEERFULLY. " God loveth a cheerful giver " (2 Cor. 9: 7), literally a " hilarious " giver. A faithful consecration of the Lord's portion of our time (one-seventh) makes the other six more blessed and fruitful. The same is true of His portion of our income. Giving is not a matter of raising enough money for current expenses; it is a means of grace. Therefore we ought not to stop because there is no special call for money, but keep on putting aside the Lord's tenth, the holy tithe, just as we keep the Lord's day sacred whether there is preaching or not. Thus entering into the purpose and spirit of giving, what has been a tax will become a joyful offering.

5. THE REWARD is according to willingness to give rather

than the amount given (2 Cor. 8: 12), and includes both temporal prosperity (Psa. 41: 1; Psa. 37: 3; Prov. 3: 9, 10; Prov. 11: 24; Mal. 3: 10, 11; Luke 6: 38) and eternal reward (Matt. 25: 1; 1 Cor. 3: 14; Rev. 22: 12);—as Jesus said, " In this world an hundredfold with persecutions and in the world to come eternal life " (Mark 10: 29, 30). It is for us to do what we can. God asks nothing more, but *also nothing less.* Many will hesitate to adopt this standard fearing they cannot afford it. Truly one cannot afford not to adopt it. The right way is the best way. The Gospel plan is the only plan. Only try it and you will bless the day you began.

Christian Stewardship.

The servant who knew his Lord's will and made not ready, nor did according to His will shall be beaten with many *stripes.*—Luke 12: 47.

YOU Are a Steward.	If you are a Christian. Or if you are not.	Matt. 25: 14. Luke 19: 14, 27.
The Evil Steward.	Rejects his Master. Embezzles his property. Comes to bad end.	Luke 20: 9-16.
The Careless Steward.	Delays his service. Lives in selfishness. Is surprised and punished.	Luke 12: 41-48.
The Idle Steward.	Buries his talent. Excuses his laziness. Is unexcused in judgment.	Matt. 25: 24-30.
The Faithful Steward.	Uses all for the Master. Returns all with interest. Is amply rewarded.	Luke 19: 12-19.

Your Duty as a Steward.

1. Recognize all as the Lord's. Matt. 25: 14.
2. With a portion in your care. Matt. 25: 14.

The Tithe

3. According to your ability. Matt. 25: 15.

4. To be used for Him. Matt. 25: 27.

5. Reserving a living. 1 Tim. 5: 8; Luke 10: 7.

6. Observing the tithe. Lev. 27: 30; Matt. 23: 23; 1 Cor. 9: 13, 14.

7. With weekly offerings as prospered. 1 Cor. 16: 2.

8. Accepted according to willingness. 2 Cor. 8: 12.

9. Rewarded according to faithfulness. Rev. 22: 12.

10. When you give account at His coming. Luke 19: 15-28.

CONCLUSION: Our Father has given us all things (Acts 17: 25) that He may lead us to Himself (Acts 17: 27; Rom. 2: 4) and make us children (John 1: 12). The Master has given to each a stewardship according to ability (Matt. 25: 15). The tithe is a recognition of this stewardship, but all we have we are to use for Him (Matt. 25: 27) till He comes (Luke 19: 13), when we shall give an account of our stewardship (Matt. 25: 20), and receive our eternal reward (Matt. 16: 27).

O the peace that comes from the consciousness that whether the Lord shall return at night or at noonday we are ready! O the faith that will look at the things of the world and say, "I suffer the loss of all things and do count them but refuse, that I may gain Christ" (Philpp. 3: 8.)! Herein is love. Herein is the secret of the blessed life. Herein is the gospel of giving. May you, dear reader, practice it more and more as a faithful and wise steward (Luke 12: 42, 44), that having been faithful over a few things you may be made ruler over many things in the kingdom of our coming Lord (Matt. 25: 23; Rev. 22: 12).

Consecration.

Lord all is thine
Nor aught is mine
   To claim;
Thou gavest me
I give to thee
   The same.

A tithe to show
The debt I owe
   I pay;
With this I bring
Love's offering
   Each day.

Not half but all
E'en that is small
   To give;
For thee alone
Till life is gone
   I'll live.

THE PURIFYING HOPE: THE COMING OF THE LORD.

In attempting to assist in restoring the ordinances of the church to their proper place, we do not fail to recognize that, after all, they are means of grace adapted to this earth life of God's people. As such they are of vital importance to us, and we do right to contend earnestly for their proper observance, but when John saw the vision of the heavenly Jerusalem coming down he wrote, "I saw no temple therein" (Rev. 21: 22). Coming dispensations will not need these means of grace, because the glorified bodies will not be dominated by the appetites of the flesh. We long for that day. What millennial joys may follow the coming of our Lord we may not fully know until the time, but this we know, that His kingdom which is coming, coming, coming, must have a consummation. And though our Lord reminded us that He might delay His coming, yet the longest delay must have an end. He is coming, coming, and we may not do better in closing the message of this book than to speak of that "blessed hope" (Titus 2: 13), that purifying hope (1 John 3: 3), the coming of our Lord. The hope of His coming was one of the greatest incentives to faithfulness in the apostolic church, and should be in the church to-day.

The most effective way for Satan to get rid of a weapon that wounds him sorely is to get the church to arguing about it instead of using it. Thus the ordinances were first perverted in meaning, then discarded or altered in form, and then the truths for which they stood were largely lost, while the church argued about the forms. The doctrine of the second coming of Christ has also been the subject of argument rather than the inspiration of evangelization. Mr. Moody said concerning it:

> The devil does not want us to see this truth, for nothing would wake up the church so much. The moment a man realizes that Jesus Christ is coming back again to receive His followers to Himself, the world loses its hold on him. Gas stocks and water stocks, and stocks in banks and railroads are of very much less consequence to him then. His heart is free, and he looks for the blessed appearing of his Lord, who at His coming will take him into His blessed kingdom.

I. Seven Difficulties Considered.

Let us prepare the way of the Lord by first considering the difficulties faith in His return must encounter:

1. THE SLOW GROWTH OF THE KINGDOM. Did not Jesus liken the kingdom of heaven to leaven hid in the meal till all was leavened (Matt. 13: 33)? He did, and Christians are leavening the world, but not all the meal becomes leaven. Did He not say, "If I be lifted up I will draw all men unto myself" (John 12: 32)? He did, but so far from converting all before His coming, He says, "When the Son of man cometh shall he find faith on the earth?" (Luke 18: 8.) The kingdom is growing gloriously, but that only prepares the way for the coming of the King, by drawing the line more clearly between the good and the evil. The brighter the light the blinder the heart that rejects it, and soon "He shall gather out of his kingdom all things that cause stumbling, and them that do iniquity" (Matt. 13: 41).

2. CHARACTER MUST BE A GROWTH. The kingdom must be natural, not artificial; a growth, not a product of manufacture. True, but the coming of the Lord is not to compel conversion. It will increase the light, but while many will believe, some will be hardened the more. If miracles were proper to establish faith in Moses (Ex. 4: 9, 17, 28),

The Return of Our Lord

and in Christ and the apostles at the first advent (Acts 2: 22, 43; 14: 3), it can scarcely be said that the return of our Lord will be of no value to faith.

3. HIS COMING ABSURD. So it seems to the scoffer, or to those who localize the Deity, but to those who have faith in His omnipresence, it is easy to think of His coming without any other part of the universe being robbed of His spiritual presence. If we believe that Jesus came in humiliation, it ought not to be impossible to believe that He can come in glory.

4. THE MILLENNIUM MENTIONED ONLY IN REV. 20. The fact of the return does not depend upon this passage. Besides, many find hints at least of the millennium in other passages. See 2 Tim. 2: 12; Zech. 8: 20-23; 14: 16-21; Isa. 2: 2-5; 4; 11: 1-12; 25; 65: 18-25; Mic. 4: 1-44.

5. THE APOCALYPTIC LANGUAGE OF SOME PROPHECIES. The *fact* of the coming does not depend on whether the language describing it is literal or figurative. The manner may be affected, but the fact remains.

6. JESUS PREDICTED HIS RETURN IN THAT GENERATION (Matt. 24: 32-34). It is not certain that He did. The disciples asked Him three things (Matt. 24: 3) : (1) the end of the (Jewish) age, (2) His own coming, and (3) the end of the world. His reply dealt with three questions, but what He said is not clearly divided in the account. If we had it complete, there probably would be no difficulty. However even Jesus did not know the *time* of His return (Matt. 24: 36), and though He spoke of His coming "in His kingdom" as near (Matt. 16: 28) He may have referred there to the spiritual coming. On the other hand, He gives many intimations that His personal return might be long delayed. He is the Master who returned "after a long time" to reward His servants (Matt. 25: 19), the one of whom they said, "he delayeth his com-

ing" (Matt. 24: 48), and again "the bridegroom tarried" (Matt. 25: 5) and the nobleman went "into a far country" to receive a kingdom (Luke 19: 12). Jesus purposely left the time of His coming so vague, that every generation might be expecting it.

7. THE APOSTLES EXPECTED IT IN THEIR DAY. That was perfectly consistent with their inspiration in other things, because they were expressly told that they were not to know the time of this event (Matt. 24: 36; Acts 1: 7), but were to watch and be ready, and to teach the church to do likewise.

II. Seven Errors Corrected.

Many say, "O yes, I believe in the coming, but not a personal coming; He comes in other ways." Very true, but these other ways do not take the place of the coming at the end of this age.

1. NOT THE RESURRECTION OF JESUS. The return is not the resurrection of Jesus, because it was announced after that event (Acts 1: 11).

2. NOT PENTECOST. Jesus is here in spirit, but He is not to be identified in person with the Holy Spirit (John 14: 26, &c.). His coming was also predicted after Pentecost (1 Thess. 1: 9, 10; 3: 13; Heb. 9: 24-28, &c.).

3. NOT THE DESTRUCTION OF JERUSALEM. That event did not exhaust the promise, because, while many prophetic passages refer to this event, yet Jerusalem did not say "Blessed is he" at its destruction (Matt. 23: 39), nor did Jesus then receive the disciples to Himself (John 14: 3). The end of the Jewish age was the beginning of the "times of the Gentiles" (Luke 21: 24), but they shall have an end and the Lord shall come again, at the "times of restoration of all things" (Acts 3: 21).

4. NOT THE GROWTH OF THE KINGDOM. In a very real

The Return of Our Lord

sense, Christ comes in this way, but this coming cannot answer to the " like manner in which ye have seen him go " of Acts 1: 11 or to the rapture of 1 Thess. 4: 13 or to the implications of many other passages. The gradual coming of the kingdom must have its consummation at some time, in some way; and when, unless " when he shall appear " ?

5. IT IS NOT CONVERSION. Conversion only gives the greater joy to the hope of Christ's final coming. The apostles were converted, but they hoped for another coming of the Lord. Thus did Paul (Philpp. 3: 20, 21), Peter (1 Pet. 5: 1-4), Jude (Jude 14, 15), James (Jas. 5: 7, 8), and the author of Hebrews (ch. 9: 28).

6. IT IS NOT DEATH. The Scriptures speak of death as a going to Jesus (Philpp. 1: 23). They call death an enemy (1 Cor. 15: 25), but hail the coming of Jesus as the dearest event on the calendar of time, because at His coming shall death, the last great enemy, be destroyed.

7. IT IS NOT THE RESURRECTION. The resurrection ("each in his own order"), is connected with His coming (1 Cor. 15: 50, 51), but this is only one of the events and is not to be identified as the coming itself.

Is there any other way than these seven, in which Jesus comes, save that which was the comfort and hope of the apostles, and should be of the church to-day? Consider the following passages, and see if they can be consistently referred to any of these seven comings just mentioned, or if they must be referred to another coming, yet future, but near.

If I go away I will come again and receive you unto myself.—John 14: 3.

This Jesus, who was received up into heaven, shall so come in like manner as ye beheld him going into heaven.—Acts 1: 11.

But each in his own order: Christ the first fruits; then they that are Christ's, at his coming.—1 Cor. 15: 23.

So Christ also having been once offered to bear the sins of many, shall appear the second time, apart from sin, to them that wait for him, unto salvation.—Heb. 9: 28.

For many deceivers are gone forth into the world, **even** they that confess not that Jesus Christ cometh in the flesh.—2 John 7.

For this we say unto you by the word of the Lord, that we that are alive, that are left unto the coming of the Lord, shall in nowise precede them that are fallen asleep. For the Lord himself shall descend from heaven, with a shout, with the voice of the archangel, and with the trump of God; and the dead in Christ shall rise first; then we that are alive, that are left, shall together with them be caught up in the clouds, to meet the Lord in the air: and so shall we be ever with the Lord.— 1 Thess. 4: 15-17.

III. Seven Signs of His Coming.

It is not for us to know the day nor the hour (Matt. 24: 36) nor "the times and seasons which the Father hath set within his own authority" (Acts 1: 7), but there are certain signs of Christ's coming which may be recognized when it is near at hand. They are such that every generation has believed their fulfillment at hand, and hence has sustained the attitude of expectancy, but it is for us to know them and to learn from them. From the parable of the fig tree (Luke 21: 29-33) we learn that as the putting forth of leaves indicates the coming of summer, so the natural growth of the kingdom to a certain stage will cause it to put forth the leaves that indicate the approach of the millennial summer of the world. And the coming of the leaves of the fig tree is no more in conformity to natural law than is the coming of our Lord in the fulness of time. The dispensations move on with the rhythm of the universe and when the clock of eternity strikes the hour (Acts 3: 20, 21) the Lord Himself will appear.

1. THE SIGN OF TRAVEL AND KNOWLEDGE.

The Return of Our Lord

Seal up the book until the time of the end: many shall run to and fro and knowledge shall be increased.—Dan. 12: 4.

The use of steam and electricity has revolutionized travel. Where one person made a journey of a hundred miles fifty years ago, a hundred persons go a thousand miles now. It is estimated that the number of railroad passengers of the world in one year is about three billion, while the mileage is about thirty billion miles. Add to this the travel by steamboat, automobile and other conveyance, and note that the rate is increasing by leaps and bounds. Only recently the principle of the gyroscope has been applied to ships and railway cars, and it is predicted that it will again revolutionize travel. Balanced by a mighty fly wheel revolving at high velocity there will be palaces on wheels flying across country on single rails, at treble the speed of present trains. And with the progress that is being made in aeroplanes and air ships, who does not expect to see the aerial ocean traversed with greater ease and speed than now we sail over the briny deep?

And mark that this sign is seen in all the world. The Cape to Cairo railway is about to deliver passengers from one end of Africa to the other. A railroad is building from Jerusalem in Judea to Mecca in Arabia. Russia is double-tracking across Siberia and pushing down through Persia. France with the iron horse is crossing the desert of Sahara. China is granting railway franchises throughout her vast empire. South America has two transcontinental railroads about completed.

Travel means the distribution of knowledge. As the nations of the world get together they learn from each other. It is not surprising, therefore, that China is opening up schools of modern learning by the thousand, and sending her young people abroad to fit themselves for teachers. Several of the South American republics have appealed to

Protestant Mission Boards of the United States to help to supply them with school teachers. The American Government is calling for hundreds of teachers for the Philippines. At a recent conference of Mohammedans at Mecca, it was declared that their missions had failed because they fail to educate their women. They, too, are turning to modern learning.

The printing press has revolutionized learning. As some one has said, "We can buy more now for fifty cents than all the ancient philosophers ever knew." Newspapers and magazines, Chautauqua assemblies and reading circles, lecture courses and travel clubs, colleges and universities,— there is no end to the opportunities for knowledge that are before the youth of this generation. And there are other things, as the spread of a universal language, and increasing ease of travel and communication, that will vastly increase these facilities for knowledge in the years before us.

2. THE SIGN OF APOSTASY.

In the last days grievous (kalepoi, "hard to bear") times shall come. For men shall be lovers of self, lovers of money, boastful, haughty, railers, disobedient to parents, unthankful, unholy, without natural affection, implacable, slanderers, without self-control, fierce, no lovers of good, traitors, headstrong, puffed up, lovers of pleasure rather than lovers of God; holding a form of godliness, but denying the power thereof (2 Tim. 3: 1-5).

This sign might perhaps more than any other be applied to every age, for as the light of knowledge and the Gospel grows brighter they who resist it make themselves that much the worse. In many ways, the world is better now than it ever was before, but this only makes the wickedness of the wicked the more inexcusable, and their apostasy the more apparent. In spite of the growth of the kingdom there has also been a growth of crime. Statistics show that the number of suicides, murders, divorces and crimes of all kinds is increasing faster than the population, even in America. So noticeable is the disobedience of children that the National Teachers' Association, numbering many thousands, at its meeting at Los Angeles (1907) passed a resolution deploring the fact and calling for more instruction along this line in the public schools. The operation of many causes has made it impossible for most of the denominations to secure sufficient pastors for their churches. The mystery of iniquity was at work in Paul's day (2 Thess. 2: 8), but has been going on toward its culmination, and the long "last hour" marked by the "many antichrists of 1 John 2: 18, must sometime end." The church will be in a lukewarm state when Jesus comes. It certainly will be in that state soon if the present tendency to slight whatever commandments are not agreed upon continues. The evangelical forces are federating, and some that are not evangelical are clamoring to join the federation. We hear of "labor churches" being organized, and many consider their lodges as on a level with the church. When we have a union of all of these, as some propose, there will be indeed a Babylon such as is described as a part of the apostasy of the last times. Deplore it though we may, the very thing that will seem to many to be good, will be the delusion of the antichrist.

3. THE SIGN OF RENEWED DEMONIACAL ACTIVITY.

But the Spirit saith expressly that in later times some shall fall away from the faith, giving heed to seducing spirits and dictrines of demons, through the hypocrisy of men that speak lies, branded in their own consciences as with a hot iron; forbidding to marry, &c.—1 Tim. 4: 1-3.

This is worthy of mention as a special sign because it is one of the things that the Spirit mentioned "expressly." Spiritualism is an ancient evil (Lev. 20: 27), but it has had its revival in our own day. Beginning a generation ago, Spiritualism has grown until it claims over a million of adherents. We would not include in it the number of those who for the sake of science are making honest investigations of psychic phenomena, but refer to that host of charlatans who feed on the credulity of the public which they delude. If it is the will of God that the living should communicate with the dead, the way will open to do so in creditable ways, but the fruit of modern spiritualism is such that it cannot stand the Gospel test (1 John 4: 1-3) "Prove the spirits * * * Every spirit that confesseth not Jesus is not of God." The leading spiritualist papers are filled with blasphemies against Christ and the Bible. And yet one of them, *The Progressive Thinker,* confesses that "ninety-nine times out of a hundred if you catch the spirit at a materializing seance you will have the medium or a confederate." One time at a regular open service, we heard the worshipers(?) use Gospel hymn tunes to free-love songs. That there are devout Christians who believe in spiritualism we do not deny, but we only state facts and submit them to the judgment of all. In a mass of trickery there are phenomena by a few abnormal persons that are mysterious, but because the fruit of the movement is evil we must class it where the Gospel puts it, and beware of its recrudescence as a sign of the last days.

4. THE SIGN OF THE MASSING OF WEALTH.

Come now ye rich, weep and howl for your miseries that are coming upon you. Your riches are corrupted, and your garments are moth-eaten. Your gold and silver are rusted; and their rust shall be for a testimony against you, and shall eat your flesh as fire. Ye have laid up your treasure in the last days (Jas. 5: 1-8).

Increase in travel and invention has opened up the treasure chest of the world and the consequent massing of wealth is a phenomenon of this present generation. Ten men in America are estimated to be worth $200,000,000 apiece, which means an income of a million a month. Seventy other men have fortunes averaging $35,000,000 while 5,000 men together are rated at $15,000,000,000, or one sixth of the wealth of the country.

On the other hand one-third of the people have incomes of less than $400, one-half less than $600, and two-thirds of less than $900.

Patrick Henry said: "When Egypt went down 3 per cent of the people owned 97 per cent of the wealth. When Babylon went down 2 per cent of the people owned all of the wealth. When Persia went down 1 per cent of the people owned all of the land. When Rome went down 1800 men owned the world." We may apply his words to the world to-day. The significance of the figures as to the wealth of a few is chiefly in the fact that the massing of wealth is rapidly increasing. If, even in America, the land of equality and opportunity, these conditions have become alarming, what shall be said of other lands where they are very much worse?

5. THE SIGN OF THE RESTORATION OF ISRAEL.

A hardening in part hath befallen Israel until the fulness of the Gentiles be come in: and so all Israel shall be saved; even as it is written. (cf. Isa. 59: 19-21.)

Advocates of the advent may sometimes use passages to show a future restoration of Israel, which were not so intended, but there are some which, by accepted rules of interpretation, we can not easily refer to any past return, or even to the spiritual Israel composed of Christian believers (Rom. 4: 16, 17). Such, for instance, is the statement of Jesus, "Jerusalem shall be trodden down of the Gentiles until the times of the Gentiles be fulfilled" (Luke

21: 24). Such also is the prophecy of Amos (ch. 9: 14, 15 and Isaiah 66: 20-22. See also Ezekiel, chapters 36 and 37).

Is Israel being restored in our day? Just 1260 years after the capture of Jerusalem by the Mohammedans, the Zionist congress met, and organized and authorized the raising of $50,000,000 to buy back the Holy Land. It is said that they now have $200,000,000 in the banks of Europe ready for the purchase. Meanwhile the Turkish government is in the toils of debt, and it is likely that at any time the world may witness the Jews, by common agreement of the nations, being allowed to possess once more the land that was promised to their fathers four thousand years ago. It is true there is a "liberal" branch of the Jews that scoff in unbelief, but as the promises of old were fulfilled through the righteous remnant, so now the restoration will be through that vast mass of orthodox Jews who pray every morning, "Save us, O God of our salvation, and gather us together and deliver us from the nations." Already they are gathering into Palestine in great numbers. Already the fig tree is budding. Soon the leaves shall be apparent to all, and then, "Know you that he is nigh, even at the door."

6. THE SIGN OF THE UNIFICATION OF THE WORLD.

Making known unto us the mystery of his will, according to his good pleasure which he purposed in him, unto a dispensation of the fulness of times, to sum up all things in Christ (Eph. 1: 10).

The God of the Bible is also the God of the world. He guides the destinies of all nations, and not of the Jews only. The busy world has not known Him, yet unconsciously has been preparing for the universal empire which has been the dream of ages. Geniuses of the past have tried to establish such an empire, but one and all have failed. Is it coming now? What are the signs of the unification of the world and preparation for one universal empire, such as is to exist under the reign of our Lord?

(1) *Commerce* is uniting the world. The commercial interests of the nations is one of the strongest factors in bringing about a federation of the world.

(2) The world is moving toward a *universal language,* which shall undo the mischief of Babel. What shall it be? Of all the existing languages, the noble *English* is far in advance and is forging still farther ahead. The English flag floats in all seas, and in all Anglo-Saxon colonies is supplanting the native languages. In India it is taking the place of the three hundred or more native dialects. In China there is a mania for learning English. It is the richest and best of languages and may yet win its way to all nations.

Or it may be that *Esperanto* will prevail as a secondary language. It is a new and artificial language that is so simple that one can buy a grammar for a penny, learn it in a week and in two or three months be able to read and speak with ease. Moreover, it is precise and elegant and rich. There are already many journals published in this language and many clubs for study in all parts of the civilized world. Part of the World's Christian Endeavor Convention at Geneva, Switzerland, in 1905, was held in Esperanto, and Esperanto congresses have brought enthusiastic delegates from all the leading nations. It is recognized as a modern language in Europe and therefore may be used for letters and telegrams. The name Esperanto means "hope" and is significant of the larger hope of the universal reign of our Lord. The use of one language by all nations will do much to unify the world.

(3) *Invention* has been the handmaid of Christianity.

Under the providence of God, invention has not been allowed to run ahead of the moral progress of the world, but has kept pace with it. When the time was ripe for the Reformation, the compass enabled Columbus to sail to America, and the printing press afforded a means of propagating the Gospel. Now that the world is ripening for universal brotherhood, invention has made possible the material side of it. We are talking across oceans and continents without wires and soon, perhaps, shall see as well. The world has become a community, and needs only the Gospel leaven to complete the preparation for the coming of the Lord.

7. THE SIGN OF THE EVANGELIZATION OF THE WORLD.

And this Gospel of the kingdom shall be preached in the whole world for a testimony unto all the nations: and then shall the end come (Matt. 24: 14).

The other signs give cumulative evidence that is very strong, but when this one is fulfilled *THEN SHALL THE END COME*. Is it about fulfilled?

Silently and steadily as the morning light advances, the Gospel has been moving into all the world with light and life. At the end of the first five hundred years, there were ten million Christians; at the end of one thousand years, there were fifty millions; at the end of fifteen hundred years, there were one hundred millions, and now, at less than two thousand years, there are about five hundred millions of nominal Christians, while Christian nations govern five hundred million of the one billion heathen.

Note how the growth has not only been continuous, but has been gathering momentum. During the past five hundred years, Christianity has gained five times as many adherents as in the previous fifteen hundred years. That means that the rate of growth has been fifteen times as rapid. Moreover, most of this great increase has come in the present century. Professor Gulick shows by statistics that *more people have come under the influence of Christianity during the past century than in all the first thousand years.*

Now look at the map and you will see that Christianity has spread over most of the territory of the world. According to the *Statesmen's Year Book* for 1894, the area under the rule of the various governments is 49,100,000 square miles. Of this, 17,417,000 square miles are ruled by Protestant nations; 14,147,100 are under Roman Catholic rule; 8,852,700 are under the Greek Church, and 8,782,800 are under heathen rulers. That means that about eighty-two per cent of the land surface of the world is under Christian governments, and the Protestants alone rule twice as much as all the heathen. What is more, the remaining heathen governments are, for the most part, so incompetent that they must be regenerated by the Gospel or soon pass under the control of Christian nations More than that, two thirds of the population of the world to-day is under governments which are Christian at least in name.

More than that, the strategic points in the world's conquest are in the hands of Christians. Christian nations possess the richest lands, and those located in the temperate zone. In Asia, England holds India, and in alliance with Japan will exert an enormous influence in the regeneration of China. In Africa, England holds Egypt at one end and the Transvaal at the other, and is building a railroad from Cairo to Capetown which will help to bind the dark continent with the bands of Christian civilization. The United States is sure to have a moulding influence over all of Central and South America and already has a large influence over China and Japan, while students by the hundreds are coming from these countries to be educated in our universities. Protestant Christianity occupies a stragetic place, because it has possession of most of the colleges of the world and is winning the educated classes. Protestant teachers are being called to positions in the countries that are just awakening, such as China and Japan. When modern education permeates the heathen lands, the idols will totter and the cross shall be exalted.

But what of the character of the Christianity that is folding the world like a garment? It is charged that the Church is losing its purity and power. It would be of little value to the world to be dominated by a paganized type of Christianity like that of South America or Russia, but it is not that type that is coming to dominate. It is the Anglo-Saxon and Teutonic races that are dominant, and these hold to the Protestant form of Christianity. Protestantism is already far in the lead and is growing more rapidly than Catholicism, Greek and Roman combined. Under aggressive Protestant missionary work South America and Russia are destined to undergo a reformation.

Heathen religions grow old and die, but Christianity purges itself, and, like a vine that is trimmed, springs up to greater power and beauty, because the divine Spirit is in it. The most spiritual portion of the church is most missionary in spirit, and therefore it is this portion that is destined to prevail.

We point to the early church as a model, but even it had its disorders and divisions and incompleteness of organization. We speak of the devotion of the Pilgrims and Puritans, but they were a chosen few out of a mass of different spirit, and even they had their lotteries for raising church money, their bear-baiting and liquor drinking, their witchcraft and slavery. With all the follies and avarice and pride and heresy and apostasy that curse the church to-day, it is (the faithful part of it) a better church than the world has ever seen since the days of the apostles.

The Christianity of to-day is *more rational* than ever before. Some of the errors and superstitions of the Dark Ages still persist, but the wide diffusion of the Scriptures and more intelligent methods of study are causing truth to prevail. The authority of the Bible is the authority of truth, and the best apology for the church is its good works and intrinsic worth. The searchlight of criticism turned on the foundations of Christianity reveals the fact that they are firm. There is a larger percentage of Christians among scientific students and educated men than among any other class.

With faith in Christianity resting on a firm and rational basis, and backed by the testimony of experience, there has come a *larger liberality*. Formerly, men were burned at the stake because they opposed the Pope. In European museums, we saw the instruments of torture used in the inquisition. They have no place now save in museums.

And then Christianity is *more practical* than in the past. It has passed through the period of speculation and organization and is entering the period of application. A few years ago, Josiah Strong wrote a little book called *The Next Great Revival,* in which he pointed out that evangelistic work in this century would likely transform social and business life. We are seeing his words come true. In the world-wide kingdom, whose morning streamers tint the sky, the Gospel of love shall rule in every department of life.

In the study of natural science, we have watched the development of a fish from the egg, and have seen the formation of the veins and heart, the coloration of the blood and the first pulsations of the heart sending the red blood into all parts of the body, giving it the power of sensation and motion. So we may witness the work of the Spirit of God in quickening the public conscience; and from the tinglings and first weak pulsations see the coming of the day when the kingdoms of this world shall become the kingdom of our Lord.

And what an array of *organizations* have sprung up to help in the application of Christian love, which in various ways are making real in life the spirit of caring for more than self. It is this orthodox, active, Christo-centric, practical Protestant form of Christianity that is leading in the conquest of the world. In the midst of the final apostasy, this is the " righteous remnant " that shall prevail. International organizations also are binding the nations together with ties so strong that they cannot be severed by the sword. At the World's Christian Endeavor Conventions we have seen the flags of all nations floating over the young people gathered from the four corners of the earth to promote the kingdom of God, and have heard the different national songs followed by " Blest be the tie that binds." With such forces behind the thrones of this world, it is not strange that arbitration is the watchword of the present hour, and disarmament shall be that of the next, even though the long expected final war may intervene.

Let us notice also how the *barriers to mission work have been removed*. A hundred years ago there were very few places open to mission work on account of the hostility of the heathen; now, there are few places that are closed. The doors that are opening in great China and Russia and South America are a challenge to the church to enter in. Even Thibet is now wide open. Afghanistan, Turkey, with parts of Arabia and Persia, are still partly closed to the missionary, but in various ways the leaven is working even in these places.

Bible colporters are often allowed to go where preachers

of the Gospel are not, and they are opening the way. At the Nashvillle Student Volunteer Convention, we saw a table on which lay Bibles in over four hundred fifty languages. This is the modern miracle of Pentecost, the Spirit speaking in many tongues.

The barrier of poverty has also been removed and the church has all the wealth needed to complete the evangelization of the world in this generation. God has placed in the hands of the Protestant Christian nations the bulk of the wealth of the world. Is not this a stewardship for which we must give an account?

God has also raised up *workers* willing to carry the message. A hundred years ago, William Carey pleaded in vain for a missionary society to send him to India. The church ridiculed the very idea of missions. But now there are twenty-five thousand missionaries on the field and other thousands ready to go.

At Nashville, Tennessee, in 1906, the representatives of the Foreign Boards of forty-seven denominations met, and after comparing notes declared that in order to complete the evangelization of the world in this generation it is only necessary to double our present force. Twenty-five thousand more missionaries on the field in a generation,—is that visionary and absurd? Our government could issue a call to battle and a million men would spring to arms. Will the church for which Christ died do less for Him?

The *money needed* for the missions is also coming. The Layman's Missionary Movement has spread with great rapidity throughout the denominations, and has resulted in interesting the business men in their responsibility. A large committee of wealthy men, at their own charges have visited the mission fields and reported as to their needs. They are gathering in groups in various centers and taking upon their shoulders the task they have so long neglected. The result must be such an increase of funds as will enable the mission boards to meet the demands of their fields.

Above all, the faithful portion of the church is beginning to pray and to watch and to work for Christ's coming as never before. We have already related how in 1902 at the Student Volunteer Convention at Toronto, there was prayer, by the convention that during the four years following there might be a thousand students to volunteer to go to the foreign field, and that at the convention at Nashville four years later it was announced that exactly one thousand had volunteered. Then the convention prayed, not for a thousand in four years, but a thousand every year; and if God answers that prayer, the twenty-five thousand needed to complete the evangelization of the world will be on the field in twenty-five years. Shall it not be done? God honors great faith. He is stirring up the hearts of men, and all around the world to-day there are outbursts of revival flame that are nothing less than Pentecostal in power. From Wales, the outpouring of the Spirit spread through Norway and Sweden. To Australia God called Torrey and Alexander, and around the world the revival has gone like a flame of celestial fire. In India and China, in Burma and Korea, in New Zealand and Madagascar, there are thousands accepting the Gospel. One missionary from Korea said at Nashville that he had won over three thousand converts during the year.

Every Foreign Mission Board is now calling for a large increase of forces to meet the opportunities of their fields. The fourteen million young people in the churches of America are organizing for study and preparation for mission work. Does it not seem possible, nay, even probable, that in spite of the apostasy of a large part of the church this generation shall witness the completion of the evangelization of the world? And does not the coming of such striking fulfillment of all these signs at once mark such an epoch as to cause us to lift up our heads and rejoice for the coming of the Lord draweth nigh! *Marana Tha! The Lord cometh!*

The following passage from the *Teaching of the Apostles*, written while some of them were yet living, is a fitting closing exhortation for us:

Watch for your life's sake. Let not your lamps be quenched, nor your loins unloosed; but be ye ready, for ye know not the hour in which our Lord cometh. But often shall ye come together, seeking the things which are befitting to your souls: for the whole of your faith will not profit you, if ye be not made perfect in the last time. For in the last days false prophets and corruptors shall be multiplied, and the sheep shall be turned into wolves, and love shall be turned into hate; for when lawlessness increaseth, they shall hate and persecute and betray one another, and then shall appear the world-deceiver as the Son of God, and shall do signs and wonders, and the earth shall be delivered into his hands, and he shall do iniquitous things which have never yet come to pass since the beginning. Then shall the creation of men come into the fire of trial, and many shall be made to stumble and shall perish; but they that endure in their faith shall be saved from under the curse itself. And then shall appear **the signs of the truth:** first the sign of an outspreading in heaven; then the sign of the trumpet; and the third, the resurrection of the dead; yet not of all, but as it is said: "The Lord shall come and all his saints with Him." Then shall the world see the Lord coming upon the clouds of heaven.

We will miss the benefit of this discussion of the return of our Lord if we fail to remember that the promise is given as a means of grace. Theories concerning the time and manner of the return may be partly speculative, but the duties which are ours as a result of this hope are very clear.

But suppose that the pre-millennial coloring of this closing chapter should prove to be an illusive vision? Suppose that the apocalyptic expression " coming in the clouds of heaven " should prove to mean only " coming in divine power in the majestic growth of the kingdom, which is ' righteousness and peace and joy in the Holy Spirit ' " (Rom. 14: 17)? What then? Then no message of this book needs to be retracted. Then it is equally our duty to keep the commandments, " God's Means of Grace," that thereby we may attain unto this righteousness and peace and joy in the Holy Spirit. Whether the Master comes in one way or the other, " Blessed are those servants who when the Lord cometh, he shall find watching." And whether the present world crisis means the opening of the portals for our King to reign a thousand years in person, or ten thousand years in His spiritual kingdom,—whether the New Jerusalem is a literal city or a figure of the kingdom, it remains our duty to pray, " Thy kingdom come. Thy will be done on earth as it is in heaven," and then to work in the direction of our prayers by yielding loving obedience ourselves, and pressing the evangelization of the world as the one great mission in life, and to rejoice that in one way or the other the earth shall soon be filled with the glory of God.

In the stillness of an October night we have seen the aurora borealis suddenly flame from horizon to zenith and play about it as it were a throne of glory. Beautiful beyond description was the scene, yet these waves of the electric ocean enfold the world all the while, and needed only a slight change in temperature to make them manifest. So our Lord is with us " all the days " (Matt. 28: 20 Gr.) and it needs only a little more leavening of the Gospel to make Him manifest in glory. Many scientists now teach the vibration theory of existence:—that different forms (as ice, water, steam and vapor, or matter, electricity and life) are possible because of different rates of vibration, the rate increasing from lower to higher forms, and the higher thus being able to penetrate and invest the lower, as water passes through a screen, or light through a glass, or the X-rays through a body, or high tones through lower tones. May it not be that thus it is that the Spirit of God is " over all, and through all, and in all " (Eph. 4: 6)? and that as conversion awakens the organ of the mind by which we perceive the Spirit's influence, so the present awakening of the world-conscience marks the growth of the supremacy of the spiritual to a stage which makes possible the aurora of His presence in glory?

We may admit the gradual growth of the kingdom of God, but we may not deny its crises, and the greatest crisis of its history is upon us.

The world is in its period of adolescence. Beginning with infant innocency, and passing thence through the patriarchal age of dawning conscience, and the age of restraining law, it has come through the Gospel age of grace to the period of the quickening of the new life of the dawning consciousness of maturity. As the adolescent period is the most critical in the life of the child, so it is in the history of the race. When scientists wish to produce a new and more perfect type of plant or animal life they first cross existing varieties and thus produce a hybrid, which, being a mixture is unstable in its tendencies and may thus be easily developed in the desired direction. Luther T. Burbank, the leading demonstrator of this truth, says that by observing the laws of heredity the race can be transformed in a few generations. This means, not only that special care should be given to the boys and girls in the adolescent period, which is the time of change, of apparent fickleness, of strong impressions, and especially of greatest religious susceptibility; but also that we should mark the progress of the race at this period. Invention has made the world a neighborhood, and it is the opportunity of the church to make it a brotherhood. The mingling of the races has produced a hybrid condition of religion. It is an age of change, of fads, of falling away, but also of rising to new heights of faith. It is a time of crisis. It is the dawning of a new age.

And what more can we say? We can but close as we began, with the plea for fidelity to Him " who is and was and is to come ", that when He comes we may be found with the wedding garment of righteousness, with lamps trimmed and burning, and may enter through the gates to sit down with Him at the marriage supper in the city of our God. Ten years ago a Buddhist paper in Japan declared,

"The greatest movement of the twentieth century will be the coming of a vast army of Christian missionaries to invade the east, backed by the wealth of Christendom, and we must prepare to meet them."

May not our Christian faith see not only the going of the church with the Gospel, but the coming of the nations into the kingdom of God, and crowning all, the coming of our Lord Himself. Surely among all the blessed means of grace we must retain this purifying hope.

The following Scriptures should be treasured up as memory gems for times of need.

Seven Duties in View of His Coming.

1. *Holiness.* " Every one that hath this hope set on him purifieth himself even as he is pure."—1 John 3: 1-3.

2. *Patience.* " Be patient therefore brethren, until the coming of the Lord."—James 5: 7, 8.

3. *Forbearance.* " Judge nothing before the time, until the Lord come."—1 Cor. 4: 5.

4. *Faithfulness.* " I charge *thee* in the sight of God, and of Christ Jesus, who shall judge the living and the dead, and by his appearing and his kingdom: preach the word; be urgent in season, out of season; reprove, rebuke, exhort. with all long-suffering and teaching."—2 Tim. 4: 1-4.

5. *Soul-winning.* " For what is our hope, or joy, or crown of rejoicing? Are not even ye, before our Lord Jesus at his coming?" 1 Thess. 2: 19, 20.

6. *Hope.* " Henceforth there is laid up for me the crown of righteousness which the Lord, the righteous judge shall give me at that day, and not for me only, but for all them that love his appearing."—2 Tim. 4: 8.

7. *Comfort.* " So shall we ever be with the Lord. Wherefore comfort one another with these words,"—1 Thess. 4: 17, 18.

The Sevenfold Warning to Watch.

Watch therefore; for ye know not on what day your Lord cometh (Matt. 24: 42). **Watch** therefore, for ye know not the day nor the hour (Matt. 25: 13). Take ye heed, **watch** and pray; for ye know not when the time is. . . . **Watch,** therefore: for ye know not when the lord of the house cometh, whether at even, or at midnight, or at cock crowing, or in the morning; lest coming suddenly he find you sleeping. And what I say unto you I say unto all, **watch** (Mark 13: 33-37). If therefore thou shalt not **watch,** I will come on thee as a thief (Rev. 3: 3, 11). Blessed is he that **watcheth,** and keepeth his garments (Rev. 16: 15).

AS SEEING HIM WHO IS INVISIBLE. Heb. 11: 27.

"He endured as seeing Him who is invisible,"
   And you, my soul, endure as seeing Him!
What though the way be rough with bitter trial,
   And joys of life be clouded o'er and dim?
What though your earthly hopes are torn and shattered?
   What though your earthly plans must each one fail?
Endure, as seeing Him, as yet invisible,
   Save as the soul meets Him within the veil.

O soul, get free from all the weight and bondage
   Of selfish flesh, of clinging worldly cares;
The Father, coming out to meet thy yielding,
   Doth heed thy supplicating tears and prayers.
This span of time in God's great arch eternal
   Is passing swiftly onward from our view;
O rise to see **Him**,—Him who **never** passes,
   Whose love is endless as His Word is true.

Endure unto the end. Night passes; dawn is breaking.
   Be ready, for thy Savior's call to thee:
What matter **then** what trials have crossed thy pathway,
   What stormy billows tossed thee on life's sea?
Behold He cometh! O my soul! As, clothed upon
   With immortality you meet Him in the skies,
And see Him as He is, 'twill well reward thee
   To have one glance of welcome from His eye.

So may I live as seeing Him invisible
   To mortal eye, but present with the soul;
As unto Him perform each humble duty,
   The daily task, or seeming fruitless toil.
Each uttered word, as heard by Him who listens;
   Each simple act as guided by His Word,
That when He comes, my soul may, earth forgetting
   Leap forth to be forever with the Lord.

                       —Mrs. H. W. Robinson.

SUBJECT INDEX

A Clean Heart (poem). 532.
Adornment. 470.
Agape. 361. See Love-Feast.
Altar of Sacrifice. 45.
American Revised Bible. 14.
Anointing the Sick. 436.
Antitypes of Tabernacle. 45.
Apostasy. 597.
Arbitration. 500, 509.
Archæology and Baptism. 156.
Ark and Baptism. 120.
Arius. 251.
Asecticism. 461.
Atonement. Taught in O. T., 37; 45; triple dipping before, 122.

Backsliders. 326.
Baptism. Discussion of, 120; Foreshadowings of, 120; Jewish trine immersion, 123; of proselytes, 124; by John, 125; Christian, 126; Meaning of, 127; Subjects of, 133; of infants, 134; of households, 138; Mode, 148; causes of confusion, 149; Ten lines of evidence, 150; Meaning of **baptizo**, 151; Figurative use, 155; Greek words for sprinkle and pour, 157; Meaning and mode, 183; Spirit and water, 189; Scripture examples, 190; Scripture objections, 204; Early church examples, 216; Historical objections, 204; Greek church, 243; Early baptistries, 244; Origin of single immersion, 248; of pouring, 254; of sprinkling, 255; Combination of modes, 258; Tri-une immersion the dominant mode, 259; Proper place, 261; Time, 262; Administrator, 264; Attendant ceremonies, 266; Rebaptism, 267; poem, 273.
Bazaleel. 45.
Beauty. 473.
Beecher. On the church, 28; On feet-washing, 345.
Bible. A. R. V., 14; Relation of O. T. and N. T., 38; Discussion, 51; God's message, 56; Compared with nature, 57; Purpose of, 66; How to study, 70; How to mark, 71; How to understand, 74.
Books. God's two, 57.
Brotherhood. 465.

Caste. 491.
Charity. 477, 486, 496.
Children. 146, 431, 530, 586.
Christ. And the church, 24; Ordinances a memorial of, 31; Reveals God, 54; Our Passover, 293; Work in baptism, 130; Return of, 391, 590.
Christian Science. 451.
Church. Union, 10; Two essentials of, 11; Not to make or change laws, 12; necessity of membership, 21; The bride of Christ, 22, 282, 368, 464, 531; Relation to lodges, 494; wealth of, 560; growth of, 604, character of, 605; in the wilderness, 43, 391.
Circumcision. 121.
Cleansing. Taught in O. T., 38.
Consecration. Of infants, 147; poem, 589.
Confession. 115, 132.

Conscience. 52.
Commission. 164; Authenticity, 165; Meaning, 176.
Conversation. 467.
Covenant. Relation of old and new, 40; Old fulfilled in Christ, 43.
Customs, worldly, 471.

Day of the Lord. 550.
Death. 594.
Debt. 585
Divorce. 532.
Dress. 409.

Enduement for service. 423.
Equality in Christ. 527.
Eucharist. 387; Meaning of, 389; Elements of, 408.
Esperanto. 602.
Eunomius. 248.
Evangelization. 603.
Exercise in the church, 27.

Faith. 30, 131.
Family worship, 94.
Father. 130.
Fathers. Dates of birth given, 14.
Feet-washing. 45, 296. The custom, 297; The contention, 302; The ordinance, 312; Significance, 317; Early church practise, 336; Objections to, 347; Blessings of, 349.
Fellowship. 31.

Gifts of the Spirit. 424, 430, 462.
Girard. 68.
Golden Candlestick. 45.
Grace at meals. 94.
Guidance. 27.

Healing. 438-448.
Heaven and Home (poem) 535.
Holiness. 37, 327.
Holy Kiss. 273; 406.
Holy Spirit. Leads to God, 55; Sin against, 55; Work in regeneration, 130; Symbols of, 418; Being of, 419, Conditions of receiving, 425.
Households. 138.
Husband and wife. 521.
Hypocrites. 23.

Infants. Baptism of, 133; Conversion of, 146; Consecration of, 147.
Inductive method. 33.
Invention. 602.
Israel. To be restored, 600.

Jerusalem. Water supply, 195; Destruction of, 543.

Kingdom of Heaven. 36, 100, 134, 591, 593, 594.

Laver. 45, 313.
Law. 39, 540.
Lawsuits. 499.
Laymen's Missionary Movement. 607.
Laying on of Hands. 423.
Lodges. 476.
Lord's Day. 544.
Lord's Prayer. 98.
Lord's Supper. 285; Not Jewish Passover, 286; Conditions of sharing, 393; Time of observing, 397; Suggestions on, 404; A unit, 404.
Love Feast. 353; New name, 361; Early church observance, 370; Practical value of, 384; Poem, 415.

Manna. 288.
Marriage. 517.
Marriage Supper. 282, 367, 392, 405.
Means of grace. 12, 13, 31. See **Value.**
Medicine. 441.
Memory. 33.
Mercy. 37.
Millennium. 552, 592.
Mingled Cup. 409.
Missions. 607.
Ministry. 433, 493.
Monasticism. 460.
Money. 559.

Subject Index

Mormons. 268.
Müller. 104.
Moody. On secretism, 498; On Christ's coming, 591.
Morality. 453, 485, 495.
Morning Watch. 95.

Nature. 51.
Nonconformity. 467.
Non-resistance. 499.
Non-secrecy. 476.

Oaths. 480.
Obedience. 30, 37, 47.
Occupation. 468.
Offerings. 582.
Ordination. 430.
Ordinances. Value of, 30; Types of, 36; Fundamental, 46.
Original Sin. 136, 531.
Outlines (Tables of Scriptures). Of the spiritual feast, 25; of types and antitypes, 45; of the meaning of baptism, 188; of the Scriptures on baptism, 203; of the Lord's Supper, 282; of Christ our Passover, 293; of Christian Science errors, 451; of the Ten Commandments in O. T. and N. T., 541; of Christian Stewardship, 587.

Papacy. And baptism, 252.
Parents. 529.
Passover, 286, 387, 407.
Pouring. 209.
Praise. 106; In the church, 107; Use of instruments, 108; Spirit of, 110.
Prayer. 79; Can God answer, 80; Will God answer, 83; Conditions of, 83; Example of Jesus, 93; Externals of, 94; Lord's Prayer, 98; Answers to, 102; for healing, 444; in lodges, 488.
Probation. 263.
Purification. 161.
Polygamy. 520.

Rich, warning to, 599.
Re-marriage, 533.
Romanism. 12, 252.

Sabbath. A symbol, 37; Creation, 536; Old covenant, 538; The Lord's Day, 544; Texts explained, 552.
Sacraments. 13.
Sacrifices. 40, 315.
Secrecy. 482.
Sectarianism. 14.
Seeing Him Who is Invisible. 612.
Separation. 457; Principles of, 463; Rewards of, 474.
Sickness. Causes of, 438; How to use, 439, 443; Prayer for, 444.
Signs of Christ's Coming. 595.
Sincerity. 11.
Single Immersion. Origin of, 248, 253.
Spiritualism. 598.
Sprinkling. 209, 210, 211, 212.
Stewardship. 564; Tithe a Symbol of, 576; Offerings, 582; Spirit of, 584.
Student Volunteers. 609.
Symbols. As aids in teaching, 32; In O. T., 36.

Tabernacle. Type of church, 44, 312, 353, 368, 388, 421.
Table of Show-bread. 45, 368.
Ten commandments. 541.
The Rose's Thorn (poem). 440.
The Tempted Bride (poem). 512.
Tithe. 558; A symbol, 37, 566, 576; Taught in N. T., 571; Value of observance, 578.
Tobacco. 465, 561, 583.
Trinity, represented in baptism. 129.
Titles of Honor. 491.
Torrey. On the Tabernacle, 45; On the Lord's Supper, 294.
Truth. Taught by Symbols, 32.

Uniformity. 462.
Unfermented wine. 408.
Unleavened bread. 407.
Unpardonable sin. 55.

Value. Of the church, 24; of the ordinances, 30; of the Bible, 66; of prayer, 102; of praise, 106; of confession, 115; of baptism, 127; of the holy kiss, 276; of feet-washing, 349; of the love-feast, 384; of the cup and loaf, 389; of the laying on of hands, 428; of ordination, 430; of anointing, 437; of separation from the world, 474; of marriage, 534; of the sabbath, 555; of the tithe, 578; of the hope of Christ's coming, 610.

Veil. 521.
Voltaire. On Christianity, 22.

Waldensians. 296, 450.
War. 502.
Washing. 209, 221.
Wealth of the church, 559; A sign, 599.
Wedding garment. 329.
Will. Aided by the means of grace, 34.
Woman. Relation to man, 527; The covering, 521; Silence in church, 527.
World. Separation from, 457; or organization of, 478; pleasures of, 478, 583. Unification of, 601.

Youth, and salvation. 147.

INDEX OF PRINCIPAL SCRIPTURE QUOTATIONS.

Of the more than twenty-two hundred Scripture references cited or quoted in this book the following are accompanied by more or less extended explanations and are therefore indexed.

Genesis
2: 1-3 (536)
4: 3 (566)
17: 9-14 (134)
Exodus
12: 6 (286)
15: 26 (445)
25: 23-28 (285)
30: 1-11 (79)
    19-21 (313, 323)
31: 1-5 (45)
    17 (68)
Leviticus
25: 23 (45)
27: 30 (570)
Numbers
18: 21-26 (578)
Deuteronomy
31: 12 (77)
Psalms
19: 1 (52)
119: 71 (439)
Isaiah
43: 10 (53)
52: 15 (210)
Jeremiah
18: 7-9 (503)
Ezekiel
26: 35 (211)
Daniel
12: 4 (596)
Malachi
3: 8 (558)
    10 (579)
Matthew
3: 11 (190)
    15 (268)
5: 31, 32 (532)
    33-38 (481)
6: 9-14 (98)
    33 (562)
8: 11 (178)
    17 (446)
11: 33 (591)
16: 18 (21, 177)
17: 14-21 (88)
18: 19 (91)
22: 11-13 (23)
    21 (572)
23: 23 (571)
24: 14 (603)
    20 (553)
    36 (595)
26: 17 (288, 290)
27: 46 (409)
28: 19 (129, 137, 164, 176, 181)
Mark
1: 4 (192)
3: 29 (55, 444)
7: 4 (214)
11: 24 (85)
    25 (86)
16: 16 (131)
Luke
9: 26 (179)
10: 5 (277)
18: 41 (89)
22: 1 (408)
    13-15 (289)
    19, 20 (389)
    24-29 (303)
    29, 30 (369)
John
3: 5 (128, 207)
3: 23 (192)
4: 23 (84)
10: 9 (25)
    29 (26)
13: 1 (364)
    3-5 (314, 354)
    12-16 (318)
    35 (365)
14: 4 (92)
16: 8-11 (55)
17: 15 (461, 478)
    17 (68)
    21-23 (170)
18: 20 (484)
Acts
2: 38-41 (193)
    44-46 (397)
    47 (23)
8: 12-16 (197)
    36-38 (198)
9: 18 (200)
10: 47, 48 (201)
16: 15 (138, 202)
    33, 34 (139, 202)
17: 28 (445)
18: 4 (554)
Romans
2: 4 (52)
    15 (53)
4: 3 (68)
6: 3-5 (128, 184)
10: 4 (41)
    14-17 (67)
11: 25, 26 (600)
13: 3-5 (503)
14: 13 (465)
    17 (406)
16: 16 (275)
1 Corinthians
1: 16 (139)
3: 16 (440)
5: 7, 8 (335, 387)
6: 1-12 (499)
9: 7-14 (572)

10: 1, 2 (121)
6-12 (440)
11: 1-17 (521)
17-34 (356, 391,
392, 395)
12: 13 (206)
16: 2 (545, 586)
II Corinthians
1: 4 (440)
3: 6-11 (54)
18 (69)
4: 17 (440)
Galations
3: 24, 25 (39)
28 (527)
Ephesians
1: 10 (601)
4: 5 (204)
5: 11, 12 (483)
25-33 (22, 393)
6: 4 (530)
18 (92)
Collossians
2: 12 (208)
11-14 (39, 121)
I Thessalonians
5: 16 (275)

I Timothy
4: 1-3 (598)
5: 8 (565)
10 (333)
II Timothy
2: 12 (116)
3: 1-5 (597)
16 (56)
Titus
3: 4-8 (133)
Hebrews
1: 1 (54)
4: 3-11 (539)
6: 1, 2 (206, 426)
7: 19 (39)
26 (40)
8: 6 (40)
9: 1 (43)
9 (44)
10 (212)
10: 1 (39)
22 (122, 212)
11: 4 (564)
10 (40)
13 (564)
35 (41)
40 (41)

13: 14 (577)
James
1: 7 (86)
25 (553)
5: 1-8 (599)
14, 15 (437)
16 (88)
I Peter
1: 23 (67)
3: 3, 4 (470)
21 (120)
1 John
1: 8, 9 (324)
3: 22 (86)
4: 2 (116)
5: 14, 15 (90)
16 (55)
II John
7 (585)
Jude
12 (361)
Revelation
15: 2 (109)
19: 6-9 (22, 330, 368)
20: 1-15 (592)

INDEX OF AUTHORS QUOTED.

In the study of God's means of grace, the Bible, of course, is the chief authority, and the references in this book are mainly from it; but other sources of information have also been helpful. A list of sources from which quotations have been made is given below, the chapter or page being given, in most instances, with the credit in the body of the work. Of course the authorities quoted are few, compared with the number consulted. The literature available on part of the subjects is very extensive, one author having collected a list of over three thousand treatises on baptism alone, but on other subjects it is scarce and unsatisfactory. For example, there is need of further research on the history of feet-washing in the writings of the early Christians which are not included in the usual volumes of the church "Fathers." The writer has been fortunate in having extended access to the large libraries in Chicago and elsewhere, but much remains to be done, and this work will probably need to be revised in some points and enlarged in others as new light is discovered.

Early Writers: First Century; Didache or Teachings of the Apostles (140, 165, 175, 194, 216, 254, 266, 270, 338, 370, 389, 398, 546, 574, 610), Shepherd of Hermas (142, 218), Epistle of Barnabas (218, 547), Dionysius (278), Mathetes (471), Clement of Rome (218, 400, 449), Pliny (371, 398). **Second Century:** Ignatius (165, 205, 370, 546), Polycrates (402), Irenaeus (141, 219, 225, 337, 449, 548, 574), Diognetus (547), Justin Martyr (140, 165, 179, 201, 221, 266, 279, 389, 394, 547), Tertullian (140, 165, 175, 222, 278, 338, 373, 385, 401, 427, 449, 523, 548), Theophylus (402), Melito (402), Origen (142, 226, 374, 401, 449, 548), Apostolic Canons and Constitutions (118, 165, 221, 270, 278, 319, 374, 396, 399, 403, 427, 548, 574, 584). **Third Century:** Anatolius (401), Clement of Alexandria (338, 372, 450), Cyprian (141, 194, 227, 254, 255, 270, 374, 398, 427, 470, 472, 524), Hippolytus (227), Eusebius (255, 403), Athanasius (227, 340), Minucius Felix (372), Monulus (226). **Fourth Century:** Augustine (194, 229, 278, 279, 341, 397, 403, 450, 574), Basil (228, 230), Cyril (228, 339), Gregory Nanzianzen (248, 270), Ambrose

(228), Jerome (232, 266, 427, 471), Chrysostom (195, 234, 263, 278, 375, 339, 385, 410, 574), Optatus (228), Philostargius (249), Theodoret (249), Gregory of Nyssa (180, 229), Julian (375). **Fifth Century:** Socrates (250, 376, 398), Sozomen (249). **Sixth Century:** Pelagius (251).

Versions: Septuagint (150), Latin (158), Syriac (158, 206), Egyptian (158), Armenian (158), Gothic (158), Slavonic (158), Arabic (159), Persic (159), Old Anglo-Saxon (159), Emphatic Diaglott (205).

Canons of Church Councils: Elvira, 307 A. D. (342), Nicea, 325 A. D. (231), Antioch, 341 A. D. (404), Gangra, 360 A. D. (400), Neo-Ceserea, 315 A. D. (254), Constantinople, 381 A. D. (270), Carthage, 397 A. D. (270), Toledo, 633 A. D. (251, 694), Cologne (140).

Historians and Histories: Allan—Christian Institutions (380); Bartlett—Apostolic Age (143, 382); Bapheidos—Church History (239); Bingham—Christian Antiquities (229, 379, 385); Coleman—Ancient Christianity Exemplified (257); Fisher—Beginnings of Christianity (383); Garruci—Christian Antiquities (245); Gibbon—History of Rome (379); Grotius (567); Henson—Apostolic Christianity (383); Josephus—History of the Jews (195, 286); Kurtz—Church History (381); McGiffert—Church History (211); Mospero—Dawn of Civilization (567); Mosheim—Church History (382); Moxom—From Jerusalem to Nicea (383); Neander—Church History (142, 238, 378); Pressence—Early Years of Christianity (239); Probst—Liturgie (367); Pullan—Early History of Christianity (383); Robinson—History of the Baptists (253); Sayce—Struggle of the Nations (567); Schaaf—Lessons from the Didache (239, 280); Stanley—Christian Institutions (143, 279, 380); Thucydides (568); Warren—Liturgy of Ante-Nicene Church (165, 280); West—Ancient History (372); Weizacker—Apostolic Age (382); Xenophon—Anabasis (568).

Cyclopedias: The American Encyclopedia (244), The Americana (154, 238), Biblical Encyclopedia (381), Browne's Bible Dictionary (191), Chambers' Encyclopedia (237), Dictionary of Christ and the Gospels (363), The Edinburgh Cyclopedia (256), The Encyclopedia Britannica (236, 257), Hastings' Bible Dictionary (125, 143, 154, 166, 196, 239, 427), The International Cyclopedia (238, 343), McClintock and Strong (344), The Jew-

Authors Quoted

ish Cyclopedia (123, 299, 323, 358), Kitto's Bible Encyclopedia (182, 343, 378), The Schaaf-Herzog Cyclopedia (237), Smith's Dictionary of Antiquity (236, 247), Smith and Cheatham (344),

Lexicons and Authorities on Language: Adler (151), Bars (151), Bretschneider (153), Buttman (153), Burton (153), Bullion (153), Cremer (153, 156), Century Dictionary (158), Dunbar (151), Donegan (151), DeStourdza (152), Gaza (154), Gesenius (158), Goodwin (191), Greene (156), Greenleaf (151), Komma (152), Leigh (152), Liddel and Scott (151), Parkhurst (151), Passow (154), Richardson (154), Rost and Palm (151), Robinson (151), Schleusner (151), Sophocles (151), Stephanus (151), Stevens and Vosius (153), Thayer (152, 156), Wilke (153), Wright (152).

Commentaries and Miscellaneous Works: Beer—The Lord's Supper (290); Bennet—Christian Archaeology (376); Beverage's Works (252); Binney—Theological Compend (200); Cathcart—Baptism of the Ages and Nations (241, 245); Chrystal—History of the Modes of Baptism (224); Cote—Archaeology of Baptism (245); Campbell and Rice Debate (224); Conant on Baptism (153, 174); Conybeare and Howson—Life and Epistles of St. Paul (241); Dale—Classic Baptism (196); Eddy—Key to the Scriptures (451); Edersheim—Life of Christ (124, 126, 215); Farrar—Texts Explained (381); Ford—Studies in Baptism (197, 235, 246, 258); Good and Gregory—Pantalogia (243); International Critical Commentary (132); Guericke—Manual of Antiquity (381); Geike—Hours with the Bible (523); Gulick—Growth of the Kingdom (601); Jamieson, Fausset and Brown —Commentary (324); Judson on Baptism (253); Keating—The Agape and the Eucharist (367, 383); Lundy—Monumental Christianity (247); Lange—Commentary (358); Lansdell—The Sacred Tenth (568); Moody—The Second Coming of Christ (591); Moore—Life of Wesley (241); Orchard—History of Foreign Baptists (225); Prayer Book of Episcopal Church (142); Report of Palestine Exploration Society (196); Stearns—Manual of Patrology (15); Torrey—Difficulties in the Bible (294); Vincent —Word Studies (314).

Papers and Tracts: The Christian Endeavor World (454); The Christian Advocate (144, 346); Christian Cynosure (488); Current Anecdotes (453); The Edinburg Review (380); The Homiletic Review (453); The Christian (386); The Gospel Messenger (262); The Missionary Visitor (569); **The Golden Baptism** (272); Gnagey—Baptism (202); Wampler—The Law of Baptism (259); Sunday School Times (298, 326); Martyr's Mirror (345); Donneldson's Pocket Companion of Oddfellowship (489); Grosh—Manual of Oddfellowship (490).

Other Authorities: Alford (343), Lyman Abbott (345), Arnold (344), Beery (353), Beecher (28, 345), Mrs. Booth (345), J. M. Buckley (346), Horace Bushnell (146), John Calvin (142, 345), Alexander Campbell (239), Delitsch (152), D'Ooge (152), Henry Drummond (320), Durbin (196), Professor Flagg (152), Professor Fox (257), Haefele (165), Harnack (152, 165, 219, 238), Professor Humphreys (152), Jacobs (377), Jackson (344), Judson (146), Professor Kyriasko (152), Lightfoot (382), Martin Luther (187), Moody (498), John R. Mott (104), Max Muller (575), Marriot (238), Chaplain McCabe (575), Dr. Miller (579), Dr. Owen (575), Orr, (379), Wendell Phillips (496), James Quinter (196, 213), Robert E. Speer (103), Strabo (196), Professor Sandy (131), Professor Stuart (142), Schmidt (345), Charles Sumner (506), Dr. Terry (211), Professor Timayenis (152), Professor Tyler (152), Rabbi Wise (103), Daniel Webster (497). The Talmud (335).

TESTING QUESTIONS.

The following questions are given for the guidance of parents who may wish to give instruction in these subjects in the home; and of teachers of Sunday-school classes which may use the book for supplemental study, or of leaders of other Bible classes; and for private readers who may wish to be sure that they remember the contents.

INTRODUCTION AND PREFACE.

1. Upon what two things, does Professor Haines say, does the merit of a book depend? 2. Is there need of information on the subjects discussed in this book? 3. What are the author's reasons for writing? 4. Why is it entitled "God's Means of Grace" (p. 13)? 5. Can you accept the closing caution (p. 15)? 6. Give the outline of contents.

THE CHURCH (pp. 21-48).

1. What are the five reasons for the necessity of church membership? 2. What five benefits of church membership are mentioned? 3. What sixteen reasons combine to make the ordinances of such great value? 4. Give examples of how God taught His people in Old Testament times. 5. How is the Old Testament related to the New? 6. How is the new covenant better than the old? 7. What became of the old? 8. What does the new have, corresponding to things of the old?

THE BIBLE (pp. 51-78).

1. In what seven ways does God speak to us? 2. In what seven ways do the Book of Nature and the Book of Revelation show that they were written by the same Divine Author? 3. What is the purpose of the Bible? 4. What five things does it do for the spiritual life? 5. What suggestions are given as to Bible helps and methods of study?

PRAYER (pp. 79-105).

1. What are some difficulties in the way of faith in prayer, and how are they answered? 2. Why do we believe that God

is both able and willing to answer true prayer? 3. What seven conditions as to attitude of heart do the Scriptures teach as essential to prevailing prayer? 4. What seven conditions of right asking? 5. What may we learn from the example of Jesus in prayer? 6. What suggestions are given as to the externals of prayer? 7. Explain the Lord's Prayer. 8. Give instances of answer to prayer.

PRAISE (pp. 106-115).

1. Why is praise necessary to the Christian? 2. How did God's people praise Him under the Old Covenant? Under the new? 3. What do the Scriptures teach as to the use of instruments? 4. As to the true spirit of praise?

CONFESSION (pp. 115-120).

1. In what five ways is public confession of Christ valuable? 2. What three things are essential to true confession?

BAPTISM (pp. 120-173).

1. Explain how Christian baptism was foreshadowed by the following: The ark, the passage of the Red sea, circumcision, bathing before atonement, the Jewish triune immersion, proselyte baptism. 2. What was the form and meaning of John's baptism? 3. When and how was Christian baptism instituted? 4. How do we know it is water baptism rather than Spirit baptism merely? 5. What five things are signified by Christian baptism? 6. What do the Scriptures teach as conditions of baptism? 7. Why are infants not proper subjects for baptism? 8. Why is it important to preserve the proper mode of baptism? 9. What are the ten lines of evidence as to mode? 10. What seven proofs combine to show that the word baptism primarily means only to dip or immerse in classical Greek? 11. What seven additional arguments prove that this is also the meaning in the Gospel? 12. What prepositions are used with the word in the Gospel, and why? 13. How does a grammatical study of Matt. 28: 19 prove triune immersion? 14. How may the mode of baptism be inferred from its meaning? 15. What is the relation of water and Spirit baptism? 16. What are the Scripture examples of baptism and what may we learn from them? 17. What scriptures are used against triune immersion, and how are they to be explained? 18. What historical

testimony is there concerning baptism? 19. What churches have practiced triune immersion continuously from the apostles? 20. What was the origin of single immersion? Of pouring? Of sprinkling? 21. When, where and by whom should baptism be administered? 22. How should errors in baptism be corrected?

THE HOLY KISS (pp. 274-281).

1. What scriptures teach the observance of the holy kiss? 2. How was it observed by the early church?

FEET-WASHING (pp. 285-352).

1. How do we know that the last supper of Jesus and the disciples was not the Jewish Passover? 2. How do we know that the feet-washing at this supper was not for physical cleansing? 3. How do we know that it was not caused by the contention that occurred? 4. How do we know that it was intended to be perpetuated? 5. What is the significance of the rite? Of what practical value is it?

THE LOVE-FEAST (pp. 353-386).

1. What ten reasons are given for observing the love-feast as an ordinance? 2. What is the meaning of the love-feast? 3. Where did it get this name? 4. Of what practical value is it?

EUCHARIST (pp. 387-415).

1. What is the significance of the eucharist? 2. What are the conditions of sharing in the Lord's supper? 3. How often should it be observed? 4. Why should unleavened bread and unfermented wine be used in the eucharist? 5. How is the Lord's supper, including feet-washing, the love-feast and the eucharist, a unity?

THE LAYING ON OF HANDS (pp. 419-430).

1. What do the Scriptures teach as to the being of the Holy Spirit? 2. What is the Scripture authority for the laying on of hands? 3. What is the meaning of the rite?

ORDINATION (pp. 430-435).

1. What was the form of ordination in the Old Testament? 2. What precedents are there for ordination in the Gospel? 3. What is the meaning of ordination? 4. Why should the church call all who are adapted to it to the work of the min-

istry? 5. Why should every youth seek the ministry as first choice of occupations?

ANOINTING THE SICK (pp. 436-455).

1. What Scripture authority is there for the anointing of the sick with oil for healing? 2. What is the purpose of affliction? 3. What should we do in time of sickness? 4. What is the basis for faith in God for healing?

SEPARATION FROM THE WORLD (pp. 459--513).

1. What is said of the principle of separation (a) in nature (b) in the kingdom of God? 2. What three errors as to separation are corrected? 3. What seven principles of separation are given? 4. What principles of non-conformity are given? 5. What seven principles are given with reference to lodges? 6. How should the church prevent any excuse for the lodge substitute? 7. What do the Scriptures teach about lawsuits? 8. What about war?

MARRIAGE (pp. 517-535).

1. When and why was marriage instituted? 2. Who should not marry? 3. What do the Scriptures teach as to the relation of husband and wife? 4. Of parents and children? 5. What has the State to do with marriage? 6. What did Jesus teach as to divorce? 7. When may separation be permitted? 8. Of what is marriage a type? 9. What is its practical value?

THE SABBATH (pp. 536-557).

1. When and why was the creation Sabbath instituted? 2. How long will it continue? 3. What proof is there that the Saturday Sabbath of the Jewish law was for that dispensation only? 4. What was the significance of the Jewish Sabbath? 5. When and how did the Lord's day come to be observed? 6. What is the significance of the Lord's day? 7. What is the value of observing the Sabbath?

THE TITHE (pp. 558-589).

1. How is stewardship taught in the Old Testament? In the New? 2. What proof is there that the holy tithe was taught along with the Sabbath and marriage from the beginning? 3. What Gospel authority is there for observing it now? 4. Of what is it a symbol? 5. What blessings attend its observance? 6. What do the Scriptures teach concerning offerings?

THE COMING OF THE LORD (pp. 590-612).

1. What objections are there to faith in the return of the Lord, and how are they answered? 2. In what seven ways is Jesus said to come again? 3. What are some scriptures that cannot be referred to any of these ways? 4. What are the seven signs of His coming? 5. What seven duties are taught in view of His coming? 6. What special help have you gotten from the study of this book? 7. How may you make it of help to others also?